Innovation, Competitiveness, and Development in Latin America

Innovation, Competitiveness, and Development in Latin America

Lessons from the Past and Perspectives for the Future

EDITED BY EDMUND AMANN AND PAULO N. FIGUEIREDO

OXFORD UNIVERSITY PRESS

OXFORD
UNIVERSITY PRESS

Oxford University Press is a department of the University of Oxford. It furthers the University's objective of excellence in research, scholarship, and education by publishing worldwide. Oxford is a registered trade mark of Oxford University Press in the UK and certain other countries.

Published in the United States of America by Oxford University Press
198 Madison Avenue, New York, NY 10016, United States of America.

CIP data is on file at the Library of Congress

ISBN 978-0-19-764807-0

DOI: 10.1093/oso/9780197648070.001.0001

Printed by Integrated Books International, United States of America

Contents

Contributors

André Pineli is a Researcher at the Henley Business School of Business, University of Reading.

Gabriela Arona is a Researcher in the Institute of Economics at the Federal University of Rio de Janeiro.

Ari Van Assche is Professor of International Business, HEC, Montréal.

Edmund Amann is Professor of Brazilian Studies at Leiden University and Adjunct Professor at the School for Advanced International Studies at Johns Hopkins University.

Carlos Azzoni is Professor of Economics in the Faculty of Economics and Administration, University of São Paulo.

Moises Balestro is Associate Professor at the University of Brasilia in the Graduate Program of Comparative Studies on the Americas at the Department of Latin American Studies.

Rodrigo A. Bellezoni is a Researcher at the São Paulo School of Management (FGV/EAESP), Department of Public Management (GEP), Fundação Getulio Vargas (FGV), São Paulo, Brazil.

Carlos Bianchi is Assistant Professor at the Institute of Economics, Universidad de la República (UdelaR), Uruguay.

Tereza Bicalho is a Researcher based at the World Wildlife Fund, Paris.

Claudio Bravo-Ortega is Associate Professor at the School of Business, Universidad Adolfo Ibañez, Chile.

John Crabtree is a Research Associate at the Latin American Centre, University of Oxford.

Mahrukh Doctor is Professor of Comparative Political Economy at the University of Hull.

Nicolas Eterovic is a Senior Economist at the Banco Central de Chile.

Paul Fenton Villar is an Associate Researcher in the School of International Development, University of East Anglia.

João Carlos Ferraz is Professor at the Institute of Economics, Federal University of Rio de Janeiro.

Paulo N. Figueiredo is Professor of Technology and Innovation Management at the Brazilian School of Public and Business Administration (EBAPE) at the Getulio Vargas Foundation (FGV).

Mariana Fuchs is a Researcher at the Universidad de Buenos Aires.

Fernando Isabella is a Researcher at the Institute of Economics, Universidad de la República (UdelaR), Uruguay.

Rhys Jenkins is Emeritus Professor of International Development at the University of East Anglia.

Bernardo Kosacoff is Professor of Economics at the Universidad de Buenos Aires, Universidad Nacional de Quilmes and Universidad Di Tella.

Ivan Luzardo-Luna is a Postdoctoral Fellow at the Department of Economics, University of Pennsylvania.

Rajneesh Narula is Professor and Director of the John H. Dunning Centre for International Business, Henley Business School, University of Reading.

Jeffrey Orozco is Professor and Director of the International Centre for Political Economy, Universidad Nacional de Costa Rica.

Elissaios Papyrakis is Senior Lecturer in Development Economics at the Institute of Social Studies (ISS), Erasmus University.

Lorenzo Pellegrini is Professor of Economics of Environment and Development at the International Institute of Social Studies (ISS), Erasmus University.

Wilson Peres is Senior Economic Affairs Officer at the Division of Production, Productivity and Management of the UN Economic Commission for Latin America and the Caribbean (ECLAC) in Santiago, Chile.

Carlo Pietrobelli is Professor of Economics at the Università Roma Tre.

José A. Puppim de Oliveira is Research Professor at the Brazilian School of Public and Business Administration (EBAPE) at the Getulio Vargas Foundation (FGV).

Roberta Rabellotti is Professor of Economics in the Department of Political and Social Science at the Università di Pavia.

Keynor Ruiz is a Researcher at the International Centre for Political Economy, Universidad Nacional de Costa Rica.

Clemente Ruiz Durán is Professor at the Faculty of Economics of the National Autonomous University of Mexico (UNAM).

Milene Tessarin is a Researcher in the Economic Geography Section at the University of Utrecht.

Julia Torracca is Professor at the Institute of Economics, Federal University of Rio de Janeiro.

SECTION I

INTRODUCTION AND CONTEXT

1
Introduction

Edmund Amann and Paulo N. Figueiredo

1.1. Introduction

Since World War II, Latin America has experienced two broad development policy epochs. The first, which lasted until the start of the 1980s, saw the rise of state-driven industrialization in an attempt to foster development through structural transformation and a changed role for the region in the global division of labour. The second, pursued subsequently, has de-emphasized wholesale structural shift in favour of a quest for efficiency and more intensive integration into global markets. In a few instances, left-populist governments disaffected by these policies have followed alternative statist approaches with distinctly mixed results. Despite more than six decades of these contrasting regimes, the Latin American economies have failed to close the development gap with the West. Compared with other emerging regions, the underperformance, whether in terms of income, productivity, or innovation, has been even greater. Two decades into the twenty-first century, it is hard to escape a sense of frustration, of potential thwarted, of opportunities missed.

One interpretation of this malaise is that Latin America has fallen into a middle-income trap where developmental progress has become impeded by structural constraints. These would principally include low levels of industrial technological capabilities, stemming from a lack of technological learning and underinvestment in human capital. These features also relate to over-reliance on commodities exports, poor infrastructure, and lack of articulation between sectors. The COVID-19 pandemic has shone further light on the challenges faced. The pandemic saw gross domestic product (GDP) across Latin America contracting in 2020 more than that of any other emerging market region. This seemed to underscore the region's relative lack of economic resilience in the face of shocks, perhaps another dimension of the middle-income trap.

Yet, despite all this, domestic developments, as well as those in the global economy, present opportunities for escape, if only the constraints of the past can be overcome. The need to find a way forward in this challenging, yet promising landscape provides the context for this volume.

Edmund Amann and Paulo N. Figueiredo, *Introduction* In: *Innovation, Competitiveness, and Development in Latin America.* Edited by: Edmund Amann and Paulo N. Figueiredo, Oxford University Press.
DOI: 10.1093/oso/9780197648070.003.0001

This book concerns itself with the key puzzle of the postwar political economy of Latin America: why has the pursuit of development proved so elusive? Specifically, the volume seeks to explore the key factors comprising Latin America's middle technology and income trap and what steps might be taken to help the region escape it. Engaging with this central question and determining ways forward, this volume emphasizes the role of policy and (potentially hidden) opportunities arising from productive and technological capabilities which have already been built up, or which could be realistically soon be developed.

One of the key focal points here concerns the role of natural-resource-intensive sectors and their potential role in reigniting growth. Examining these sectors and others, this book aims to establish what has worked, what has failed, and what needs to be done. What are the best forms of policy intervention to help Latin America overcome its structural impediments and seize emerging global opportunities? What institutional obstacles lie in the path of the implementation of effective policies? How, in the future, could the region avoid 'missing the boat' in terms of new windows of technological, learning, or sectoral opportunity? The questions this book addresses will be set out in more detail very shortly. First, though, at a time of wrenching change in both the regional and global economies, it is worth setting out the economic context which Latin America faces, and in which it must configure a new way forward.

1.2. The Overall Economic Context

The region's economies presently face a unique combination of circumstances. Some of these are structural in nature. Others are conjunctural, stemming from more ephemeral factors in the economic and political environment. Collectively, these circumstances exercise obvious constraints on investment or policy choices. However, they also open up promising and underexplored avenues for building competitiveness and capabilities. The key elements forming this crossroads begin with the region's long-established susceptibility to commodities cycles.

As far back as the colonial period, Latin America's position in the international division of labour has comprised a significant relative dependence on exports of natural-resource-intensive products. For example, the region ranks amongst the world's very largest producers of agricultural products such as beef and soya, minerals such as copper and lithium ores, and other key commodities, notably oil. Over recent years, as will become apparent later in the volume, many Latin American countries have built upon natural comparative advantages in these areas. This has occurred both in terms of downstream processing, and in relation to developing innovative techniques in exploration, extraction, and production.

These advances have placed many of the region's economies, notably Brazil, Chile, and Peru, in an advantageous position to benefit from the rise of China as a key export market. More generally, Latin America has been able to capitalize on surges in commodity prices such as that which peaked around 2012–2013 (UNCTAD, 2021). The unwinding of the latter contributed to the outbreak of recessions across the region over the subsequent five to six years. Although commodity prices are currently recovering, they will remain volatile. Against this background, one key issue faced by the region centres on building on and—where necessary—supplementing existing natural and developed comparative advantages. This will occur in the face of a challenging global market environment for natural-resource-intensive products. It will require the pursuit of appropriate capabilities in building strategies that facilitate the leveraging of existing strengths or, in some cases, the forging of completely new centres of specialization.

Volatility in global demand for natural-resource-intensive products is, of course, a timeless and unavoidable challenge faced by the region. At the same time, though, there exist other developments which are arguably more transitory, yet which nevertheless present serious policy dilemmas. One of the most important developments centres on the challenge to globalization which has emerged over the past decade. During the 1980s and 1990s the region's economies embarked on a course of ever-intensifying trade reform in lockstep with similar liberalization in key global markets (Ventura Dias et al., 1999). However, the prospective trade landscape is now more uncertain. While Latin American economies appear to have recommitted to trade reform (following rollbacks in Argentina and Brazil, for example), it seems unlikely that the Biden administration in the United States will resume progress towards the hemispheric trade integration that characterized the very early years of this century.

An indication of the posture of the United States towards the extension of freer trade through fresh multilateral agreements was given by the refusal of Washington to join the Comprehensive and Progressive Agreement for Trans-Pacific Partnership (CPTPP). This trade agreement, signed in March 2018, includes Chile, Mexico, and Peru in its membership, alongside Canada and seven Asian and Australasian economies. An earlier version of the CPTPP, the Trans-Pacific Partnership (TPP) was set aside following President Trump's decision to end US participation in 2017 (*The Economist*, March 7, 2023). Still, the emergence of the CPTPP shows that the region's key Asian trading partners, at least, remain keen on free trade agreements. Separate to the CPTPP for the time being, China, in particular, is keen to expand trading (and investment) relationships wherever possible. In this connection, it has been making special efforts in the case of Argentina, a country not traditionally the focus of China's efforts to forge global economic ties.

The complexity of the global trade policy environment facing Latin America is further highlighted in the case of the region's relationship with the European Union. Years in the making and agreed in principle in 2019, an agreement has been signed between Mercosul[1] and the European Union that promises to open up trade considerably. No fewer than 93% of tariffs facing Mercosul exports to the European Union would be abolished, with the exports subject to the remaining 7% being given preferential treatment (EU, 2019). The agreement would offer significant opportunities for Mercosul-based agricultural exporters, in particular.

The main access benefit from the EU perspective would centre on sales of its manufactures which, hitherto, have faced comparatively heavy protective barriers. Since the signing of the agreement, though, progress in implementing it has been very slow. In particular, given concerns over Brazilian deforestation, there have been severe doubts over whether the accord would ever be ratified by EU member states, especially France. Now that Brazil's Bolsonaro administration has departed and has been replaced by that of President Lula (who is committed to seriously tackling deforestation), it is possible that the agreement will finally enter force. However, this cannot be guaranteed, and doubts continue to surround the future shape of Latin America's access to Europe's vast markets. The challenge for the region's economies therefore centres on navigating this uncertainty. This will possibly involve expanding trade links in fresh directions, with perhaps a growing emphasis on the Asia Pacific region and the Global South. From this would stem important implications for the choice of sectors in which to specialize, where competitiveness and capabilities can be usefully built upon or developed from scratch.

Uncertainty around the future trajectory of trade policy coincides with another important element. This is more structural in nature and is likely to have profound effects on the future course of Latin America's productive sector, the nature of growth strategy, and the region's position within the global division of labour. This element—the new landscape of enterprise organization—has been emerging over the past four decades. It is characterized by more geographically dispersed global value chains. However, as Amann and Cantwell (2012) suggest, the process also involves changes in the conduct of innovative activities within multinational enterprises. This is leading to accelerated geographical dispersion of activities and a deconcentration of research and development (R&D) activity. In turn, this is offering Latin American economies fresh opportunities to capture elements of multinational corporation (MNC) activities that were more traditionally the province of Europe, North Asia, and North America. At the same time, innovation in enterprise organization structures globally offers Latin

[1] A customs union whose primary members are Argentina, Brazil, Paraguay, and Uruguay.

American enterprises significant learning opportunities to improve agility, innovativeness, and business-process efficiency. The question is, which enterprises or countries in the region are best disposed or able to capitalize on this? As will become clear, some Latin American economies, with more developed national systems of innovation (and established technological capabilities in lead sectors and enterprises), may be better placed than others.

As suggested in the earlier discussion regarding trade and trade policy, the global economic environment shaping Latin America's future will be strongly affected by the evolution of China. In particular, it is likely that the region will be increasingly an arena in which economic—and geopolitical—competition is played out between China and the traditional hegemon, the United States. The rise of China over recent decades has already profoundly affected Latin America's global trading patterns and sources of foreign direct investment (FDI). According to Roy (2022), China by 2021 had become South America's top trading partner. So far, patterns of trade have concentrated on natural-resource-intensive product exports from the region with a counterflow of manufactured-product imports from China. Over time, however, as China's cost advantages in certain parts of the industrial and manufacturing value chain erode, it is possible that the qualitative nature of the trade relationship might change. This is provided, of course, that Latin American enterprises are able to seize the relevant opportunities. This heralds the prospect of export diversification.

Turning to the investment relationship, China has already built up significant FDI holdings in Latin America, especially in natural resources. Over the future, it is quite possible that, as in the case of trade, the sectoral basis of the investment relationship might change. In particular, if China's MNCs continue to extend activities in Latin America, there may be considerable scope for capturing locally additional elements of their value chains. In addition, the expansion of the controversial Belt and Road initiative to the Latin American region raises the prospect of generating much-needed investment in critical infrastructure. However, the extension of Chinese economic influence in the region is unlikely to go unchallenged as Washington seeks to protect its traditional interests. This may translate into diplomatic pressure to limit Chinese investment in strategic sectors (*The Economist*, March 7, 2023).

Another critical structural issue which will increasingly impinge on Latin America's options for growth and development concerns demographic change. As among the advanced industrialized countries, Latin America is now having to confront the consequences of an ageing population (Cottlear, 2011). This poses challenges, in terms of labour supply, pension provision, and healthcare. All of these issues will require innovative solutions to address effectively. One of the key challenges that arises here surrounds how the region may have to renegotiate its position in the global division of labour in response to labour supply constraints that will become more binding as the population ages. Growing scarcity in the supply of labour is likely to drive up unit labour costs, harming competitiveness, unless efforts are intensified to increase labour productivity. One response to this is likely to involve enterprises in the region moving up the value chain in such a way that higher labour costs can be more readily absorbed and passed on. The latter, of course, is a development which has been widely witnessed in the advanced industrial economies. To succeed here, Latin American countries will be obliged to intensify innovation, build technological capabilities, and redouble efforts to improve the quality of human capital.

From the discussion so far, it should be clear that Latin America will face a series of challenges arising from conjunctural and structural factors, many of which are global in nature and essentially beyond the ability of actors in the region to effectively control. However, side by side with this, enterprises across all sectors will have to contend with the consequences of domestic change. This will be especially true in terms of changes relating to the political environment. In this connection, the region appears to have arrived at a turning point in its own affairs.

With the exception of Venezuela, prior to the pandemic, Latin American economies had embarked on a modest recovery following the commodity price shock of 2012–2014. This rebound was stopped in its tracks after 2019 and the arrival of the COVID-19 pandemic. In parallel with these developments, the wave of left populism, which appeared to have slowed, has gained ground. On the eve of the pandemic, in late 2019, mass protests in Chile gave vent to a surge in popular opposition to the country's centre-right administration and its policies of market liberalization. The protests laid the ground for the election of a leftist president, Gabriel Boric, in 2021, and the drafting of a new, more socially inclusive constitution (subsequently rejected in a plebiscite). In the following year, Colombia (another erstwhile bulwark of the centre right and market-orientated economic policies) saw the election of a left-wing president, Gustavo Petro. The election of President Petro also followed a wave of popular protests concerning economic issues. Brazil, shortly afterwards, continued with this trend. In October 2022, left-wing candidate Luiz Inácio Lula da Silva secured an unprecedented third presidential term, defeating right-wing candidate President Jair Bolsonaro.

These events signal a leftward alignment in Latin American politics which has been gathering momentum over recent years (Pickup, 2019). Alongside Brazil, Chile, and Colombia, Latin America's other largest economies, Argentina and Mexico, are also governed by centre-left administrations. This development has clear implications for the types of policies and approaches which are likely to find favour as the region attempts to confront its growth challenges and break out of the middle-income trap. At the very least, it is fair to say that the region-wide political consensus underpinning market liberalization is fragile. Indeed, it can be argued that liberal market reforms and their failure, as implemented, to thoroughly address issues of stagnating living standards and income concentration, have provided the impetus for the recent shift leftwards.

Against this background, major economies across the region are likely to prove more open towards development policies which favour an activist state. Thus, attempts to rekindle growth will probably involve close interaction between the state and the private sector, whether this involves the articulation of national or sectoral systems of innovation, the creation of new capacity through the provision of official finance, directed efforts at human capital formation, or, possibly, the implementation of activist trade policy. To the extent that the state returns to the centre stage as a prime mover in engineering structural reform and promoting development, risks will arise centring on issues of state capture, rent-seeking activity, and other dangers. These would include those associated with what is colloquially known as 'crony capitalism'. This volume addresses these issues in Chapter 3 and considers the extent to which they can be mitigated by better institutional and policy design.

Turning to a final feature of the landscape, at the time of writing the COVID-19 pandemic had subsided and most of the restrictions associated with it had been abolished across the region. The pandemic hit Latin America harder than any other developing or emerging market region in terms of output lost and mortality (on a per capita basis). Peru—a country featured in this volume—has the unwelcome distinction of witnessing more COVID-related deaths per capita than any country on Earth.[2] This occurred in the face of one of the strictest lockdowns in the region. In Peru, as in neighbouring countries, the pandemic has laid bare the structural failings and rigidities that have afflicted Latin America for years. In so painfully highlighting these, it may have sown the seeds for a more purposeful, region-wide attempt to tackle the factors which continue to hold back economic growth and human development.

1.3. The Conceptual Approach

This book is motivated by a major growth and development challenge which has overtaken Latin America in recent years. Conceptually, many analysts have characterized this challenge as a 'middle-income trap' and argue that, in the absence of concerted policy interventions, countries caught in it will forever face below-par growth and a failure of standards of living to take off. Perhaps more

[2] Source: Johns Hopkins Coronavirus Resource Center (https://coronavirus.jhu.edu/data/mortality).

broadly, in a comparative context, the existence of a middle-income trap could prevent countries snared in it ever catching up with their advanced industrial counterparts. Given the sobering implications of this prospect, it is not surprising that the middle-income trap has received considerable attention from analysts and policymakers alike. But what exactly is the middle-income trap, and how does it relate to the conceptual orientation of this volume?

The term 'middle-income trap' is comparatively recent and was first coined by Gill and Kharas in their seminal 2007 paper. The authors were motivated in formulating the concept by the empirical observation that some countries, notably in Latin America, had suddenly slowed down after a period of comparatively rapid growth (Gill and Kharas, 2015). For the authors, the key problem seemed to be that such economies were 'squeezed between the low-wage poor country competitors that dominate in mature industries and the rich-country innovators that dominate in industries undergoing rapid technological change' (Gill and Kharas, 2007, p. 1). In the explosion in the literature that has followed, many empirical studies of the trap have emerged. However, there is little agreement as to the precise definition of the trap, either in terms of the income thresholds that might define it, or to the structural or other factors that might serve as the underlying causes.

In a very useful survey of the literature and its relevance to the Latin American context, Paus (2014) identifies two broad theoretical approaches to the trap which are not necessarily mutually inconsistent with one another. In the first, towards which this book is broadly aligned, the middle-income trap can be understood as a structural phenomenon in which the growth 'problem' resides in a failure to engage in 'structural change towards higher value activities' (Paus, 2014, p. 13). Accordingly, attempts to accelerate growth face increasing headwinds. This happens as the economy sees its competitiveness in mature activities eroded by competition from lower-income countries. At the same time, the country concerned cannot, or will not, move into higher value-added sectors, or activities where market demand is more buoyant. For this reason, rising costs (especially labour costs) cannot be more readily absorbed and passed on to consumers.

The second broad approach to the middle-income trap places less emphasis on failure to engage in structural transformation or to move along a value chain. Instead, the focus rests on a 'growth slowdown', often analysed in terms of a neo-classical growth model (Paus. 2014). This approach also rests on extensive cross-country empirical studies (e.g. Eichengreen et al., 2013), the objective being to identify which groups of countries appear to have exhausted their rapid growth phase and at what income level this phenomenon arose. As Paus (2014) argues, the policy implications of the 'growth slowdown' literature are less readily apparent, but, given its rootedness in the neo-classical growth model literature, generic interventions such as investment in infrastructure and human capital are likely to be beneficial. To the extent that such interventions will have across-the-board positive effects, they would also assist in the development of new capabilities and higher-value activities. In this sense, from a policy perspective at least, both structural and growth slowdown approaches share a certain consistency.

Turning back to the 'structural' approach to analysing the middle-income trap, the literature places a heavy emphasis on technological upgrading and incremental structural transformation. An important element here, as described by Amann and Cantwell (2012) and Ohno (2009), centres on catching up with advanced economies through systematic capability building and technological learning. As capabilities are accumulated it becomes viable for enterprises (or productive sectors) to approach and possibly eventually define the global frontier. This allows for the possibility of enhanced ability to engage in price setting, product differentiation, and the application of acquired technological and productive capabilities into other sectoral settings.

However, the accumulation of such productive capabilities, with the structural shifts that they facilitate, is not a straightforward process. Their acquisition can be, and often is, capital- and knowledge-intensive. The risks involved can be high and progress, if any is made, is nonlinear. Reversals, outright failures, and capabilities erosion always remain possibilities. Whether success is achieved and growth-enhancing structural change is realized depend on a number of factors, including the strength and consistency of the policy environment, the pre-existence of relevant capabilities, the extent to which effective learning occurs as a result of interactions with foreign MNCs and capital equipment, and the quality of the education and training systems (Paus, 2014; Amann and Cantwell, 2012).

A critical issue concerning the structural nature of the middle-income trap and strategies to break out of it centres on the role of the natural-resource-intensive sectors. For some authors (e.g. Ohno, 2009), the middle-income trap is seen as being the end state of a growth strategy which has natural limits, especially one based on natural resources or FDI inflows (Gill and Kheras, 2015, p. 11). In this connection, the route out centres on a technocratic industrial strategy and strategic state alliances with business (Gill and Kheras, 2015). While not in any way discounting the potential of industrial policy, or the fomenting of industrial activity more generally, this book would like to emphasize that valid approaches to addressing the middle-income trap can also rest with alternative strategies. These can involve building on established strengths in the natural-resource-intensive sectors. It is to this issue that the discussion now turns.

Concern with low growth and vulnerability in the face of a turbulent global economy are hardly novel factors in the Latin American context. During the 1940s and 1950s, reflecting back on the lessons of the interwar global depression, an intellectual project known as structuralism gained real policy traction. This was to set the region on a different course for the next four decades, resulting in large-scale industrialization and urbanization. Adherents of the structuralist school, famously Hans Singer and Raul Prebisch, identified Latin America's traditional role in the global division of labour as prejudicial to the region's long-term economic interests (Love, 1980). Their argument centred on the notion that specialization in primary products exports (the region's traditional export focus) exposed economies to the volatility associated with global commodities markets.

Critically, over time, such specialization would also bring about a deteriorating terms of trade vis-à-vis countries that had specialized in the production of industrial products, especially manufactured goods. Combined, these two features would confine Latin America's economies to low, volatile growth. According to the structuralists, the remedy for breaking out of this trap centred on economic diversification, in particular the promotion of industrial activities (that could later be expected to transform the profile of exports). This ambitious goal was to be achieved via a policy of import substitution industrialization (ISI) which was implemented across the region between the 1930s and the end of the 1980s (Thorp, 1998). ISI involved a combination of protectionist trade measures and direct state participation in selected industrial sectors.

As the decades wore on, the achievements and limitations of the ISI strategy became readily apparent. On the positive side, ISI gave rise to a remarkable transformation in the structures of Latin America's major economies, elevating the share of industry in total output and giving rise to export diversification in favour of non-traditional (i.e. industrial) exports. For a while this was accompanied by accelerated growth. However, the momentum of ISI could not be maintained, as the productive inefficiencies and import dependencies[3] associated with the strategy produced recurrent deficits on the trade balance (Baer, 2013). By the early 1980s these could no longer be financed with cost-effective capital inflows. This occurred as global interest rates rose sharply and the deficits themselves were widened by the jump in oil prices following OPEC II in 1979. Under the terms of structural adjustment packages furnished by the IMF and the World Bank, ISI structures were progressively abandoned in the 1980s and 1990s as the so-called Washington Consensus gained hold.

The departure from ISI and the sidelining of associated structuralist viewpoints surrounding the future course of Latin Americas economies has had profound effects. In retrospect, the 1980s and early 1990s, when ISI was dismantled, can be seen as a point of policy rupture. Not only was the role of the state in the economy recast in a more liberal vein; Latin American countries were made to

[3] The key issue being that protectionism associated with the strategy limited the ability of countries that adopted it to export competitively, while reliance on imports (especially in terms of capital goods and fossil fuels) remained very high.

abandon decades of tariff and non-tariff protection in favour of a much more open trade regime. In some cases, this was reinforced by participation in multilateral trade agreements, as with the North American Free Trade Agreement (NAFTA) and Mercosul. These both came into being at the start of the 1990s. One consequence of the more liberal trade policy order which has been in place since the end of the past century has been the much-discussed 're-primarization' of the region (Ocampo, 2019). This phenomenon has seen the region fall back on traditional sources of comparative advantage in the natural-resource-intensive sectors. This process has occurred in the wake of deindustrialization, as many manufacturing and industrial sectors established under ISI struggled to compete in the new environment of diminished state support and much more open trade. Some authors have specifically linked re-primarization to the growth in trade with China (Delgado and Azuaje, 2022). As is well established in this literature, patterns of Latin America–China trade are strongly associated with a surge in commodities exports from the former, with countervailing flows of industrial exports (including manufactures) from the latter.

An important question stems from the concern over the re-primarization issue: to what extent should confronting it form a centrepiece of strategies to escape the middle-income trap? One approach to this question might be to engage in a traditional structuralist policy discourse whereby efforts should be made to diversify the export base, principally by rebuilding elements of the industrial sector. This might involve reintroducing elements of earlier ISI policy regimes, albeit selectively and with closer engagement with the private sector. One can see elements of such an approach undertaken by the Kirchner administrations in Argentina during the first decade of the twenty-first century and the Rousseff administration in Brazil during the 2010s (Amann, 2021). In the case of Brazil, much effort was made to build up domestic industrial capacity in the oil and gas sector, for example. Such a policy approach is also detectable in other settings, notably the United States, where the 2022 Inflation Reduction Act provides subsidies for the domestic production of electric vehicles and batteries.

While selectively promoting (or defending) industrial capacity and associated capabilities is likely to play a role in future growth strategies for Latin America, we stress that it is important for the region not to become caught up in traditional preoccupations concerning the supposed binary divide between natural-resource-intensive and industrial sectors (or, for that matter, services). As a growing literature attests (e.g. Figueiredo and Cohen, 2019), the natural-resource-intensive sectors in which Latin America abounds have enormous strengths. These include the accumulation of significant technological capabilities and the ability thereby to move up the value chain and engage in product differentiation. Such attributes have traditionally been associated with the industrial sector. The Latin American experience indicates that pathways to growth and value creation can also flow from activities sometimes misleadingly viewed as 'traditional' and (often mistakenly) associated with growth stagnation. Flowing from this, the volume will focus on activities and reforms which might kick-start growth, but with a key preoccupation centring on re-primarization and the opportunities (not just obstacles) that it presents.

1.4. The Key Objectives and Questions of This Book

As suggested at the beginning of this chapter, this book concerns itself with trying to understand why it has proven so difficult for Latin America to close the development gap which has opened up between it and the advanced industrial countries. To achieve this objective, the volume seeks to explore some of the realities around Latin America's middle-income trap, as well as possible solutions to it. What forms of policy intervention might help Latin America overcome its structural impediments? How, in the future, could the region seize fresh opportunities in terms of new windows of technological achievement, learning, or emerging sectors?

With all of this in mind, four broad questions arise which our book sets out to address. These are as follows. In first place, what factors characterize Latin America's middle technology and income trap, and how do they impact the region's ability to break out of it? Second, how are these issues reflected in the experience of individual countries, as well as across the region? Third, nationally and across the region, which policies are proving effective in addressing the middle technology and income trap? Finally, given the region's current situation and the lessons of policy experience, what are the best ways forward for the future regarding Latin America's prospect of breaking out of the trap?

From these central questions emerge vital issues which the book's chapters variously address. A key concern centres on where the region's strengths, weaknesses, and opportunities lie in relation to established or emerging sources of competitive advantage and technological capability. Identification of these elements, however, is only a first step in generating a policy set that might prove effective in levering the region out of its current impasse and ushering a future of more rapid, inclusive, and sustainable growth. Therefore, it is also important to understand the structural factors which are impeding or assisting the development of growth opportunities, competitive advantage and technological capability. As well as public policy, what are the roles of inward FDI and connection to global value chains? In reality, how important have been issues around investment in infrastructure, education and skills, and fixed capital? What opportunities and constraints does the transition to renewable energy sources, especially biofuels, present? Whether in terms of an obstacle or facilitating factor, what roles do institutions play? Are contemporary institutional structures and norms fit for the purpose, or are they holding the region back, preventing much-needed structural change?

In relation to the theme of institutions, it is also important to consider the role which the political process plays. Have patterns of political debate and decision-making proved conducive or inimical to the building of capabilities and the tackling of obstacles to growth? Latin America is often regarded as a region notable for political rupture rather than continuity. Accordingly, the economic and business environments have witnessed wrenching change in many countries, whether in the form of different monetary regimes, the switch from protectionist trade policy to a more open environment (and sometimes back again), or periods in which the role of the state has rapidly multiplied or contracted. What impacts has all of this had on the region's ability to develop new sources of competitiveness and avenues to accelerated, sustainable, and inclusive growth? In particular, can it be said, as is often supposed, that political volatility and sudden economic regime change are holding the region back? Or could it be the case, conversely, that policy experimentation and the fast-changing environment of recent decades have proven effective stimulants for innovation, supply-side responsiveness, and competitive agility?

In order to address these wide-ranging issues, the book adopts the following structure. Following this introduction (Chapter 1), Section II of this volume incorporates a range of chapters with a strong thematic emphasis. In Chapter 2, Mahrukh Doctor analyses the role of institutions and the constraints they may place on the ability of countries to engage in much-needed reform and structural change. Next, Chapter 3, by Rhys Jenkins, considers the role of China and whether its economic links with the region are hastening or lessening the prospects of a breakout from the middle-income trap. Following this, in Chapter 4, Claudio Bravo Ortega and Nicolas Eterovic explore similarities and differences between growth strategies pursued in Scandinavia and Latin America, two regions in which natural-resource-intensive sectors have played a critical role.

Chapter 5, by André Pineli and Rajneesh Narula, then moves on to consider the role of FDI and the role of MNCs in the development process, with special reference to the evolution of output and export structures. Keeping with the MNC theme, Chapter 6, by Carlo Pietrobelli, Roberta Rabellotti, and Ari Van Assache, focuses on the role of global value chains (GVCs), policy towards them, and the development opportunities which they continue to present the region. Chapter 7, by Carlos Azzoni and Milene Tessarin, investigates the often overlooked regional and spatial aspects of innovation, competitiveness, and capabilities building. Next, Chapter 8, by Paul Fenton Villar, Elissaios Papyrakis, and Lorenzo Pellegrini, explores institutional and policy interventions that can enhance the long-term development impacts of natural-resource-intensive sectors on the economies in which they are hosted. Chapter 9, by Tereza Bicalho, Rodrigo Bellezoni, and José Puppim de Oliveira, analyses the potential for environmental, energy, and sustainability technological transitions in Latin America with a focus on biofuels. Maintaining the focus on this key sector, Paulo Figueiredo in Chapter 10 focuses on the complexities and policy implications of capabilities-building in the biofuels complex. Rounding off Section I, Chapter 11, by João Carlos Ferraz, Julia Torracca, Gabriela Arona, and Wilson Peres, investigates the extent to which the diffusion of digital-related technologies may contribute to development and catching-up processes in Latin America.

Moving on from the thematic focus of its predecessor, Section III considers individual country experiences. The focus is placed on attempts to identify successful growth and development strategies, and how Latin American economies have continued to confront facets of the middle-income trap. Country cases from across the region are analysed in this section, starting with Chapter 12, by Bernado Kosacoff and Marianna Fuchs, on Argentina. This is followed by Chapter 13 on Brazil, by Edmund Amann; Chapter 14 on Colombia, by Ivan Luzardo-Luna; Chapter 15 on Mexico, by Clemente Ruiz Durán and Moises Balestro; Chapter 16 on Peru, by John Crabtree; Chapter 17 on Uruguay, by Carlos Bianchi and Fernando Isabella; and Chapter 18 on Costa Rica, by Jeffrey Orozco and Keynor Ruiz. Finally, in Section IV, Chapter 19, 'Final Remarks', by Edmund Amann and Paulo Figueiredo, draws together the main currents of the analysis and considers key policy lessons and potential ways forward.

References

Amann, E. 2021. *The Brazilian Economy: Confronting Structural Challenges.* Abingdon, UK: Routledge.

Amann, E., and Cantwell, J. 2012. *Innovative Firms in Emerging Market Countries.* New York: Oxford University Press.

Baer, W. 2013. *The Brazilian Economy: Growth and Development.* Boulder, CO: Lynne Rienner.

Cottlear, D. 2011. *Population Aging: Is Latin America Ready?* Washington, DC: World Bank.

Delgado, R., and Azuaje, C. 2022. 'Economic Growth in Latin America and the Role of China: An Analysis of Latin American Neo-Structuralism', *Janus.net: An e-journal of International Relations*, 13(2), 76–102.

The Economist. March 7, 2023. 'How Donald Trump Damaged America's Interests in Asia'. https://www.economist.com/asia/2023/03/07/how-donald-trump-damaged-americas-interests-in-asia?

The Economist. March 7, 2023. 'Argentina Is Wasting the Vast Opportunities China Offers It'. https://www.economist.com/the-americas/2023/03/07/argentina-is-wasting-the-vast-opportunities-china-offers-it.

Eichengreen, B., Park, D., and Shin, K. 2013. 'Growth Slowdowns Redux: New Evidence on the Middle-Income Trap'. *NBER Working Paper* No. 18673.

European Union. 2019. 'New Mercosul-EU Trade Agreement: The Agreement in Principle.' http://www.sice.oas.org/TPD/MER_EU/Texts/Agt_in_Principle_e.pdf.

Figueiredo, P., and Cohen, M. 2019. 'Explaining Early Entry into Path-Creation Technological Catch-Up in the Forestry and Pulp Industry: Evidence from Brazil', *Research Policy*, 48(7), 1694–1713.

Gill, I., and Kharas, H. 2007. *An East Asian Renaissance*. Washington, DC: World Bank.

Gill, I., and Kharas, H. 2015. 'The Middle-Income Trap Turns Ten.' *World Bank Research Policy Working Paper* No. 7403, pp. 1–27.

Love, J. 1980. 'Raul Prebisch and the Origins of the Doctrine of Unequal Exchange', *Latin American Economic Review*, 15(3), 45–72.

Ocampo, J. 2019. 'Latin America's Structural Transformation Patterns', in C. Monga and J. Lin, eds., *The Oxford Handbook of Structural Transformation*. New York: Oxford University Press, 439–464.

Ohno, K. 2009. 'Avoiding the Middle-Income Trap: Renovating Industrial Policy Formulation in Vietnam', *Asean Economic Bulletin*, 26(1), 25–43.

Paus, E. 2014. *Latin America and the Middle-Income Trap*. Santiago: CEPAL.

Pickup, M. 2019. 'The Political Economy of the New Left', *Journal of Latin American Perspectives*, 46(1), 23–45.

Roy, D. 2022. *China's Growing Influence in Latin America*. New York: Council on Foreign Relations.

Thorp, R. 1998. *Progress, Poverty and Exclusion: An Economic History of Latin America in the 20th Century*. Washington, DC: Inter-American Development Bank.

UNCTAD. 2021. *The Recent Commodity Price Surge: A Boon for Latin America and the Caribbean?* Geneva: UNCTAD.

Ventura-Dias, V., Cabezas, M., and Contador, J. 1999. *Trade Reforms and Trade Patterns in Latin America*. Santiago: CEPAL.

SECTION II
THEMATIC ISSUES

2

Institutional Challenges, the Middle-Income Trap, and the Pursuit of Global Economic Integration in Latin America

Mahrukh Doctor

2.1. Introduction

When states pursue development that is transformational, inclusive, and sustainable, the institutional context within which policies are formulated and implemented is central to understanding how success is achieved. This is because, simply put, institutions embody the 'rules of the game' in the economy and society (North, 1990). Rules and conventions of behaviour can be both formal and informal (the definition is explored further later) while organizations are the formal structures created to pursue an explicit purpose. They can be viewed as the actors or players in the system (Edquist 1997; Edquist 2006).

Successful development often implies parallel changes in institutions and organizations to support desired social and economic transformation. Most Latin American countries have emphatically embraced the pursuit of development in their political discourse and policy agendas. Both public and private sector decision-makers often envision development as a process of 'upgrading' and 'catching up,'[1] and as such, subject to changing policy objectives and outcomes over time. However, support for institutional change has been more ambiguous, especially where political and economic elites (often represented in key organizations of the public and private sectors) have been wary of losing status and influence as a consequence.

Both development and institutional change are inherently political processes. If one accepts that institutions are shaped by (previously prevailing) ideas and

[1] 'Up-grading' in the sense of producing goods and services with increasing value added and sustained productivity growth in a context of greater domestic linkages, as well as international competitiveness; 'catching-up' in the sense of getting closer to the development, technological, and income standards of the advanced economies and/or high-income countries.

Mahrukh Doctor, *Institutional Challenges, the Middle-Income Trap, and the Pursuit of Global Economic Integration in Latin America* In: *Innovation, Competitiveness, and Development in Latin America.* Edited by: Edmund Amann and Paulo N. Figueiredo, Oxford University Press. © Oxford University Press 2024. DOI: 10.1093/oso/9780197648070.003.0002

interests, then institutional change (whether abrupt or incremental) is shaped by evolving preferences with respect to ideas and interests. Moreover, institutional change does not occur from a *tabula rasa* starting point. If institutions are seen to reflect past and ongoing power relations, then understanding the prospects for institutional change benefits from analysing coalition formation and mobilization capacity of the relevant organizations or actors. Thus, examining both structural factors inhibiting institutional change and opportunities for agency within existing institutions and organizations is key to understanding the challenges ahead for Latin America.

Intriguingly, the academic literature has long focused on studying successes and failures of development policies in Latin America. However, it has not dedicated equal effort to understanding the challenges of institutional modernization in the region. When Latin American institutions are studied, the focus tends to be on institutional deficiencies or failures (Brinks, Levitsky, and Murillo, 2019). However, my research shows that at the heart of many of the development problems in Latin America lies the difficulty of not just building institutions conducive to inclusive and sustainable development, but actually overcoming the stubborn persistence and stickiness of those that block development, innovation, and competitive integration (Doctor 2017). The stickiness of institutions also exposes their different purposes: not just reducing transaction costs, improving the business climate, or enhancing development outcomes; but instead supporting the extraction of rents, protecting power and entrenching privileges of the few, and inhibiting the participation and voice of others.

The main puzzle this chapter addresses concerns how and why institutions have posed an obstacle to implementing policies that support innovation and the competitive integration of Latin America into the global economy. It presents an overview of the impediments to institutional change at the heart of the challenges of development, and a lens through which to understand these challenges. After this introduction (2.1), the chapter divides into the following sections: 2.2, an overview of regional economic performance with a focus on levels of integration into the global economy and innovation efforts to support competitive integration; 2.3, evolving approaches to development policy; 2.4, theories of institutional change, with a focus on the challenges facing the region; 2.5, issues related to developing institutions that foster innovation and competitive integration; and 2.6, some lessons for escaping the middle-income trap.

2.2. Overview of Regional Economic Performance

Over the past four decades, economic indicators across the board confirm that Latin America has failed to close the development gap with advanced high-income economies. Latin America typically performs poorly in the various global rankings that measure economic competitiveness and performance, such as the Global Competitiveness Report, the Global Innovation Index, and the World Bank's Doing Business Report.[2] Unsurprisingly, there is a palpable sense of increasing frustration with the region's underperformance. Economists argue that many of the larger economies in the region (Argentina, Brazil, Chile,[3] Colombia, Mexico, and Peru) seem to have fallen into a middle-income trap. Adopting a comparative political economy approach this chapter seeks to provide additional understanding of the dilemmas faced by policymakers in climbing out of it.

One of the most outstanding features of the region is the high level of income inequality and concentration of wealth (Sanchez-Ancochea 2020; Thorpe 1998). Strikingly, many of the economies considered to be stuck in the middle-income trap have very high Gini coefficients, as well as considerable issues of sociopolitical marginalization experienced by their populations. The commodity boom might have briefly raised growth rates in the region, but it also exacerbated difficulties related to improving both enterprise productivity and social inclusion (Foxley and Stallings 2016). As Doner and Schneider (2016) point out, inequality makes politics more fractious and discordant, increasing the likelihood of elite capture, clientelism, and populism. As discussed later, these features also make institutional change for innovation and inclusion more difficult to implement and manage.

Although the region is well integrated into global markets, mainly as a commodity supplier, it has a more modest presence as an exporter of manufactured goods and services, especially in high-tech segments. Trade in Latin America and the Caribbean (LAC) represents a relatively low percentage of gross domestic product (GDP) (at around 45% since the global financial crisis in 2009). It is highest in Mexico (78.2% in 2020), followed by Costa Rica (61.3%) and Chile (57.8%), and only 32.4% in the region's largest economy, Brazil (World Bank 2022).

The region performs poorly when considering participation in global value chains (GVC). Chile has the strongest GVC links (52% of its gross exports), followed by Mexico (47%) and Costa Rica (45%) (Cadestin, Gourdon, and Kowalski 2016, p. 11; also see Blyde and Trachtenberg 2020). Enterprise upgrading to better compete has been affected not only by firm-specific factors

[2] Although there may be some methodological questions related to these rankings, the point here is that they show a broad picture of general and relative underperformance of the region.

[3] Note, although Chile is listed as a high-income country, it still has high levels of income inequality and some 30% of its population are economically vulnerable. According to the World Bank (2021, n.p.), 'the existing policy framework has been insufficient to continue fostering productivity growth and economic diversification . . .'. In effect, it still exhibits features of the middle-income trap.

and actions, but also by the environment within which they operate, including the pattern of value chain governance, efficiency of public-private coordination, trade regimes, intellectual property rights and innovation policy, and availability of skilled personnel (Pietrobelli and Rabelotti 2006).

The region also underperforms in terms of various science, technology, and innovation (STI) indicators. Research and development (R&D) spending is very low in the region—only 0.56% of total regional GDP in 2019, down from 0.65% in 2013 (ECLAC, 2022). Brazil's R&D spending, at 1.16% of GDP, is the highest in the region, and it accounts for 62% of total Latin American R&D spending (Brazil, Cuba, and Uruguay were the only economies with R&D spending over 0.5% of GDP in 2019). Also, most R&D spending is undertaken by public-sector organizations and public universities, with the private sector rarely contributing even a third of the total. The region has an average of 1.21 researchers per 1,000 population (Argentina was highest at 3/1,000), with a positive feature being that 46% of researchers are women (the global average is 28%). In terms of research outputs, the region's participation in global scientific publications rose from 3.85% in 2009 to 5.02% in 2019, but the share of LAC residents in global patents was only 1.6% (ECLAC, 2022, pp. 25–27). Four Latin American universities feature among the top ten from middle- and low-income countries in the Quacquarelli Symonds university rankings (QS, 2019).[4]

According to the Global Innovation Index (WIPO, 2021), not a single Latin American economy features in the top quartile of its ranking (132 economies were assessed). The best in the region were Chile (53rd), Mexico (55th), Costa Rica (56th), and Brazil (57th). Chile and Mexico were the only two countries to score above the regional average on all six pillars of the index. As Barceló and Higuera-Cota (2019) point out, efficiency of innovation management is a key challenge, especially the need to improve market functioning (competition, credit, and investment), as well as increasing knowledge absorption capacity (both human capital formation and institutional aspects).

The Economic Commission for Latin America and the Caribbean (ECLAC) noted that the COVID-19 pandemic hit the region's economies hard in 2020 (regional GDP contracted 6.8%, export earnings fell 13%, 2.7 million businesses closed, and poverty increased by 22 million to 209 million (i.e. 33% of regional population) (ECLAC, 2022). The organization argues that one of the positive outcomes of the pandemic was a greater appreciation for the importance of STI polices in achieving the United Nations' Agenda 2030/the Sustainable Development Goals, and an elevated inclination to formulate more ambitious STI strategies. However, increasing capacity to formulate and manage

[4] University of Buenos Aires (overall 74th), National Autonomous University of Mexico (103), University of Sao Paulo (116), and Monterrey Institute of Technology (158).

STI policies will require more coordination among stakeholders (government, academia, private sector, and civil society) and more effective institutional arrangements (ECLAC, 2022, p. 13).

2.3. Evolving Approaches to Development

The region has been through significant shifts in its approach to development from the latter half of the twentieth century to the COVID-19 pandemic. During those seven decades, it went from reliance on commodity exports to pay for its industrial imports to import substitution industrialization (ISI), to export-oriented growth; from state-led development to market-oriented reforms to neo-structural 'new developmentalism'; from structural adjustment to sustainable development; and from economically-focused measures to more inclusive and socially-focused policies for development. There is a rich academic literature analysing these processes (Amann, Azzoni, and Baer 2018; Birdsal, de la Torre, and Calceido 2010; Bresser Pereira, 2016; Evans, 1979; Foxley and Stallings, 2016; Huber and Stephens, 2012; Kingstone, 2018; Leiva, 2008; Petras and Veltmeyer, 2014; Sicsú, Paula, and Michel, 2007; Thorpe, 1998; Weyland, 2004).

The early stages of ISI had contributed to creating a diversified industrial sector and robust growth rates (albeit with distributive inequality) in many of the larger economics of Latin America. State developmentalism was a fundamental feature of the region's industrialization process (as it was elsewhere too), but it never achieved the ideal type of developmental state that Evans (1995) discusses in terms of 'embedded autonomy' or Kohli (2004) refers to as a 'capital-cohesive state'. In Latin America, politicians rather than technocratic bureaucracies directed development policymaking. High dependence on foreign markets, the challenges of peripheral economic dependency, and stark inequalities hampered embedding of a true developmental state (Orihuela 2019).

After some successes in industrialization and productive development, the debt crisis of the 1980s ended the state's high spending ways. This was followed by a massive restructuring of industry and deep structural reforms in the 1990s. The main feature of these two decades was a move to market-oriented Washington Consensus–prescribed policy reform. This brought about macro-economic stabilization, trade opening, and privatization, and eventually more focus on augmenting the productivity and competitiveness of enterprises.

Two main impacts of these economic reforms were: (i) the drastic narrowing of space for domestic capital and state-owned enterprise, with a concomitant rise in the influence of foreign capital; and (ii) a severe drop in public spending due to the focus on macro-economic stabilization, fiscal and monetary austerity, and balanced public accounts. The former meant the state had less control over the definition of investment strategies and decisions (many of which were now taken outside the region). Also, the division in capital ownership between domestic and foreign made it more difficult to organize business collective action. Shrinking the state often went hand in hand with shrinking state capacity. It also exacerbated economic marginalization: unlike elsewhere in the world, industrialization and urbanization did not lead to the creation of more formal jobs in the region. Rather, it resulted in a growing proportion of informal workers among the economically-active population (often well above 50%).

Even at the height of market-oriented reforms, pro-interventionist and state developmentalist elements were often represented in governments across the region. This was especially true in the case of Brazil. Here, it remained so even in the 1990s, becoming openly acknowledged policy during the Workers' Party (PT) presidencies from 2003 to 2016. Neoliberal market fundamentalism never held great appeal, and the counter discourse of neo-structuralism soon proved much more attractive in the region (Leiva 2008). The dropping of market fundamentalist approaches to development became widespread during the so-called 'Pink Tide' from the early years of the twenty-first century (e.g. see Huber and Stephens, 2012; Kapiszewski, Levitsky, and Yasher, 2021). Although policymakers recognized that ISI was exhausted and the old instruments of development policy were inadequate for dealing with the challenges of the modern knowledge-based innovation-led globalized economy, many of the outdated institutional configurations seemingly survived into the twenty-first century. Arguably, this slowed upgrading and catch-up efforts.

Two more recent approaches to development policy have gained attention in Latin America in recent years, both engaging with the issue of institutional weaknesses that inhibit good governance in the area of innovation and competitive integration into the global economy.

First, the evolutionary economics approach provides valuable insights. This notes the importance of developing a national system of innovation (NSI), which is focused on innovation, learning, and capability-building at the microeconomic level. It also emphasizes creating appropriate institutions and a role for industrial policy to foster development at the macro-economic level (Edquist, 1997; Lundvall, Johnson, Anderson, and Dalum, 2002; Nelson and Winter, 1982). The NSI involves a range of organizations, including public-sector agencies, private-sector firms, and venture capital organizations, as well as universities and research institutes. There are three main types of innovation policy instruments (regulatory; economic and financial; 'soft instruments') and the particular mix of policies applied are typically unique to the case (Borrás and Edquist, 2013). Where does the NSI literature fit amid the broader debates on development policy in Latin America? There is a striking closeness in the positions of the innovation system perspective and Latin American neo-structuralism on issues of technological change and development (see Cassiolato et al., 2005, for a comparison of themes related to development and innovation in the two literatures). Both emphasize non-economic factors, such as history, culture, and institutions, as well as position in the global hierarchy in driving technological progress and development. Both also draw out the implications of the asymmetrical character of international technological development on uneven distribution of gains from new knowledge and a growing gap between the leaders and the rest. Both understand that the role of government must change from simply being a provider and regulator to that of a coordinator and facilitator of innovation and development (Borrás and Edquist, 2013).

A second key perspective is formatted by the 'mission economy' approach (Mazzucato 2022). This argues that we need to rethink the role and capacities of government within economy and society to come up with innovative, inclusive, and sustainable solutions for the fundamental problems of contemporary capitalism (also see Mazzucato, Kattel, and Ryan-Collins, 2019). Mazzucato notes the urgent need for all stakeholders, both public and private sector, to share risks and rewards to find solutions to the most 'wicked' societal problems. She argues that success entails innovation and investment being directed in practical mission-oriented ways and 'also truly confronting the "ways of doing things" that currently exist in government' (Mazzucato 2020, p. 1).

The last point reflects the importance of addressing institutional configurations and institutionalized practices that might hamper upgrading and catching up. The mission economy approach also reflects the NSI approach in the importance of identifying core problems and finding a holistic approach based on a customized mix of policy instruments to resolving them. These are the type of approaches that are gradually gaining attention in Latin American policy circles. Before examining them in more detail, it is important to consider theoretical aspects and practical challenges related to institutional change.

2.4. Theories of Institutional Change

The analysis that follows applies two complementary definitions of institutions. First, institutions are 'the formal or informal procedures, routines, norms and conventions embedded in the organizational structure of the polity or political economy' (Hall and Taylor, 1996, p. 938; also see Edquist, 2006), i.e. they are the 'rules of the game' in society and the economy, also creating incentives and constraints on behaviour (North 1990). Second, political institutions refer to 'the norms that regulate the formation of binding policy decisions and the selection of the people in charge of such decisions in a polity' (Pérez-Liñán and Castañeda Angarita, 2012, p. 395). In contexts of high inequality, this often results in economic elites creating extractive institutions that secure their rents even if it undercuts programmatic politics and dilutes upgrading efforts of governments (Acemoglu and Robinson, 2012; Doner and Schneider, 2016). It can also result in 'institutionalized crime', i.e. corruption (Pontes and Anselmo, 2022). Thus, institutional arrangements should not be seen in isolation from the political setting in which they are embedded. Instead, changes in one arena could affect ongoing processes elsewhere leading to 'unintended consequences' (Thelen, 1999, pp. 382–383).

Crucially, even codified institutions retain elements of interpretation in what are 'contested settlements' (Mahoney and Thelen, 2010, p. 8). Thus, institutions relevant to political economy are not neutral or passive coordination mechanisms. They may decide the distribution of political resources, shape incentives and behaviour among state and societal actors, and create long-term historical legacies (sometimes including unintended consequences) subject to path dependencies.

In terms of types of institutional change, Latin American countries have experienced critical junctures (Collier and Collier, 1991), serial displacement (Levitsky and Murillo, 2013) as well as incremental institutional change (Mahoney and Thelen, 2010; Doctor, 2017). Given the high costs of abrupt institutional change, Lindblom (1959) argued that rational decision-making processes of political actors were likely to favour incremental institutional change. Some of these changes have been an outcome of shifting domestic coalitions around development objectives and policy reform, whereas others have been triggered by external shocks or contagion from international crises. Also, there tends to be a lag between changing exogenous conditions and a realization among agents that they must act to change institutions—what March and Olsen (1996) describe as converting history into a meander.

Historical institutionalism examines institutional development with reference to the concept of critical junctures, which are seen as 'starting points' or 'bookends' explaining relatively long periods of path-dependent institutional stability with brief phases of institutional flux where more dramatic changes with 'momentous impact' might occur (Capoccia and Keleman, 2007, p. 343). Thus, a critical juncture produces a distinct legacy in terms of throwing up new actors and reorganizing relationships in the political economy. For example, Mexico's announcement of a debt default in 1982 can be seen to have triggered a critical juncture, namely the Latin American debt crisis of the 1980s. This led to subsequent implementation of market liberalization and structural reforms. The latter can be seen as path dependent outcomes of the former, albeit not the only path that could have been taken. As Mahoney (2001) notes in his study of liberalization in Central America, critical junctures are 'choice points' where actors exercise agency. However, once a policy option/response is selected, it becomes more difficult to return to the original point.

Meanwhile, incremental forms of institutional change can be conceived of in terms of four types (Streeck and Thelen, 2005): displacement, layering, drift, and conversion. In the first two types, old rules are replaced or new ones added without removing the old, but their implementation is gradual, often due to a process of resistance/contestation. In the latter two types, there are no formal changes in the rules, but shifting conditions and interpretations, respectively, which see alterations in patterns of behaviour. For example, Chile's Open Innovation Programme in Mining was part of a broader response to the *Ley Alta* of 2015, which saw a *layering* of new responsibilities on Chile's Production Development Corporation (CORFO); similarly, the Brazilian National Development Bank (BNDES) experienced a *conversion* in its mission as it shifted the focus of its credit operations from state-owned enterprises to private enterprises in the aftermath of privatizations it led and carried out in the 1990s.

When looking at institutional change, there is often an assumption that abrupt shifts triggered by exogenous shocks lead to critical junctures that are more consequential. However, this is not necessarily the case, as pointed out by Mahoney and Thelen (2010). They argue that path-dependent lock-in is rare and that institutions often evolve incrementally and not via 'punctuated equilibria'. Instead, 'institutional change often occurs precisely when problems of rule interpretation and enforcement open up space for actors to implement rules in new ways' (Mahoney and Thelen, 2010, p. 4). Tensions arising from competition for resources or distributional consequences of reform suggest that the necessary 'ambiguous compromises' made initially might jeopardize self-perpetuating institutional stability in the longer run. In this sense, compliance with the rules becomes a variable.

Hence, many of the challenges of fostering innovation and creating an NSI in LAC economies stem from (i) shifting coalitions around institution creation, modification, or demise; (ii) issues of rule and role interpretation; as well as (iii) development-enhancing implementation and enforcement of policies. As Mahoney and Thelen (2010, pp. 12–13) point out, ambiguity in expectations regarding compliance with codified rules allows creativity and agency as well as 'slippage' and 'expansive applications'. Levitsky and Murillo (2013) go so far as to argue that non-compliance can actually enhance institutional stability in some contexts in Latin America. Here powerful veto players are often allowed to get away with ignoring rules with impunity or threaten another instance of serial replacement. In this type of stable unstable setting, where uncertainty is a certainty, long-term investment strategies based on continuous innovation and greater integration into the global economy become very difficult.

Based on the above, Mahoney and Thelen present a model for institutional change in terms of character of the political context (seen in terms of veto players and veto points) and character of the institution (seen in terms of level of discretion in interpretation and/or enforcement). Displacement is a likely strategy among change agents when they face weak veto players or few veto points. Drift and layering are more promising pathways to institutional change where there are strong veto players. Conversion normally occurs where institutions allow for high levels of discretion in interpretation and there are weak veto possibilities. Drift and conversion are easier where there are situations of bureaucratic ineptitude and weak administrative capacity. Research shows that all four types of incremental institutional change feature across the economies of LAC (as discussed in the next section). Notably, critical junctures are less likely to come into play when creating and embedding institutions that foster innovation and integration into the global economy.

Finally, who are the agents who carry out these changes? It is too simplistic to discuss them in terms of winners and losers, since most actors are involved in more than one arena or set of institutions (possibly winning in some, losing in others). It is important to identify the actors involved and the coalitions that they form in processes of institutional transformation, especially when defining their preferences and resources. It is in this context that Mahoney and Thelen (2010) name four types of change agents (note this is a role, not a fixed identity): insurrectionaries, symbionts, subversives, and opportunists. Importantly, change agents rarely work alone and often ally with either institutional supporters or challengers, depending on their aims. As their name suggests, insurrectionaries and subversives are most likely to ally with those who seek to change the status quo, whereas symbionts are more likely to support those who resist change (opportunists could swing either way, depending on what is on offer). Keeping these roles in mind, we can now turn to identifying the political and institutional conditions where institutions for innovation and competitive integration could flourish in the region.

2.5. Institutions for Innovation and Competitive Integration in Latin America

The competitive pressures of globalization paradoxically require ever more focused national efforts for economic success, including complementary non-market-based mechanisms to deal with them. The biggest shift in development thinking required of the region's governments and business is to move from conceiving of the economy as a system of production to a system of innovation.

Innovation can be defined as the transformation of new ideas and technologies into economic and social solutions. It encompasses both new products and new processes for production and delivery of goods and services. Thus, innovation should be seen as a systemic process which involves multiple actors, institutions, and inputs. From a knowledge and innovation point of view, the institutional framework is central to providing the rules of the environment within which knowledge and innovation are disseminated in an NSI. The innovation environment encompasses various aspects, including the general business environment, but also the scientific, technological, financial, and regulatory environments. These environments have interconnecting impacts, which means that coordination between them is crucial for successful innovation-led growth and development.

An NSI implies state allocation of resources based on identifying national strategic priorities and not simply responding to market demands for funding. The task is made more difficult because structural conditions in Latin America have so far discouraged the development of interactive learning spaces or of a knowledge- and innovation-driven society (Arocena and Sutz, 2000). There are also few resources tied to developing mechanisms to transfer technological innovation from research institutes/universities to the productive sector, much less to monitor its take-up by the private sector. For example, researchers in the internationally-respected Brazilian Agricultural Research Corporation (EMBRAPA) noted that their research often struggled to get transferred to practical application among agricultural sector producers (dos Santos et al., 2012).

Moreover, companies operating in the oligopolistic market conditions often found in the region have benefited from protectionist and extractive institutions that sustained rent-seeking coalitions with political elites. Such institutions stifle local competition and global competitiveness. Additionally, the hierarchical nature of capitalism in the region throws up many further challenges related to these issues (Schneider, 2013). For example, it is often linked to the lack of high-skilled labour and low levels of human capital development, as well as lax corporate governance institutions and weak capital markets and credit-related institutions.

Evidence shows that success of reform policies also strongly depends on 'fundamental state capabilities' (Ardanaz, Scartascini, and Tommasi, 2010), and the negotiating arenas (formal and informal) where key participants interact. Innovation is a policy area that involves extensive coordination across many parts of the state. This calls for institutional arrangements that facilitate coordination and strengthen capacity-building and policy management (ECLAC, 2022, p. 33). According to ECLAC, conceiving industrial policy in terms of a mission to overcome national challenges could lead to a more holistic post-pandemic transformative recovery (some positive steps already taken include Colombia's

'Mission for the Wise' and Chile's National Green Hydrogen Strategy). Let us now consider some examples of how business-state relations evolved around issues of institutional innovation and reform in Latin America and how institutional change (or lack thereof) has impacted the region's competitive integration into the global economy.

As Navarro, Benavente, and Crespi (2016) note, markets tend to generate a sub-optimal level of innovation, if left alone. This is why institutions to overcome coordination failures and asymmetric information are essential for tech-based entrepreneurship to flourish. Market-oriented reforms, such as privatization, trade liberalization, or deregulation, are not enough to boost innovation. For example, the privatization of Brazilian aircraft manufacturer EMBRAER opened opportunities for technology collaborations abroad and saw both product and process innovations, and these were the result of post-privatization management's choices and strategies. Conversely, Mexico did not experience a jump in innovation from signing the North American Free Trade Agreement (NAFTA), because NAFTA's initial '*maquila*' manufacturing model was based on cheap labour, not high technology or innovation (Rullán Rosanis and Casanova, 2016). Subsequently, Mexican competitiveness did benefit from access to North American value chains, even more so in the context of rising trade tensions between the United States and China. Following on from this, the evolutionary economics literature argues that active industrial policy measures are important in fostering innovation (e.g. tax incentives for R&D, organizing technology missions, supporting international technology collaborations, encouraging use of technology licensing, and fast-tracking entrepreneurial immigration) (Alvarez, Benavente, and Crespi 2019).

So, what are the institutions and instruments relevant to the NSI? Clearly, some can be seen as background institutions that shape the general political and economic context, whereas others directly involve instruments of innovation policy and activities. Also, institutions could be characterized in terms of their impacts—effective or detrimental—on innovation and the competitive integration of LAC into the global economy. Borrás and Edquist (2013) note that innovation institutions and instruments benefit from a holistic approach, and these can occur across different levels of government. Also, there is no optimal mix, but rather it depends on the concrete problems and bottlenecks found in a particular national context. Often new policy instruments are more difficult to get off the ground than redesigning or adapting already existing ones.

There are four types of innovation system activities, including (i) provision of knowledge inputs (R&D, education, and training); (ii) demand side activities (quality standards, public procurement); (iii) provision of innovation system constituents (organizing networking activities, creating innovation-focused organizations); and (iv) support services for innovative firms (incubation and start-up activities, financing of innovation and entrepreneurship). Some form of all these activities can be found in all the bigger economies of LAC, as discussed below. We also will see that it is not only the type, but also the quality of institutions that matters.

The cases of Brazil, Chile, and Mexico are appropriate for considering the main challenges of implementing STI policies in a context of relatively inflexible and hierarchical institutions. We will also find that whereas key actors recognize the general challenge, they can be unwilling to take the necessary action because it might reduce their power and hurt their immediate short-term interests.

2.5.1. Brazil

Here the attitudinal and structural legacies of mature relatively successful inwardly-oriented ISI policies endured well past the market reforms and monetary stabilization of the 1990s. Sometimes these legacies locked actors into inferior institutional arrangements that inhibited innovation and development. When the Workers' Party (PT) President Luiz Inácio Lula da Silva (2003–2010) first took office, he understood the tight macroeconomic constraints on his government and instead focused efforts on the microeconomy, putting in place institutions and policies that aimed to boost innovation. Although labels signalling industrial policy were still unfashionable, the focus on innovation was found to be acceptable. Hence, the two main policy statements emphasized innovation, technology, and productivity: the *Política Industrial, Tecnológica e de Comércio Exterior* (Policy for Industry, Technology and Foreign Trade, PITCE) announced in November 2003 and the *Plano de Desenvolvimento da Produção* (Production Development Plan, PDP) announced in May 2008. They were complemented with two key pieces of legislation: *Lei de Inovação* (Innovation Law; Law 10,973/2004) and the *Lei do Bem* (The Good Law; Law 11,196/2005). The latter incentivized investment in STI and provided tax benefits and other support to encourage business innovation to increase productivity and competitiveness. These policies were backed by public financing from mainly BNDES and the Funding Authority for Studies and Projects (FINEP). During the Lula years, institutional support for innovation received strong government backing, and inter-agency coordination improved. Although the policy statements and legal instruments were new, they often made use of layering and conversion forms of institutional change to get early results (e.g. the shifting focus of BNDES and FINEP financing from public to private sector projects, as well as boosting funding and capabilities in university-led R&D).

The PT governments were well aware of the need to engage potential veto players constructively to win business backing. Various consultative mechanisms and bodies were set up to create supportive coalitions around productivity- and competitiveness-enhancing objectives. Two key new state organs, the *Conselho Nacional de Desenvolvimento Industrial* (National Industrial Development Council, CNDI) and the *Conselho de Desenvolvimento Economico e Social* (Economic and Social Development Council, CDES) were specifically set up to institutionalize arenas of public-private consultation on economic matters (Doctor, 2007). In addition, the *Agência Brasileira de Desenvolvimento Industrial* (Brazilian Industrial Development Agency, ABDI) worked towards better coordination between government, business, and regional trade partners. The ABDI and CNDI were particularly important in providing the necessary strategic overview and inter-bureaucratic coordination, as well as establishing links within business and civil society.

With respect to identifying strategic options (software, semi-conductors, capital goods, and pharmaceuticals) and key technologies of the future (biotechnology, nano-technology, renewable energy), the PITCE tried to avoid the past industrial policy practice of targeting specific firms and/or picking winners. The government recognized the need to concentrate efforts on sectors that were knowledge intensive and/or could generate valuable spillovers into others of importance to economic growth and citizen welfare. For example, the capital goods and information technology sectors had clear links to infrastructure (policies for energy, logistics, telecommunications, etc.). Similarly, pharmaceuticals had important links with health policy. EMBRAPA was key to fostering innovation in and the competitiveness of Brazilian agricultural sector exports. All the same, many research institutes linked to these sectors often were not driven by market demand for their research and technological innovations, and hence often found low interest in commercialization of their ideas and innovations (e.g. dos Santos et al., 2012, found that for EMBRAPA Agrobiology about 40% of research demands originated in the government/public sector and only 9.1% from the market/private sector).

Brazilian business associations also took up the call for developing an NSI and encouraging technological upgrading and competitive integration; for example, the National Confederation of Industry (CNI) periodically publishes a report comparing Brazil to some 17 other economies in terms of various measures of competitiveness (see CNI, 2020). However, it would be erroneous to think that innovation and an effective NSI were a purely positive sum game. An innovation-driven industrial strategy could actually destroy some skills and competencies, aggravate income polarization and employment problems in the short and medium term, and redistribute power in ways that may not be perceived as equitable by the market and/or society.

Brazil seemed to have found an attractive niche for active intervention in the area of technology development and innovation in the first decade of the twenty-first century (Diniz, 2011). It also seemed to benefit from a history/institutional legacy of deliberative councils (Schneider, 2010). However, both policies and councils often suffered from funding difficulties, personnel deficiencies, and institutional coordination issues. It left them vulnerable to charges of too much rhetoric, insufficient action, and paltry results. Also, given continuing low investment in R&D, business remained far from convinced about adopting a long-term productivity and innovation-led approach. Their rather instrumental engagement in these councils and innovation-focused policies meant that once recession hit Brazil in late 2014, the many efforts towards developing a stable NSI took a backseat or were completely abandoned. Nonetheless, in the run-up to the 2018 elections, the CNI (2018) published its wish-list agenda for the next government. As usual, innovation, education and training, infrastructure, and competitiveness were issues that were raised in the document, but there was also emphasis on environmental issues and sustainable development.

Here again, the state should have had a central role in minimizing the deleterious effects of these problems. However, this would require it to strengthen its institutional presence and capabilities for which there seemed neither appetite nor resources once recession hit Brazil. Moreover, entrepreneurs and enterprise managers had failed to do their part in moving towards a technological innovation-inspired strategy in the boom years. It is the short-termism (of both political and economic actors) and the far from embedded nature of public-private coordination on STI issues that lie at the heart of the institutional challenges facing innovation and productivity rises in Brazil (and more widely in the region too).

2.5.2. Chile

While Chile had a head-start in implementing neoliberal reforms, this (perhaps expectedly) hampered it in developing institutions with a mindset of engaging in industrial policy. Despite its relative prosperity, Chile's R&D spending and innovation profile have not fared better than elsewhere in Latin America. In fact, R&D spending has remained uncomfortably stable, at a low 0.4% of GDP, for decades (Alvarez et al., 2019). Also, Chile has lagged in taking advantage of its competitive and dominant position in resource-based export sectors, such as copper, to develop backward and/or forward value chains. For example, it is only recently that a local mining goods and services industry is starting to take shape. The first move here came from the private mining company BHP, when it set up the World Class Supplier Program in 2008 (see Anzolin, 2021, for details). Only afterwards did the long-standing *Fondacion Chile* (Chile Foundation) and CORFO become involved in the project. The aim here was to foster innovation and exports by encouraging spin-off companies to develop local mining services and equipment suppliers. The initial format of the programme left all the risk to the small firms. In 2017 a revised version with state support required more commitment (and risk-taking) from the big mining companies. This initiative became the Open Innovation Program in Mining, which also received additional support from CORFO. Subsequently, the Mining and Development Commission of Chile noted that its objective was to create 150 local suppliers in the mining sector and exports of US$10 billion by 2035 (Anzolin, 2021). Chile's innovation agency, Innova, is also active in supporting other initiatives, such as 'Start Up Chile' to fast-track immigration for those bringing know-how and boosting the domestic entrepreneurial culture.

Another bottleneck has been the shortage of skilled human resources, and it was clear that more needed to be done to boost supply of not only specific human capital development courses at university level, but also worker vocational training. A Mining Skills Council was set up, and a general review of education policies with the aim of supporting national development needs has remained high on the government agenda.

As such, the Chilean case shows the importance of not just designing and implementing human-resource-related policies, but also wider complementary policies related to sector regulation, sustainability and green growth, R&D support, innovation financing, and inclusive access to technical and higher education. It also points to the importance of distributional issues in the wider economy, not least the coalitions of power that block a root-and-branch reform of both formal and informal institutions that need to be in place to build up the NSI. Chile's efforts to write a new constitution could be viewed as a step in the right direction.

2.5.3. Mexico

Government and business leaders have shown growing awareness of the importance of innovation to further Mexican competitiveness, as well as successful integration into GVCs. R&D spending has remained stubbornly low at around 0.5% of GDP. After the launch of Mexico's neoliberal reform programmes in the 1980s and regional integration efforts in the 1990s, the National Council for Science and Technology (CONACYT) organized efforts at boosting innovation and the knowledge economy in Mexico. Although CONACYT was created in 1970, its modern iteration emerged after a restructuring in 2002 as part of the new Science and Technology Law. It also set up a National Conference on Science and Technology, which includes representatives of state governments working alongside CONACYT. The latter is also involved in supporting a number of research centres and has prioritized graduate programmes in engineering, science, manufacturing, and construction. In 2013, it helped launch the Mexican Energy Innovation Centres (CEMIE) for R&D in bio-energy, geo-thermal, solar, and wind energy.

In 2012, in recognition of the importance of boosting innovation, Mexico launched a 25-year Special Programme for STI (PECiTI). At the time, only 5% of Mexican businesses conducted any R&D activity. PECiTI is updated every three years to reflect evolving conditions in global and local markets. Run in four phases, it identified six main strategies for STI contributing to Mexico's social and economic development objectives, including raising R&D spending to 1% of GDP, improving human capital formation, better links between stakeholders in the NSI both national and local (see Rullán Rosanis and Casanova, 2016. for more details). The programme is presented as a horizontal industrial policy, although biosecurity is the one area that gets special mention.

Crucially, Mexico's most influential business association, the *Consejo Mexicano de Hombres de Negocios* (Mexican Council of Businessmen, CMHN), was made up of the top businesspeople representing national industry, but with no representation of the many foreign investors operating in the country. The role of CMHN in policymaking is debated in the literature (Schneider 2004), but undoubtedly their connection to government, both individually and collectively, was central to ensuring only incremental institutional change in the orientation of economic policymaking. The fact that it did not have representatives of transnational corporations (TNC) meant the exclusion of the very firms most likely to create backward and forward linkages for Mexican production in GVCs. At the other end of the spectrum was the need to foster innovation in small and medium enterprises (SMEs), including potential suppliers to the TNCs. Governments increasingly recognized that local efforts fostering innovation for social inclusion and targeting SMEs were essential ingredients for success (e.g. the Innovation Incentive Programme for SMEs (PEI).

Mexico has gradually created a science and technology platform based on setting up public agencies specialized in R&D, formation of scientific communities and research centres, political institutions to coordinate and promote an NSI, legislation and regulatory structures that boost private-sector STI investments. All the same, Mexico has been extremely slow in managing to boost private-sector R&D efforts in collaboration with universities, leaving the nascent NSI rather lopsided. It has also much to do to establish conditions where R&D is converted into commercial applications (Feria and Hidalgo 2008), not to mention creating more good-quality jobs that could support the economy's emergence from the middle-income trap.

The empirical details of the three cases allow a comparison of the institutional features of Latin American innovation systems. Typically, Latin American economies take a national level and top-down approach to setting STI policies, even though research institutes might be territorially dispersed, and education and training are often in the hands of sub-national levels of government. The evidence also suggests that the region's governments are eager to develop a culture of innovation and competitive integration into the global economy with all having various STI policies to support these aims. Although they adopt the language of a 'mission approach', institutional change in STI policy has tended to be incremental, with layering and conversion featuring heavily. Also, after years of neoliberal market prescriptions being hammered home, many governments remain wary about anything that could be labelled 'industrial policy'. Overcoming this mindset (partly due to a crude understanding about the NSI approach itself) is one of the biggest challenges related to innovation in the region.

Latin American economies show heavy reliance on public-sector resources (finance and personnel) for generating technological advances, even in a context of restricted or dwindling fiscal space. Public policies related to tax, intellectual property, research infrastructure, human resources, and so on, as well as bureaucratic inefficiency in implementing these policies, often are noted as weaknesses across the region. Official reports and the academic literature also suggest that problems often arise in policy execution—not just due to weak government coordination and follow-up on policies, but also due to the impacts of institutions that are harmful for successful innovation, most notably corruption (sometimes even referred to as 'institutionalized crime') as well as fluid interpretation of the law (often benefiting vested interests and/or potential veto players).

The region's firms also share many features with respect to innovation. Oligopolistic market structures, strong presence of TNCs in key sectors, a short-term mindset informed by a history of economic volatility, as well as low business confidence, also hinder firms from committing resources to investment in R&D and innovation. Extractive institutions that favour rent-seeking behaviour and informal particularistic access to the state further limit incentives for innovation. The low uptake of publicly funded research and technological development is a puzzling feature that repeatedly shows up across LAC, where there seems to be little coordination between business innovation needs and university researchers' efforts and outputs. The triple helix discussed in the NSI literature rarely consolidates in the region. Other chapters in this volume discuss various country case studies in more detail.

2.6. Conclusions

This chapter has called attention to the significance of institutional failures and how related issues also feed into the middle-income trap. Perhaps most important is the inadequate level of education and human capital formation, with a special focus on STI-related areas. Latin America's focus on natural-resource-based integration into the global economy, which requires relatively few high-skilled workers, has in some cases discouraged investing in human capital development. The region's over-reliance on investment from TNCs for developing higher-tech production has seen national innovation-led activities given relatively low priority, which further reduced opportunities for higher skilled (and higher paying) jobs. The elevated levels of income inequality and minimal level of social cohesion have meant that institutions that foster inclusive development policy, although urgently needed, take a back seat in the minds of political and economic elites.

The analysis also pointed to the issue of how institutional frameworks set up for conditions of inwardly-oriented development and pre-globalization patterns of international trade are not conducive to managing participation in an innovation-driven and knowledge-intensive global economy. Competitive integration into global markets is most likely to drive improved outcomes in terms of rising productivity, income, and standards of living, and eventually to more inclusive forms of social and political engagement. However, this requires sustained investment in human capital formation, as well as public-private coordination around institutions and policies that support good governance. Most multilateral development agencies pay little attention to cleavages in the business community (foreign-owned vs. domestic-owned; large conglomerates vs. SMEs), but these are key to understanding the potential for creation of coalitions that might support the necessary institutional change and policy reforms (Doner and Schneider, 2016). The fragmented production structure also makes it difficult to create social cohesion around collective development objectives, including policies that could help LAC emerge from the middle-income trap.

Where political elites face polarized societal actors (whether divided labour or divided business sectors), they are much more able to block processes of institutional reform. It also makes it easier to entrench rent-seeking and draw on their long-standing privileges. However, their powers do not extend to control over the direction of institutional change. On the one hand, these elites struggle to keep up with the shifting coalitions and distributional negotiating strategies of often polarized societal actors. On the other hand, those favouring institutional modernization might find that relying on modes of institutional change that do not directly challenge the status quo supporters might be the only way forward. However, relying on layering, drift, and conversion in the absence of wholesale systemic structural reform can be a highly resource-consuming (time and money) way of achieving higher productivity, better innovation, and deeper global economic integration outcomes. The extensive negotiations required to win over opponents, but also ambivalent or opportunist actors, often delay change and jeopardize more inclusive and sustainable development outcomes. They also contribute to holding economies captive in the middle-income trap.

References

Acemoglu, D., and Robinson, J. 2012. *Why Nations Fail: The Origins of Power, Prosperity and Poverty*. New York: Crown Books.

Alvarez, R., Benavente, J. M., and Crespi, G. 2019. 'Innovation in the Global Economy: Opening-Up Latin American Innovation Systems', *IDB Discussion Paper*, No. IDB-DP-729. Washington, DC: Inter-American Development Bank.

Amann, E., Azzioni, C., and Baer, W. 2018. *The Oxford Handbook of the Brazilian Economy*. Oxford: Oxford University Press.

Anzolin, G. 2021. 'Productive Development Policies in the Mining Value Chain: Policy Opportunity and Alignment', *IDB Discussion Paper*, No. IDB-D-918. Washington, DC: Inter-American Development Bank.

Ardanez, M., Scartascini, C., and Tommasi, M. 2010. 'Political Institutions, Policy-Making and Economic Policy in Latin America', *IDB Working Paper Series*, No. IDB-WP-158. Washington, DC: Inter-American Development Bank.

Arocena, R., and Sutz, J. 2000. 'Interactive Learning Spaces and Development Policy in Latin America', *DRUID Working Paper*, No. 00-13. Copenhagen: Danish Research Unit for Industrial Dynamics.

Barceló, J. G. A., and Higuera-Cota, F. 2019. 'Challenges in Innovation Management in LAC: An Efficiency Analysis', *CEPAL Review* 127, 7–23.

Birdsall, N., de la Torre, A., and Valencia Calceido, F. 2010. 'The Washington Consensus: Assessing a "Damaged Brand"', in J. A. Ocampo and J. Ros, eds., *Oxford Handbook of Latin American Economics*. Oxford: Oxford University Press, 79–107.

Blyde, J., and Trachtenberg, D. 2020. 'Global Value Chains and Latin America: A Technical Note', *IDB Technical Note*, No. IDB-TN-1853. Washington, DC: Inter-American Development Bank.

Borrás, S., and Edquist, C. 2013. 'The Choice of Innovation Policy Instruments', *Technological Forecasting and Social Change*, 80(8), 1513–1522.

Bresser Pereira, L. C. 2016. *The Political Construction of Brazil: Society, Economy and State since Independence*. Boulder, CO: Lynne Rienner Publishers.

Brinks, D., Steven L., and Victoria Murillo, M. 2019. *Understanding Institutional Weakness: Power and Design in Latin American Institutions*. Cambridge Elements. Cambridge: Cambridge University Press.

Cadestin, C., Julien Gourdon, J., and Kowalski, P. 2016. 'Participation in Global Value Chains in Latin America: Implications for Trade and Trade-Related Policy', *OECD Trade Policy Papers*, No. 192. Paris: OECD Publishing.

Capoccia, G., and Keleman, D. 2007. 'The Study of Critical Junctures: Theory, Narratives and Counterfactuals in Historical Institutionalism', *World Politics*, 59(3), 341–369.

Cassiolato, J., Guimarães, V., Peixoto, F., and Lastres, H. 2005. *Innovation Systems and Development: What Can We Learn from the Latin American Experience?* Paper for III Globelics Conference, Pretoria.

CNI. 2018. *Agenda da indústria para o Poder Executivo 2018*. Brasilia: Confederação Nacional da Indústria.

CNI. 2020. *The Brazilian Competitiveness Report 2019–2020*. Brasilia: Confederação Nacional da Indústria.

Collier, P., and Berens Collier, R. 1991. *Shaping the Political Arena*. Princeton, NJ: Princeton University Press.

Diniz, E. 2011. 'Democracy, State and Industry: Continuity and Change between the Cardoso and Lula Administrations', *Latin American Perspectives*, 38(3), 59–77.

Doctor, M. 2017. *Business-State Relations in Brazil: Challenges of the Port Reform Lobby*. New York: Routledge.

Doner, R., and Schneider, B. R. 2016. 'The Middle-Income Trap: More Politics than Economics', *World Politics*, 68(4), 608–644.

Dos Santos, J. A. M., Mauro C. Tavares M. C., de Vasconcelos, M. C. R. L., and Afonso, T. 2012. 'O processo de inovação tecnológica na Embrapa e na Embrapa Agrobiologia: Desafios e perspectivas', *Perspectivas em Ciencia da Informação*, 17(4), 175–194. https://doi.org/10.1590/S1413-99362012000400011.

ECLAC. 2022. *Innovation for Development: The Key to a Transformative Recovery in Latin America and the Caribbean*. Santiago: UN Publications.

Edquist, C. 1997. *Systems of Innovation: Technologies, Institutions and Organisations*. London: Pinter.

Edquist, C. 2006. 'Systems of Innovation: Perspectives and Challenges', in J. Fagerberg and D. Mowrey, eds., *The Oxford Handbook of Innovation*. Oxford: Oxford University Press, 182–209.

Evans, P. 1979. *Dependent Development: The Alliance of Multinational, State and Local Capital in Brazil*. Princeton, NJ: Princeton University Press.

Evans, P. 1995. *Embedded Autonomy: States and Industrial Transformation*. Princeton, NJ: Princeton University Press.

Feria, V., and Hidalgo, A. 2008. 'Towards a National Innovation System in México Based on Knowledge', *The International Journal of Technology, Knowledge And Society*, 4, 225–233.

Foxley, A., and Stallings, B., eds. 2016. *Innovation and Inclusion in Latin America: Strategies to Avoid the Middle-Income Trap*. Abingdon, UK: Palgrave Macmillan.

Hall, P., and Taylor, R. 1996. 'Political Science and the Three New Institutionalisms', *Political Studies*, 44(4), 936–957.

Huber, E., and Stephens, J. 2012. *Democracy and the Left: Social Policy and Inequality in Latin America*. Chicago: University of Chicago Press.

Kapiszewski, D., Levitsky, S., and Yasher, D., eds. 2021. *The Inclusionary Turn in Latin American Politics*. Cambridge: Cambridge University Press.

Kingstone, P. 2018. *The Political Economy of Latin America: Reflections on Neoliberalism and Development after the Commodity Boom*, 2nd edition. New York: Routledge.

Kohli, A. 2004. *State-Directed Development: Political Power and Industrialization in the Global Periphery*. Cambridge: Cambridge University Press.

Leiva, F. 2008. 'Toward a Critique of Latin American Neo-Structuralism', *Latin American Politics and Society*, 50(4), 1–25.

Levitsky, S., and Murillo, M. V. 2013. 'Lessons from Latin America: Building Institutions on Weak Foundations', *Journal of Democracy*, 24(2), 93–107.

Lindblom, Charles E. 1959. 'The Science of "Muddling Through"', *Public Administration Review*, 19(2), 79–88. *JSTOR*, https://doi.org/10.2307/973677. Accessed 20 Sept. 2023.

Lundvall, B., Johnson, B., Anderson, E. S., and Dalum, B. 2002. 'National Systems of Production, Innovation and Competence Building', *Research Policy*, 31, 213–231.

Mahoney, J. 2001. *The Legacies of Liberalism: Path Dependence and Political Regimes in Central America*. Baltimore, MD: Johns Hopkins University Press.

Mahoney, J., and Thelen, K. 2010. 'A Theory of Gradual Institutional Change', in J. Mahoney and K. Thelen, eds., *Explaining Institutional Change: Ambiguity, Agency, and Power*. Cambridge: Cambridge University Press, 1–37.

March, J., and Olsen, J. 1996. 'Institutional Perspectives on Political Institutions', *Governance*, 9(3), 247–264.

Mazzucato, M. 2020. 'Mission Oriented Innovation and Industrial Policy', *Opinion Piece, World Trade Report 2020*. Geneva: World Trade Organisation, 101.

Mazzucato, M. 2022. *Mission Economy: A Moonshot Guide to Changing Capitalism*. London: Penguin.

Mazzucato M., Rainer K., and Josh Ryan-Collins. 2020. 'Challenge-Driven Innovation Policy: Towards a New Policy Toolkit', *Journal of Industry, Competition and Trade*, 20(2), 421–437, Springer June.

Mendonça de Barros, J., and Goldenstein, L. 1997. 'Avaliação do proceso de reestruturação industrial brasileiro', *Revista de Economia Política*, 17(2), 11–31.

Navarro, J. C., Benevente, J. M., and Crespi, G. 2016. *The New Imperative of Innovation: Policy Perspectives for Latin America and the Caribbean*, IDB Monograph, IDB-MG-396. Washington, DC: Inter-American Development Bank.

Nelson, R., and Winter, S. 1982. *An Evolutionary Theory of Economic Change*. Cambridge, MA: Harvard University Press.

North, D. 1990. *Institutions, Institutional Change and Economic Performance*. Cambridge: Cambridge University Press.

Orihuela, J. C. 2019. 'The Political Economy of the Developmental State in Latin America', in Harry E. Vanden and Gary Prevost, eds., *Oxford Research Encyclopaedia in Politics: Latin America*. Oxford: Oxford University Press, 1–25.

Pérez-Liñán, A., and Castañeda Angarita, N. 2012. 'Institutionalism', in P. Kingstone and D. Yasher, eds., *Routledge Handbook of Latin American Politics*. New York: Routledge, 395–406.

Petras, J., and Veltmeyer, H. 2014. *The New Extractivism: A Post-Neoliberal Development Model or Imperialism of the Twenty-First Century?* London: Zed Books.

Pietrobelli, C., and Rabelotti, R., eds. 2006. *Upgrading to Compete: Global Value Chains, Clusters and SMEs in Latin America*. Washington, DC: Inter-American Development Bank.

Pontes, J., and Anselmo, M. 2022. *Operation Car Wash: Brazil's Institutionalised Crime and the Inside Story of the Biggest Corruption Scandal in History*. London: Bloomsbury. Translated by Anthony Doyle.

Sanchez-Ancochea, D. 2020. *The Costs of Inequality in Latin America: Lessons and Warnings for the Rest of the World*. London: I. B. mTaurus.

Schneider, B. R. 2004. *Business Politics and the State in Twentieth-Century Latin America*. Cambridge: Cambridge University Press.

Schneider, B. R. 2010. *Business-Government Interaction in Policy Councils in Latin America: Cheap Talk, Expensive Exchanges, or Collaborative Learning?* Working Paper IDB-WP-167. Washington, DC: Inter-American Development Bank.

Schneider, B. R. 2013. *Hierarchical Capitalism in Latin America: Business, Labor, and the Challenges of Equitable Development*. Cambridge: Cambridge University Press.

Sicsú, J., de Paula, L. F., and Michel, R. 2007. 'Por que novo-desenvolvimento?', *Revista de Economia Política*, 27(4), 507–524.

Streeck, W., and Thelen, K. 2005. *Beyond Continuity: Institutional Change in Advanced Political Economies*. Oxford: Oxford University Press.

Thelen, K. 1999. 'Historical Institutionalism in Comparative Politics', *American Review of Political Science*, 2, 369–404.

Thorpe, R. 1998. *Progress, Poverty and Exclusion: An Economic History of Latin America in the Twentieth Century*. Oxford: Oxford University Press.

Weyland, K. 2004. *The Politics of Market Reform in Fragile Democracies*. Princeton, NJ: Princeton University Press.

WIPO. 2021, 'Indicator Rankings and Analysis', in *Global Innovation Index 2021*. Geneva: World Intellectual Property Organisation, https://www.globalinnovationindex.org/analysis-indicator (accessed on 6 July 2022).

World Bank. 2022. *Trade as a % of GDP, World Bank Data* (online). https://databank.worldbank.org/.

World Bank. 2021. *The World Bank in Chile: Overview*. Washington DC.https://www.worldbank.org/en/country/chile/overview#1 (accessed on 22 April 2022).

3
China and the Middle-Income Trap in Latin America
Constraints and Opportunities

Rhys Jenkins

3.1. Introduction

Latin America's development problems have in recent years often been discussed in terms of the 'middle-income trap' (Foxley and Stallings, eds., 2016; Lin and Treichel, 2012; Paus, 2014, 2020; Melguizo et al., 2017). It is argued that middle-income countries find it difficult to compete with lower-wage countries in low technology, labour-intensive sectors, while they cannot compete with more advanced economies in high-technology sectors. The causes of such a trap have been identified as an overreliance on commodity exports, low levels of industrial technological capabilities, poor infrastructure, and a lack of integration between sectors.

One of the most important economic changes in Latin America over the past two decades has been the growing presence of China, which is now the major trade partner of a number of countries in the region and has become an important source of foreign direct investment (FDI) and loans for several. China has also extended its diplomatic relations in the region, with a number of Central American and Caribbean countries switching relations from Taiwan over the past five years.

The rise of China to become the second-largest economy in the world in terms of current GDP has shifted the goal posts for the Latin American and Caribbean (LAC) countries in terms of the challenges that they face in overcoming the 'middle-income trap' (Paus, 2020). Since embarking on economic reform under Deng Xiaoping in the late 1970s, China has continuously upgraded its manufacturing industry, becoming internationally competitive in an ever-widening range of industries and investing heavily in research and development (R&D) (Jenkins, 2018, ch. 2). China has also become a major market for commodities to supply its expanding manufacturing sector with inputs and to

Rhys Jenkins, *China and the Middle-Income Trap in Latin America* In: *Innovation, Competitiveness, and Development in Latin America.* Edited by: Edmund Amann and Paulo N. Figueiredo, Oxford University Press.
 DOI: 10.1093/oso/9780197648070.003.0003

feed its more affluent population (Jenkins, 2018, ch. 3). Since the beginning of the twenty-first century, the Chinese government has encouraged Chinese firms to 'go out' through FDI and construction and engineering projects, often funded through the Chinese policy banks (Jenkins, 2018, ch. 4).

This chapter considers the implications of the growing presence of China for Latin America's prospects of breaking out of the 'middle-income trap'. The next section (section 3.2) provides a brief summary of the growth of economic relations between China and LAC, focussing on trade, bilateral FDI flows, infrastructure projects, and Chinese finance. The following section (section 3.3) considers whether Chinese involvement has reinforced the region's over-dependence on primary commodities.

One of the routes out of the 'middle-income trap' is to upgrade to higher technology and more advanced products in order to avoid competition from countries with lower wage levels. However, it has been argued that China makes this more difficult because it has itself moved into these sectors. Section 3.4 analyses the pattern of competition between China and Latin America in world markets. The rapid level of technological change in China could offer opportunities for Latin America to upgrade technologically both through integration with Chinese-led global value chains (GVCs), and by importing Chinese technology through FDI. Section 3.5 examines the evidence that such opportunities have materialized in Latin America.

Finally, it is generally recognized that poor infrastructure has been an obstacle to development in the region (Kohli, 2013). China has both the expertise in its construction companies and the finance available to undertake major infrastructure investment, as has been shown in Asia and Africa. With the extension of the Belt and Road Initiative (BRI) to Latin America in 2018, considerable expectations have been raised regarding the prospects for major Chinese infrastructure projects in the region. These offer the possibility of enabling it to take a significant step towards escaping the 'middle income trap'. Section 3.6 examines these possibilities before a conclusion is reached in section 3.7.

3.2. The Growth of Economic Relations between China and Latin America

Economic relations between China and Latin America have only become a major factor in the region's economic development since the turn of the century. Initially this was almost exclusively based on bilateral trade, but in recent years Chinese FDI and loans have become increasingly significant, and there has also been some investment by Latin American firms in China.

3.2.1. Trade Relations

Trade has played a central role in Sino-LAC economic relations. In the late 1990s total trade between China and the region was only around US$5–8 billion a year but grew rapidly in the twenty-first century to reach more than US$300 billion by 2018 (UNCTADStat). Despite a fall in the value of bilateral trade after 2018, reflecting the slowdown in growth in Latin America and the COVID-19 epidemic, China's share of LAC trade continued to rise. By 2020, a sixth of all Latin American trade was with China, up from around 2% in the mid-1990s.

As many observers have commented, the pattern of trade between China and the region is highly asymmetrical, with China's exports virtually entirely made up of manufactured goods, while almost 90% of Latin American exports to China are primary products and resource-based manufactures with limited processing (UNCTADStat). The main products which China imports from the region are soybeans, iron ore, oil, and copper, while its exports consist of a wide range of manufactured goods, including labour-intensive products such as clothing and footwear, and higher technology products such as transport equipment and machinery.

3.2.2. Chinese FDI in Latin America

Any discussion of Chinese FDI in Latin America faces difficulties in obtaining reliable information on the scale of such investment. The official Chinese statistics on outward FDI only give the immediate destination of the investment, and since so much of Chinese FDI goes through Hong Kong or tax havens such as the Cayman Islands, the British Virgin Islands, and Luxembourg, it is unclear how much ends up in Latin America. Equally, what is reported by the host countries as inward investment from China can suffer from the same problem when the investment is made through Chinese subsidiaries in third countries. A study by the Brazilian Central Bank estimated that around 90% of investment by Chinese firms in Brazil between 2010 and 2016 was made through third countries (BCB, 2018, fig. 14).

Faced with the underestimation of Chinese FDI in official statistics, there have been several estimates made on the basis of media reports and announcements of Chinese FDI in the region. These are also problematic since planned projects may not be carried out in the end, and the amounts of investment quoted may not be reliable. This approach is also biased towards large projects and tends to miss smaller investments.

Despite these caveats, it is clear that Chinese firms only began to invest on a significant scale in Latin America towards the end of the first decade of the twenty-first century. It is also clear that despite recent growth, China is far less significant for the region as a source of FDI than it is in terms of trade. It was not ranked amongst the top 10 investors in the region in 2017 according to the UNCTAD, *World Investment Report, 2019*. Even if the higher, unofficial estimates of Chinese FDI are used, China still lags a long way behind the European Union and the United States as a source of FDI for LAC (Jenkins, 2018, p. 229).

The major sectors in which Chinese firms have invested in Latin America are oil and gas, mining, and electric power. Estimates of the share of total Chinese FDI going to the manufacturing sector, despite increasing over time, remain low, accounting for less than 10% of inflows between 2010 and 2018.[1]

3.2.3. Chinese Contracts in Latin America

Another area of activity by Chinese companies in Latin America has been construction and engineering projects, which are not classified as FDI because they do not establish a permanent foreign presence in the host country. These grew rapidly from the time of the global financial crisis to 2015, although the economic slowdown in the region in the second half of the decade led to a drop in Chinese activity and the cancellation of a number of projects.[2] Despite this, Chinese firms have increased their relative significance in infrastructure in LAC in recent years. Figures for the largest 250 international contractors show that the share of Chinese firms in the region almost doubled, from 12.9% in 2014 to 23.7% five years later (ENR, 2015, p. 40; ENR, 2020, p. 40).

Energy has been the most important sector for contracts in the region, followed by transport. Between them, these account for over 80% of the total value of projects contracted between 2005 and 2019.[3] Energy accounts for more than half of the value of contracts, and the most important subsector is hydropower. The main sector for transport contracts is railways, with large deals in Venezuela and Argentina.

3.2.4. Chinese Loans to Latin America

China does not publish data on official financial flows on either a country or a regional basis, so that the only information available is based on announcements

[1] Own calculation from Dussel (2019), Tables 1 and 3.
[2] Two major high-speed rail projects were cancelled in Venezuela and Mexico.
[3] Own elaboration from *China Global Investment Tracker*.

of loans made. The Inter-American Dialogue *China-Latin America Finance Data Base* provides information on loans from the China Exim Bank and the China Development Bank to the region (available at: https://www.thedialogue.org/map_list/). It estimates that the two Chinese policy banks have lent more than $140 billion to LAC since 2005. Venezuela has been the major recipient of these loans, accounting for almost half the total, followed by Brazil, Ecuador, and Argentina.

To put this in context, China has provided the region with more official finance than either the World Bank or the Inter-American Development Bank over the period. However, in recent years new lending from China has declined, partly reflecting the economic crisis in Venezuela and the slowdown in growth in the region more generally.

3.3. China's Impact on Latin America's Dependence on Commodities

It is widely believed that one of the major obstacles preventing LAC from escaping the 'middle-income trap' has been an excessive dependence on commodity exports. As noted earlier, the bulk of Latin America's exports to China have been primary commodities, which have also been an important target for Chinese FDI in the region. The rapid growth of trade relations with China coincided with the commodity boom, to which China's growth contributed. Although the region benefitted both directly, from increased exports to China, and indirectly through the higher prices of key commodities, such as copper, iron ore, and oil, on world markets, concerns were raised over the longer-term impacts. These focussed on the 're-primarization' of Latin American exports and fears over the 'resource curse' (Rosales and Kuwayama, 2012, pp. 92–107; Su, 2017, pp. 582–586).

There were several ways in which the growth of China contributed to Latin America's increased dependence on commodity exports. First the share of primary products in the region's exports to China was higher than in the case of exports to its other major markets, the United States and the European Union, so that as the share of exports going to China increased, the share of primary products in total exports also rose (Jenkins, 2018, fig. 9.2). Second, higher commodity prices also increased the share of primary products in the value of exports and at the same time made it more profitable to produce such products for export. Finally, Latin American exporters of manufactured goods faced increased competition from China in both developed-country and regional markets, which reduced their market shares and made them more dependent on commodity exports (Jenkins, 2010, 2014; Dussel-Peters, ed.,

2016). It is not surprising therefore that the share of primary products in Latin American exports increased from just over 40% in 2001 to a peak of 57% in 2011 (UNCTADStat).

The issue of 're-primarization' has particular resonance in Latin America, where the Prebisch-Singer thesis of the deterioration of the terms of trade of primary commodity exporters was such a central part of structuralist economic thinking. Although most Latin American countries saw their terms of trade improve during the commodity boom, this could still be viewed as a temporary interruption to the long-term trend, so that concerns remained, and these were reinforced by the fall in commodity prices after 2011.

A second concern is that the increased demand for commodities from China would lead to 'Dutch disease' effects. This is associated with an appreciation of the real exchange rate, making other exports (particularly of manufactures) uncompetitive on international markets and leading to increased competition from imports. The country in Latin America where the exchange rate appreciated most between 2002 and 2011 was Brazil. Although this was partly the result of high capital inflows and other factors, increased trade with China was also a factor (Jenkins, 2015). In contrast, Chile, whose exports also benefitted from demand in China and whose terms of trade improved as much as Brazil's between 2002 and 2011, experienced far less appreciation of the exchange rate over that period,[4] reflecting its success in developing effective policies to deal with the problems generated by a commodity boom. This indicates that the effect of China on commodity exports does not necessarily lead to Dutch disease.

Overreliance on commodities is also seen as an obstacle to escaping the middle-income trap because it is believed that natural resource sectors are not as technologically dynamic as other sectors, particularly manufacturing. The view that resource-based industries do not have much potential for technological change has, however, been challenged by recent research showing significant innovation in some sectors in Latin America (Andersen et. al., 2018). A very relevant example of innovation in relation to Sino-LAC trade is the introduction of zero-tillage technology and genetically modified (GM) varieties for soybeans in Brazil and Argentina.

A final issue is the 'enclave' nature of natural resource industries, which implies a lack of inter-sectoral linkages with the local economy. This is a particular problem with the region's exports of primary products to China because the Chinese state has used various mechanisms to ensure that downstream processing of resources takes place in China. A vivid example of this is China's

[4] Whereas Brazil's real effective exchange rate appreciated by over 80% between 2002 and 2011, Chile's increased by only 12%.

imports of soybeans from Argentina. In the 1990s China promoted its own crushing industry through a variety of incentives and protectionist policies, so that imports of soybean flour virtually ended, to be replaced by imports of unprocessed soybeans (Jenkins, 2018, box 9.1).

There is clear evidence that the growth of China has contributed to an increased reliance on commodity exports in Latin America. This has accentuated the challenges that the countries of the region face in trying to escape the middle-income trap. However, it is not the case that negative ('resource curse') outcomes have been inevitable. Whether or not they occur depends on the policies both of Latin American governments and of China.

3.4. Chinese Competition and Structural Change in Manufacturing

From a structuralist perspective, a key aspect of escaping the middle-income trap is bringing about changes in the structure of the economy towards more technologically advanced manufacturing sectors (Paus, 2020). A country's international trade structure provides a good indication of the extent to which it has been successful in doing this.

One common indicator of the sophistication of a country's exports is the Export Complexity Index (ECI).[5] Latin America as a whole has performed poorly in terms of the ECI over the past two decades. Most of the countries of the region have seen their position in the rankings decline. Only Mexico and Costa Rica have shown a significant improvement. In contrast, over the same period China's export sophistication has increased dramatically, overtaking both Mexico and Brazil (see Table 3.1).

A more direct indicator of the success of a country in terms of moving into more technologically advanced sectors is its international competitiveness in different types of industries. Table 3.2 classifies the region's non-resource-based manufactured exports into low-, medium-, and high-technology products based on the classification developed by Lall (2000). It shows that Latin America has seen its international competitiveness decline in both low- and high-technology products since 2000, reflected in a fall in the region's share of world exports and a decline in the Balassa Revealed Comparative Advantage (RCA).[6] The

[5] The economic complexity of a country is calculated based on the diversity of exports a country produces and their ubiquity, or the number of countries able to produce them (and those countries' complexity) (Atlas of Economic Complexity, 2022a).

[6] The Balassa measure of RCA compares a product's share in a country's exports with that product's share in world trade. An RCA >1 indicates that a country has a comparative advantage in that product.

Table 3.1 Economic Complexity Rankings of Latin American Countries and China, 2000 and 2019

Country	2000 Rank	2019 Rank
Argentina	54	73
Brazil	26	53
Chile	65	71
Colombia	57	55
Costa Rica	70	44
Ecuador	115	117
Mexico	25	18
Peru	79	100
Uruguay	51	62
Venezuela	69	128
China	39	16

Source: Elaborated from Atlas of Economic Complexity (2022b).

Table 3.2 Latin American Competitiveness by Type of Product

	Latin America		China	
	2000	**2019**	**2000**	**2019**
Share of World Exports				
LT	5.1%	2.9%	10.8%	27.9%
MT	4.8%	5.5%	2.6%	11.8%
HT	4.0%	2.9%	3.8%	21.0%
Total*	5.7%	5.6%	3.9%	13.3%
Balassa RCA				
LT	0.89	0.52	2.77	2.10
MT	0.84	0.98	0.66	0.89
HT	0.70	0.52	0.99	1.58

* Including primary products and resource-based manufactures.
LT: Low Technology
MT: Medium Technology
HT: High Technology
RCA: Revealed Comparative Advantage
Source: Author's calculation from UNCTADStat.

region has clearly found it difficult to upgrade into more technology-intensive sectors to offset the loss of competitiveness in low-tech sectors. It was only in medium technology industries where there was an improvement in the region's competitiveness.

In contrast, China has seen its share of world exports increase in all types of manufactured products, particularly in low- and high-technology goods. China also increased its share of world exports of medium-technology products, but this is the area in which its performance is less spectacular and where LAC has performed best.

Although the decline in Latin American competitiveness and the rise in China's does not necessarily indicate a causal relationship, it does suggest that the latter has made it more difficult for the region to upgrade into high technology sectors (Gallagher and Porzecanski, 2010, ch. 4). Since intra-regional exports tend to have higher technological content than those to developed-country markets, Chinese competition within Latin America is making it even more difficult for the countries of the region to upgrade their manufactured exports (Dussel-Peters, ed., 2016).

In an early article analysing the competitive threat posed by China for Latin America, Lall and Weiss (2005) developed a matrix of competitive interactions between China and other countries in export markets. They identified two categories in which China posed a threat to Latin American exports. Those products in which China's share of the world market increased while LAC's fell were referred to as being under *direct threat*, while products where LAC's share was increasing, but at a slower rate than China's, were categorized as under *partial threat* (Lall and Weiss, 2005, table 1).

Lall and Weiss analysed trade between 1990 and 2002, covering the period leading up to China's accession to the World Trade Organization (WTO) at the end of 2001. Since 2000, China's share of world export markets has increased significantly from less than 4% to over 13%, and its share of high-technology product exports has gone up from 3.8% to 21%. Over the same period, LAC's share of high-technology exports has fallen from 4% to less than 3% (Table 3.2).

Focussing on high-technology products in the period since 2000, over four-fifths of Latin American exports were in the 'direct threat' category, where the growing market share of China was accompanied by a fall in the share of LAC exports. The remainder of the region's high-technology exports were under 'partial threat', where the region's exports have increased their share of the global market, although not as fast as China.[7] There were no high-technology products where LAC gained market share relative to China during the period. The overall

[7] Own calculation from UNCTADStat data on exports at the 3-digit SITC level.

picture in high-technology industries does support the view that Chinese competition has made it more difficult for the region to upgrade its export structure.

3.5. China and the Development of Technological Capabilities

The development of technological capabilities is central to any attempt at overcoming the middle-income trap. Although increased competition from China may be making it more difficult for Latin America to compete in high-technology industries, does the increased presence of China in the region also present an opportunity to upgrade technologically?

The potential technological impacts of China on the region can be direct or indirect. Direct impacts occur through the introduction of more advanced technologies by Chinese firms through FDI, joint ventures or licensing agreements, and the training that the labour force is given. Indirect effects involve 'spillovers' from Chinese activities either horizontally to competing firms in the same line of business, or vertically to suppliers or customers. Such 'spillovers' can be negative, leading to technological downgrading, as well as positive. Vertical spillovers have often been found when firms are integrated into GVCs.

3.5.1. Chinese Technology Transfer to Latin America

Chinese manufacturing has undergone a process of rapid technological upgrading since China joined the WTO. China is aiming to become a world leader in technological innovation. The 'Made in China 2025' plan, launched in 2015, is an ambitious effort to develop an advanced manufacturing industry based on innovative technologies (Wubbeke et al., 2016). The share of R&D in GDP in China increased from less than 1% in 2000 to over 2% by 2017. In contrast, Latin America allocates a mere 0.7% of GDP to R&D, and the only country in the region that spends more than 1% of GDP on R&D is Brazil. In most of the other countries, R&D spending accounts for less than half a per cent of GDP (ECLAC, 2018, p. 81).

Official Chinese documents identify technology transfer and R&D as important areas for cooperation between China and Latin America. China's 2016 Policy Paper refers to 'the expansion of cooperation with Latin American and Caribbean countries in high-tech fields such as information industry, civil aviation, civil nuclear industry and new energy, to build more joint laboratories, R&D centres and high-tech parks' (PRC, 2016, para 2.8), and to helping Latin American and Caribbean countries in their industrial upgrading. The China and Community of Latin American and Caribbean States (CELAC) Forum

Cooperation Plan, adopted in Beijing in 2015, also refers to increasing the transfer of technology and know-how between the two sides (CELAC, 2015).

These statements are a reflection of aspirations rather than achievements in terms of technology transfer from China to Latin America. Although China has invested heavily in R&D at home, there is little evidence that Chinese firms are transferring technology to Latin America on a significant scale. A recent report by ECLAC concluded that 'the results in terms of transferring technology, promoting research and development and creating good-quality jobs have, in most cases, fallen short of expectations' (ECLAC, 2018, p. 96). Most of the collaboration that is taking place between China and Latin America in science and technology has been at the inter-governmental level in areas such as aerospace, where there has been cooperation on satellites with Brazil and astronomical observation with Chile and Argentina.

The nature of the economic relations between China and LAC has limited the extent of technology transfer in the productive sectors. As was noted earlier, much of Chinese FDI in Latin America has been in the energy and mining sectors. A study of technology transfer between China and Brazil in the energy sector concluded that so far, the extent of transfers has been limited, despite the objectives set out in high-level agreements between the two governments (Husar and Best, 2013). There is some evidence of Chinese technology in renewable energy being transferred to Latin America (see Borregaard et al., 2017, on Chile), but Chinese companies only accounted for 2% of total investment in alternative energy in LAC between 2005 and 2017 (Salazar-Xirinachs, 2019, p. 6).

The overall picture does not suggest that China is making a significant contribution to developing technological capabilities in the industrial sector either. The fact that investment in manufacturing in the region has tended to be market-seeking and mainly in assembly activities means that it has not involved advanced technology or extensive R&D in the region. Recently some Chinese internet companies, such as Alibaba, Baidu, and Tencent, and telecommunications infrastructure firms, such as Huawei and ZTE, have entered Latin America (Guzman, 2019; ECLAC, 2021, ch. II D.3), but there are questions over the extent of technology that is transferred and the amount of real R&D that they do in the region. As a recent ECLAC report discussing Chinese technology companies' activities in the region concluded, 'In terms of scale and scope, however, these investments are minor and focus mainly on marketing or assembly activities rather than manufacturing or research and development' (ECLAC, 2021, p. 110). For example, although Huawei has an R&D centre in Mexico, it is reported that it has only 14 employees and is mainly involved in modifying software for local clients (Micheli and Carrillo, 2016, pp. 52–53).

This does not rule out the possibility that technology transfer from China will increase in the future, but past experience suggests that it will not lead to significant upgrading of technological capabilities within Latin America unless governments adopt measures of the kind that China itself has used in order to develop its own technological base.

3.5.2. Technology 'Spillovers' and Chinese-Led Value Chains

One possible way in which China could facilitate Latin America overcoming the middle-income trap would be through increased integration into Chinese-led value chains. There is an extensive literature on the links between GVCs and the development of technological capabilities (Lema et al., 2019; Morrison et al., 2008; Staritz and Whitfield, 2019), and although such integration does not automatically lead to technological upgrading, it does open up possibilities for local firms.

There are two types of integration into GVCs:

- Backward (upstream linkages), where a country uses imported inputs to produce the products that it exports
- Forward (downstream linkages), where a country's exports are used in the importing country as inputs to produce exports.

In Latin America, Mexico and Costa Rica are two examples of countries with significant backward participation in GVCs, particularly with the United States and Canada.[8] In contrast, Chile and Peru have significant forward linkages since their exports are processed abroad and then are exported to third countries. Although statistically both backward and forward types are regarded as forms of integration into GVCs, they represent quite different situations. The latter in Latin America usually involves the export of primary products that are then incorporated into manufactured goods exported by the importing country. These are usually products which are sold in global markets and do not involve the kind of governance that is more commonly associated with GVCs. On the other hand, the cases of backward participation in GVCs in the region are examples where imports are further processed or assembled by manufacturers who then export the product. This is more likely to involve the kind of fragmented international production that is typical of GVCs.

The evidence suggests that LAC is less integrated into GVCs than other regions such as the European Union or Asia, particularly in terms of the kind of

[8] The discussion on LAC integration into GVCs is based on Blyde (2014), chapter 2; Blyde and Trachtenberg (2020); and Cadestin et al. (2016).

upstream linkages that characterize fragmented global production (Blyde, 2014, fig. 2.2; Blyde and Trachtenberg, 2020, fig.1). The countries that are most integrated, such as Mexico and Costa Rica, are mainly involved in GVCs centred on North America (Cadestin et al., 2016, fig. 5).

Despite the rapid growth of trade between China and Latin America over the past two decades, the extent to which this has involved integration into Chinese-led GVCs has been limited. The OECD/WTO TiVA database provides estimates of the share of Chinese inputs in LAC exports for seven countries in the region (see Table 3.3). At the start of the millennium there was virtually no involvement by the Latin American countries in Chinese-led value chains, reflecting the low level of trade that existed with China before it joined the WTO. Even in 2018, the latest year for which data are available, the extent of backward integration remained very limited, with imports from China accounting for less than 2% of the value of exports in all countries apart from Mexico.

Looking at downstream integration, the countries with the most significant relations with China are Chile and Peru. In 2018 between 6% and 7% of domestic value added in their worldwide exports were incorporated into products that were then exported from China. The extent of forward integration depends to a significant extent on the type of products exported by different countries in the region. Chile and Peru, with significant exports of minerals (particularly copper) to China, have relatively high levels because China is a significant exporter of copper products. In contrast, Argentina exports mainly soybeans, which are used to produce feed for the Chinese livestock industry, so that incorporation into Chinese exports is minimal.

Table 3.3 Backward and Forward Integration with China, 2000 and 2018

	Backward Integration		Forward Integration	
	2000	2018	2000	2018
Argentina	0.1%	1.4%	0,5%	1.3%
Brazil	0.2%	1.5%	0.4%	3.7%
Chile	0.4%	1.9%	0.9%	6.2%
Colombia	0.2%	1.4%	0.1%	2.6%
Costa Rica	0.3%	1.7%	0.0%	0.5%
Mexico	0.5%	6.5%	0.1%	0.6%
Peru	0.2%	1.8%	0.8%	4.5%

Source: Author's elaboration from OECD/WTO, *TiVA Database.*

Given the low level of integration of Latin American producers into Chinese value chains, it is unlikely that this would have been a significant source of technological upgrading for the region.

3.6. Infrastructure

One of the key obstacles to escaping the middle-income trap in Latin America is the poor state of infrastructure in the region. The Inter-American Development Bank (IDB) estimates that the infrastructure deficit comes to some US$150 billion a year, or around 2.5% of the region's GDP (Serebrisky et al., 2015; Cavallo and Powell, 2019, ch. 6). The lack of infrastructure investment in a sample of six LAC countries has been estimated to have reduced the rate of GDP growth by around 1% a year (Cavallo and Powell, 2019, ch. 7).

A high level of infrastructure expenditure played a crucial role in China's own development, and as a result, Chinese companies gained significant capabilities in project design and implementation. They were able to leverage these capabilities to expand internationally and are now among the largest international contractors, establishing a significant presence in Asia and Africa.

In 2013 the global expansion of Chinese construction companies was given a further push by the launch of the BRI. The BRI had its origins in two speeches made by President Xi Jinping in 2013 in Kazakhstan and Indonesia. In Kazakhstan, he proposed the development of a new Silk Road Economic Belt linking China, Central Asia, South Asia, Russia, and Europe by land. In Indonesia he announced a plan for a twenty-first-century Maritime Silk Road, linking China with South-East Asia, South Asia, the South Pacific, the Middle East, and East Africa by sea. These initiatives were brought together in 2014 under the 'One Belt, One Road' (OBOR) label. In 2016, the official English translation from the Chinese was changed to the Belt and Road Initiative. One of the 'Five Cooperation Priorities' of the BRI is to develop 'facilities connectivity' to which China has contributed substantial resources.

Latin America was not originally included as part of the BRI, but over time the number of countries to which the initiative was applied widened considerably. In 2018 at the China-CELAC Summit in Santiago, China extended an invitation to all Latin American and Caribbean countries with which it had diplomatic relations to take part. As a result, 19 countries signed BRI memoranda of understanding with China in 2018 and 2019. Given the BRI's emphasis on infrastructure connectivity and the global expansion of Chinese firms in the sector, particularly in Africa, it is not surprising that it has been seen as a major potential benefit from LAC participation. The executive secretary of Economic Commission for Latin America and the Caribbean (ECLAC), Alicia Barcena, said at the 2018 Silk Road Forum in Paris, that for LAC, 'BRI offers opportunities to diversify and improve the quality of its economic links with China and, more specifically, it can help attract much-needed investment in infrastructure, industry and services' (CEPAL, 2018, n.p.). Such investment in infrastructure could play a key role in helping Latin America break out of the middle-income trap.

However, the extent of Chinese involvement in infrastructure projects in the region so far has been quite limited. The most ambitious projects that have been proposed—linking the Caribbean with the Pacific via a canal through Nicaragua, and the Bio-oceanic railway from Brazil to Peru—have not gotten off the ground. In recent years the annual value of Chinese contracts has been in the range of US$10–15 billion, less than 10% of the amount required to close the region's infrastructure gap. Chinese involvement in infrastructure in Latin America has not been on the same scale as in Sub-Saharan Africa (Jenkins, 2018, pp. 258–259). There is also no sign that infrastructure investment in the region has increased since it began to participate in the BRI (Jenkins, 2021).

3.7. Conclusions

Several obstacles have been identified to Latin America getting out of the 'middle income trap'. The changing international context faced by the region as a result of the rise of China and its increased engagement with LAC presents new challenges and opportunities. There is a clear increase in the region's dependence on a narrow range of commodity exports that has been identified as one of the main causes of the 'middle income trap'. Chinese competition has also posed a challenge to the development of manufacturing and technological upgrading through exports of more sophisticated industrial products. Potential opportunities to increase technological capabilities through inward investment from China and integration into Chinese-led GVCs have not materialized on a significant scale. Moreover, despite the hopes generated by the extension of the BRI to LAC, the contribution of China to infrastructure construction in the region has so far remained limited. It is unlikely that this will change without more effective industrial and technology policies on the part of Latin American governments.

References

Andersen, A. D., Marìn, A., and Simensen, E. O. 2018. 'Innovation in Natural Resource-Based Industries: A Pathway to Development? Introduction to Special Issue', *Innovation and Development*, 8(1), 1–27.

Atlas of Economic Complexity. 2022a. *Glossary*. Cambridge, Mass. Harvard Growth Lab. available at: https://atlas.cid.harvard.edu/glossary (accessed 28/3/22).

Atlas of Economic Complexity. 2022b. *Country and Product Complexity Rankings*. Cambridge, Mass. Harvard Growth Lab available at: https://atlas.cid.harvard.edu/rankings (accessed 17/1/22).

BCB. 2018. *Relatório de Investímento Direto no País*. Brasilia: Banco Central do Brasil.

Blyde, J. S. 2014. *Synchronized Factories: Latin America and the Caribbean in the Era of Global Value Chains*. Cham: Springer Open.

Blyde, J., and Trachtenberg, D. 2020. 'Global Value Chains and Latin America: A Technical Note', *Inter-American Development Bank*. Washington DC.

Borregaard, N., Dufey, A., Ruiz-Tagle, M. T., and Sinclair, S. 2017. 'Chinese Incidence on the Chilean Solar Power Sector', in R. Ray, K. Gallagher, A. López, and C. Sanborn, eds., *China and Sustainable Development in Latin America: The Social and Environmental Dimension*. London: Anthem Press, 269–320.

Cadestin, C., Gourdon, J., and Kowalski, P. 2016. 'Participation in Global Value Chains in Latin America. Participation in Global Value: Implications for Trade and Trade-Related Policy', *OECD Trade Policy Papers*, No. 192. Paris: OECD Publishing, http://dx.doi.org/10.1787/5jlpq80ts8f2-en.

Cavallo, E., and Powell, A. 2019. *Building Opportunities for Growth in a Challenging World*. Washington, DC: Inter-American Development Bank.

CELAC (China and the Community of Latin American and Caribbean States). 2015. *Cooperation Plan (2015–2019)*. China-CELAC Forum, available at: http://www.chinacelacforum.org/eng/zywj_3/t1230944.htm (accessed 20/2/17).

CEPAL. 2018. *Chinese Belt and Road Initiative Is an Opportunity for Inclusive and Sustainable Investments: ECLAC*. Santiago de Chile: Economic Commission for Latin America and the Caribbean, available at: https://www.cepal.org/en/news/chinese-belt-and-road-initiative-opportunity-inclusive-and-sustainable-investments-eclac (accessed 15/4/21).

Dussel-Peters, E., ed. 2016. *La nueva relación commercial entre América Latina y el Caribe y China: Integración o desintegración regional?* Mexico City: Unión de Universidades de América Latina y el Caribe.

ECLAC. 2018. *Exploring New Forms of Cooperation between China and Latin America and the Caribbean*, January 2018, available at: https://repositorio.cepal.org/bitstream/handle/11362/43214/1/S1701249_en.pdf.

ECLAC. 2021. *Foreign Direct Investment In Latin America and the Caribbean, 2021*. Santiago, Chile: UN.

ENR (Engineering News Record). 2015. 'How the Top International Contractors Shared the 2014 Market', *Engineering News Record*, (16), 1–77. 24/31 August 2015.

ENR (Engineering News Record). 2020. 'How the Top International Contractors Shared the 2019 Market', *Engineering News Record*, (170), 1–44. 17/24 August 2020.

Foxley, A., and Stallings, B. eds. 2016. *Innovation and Inclusion in Latin America: Strategies to Avoid the Middle-Income Trap*. New York: Palgrave Macmillan.

Gallagher, K., and Porzecanski, R. 2010. *The Dragon in the Room: China and the Future of Latin American Industrialization*. Stanford, CA: Stanford University Press.

Guzman, D. 2019. 'China's Billions Are Powering Latin America's Tech Boom', *Bloomberg*, available at: https://www.bloomberg.com/news/articles/2019-01-08/guess-who-s-behind-latin-america-s-tech-boom-china-of-course (accessed 28/10/19).

Husar, J., and Best, D., 2013. *Energy Investments and Technology Transfer across Emerging Economies: The Case of Brazil and China*. Paris: International Energy Agency.

Jenkins, R., 2010. 'China's Global Growth and Latin American Exports', in A. Santos Paulino and G. Wan, eds., *The Rise of China and India*. Houndsmill: Palgrave, 220–240.

Jenkins, R. 2014. 'Chinese Competition and Brazilian Exports of Manufactures', *Oxford Development Studies*, 42(3), 395–418.

Jenkins, R. 2015. 'Is Chinese Competition Causing Deindustrialization in Brazil?', *Latin American Perspectives*, 42(6), 42–63.

Jenkins, R. 2018. *How China Is Reshaping the Global Economy: Development Impacts in Africa and Latin America*. Oxford: Oxford University Press.

Jenkins, R. 2022. 'China's Belt and Road Initiative in Latin America: What Has Changed?', *Journal of Current Chinese Affairs*, 51(1), 13–3918681026211047871. https://doi.org/10.1177/18681026211047871.

Kohli, H. A. 2013. 'Infrastructure Needs for a Resurgent Latin America', in H. Kohli, C. Loser, and A. Sood, eds., *Latin America 2040—Breaking Away from Complacency: An Agenda for Resurgence*, 2nd edition. New Delhi: Sage, 229–238.

Lall, S. 2000. 'The Technological Structure and Performance of Developing Country Manufactured Exports, 1985–98', *Oxford Development Studies*, 28(3), 337–369.

Lall, S., Weiss, J., and Oikawa, H. 2005. 'China's Competitive Threat to Latin America: An Analysis for 1990–2002', *Oxford Development Studies*, 33(2), 163–194.

Lema, R., Pietrobelli, C., and Rabellotti, R. 2019. 'Innovation in Global Value Chains', in G. Gereffi, S. Ponte, and G. Raj-Reichert, eds., *Handbook on Global Value Chains*. Cheltenham: Edward Elgar, 370–384.

Lin, J. Y., and Treichel, V. 2012. 'Learning from China's Rise to Escape the Middle-Income Trap: A New Structural Economics Approach to Latin America', *World Bank Policy Research Working Paper*, 6165.

Melguizo, Á., et al. 2017. 'No Sympathy for the Devil! Policy Priorities to Overcome the Middle-Income Trap in Latin America', *OECD Development Centre Working Papers*, No. 340. Paris: OECD Publishing, https://doi.org/10.1787/26b78724-en.

Micheli, J., and Carrillo, J. 2016. 'The Globalization Strategy of a Chinese Multinational: Huawei in Mexico', *Frontera Norte*, 28(56), 35–58.

Morrison, A., Pietrobelli, C., and Rabellotti, R. 2008. 'Global Value Chains and Technological Capabilities: A Framework to Study Learning and Innovation in Developing Countries', *Oxford Development Studies*, 36(1), 39–58.

Paus, E. 2014. 'Latin America and the Middle Income Trap', *ECLAC, Financing for Development Series*, (250). Available at SSRN: https://ssrn.com/abstract=2473823 or http://dx.doi.org/10.2139/ssrn.2473823.

Paus, E. 2020. 'Innovation Strategies Matter: Latin America's Middle-Income Trap Meets China and Globalisation', *The Journal of Development Studies*, 56(4), 657–659.

PRC. 2016. *China's Policy Paper on Latin America and the Caribbean*. Beijing: Foreign Ministry of the People's Republic of China.

Rosales, O., and Kuwayama, M. 2012. *China and Latin America and the Caribbean: Building a Strategic Economic Relationship*. Santiago, Chile: UN ECLAC.

Salazar-Xirinachs, J. M. 2019. *A New Phase in China-Latin America Relations: Cooperation on Science, Technology and Innovation*. 2019 Forum on Innovation and Cooperation for Development, Xi'an, China, 17 June.

Serebrisky, T., Suárez-Alemán, A., Margot, D., and Ramirez, M. C. 2015. *Financing Infrastructure in Latin America and the Caribbean: How, How Much and by Whom*. Washington, DC: Inter-American Development Bank.

Staritz, C., and Whitfield, L. 2019. 'Local Firm-Level Learning and Capability Building in Global Value Chains', in *Handbook on Global Value Chains*. Cheltenham: Edward Elgar, 385–402.

Su, Z. 2017. 'Continuing to Deepen the Cooperation and Realizing Common Development', in Z. Su, ed., *China and Latin America: Economic and Trade Cooperation in the Next Ten Years*. Singapore: World Scientific, 604–649.

Wübbeke, J., Meissner, M., Zenglein, M. J., Ives, J., and Conrad, B. 2016. *Made in China 2025: The Making of a High-Tech Superpower and Consequences for Industrial Countries*. Mercator Institute for China Studies, 17, Berlin, available at: https://espas.secure.europarl.europa.eu/orbis/sites/default/files/generated/document/en/MPOC_No.2_MadeinChina_2025.pdf. (accessed 26/6/18).

4

Development, Trajectories, and Catch-Up

Lessons from the Latin American and Scandinavian Experiences

Claudio Bravo-Ortega and Nicolas Eterovic

4.1. Introduction

Have Latin American countries learned enough about their own—and similar—experiences of development? Does there exist a natural experiment from which Latin American countries could extract some lessons? It would seem the answer to these questions is 'no' and 'yes,' respectively. During the late nineteenth century and the beginning of twentieth, Scandinavian and Latin American countries registered similar levels of GDP per capita, and both were mostly exporters of natural resources. In fact, in 1870, Finland, Norway, and Sweden had per capita incomes of $1,107, $1,303, and $1,664, respectively, while Argentina and Chile had per capita incomes of $1,311 and $1,153, respectively[1] (see Table 4.1).

What factors drove the industrialization of one and not the other group of countries? Why did both groups diverge?[2] Theoretical approaches suggest that special conditions are needed for the industrialization of an economy, which in most cases is generated by taking advantage of scale economies. According with this view, Murphy, Schleiffer, and Vishny (1989a, 1989b) present several models following the idea of the 'big push' introduced by Rosenstein-Rodan (1943),[3] where the development of one industrial sector can benefit other industrial sectors by enlarging the size of the market.

Why were Scandinavian countries placed to benefit from a 'big push' and not those of Latin America? We can approach this question, noting that the big push relies not only in the coordination among productive agents, but also in the initial and further size of the market and the distribution of earnings among the population.[4] Thus, countries with little population or marked inequality would not be

[1] All the figures in 1990 Geary Khamis dollars extracted from Maddison (1995).

[2] The idea of divergent paths and the interest arose to the authors after reading Blomstrom and Meller (1990), *Trayectorias Divergentes* (Divergent Paths).

[3] Cited by Murphy, Vishny, and Schleifer (1989a, 1989b); hereafter, MSV.

[4] MSV (1989b).

Claudio Bravo-Ortega and Nicolas Eterovic, *Development, Trajectories, and Catch-Up* In: *Innovation, Competitiveness, and Development in Latin America.* Edited by: Edmund Amann and Paulo N. Figueiredo, Oxford University Press.
 DOI: 10.1093/oso/9780197648070.003.0004

Table 4.1 Comparative Evolution of Income and Exports Per Capita (1990 Geary Khamis Dollars)

	GDP per capita			Annual Growth Rate	Exports per capita		Annual Rate of Growth Export Volume
	1870	1900	1913	1870–1913	1870	1913	1870–1913
Austria	1875	2901	3488	1.5	103	299	3.5
Belgium	2640	3652	4130	1.0	243	955	4.2
Denmark	1927	2902	3764	1.6	166	501	3.3
Finland	1107	1620	2050	1.4	177	528	3.9
France	1858	2849	3452	1.5	91	272	2.8
Germany	1913	3134	3833	1.6	293	1009	4.1
Italy	1467	1746	2507	1.3	64	124	2.2
Netherlands	2640	3533	3950	0.9	478	702	2.3
Norway	1303	1762	2275	1.3	129	349	3.2
Sweden	1664	2561	3096	1.5	171	475	3.1
Switzerland	2172	3531	4207	1.5	416	1484	3.9
UK	3263	4593	5032	1.0	417	923	2.8
Australia	3801	4299	5505	0.9	281	704	4.8
Canada	1620	2758	4213	2.2	194	515	4.1
New Zealand	3115	4320	5178	1.2	344	729	
USA	2457	4096	5307	1.8	62	197	2.2
Portugal	1085	1408	1354	0.5	31	46	
Spain	1376	2040	2255	1.2	52	182	3.5
Argentina	1311	2756	3797	2.5	124	257	5.2
Brazil	740	704	839	0.3	87	80	1.9
Chile	1153	1949	2653	2.0	85	201	3.4
Colombia		973	1236		48	51	2.0
Mexico	710	1157	1467	1.7	26	158	5.4
Peru	676	817	1037	1.0	78	94	5.3

Source: Elaborated using data from Maddison (1995), except for Portuguese exports and Peruvian and Chilean GDP, whose source is discussed in the Appendix.

well positioned for developing their big push. However, under such conditions international trade could play an important role, by taking the place of internal demand in stimulating the development of the industrial sectors.

This chapter intends to assess whether or not the exposure to international trade would have played an important role in the trajectories of growth followed by Scandinavian and Latin American countries for the period 1870–2010. The structure of the chapter is as follows. The next section (section 4.2) discusses the theoretical background of the chapter. Following this, section 4.3 employs cross-sectional regressions to test whether or not the access to international markets played an important role in explaining the long-term paths of growth for the Latin American countries. Section 4.4 then assesses and reviews the evolution of trade and industrial policies in Chile over the long term. In conclusion, these main threads of the argument are the drawn together in section 4.5.

4.2. The Conceptual Framework

The main idea developed by Rosenstein-Rodan (1943) and utilized by Murphy, Schleifer & Vishny (1989a) is that the development of one industrial sector can benefit other industrial sectors by enlarging the size of the market. This external effect of the firm's investment decisions gives a crucial role to the coordination among productive agents, whose simultaneous investing decisions make profitable the change from technologies with decreasing marginal returns to technologies with economies of scale. The link between the technological change and the further growth is given by the distribution of the firm's earnings among the population, which stimulates the internal demand, generating subsequent economic growth.[5]

The fact that the big push relies not only on the coordination among productive agents, but also on the size of the market and the distribution of earnings among the population is discussed in Murphy, Schleifer & Vishny (1989b). Thus, countries with scarce population or deep inequality would not be well placed for developing their big push. The new model of Murphy, Schleifer & Vishny (1989b) establishes that industrialization is caused by an increase in agricultural productivity, or by an exports boom that raises the income and therefore demand for domestic manufactures. Despite this, the role of the leading sector is not always enough for realizing industrialization. Under certain circumstances, although extra income is generated, it may not go to potential customers of domestic industry.

The expansion of industrial markets requires concentration of buying power in the hands of consumers. In fact, in the Murphy, Schleifer & Vishny (1989b) model, the exportation of minerals or crops enables a country to substitute efficient export production and food imports for inefficient domestic food production. Indeed, they sustain: 'The net result of this productive roundabout means of obtaining food can often be more profits in the hands of the middle class and even food wages which are high enough that wage earners begin to demand

[5] See Table 4.2 for a quick assessment of inequality in Latin America based on data on indigenous and mestizo population.

manufactures. In this way, a productive export sector can raise the extent of domestic industrialization' (1989b, p. 557).

So, why would Scandinavian countries have been appropriately placed for the 'big push' and not Latin America? It has been widely claimed that the success of the Scandinavian transformation relies in how open these economies were. O'Rourke and Williamson (1995) establish that Sweden's catch-up was due mostly to mass migration, international capital flows, and trade, and that this experience does appear to apply to the rest of Scandinavia. Surprisingly, this explanation attributes a modest importance to the role played by the relatively high level of educated population in the Scandinavian countries (see Table 4.2). Therefore, considering that the Scandinavian countries were relatively small with respect to the European population, it may be possible that international trade had played a role, as suggested by the big push theory. In this sense, it is highly probable that Latin American countries would have been in an unfavorable situation just because of their geographical location, apart from what might be said about their trade policies.[6]

Despite this, it should be claimed that the effects of the openness of one economy depend not only on the comparative advantages it has, but also on the distribution of the factors of production in the population, and movement in their relative prices as a consequence of international trade. According to this, in Latin American economies, where the land was highly unevenly distributed, the effect of trade should have raised the returns to the land. This finally should have increased inequality among the population, reducing the 'effective size' of the internal markets. Assuming that the land was equitably distributed in the Scandinavian countries and that they also had agricultural comparative advantage, the effect of the openness would have been to enlarge the size of domestic markets.[7]

4.2.1. Late Nineteenth-Century Catch-Up?

Less than widely discussed in the literature is the fact that only not did Scandinavia experience high rates of growth during the late nineteenth century (the so-called Scandinavian catch-up), but that this also occurred in also some Latin American countries. Despite the fact that Latin America as a whole did not catch up to the European countries, Argentina and Chile experienced high rates of growth. By the late 1920s their income per capita was higher than that of Italy, Finland, Norway, and Spain. But how was it possible for Argentina and Chile to

[6] For a detailed description of the evolution of transport costs for Latin American countries in this period, see Williamson (1998).

[7] In the next section we will see that this scenario is highly probable.

Table 4.2 Social Infrastructure Indicators

	Railroad (Kilometres)			Annual Growth Rate	Enrolment Rates Primary Education (% of relevant population)			Literacy Rate (percent)	Students in Universities (Thousands)		Population (Thousands)		Population Annual Growth Rate
	1870	1890	1910	(%; 1870–1910)	1870	1890	1910	1870-90	1870	1910	1870	1910	(%; 1870–1910)
Austria	6,612	15,273	22,642	3.1	40	63	70	66	11.6	39.4	4,520	6,614	1
Belgium	2,897	4,526	4,679	1.2	63	46	62	86	2.6	7.9	5,096	7,498	1
Denmark	770	2,033	3,445	3.8	58	61	66	99		0.8	1,888	2,882	1.1
Finland	483	1,897	3,356	5		10	26	89	0.7	3.2	1,754	2,929	1.3
France	15,544	33,878	40,484	2.4	57	83	86	96		41.2	38,440	41,224	0.2
Germany	18,876	42,869	61,209	3	67	74	73	97	20.6	70.2	23,055	36,481	1.2
Italy	6,429	13,629	18,090	2.6	29	37	45	47	12.1	26.9	27,888	36,572	0.7
Netherlands	1,419	2,610	3,190	2	59	64	70	97	1.2	4.1	3,615	5,902	1.2
Norway	359	1,562	2,976	5.4	61	65	69	98	1	1.5	1,735	2,384	0.8
Sweden	1,727	8,018	13,829	5.3	57	75	67	98		7.7	4,164	5,449	0.7
Switzerland	1,421	3,243	4,463	2.9	76	76	71	99		6.8	2,664	3,735	0.8
UK	21,558	27,827	32,184	1	49	56	79	96			29,312	41,938	0.9
Australia					70	76	89	97			1,620	4,375	2.5
Canada	4,211	21,164	39,799	5.8	75	84	88	90			3,736	7,188	1.6

New Zealand					50	80	91				291	1,045	3.2
USA	85,170	268,282	386,714	3.9	72	97	97	88	52	355	40,066	92,767	2.1
Portugal	714	1,932	2,448	3.1	13	22	19	38			4,553	5,937	0.7
Spain	5,454	10,163	14,694	2.5	42	52	35	42		20.5	16,201	19,858	0.5
Argentina	732	9,254	27,713	9.5	21	26	37	46		10	1,796	6,836	3.4
Brazil	745	9,973	21,326	8.7	6	8	11			8.8	9,797	22,216	2.1
Chile	732	2,747	5,944	5.4	19	20	39			2.4	1,943	3,364	1.4
Colombia	0	282	988		6	9	21			1.6	2,392	4,890	1.8
Mexico	349	9,718	19,748	10.6	16	19	25				9,217	15,000	1.2
Peru	669	1,599	2,995	3.8		10	15				2,606	4,206	1.2

Source: Elaborated using the following data: Railroad and university students, Mitchell (1992); enrolment rates from Benavot and Riddle (1988); population from Maddison (1995); literacy from O'Rourke et al. (1995).

Some years have been replaced using the closest available year of information, that is the case for university students for Germany in 1872 and Colombia in 1914.

experience such growth? The answer is not clear; neither is it clear why Brazil, Mexico, and Peru failed to experience such growth rates. For Argentina and Chile it would seem that international trade played a fundamental role, specifically the comparative advantages they enjoyed in the production of meat, wheat, and nitrates.

Available research suggests that during the 1870–1914 period, Latin American countries applied more protectionist policies than did the Scandinavian countries. These protectionist policies were applied to help financing social infrastructure (railroads and education), and not for protecting nascent industries.[8] In fact, in most countries tariffs were one of the key sources of government funds. Given the levels of existing tariff protection, Latin America might have experienced the distributive effects connected with international trade.

The Hecksher Ohlin theorem establishes that under presence of trade, each country specializes in the production of goods with intensive use of its relative abundant factor of production. Thus, in Latin America, where the land was the most abundant productive factor, we find that most the exports were agricultural, mining, or livestock products. This situation would have increased returns to landowners. Now considering that in Latin American countries the ownership of the land was highly unequally distributed (see Table 4.3), this situation would have skewed the income distribution, shrinking the size of the domestic markets. This would have made conditions less propitious for a big push. In this regard, contrasting the distribution of the land in Chile and Finland in Table 4.3 is telling.

Furthermore, if we consider that in Latin America an important part of the population was indigenous, with lower rights, then social inequality in the region may have been more extreme than figures on land distribution would suggest. This would certainly stand in contrast with the Scandinavian situation which was marked by early agricultural and educational reforms.

With respect to the protectionist policies applied in the Scandinavian countries, it can be argued that such policies appeared after almost 50 years of free trade. During this time free trade, in contrast with what happened in Latin American countries, would have enlarged the size of the internal markets, creating the internal demand for further nascent industries.[9]

[8] Maybe Mexico is the exception to this situation; during the Porfiriato it would have imposed tariffs with protectionist interest for supporting nascent industries in the manufacture sector (Marquez, 1998).

[9] This point can be understood following Williamson (1996, p. 301), who asserts: 'Suppose the source of convergence lay instead with the two open economy and globalization forces that I have already stressed, namely, international labour migration and factor price convergence induced by global commodity market integration and trade booms. Here the distributional impact is even clearer and probably more powerful. Unskilled labour migration raised the real wage of unskilled

Table 4.3 Land Distribution in Finland and Chile

Finland, 1910.		Chile, 1925.		
ha	Ownership of total %	ha	Ownership of total %	hectares as a % of total
0.5–5	54			
5–10	23	0–50	80	3.3
10–25	17			
25–100	6	51–200	11	5.1
>100	0			
		>200	9	91.6
Total of Properties	221,239		109,853	

Source: Elaborated from Kokko et al. (1990), p. 205; Meller (1996), p. 88.
Note: 1 hectare corresponds to 10,000 square meters.

4.3. Empirical Approach and Results

To determine the factors underpinning the different growth trajectories of Latin America and Scandinavia, this section presents several cross-section regressions. The analysis employs an approach similar to that of Barro and Sala i Martin (1995). For our estimation, we will employ series on GDP per capita and exports from Maddison (1995), enrolment rates from Benavot and Riddle (1988), literacy from O'Rourke and Williamson (1995), railroad kilometres from Mitchell (1992), and distance between countries from Frankel and Romer (1999). The area for each country in 1961 is used as proxy for the area 1870, the date being drawn from the WDI 1998 CD-Rom.

Using the data from Romer and Frankel (1999) of the distance between countries and the data from Maddison (1995) for the GDP, distance was constructed to the 'gravitational centre of the world', using GDP of the countries as weights.

labour in poor emigrating countries [Scandinavian] and lowered it in rich immigrating countries. These forces were reinforced by trade. Recall that powerful forces of global commodity markets integration were at work in the late nineteenth century: the resulting trade booms shifted unskilled labour demand to the right in poor countries (compared with other factors) and to the left in rich countries (compared with other factors). These trade-induced forces tended to have the same effect as the mass migrations: the relative price of unskilled labour tended to rise in poor countries [Scandinavia] and to fall in rich countries [Latin America]. It follows that the skill premium, earnings inequality, and income inequality should, ceteris paribus, have falling in the poor European countries that were catching up. The faster the catch-up, the bigger the fall. In contrast, the skill premium, earnings inequality, and income inequality should, ceteris paribus, have been rising in the New World countries.'

The idea is to capture, in an approximate way, the transport cost that each country faced, or real access to the world market that each had. More formally the distance to 'the market' for the country *i* at time *t* is given by:

$$d_{iW,t} = \frac{\sum_{j \neq i} GDP_j,t \cdot d_{ij}}{\sum_j GDP_j,t} = \frac{\sum_{j \neq i} GDPpc_{j,t} \cdot Pop_{j,t} \cdot d_{ij}}{\sum_j GDP_{j,t}} \tag{4.1}$$

The hypothesis to be tested sustains that this limited access to the world market played an important role in the development of the Latin American and Scandinavian countries in the nineteenth century.[10] Thus, at the light of the big push theory, it is expected that countries more distant from the 'world market' will grow less. A similar approach has been used by Frankel and Romer (1999) to explain the levels of trade and economic growth for a panel of countries in 1995. Luke, Sachs, and Mellinger (1998) report similar results for the growth rates of GDP per capita and other geographical variables distinct of our 'gravitational' measure.[11] Table 4.4 shows a summary of exports and our gravitational measure, while Table 4.5 shows the values of the remaining variables used in our estimations. The data used to derive these estimations are described in the Appendix.

Table 4.5 also summarizes the results for the determinants of the growth of the GDP per capita in the period 1870–1913, enlightened by the big push theory. The first fact that is interesting to note is that for the period unconditional convergence does not exist.[12] Indeed, Table 4.5 reports just the regressions that *explain* conditional convergence. Regression 1 in Table 4.5 utilizes as explanatory variables income per capita in 1870, exports growth, and primary enrolment rates. According with the unconditional divergence reported, this time the income per capita and enrolment rates do not appear statistically significant; however, the export growth variable is statistically significant at 90% confidence. Incorporating an intercept-dummy variable for the Latin America countries does not improve the results. Regression 2 in Table 4.5 incorporates a dummy variable for the export growth of the Latin American countries, and was obtained after verifying that the exports growth was not significant for the rest of the sample; this fact improves the

[10] The distance to the market affects not just the export dynamism, but also the cost of import goods, particularly goods of capital. Also, at that time the distance to the market could also have implied more difficulties for the diffusion of technologies.

[11] For Luke et al. (1998), the variable L distance, defined as the distance between each country to one of the three core areas, is not statistically significant.

[12] Similar result is reported by De Long (1988) and Williamson (1996).

Table 4.4 Gravitational Information

	Exports as fraction of GDP		Distance to Gravitational Center. (Thousand Kilometers)		
	1870	1913	1870	1913	% Change
Austria	6	9	3150	4434	41
Belgium	9	23	2548	3798	49
Denmark	9	13	2989	4166	39
Finland	16	26	3649	4734	30
France	5	8	2525	3788	50
Germany	15	26	2631	3889	48
Italy	4	5	3226	4536	41
Netherlands	18	18	2594	3820	47
Norway	10	15	3124	4200	34
Sweden	10	15	3336	4441	33
Switzerland	19	35	2752	4035	47
UK	13	18	2492	3699	48
Australia	7	13	16001	15478	-3
Canada	12	12	4868	4266	-12
New Zealand	11	14	17030	15907	-7
USA	3	4	5348	4419	-17
Portugal	3	3	3053	4197	37
Spain	4	8	3214	4249	32
Argentina	9	7	10361	9853	-5
Brazil	12	10	9047	8785	-3
Chile	7	8	10689	10011	-6
Colombia		4	7646	6921	-9
Mexico	4	11	7694	6667	-13
Peru	11	9	9165	8384	-9

Source: Elaborated using data from Maddison (1995), except for Portuguese exports and Peruvian and Chilean GDP, whose source is discussed in the Appendix.

statistical significance of this variable to the 98%, and increases those of enrolment rates to 99%, and also improves the explanatory power of the regression to 36%.[13]

Regressions 3-10 in Table 4.5 incorporate the variables used to test the hypothesis that geographical location mattered for the big push. Regression 3 shows the correct

13 The exports growth is not significant for the rest of the countries or for the Scandinavian countries.

Table 4.5 Economic Growth and Its Determinants Dependent Variable Growth Rate of GDP per capita 1870–1913

	1	2	3	4	5	6	7	8	9	10	11
Log (Ypc70)	−0.434	−0.265	−0.219	0.015		−0.415	−0.753	−0.749	−0.0877	−1.1	−0.819
	(0.377)	(0.332)	(0.343)	(0.39)		(0.313)	(0.240)	(0.234)	(0.245)	(0.172)	(0.245)
X per Capita											
Growth of Export Volume	0.225										0.066
	(0.111)										(0.054)
Growth of Export Volume		0.266	0.3	0.284	0.284	0.347	0.349	0.278	0.326	0.218	0.336
Latin America		(0.007)	(0.096)	(0.095)	(0.090)	(0.083)	(0.059)	(0.069)	(0.058)	(0.04)	(0.058)
Primary Enrolment Rate	0.008	0.021	0.021	0.016	0.016	0.025	0.012		0.013		0.011
	(0.008)	(0.007)	(0.008)	(0.008)	(0.006)	(0.007)	(0.006)		(0.005)		(0.005)
Literacy								0.263		0.5	
								(0.567)		(0.278)	
Log (Distance to 'Gravitational'			−0.159	−0.562	−0.554				−0.327	−0.103	−0.325
Centre)			(0.215)	(0.396)	(0.329)				(0.137)	(0.109)	(0.134)
Change in Distance				−0.011	−0.011						
				(0.009)	(0.007)						
Log(Distance to 'Gravitational'						−0.109	−0.524	−0.449			
Centre / Railroad)						(0.063)	(0.120)	(0.175)			
Log(Rail per capita)									0.577	0.568	0.608
									(0.122)	(0.097)	(0.122)
Log (Population)							−0.591	−0.504			
							(0.159)	(0.242)			
R^2	0.29	0.47	0.49	0.54	0.54	0.61	0.82	0.76	0.84	0.9	0.86
R^2 Adj	0.15	0.36	0.35	0.37	0.41	0.5	0.74	0.64	0.77	0.85	0.78
Obs	19	19	19	19	19	18	18	16	18	16	18

Source: Authors' calculations.

… multiplied for a dummy variable for Scandinavia.

sign for the distance to the market, but is not statistically meaningful. The variables enrolment and export growth maintain their statistical significance. Regression 4 also incorporates also the rate of change in the distance to the market for the period 1870–1913. The latter again shows the correct sign, but fails in its statistical meaningfulness, as does the rate of change of the distance. In short, the effect of distance can affect growth rates, but is not an explanation; in fact, transport cost or the access to the world market involves not only distances but also infrastructure.

Regression 5 tests for the robustness of this result, omitting the initial income per capita. In regression 6 our gravitational variable to the ratio of the distance to the market changes to become kilometres of railroad. This takes into account the fact the growing importance of ground transportation over the period.[14] With respect to the new gravitational variable, this ratio appears statistically meaningful, which would imply that countries with better infrastructure and shorter distance to the gravitational centre grew more. Enrolment rates and export growth are still significant and with correct signs; in addition, the significance of the initial income increases notably.

Regression 7 also incorporates the population of each country as an explanatory variable. Despite the fact that a larger population could imply larger markets, it could also imply that the social infrastructure in per capita terms is lower. Thus, the expected sign for this variable is not clear. In fact, in regression 7 the coefficient for population is negative and statistically meaningful. Now all the variables are statistically significant at 95%, with the exception of enrolment rate, which is significant to 90%. Regression 8 just changes our educational variable (to literacy rates) which reduces the sample to 16 countries. This variable is less significant, perhaps because of the reduction on degrees of freedom, but also because it has lower variance among the countries of the reduced sample, which are mostly European. In fact, the only Latin American country present now in the sample is Argentina, which has had traditionally superior educational indicators in the region, and is closer to European average.

Finally, regression 9 considers the fact that the population variable is statistically meaningful and that it may have the dominating effect of reducing capital invested per capita. It is incorporated into the regression by dividing by kilometres of railroad. In this way, given the restricted number of observations, we do not decrease the degrees of freedom of the sample. The railroad per capita variable can be thought as a proxy for the access of the average person to the formal market, whether as consumer or producer. The expected sign for this variable is positive. Regression 9 incorporates the distance to the market as gravitational variable.

[14] Given the range of the variable distance to the market, we can think that the distance to the gravitational centre is a trip made mostly by sea; as in fact was most of the international trade of the era.

The result for the regression 9 is relatively good; conditional convergence appears, the enrolment variable is significant, the distance to the world market is also important, and the railroad per capita as facilitating access to the market also is statistically significant. Regressions 10 and 11 are displayed to indicate the robustness of the result; regression 10 replaces literacy with enrolment, while 11 incorporates a dummy for the export growth of the Scandinavian countries, these variables being not statistically significant. Despite this, the last three equations have an explanatory power of 77%, 85%, and 78%, and the signs and the statistical significance of the remaining variables are held.

4.3.1. Beyond the Results: Some Implications

The results found show that the access to the 'world market' matters for economic growth. In fact, the two Latin American countries with the highest exports per capita—Argentina and Chile—showed the best economic performance (see Table 4.1). But it remains an open question why these two countries, and with them the region, diverged with respect to the advanced industrial countries. However, our results tentatively suggest that mechanisms aligned to the big push theory will likely have played a role.

Notwithstanding the advantages of having been able to export and being connected with the world market, this also could have generated certain strong dependence on it. In a context of world openness to international trade, this fact could have not represented any kind of unavoidable disadvantage except for the high degree of specialization that characterized Latin American export patterns at the time (see Table 4.6). This high specialization implied serious problems for getting equilibrium in the fiscal accounts and balance of payments; as a result, Latin American countries frequently faced problems for serving their debt, which also created significant degrees of political instability.[15] This kind of problem has been contemporaneously solved in some of them with the creation of stabilizing funds; unfortunately this kind of policy tool was not available for the Latin American policymakers at that time.[16]

The high degree of specialization in the export patterns could have been the consequence of at least two main issues: distance to the world market and the degrees of human capital accumulation. The costly access to the market could have diminished the range of goods over which Latin America had comparative

[15] Cortes Conde (1985); Bordo and Rokoff (1996)

[16] For more details on stabilizing funds, see Engel and Meller (1993); for Latin American policy makers and its 'money doctors' see Caldentey and Vernengo (2019).

Table 4.6 Composition of Exports (Participation on total Exports: %)

Chile		Colombia			Argentine		
	Nitrate		Coffee	Precious Metals		Livestock Products	Agricultural
1880	26	1874–1879	7	28	1880	85.7	0.7
1890	57	1905–1909	39	21	1890	65.5	25.8
1900	68	1910–1914	46	19	1901	45	35.4
1910	79				1911	41.7	34.8
1915	76						

Norway			Sweden		
	Fish	Timber		Grain	Livestock
1866–1870	37	42	1871–1880	19	4
1901–1905	32	36	1881–1890	10	12
1920	18	27	1891–1900	3	17
			1901–1910	0.4	10

Source: Elaborated using data from Chile, Cariola (1985); Colombia, Mc Greevey (1971); Argentina, Cortes Conde (1985).

Source: Elaborated using data from Hvee (1990) and Drachmann (1915).

Shares obtained as simple averages using the data reported by Drachmann (1915).

advantages, creating strong dependence on a few products, and making the region more vulnerable to external shocks.[17]

The role played by the levels of human capital is striking when the historical development of the Scandinavian export and industrial sector is analysed. Despite the fact that Scandinavian countries also exported natural resources, their degree of specialization was lower than that for Latin America. One possibility is that because of their closeness to Europe and higher levels of human capital, Scandinavian countries could also develop comparative advantages in the production of goods related to their 'leading sectors' (backward and forward linkages).

The greater openness of Scandinavia exposed it to frequent external shocks that were accommodated by changing the mix of exports. Thus, once again higher levels of human capital would have facilitated this shifting process. Some

[17] This analysis could be understood working in some extension of the model presented by Krugman (1990), and assuming that changes in transport costs or distance will have effects in the range of goods produced in each country shifting the 'trade balance equilibrium'. Unfortunately to formalize this aspect deserves more attention. Here this idea is presented just as a possible explanation for connecting transport cost and specialization.

examples of this flexibility are the move of Denmark from the exportation of grains in the 1870s to livestock;[18] the change from lumber exports to pulp made by the Sweden and Norway at different times;[19] the development and enhancement of British metallurgical techniques by Sweden for developing the iron and steel industries;[20] the change from sail vessels to steamships in the shipping industry; and the development of early electrical power for Norwegian industries.[21] In short, human capital would have allowed to the Scandinavian countries to face external shocks with lower social costs, and in the long run positive growth effects. What for Latin America would have been a serious social crisis was for Scandinavia no more than another 'Schumpeterian' crisis.

4.4. Chile: From Lagging Behind to Catching Up with Scandinavia

In this section, we expand the model presented in section 4.2, adding the role of creation and expansion of productive and innovative capabilities in Chile. This shows how the openness process allowed the country to initiate a second period of catch-up with Scandinavian countries. We also highlight the need to deepen the international economic integration of Chile in order to accelerate its economic growth. Our data show that Scandinavian and Latin American countries experienced a short period of significant growth at the end of the nineteenth century. They then diverged regarding growth performance in the mid-twentieth century as a consequence of import substitution industrialization trade protectionist policies pursued in Latin America. However, Chile initiated a convergence process without comparison in Latin America as a consequence of unilateral and multilateral trade liberalization implemented in the last quarter of the twentieth century and beyond.

4.4.1. Chile's Access to International Markets: Confirming the Big Push Hypothesis

During the nineteenth century the Chilean economy faced two export booms that were of increasing magnitude and consequence. The first was connected with the increment in the level of the exports of gold, silver, and cooper in the period

[18] Drachmann (1915), pp. 18–19.

[19] Sweden developed the first plant for industrial processing of pulp in the world. Heckscher (1968), p. 229.

[20] Hecksher (1968), p. 216.

[21] Hveen (1990), p. 149.

1840–1870; between these years Chile also experienced a little boom in its exports of wheat and flour as consequence of temporary demand surges from California and Australia. These booms were important because they were the first experience of this kind for the country, particularly for its entrepreneurs and its government. They permitted the start of the construction of the Chilean railroad system. But despite this, at the end of the 1870s the Chilean economy began to experience the most important boom of its history at that time, the nitrate boom.

The nitrate boom was possible after the Pacific War, after which the nitrate mines passed to Chilean control. The exploitation and exportation of nitrates in the Atacama and Antofagasta regions were initiated in the early 1860s by British, German, and Chilean entrepreneurs and Chilean workers.[22] Given that the mines where relatively close to the sea, Chile rapidly became the number one exporter of nitrates in the world.[23] The development of this sector provided the Chilean state with important amounts of income that were fundamental for providing the country with physical and social infrastructure for further development. The state came to play an important role, not just in the appropriation of the mines, but also in collecting taxes and allocating recourses within the economy.

4.4.2. The Twentieth Century in Detail: Trade and Industrial Policies

4.4.2.1. Trade

During the government of Alessandri in the 1920s, the Chilean parliament raised import duties by 50% and special levies (sometimes up to 100%) on a range of specific items.[24] As pointed out by Lederman (2005), the evidence indicates that this change in trade policy was an important episode in Chilean history because it represented, along with the general modifications to import tariffs implemented in 1914 and 1916, an increase in protectionist policies.

The tariff structure was revised several times during the 1920s. The revision of 1928 was the last before the crisis increased the tariffs on a number of manufactured goods. In addition, it authorized the president to increase, at his discretion, the tariffs on any product by up to 35%. Two years later, Ibanez would employ this instrument to raise the tariffs on products included in 440 custom classifications. Thus, import taxes increased from 12% of total public revenue in 1915, to 20% in

[22] See Cariola et al. (1985) for further details on composition of the population for these regions at that time.

[23] See Meller (1996).

[24] Part of the following sections are taken from Bravo-Ortega and Eterovic (2015), unpublished working paper.

1925, and 28% in 1930 (Palma, 1979; Ellsworth, 1945). A second set of economic measures that affected the transition from one model to another is related to the exchange rate. As documented by Palma (1984), between 1913 and 1929, the peso suffered a real devaluation of 60%. This constituted another important stimulus causing aggregate demand to be increasingly oriented towards local markets.

During the recovery years, starting in 1933, import tariffs were increased to 50% across the board (Butelmann, 1981). Additionally, import quotas and licenses were set, and administered by the Comisión de Licencias de Importación (Lederman, 2005). This was followed by a replacement of the aforementioned tariffs with general surcharges of 100% applied in the gold standard of 1934 (Palma, 1984). After 1935, there were no more general revisions to the tariff system.[25]

During the presidency of Pedro Aguirre Cerda, there was a period of increasing controls over trade in the form of import quotas, prohibitions, a number of different exchange rates, and, to a lesser extent, tariffs starting in 1938. The regime of quotas served multiple purposes, including the rationing of foreign exchange and protection. It also constituted an instrument to favour the import of 'normal' goods at the expense of 'luxury' ones. However, there were certain difficulties in establishing such quota practices. On many occasions, the total number of quotas granted surpassed the quantity of foreign exchange available, thereby preventing the clearance of the merchandise.[26]

As mentioned above, there were three attempts to liberalize the Chilean economy before 1973. As we will see in the forthcoming sections, all of them failed for a number of reasons, varying from the inability to cope with external shocks to copper prices, to the lack of a consistent monetary policy with a fixed exchange rate, or due to incomplete policies as seen in Frei's government.

The initial attempt was during Ibanez's government with the Klein-Saks Mission, which proposed a modest liberalization programme.[27] The list of

[25] In general, during the period between 1928 and 1935, there were not any major variations in the tariff policy established in 1928. However, in 1936, an *ad valorem* tax on imports was set (over customs, insurance, and freight [CIF] value). This tax involved a number of modifications; until 1943, the Ministry of Finance set the structure that would remain in force until 1967, namely: 2.5% for primary goods, 10% for goods of 'ordinary use', and 20% for 'luxury goods' (Butelmann, 1981; Lederman, 2005).

[26] Facing these constraints, in 1947 the government established a 'Foreign Exchange Budget', which consisted of estimates of the available foreign exchange to import the incoming year, to be assigned among the different groups of products. The idea of this 'Foreign Exchange Budget' was to avoid deficits in the balance of payments (BoP); however, it did not achieve this end. Until 1952, it coexisted with the free acquisition of many goods at a higher exchange rate. That same year there was a BoP crisis and the authorities decided to subject all imports to the quotas set by the 'Foreign Exchange Budget'.

[27] As pointed out by Lüders (2012), the structural reforms recommended by this Mission were not significantly different from those implemented later by the 'Chicago Boys' during the military regime.

permitted imports was expanded throughout this period, from 530 goods in April 1956 to 958 two years later. Capital goods were the most common, and represented 20% of the list. However, they decreased in importance over time, representing only 5% by 1956. However, in 1957, copper prices decreased by a third, generating a 14% deficit. This, in turn, caused the government to discourage imports in order to balance the BoP. This would be the first sign of the end of liberalization.

A second attempt at liberalization was during the tenure of Jorge Alessandri. This liberalization programme was similar to the one instituted in 1974. Basically, it established a fixed exchange regime, liberalized foreign exchange markets, and also expanded the list of permitted imports to include most goods. However, this process was not accompanied by a monetary policy consistent with a fixed exchange regime, which generated a substantial credit expansion that culminated with the depletion of international reserves in 1961. Thus, the government was obliged, once again, to set controls over trade. Like the first attempt, liberalization had failed and a number of different mechanisms were used in order to prevent local demand from turning to external markets.

Finally, during the government of Eduardo Frei Montalva, the liberalization programme was postponed, justified by the pressing foreign debt problem. Later, in the context of high copper prices and restructured foreign debt, the government launched a modest liberalization programme by adding 100 items to the list of permitted imports. However, the prior import deposits were abnormally large, by the order of 10,000%, and machinery and capital goods were the most privileged.

Despite the fact that the foreign exchange market was unified, copper exports were significantly limited by a discriminatory exchange rate applied to copper exports. The most important event in this sector was the 'Chilenization of copper,' whereby, after long negotiations, the government became a majority shareholder of the large-scale copper mining companies.

Other exports were widely favored through the drawback (which amounted to 30% of the value), exchange rate guarantees, and special credit lines. The industrial sector benefited the most; by 1969, half of the total funds were designated to manufacturing, distributed among 331 items. However, this system of incentives for exports did not turn out to be very efficient.

In October 1973, right after the military intervention, the Minister of Finance suggested that the country's best prospects for growth were to open its market to international competition. During this period, political authorities did not know precisely how deep and how fast the liberalization process should be. In fact, as documented by Lederman (2005), it was only after Chile withdrew from the Andean Pact in December 1977 that the government's chief economic strategist, Minister Sergio de Castro, declared that the main goal was to reduce tariffs to a uniform rate of 10% by mid-1979. This change in tariff policy was justified based on the disparate tariff structure in 1977, with rates between 10% and 35%, because it generated unjustifiable discrimination across sectors.

The first stage of liberalization was sudden. By June 1976, the average tariff was 33%, equivalent to a reduction of more than 60% compared to the average tariff in December 1973. This result was particularly noteworthy since quantitative import restrictions had been eliminated by August 1976. By June 1979, when the first stage of liberalization came to an end, all items had a nominal import tariff of 10%, with the exception of automobiles. As pointed out by Lederman (2005), the impacts of this stage of liberalization varied across sectors.

The third stage of Chile's trade liberalization occurred during the period between March 1983 and June 1985. Uniform tariffs were set from 10% to 35%, aiming to accelerate the adjustment process. Along with this, the government reintroduced price bands for certain commodities, such as wheat, sugar, and edible oils in 1983. This provided an equivalent protection to the uniform tariff rate. Between 1982 and 1983, Chile experienced a severe economic contraction, together with a fast adjustment of its current account. As opposed to previous historical experiences where trade protection was used to correct external imbalances, such as those undertaken during the Great Depression, this time the tariff hike was temporary (e.g. no quantitative restrictions were applied). Notably, price bands still exist today (Lederman, 2005).

The process of unilateral liberalization ended in June 1985, when the uniform tariff was reduced again to 20%. Later, in May 1988, the tariff was again reduced to 15%. As documented by Lederman (2005), this was the last trade reform carried out by the military, as Pinochet lost the referendum or plebiscite vote of 1988. The result was the democratic elections of 1989, in which Patricio Aylwin of the Christian Democrats won the election in March 1990. During this time, there was a high degree of uncertainty regarding the future economic policies of a democratically elected government. Consequently, several important economic measures were undertaken, including the establishment of an independent Central Bank, which aimed to reassure markets that a dramatic change in economic orientation would not take place after the political transition.

The uncertainty regarding future trade policies under the newly elected democratic government of Aylwin was mitigated by further reductions of the uniform tariffs, from 15% to 11% in June 1991. This latter confirmed that the liberalizing trend would continue during the new democratic regime. Nonetheless, this did not mean that the new administration would pursue a similar strategy as the military. It was indeed similar, yet focused more on preferential trade agreements (PTA). Most heated domestic debates have spun around Chile's free-trade negotiations with the Common Market of the Southern Cone (Mercosur), implemented in 1997, and, to a lesser extent, the free trade agreement with the United States. A number of Chilean economists, particularly those from the Universidad Catolica, as well as some members of the National Society of Agriculture (SNA), have advocated the idea of unilaterally reducing the uniform tariff (Lederman, 2005).

As pointed out by Lederman (2005), there are a number of reasons for this renewed interest in unilateral liberalization, as well as growing concerns. For instance, PTAs may increase the degree of trade diversion and affect producers of traditional agricultural products in terms of the real appreciation of the currency. Another challenge is the increasing competition from Argentine and Brazilian exports of wheat and edible oil. In addition, the associate membership agreement with Mercosur stipulates the elimination of the price bands approximately 18 years after the implementation of the agreement in 1997. In addition, the PTAs indicate that the 'tariff structure has again become differentiated in the range of 0–11%, depending on the country of origin' (Corbo 1997, p. 75).

After a long debate during 1997 and 1998, the government put forward a new bill to reduce uniform tariffs in November 1998. By the beginning of 1999, the tariff was reduced to 10% and was scheduled to be further reduced 1% annually, up to 6% during 2003. Following this shift towards unilateral liberalization, Chile's relationship with Mercosur improved during the presidency of Ricardo Lagos, who was a personal friend of Brazil's President Fernando Henrique Cardoso. In 1999, President Lagos travelled to Brasilia and officially announced his intention for Chile to become a full member of the South American Trade Bloc (Lederman, 2005).

Nevertheless, as pointed out by Lederman (2005), it was never clear what 'full membership' meant because Lagos received Brazil's blessing to maintain its own external tariff. In December 2000, the government surprised the public by announcing the formal initiation of trade-agreement negotiations with the United States. That trade agreement came into effect on January 1, 2004. As pointed out by Lederman (2005), it is also unclear whether Chile will move forward with its intention to achieve full membership status with Mercosur.

Two other factors that have been detrimental to this new phase of unilateral liberalization in Chile are the ongoing use of price bands for agricultural products and the increased difficulty in the use of anti-dumping and countervailing duties (Fischer and Meller, 1999). As documented by Lederman (2005), on August 20, 1993, the government implemented Decree No. 575, which established regulations concerning anti-dumping and countervailing duties. According to the World Trade Organization (WTO), these regulations were not fully compliant with WTO standards. In particular, the national legislation lacked: (1) a government accountability system of judicial review that could challenge administrative decisions, (2) a system of refunds of duties paid in case decisions are reversed, and (3) accelerated investigations for new exporters (WTO, 1997).

4.4.2.2. Industrial Policy

As mentioned previously, the turn towards greater protectionism started just after World War I and was mainly characterized by controls over trade and a number of revisions to import tariffs, quotas, and exchange rate controls. This economic reality coexisted with some attempts to modernize the apparatus of public administration in Chile during the government of Ibanez, with the creation of developmental agencies aimed to boost the national industry, such as the Ministry of Promotion.[28] However, these attempts were interrupted by the Great Depression and the political turmoil that came with it.

Specifically, there were a number of different short-lived governments, whose efforts were not always sufficient to alleviate the economic situation of the country and thus, implement industrial policies with long-term prospects. Only by 1939, with the creation of CORFO, did the state participate in the economic activity of a number of sectors. Through CORFO, the state quickly began to dominate economic activity in the country, participating in most of the largest investments in the Chilean economy. This institution was financed mainly by the tax revenues of the large-scale copper mining industry and credits from the Central Bank, which was subordinated to the needs of CORFO. As such, CORFO became the main instrument for promoting growth through development policies. In this regard, it provided technical assistance and financing to the private sector through credit policies. It played either a direct or indirect role in these firms, delivered them in concession to private or public institutions, but only when they were oriented to promote the progress of the country in the absence of the cooperation of private capital.[29] After a thorough analysis of imported manufacturing goods that could be produced by Chilean industries, CORFO isolated four sectors to orient its promotion policy: metallurgy, textiles, chemicals, and fishing.

The results of these policies, as we will see, changed the economic reality of the country. The development of metallurgy and the subsequent creation of a national iron and steel company, CAP, paved the way for further developments in this sector. Also significant in this sense was the creation of the National Electricity Company (ENDESA) of Chile, which carried out the national electricity plan that provided the necessary infrastructure for the development of a number of sectors of production. Basically, these would constitute the main

[28] In order to finance this promotion plan, the government was highly indebted to other countries. The plan was executed by the Institute of Industrial Credit, created in 1928, which used pension funds and government money to stimulate the manufacturing industry. By accepting plant equipment as collateral, it also acted as a lender to industrialists, providing technical assistance and financing the modernization or expansion of plants. It also channeled credit to the metallurgical, furniture, textile, food, and beverage industries (see Lederman, 2005).

[29] CORFO (1989).

successes of government intervention during the 1940s. However, as will be noted throughout this section, not all interventions were successful. The government made a number of efforts in other sectors, including forestry, fisheries, livestock farming, and training. In the case of forestry, the interventions had no immediate effects. Meanwhile, some of the other industries, such as fisheries and livestock farming, were mainly stagnant during the period. Other noteworthy efforts were those intended to boost the agricultural sector, but again these would be in vain, given the high concentration of land in the so-called Chilean Hacienda during this period.

By 1952, most national companies were dedicated to supplying basic industrial inputs, and energy and steel were already consolidated. During the difficult years to follow, there were no new initiatives in these sectors. This did not mean that the existing industries stagnated; rather, these continued to grow and modernize. A clear example of this is the case of Empresa Nacional de Petroleo, where the state monopoly was stipulated by law. It was during these years that the expansion in terms of the scale and the variety of operations made it possible to talk about a maturation process. It is also important to mention that ENAP achieved full self-financing during this period and, therefore, did not require state contributions.

Another sector illustrating the legitimacy of state intervention was the outstanding growth in electricity. By 1964, ENDESA contributed 68% of the total production. Unlike ENAP, however, the elevated costs of investment prevented ENDESA from self-financing. Therefore, it was subject to continuous state contributions and external financing.

The case of CAP provides a distinct contrast, given that it continued with an expansive trend. From the start, CAP was defined as a mixed enterprise with both private and public participation. This decision was justified by the need to manage a number of international loans for the construction of Huachipato, and the preference of giving capital to private firms. This generated a debate between those who were in favour of public administration, versus those who were against it. This discussion reached its zenith in 1955, and ended with the prevalence of the privatizing trend of the period that was recommended by the Klein-Saks Mission.

During Alessandri's government, CORFO was instructed to move away from its entrepreneurial role to a more subsidiary role, with a very active credit policy and greater financial support to the private sector. In the National Development Plan of 1961, emphasis was placed on sectors such as food; wood, leather, and chemical products; construction materials; ceramics and porcelain; non-metal foundries; metallurgy; and others. The credit policy was fairly generous for these sectors. One of the few sectoral policies during this period was the Livestock Development Program and Transport Program in 1961. These included credit lines for the creation of artificial grasslands, the acquisition of fine livestock, the construction of facilities and inner roads, and machinery.

Also provided was technical assistance in the form of the provision of forage seeds, livestock sanitary control, improvement of breeds, poultry promotion, and investment in dairy plants and slaughterhouses. As expected, the National Development Program performed relatively well between 1961 and 1962, the first years of its execution. However, the economic deterioration of the country that followed made it difficult to sustain improvements. This situation worsened with the inability to promote the domestic savings required to finance the plan, therefore increasing external debt and causing inflationary pressures at the end of 1962. This led to a contraction in public expenditure that prevented the continuation of the plan.

During the government of Eduardo Frei Montalva in 1967, the state-planning agency Oficina de Planificacion Nacional (ODEPLAN) was established based on the importance of social and economic planning. With the creation of ODEPLAN, CORFO stepped out in its planning role and was redefined as a coordinator of a number of sectoral programmes carried out by specialized state institutions. This entailed the creation of a number of state organizations dependent on CORFO, such as the National Vocational Training Institute (INACAP) created in 1966, and the National Commission for Scientific and Technological Research (CONICYT) in 1967, which was in charge of basic research and policy proposals on a variety of subjects.

It becomes clear that most of the policies carried out during Frei's government were vertical, in line with an import substitution strategy, and aimed to strengthen national industries while prioritizing income redistribution. This was attempted in a number of ways, starting with the development of a new plan for agrarian reform, and the so-called Chilenization of the large-scale copper mining (LSCM) industry.

Under the government of President Allende, an attempt was made to implement an industrial strategy conducive to the establishment of a socialist economy. In order to achieve this goal, CORFO was of central importance. As we will see in the following sections, the Allende government was not concerned with creating new firms. Instead, the administration was characterized by the massive acquisition of a number of firms under its control to form the social property area. This entailed a major administrative effort for CORFO, which included the management of firms under its control, as well as the transformation and reorientation of production units.

As previously discussed, most of the reforms implemented during the military government and those that continued into the next administration were horizontal. This does not mean that the government did not apply vertical policies; however, there are significant opposing trends between horizontal and vertical policies.

Under the government of the military junta (1973–1990), part of the reactivation policy was to increase exports, mainly of non-traditional products. This was an export-oriented system aimed at making better use of domestic resources and the labour force. Since the beginning, CORFO had carried out a multisectoral role. This had to continue under the military since there were no other institutions that could replace it in certain fields. In light of this, CORFO's functions were oriented towards the management of companies, promotion, and development, along with a normalization function of transitory character (CORFO, 1989).

In the spirit of this new role, CORFO created the Fondo de Desarrollo Productivo in 1983, whose objective was to collaborate with the private sector for achieving greater technological development. This would happen through national funding of technological and prospecting research projects on natural resources, while subsidizing part of the costs of executing any initiatives coming from that research. The basic principle of self-financing created surpluses to fund new investment projects. Together with the improvement of administrative efficiency, this delivered surpluses greater than US$1 billion between 1978 and 1987. Notably, after 1978 it became fiscally self-sufficient. In turn, this made it possible to expand access to hydro-electric power throughout the country, satisfying both popular and economic demand. The expansion of available electricity entailed the construction of hydro-electrical plants in the tenth and eleventh regions.

A number of credit programmes established by CORFO have been very important in promoting these development initiatives, including the following: the Global Multisectoral Credit Program, CORFO–Inter-American Development Bank (IADB) I; Global Multisectoral Credit Program, CORFO-IADB II; Programa de Recuperaciones de Colocaciones, CORFO-IDB I; CORFO–World Bank–SERCOTEC Program; and the Financial Intermediation Program, the International Bank for Reconstruction and Development, BIRF–CORFO–Central Bank.

In the first transitory stage, the normalization function was the privatization of the majority of state firms. Of the 259 firms dependent on CORFO in 1973, when CORFO did not have capital participation, 251 had been privatized by 1976, with only 8 left to be normalized. CORFO played a role in an additional 235 firms. Summarizing this period, CORFO performed a fundamental role in the application of the government's growth strategy, mainly by implementing the concept of the subsidiary state (CORFO, 1989).

As we will see shortly, the industrial policy reforms carried out by the military were mainly horizontal, consistent with the subsidiary role of the state that was embraced by the military. There are some exceptions to this rule, which turned out to be very successful, as in the case of Decree Law 701 (1974) in the forestry sector. Under this decree, the government granted a number of subsidies and also intervened directly through CORFO by increasing the area of planted surfaces. Another interesting case is the large-scale copper mining industry (LSCM), which, after a process of massive nationalization during the Popular Unity government, was completely controlled by the military, which decided to create CODELCO (1976). Thus, the military kept control over the mining industry, instead of handing it over to private firms. While there has been tremendous debate regarding whether CODELCO should have been privatized, or whether its strategies should have been bolder, it has certainly proven to be very efficient and continues to be a world leader in the exploitation and production of refined copper.

Other defining policies of the military that are worth mentioning are the creation of the Foreign Investment Statute in 1974, which certainly improved Chile's image internationally. It also provided necessary guarantees to foreign investors that further expropriations would not take place, positioning Chile positively when compared to the rest of the region. In addition, the role of some state institutions has also been very important, such as the creation of ProChile in 1975, with the purpose of promoting export activities, and Fundacion Chile (FCh) in 1976, in order to carry out research and technology transfers.

Regarding credit and financing, during the 1980s CORFO was a direct lender, that is, it operated as a first lending institution. This situation, however, changed dramatically when this role resulted in significant losses. In 1990, all the direct credit mechanisms of CORFO were terminated and their debt portfolios were auctioned with a nominal value of US$714 million. The difference between the sale value and the nominal value resulted in a loss of US$514 million.

As documented by Dini and Stumpo (2002), CORFO started operating as a second lending institution in 1991, following a scheme in which direct credits to final users were replaced by bank funding and other specialized funding intermediaries that allocated resources to final clients. This substantially reduced the risk of financial losses for the state.[30]

As pointed out by Zahler et al. (2014), most instruments used by CORFO during this period were horizontal. Basically, this approach was inherited from the military regime in line with the subsidiary role of the state advocated by most of the opposition. Taking these constraints into account, in the first half of 1990, CORFO developed broad-based innovation programmes (a, b),

[30] Currently, CORFO's main credit lines are the following: (a) investment funding for SME (credit line B.11); (b) investment funding for small industries, CORFO-Germany (credit line b.12); (c) credit for liability reprograming for small firms (credit line B.13); (d) Input and Foreign Commercialization Fund (credit line B.22); (e) Risk Hedging for Exporters (COBEX); (f) Quasi-Capital Program; (g) programme of 'purchase of subordinated bonds to banks for funding the SME'; (h) programme 'FIDES funding for risky capital'; (i) leasing; (j) refunding leasing operations for the SME (credit line a.3); (k) subsidies; and (l) debt renegotiation programme for SME. For further details, see Dini and Stumpo (2002).

the improvement of processes and associative promotion programmes (c, d), programmes targeted to small and medium enterprises (SMEs) (e, f, g), and a programme to attract foreign direct investment (FDI) (f). Later, this horizontal orientation would become more flexible, creating space for more vertical policies. As we will see from the description of these programmes, these entailed clear cooperation between the private sector and CORFO, in particular those related to associativity and technical assistance, requiring human resources, knowledge, and capabilities from the private sector. This is why CORFO initiated an externalization process of functions, which led to the creation of the current network of intermediary institutions of promotion (Dini and Stumpo, 2002).

In this period, most of policy efforts have been horizontal policies with various degrees of success. For example, the Scientific and Technological Development Fund (FONDEF) was created in 1991 to strengthen the scientific and technological capabilities of universities, technological firms, and other institutes aimed at increasing the competitiveness of firms (FONDEF website, 2012). The Suppliers Development Program (PDP) was created in 1998 and operational regulations were incorporated in 2000. The objective of this instrument is to support the evaluation, development, and execution of projects between firms, with the goal of improving the quality and productivity of small-sized suppliers. The Support Program for the Management of Export Firms (PREMEX) is an instrument used by CORFO to target SMEs, with the objective of promoting the exporting capacity of manufacturing firms and computational programmes. PREMEX was discontinued because authorities feared that it could be considered incompatible with the norms of the WTO (Macario, 1998).

The Pre-investment Program (PI) supports pre-investment studies with the goal that firms can make the best decisions regarding a number of investment alternatives that can be identified and assessed technologically, economically, and financially. This instrument is composed of five areas: (i) environment (2000); (ii) irrigation (2001); (iii) movie industry (2005); (iv) small-scale fishing projects (2006); (v) non-conventional renewable energies (2006).

The Guarantee Fund for Small Businesses (FOGAPE), created in 2000, is aimed to guarantee a minimum percentage of credit that public or private financial institutions grant to micro and small enterprises (MSEs), small exporters, and small associations of businesses (Agosin, Larraín, and Grau, 2006). FOGAPE is run as a separate entity through BancoEstado. A similar programme run by CORFO, the Investment Guarantee Fund (FOGAIN), is addressed to firms that do not qualify for FOGAPE (Agosin, Larraín, and Grau, 2010). The Quality Promotion programme was created in 2004, and its main objective is to support firms in improving quality and productivity through specialized consultancy projects meant to integrate systems or management standards with performance assessments that can be certified or verifiable. The advantage of using this instrument is that, as opposed to other instruments such as the Technical Assistance Fund (FAT), FOCAL is a model of technical assistance that is highly standardized that allows for the verification of final results (Ministry of Economy, 2011, cited by Zahler et al., 2014).

But not all horizontal policies implemented since the 1990s have been considered successful. The FAT incorporated, through specialized consultancies, technical management for firm operations and new technologies for productive processes, enabling firms to improve their competitiveness (Zahler et al., 2014). Similarly, the evaluations of the Integrated Territorial Program (2000) that tried to organize production clusters in specific geographical locations were not good. The main goal of this instrument is to support the coordination and direction of projects related to entrepreneurial development, oriented to improving competitiveness in a certain territory/geographical location. The Associative Development Programs (PROFO) is a subsidy to finance collective projects for SMEs. It is designed to improve competitiveness for groups of firms that are willing to be involved in collective actions aimed at solving management and merchandising problems, which because of their very nature or magnitude may be tackled more efficiently as a group.

Since the 1990s there have also been a small number of policies that can be considered vertical. As pointed out by Zahler et al. (2014), the foreign investment attraction programme was among the first formal vertical industrial policies in Chile following the military regime. This programme was launched by CORFO to attract FDI. It was aimed at the information and communication technologies (ICT) sector. As pointed out by Agosin et al. (2010), the results of this programme are quite promising.

Another vertical successful policy, until recently, was the irrigation policy (1992). The Ministry of Public Infrastructure carried out the Rehabilitation and Construction Program for Small- and Medium-Scale Irrigation Schemes (PROMM), investing more than US$100 million. Also in the agricultural sector the resources of INDAP, the main agricultural institution dedicated to small-scale agriculture, have increased by a factor of 2.6 since 1990, and represent more than 50% of the budget of the Ministry of Agriculture. A programme for soil recovery was launched in 1993 by INIA and the Ministry of Agriculture for the XI and XII regions (Portilla, 2000). Also considered successful is the creation of the Technological Institute of Salmon (1994) (INTESAL) established by the Salmon Industry Association (SalmonChile) and the government, through CORFO's technological transfer programmes.

CORFO also participated in the Technology Consortia Program. The programme was created to bring together the innovation efforts of the private sector and increase their collaboration with universities. The programme was launched as an initiative of the Bicentennial Program of Science and Technology

(PBCT), a World Bank programme that provided the Chilean government with technical assistance and a loan (matched by the government) to fund these types of programmes (Ramirez et al., 2008, cited by Zahler et al., 2014).

After the Science and Technology Program (PCT), which operated between 1992 and 1995, the Technological Innovation Program (PIT) was launched, lasting from 1996 to 2000. Then, in 2001, the Development and Technological Innovation Program (PDIT) was established, lasting until 2004. PDIT was explicitly oriented towards the promotion of innovation in a number of important sectors for Chile, namely forestry and agricultural biotechnology, ICT, and clean technologies. It was also the first explicit policy measure aimed at small enterprises. FONTEC was created in 1991 and was financed by the IADB and the Ministry of Finance. It is an institution dependent on CORFO whose objective is to promote, orient, finance, and co-finance the execution of technological innovation projects.

In late 1980s and early 1990s, SERCOTEC initiated a phase of changes to its management structure that weakened its capacity for action. This continued until the arrival of the new democratic government. Political changes also redefined the institutional mission of SERCOTEC, which is to contribute to the development of SMI by creating a modern entrepreneurial culture through innovation and the development of appropriate conditions. The trajectory of interventions implies that the goals of this mission are: (i) to improve environmental conditions, emphasizing the creation and/or development of a sector service market; (ii) to change the thinking of the players; and (iii) to support the production chain, stressing the local and regional dimension. As can be clearly seen from this mission, the new administration strongly emphasized instruments that promote associativity and the joint actions of firms (Molsalves, 2002).

During the government of President Bachelet, great attention was given to the development of regional production clusters. This crystallized into the National Cluster Program, coordinated by INNOVA. The programme was developed with the consultation of independent experts[31] who looked for sectors with high potential. After assessing a number of sectors conducive to development, the government selected: (i) global services, (ii) special interest tourism, (iii) mining, (iv) agriculture, and (v) aquaculture. These sectors were then analysed in depth in order to identify potential gaps and bottlenecks that could be addressed by policy intervention. In a third stage, a number of actions were set up to promote these industries, in which the government coordinated different institutions to address these bottlenecks (see Zahler et al., 2014).

[31] Boston Consulting Group.

The period between 2003 and 2006 was very important for innovation policy. A mining royalty was legally passed, whereby all of proceeds would be devoted to innovation programmes. Around 25% of funding would be directly allocated to regional governments for innovation programmes. This led to the creation of CNIC (Consejo Nacional de Innovacion para la Competitividad), a national council for managing these new resources, established in 2005 by presidential decree. Although it had more limited faculties than initially thought, the CNIC is in charge of elaborating innovation strategies by proposing how to spend available resources and also by providing general guidelines on public spending on science and technology.

Before the creation of the CNIC, key loans were made by international institutions to enhance firm innovation and their connection to science and basic research, and to enhance the quality of applied university research. Three programmes began with such loans: the Millennium Scientific Initiative (MIDEPLAN) with a World Bank loan, the CORFO-affiliated Chile Innova programme with an IADB loan, and the CONICYT-affiliated Bicentennial Program for Science and Technology (PBCT) with a World Bank loan (Zahler et al., 2014).With the creation of the National Innovation Council for Competitiveness in 2005, CORFO restructured its instruments and fused them into INNOVA Chile instruments, reforming its 'Consejos' and creating a new 'macro Consejo', INNOVA, therefore simplifying its innovation role (Zahler et al, 20142).

During the past decade many of the policy instruments implemented since 2000 have continued to be used; however, those with a cluster focus were implemented by Bachelet`s government and cancelled by Piñera's government.

Perhaps the most important change in the implementation of industrial policy tools has been the modernization of CORFO`s structure and programmes (see Correa, Dini, and Letelier, 2021), for detailed information, some of which is summarized and presented below). In particular, since the year 2015, CORFO's objectives have continued to be the promotion of entrepreneurship and innovation, but now are aligned with sustainable development goals and are territorially balanced across the country. By 2021, CORFO had six divisions: Investment and Funding, Entrepreneurship, Innovation, Technological Capabilities, Networks and Territory, and the best known, Start Up Chile.

The innovation division has programmes such as Sum to Innovation, Connect and Collaborate, Create and Validate, Consolidation and Expansion. The programme names are self-explanatory and are aimed to support innovation at their different stages. Moreover, there are regional innovation programmes. There are also 13 centres aimed at the provision of public goods that encourage firms' associativity. Since 2020 this programme depends on the Networks and Territory division. The Entrepreneurship division has mainly two types of instruments: those that provide funding, and those that provide support to the entrepreneurial ecosystem. In the first category we find seed capital, scaling seed capital, and challenge-oriented subsidies. In the second category we find support for networking, workshops, and so on. Furthermore, there is funding to accelerators.

Maybe the most important current programme for support entrepreneurs is the Start Up Chile programme, today a new division of CORFO, which was implemented by Piñera`s government. The aim of this programme is to foster technological entrepreneurs who are globally oriented, and it offers supports not only to Chilean entrepreneurs but also to foreigners. The other CORFO divisions have programmes that offer state warranties to help firms with low collateral, green credits, SMEs credits, support to engineering schools, territorially oriented programmes, and funding for technological centres for innovation, among others.

Also, among the most innovative new programmes of the last decade is the Business Centres programme implemented under Bachelet's government, which is the Chilean version of the business development centres of the United States. Currently, there are 53 centres operating all across the country. Finally, another institution that keeps supporting entrepreneurs is BancoEstado, which operates programmes that offer state warranties as FOGAPE, FOGAIN, and COBEX. However, the most successful and relevant programme from BancoEstado during the past decades is CUENTA RUT, a debit account with a DNI number that nearly 10 million people use. This programme has greatly improved the access to financial services to independent workers and microentrepreneurs.

4.5. Conclusions

This chapter has examined the development trajectories of two resource-rich regions, Scandinavia and Latin America. With regard to the latter, special reference was made to the Chilean case. Through the use of econometric analysis, it was argued that openness and proximity to key markets have been extremely important drivers of growth. During the late nineteenth and early twentieth centuries, Latin American countries pursuing such openness were able to perform well. Still, they eventually saw an income gap open up between themselves, Scandinavia, and the advanced industrialized economies.

The Scandinavian countries proved more adept at managing the external buffeting effects of commodity price swings than did their Latin American counterparts. This was in part due to superior human and social capital and their capacity to innovate. This created new market opportunities and provided a better basis for sustaining good growth performance. Still, when, once more,

Latin American countries pursued economic openness (as they did beginning in the 1980s), better outcomes did result. The widening income gap between Latin America and Scandinavia that had started at the beginning of the twentieth century began to close once more at the beginning of the twenty-first.

Turning more specifically to the case of Chile, does the income gap remain insuperable? The chapter has argued that while industrial and sectoral policies may have had their failures, economic opening allowed Chile to capitalize on human capital and learning accumulated from a more interventionist era. Consistent with the big push hypothesis, more access to international trade enlarged the size of the market for Chilean firms. It enabled them to deploy resources and capabilities bequeathed by the import substitution period. Firms were able to ramp up exports, with GDP rising accordingly. When one examines the data on income and exports in Chile and Sweden, the findings are noteworthy. Once a more open strategy was adopted in Chile from the mid-1970s onwards, the share of its exports as a proportion of those of Sweden recovered. In tandem with this, the income per capita gap began to narrow appreciably, with Chile gaining ground on Sweden. All of this suggests that export performance and the policy framework that supports it have a vital role to play in helping Latin American countries address the income gap separating them from more advanced economies.

References

Agosin, M., Larraín, C., and Grau, N. 2010. 'Industrial Policy in Chile', *IDB Working Paper Series*. https://publications.iadb.org/publications/english/document/Industrial-Policy-in-Chile.pdf.

Barro, R., and Sala i Martin, X. 1995. *Economic Growth*. New York: McGraw Hill, 1995.

Benavot, A., and Riddle, P. 1988. 'The Expansion of Primary Education, 1870–1940: Trends and Issues', *Sociology of Education*, 61(3) July, 191–210.

Blomstróm, M., and Meller Bock, P. 1990. *Trayectorias divergentes: Comparación de un siglo de desarrollo económico latinoamericano y escandinavo*. Santiago de Chile: CIEPLAN: Hachette.

Blomström, M., and Meller, P. 1991. *Diverging Paths: Comparing a Century of Scandinavian and Latin American Economic Development*. Washington, DC: Inter-American Development Bank.

Braun, L. J. 2000. *Economía Chilena 1810–1995: Estadísticas Históricas*. Santiago: Pontificia Universidad Católica de Chile, Instituto de Economía.

Bravo-Ortega, C., and Eterovic, N. 2015. 'A Historical Perspective of a Hundred Years of Industrialization: From Vertical to Horizontal Policies in Chile,' *Working Papers* wp399, Department of Economics, University of Chile. https://ideas.repec.org/p/udc/wpaper/wp399.html

Butelmann, A. Cortés, H., and Videla, P. 1981. 'Proteccionismo en Chile: Una visión retrospectiva', *Cuadernos de Economía* No. 54–55, Instituto de Economía, Universidad Católica de Chile.

Caldentey, E., and Vernengo, M. 2019. 'The historical evolution of monetary policy in Latin America', in S. Battilossi et al., eds., *Handbook of the History of Money and Currency*: Singapore: Springer, 1–28.

Cariola, C., and Sunkel, O. 1985. 'The Growth of the Nitrate Industry and Socioeconomic Change in Chile 1880–1930', in R. Cortes-Conde and S. J. Hunt, eds., *The Latin American Economies: Growth and the Export Sector 1880–1930* .New York and London: Holmes & Meier, 137–254.

Chenery, H., and Syrquin, M. 1975. *Patterns of Development 1950–1970*. Oxford: Oxford University Press.

Chenery, H., Syrquin, M., and Robinson, S. 1987. *Industrialization and Growth: A Comparative Study*. Oxford: Oxford University Press.

Corbo, Vittorio. 1997. 'Trade Reform and Uniform Import Tariffs: The Chilean Experience', *American Economic Review*, 87(2), 73–77.

Correa Mautz, F., Dini, M., and Letelier, L. April 2022. 'Análisis del sistema público de apoyo al desarrollo productivo en Chile desde un enfoque multinivel', *Serie Documentos de Proyectos*. https://hdl.handle.net/11362/47668.

Cortes Conde, R. 1985. 'The Export Economy of Argentina 1880–1920', in Cortes Conde, R., ed., *The Latin American Economies*. New York: Holmes & Meier, 319–381.

Cortés Douglas, H., Butelmann, A., and Videla, P. 1981. 'Proteccionismo en Chile: Una visión retrospectiva', *Cuadernos de Economía*, 18(54–55), 141–194.

Diaz Alejandro, C. 1970. *Essays on the Economic History of Argentine Republic*. New Haven, CT: Yale University Press.

Dini, M., and Stumpo, G. 2002. 'Análisis de la política de fomento a las pequeñas y medianas empresas en Chile', *Serie Desarrollo Productivo*, no. 136 (December). http://hdl.handle.net/11362/4526.

Drachmann, P., and Westergaard, H. 1915. *The Industrial Development and Commercial Policies of the Three Scandinavian Countries*. Oxford: Clarendon Press.

Ellsworth, P. T. 1945. *Chile: An Economy in Transition*. New York: Macmillan.

Engel, E., and Melle, P. 1993. *External Shocks and Stabilization Mechanisms*. Washington, DC: Inter-American Development Bank.

Engerman, S., and Sokoloff, K. 1997. 'Factor Endowments, Institutions and Differential Paths of Growth among New World Economies', in Harber, S., ed., *How Latin America Fell Behind: Essays on the Economic Histories of Brazil and Mexico, 1800–1914*. Stanford, CA: Stanford University Press, 260–306).

Frankel, J., and Romer, D. 1996. 'Trade and Growth: An Empirical Investigation', *NBER Working Paper Series*.

Frankel, J., and Romer, D. 1999. 'Does Trade Cause Growth?', *American Economic Review*, 89(3), 379–399.

Gallup, J. L., Sachs, J. D., and Mellinger, A. D. 1999. 'Geography and Economic Development', Harvard University Centre for Economics Development Working Paper No. 1 p. 1–57.

Heckscher, E. 1968. *An Economic History of Sweden*. Cambridge, MA: Harvard University Press.

Hveen, H. 1990. 'Desarrollo de una economia abierta: La transformacion de Noruega, 1845–1975', in M. Blomström and P. Meller, eds., *Trayectorias divergentes: Comparación de un siglo de desarrollo económico latinoamericano y escandinavo*, Santiago: Cieplan, 228–232.

Krugman, P. 1990. 'The Narrow Moving Band, the Dutch Disease, and the Competitive Consequences of Mrs Thatcher: Notes on Trade of Scale Dynamic Economies', *Journal of Development Economics*, 27(1–2), October 41–55.

Lederman, D. 2005. *The Political Economy of Protection: Theory and the Chilean Experience* Stanford, CA:tanford University Press.

Long, B. D. 1988. 'Productivity Growth, Convergence, and Welfare: Comment', *American Economic Review*, 78(5), 1138–1154.

Lüders, R. 2012. 'La Misión Klein-Saks, Los Chicago Boys y la política económica', *Documento de Trabajo, Instituto de Economía, Pontificia Universidad Católica*, no. 411 (January), 1–34. https://www.economia.uc.cl/docs/doctra/dt-411.pdf.

Macario, C. 1998. 'Chile: De las políticas de subsidio a las exportaciones a las políticas de desarrollo de la competitividad', *Sede de la CEPAL en Santiago (Estudios e Investigaciones*, 1–42. http://hdl.handle.net/11362/34634.

Maddison, A. 1995. *Monitoring the World Economy 1820–1992*. Paris: OECD.

Marquez, G. 1998. 'Tariff Protection in Mexico, 1892–1909: Ad Valorem Tariff Rates and Sources of Variation', in A. Taylor and J. Coastworth, eds., *Latin America and the World Economy since 1800 (Series on Latin American Studies)*. David Rockefeller Center for Latin American Studies, 407–442.

Matsuyama, K. 1991. 'Increasing Returns, Industrialization and Indeterminacy of Equilibrium', *The Quarterly Journal of Economics*, 106(2), 617–650.

McGreevey, W. 1971. *An Economic History of Colombia*. Cambridge: Cambridge University Press.

Meller, P. 1996. *Un siglo de economia politica chilena (1890–1990)*. Santiago: Editorial Andres Bello.

Mitchell, B. R. 1992. *International Historical Statistics Europe 1750–1988*. New York: Stockton Press.

Monsalves, M. 2002. 'Las PYME y los sistemas de apoyo a la innovación tecnológica en Chile', Working paper 126, Red de Reestructuración y Competitividad Unidad de Desarrollo Industrial y Tecnológico División de Desarrollo Productivo y Empresarial desarrollo productivo 126 Santiago de Chile, July 2002. https://www.cepal.org/sites/default/files/publication/files/4512/S026456_es.pdf.

Murphy, K., Schleifer, A., and Vishny, R. 1989a. 'Income Distribution, Market Size, and Industrialization', *The Quarterly Journal of Economics*, 104(3) 537–564.

Murphy, K., Schleifer, A., and Vishny, R. 1989b. 'Industrialization and the Big Push', *Journal of Political Economy*, 97(5), 1003–1026.

O'Rourke, K., and Williamson, J. 1995. 'Education, Globalization and Catch up: Scandinavia in the Swedish Mirror', *Scandinavian Economic History Review*, 43(3), 287–309.

O'Rourke, K., and Williamson, J. 1999. *Globalization and History*. Cambridge, MA: MIT Press.

Ortega Martínez, L. 1989. *Corporación de fomento de la producción: 50 años de realizaciones 1939–1989*. Santiago: Universidad de Santiago de Chile.

Palma, J. G. 1979. 'Growth and Structure of Chilean Manufacturing Industry from 1830 to 1935: Origins and Development of a Process of Industrialization in an Export Economy'. PhD thesis. University of Oxford.

Palma, J. G. March 1984. 'Chile 1914–1935: De economía exportadora a sustitutiva de importaciones', Estudio No. 81, *Colección de Estudios*.

Portilla R., Belfor. 2000. 'La politica agrícola en Chile: Lecciones de tres décadas', *Serie Desarrollo Productivo*. Santiago,.

Rosenblat, A. 1954. *La población indígena y el mestizaje en América*. Vol. 1. Buenos Aires: Editorial Nova.

Rosenstein-Rodan, P. N. 1943. 'Problems of Industrialisation of Eastern and South-Eastern Europe', *The Economic Journal*, 53, 202–211.

Sala-i-Martin, X., and Barro, R. J. 2004. *Economic Growth*. 2nd ed. Cambridge, MA: MIT Press.
Sunkel, O., and Paz, P. 1975. *El subdesarrollo latinoamericano y la teoría del desarrollo*. 8th ed. Mexico: Instituto Latinoamericano de planificación economica y social, Economía y demografía.
Williamson, J. 1996. 'Globalization, Convergence and History', *The Journal of Economic History*, 56(2), 277–306.
Williamson, J. 1999. 'Real Wages and Relative Factor Prices in the Third World 1820–1940: Latin America (Real Wages, Inequality, and Globalization in Latin America before 1940)', *Revista de Historia Económica* 17, 101–142.
Zahler, A., Benavente, J. M., Ortega, C. B., and Goya, D. 2014. 'Public-Private Cooperation in Productive Development Policies: Case Studies from Chile', *IDB Working Paper Series*.

Appendix

Construction of Data

Exports: For export current exports data are used withimplicit regional exports deflators applied deriving from from Lewis (1981). For converting exports into 1990 iGeary Khamy dollars, the implicit exchange rate was used, this being obtained from Maddison (1995) (who also utilizes Lewis (1981) as a source).

GDP: Per capita GDP data were constructed for Peru and Chile in 1870. For Chilean case, use was made of Maddison's GDP dataset (Maddison, 1995) with the growth rates of real GDP obtained from Brauwn et al. (1999). For the Peruvian case use was made of the average rate of growth reported by Engerman and Sokoloff (1997), combined with Maddison's series.

5
The Co-Evolution of FDI and the Output and Export Structures of Brazil and Mexico, 2000–2015

André Pineli and Rajneesh Narula

5.1. Introduction

Since the 1970s, scholars and international organizations have been promoting foreign direct investment (FDI) as a catalyst for economic development. A key assumption is that FDI is a vehicle for knowledge and technology transfer. This is supposed to make the host country more productive, not only directly—that is, through the affiliate's activities—but also indirectly because it is assumed that FDI generates positive spillovers to domestic firms.

Both economists and international business (IB) specialists have sought to unravel the socioeconomic impact of the multinational enterprises (MNEs) (Narula, Giuliani, and van der Straaten, 2022). Much of the work over the past five decades in the field noted that the presence of MNE activity per se is not a *sine qua non* for economic development, and indeed, the net effect can be negative, and may evolve over time due to a variety of factors.

John Dunning's early work on understanding the co-evolution of FDI and economic structures has been particularly influential. Shaped by the stages of development literature that emphasized that economic development was not simply a synonym of GDP growth but entailed qualitative changes in the structures of production employment and consumption (Kuznets, 1957; Chenery, 1960), 'the investment development path' described how a country's inward and outward FDI position evolved according to its level of development (Dunning, 1981a, 1988; Dunning and Narula, 1996; Narula, 1996; Narula and Dunning, 2010).

This body of work explained that the development effects of a specific investment depended upon a number of factors. The extent to which MNE investments influenced the development of its host location was primarily determined by the characteristics of its affiliates operating in the country (in the form of the MNE's

André Pineli and Rajneesh Narula, *The Co-Evolution of FDI and the Output and Export Structures of Brazil and Mexico, 2000–2015* In: *Innovation, Competitiveness, and Development in Latin America.* Edited by: Edmund Amann and Paulo N. Figueiredo, Oxford University Press. © Oxford University Press 2024. DOI: 10.1093/oso/9780197648070.003.0005

ownership advantages[1]) and the characteristics of the host country, as reflected in its location advantages. Both advantages are not immutable and tend to influence each other—that is, the presence of MNEs may contribute to alter the country's location advantages, while the country's characteristics may affect the affiliates' advantages.

The impacts on host economy also depended on the fundamental motives that led the MNE to engage in that specific investment. Cuervo-Cazurra, Narula, and Un (2015) list four broad (and non-mutually exclusive) motives that lead a firm to invest abroad: sell more, buy better (reduce costs of inputs), upgrade (increase the pool of assets that compounds the firm's competitive advantages), or escape (from an adverse environment in the home country).[2]

The development effects of any given affiliate within an MNE's network of affiliates are not constant, and indeed change over time. The choice of the activities performed in a country is connected to an MNE's overall strategy. To some extent, affiliates of the same MNE located in different countries may well compete against each other for tasks and functions within the overall corporate structure. Thus, the role of any given affiliate evolves over time, and may become increasingly specialized and upgraded, or downgraded. Such a change in scope, scale, and intensity will reflect on its economic impact to the host economy. A subsidiary, a region, or a country can remain locked in to low value-adding activities, and may have a negligible multiplier effect, reflecting weak backward and forward linkages by the MNE affiliate.

Although many studies have investigated the impact of FDI on host economies, fewer studies investigate the relationship between FDI and GDP growth (for a review, see Narula and Pineli, 2017, 2019). There are fewer studies that examine the co-evolution between FDI and economic structure, with Pineli, Narula, and Belderbos (2021) and Pineli (2022) being two recent attempts to advance the literature on FDI and structural change, but in general such analyses require data that are not usually available.

We seek to bridge this gap by investigating the co-evolution between FDI, economic structure, and export structures in the two largest Latin American economies, Brazil and Mexico, over the period 2000–2015. Prior to this period, these countries had followed quite similar development strategies, focusing on

[1] To explain 'why', 'where', and 'how' a firm performs activities overseas, Dunning (1981b) put forward the 'eclectic paradigm' of international production. According to this approach, FDI requires the fulfilment of three preconditions: (a) an investing firm must own some kind of proprietary assets capable to yield extraordinary rents as a means to overcome the cost advantages of being an outsider (ownership advantage); (b) there must be an advantage in producing in chosen location, otherwise the firm would produce and export from home country (location advantage); (c) there must be a justification for carrying out the activity within the firm, otherwise a market transaction (such as the licensing of the firm's brand or technology to a third party) would be preferred (internalization advantage).

[2] These motives are similar, but not identical, to Dunning's (1988, 1993) better-known classification.

inward-oriented industrialization as a path to economic prosperity. At the end of the import-substitution era, and accelerated by huge foreign debts, both adjusted their strategies, but in differing ways. While Brazil remained largely oriented towards its domestic market, Mexico made a radical shift towards an export-led model. Despite these differences, both countries converged in (at least) one thing: the disappointing results in terms of GDP growth.

In addition to the analysis of the key indicators, we briefly discuss the role played by industrial policies—or their absence—within Brazil's and Mexico's development strategies. We take the view that industrial policy has the objective of changing the structure of an economy in either direction, magnitude, or speed, in a way that market forces alone would not be able to achieve. Our analysis implicitly assumes that what an economy produces and exports matters for its long-term growth trajectory (Hausmann, Huang, and Rodrik, 2006). Industrial policy instruments, such as infant industry protection, subsidies, tax and financial incentives, as well as performance requirements, may be crucial to shift the economic structure in the direction of the desired industries. Nonetheless, industrial policy may also be the source of distortions and inefficiencies that, in the end, hamper economic growth. Therefore, industrial policy incentives must be temporary, transparent, and evaluated on measurable performance criteria defined in advance (Moreno-Brid, 2016).

The chapter is organized as follows: the next section (section 5.2) presents the antecedents of the period under analysis, discussing the role and the effects of FDI during the import substitution industrialization (ISI) phase and the following period of market-oriented reforms. The period 2000–2015 is analysed in section 5.3, which is followed by the concluding remarks (section 5.4).

5.2. Antecedents: Import Substitution Industrialization and the Market Reforms of the 1980s and 1990s

For (at least) three decades of the twentieth century—from the 1950s to the 1970s—Brazil and Mexico (like much of Latin America) followed very similar strategies of import substitution in their pursuit of prosperity. Industrialization was considered crucial to escape the development trap arguably imposed by continued reliance on primary product exports and the import of manufactures and industrial products. Given the inability of the import substitution industries to compete globally, domestic manufacturers targeted the domestic markets, which were protected from foreign competitors (Prebisch, 1949; Singer, 1950). The belief was that the exposure to novelty in the form of new products, new processes, new technologies, and new knowledge would induce learning and the development of upgraded domestic capabilities (Bruton, 1989).

State-led ISI was the engine of Brazilian and Mexican growth. Key industries, such as petroleum, electricity, and telecommunications, were kept under strict state control. However, FDI was allowed in non-strategic manufacturing and services industries, although occasionally subject to minority stakes and performance requirements.

In Brazil, foreign MNEs became the market leaders in industries like automobiles, pharmaceuticals, and electrical equipment (Morley and Smith, 1971; Bonelli, 1980; Willmore, 1987; Nonnenberg, 2003). In Mexico, foreign MNEs dominated industries like automobiles, chemicals, and electrical equipment (Newfarmer and Mueller, 1975), but Mexican laws were considerably less permissive than Brazilian laws as they imposed restrictions on wholly-owned MNE subsidiaries, with a preference for joint ventures with national private capital or even with state-owned enterprises (Vidal, 1986). In Mexico, further stimulus for inward FDI was given in the mid-1960s by the introduction of a program aimed at creating export-processing industries in states that bordered the United States, and were suffering from high unemployment rates, giving rise to the *maquiladora*—or simply *maquila*—system.[3] Similarly, in Brazil inward FDI was encouraged by the implementation of the Second National Development Plan (*II Plano Nacional de Desenvolvimento*, II PND) (1975–1979). The first oil shock saw a balance of payments constriction imposed in Brazil, aimed at deepening import substitution of basic materials (steel, cement, cellulose, fertilizers, petrochemicals) and capital goods, among other ambitious targets[4] (Suzigan, 1988).

The results of the ISI are controversial—evaluations were initially favourable but became increasingly negative as the distortions and inefficiencies became clear, although under a heavily protectionist regime, manufacturing shares in GDP rose substantially in both countries.[5]

During the ISI phase, the ultimate motive for FDI was tariff-jumping, and this inevitably affected the way the relationship between the MNE affiliates and the headquarters evolved. Moreira (1999) argues that in Brazil most MNEs were operating in capital- and technology-intensive industries, due to overprotection against imports, and the ownership advantages of the MNEs were underutilized by their Brazilian affiliates, as demonstrated by their outdated products and processes.

[3] The *maquila* system is further detailed in the next section.

[4] One of the II PND's central objectives was rebalancing the tripod formed by the state-owned, the foreign multinational, and the private national enterprise, strengthening the latter's position in the country's economy (Lessa, 1978). Thus, the FDI policy became more selective, prioritizing, for example, industries capable of contributing to diversify the country's export structure (Nonnenberg, 2003).

[5] In Brazil, aside from macroeconomic tools such as multiple exchange rates, the protectionist arsenal included high tariffs, restrictive import licences, and prohibition of imports when a similar domestically made good was available (Colistete, 2003).

After the early 1980s debt crises, and the exhaustion of the ISI model, Brazil and Mexico had to reset their development strategies. Mexico soon embarked in a radical shift, characterized by unilateral trade liberalization, relaxation of FDI restrictions, privatization of state-owned enterprises, deregulation, and reduction of state intervention in the economy, making the country a posterchild of what came to be known as the Washington Consensus. The same set of reforms were undertaken by Brazil, mostly in the 1990s, although often in a softer version than in Mexico.[6]

In Mexico, the previous inward orientation gave way to an economy in which export production became the main driver of economic growth (Hanson, 2002). Merchandise trade (exports plus imports) increased from 10.6% of GDP, in 1976, to 67.1% in 2015. In addition, there was an impressive change in their composition: crude petroleum, which used to account for a large part of Mexican exports until the early 1980s, now accounted for less than 15%, meaning that *Mexico's role in the international division of labour was now related to manufacturing.* In addition, the country was able to increase the share of medium- and high-technology goods in its export basket. Nonetheless, the subtle abandonment of the ISI model caused the dismantling of the linkages within the manufacturing sector and the explosion of imports, which was never reversed. The culmination of the radical shift was the signature of the North American Free Trade Agreement (NAFTA), in force from December 1994, which definitively tied the Mexican economy to its major trade partner, the United States.[7]

FDI attraction was given a central role in the new development agenda. In Mexico, it went mostly to the manufacturing sector, particularly to the *maquilas* (Máttar, Moreno-Brid, and Peres, 2003), but privatization was also an important pull factor, especially in the early 1990s (Dussel Peters, 2000). According to Máttar, Moreno-Brid, and Peres (2003), Mexico's export drive was led by subsidiaries of foreign MNEs. More than this, the reconversion of the Mexican economy from an inward-oriented to an export-led one was largely the result of efficiency-seeking FDI led by US MNEs, because trade growth was essentially intra-firm trade growth.

In Brazil, inward FDI decreased to negligible levels during the turbulent 1980s. Only after the Real Plan (*Plano Real*), the currency stabilization program put in place in 1994, did FDI surge, reaching a first peak in the period 1997–2000, when

[6] An amendment to the Brazilian Constitution sanctioned in 1994 extinguished legal differentiation between national and foreign enterprises. This not only broadened the scope for MNEs' activities but also gave them access to industrial policy instruments formerly reserved for national firms (Bielschowsky, 1999). In addition, restrictions to FDI in oil and gas extraction, mining, banking, and telecommunications were lifted in 1995 (Nonnenberg, 2003).

[7] The synchronization with US economic cycles is clearly exemplified by the deep Mexican recession of 2009, following the subprime crisis in the United States.

several energy and telecommunications companies were privatized. Differently from Mexico, where historically more than two-thirds of FDI come from the United States, in Brazil the sources of FDI were more diversified—in 1990, for example, half of the FDI stock came from Europe, while the United States accounted for roughly a third (Bielschowsky, 1994).

In contrast to Mexico, Brazil remained largely an inward-oriented economy, as demonstrated by indicators like merchandise trade/GDP, one of the lowest in the world (13.8% in 1990, and 20.4% in 2015). Despite this, trade liberalization—along with other reforms—radically altered MNE activity in Brazil. Increased competition forced rationalization and restructuring—MNEs were predominant in industries in which scale matters, such as consumer durable goods, but they were often operating at rather inefficient scales. In the new scenario, location advantages became more important, leading to a correction of the prior excessive degree of verticalization and a greater integration of the Brazilian affiliates into MNE networks, which implied rationalization of production—that is, reduction in product portfolios, outsourcing, and increase of imports from the parent and from other affiliates (Moreira, 1999; Nonnenberg, 2003). Nonetheless, MNE strategies remained largely unaltered, as they continued to target the domestic market, with few exceptions.[8]

Despite the diverging strategies followed since the foreign debt crises, Brazil and Mexico converged in terms of the disappointing growth performance. Indeed, since the 1980s, Brazil and Mexico are the typical stop-and-go economies. Growth spurts are promptly followed by recessions and crises—in Brazil, growth episodes are sardonically called 'chicken flights' due to their short length (Leahy, 2012). The next section analyses the co-evolution between FDI and output and export structures in the period 2000–2015.

5.3. The Co-Evolution of FDI and Output and Export Structures in Brazil and Mexico, 2000–2015

In what follows, this section seeks to trace the co-evolution between FDI and economic structures. It begins by describing Brazil's and Mexico's economies at the turn of the twenty-first century. Next, it indicates to which sectors and industries FDI was directed to over the period 2000–2015. Finally, it investigates whether production and export structures shifted towards sectors that received most

[8] Due to arrangements made within Mercosur, MNEs in the automotive sector integrated their operations in the bloc. Apart from this, only MNE affiliates in natural-resource-intensive industries, such as mining, paper and pulp, and wood products, had an unequivocal outward orientation (Sarti and Laplane, 2002).

FDI. With respect to production, the chapter extends the analysis beyond the industry directly related to FDI, as a means of searching for additional FDI effects through backward linkages. It also assesses whether FDI may have contributed to diversifying export structures, especially in the direction of more sophisticated products.

Three sets of data are employed: FDI statistics, provided by national sources (Central Bank of Brazil and Department of Economy of the Government of Mexico); production (value-added) and input-output relations, provided by the Organisation for Economic Co-operation and Development (OECD) and by the Brazilian Statistical Office (IBGE); and export statistics, including revealed comparative advantage (RCA), provided by the OECD's Trade in Value Added (TiVA) database and by the Observatory of Economic Complexity (OEC).

5.3.1. The Brazilian and Mexican Economies in 2000

In 2000, 67.7% of the value-added in the Brazilian economy came from the services sector, 15.3% came from manufacturing, 10.1% from utilities and construction, 5.5% from agriculture, and 1.4% from the extractive mineral sector. In Mexico, the services sector accounted for 60.5% of value-added, the manufacturing sector for 20%, utilities and construction for 9.3%, the extractive sector for 6.7%, and agriculture for 3.5%. Therefore, at the turn of the twenty-first century, Mexico was considerably more industrialized than Brazil, was more dependent on the extractive sectors, especially the oil sector, while in Brazil a larger share of the value-added came from services and from the agricultural sector.

FDI stocks grew substantially during the 1990s in both economies, following processes of liberalization and regional integration (NAFTA and Mercosur), besides large privatizations. Data on FDI stocks with sectoral disaggregation are available for Brazil but not for Mexico. As shown in Table 5.1,[9] the subtle growth in Brazilian inward FDI stock in the late 1990s was accompanied by an impressive change in its sectoral distribution. The share of manufacturing fell from two-thirds of total FDI stock to one-third. In turn, FDI in energy, telecommunications, and banking skyrocketed, following privatization of state-owned enterprises. In 2000, Brazil and Mexico had quite similar inward FDI stocks in relative terms. In Brazil, FDI stock was equivalent to 15.8% of GDP. In Mexico, it was 17.2%.

[9] The sectors/industries utilized in these tables are described in the Appendix.

Table 5.1 Brazil: FDI Stocks

Sector	1995			2000		
	Annual Aver. US$ Mi	Share (% of Total)	% of GDP	Annual Aver. US$ Mi	Share (% of Total)	% of GDP
Agriculture and mining	925	2.22	0.119	2,401	2.33	0.368
01–03	246	0.59	0.032	384	0.37	0.059
05–06	72	0.17	0.009	1,022	0.99	0.157
07–09	607	1.46	0.078	995	0.97	0.153
Manufacturing	27,907	66.93	3.587	34,726	33.71	5.323
10–12	3,543	8.50	0.455	5,342	5.19	0.819
13–15	1,036	2.49	0.133	874	0.85	0.134
16	29	0.07	0.004	240	0.23	0.037
17–18	1,772	4.25	0.228	1,764	1.71	0.270
19	0	0.00	0.000	1	0.00	0.000
20–21	5,331	12.79	0.685	6,043	5.87	0.926
22	1,539	3.69	0.198	1,782	1.73	0.273
23	854	2.05	0.110	1,170	1.14	0.179
24	3,005	7.21	0.386	2,513	2.44	0.385
25	573	1.37	0.074	593	0.58	0.091
28	2,345	5.62	0.301	3,324	3.23	0.510
26	1,412	3.39	0.181	3,186	3.09	0.488
27	1,101	2.64	0.141	990	0.96	0.152
29	4,838	11.60	0.622	6,351	6.17	0.974
30	223	0.53	0.029	356	0.35	0.055
31–33	308	0.74	0.040	195	0.19	0.030
Utilities, construction and services	12,864	30.85	1.653	65,888	63.96	10.100
35–39	4	0.01	0.001	7,384	7.17	1.132
41–43	203	0.49	0.026	416	0.40	0.064
45–47	2,886	6.92	0.371	10,240	9.94	1.570
49–53	193	0.87	0.047	495	0.48	0.049
55–56	364	0.46	0.025	317	0.31	0.076
61	399	0.96	0.051	18,762	18.21	2.876
62–63	115	5.22	0.280	2,543	2.47	1.939
64–66	2,178	2.66	0.143	12,652	12.28	0.122
68	1,109	0.28	0.015	798	0.77	0.390
69–82	5,322	12.76	0.684	11,838	11.49	1.815

(continued)

Table 5.1 Continued

Sector	1995			2000		
	Annual Aver. US$ Mi	Share (% of Total)	% of GDP	Annual Aver. US$ Mi	Share (% of Total)	% of GDP
85	1	0.00	0.000	6	0.01	0.001
86–88	18	0.04	0.002	70	0.07	0.011
Other services	72	0.17	0.009	369	0.36	0.056
Total	41,696	—	5.359	1,03,015	—	15.791

Source: Central Bank of Brazil (CBB). https://www.bcb.gov.br/rex/censoce/port/censo.asp?frame=1. The source of GDP used in this table is UNCTAD (https://unctadstat.unctad.org/EN/) Author's elaboration.

Note: Other services include sectors 90–98.

5.3.2. Where Has FDI Been Destined since 2000?

Table 5.2 shows the sectoral distribution of inward FDI flows to Brazil over the period 2001–2014. We note that, after the period of large privatizations, the manufacturing sector increased its share in FDI flows, while the shares of the energy and, especially, the telecommunications sectors decreased substantially, particularly from 2006 onwards. FDI in extractive sectors jumped after 2000, after the end of severe restrictions to foreign activity (a state monopoly prevailed until 1995). Within the manufacturing sector, investments occurred in food and beverages, chemical and basic metals. In turn, the relative weight of the car industry declined over the period.

The evolution of sectoral FDI flows to Mexico is displayed in Table 5.3. The picture in Mexico is quite different from Brazil. Not only is the share of the manufacturing sector in total FDI larger than in Brazil, but it increased over the period, accounting for 56% of FDI in 2010–2014. Within the manufacturing sector, substantial growth in the importance of the food and beverages sector can be noted, together with an increase in the share of the automotive industry. Other significant manufacturing sectors are chemicals and the computer and electronics industry, which retained their relevance over the period. The mining sector, which was irrelevant in the beginning of the new century, became a key recipient of FDI from the second half of first decade of the twenty-first century. In turn, FDI in services declined over the period, largely due to the large reduction in FDI in the financial sector.

Table 5.2 Brazil: FDI Flows

Sector	2001–2005			Sector	2006–2009			2010–2014		
	Annual Aver. US$ Mi	Share (% of Total)	% of GDP		Annual Aver. US$ Mi	Share (% of Total)	% of GDP	Annual Aver. US$ Mi	Share (% of Total)	% of GDP
Agriculture and mining	*1,376*	*7.19*	*0.215*		*5,971*	*17.93*	*0.407*	*9,739*	*16.86*	*0.399*
01–03	190	0.99	0.030	01–03	500	1.50	0.034	671	1.16	0.027
05–06	683	3.57	0.107	05–06	1,331	4.00	0.091	5,770	9.99	0.236
07–09	503	2.63	0.079	07–09	4,140	12.43	0.282	3,298	5.71	0.135
Manufacturing	*7,265*	*37.95*	*1.138*		*12,359*	*37.10*	*0.843*	*20,491*	*35.46*	*0.838*
10–12	2,053	10.72	0.322	10–12	1,375	4.13	0.094	3,755	6.50	0.154
13–15	73	0.38	0.011	13–15	215	0.65	0.015	67	0.12	0.003
16	59	0.31	0.009	16	101	0.30	0.007	123	0.21	0.005
17–18	267	1.39	0.042	17–18	892	2.68	0.061	576	1.00	0.024
20–21	1,232	6.44	0.193	19	1,204	3.61	0.082	1,078	1.87	0.044
22	236	1.23	0.037	20–21	1,515	4.55	0.103	3,990	6.91	0.163
23	108	0.56	0.017	22	455	1.37	0.031	695	1.20	0.028
24	410	2.14	0.064	23	370	1.11	0.025	771	1.33	0.032
25	98	0.51	0.015	24	3,787	11.37	0.258	4,391	7.60	0.180
26	579	3.03	0.091	25	105	0.31	0.007	315	0.55	0.013
27	259	1.35	0.041	26	247	0.74	0.017	1,097	1.90	0.045
28	312	1.63	0.049	27	337	1.01	0.023	610	1.06	0.025
29	1,246	6.51	0.195	28	421	1.26	0.029	726	1.26	0.030

(continued)

Table 5.2 Continued

Sector	2001–2005			Sector	2006–2009			2010–2014		
	Annual Aver. US$ Mi	Share (% of Total)	% of GDP		Annual Aver. US$ Mi	Share (% of Total)	% of GDP	Annual Aver. US$ Mi	Share (% of Total)	% of GDP
Other manuf.	334	1.74	0.052	29	1,070	3.21	0.073	1,593	2.76	0.065
				30	63	0.19	0.004	237	0.41	0.010
				31–33	202	0.61	0.014	466	0.81	0.019
Utilities, construction and services	*10,504*	*54.87*	*1.645*		*14,980*	*44.97*	*1.021*	*27,551*	*47.68*	*1.127*
35–39	1,314	6.86	0.206	35–39	1,353	4.06	0.092	2,139	3.70	0.088
41–43	223	1.17	0.035	41–43	1,263	3.79	0.086	1,566	2.71	0.064
45–47	1,617	8.45	0.253	45–47	2,364	7.10	0.161	5,448	9.43	0.223
49–53	184	0.96	0.029	49–53	676	2.03	0.046	1,647	2.85	0.067
55–56	155	0.81	0.024	55–56	246	0.74	0.017	307	0.53	0.013
61	3,612	18.87	0.566	58–60	0	0.00	0.000	103	0.18	0.004
62–63	265	1.38	0.041	61	630	1.89	0.043	2,587	4.48	0.106
64–66	1,645	8.59	0.258	62–63	395	1.19	0.027	747	1.29	0.031
68	203	1.06	0.032	64–66	4,519	13.57	0.308	5,941	10.28	0.243
69–82	809	4.23	0.127	68	1,007	3.02	0.069	2,216	3.84	0.091

Other services	478	2.50	0.075	69–82	1,598	4.80	0.109	3,139	5.43	0.128
				85	80	0.24	0.005	340	0.59	0.014
				Other services	847	2.54	0.058	1,372	2.37	0.056
Total	19,145	—	2.9983296046	Total	33,310	100.00	2.271	57,782	—	2.364

Source: Central Bank of Brazil (CBB). https://www.bcb.gov.br/htms/infecon/seriehistfluxoinvdir.asp?frame=1.

The source of GDP used in this table is UNCTAD (https://unctadstat.unctad.org/EN/).

Author's elaboration.

Notes:

1. The data used in this table refer to equity investment only, that is, do not include intercompany loans.
2. CBB changed the level of disaggregation of FDI flows data from 2006 onwards.
3. For the purpose of this study, all the FDI in the primary sector not included explicitly in mining was considered in sector 01–03.
4. For the period 2001–2005, other manufacturing probably includes all the sectors not explicitly identified, which include sectors 19 and 30–33.
5. For the period 2001–2005, other services probably include all the sectors not explicitly identified, which include sectors 84 onwards.
6. For the period 2006–2014, other services probably include all the sectors not explicitly identified, which include sector 84 and 86 onwards.

Table 5.3 Mexico: FDI Flows

Sector	2000–2004			2005–2009			2010–2014		
	Annual Aver. US$ Mi	Share (% of Total)	% of GDP	Annual Aver. US$ Mi	Share (% of Total)	% of GDP	Annual Aver. US$ Mi	Share (% of Total)	% of GDP
Agriculture and mining	*241*	*1.04*	*0.032*	*1,744*	*6.85*	*0.177*	*2,886*	*9.41*	*0.239*
01–03	43	0.19	0.006	34	0.13	0.003	158	0.52	0.013
05–06	4	0.02	0.001	6	0.02	0.001	59	0.19	0.005
07–08	186	0.80	0.025	1,658	6.52	0.169	2,568	8.38	0.213
09	7	0.03	0.001	46	0.18	0.005	101	0.33	0.008
Manufacturing	*9,797*	*42.33*	*1.307*	*10,899*	*42.85*	*1.109*	*17,195*	*56.08*	*1.426*
10–12	1,958	8.46	0.261	1,738	6.83	0.177	6,127	19.98	0.508
13–15	398	1.72	0.053	258	1.01	0.026	172	0.56	0.014
16	2	0.01	0.000	4	0.02	0.000	28	0.09	0.002
17–18	288	1.24	0.038	226	0.89	0.023	317	1.03	0.026
19	26	0.11	0.003	–13	–0.05	–0.001	21	0.07	0.002
20–21	1,508	6.52	0.201	1,631	6.41	0.166	2,233	7.28	0.185
22	204	0.88	0.027	539	2.12	0.055	724	2.36	0.060
23	327	1.41	0.044	169	0.66	0.017	129	0.42	0.011
24	227	0.98	0.030	1,501	5.90	0.153	670	2.19	0.056
25	177	0.76	0.024	249	0.98	0.025	313	1.02	0.026
26	962	4.16	0.128	1,186	4.66	0.121	1,128	3.68	0.094
27	674	2.91	0.090	550	2.16	0.056	574	1.87	0.048
28	529	2.29	0.071	351	1.38	0.036	574	1.87	0.048
29	2,078	8.98	0.277	2,039	8.02	0.207	3,489	11.38	0.289
30	82	0.35	0.011	217	0.85	0.022	265	0.87	0.022
Other manuf.	357	1.54	0.048	255	1.00	0.026	431	1.41	0.036

Utilities, construction and services	*13,104*	*56.63*	*1.748*	*12,794*	*50.30*	*1.301*	*10,578*	*34.50*	*0.877*
35–39	468	2.02	0.062	429	1.69	0.044	853	2.78	0.071
41–43	268	1.16	0.036	1,015	3.99	0.103	1,116	3.64	0.093
45–47	1,796	7.76	0.240	1,437	5.65	0.146	2,323	7.58	0.193
49–53	221	0.95	0.029	820	3.22	0.083	1,161	3.79	0.096
55–56	652	2.82	0.087	1,249	4.91	0.127	1,166	3.80	0.097
58–60	189	0.82	0.025	–35	–0.14	–0.004	331	1.08	0.027
61	1,629	7.04	0.217	872	3.43	0.089	399	1.30	0.033
62–63	35	0.15	0.005	0	0.00	0.000	41	0.13	0.003
64–66	6,857	29.63	0.915	4,545	17.87	0.462	1,446	4.72	0.120
68	516	2.23	0.069	1,524	5.99	0.155	738	2.41	0.061
69–82	412	1.78	0.055	774	3.04	0.079	817	2.66	0.068
85	10	0.04	0.001	47	0.19	0.005	10	0.03	0.001
86–88	5	0.02	0.001	11	0.04	0.001	16	0.05	0.001
90–96	11	0.05	0.002	74	0.29	0.008	68	0.22	0.006
Other services	36	0.15	0.005	32	0.12	0.003	95	0.31	0.008
Total	23,142	–	3.087	25,436	–	2.587	30,659	–	2.543

Source: Government of Mexico, Department of Economy, Open Data. https://datos.gob.mx/busca/dataset/informacion-estadistica-de-la-inversion-extranjera-directa/resource/06ad9dbb-cbd2-4b17-9586-daf78326308a.

The source of GDP used in this table is UNCTAD (https://unctadstat.unctad.org/EN/).

Author's elaboration.

Notes:

1. Other manufacturing includes undisclosed values due to confidentiality.
2. Other services includes undisclosed values due to confidentiality.

5.3.3. How Have the Economic Structures Evolved since 2000?

The evolution of economic structure (understood to mean changes in the sectoral distribution of output over time) depends on the growth of each sector's physical production, and on changes in relative prices. In this context, the first decade of the twenty-first century was marked by a 'double China effect'. On the one hand, international prices of mineral commodities soared in response to the enormous growth in Chinese demand. On the other hand, the relocation of part of the world's manufacturing capacity to developing Asia, especially China, introduced a deflationary trend in the market for certain types of manufactures, particularly those intensive in semi-skilled labour and in assembling activities.

Like most Latin American economies, Brazil benefited from China's growth, especially in the period 2003–2008, when Chinese demand for raw materials and food boosted prices, raising the country's terms of trade. Such an export boom not only alleviated Brazil's chronic balance of payments problem but also pushed the domestic-oriented sectors through wealth effects. For Mexico, however, China's rise was not so beneficial. The benefits stemming from the upsurge in oil prices were counterbalanced by increased competition imposed by Chinese exports in US manufactures markets. Hanson (2010) argues that Mexico has the bad luck of exporting goods that China sells, instead of goods that China buys.

5.3.4. Brazil: The Co-Evolution between FDI and Output Structure

According to Table 5.4, the share of the extractive sector in Brazilian economy increased substantially in the period 2000–2005. As mentioned, even though production expanded, most of the sector's gain in terms of GDP share was due to price rises. The opposite occurred in the period 2010–2015, as declines in prices overrode the increases in production. The oil and gas and mining sectors were not historically significant recipients of FDI in Brazil, largely due to state monopoly and other restrictions to foreign activity. As shown in Table 5.1, they accounted for less than 1% (each) of FDI stock in 2000. However, this picture changed in the two decades after. In the period 2006–2009, 12.4% of inward FDI went to the mining sector. Likewise, 10% went to oil and gas in the period 2010–2014.

These flows were not only attracted by the record prices and the removal of restrictions, but also—in the case of oil and gas—by the discovery of large reserves in the pre-salt layer. These sectors, which received disproportionate FDI flows (relative to the weight in the economy), grew considerably faster than the rest of the economy and—what is particularly important for this study—created

Table 5.4 Brazil: The Evolution of Economic Structure and Input-Output Relations

Sector	Sector share in VA (% of Total)				Sector VA real growth (%)			Sector's domestic demand of inputs – real growth (%)		
	2000	2005	2010	2015	2000–2005	2005–2010	2010–2015	2000–2005	2005–2010	2010–2015
01–03	5.52	5.48	4.84	5.02	26.94	17.38	17.82	31.02	−3.57	30.80
05–06	1.01	2.36	1.92	1.43	38.49	26.89	13.76	139.01	−8.60	27.66
07–09	0.37	0.79	1.41	0.72	22.23	28.15	10.57	26.73	7.10	0.77
10–12	1.75	2.38	2.38	2.40	20.78	4.88	−8.01	28.35	3.80	8.93
13–15	1.81	1.34	1.32	1.01	−5.67	4.66	−14.44	1.77	−9.73	−9.72
16	0.32	0.35	0.26	0.19	8.39	−16.71	−2.74	42.62	−29.17	−0.73
17–18	1.13	0.89	0.69	0.60	28.00	7.28	−7.63	15.95	−8.43	−7.20
19	1.10	1.50	0.66	0.87	22.85	−22.23	0.20	−8.36	68.53	−0.46
20–21	2.00	2.30	1.52	1.40	12.57	12.84	2.22	9.60	2.02	8.26
22	0.58	0.65	0.65	0.51	4.83	12.07	−14.85	7.75	24.46	0.69
23	0.58	0.47	0.68	0.54	7.14	20.75	−4.81	−10.40	29.89	8.23
24	0.53	1.27	0.73	0.67	16.58	0.02	−11.68	18.10	4.97	−8.57
25	0.90	1.13	0.89	0.67	24.91	21.95	−7.55	−15.20	28.67	−18.47
26	0.53	0.62	0.60	0.44	29.72	13.94	31.60	4.17	−26.69	31.80
27	0.41	0.40	0.44	0.33	22.76	13.47	−8.52	−5.99	18.88	−13.54
28	1.11	1.33	1.45	1.16	18.98	22.81	−11.41	13.04	21.67	−14.68
29	1.33	1.58	1.88	0.79	43.46	34.38	−38.32	53.47	10.24	−23.24
30	0.35	0.47	0.29	0.23	46.72	55.94	6.28	48.81	25.21	25.97
31–33	0.83	0.67	0.54	0.44	6.03	22.98	−14.70	−8.60	98.85	9.05
35–39	3.14	3.37	2.81	2.39	9.16	21.38	5.51	11.92	26.90	46.09
41–43	6.96	4.59	6.27	5.74	1.76	39.03	3.93	−20.84	87.95	0.96

(continued)

Table 5.4 Continued

Sector	Sector share in VA (% of Total)				Sector VA real growth (%)			Sector's domestic demand of inputs – real growth (%)		
	2000	2005	2010	2015	2000–2005	2005–2010	2010–2015	2000–2005	2005–2010	2010–2015
45–47	8.11	10.76	12.60	13.30	11.60	29.94	0.99	24.26	80.82	22.08
49–53	3.67	3.49	4.29	4.39	11.27	23.18	6.04	25.90	45.78	-3.22
55–56	2.19	1.60	2.13	2.38	18.08	23.82	6.49	-15.11	8.81	9.32
58–63	4.28	4.56	3.83	3.41	27.70	24.02	23.57	35.36	35.69	2.90
64–66	6.83	7.14	6.80	7.09	11.64	67.78	7.86	-8.85	55.96	4.01
68	12.23	9.32	8.31	9.68	22.31	21.54	13.00	28.28	36.20	48.87
69–82	6.15	5.78	6.71	7.02	11.16	29.24	8.02	6.32	71.03	16.57
84	10.10	10.80	10.39	9.88	16.12	15.94	7.77	31.30	-1.56	1.87
85	5.37	4.59	4.97	6.48	14.00	-3.51	1.49	25.76	10.44	14.18
86–88	4.04	3.75	3.92	4.90	16.35	23.40	10.18	28.96	5.37	12.30
90–96	3.57	3.06	2.62	2.74	6.93	14.92	8.20	4.22	4.59	-7.38
97–98	1.17	1.20	1.22	1.20	20.47	8.42	2.24	—	—	—
Total economy	100	100	100	100	15.85	22.72	5.51	—	—	—

Source: IBGE, Annual National Accounts and Input-Output Tables. ibge.gov.br.

Authors' elaboration.

Note: Sectoral value-added deflators were used to deflate sectoral output.

demand for upstream industries. For example, as indicated in Table 5.4, the domestic purchases of the oil and gas sector increased by an impressive 139% in the period 2000–2005 in real terms. Therefore, besides the possible effects on the sectors itself, FDI in oil and gas and mining possibly affected other industries through backward linkages. Nevertheless, the proportion of foreign inputs in total inputs used in these sectors increased over time, despite the minimum local content policy imposed by the Brazilian government to the suppliers of Petrobras and of other oil drilling operators.[10] Given the importance of this policy in the Brazilian context, it is worth analysing it in greater detail.

Regarding employment, the largest multiplier effects of oil and gas production are found in upstream industries (Piquet, Hasenclever, and Shimoda, 2016). For this reason, many oil-rich countries implement domestic content policies as a means of maximizing the benefits of resource abundance (Tordo et al., 2013). In Brazil, these policies have been in place since the 1970s (Florencio, 2016), but they acquired more relevance after the abolition of Petrobras's monopoly in 1995. Since then, all public biddings for new exploration and development blocs have included minimum local content requirements. During the Workers' Party's ruling years (2003–2016), especially after the discovery of the huge oil reserves of the pre-salt layer (2007), these policies became a central pillar of the country's overall industrial policy (Schutte, 2021). In some bidding rounds, local content commitments exceeded 85% (Schutte, 2021).

However, the results of such policies are rather controversial. Although they fostered the development of supplier industries, such as shipbuilding, prices were considerably above the international prices and the quality of goods and services typically lower. Thus, while the policy may have induced FDI in supplier industries (Piquet, Hasenclever, and Shimoda, 2016), it also made oil extraction less attractive to foreign MNEs (Clavijo et al., 2019), thus reducing competition in bids (Tordo et al., 2013). The lack of focus on a selected few industries or products with a greater potential to engender competitive producers has been pointed out as the main fault of a policy that seems to have overestimated the capacity of the domestic industry in meeting its high targets (Florencio, 2016).

Over the period 2000–2015, the manufacturing sector's share in FDI flows remained relatively unaltered, slightly above one-third of the total. Within manufacturing, the food and beverage and the chemical industries were prominent over this entire period, while the automotive industry stood out in the period 2001–2005 and the basic metals industry stood out in subsequent periods. Interestingly, the distribution of FDI was not well mirrored in the relative performances of manufacturing industries. Some of the best performing

[10] It must be noted that input-output matrix is not the best tool for evaluating the effects of sectoral minimum domestic content policies because they do not indicate the origin of second-, third-, or fourth-tier suppliers.

industries over the period 2000–2010, such as metal products and machinery, were not prominent FDI recipients. A stronger connection, however, is likely to exist between FDI flows and the economic performance of the computers, optical, and electronic equipment industry, especially in the period 2000–2005, when Brazil became an exporter of early mobile phones, a position that it lost completely after the emergence of the smart phone. It must be noted, however, that the linkages of this sector with the rest of the economy are weak (Table 5.4)—indeed, this industry's growth has been accompanied by an increasing use of imported inputs (Table 5.5).

The basic metals industry was a prominent recipient of FDI, especially after 2005. However, production did not increase, even during the booming years of the Brazilian economy. Another important FDI recipient, the chemical industry, also underperformed relative to the overall economy and even to some other manufacturing industries.

Given its substantive potential for creating backward linkages, the automotive industry deserves a detailed analysis, even though it has not been a major recipient of FDI, as revealed by official statistics. Since the 1990s, Brazil passed through three waves of FDI in the auto industry. In all of them, the new investments—both the volume and the location within Brazil—were strongly influenced by tax and financial incentives offered by sub-national governments, which were complemented by tax exemptions and trade protection offered by the federal government. The first wave took place in the second half of the 1990s, following a major rise in import tariffs in response to a surge in imports (De Negri, 1999). Several makers that were not previously present in Brazil built plants to produce locally, including some high-end brands.

The expansion in industry's capacity was initially accompanied by fast sales growth, but this movement was suddenly reversed by the 1999 crisis that led to a major devaluation of the real and a substantial decrease in domestic sales. A new cycle of investments started in the middle of the first decade of the twenty-first century—when the idle capacity of the sector was largely suppressed—involving mainly incumbent producers. Backward linkages were strengthened during these boom years—as shown in Table 5.5, the use of imported inputs decreased, while the use of domestically-sourced ones increased. Finally, the third wave took place in the 2010s, when a new industrial policy, labelled Inovar-Auto, was adopted by the federal government. For its importance within the country's industrial policy, this initiative is examined in greater detail.

Inovar-Auto was created in 2012, in response to an upsurge in car imports from China, Mexico, and South Korea. Officially, its purposes were to encourage investments, raise the domestic content in final products, and improve the international competitiveness of the industry (Sturgeon, Chagas, and Barnes, 2017). However, since its inception it has been criticized for its heavy protectionist

Table 5.5 Brazil: Decomposition of the Output (%)

Sector	Domestic Inputs				Foreign Inputs				Gross Value Added			
	2000	2005	2010	2015	2000	2005	2010	2015	2000	2005	2010	2015
01-03	35.55	41.15	37.90	39.75	1.60	1.36	3.21	5.73	59.77	54.07	58.89	54.52
05-06	40.45	47.37	39.95	45.08	8.60	7.84	9.55	14.07	49.03	42.49	50.50	40.86
07-09	52.12	52.02	30.95	45.26	2.66	2.74	6.42	9.89	42.37	42.28	62.63	44.86
10-12	73.61	74.39	59.35	57.15	3.82	2.58	2.65	3.13	19.42	19.83	38.00	39.73
13-15	53.23	55.07	37.72	35.58	6.09	5.05	6.57	7.11	37.99	36.78	55.71	57.31
16	49.10	57.92	47.34	47.61	1.78	1.75	2.80	4.68	46.68	37.25	49.86	47.71
17-18	50.47	53.55	52.14	47.00	6.27	6.56	6.89	9.66	40.82	37.05	40.97	43.34
19	66.33	65.04	53.84	54.57	14.15	15.72	9.24	7.56	12.58	13.04	36.92	37.88
20-21	55.48	55.94	43.93	43.08	14.26	15.14	15.64	19.03	28.38	26.36	40.44	37.90
22	61.41	60.00	52.44	51.34	10.19	9.16	11.99	16.90	25.36	28.05	35.57	31.76
23	57.68	56.46	51.23	51.48	3.77	4.61	5.46	6.34	37.18	36.81	43.31	42.18
24	55.16	56.01	67.05	66.17	11.05	12.45	12.89	15.16	31.15	28.69	20.07	18.67
25	52.66	51.60	45.73	43.35	6.18	3.64	6.51	7.72	38.32	42.19	47.76	48.93
26	46.27	49.00	30.09	31.18	25.52	26.58	28.92	33.49	24.76	20.13	40.99	35.33
27	57.07	57.28	48.54	45.64	12.48	9.20	11.91	13.91	27.51	30.73	39.55	40.45
28	55.59	60.00	46.97	44.67	7.15	8.30	13.54	17.45	33.88	28.38	39.49	37.88
29	58.99	68.98	54.92	53.46	15.88	12.11	9.80	16.09	20.81	15.16	35.28	30.45
30	36.26	58.05	44.49	47.18	32.29	15.72	15.82	21.50	27.62	22.73	39.68	31.33

(continued)

Table 5.5 Continued

Sector	Domestic Inputs				Foreign Inputs				Gross Value Added			
	2000	2005	2010	2015	2000	2005	2010	2015	2000	2005	2010	2015
31-33	49.65	48.70	32.41	30.93	4.97	5.02	8.13	11.05	42.11	42.22	59.46	58.03
35-39	41.47	41.27	40.76	47.05	5.11	4.16	4.73	7.75	52.06	53.05	54.52	45.20
41-43	41.72	36.84	50.48	49.43	2.63	2.79	4.47	5.77	50.02	53.81	45.05	44.80
45-47	25.05	25.19	36.65	37.89	1.18	1.47	2.63	4.06	70.10	69.88	60.72	58.05
49-53	40.79	44.40	49.64	49.70	3.64	1.46	5.87	6.62	53.92	50.56	44.48	43.67
55-56	49.05	49.11	46.14	46.37	0.57	0.69	5.16	5.95	42.36	43.02	48.70	47.68
58-63	41.43	40.89	39.31	37.63	3.97	4.41	4.22	6.71	52.26	52.20	56.47	55.66
64-66	39.86	29.49	32.79	31.71	2.02	2.10	1.92	1.92	54.74	65.19	65.29	66.37
68	4.27	5.21	6.58	7.70	0.18	0.21	0.30	0.48	95.13	94.13	93.12	91.83
69-82	34.46	30.71	29.95	29.07	2.17	2.20	2.54	3.33	59.75	62.11	67.51	67.59
84	31.92	32.72	29.88	29.36	0.95	0.88	1.81	2.57	64.05	62.31	68.31	68.07
85	21.67	24.24	25.32	20.19	0.52	0.63	1.58	2.42	75.20	71.61	73.09	77.39
86-88	35.95	39.59	39.84	35.90	2.80	3.53	5.25	5.22	57.59	52.56	54.92	58.88
90-96	33.10	31.37	42.32	41.08	1.17	1.80	6.84	7.37	60.57	61.29	50.84	51.54
97-98	0.00	0.00	0.00	0.00	0.00	0.00	0.00	0.00	100.00	100.00	100.00	100.00

Source: IBGE, Input-Output Tables. ibge.gov.br.

Authors' elaboration.

Note: For 2000 and 2005, the difference between output and the components is comprised by taxes, subsidies, trade margins and transport margins.

nature, the fiscal cost, and the lack of ambitious targets. Indeed, Inovar-Auto introduced a tricky mechanism that, in the end, imposed a surcharge of 30% on cars imported by companies that did not have a local production plant—in addition to the high regular import tariff of 35%.[11] To mask the protectionist intention, the program also included a few unambitious targets in respect to R&D expenditure and energy efficiency.

The program did not produce compelling results. Imports were curbed and a new wave of FDI effectively took place. New producers, including a few of the luxury spectre, arrived in the country, helping to expand the industry's capacity to above 5 million vehicles per year. Sturgeon, Chagas, and Barnes (2017) estimate that half of the new investments were induced by Inovar-Auto. The program, however, deepened the excess capacity problem that already existed prior to its launching, as it encouraged tariff-jumping FDI that resulted in small plants chronically unable to operate at efficient scale. The strengthening of the linkages did not take place—both investments and employment in the auto parts industry declined during the program's duration (Messa, 2017; Vargas, 2021). Likewise, exports did not expand, and the Brazilian industry did not increase its participation in the related global value chain (GVC) (Sturgeon, Chagas and Barnes, 2017). Moreover, R&D efforts did not increase—indeed, they decreased.[12] The program was even condemned by the WTO in 2016.

Electricity and telecommunications were two of the main targets of foreign investors in the Brazilian economy during the late 1990s. Most were through acquisitions of formerly state-owned enterprises. However, over the 20 years since, the acquirers have made new investments in the modernization and expansion of the existing networks, as per the privatization contracts. During the period 2001–2005, value added by the energy sector grew slower than the overall economy. However, the main reason for the unexpected slow growth were the changes in the patterns of energy demand that followed the rationing caused by the 2001 drought. For the telecommunications sector,[13] the connection between output growth and FDI is clearer, particularly in the years that followed privatization, as foreign investors had a large pool of unserved consumers to

[11] Formally, it increased in 30 percentage points the tax levied on industrial goods but reduced it by the same amount if at least 80% of the cars sold by the company were produced in the country. The program also introduced a local content requirement that would increase over time (Sturgeon, Chagas, and Barnes, 2017).

[12] Even though the industry's R&D expenditure in the period 2009–2011 corresponded to 1.57% of net sales, the program imposed a 0.5% target for 2017. In the period 2015–2017, that figure dropped to 1.25% (Vargas, 2021).

[13] Unfortunately, IBGE does not provide separate statistics for the telecommunications sector, only for the broader information services sector, which includes IT services as well as publishing, audiovisual, and broadcasting activities.

be exploited. When the Telebrás system was privatized, in 1998, Brazil had approximately 4 million mobile lines. In 2005, there were 86 million and, in 2010, 203 million lines, more than a line per capita. The expansion of information services created demand for domestic inputs, as shown in Table 5.5.

The financial sector was an important recipient of FDI over the period under analysis. However, it is hard to relate these flows to the sector's performance because the Brazilian banking market is largely dominated by domestic actors, with the largest foreign player, Santander, only the fifth-largest commercial bank. The sector's spectacular growth in the period 2005–2010 (Table 5.4) was primarily driven by the expansion of state banks' balance sheets, notably BNDES, the federal development bank. Finally, another sector that received substantial FDI flows in Brazil is wholesale and retail trade. Indeed, some of the world biggest supermarket chains, such as Wal-Mart, Carrefour, and Cassino, accelerated expansion in the country in this period, through acquisitions and the opening of new stores. Nonetheless, it is not easy to trace a relation between FDI and growth in value-added because this sector's margins are very sensitive to the business cycle.

5.3.5. Brazil: The Co-Evolution between FDI and Export Structure

Table 5.6 shows the evolution of Brazil's exports with a growing dominance of the primary sector. In addition, the share of manufactures declined over time, particularly of metals, machines, transportation, wood products, and footwear. Exports became more concentrated, as expressed by the decreasing number of products (at the HS4 6-digit level) for which Brazil possessed revealed comparative advantage (RCA).[14]

A similar pattern is revealed by Table 5.7, which displays sectoral RCA indexes based on value-added, instead of gross exports. Again, the primarization is evident—the only manufacturing segment booming was the natural-resource-intensive pulp and paper industry.

Investments in the manufacturing sector do not seem to have contributed to change Brazil's export structure toward technologically advanced manufactured goods. Indeed, FDI in this area is predominantly domestic market-seeking. Resource-seeking FDI is restricted to a few manufacturing segments

[14] The RCA index for a given industry is obtained by dividing the country's share in the world's exports of that industry by the country's share in world's total exports. It is assumed that the country's comparative advantage in a given industry is 'revealed' by the RCA index when it exceeds 1 (Balassa, 1965)

Table 5.6 Brazil: The Evolution of Export Structure and RCA, 1999–2015

Section		Number of HS4 (6-digit) with RCA >1				Share in Total Exports (%) HS4 (6-digit) with RCA >1				Share in Total Exports (%) HS4 (6-digit) with RCA ≤1			
		1999	2005	2010	2015	1999	2005	2010	2015	1999	2005	2010	2015
1	Animal Products	13	16	16	18	3.30	6.31	6.40	7.39	0.32	0.31	0.19	0.16
	Frozen bovine meat					*0.64*	*1.48*	*1.63*	*2.04*	—	—	—	—
	Poultry meat					*1.87*	*2.88*	*2.88*	*3.31*	—	—	—	—
2	Vegetable Products	16	21	16	15	8.74	7.40	9.54	17.23	0.43	0.31	0.47	0.61
	Coffee					*4.58*	*2.11*	*2.55*	*2.95*	—	—	—	—
	Corn					—	*0.22*	*1.12*	*2.65*	*0.07*	—	—	—
	Soybeans					*3.24*	*4.38*	*5.37*	*10.78*	—	—	—	—
3	Animal and Vegetable By-Products	6	10	5	5	1.67	1.25	0.74	0.75	0.09	0.05	0.10	0.14
4	Foodstuffs	21	18	18	19	14.31	10.73	13.11	11.85	0.67	0.49	0.56	0.49
	Fruit juice					*3.07*	*1.07*	*1.11*	*1.31*	—	—	—	—
	Raw sugar					*3.98*	*3.49*	*6.38*	*4.25*	—	—	—	—
	Soybean meal					*3.09*	*2.45*	*2.39*	*3.09*	—	—	—	—
5	Mineral Products	16	13	14	19	6.55	7.04	23.65	15.25	0.96	6.09	1.82	1.06
	Iron ore					*5.57*	*6.14*	*14.47*	*7.42*	—	—	—	—
	Crude petroleum					—	—	*7.96*	*6.08*	*0.05*	*3.47*	—	—
6	Chemical Products	40	37	28	30	3.59	2.67	2.90	2.95	2.26	2.13	2.34	2.53
7	Plastics and Rubbers	6	8	6	8	1.78	1.63	1.43	1.77	1.14	1.25	1.24	0.93
8	Animal Hides	6	7	8	5	1.33	1.26	0.89	1.19	0.07	0.05	0.02	0.04
9	Wood Products	13	13	7	11	2.76	2.49	0.85	1.13	0.08	0.07	0.10	0.08

(continued)

Table 5.6 Continued

	Section	Number of HS4 (6-digit) with RCA >1				Share in Total Exports (%) HS4 (6-digit) with RCA >1				Share in Total Exports (%) HS4 (6-digit) with RCA ≤1			
		1999	2005	2010	2015	1999	2005	2010	2015	1999	2005	2010	2015
10	Paper Goods	9	8	8	12	3.91	2.59	3.47	4.15	0.73	0.55	0.27	0.21
	Sulfate chemical wood pulp					*2.53*	*1.79*	*2.45*	*2.99*	—	—	—	—
11	Textiles	22	12	14	9	1.15	1.00	0.65	0.77	1.01	0.88	0.49	0.48
12	Footwear and Headwear	6	6	4	1	2.67	1.62	0.76	0.08	0.03	0.02	0.05	0.51
13	Stone and Glass	15	13	7	8	1.08	1.12	0.59	0.78	0.40	0.30	0.26	0.24
14	Precious Metals	4	3	3	1	1.56	0.12	0.11	0.09	0.17	0.74	1.12	1.45
15	Metals	41	43	23	28	9.95	10.05	5.11	5.37	1.72	1.71	2.45	2.43
	Raw aluminium					*2.48*	*1.46*	*0.71*	*0.33*	—	—	—	—
	Semi-finished iron					*2.16*	*1.62*	*1.19*	*1.35*	—	—	—	—
16	Machines	21	24	15	11	6.17	8.63	3.25	3.36	6.04	4.43	4.86	4.56
17	Transportation	32	12	10	8	8.15	6.99	4.68	5.31	3.05	6.08	4.39	3.38
	Cars					—	—	—	—	*2.28*	*3.70*	*2.25*	*1.73*
	Planes, helicopters, and spacecraft					*3.68*	*2.82*	*2.43*	*2.29*	—	—	—	—
	Vehicle parts					*2.47*	—	—	—	—	*2.03*	*1.66*	*1.18*
18	Instruments	2	1	1	0	0.35	0.04	0.04	0.00	0.58	0.43	0.38	0.47
19	Weapons	2	3	3	4	0.14	0.14	0.18	0.29	0.05	0.00	0.01	0.00
20	Miscellaneous	3	3	1	1	0.75	0.70	0.03	0.05	0.30	0.33	0.51	0.48

Source: The Observatory of Economic Complexity. https://oec.world/en.
Authors' elaboration.

Table 5.7 Brazil: RCA Index Based on Value Added

Sector	1999	2005	2010	2015
01–03	2.60	3.36	3.18	3.93
05–09	0.59	0.82	1.18	0.91
05–06	—	0.55	0.60	0.56
07–08	—	2.74	3.98	2.67
09	—	0.23	0.46	0.56
10–33	0.93	1.07	0.82	0.74
10–12	2.33	2.15	2.28	1.88
13–15	1.16	1.05	0.61	0.47
16	2.84	2.05	1.35	1.31
17–18	1.10	1.40	1.69	1.89
19	1.61	1.92	0.89	1.06
20–21	0.92	1.08	0.67	0.68
22	0.71	0.93	0.92	0.74
23	1.06	0.93	1.01	0.92
24	1.50	1.66	0.98	1.25
25	0.79	0.83	0.69	0.59
26	0.22	0.29	0.11	0.06
27	0.67	0.56	0.38	0.31
28	0.63	0.71	0.58	0.52
29	0.47	1.14	1.04	0.56
30	0.88	1.20	0.61	0.66
31–33	1.01	0.78	1.02	0.89

Source: OECD's Trade in Value Added Database. https://stats.oecd.org.

Authors' elaboration.

Note: RCA indexes were calculated using TiVA's indicator on Domestic Value Added Embodied in Foreign Final Demand.

strongly dependent on natural resources, such as basic metals, paper products, sugar, and soybean meal. In the early years of the first decade of the twenty-first century, Brazil expanded car sales to Latin American countries and was even able to export to Germany a model created in the country by Volkswagen. This movement, however, was already largely reversed by the end of the decade, and Argentina remained the sole relevant export market for vehicles and auto parts made in Brazil.

The inability of the country in expanding exports of more sophisticated products is evident when one considers how Brazil navigated within the product space[15] between 1999 and 2015. It is clear that the main products exported by Brazil are in the periphery of the product space. They are weakly connected with other products. This means that being specialized in these products creates few opportunities to competitively produce other goods, as the capabilities required to produce primary goods are often different from the capabilities required to produce most manufactured goods, particularly the more technologically sophisticated ones.

This is typical of countries that are specialized in the production of primary products, which usually takes part of the initial stages of GVCs. It would appear that Brazil has missed an opportunity of using existing capabilities to expand production and exports to nearby products (in the product space) but has also witnessed RCA vanishing in products such as vehicle parts. It can be argued that the comparatively protectionist trade policy followed by Brazil over this period tended to keep the country away from key GVCs, except for those linked to the supply of natural-resource-intensive goods.

5.3.6. Mexico: The Co-Evolution between FDI and Production Structure

The Mexican economy has historically been more dependent upon the mineral and fossil fuels extractive sector than the Brazilian economy. As shown in Table 5.8, in 2000 the oil and gas extractive industry accounted for almost 6% of value added in Mexico, whilst in Brazil its contribution was a mere 1%. However, contrary to Brazil, Mexico witnessed a substantial reduction in this sector's weight in the country's economy. During the boom years of the commodities super cycle, the oil and gas share in value-added went up, despite the substantial reduction in this sector's output in the period 2005–2010. Such an output trend continued in the following five years, but this time it was accompanied by plummeting prices. As a result, the sector's share in value-added dropped to less than half of the 2010 figure.

For several decades, a Mexican state-owned company had a monopoly in the exploitation and production of hydrocarbons. However, differently from Brazil, where monopoly was withdrawn before the discovery of overwhelming

[15] The product space is an interesting framework put forward by Hidalgo et al. (2007). Based on network techniques, it displays the relatedness between products in international trade. Related products are those that tend to be exported (with RCA) by the same group of countries. In theory, if a country exports a product *i* it is more likely to export a related product *j*—which is close to *i* within the product space—than a non-related product *k*—which is distant from *i*. Although their method is agnostic in relation to causes, we acknowledge that relatedness is likely to be associated to factor endowments as well as institutional factors.

Table 5.8 Mexico: The Evolution of Economic Structure and Input-Output Relations

Sector	Sector Share in VA (% of Total)				Setor VA Real Growth (%)			Sector's Domestic Demand of Inputs-Real Growth (%)	
	2000	2005	2010	2015	2000–2005	2005–2010	2010–2015	2005–2010	2010–2015
01–03	3.49	3.21	3.36	3.39	6.91	11.08	10.86	–10.12	7.87
05–06	5.86	6.61	5.94	2.66	8.63	–18.22	–11.21	–15.93	–5.82
07–08	0.53	0.69	0.94	0.99	19.04	9.88	35.38	–23.84	5.88
9	0.30	0.44	0.62	0.54	36.87	50.63	–2.85	17.08	–5.54
10–12	4.24	4.41	4.56	4.73	13.11	7.23	10.42	7.36	10.54
13–15	1.47	0.97	0.81	0.80	–20.88	–5.06	3.49	–21.87	–14.79
16	0.26	0.18	0.15	0.16	–21.98	–7.49	16.00	–19.76	4.58
17–18	0.46	0.41	0.42	0.42	0.65	14.32	9.47	0.84	–5.21
19	0.66	0.19	0.63	0.72	5.46	–8.68	–10.69	–9.42	–17.51
20–21	1.75	1.70	1.76	1.54	6.89	2.76	–4.99	–34.52	–6.36
22	0.55	0.48	0.46	0.54	2.41	6.37	14.52	–6.79	5.35
23	0.75	0.60	0.48	0.48	2.67	–6.79	10.24	–27.74	1.06
24	1.01	1.23	1.26	1.04	5.91	–15.95	3.64	–4.18	–4.12
25	0.61	0.57	0.57	0.64	0.51	6.24	6.86	–5.28	3.99
26	3.63	1.83	1.21	1.65	–33.16	–16.81	37.41	–12.32	–33.68
27	0.71	0.59	0.56	0.60	–7.53	–10.19	7.89	–12.58	–20.53
28	0.60	0.62	0.68	0.77	20.04	7.40	6.09	3.07	1.76
29	2.35	1.89	2.07	3.30	–0.40	21.65	56.33	8.60	35.82
30	0.15	0.15	0.12	0.31	10.58	–9.62	174.38	–22.38	134.72
31–33	0.86	0.69	0.58	0.61	0.54	–0.76	10.57	–17.89	11.18

(continued)

Table 5.8 Continued

Sector	Sector Share in VA (% of Total)				Setor VA Real Growth (%)			Sector's Domestic Demand of Inputs-Real Growth (%)	
	2000	2005	2010	2015	2000–2005	2005–2010	2010–2015	2005–2010	2010–2015
35–39	1.72	2.02	1.92	1.69	29.97	25.53	19.03	–25.15	–14.21
41–43	7.56	7.99	8.00	7.63	3.07	10.12	9.56	–4.71	–15.94
45–47	17.49	16.77	16.68	19.18	11.60	6.67	23.29	–2.41	20.20
49–53	6.67	6.34	6.49	6.79	5.16	8.00	19.66	–48.44	–4.65
55–56	2.98	2.72	2.21	2.37	–4.26	–5.43	17.50	–18.15	15.76
58–60	0.35	0.37	0.40	0.42	–1.51	16.61	24.21	8.96	9.81
61	1.33	1.78	2.02	1.47	99.73	62.36	63.82	15.33	11.01
62–63	0.12	0.13	0.11	0.10	1.25	12.54	4.17	1.87	3.84
64–66	1.90	3.18	3.54	3.69	30.35	90.42	69.58	44.40	36.49
68	12.03	12.14	12.05	11.15	16.78	15.75	11.04	14.10	4.55
69–82	6.51	6.97	6.53	6.63	9.46	6.62	16.37	–4.84	9.09
84	3.54	3.81	4.36	4.27	–4.74	12.21	8.29	10.36	14.72
85	3.45	4.04	4.17	4.34	8.56	3.43	3.99	–0.92	11.10
86–88	1.86	2.09	2.26	2.42	–1.81	13.74	4.08	3.20	24.13
90–96	1.78	1.70	1.59	1.46	2.36	4.96	6.75	–6.96	3.75
97–98	0.48	0.48	0.49	0.50	10.05	12.91	18.23	—	—
Total economy	100	100	100	100	7.26	7.53	15.52	—	—

Source: OECDStat, National Accounts and Input-Output Tables (IOTs 2018). https://stats.oecd.org/

Authors' elaboration.

Note: Sectoral value added deflators were used to deflate sectoral output.

new reserves, in Mexico the monopoly was broken as late as 2014, long after the country's peak in production and proven reserves. Thus, even considering that FDI directed to the Mexican oil sector soared from 2015 onwards—departing from very low levels—the impact on the domestic economy tends to be less relevant than in Brazil, where the attractiveness of the sector increased substantially after the discovery of the large reserves in the pre-salt layer.

Mexico underwent a period of deindustrialization, though less pronounced than in Brazil. The performances of manufacturing subsectors, however, were quite disparate. Labour-intensive activities suffered the most in the period 2000–2010, when the world was flooded by low-cost goods made in China. Even the automotive industry, one of the champions of the NAFTA-driven *maquila* wave, declined in the first half of the first decade of twenty-first century. Nonetheless, a different scenario emerged in the period 2010–2015. The manufacturing sector regained part of its previous share in GDP, with some industries, such as computers, electronics, and optical products, as well as automobiles and auto components, presenting impressive output growth.

These industries were among the largest recipients of FDI in Mexico's manufacturing sector in the period under analysis. However, the development impact of those industries, in terms of the linkages with the rest of the domestic economy, seems to have been quite different. As shown in Tables 5.8 and 5.9, the computer, electronic, and optical products industry may be called the quintessential *maquila* because even when output grew substantially (2010–2015),[16] demand for domestic inputs dropped, while the use of imported inputs went up—the ratio of imported inputs to domestic inputs jumped from 0.81 in 2005, to 1.77 in 2015. Did the same occur in the car industry? As shown in Table 5.8, the car industry expanded its purchases from the domestic producers, but the purchase of inputs did not keep the same pace of the industry itself. As a result, the share of imported inputs rose, particularly in the period 2010–2015.

[16] During the 1980s, Brazil and Mexico adopted rather similar policies in respect to the ICT industry. Both protected domestic producers against foreign competition and imposed minimum local content requirements. Protectionism was abandoned in the 1990s, but the countries followed quite different approaches since then. Brazil prioritized the domestic market, gave no attention to integration to GVCs, and maintained active industrial policy for the industry. Not surprisingly, therefore, Brazil was able to retain in the country a larger share of input purchases. Mexico, in turn, invested in greater openness and export orientation of the industry. Vertical industrial policy was practically abolished since the signing of NAFTA, even though the ICT industry has disproportionately benefited from horizontal policies aimed at fostering innovation and R&D in the whole economy. It must be noted, however, that state-level incentives to attract FDI remained in place. The state of Jalisco, for example, was able to attract major MNE plants focused on electronics export markets. According to Schatan and Enríquez (2015), over time, production in Jalisco evolved from large volumes and low value-added to smaller-scale production with higher value-added locally—what can be interpreted as an upgrading from pure *maquila* to a more knowledge- and technology-intensive stage.

Table 5.9 Mexico: Decomposition of the Output (%)

Sector	Domestic inputs			Foreign inputs			Value Added		
	2005	2010	2015	2005	2010	2015	2005	2010	2015
01–03	29.82	29.81	29.67	5.26	5.92	6.73	64.41	63.75	63.00
05–06	9.16	9.21	15.45	0.98	0.98	2.61	89.67	89.62	81.51
07–08	33.85	27.60	25.98	6.34	5.75	7.59	58.89	65.75	65.29
9	41.77	40.63	38.47	4.76	4.62	7.32	52.46	53.78	52.90
10–12	53.68	53.69	52.86	7.61	8.07	8.55	38.36	38.03	38.23
13–15	45.88	44.26	38.30	19.92	18.78	21.26	32.96	35.92	38.62
16	52.22	51.49	47.70	10.90	10.87	12.44	36.45	37.14	39.25
17–18	58.10	56.38	52.32	16.05	17.31	19.06	25.31	25.75	27.83
19	89.29	78.02	66.44	3.88	7.99	11.32	4.46	11.20	18.51
20–21	59.83	52.62	49.85	15.54	17.65	20.83	23.57	28.58	27.89
22	53.15	50.74	45.11	19.43	22.08	25.24	26.80	26.54	28.72
23	59.86	58.50	55.25	9.79	12.21	14.52	29.45	28.11	28.81
24	52.22	53.86	52.57	13.50	14.34	15.98	33.43	30.84	30.22
25	53.29	52.29	46.97	17.93	19.72	24.20	28.03	27.19	27.69
26	43.66	38.09	27.04	35.34	45.63	47.79	19.67	14.51	22.50
27	48.36	44.80	34.74	28.21	32.04	38.00	22.40	21.93	25.32
28	41.60	40.36	33.59	21.61	22.40	28.91	36.00	36.40	36.18
29	47.84	46.64	39.23	28.16	29.15	33.19	22.59	22.71	23.81
30	45.58	45.43	39.34	18.71	20.50	26.35	34.83	33.07	32.77
31–33	49.68	48.64	45.52	16.78	17.92	21.88	32.79	32.62	31.34
35–39	37.90	35.67	30.29	3.95	5.45	7.31	57.12	57.74	61.01
41–43	35.07	34.73	29.50	8.44	9.24	11.39	55.91	55.34	58.20
45–47	17.84	17.55	16.68	2.23	2.38	2.13	79.55	79.70	80.73
49–53	32.31	30.44	28.91	6.07	7.73	9.25	59.87	59.86	59.19
55–56	30.64	30.10	28.86	2.92	3.24	3.82	65.67	66.02	66.40
58–60	49.99	48.38	46.35	7.25	7.40	7.54	42.33	43.77	45.47
61	27.61	25.21	27.10	6.39	5.88	7.71	65.59	68.52	64.49
62–63	45.29	44.93	43.03	7.11	8.75	9.73	47.01	45.69	46.33
64–66	31.21	32.31	32.43	2.60	2.65	3.20	65.98	64.78	63.97
68	9.66	9.54	8.71	0.66	0.76	1.17	89.61	89.61	90.00
69–82	20.95	20.42	19.51	2.17	2.38	2.67	76.68	76.97	77.51
84	24.02	24.05	24.22	3.56	4.45	6.80	71.97	70.95	68.09
85	10.08	9.52	8.97	1.09	1.34	1.75	88.71	89.01	89.08
86–88	29.12	27.55	27.99	4.68	5.05	6.72	65.79	66.97	64.64
90–96	23.71	23.46	23.05	3.61	3.86	4.67	72.32	72.30	71.73
97–98	0.00	0.00	0.00	0.00	0.00	0.00	100.00	100.00	100.00

Source: OECD's Input Output Tables (IOTs). https://stats.oecd.org/.

Authors' elaboration.

Note: The difference between output and the components above comprises taxes and subsidies.

The infrastructure-related sectors grew considerably faster than the rest of the Mexican economy, but such improved performance was not mirrored in their share in the country's total value-added due to declining relative prices. However, unlike Brazil, where the presence of foreign MNEs in both energy and telecommunications was pervasive, FDI was not a key driver of output growth in these sectors in Mexico.

On the other hand, FDI in the financial sector was quite important in Mexico, in contrast to Brazil. After the 1994 Tequila crisis, which spread to other Latin American economies, both countries heartily welcomed foreign banks, which acquired several bankrupt domestic banks. However, the result came to be rather different. In Brazil, HSBC and Citigroup left the retail banking market after some years of struggling to compete with the largest domestic banks. In contrast, in Mexico the three largest banks by the end of 2015—the Spanish BBVA and Santander, and Banamex, a subsidiary of Citigroup—as well as the fifth and the sixth—the British HSBC and the Canadian Scotiabank—are foreign controlled. From 2001 to 2015, credit to the private sector (as a share of GDP) grew from 12.9% to 31.9%, a movement reflected in the financial sector's share in the economy's total value-added.

Nonetheless, despite such growth, credit depth remained very low in Mexico—in Brazil, which is not outstanding in this respect, that ratio reached 66.8% in 2015. The overwhelming presence of foreign actors in such a vital sector of a modern capitalist economy is not exempt from criticism. Serrano (2016), for example, argued that foreign banks in Mexico were excessively risk-averse, as demonstrated by the low level of non-performing loans. Vidal, Marshall, and Correa (2011) assign Mexico's slow recovery from the 2008 global financial crisis to the dominance of foreign banks and the minimal presence of state-owned banks that could have carried out counter-cyclical policies.

A few studies have investigated the relationship between FDI and manufacturing performance in Mexico, with a special focus on the effects of NAFTA. In this respect, Grumiller (2014) identifies a considerable gap between the ex ante projections and the ex post evaluations of the effects of NAFTA on the Mexican economy. Computable general equilibrium simulations that assumed substantial increases in greenfield FDI flows—and the correspondent rise in capital stock—seem to have overestimated employment and wage gains in Mexico.

Using highly disaggregated (4-digit) manufacturing data, Nunnenkamp and Bremont (2007) found a small positive impact of FDI on manufacturing employment in Mexico over the period 1994–2003. According to their estimates, the employment impact of FDI diminishes (or becomes more negative) the more skill-intensive the industry becomes, a result driven by blue-collar employment. White-collar employment tends to grow in response to FDI as an industry becomes more skill-intensive. Using industry-level data, Waldkirch (2010) finds a positive relationship between FDI and total factor productivity (TFP) after NAFTA, but the effect on workers' compensation was zero (or even negative). More important, the positive effect is restricted to non-*maquila* FDI—increases in *maquila* FDI does not seem to increase TFP.

5.3.7. Mexico: The Co-evolution between FDI and Export Structure

Unlike Brazil, where key export products are produced primarily by domestic firms, in Mexico exporting is associated with MNE activity, which, in turn, is associated with the *maquila* system, which accounts for a substantial part of the country's manufacture exports, especially for the US market.[17]

Mexico's export processing firms—*maquiladoras* or *maquilas*—form one of the oldest international production networks in the world[18] (Hansen, 2003). These firms import parts and components, which are assembled into final products that are later exported, mainly to the US market, which is also the main source of inputs. They are more active in electronics, automotive, and garment industries (Hanson, 2002). Until 1994, when NAFTA was put in place, the *maquilas* benefited from the US offshore assembly program, which permitted the duty-free return of domestically manufactured components that had been processed in another country—importers had to pay import tariffs only on the value added abroad (Hanson, 2002). This program, on the one hand, reduced the cost of moving assembly activities abroad for US MNEs, but, on the other hand, prevented the creation of linkages within Mexico's domestic economy as the inputs sourced locally had to pay import duties. Such distortion was eliminated by NAFTA.

[17] Until 2006, Mexico's National Institute of Statistics (INEGI) used to collect and publish data of the *maquila* system separately from the rest of the manufacturing sector. In that year, the *maquila* program was merged with another program that concede benefits to exporters (PITEX), and from that date it became impossible to distinguish the *maquilas* from other export plants in published statistics. According to Koopman, Wang, and Zei (2013), in 2006 there were 2,795 plants under the *maquila* regime and 3,620 under the PITEX. Together, these plants were responsible for 85.4% of the country's total exports and 52.7% of total imports. *Maquilas* were predominant in computer and electronics (84.9% of the exports), while PITEX were predominant in transport equipment (62.5% of the exports)

[18] The origins of the *maquilas* date back to the late 1960s, when the Mexican government instituted the (Northern) Border Industrialization Program (Hansen, 2003). The introduction of assembly plants was viewed as a way of fighting the high unemployment rates that prevailed in border cities. The program was inspired by the export processing zones that were being erected in Asia and allowed the import of raw materials, components, and capital goods duty free if the production was totally exported. Originally the companies involved in *maquila* scheme could not be controlled by foreign investors, but this restriction was lifted in 1973. With the program, US FDI in Mexico shifted from the oil sector to these assembling industrial plants. Nonetheless, the *maquila* sector only took off after the 1982 foreign debt crisis. Besides the competitiveness brought by currency devaluation, the government lifted many of the restrictions that hampered the attractiveness of the *maquilas*.

Before its implementation, there was an expectation that NAFTA would curb the *maquilas*' advantages, but they were able of remaining competitive because of wage differentials. Output and employment within the *maquila* sector expanded rapidly during the 1990s, especially in the electronics and automotive industries. NAFTA strengthened the regional value chains because it imposed an advantage for regionally sourced inputs, vis-à-vis non-NAFTA inputs, which had to pay import tariffs. NAFTA's rules of origin also created an incentive for higher value-adding in Mexico in order to export to the US market without tariffs. This incentive was reflected on domestic content of exports which, between 1995 and 2001, rose from 11% to 18% in the electronics, and from 15% to 24%, in the automotive *maquilas* (Castillo and De Vries, 2018).

Nonetheless, the scenario changed after China's accession to the WTO (Gallagher and Porzecanski, 2007). Besides being the main destinations of US MNE manufacturing offshoring, China's and Mexico's export baskets to the United States were quite similar, with the predominance of products made in export-processing zones using inputs imported from elsewhere. With China's emergence, Mexico lost one of its sources of competitive advantage—low labour costs. Nearly a quarter of the jobs in the electronics *maquilas* were lost between 2000 and 2005, while in auto parts there was a small growth in employment (Sargent and Matthews, 2008). Sargent and Matthews (2004) argue that this was partly due to relocation of export-processing plants to China in the case of goods in which proximity to the US market was not a key competitive advantage.[19]

In a study using plant-level data for the period 1990–2006, Utar and Ruiz (2013) find that a higher penetration of Chinese products in the US market is associated with a decrease in employment and in sales at Mexican *maquilas*. Plant growth and survival are also negatively affected by Chinese competition. Even considering that Mexico's exports to the United States did not fall in absolute terms, the country lost market share in favour of China in products like consumer electronics and appliances and computers. With China's entry into the WTO, proximity to the United States remained the main, if not the only, competitive advantage of Mexican *maquilas* (Sargent and Matthews, 2008).

Despite its importance for balance of payments and job creation, the *maquila* system has been, since its inception, questioned as a strategy of economic development. Linkages between the export-processing plants and the domestic firms remained very limited—the domestic value added in *maquilas*' exports fell from 27% in 1981 to 13% in 2006 (Castillo and De Vries, 2018). According to Koopman, Wang, and Wei (2013), in 2003 *maquilas* accounted for 85% of

[19] According to their definition, non-proximity-dependent products are typically high volume, highly standardized, not part of just-in-time processes, with low transportation costs relative to total costs (Sargent and Matthews, 2004, 2008).

Mexico's exports of computers and electronics, but domestic value-added was mere 14% (8.5% in the case of computers). Thus, differently from some Asian economies whose development strategies also relied upon export-processing zones—Taiwan, South Korea, and, more recently, China—Mexico has not been able to upgrade significantly within GVCs.

Table 5.10 displays the products in which Mexico exports with RCA. The contrast with Brazil is evident. Except for crude petroleum, which was impacted by the booming prices of the commodities super cycle, natural-resource-based goods are almost irrelevant within Mexico's export basket over the whole period analysed. Mexico's comparative advantages are not only localized in manufacturing, but are concentrated in two specific areas: electronics and transport equipment. The latter is usually classified as a medium-technology industry, while the former is commonly classified as high tech.

Over the period 1999–2015, Mexico's comparative advantages seem to have been concentrated in a decreasing number of products. From Table 5.10, it is clear that Mexico lost almost completely its former competitiveness in textiles. Indeed, the number of 6-digit categories in which the country has revealed advantage decreased from 37, in 1999, to 8, in 2015. In turn, transport equipment became more relevant within the country's export basket, especially auto parts and trucks.

Over the whole period, electro-electronic goods remained as the main category within Mexico's export basket, but significant shifts have taken place. Computers increased their importance, while components such as integrated circuits or office machine parts have reduced theirs. An inverted-U-shaped trend can be noted in video displays, a product that became very important in Mexico's export basket circa 2010, losing prominence since then. In turn, telephones, which were not so important in 1999, augmented their relevance over time, becoming one of the leading export products in 2015. To conclude, the increase in importance of medical instruments over the period is noteworthy.

Nonetheless, given the widely known high-import content of Mexico's exports, analysis of RCA based on gross exports can be misleading. Thus, it is important to resort to RCA based on value-added in order to have a more trustworthy picture of the country's place in the world's international division of labour. Table 5.11 confirms Mexico's RCA in computers, electronics, and automotive products, suggesting that such advantages have been increasing over time. According to these numbers, in 2015 the greatest specialization of the country was in transport equipment, followed by electronics (computers), an industry in which the country did not present RCA in 1999.

In some contrast to Brazil, Mexico is specialized in highly connected goods. According to the economic complexity literature, this means that

Table 5.10 Mexico: The Evolution of Export Structure and RCA, 1999–2015

	Section	Number of HS4 (6-digit) with RCA>1				Share in Total Exports (%) - HS4 (6-digit) with RCA>1				Share in Total Exports (%)- HS4 (6-digit) with RCA≤1			
		1999	2005	2010	2015	1999	2005	2010	2015	1999	2005	2010	2015
1	Animal Products	4	3	3	4	0.58	0.43	0.22	0.46	0.30	0.30	0.47	0.44
2	Vegetable Products	19	22	20	19	2.44	2.19	2.32	2.71	0.42	0.31	0.48	0.60
3	Animal and Vegetable By-Products	1	1	1	0	0.00	0.00	0.00	0.00	0.05	0.04	0.05	0.05
4	Foodstuffs	8	11	13	12	1.12	1.61	2.15	2.14	0.87	0.72	0.58	0.73
5	Mineral Products	13	8	9	12	6.88	13.91	12.05	6.07	0.75	1.82	2.15	1.03
	Crude petroleum					*6.45*	*13.45*	*11.58*	*4.99*	–	–	–	–
6	Chemical Products	20	23	22	19	1.03	1.04	1.18	0.91	2.18	1.99	2.01	1.98
7	Plastics and Rubbers	6	8	8	11	1.07	1.26	0.73	1.54	1.18	1.28	1.75	1.24
8	Animal Hides	6	5	3	4	0.06	0.06	0.03	0.03	0.28	0.12	0.12	0.14
9	Wood Products	3	2	0	1	0.20	0.07	0.00	0.01	0.19	0.11	0.10	0.10
10	Paper Goods	6	5	5	5	0.36	0.37	0.26	0.36	0.45	0.47	0.41	0.32
11	Textiles	37	28	15	8	6.09	3.06	1.12	0.66	1.36	1.35	1.00	1.11
12	Footwear and Headwear	4	2	2	2	0.05	0.01	0.01	0.01	0.32	0.16	0.15	0.18
13	Stone and Glass	16	20	15	12	0.92	1.04	0.80	0.71	0.40	0.16	0.16	0.28
14	Precious Metals	3	2	3	2	0.35	0.34	2.80	0.49	0.30	0.46	0.27	1.22
15	Metals	31	32	28	23	2.39	3.55	2.40	1.87	2.12	1.63	2.25	1.99

(*continued*)

Table 5.10 Continued

	Section	Number of HS4 (6-digit) with RCA>1				Share in Total Exports (%) - HS4 (6-digit) with RCA>1				Share in Total Exports (%)- HS4 (6-digit) with RCA≤1			
		1999	2005	2010	2015	1999	2005	2010	2015	1999	2005	2010	2015
16	Machines	41	45	47	44	33.15	32.30	33.00	32.30	7.29	4.85	4.16	4.68
	Computers					*4.74*	*4.07*	*3.60*	*5.15*	—	—	—	—
	Electrical transformers					*1.65*	*0.92*	*0.73*	*0.73*	—	—	—	—
	Insulated wire					*4.51*	*3.46*	*2.30*	*3.01*	—	—	—	—
	Integrated circuits					—	—	—	—	*1.17*	*0.52*	*0.34*	*0.46*
	Low-voltage protection equipment					*1.73*	*1.43*	*1.03*	*0.91*	—	—	—	—
	Office machine parts					—	—	—	—	*2.26*	*1.07*	*0.21*	*0.24*
	Telephones					*1.40*	*1.51*	*3.06*	*3.90*	—	—	—	—
	Video displays					*3.84*	*4.95*	*6.65*	*4.17*	—	—	—	—
17	Transportation	12	7	9	8	17.94	15.30	17.90	24.90	0.45	0.35	0.44	0.50
	Cars					*9.28*	*6.36*	*7.93*	*8.90*	—	—	—	—
	Delivery trucks					*3.21*	*3.49*	*3.81*	*5.82*	—	—	—	—
	Vehicle parts					*3.51*	*4.49*	*4.64*	*6.59*	—	—	—	—
18	Instruments	12	14	13	13	2.30	3.28	3.21	4.23	0.81	0.64	0.70	0.63
	Medical instruments					*0.65*	*1.57*	*1.76*	*2.13*	—	—	—	—
19	Weapons	0	0	0	0	0.00	0.00	0.00	0.00	0.01	0.01	0.01	0.01
20	Miscellaneous	11	11	9	10	2.37	2.70	1.90	2.82	0.97	0.70	0.68	0.56

Source: The Observatory of Economic Complexity. https://oec.world/en.
Authors' elaboration.

Table 5.11 Mexico: RCA Index Based on Value Added

Sector	1999	2005	2010	2015
01–03	1.01	0.77	0.81	0.96
05–09	1.86	1.90	1.57	1.04
05–06	—	2.12	1.73	0.92
07–08	—	0.83	0.95	1.51
09	—	1.20	1.25	1.28
10–33	0.61	0.81	0.88	1.10
10–12	0.63	0.69	0.88	0.95
13–15	1.87	0.92	0.58	0.58
16	1.22	0.41	0.41	0.55
17–18	0.77	0.32	0.44	0.50
19	0.49	0.30	0.60	0.58
20–21	1.98	0.47	0.50	0.43
22	1.19	0.59	0.67	0.91
23	1.41	0.81	0.70	0.81
24	1.41	1.14	1.53	1.30
25	0.41	0.55	0.61	0.72
26	0.64	1.18	1.13	1.53
27	3.46	1.23	1.19	1.41
28	1.21	0.47	0.52	0.66
29	1.46	1.62	2.24	3.41
30	0.12	0.21	0.14	0.41
31–33	2.60	0.86	0.77	0.81

Source: OECD's Trade in Value Added Database. https://stats.oecd.org.

Authors' elaboration.

Note: RCA indexes were calculated using TiVA's indicator on Domestic Value Added Embodied in Foreign Final Demand.

there is a considerable potential of expanding exports to nearby products (within the product space) as they are likely to require the same capabilities to be produced as those that Mexico already produces. This is the path that economies like South Korea and Taiwan have followed since the 1960s—that is, they moved within the product space but managed to upgrade from low value-added goods to higher value-added ones. However, this has not yet been the case of Mexico.

In sum, Mexico's post-1982 development strategy has given manufacturing exports a central role. It was expected that liberal reforms would improve efficiency and help the country to attain higher GDP growth rates. Nonetheless, the story so far is quite disappointing. Gross exports increased substantially, but their capacity to catalyse growth has proved overestimated. High use of imported inputs coupled with low integration of the *maquilas* with domestic producers limited the multiplier effects coming from foreign demand. Linkages between the export-oriented plants and the domestic-oriented economy remain scarce. For this reason, the export-oriented manufacturing sector is unable to work—borrowing from Kaldor's (1967) terminology—as a growth engine for the rest of the economy.

The emergence of China has been a great challenge to Mexico because of their similar specializations. China's share in US imports of manufactures rose sharply in the first decade of the twenty-first century, while Mexico's share, after a surge in the 1990s, declined. The inflection point, for both countries, occurred in 2001, the year China joined the WTO (Hanson, 2010). Following WTO accession and the end of the Multi-Fiber agreement, in 2005, China quickly displaced Mexico and other Latin American countries from the US apparel market. According to Chiquiar and Ramos-Francia's (2009) calculations, Mexico also lost comparative advantage vis-à-vis China in computers and electronics but maintained it in automobiles and auto parts.

The tentative emulation of export-led industrialization has not been as successful as it was in East Asia. Taiwan also started its industrialization following a model quite similar to the *maquila* system, but its firms were able to graduate and develop own-brand production—for example, two of the world's leading computer brands, Acer and Asus, are Taiwanese. Mexico has not made such a transition, remaining locked-in to labour-intensive processing of imported inputs, and having augmented the country's exposure to Chinese competition (Hanson, 2010). Among the possible explanations for Mexico's inability to upgrade in the electronics industry, Lowe and Kenney (1999) include the physical distance separating the *maquilas* from the country's major industrial and technological hubs, such as Mexico City and Guadalajara, which may have prevented the development of backward linkages. In turn, agglomeration near the US border was not sufficient to engender the positive externalities usually associated with industrial clusters.

Another possible reason for Mexico's failure to upgrade may be its approach to industrial policy. Unlike Brazil, which, despite the abandonment of ISI model, maintained and in some cases strengthened specific industrial policies, Mexico progressively forsook active industrial policy, culminating in its virtual disappearance after signing NAFTA.[20] Since then, industrialization has been promoted via trade openness, trade deals, and horizontal policies aimed at

[20] According to Calderón and Sánchez (2012), a few programs were created or maintained in the 1980s but were underfunded and hampered by the liberal macroeconomic policy.

improving the business environment (Calderón and Sánchez, 2012).[21] Indeed, despite the habitual rhetoric supportive of industrial policy, government after government has taken the view that it must not distort market signals in order to interfere in private decisions about investment, production, and so on. Instead, the focus of state action should be limited to correcting market failures (Moreno-Brid, 2016). With this narrow approach, the government may have missed the opportunity of putting in place policies aimed at upgrading within industries in which Mexico already has comparative advantage in final assembling stages, such as automobiles (Moreno-Brid, 2016).

Mexico's history also brings to the forefront an old issue that affects most developing nations that rely on FDI as a catalyst for their development: their technological dependence. Indeed, Mexico's export basket is mainly composed of mid- and high-tech goods, produced within innovation-driven value chains, whose markets are among the most dynamic in the world. However, Mexico does not engage in sufficient innovation or participate enough in truly high-tech stages of value chains. Consequently, observed market dynamism is not necessarily reflected in the construction of linkages, or the realization of higher value-added.

5.4. Conclusions

Industrialization through import substitution in Latin America has a long and complex history, which has received considerable attention in a wide literature, in many cases contrasting it with the East Asian experiences (see Gereffi and Wyman, 1990; Lall, 1996; Cárdenas, Ocampo, and Thorp, 2000; Fishwick, 2019). Brazil and Mexico both followed the import substitution path between the 1930s and the 1980s. However, the imperatives of the two economies varied considerably. In part, this reflected the relationship of Mexico to the United States, both in terms of physical proximity and political dependence. As a result of both factors, the United States became Mexico's largest trading and investment partner. Brazil, while still within the US sphere of influence, enjoyed considerably more flexibility and independence in its economic policies.

This differentiation was sustained in the wake of the 1990s Washington Consensus, with Mexico following a more orthodox path (i.e. closer to the Washington Consensus) than Brazil. Accordingly, Mexico saw greater dismantling of ISI policies

[21] It must be recognized, however, that despite the non-existence of comprehensive industrial policies, specific industries and firms, particularly foreign MNEs, benefit from incentives offered by governments, especially at the sub-national level (Calderón and Sánchez, 2012). According to Moreno-Brid, Gómez, and Garry (2020), industrial policies at the sub-national level have been crucial for the creation of new high-tech export-oriented industrial complexes such as in the state of Jalisco.

than Brazil. Whatever the differences in approach, both countries witnessed a surge of inward FDI and a consequent expansion in MNE activity. What resulted in terms of the co-evolution of FDI, exports, and economic structure?

In the case of Brazil, despite rises in inward investment across the board—including in higher-tech manufacturing—the export and economic structures did not tilt towards non-traditional (i.e. industrial) exports. Moreover, there was relatively weak interconnectedness between exports. Instead, there was a relative reversion to an emphasis on natural-resource-based activities. In Mexico, there was relatively greater export connectedness, and the share of manufacturing in economic structure and exports held up quite well. However, given the high import quotient in Mexico's industrial output, the local value-added in these activities was held back. There was also limited effort to build technological capability.

Looking ahead, if growth performance is to improve in both countries, efforts must be made to build on capabilities and sectors which have been established. This would involve sustained innovation, and attempts to build up connectivity and complementarities between export activities.

From a conceptual point of view, this is perhaps the first study that tracks the complex intertwining of policies, economic structure, and the intricate patterns of trade and investment flows, in an extended longitudinal perspective. Earlier research has tried to determine whether changes in domestic economic structures shape the patterns of FDI and trade, or vice versa. This, we have concluded in earlier studies (Pineli, Narula, and Belderbos, 2021; Pineli, 2022), is largely a futile exercise because it tends to overlook the dynamics and the feedback effects among these variables. What the comparison of Brazil and Mexico offers is an illustration of how relatively simple changes in horizontal policy frameworks towards trade and MNE investment can play a significant role in reshaping economic structure. This happens as the policy shifts alter the signals and incentives that the economic agents face. The Brazil-Mexico comparison also illustrates that industrial policy—that is, vertical selective policy interventions—matters in fostering domestic linkages, and in changing national competitiveness.

References

Arbix, G. 2010. 'Caminhos cruzados: Rumo a uma estratégia de desenvolvimento baseada na inovação', *Novos Estudos CEBRAP*, 87, 13–33.

Balassa, B. 1965. 'Trade Liberalisation and "Revealed Comparative Advantage"', *Manchester School*, 33, 99–123.

Bielschowsky, R. 1994. *Two Studies on Transnational Corporations in the Brazilian Manufacturing Sector: The 1980s and Early 1990s*. Santiago: CEPAL/ECLAC (Desarollo Productivo no. 18).

Bielschowsky, R. 1999. *Investimentos na indústria brasileira depois da abertura e do real: o mini-ciclo de modernizações, 1995–1997*. Brasília: CEPAL (Serie Reformas Económicas no. 44).

Bielschowsky, R., and Stumpo, G. 1995. 'Empresas transnacionales y cambios estructurales en la industria de Argentina, Brasil, Chile y México', *Revista de la Cepal*, 55, 139–163.

Bonelli, R. 1980. 'Concentração industrial no Brasil: Indicadores da evolução recente', *Pesquisa e Planejamento Econômico*, 10(3), 851–884.

Bruton, H. 1989. 'Import Substitution', in H. Chenery and T. Srinivasan, eds., *Handbook of Development Economics*. Amsterdam: Elsevier, 1601–1644.

Calderón, C., and Sánchez, I. 2012. 'Crecimiento económico y política industrial em México', *Problemas del Desarollo*, 170(43), 125–154.

Cárdenas, E., Ocampo, J., and Thorp, R. 2000. *An Economic History of Twentieth-Century Latin America*, Volume 3: *Industrialization and the State in Latin America: The Postwar Years*. New York: Palgrave.

Castillo, J., and De Vries, G. 2018. 'The Domestic Content of Mexico's Maquiladora Exports: A Long-Run Perspective', *Journal of International Trade & Economic Development*, 27(2), 200–219.

Chenery, H. 1960. 'Patterns of Industrial Growth', *American Economic Review*, 50(4), 624–654.

Chiquiar, D., and Ramos-Francia, M. 2009. *Competitiveness and Growth of the Mexican Economy*. Mexico City: Banco de México (Documento de Investigación no. 2009-11).

Clavijo, W., Almeida, E., Losekann, L., and Rodrigues, N. 2019. 'Impacts of the Review of the Brazilian Local Contente Policy on the Attractiveness of the Oil and Gas Projects', *Journal of World Energy Law and Business*, 12(5), 449–463.

Colistete, R. 2003. 'Was Import-Substituting Industrialisation in Brazil a Failure? Evidence from the Technological Structure of Exports, 1945–1973'. Paper presented at the 5th Brazilian Conference on Economic History (V Congresso Brasileiro de História Econômica).

Creel, L., Jr. 1968. '"Mexicanization": A Case of Creeping Expropriation', *SMU Law Review*, 22(2), 281–299.

Cuervo-Cazurra, A., Narula, R., and Un, C. 2015. 'Internationalization Motives: Sell More, Buy Better, Upgrade and Escape', *Multinational Business Review*, 23(1), 25–35.

De Negri, J. 1999. 'O custo de bem-estar do regime automotivo brasileiro', *Pesquisa e Planejamento Econômico*, 29(2), 215–242.

Dunning, J. 1981a. 'Explaining the International Direct Investment Position of Countries: Towards a Dynamic or Developmental Approach', *Weltwirtschaftliches Archiv*, 177, 30–64.

Dunning, J. 1981b. *International Production and the Multinational Enterprise*. London: Allen & Unwin.

Dunning, J. 1988. *Explaining International Production*. London: Unwin Hyman.

Dunning, J. 1993. *Multinational Enterprises and the Global Economy*. Wokingham: Addison-Wesley.

Dunning, J., and Narula, R. 1996. 'The Investment Development Path Revisited: Some Emerging Issues', in J. Dunning and R. Narula, eds., *Foreign Direct Investment and Governments: Catalysts for Economic Restructuring*. Basingstoke, UK: Edward Elgar, 1–40.

Dussel Peters, E. 2000. *La inversión extranjera em México*. Santiago: CEPAL/ECLAC.

Fishlow, A. 1972. 'Origins and Consequences of Import Substitution in Brazil', in E. Di Marco, ed., *International Economics and Development: Essays in Honor of Raúl Prebisch*. New York: Academic Press, 311–365.

Fishwick, A. 2019. 'Labour Control and Developmental State Theory: A New Perspective on Import-Substitution Industrialization in Latin America', *Development and Change*, 50(3), 655–678.

Florencio, P. 2016. 'Technology and Innovation in the Brazilian Oil Sector: Ticket to the Future or Passage to the Past?', *Journal of World Energy Law and Business*, 9(4), 237–253.

Gallagher, K., and Porzecanski, R. 2007. 'What a Difference a Few Years Makes: China and the Competitiveness of Mexican Exports', *Oxford Development Studies*, 35(2), 219–223.

Gereffi, G., and Wyman, D. 1990. *Manufacturing Miracles: Paths of Industrialization in Latin America and East Asia*. Princeton, NJ: Princeton University Press.

Grumiller, J. 2014. 'Ex-ante versus ex-post Assessments of the Economic Benefits of Free Trade Agreements: Lessons from the North American Free Trade Agreement (NAFTA)'. Vienna: Austrian Foundation for Development Research (ÖFSE) (Briefing Paper no. 10).

Guimarães, A. 2021. 'The Political Economy of Brazilian Industrial Policy (2003–2014): Main Vectors, Shortcomings and Directions', *Dados*, 64(2), 1–33.

Guimarães, E. 1996. *A experiência recente da política industrial no Brasil: Uma avaliação*. Brasília: IPEA (Texto para Discussão no. 409).

Hansen, L. 2003. 'The Origins of the Maquila Industry in Mexico', *Comercio Exterior*, 53(11), 1–16.

Hanson, G. 2002. *The Role of Maquiladoras in Mexico's Export Boom*. San Diego: University of California.

Hanson, G. 2010. 'Why Isn't Mexico Rich?', *Journal of Economic Literature*, 48(4), 987–1004.

Hausmann, R., Huang, J., and Rodrik, D. 2006. 'What You Export Matters', *Journal of Economic Growth*, 12, 1–25.

Hidalgo, C., Klinger, B., Barabási, A., and Hausmann, R. 2007. 'The Product Space Conditions the Development of Nations', *Science*, 317(5837), 482–487.

Hirschman, A. 1968. 'The Political Economy of Import-Substituting Industrialization in Latin America', *Quarterly Journal of Economics*, 82(1), 1–32.

Kaldor, N. 1967. *Strategic Factors in Economic Development*. Ithaca, NY: Cornell University Press.

Koopman, R., Wang, Z., and Wei, S. 2013. 'Estimating Foreign Value-Added in Mexico's Manufacturing Exports', in Y. Cheung and F. Westermann, eds., *Global Interdependence, Decoupling, and Recoupling*. Cambridge, MA: MIT Press, 169–212.

Koslow, L. 1992. 'Mexican Foreign Investment Laws: An Overview', *William Mitchell Law Review*, 18(2), 441–460.

Kupfer, D., Ferraz, J., and Marques, F. 2013. 'The Return of Industrial Policy in Brazil', in J. Stiglitz and J. Lin, eds., *The Industrial Policy Revolution I*. London: Springer, 327–339.

Kuznets, S. 1957. 'Quantitative Aspects of the Economic Growth of Nations: II. Industrial Distribution of National Product and Labor Force', *Economic Development and Cultural Change*, 5(4-Suppl), 1–111.

Lall, S. 1996. *Learning from the Asian Tigers: Studies in Technology and Industrial Policy*. New York: Springer.

Leahy, J. 2012. 'Brazil's "Chicken Flight" Growth', *Financial Times*, 7 March 2012.

Lessa, C. 1978. *Estratégia de desenvolvimento, 1974–1976: Sonho e fracasso*. Campinas: Unicamp.

Lowe, N., and Kenney, M. 1999. 'Foreign Investment and the Global Geography of Production: Why the Mexican Consumer Electronics Industry Failed', *World Development*, 27(8), 1427–1443.

Máttar, J., Moreno-Brid, J., and Peres, W. 2003. 'Foreign Investment in Mexico after Economic Reform', in K. Middlebrook and E. Zepeda, eds., *Confronting Development: Assessing Mexico's Economic and Social Policy Challenges*. Stanford, CA: Stanford University Press, 123–160.

Maviglia, S. 1986. 'Mexico's Guidelines for Foreign Investment: The Selective Promotion of Necessary Industries', *American Journal of International Law*, 80(2), 281–304.

Messa, A. 2017. 'Impacto de políticas de exigência de conteúdo local: o caso do programa Inovar-Auto', in A. Messa and I. Oliveira, eds., *A política comercial brasileira em análise*. Brasília: IPEA, 355–373.

Moreira, M. 1999. *Estrangeiros em uma economia aberta: Impactos recentes sobre produtividade, concentração e comércio exterior*. Rio de Janeiro: BNDES (Texto para Discussão no. 67).

Moreno-Brid, J. 2016. 'A Political and Industrial Framework for Structural Change and Growth: The Big Question for the Mexican Economy', *Problemas del Desarollo*, 47(185), 57–78.

Moreno-Brid, J., Gómez, J., and Garry, S. 2020. 'The Syncopated Dance of Mexico's Industrial Policy', in H. Veltmeyer and E. Lau, eds., *Buen Vivir and the Challenges to Capitalism in Latin America*. London: Routledge, 92–112.

Morley, S., and Smith, G. 1971. 'Import Substitution and Foreign Investment in Brazil', *Oxford Economic Papers*, 23(1), 120–135.

Morley, S., and Smith, G. 1977. 'The Choice of Technology: Multinational Firms in Brazil', *Economic Development and Cultural Change*, 25(2), 239–264.

Narula, R. 1996. *Multinational Investment and Economic Structure: Globalisation and Competitiveness*. London and New York: Routledge.

Narula, R., and Dunning, J. 2010. 'Multinational Enterprises, Development and Globalization: Some Clarifications and a Research Agenda', *Oxford Development Studies*, 38(3), 263–287.

Narula, R., and Pineli, A. 2017. 'Multinational Enterprises and Economic Development in Host Countries: What We Know and What We Don't Know', in G. Giorgioni, ed., *Development Finance: Challenges and Opportunities*. London: Palgrave, 147–188.

Narula, R., and Pineli, A. 2019. 'Improving the Developmental Impact of Multinational Enterprises: Policy and Research Challenges', *Economia e Politica Industriale*, 46, 1–24.

Newfarmer, R., and Mueller, W. 1975. *Multinational Corporations in Brazil and Mexico: Structural Sources of Economic and Noneconomic Power. Report to the Subcommittee on Multinational Corporations of the Committee on Foreign Relations, United States Senate*. Washington, DC: US Government Printing Office.

Nonnenberg, M. 2003. *Determinantes dos investimentos externos e impactos das empresas multinacionais no Brasil: As décadas de 1970 e 1990*. Rio de Janeiro: IPEA (Texto para Discussão no. 969).

Nunnenkamp, P., and Bremont, J. 2007. *FDI in Mexico: An Empirical Assessment of Employment Effects*. Kiel: Kiel Institute for the World Economy (IfW) (Working Paper no. 1328).

Pineli, A. 2022. 'FDI, Productivity Growth and Structural Change in European Post-Communist Countries: An Industry-Level Analysis', *Revista Tempo do Mundo*, 29, 335–386.

Pineli, A., Narula, R., and Belderbos, R. 2021. 'FDI, Multinationals and Structural Change in Developing Countries', in L. Alcorta, N. Foster-Mcgregor, B. Verspagen, and A. Szirmai, eds., *New Perspectives on Structural Change: Causes and Consequences of Structural Change in the Global Economy*. Oxford: Oxford University Press, 494–523.

Piquet, R., Hasenclever, L., and Shimoda, E. 2016. 'O desenvolvimento e a política de conteúdo local na indústria petrolífera: visões divergentes', *Revista Tecnologia e Sociedade*, 12(24), 45–48.

Porcile, G. 2021. 'Latin American Structuralism', in L. Alcorta, N. Foster-Mcgregor, B. Verspagen, and A. Szirmai, eds., *New Perspectives on Structural Change: Causes and Consequences of Structural Change in the Global Economy*. Oxford: Oxford University Press, 50–71.

Prebisch, R. 1949. 'O desenvolvimento econômico da América Latina e seus principais problemas', *Revista Brasileira de Economia*, 3(3), 47–111.

Sargent, J., and Matthews, L. 2004. 'What Happens When Relative Costs Increase in Export Processing Zones? Technology, Regional Production Networks, and Mexico's Maquiladoras', *World Development*, 32(12), 2015–2030.

Sargent, J., and Matthews, L. 2008. 'Capital Intensity, Technology Intensity, and Skill Development in Post China/WTO Maquiladoras', *World Development*, 36(4), 541–559.

Sarti, F., and Laplane, M. 2002. 'O investimento direto estrangeiro e a internacionalização da economia brasileira nos anos 1990', *Economia e Sociedade*, 11(1), 63–94.

Schatan, C., and Enríquez, L. 2015. 'Mexico: Industrial Policies and the Production of Information and Communication Technology Goods and Services', *CEPAL Review*, 117, 147–163.

Schutte, G. 2021. 'A economia política do conteúdo local no setor petrolífero de Lula a Temer', *Economia e Sociedade*, 30(1), 115–140.

Serrano, A. 2016. 'Foreign Banks and Credit in Mexico', *Global Finance Journal*, 30, 77–93.

Singer, H. 1950. 'The Distribution of Gains between Investing and Borrowing Countries', *American Economic Review*, 40(2), 473–485.

Stein, G., and Herrlein Júnior, R. 2016. 'Política industrial no Brasil: Uma análise das estratégias propostas na experiência recente (2003–2014)', *Planejamento e Políticas Públicas*, 47, 251–287.

Sturgeon, T., Chagas, L., and Barnes, J. 2017. *Inovar-Auto: Evaluating Brazil's Automotive Industrial Policy to Meet the Challenges of Global Value Chains*. Washington, DC: World Bank.

Suzigan, W. 1988. 'Estado e industrialização no Brasil', *Revista de Economia Política*, 8(4), 5–16.

Suzigan, W., and Furtado, J. 2006. 'Política industrial e desenvolvimento', *Revista de Economia Política*, 26(2), 163–185.

Suzigan, W., Garcia, R., and Feitosa, P. 2020. 'Institutions and Industrial Policy in Brazil after Two Decades: Have We Built the Needed Institutions?', *Economics of Innovation and New Technology*, 29(7), 799–813.

Tordo, S., Warner, M., Manzano, O., and Anouti, Y. 2013. *Local Content Policies in the Oil and Gas Sector*. Washington, DC: World Bank.

Utar, H., and Ruiz, L. 2013. 'International Competition and Industrial Evolution: Evidence from the Impact of Chinese Competition on Mexican Maquiladoras', *Journal of Development Economics*, 105, 267–287.

Vargas, T. 2021. 'Inovar-Auto: Uma nova política para velhos interesses'. PhD thesis, Universidade Federal Tecnológica do Paraná, Curitiba.

Vidal, G. 1986. 'Capital monopolista nacional y extranjero, relaciones entrelazamientos, contradicciones', in A. Aguilar, V. Sahagun, A. Guillen, and G. Vidal, eds., *El capital extranjero en Mexico*. México, D.F.: Editorial Nuestro Tiempo, 153–200.

Vidal, G., Marshall, W., and Correa, E. 2011. 'Differing Effects of the Global Financial Crisis: Why Mexico Has Been Harder Hit than Other Large Latin American Countries', *Bulletin of Latin American Research*, 30(4), 419–435.

Waldkirch, A. 2010. 'The Effects of Foreign Direct Investment in Mexico since NAFTA', *The World Economy*, 33(5), 710–745.

Willmore, L. 1987. 'Controle estrangeiro e concentração na indústria brasileira', *Pesquisa e Planejamento Econômico*, 17(1), 161–190.

Appendix

Sectors	
01-03:	Agriculture, forestry, and fishing
05-06:	Mining and extraction of energy-producing products
07-08:	Mining and quarrying of non-energy-producing products
09:	Mining support service activities
10-12:	Food products, beverages, and tobacco
13-15:	Textiles, wearing apparel, leather, and related products
16:	Wood and products of wood and cork
17-18:	Paper products and printing
19:	Coke and refined petroleum products
20-21:	Chemicals and pharmaceutical products
22:	Rubber and plastic products
23:	Other non-metallic mineral products
24:	Basic metals
25:	Fabricated metal products
26:	Computer, electronic and optical products
27:	Electrical equipment
28:	Machinery and equipment, nec
29:	Motor vehicles, trailers, and semi-trailers
30:	Other transport equipment
31-33:	Other manufacturing; repair and installation of machinery and equipment
35-39:	Electricity, gas, water supply, sewerage, waste, and remediation services
41-43:	Construction
45-47:	Wholesale and retail trade; repair of motor vehicles
49-53:	Transportation and storage
55-56:	Accommodation and food services
58-60:	Publishing, audiovisual and broadcasting activities
61:	Telecommunications

62-63:	IT and other information services
64-66:	Financial and insurance activities
68:	Real estate activities
69-82:	Other business sector services
84:	Public admin. and defence; compulsory social security
85:	Education
86-88:	Human health and social work
90-96:	Arts, entertainment, recreation, and other service activities
97-98:	Private households with employed persons

6
Global Value Chain–Oriented Policies in Latin America

Carlo Pietrobelli, Roberta Rabellotti, and Ari Van Assche

6.1. Introduction

Despite several recent major challenges to globalization, such as the COVID-19 pandemic, the Ukrainian conflict, and the increasing geopolitical tensions among China, the United States, and the European Union, global value chains (GVCs), characterized by high division of labour among firms specializing in specific tasks and located in more than one country, have marked the evolution of the global economy since the early 1990s and still dominate the world economic system.

Evidence shows that GVCs are a powerful driver for countries' economic growth (Stolzenburg, Taglioni, and Winkler, 2019; World Bank, 2019), increasing productivity (Constantinescu, Mattoo, and Ruta, 2019; Montalbano, Nenci, and Pietrobelli, 2018; Pahl and Timmer, 2020) and generating employment (Van Assche, 2017).

The low integration of Latin America in GVCs is in this respect seen as a major factor behind the slowdown in the region's economic growth in the past decade (Fernandes, Nievas, and Winkler, 2021). The region's low dynamism could be explained by its specialization mostly in commodities, with limited involvement in manufacturing GVCs, which is in contrast to the strong participation of East Asia, Europe, and North America in the more innovative stages of GVCs in advanced manufacturing and services GVCs (World Bank, 2019). According to Fernandes et al. (2021), Latin America is on average weakly integrated in GVCs, with backward and forward participation[1] lagging those of other regions

[1] Backward GVC participation is high in countries with a high portion of imported inputs used in export production. Countries specializing in manufacturing and services are highly reliant on imported inputs for exports, while backward participation is lowest for countries specialized in commodities. Forward GVC participation is high in countries with a high share of domestic value added that is re-exported by a country's trading partner (rather than consumed there), because they are used in a variety of downstream production processes that typically cross several borders. Countries with abundant natural resources and specializing in agriculture are typically characterized by high forward participation (World Bank, 2019).

Carlo Pietrobelli, Roberta Rabellotti, and Ari Van Assche, *Global Value Chain–Oriented Policies in Latin America* In: *Innovation, Competitiveness, and Development in Latin America*. Edited by: Edmund Amann and Paulo N. Figueiredo, Oxford University Press. DOI: 10.1093/oso/9780197648070.003.0006

across all sectors. However, patterns of backward and forward GVC participation differ across Latin American and Caribbean (LAC) countries, with some countries showing high integration on both metrics (e.g., Chile), and others such as Mexico with high forward but low backward participation. On the contrary Peru, Brazil, Ecuador, Colombia, Bolivia, and Venezuela exhibit low backward but high forward GVC participation rates.

The weak GVC integration of Latin America underlines the importance of exploring how policies can enhance and sustain GVC participation. So far, there has been little systematic discussion about how GVC-oriented policies work and differ from traditional industrial, innovation, and international business policies. One reason is the relatively young age of the GVC research field. With scholars only starting to pay attention to the phenomenon 25 years ago, many aspects of the GVC framework have not been fully developed theoretically or tested empirically. This is exemplified by the lack of agreement on how to conceptualize and empirically measure economic upgrading (Gereffi, 2019a; Tokatli, 2012; Van Assche and Van Biesebroeck, 2018), and points to new areas of research in which the GVC framework should expand. Another reason is the multidisciplinary character of GVC research. GVCs have attracted the attention of scholars across fields including international business, international economics, economic geography, economic sociology, development studies, and political science, but researchers have mostly analysed the phenomenon within their own discipline's frame of reference, thus making it difficult to compare their findings.

In this chapter, we explore GVC-oriented policies and categorize them according to four different policy objectives—participation, value capture, inclusiveness, and resilience. The chapter investigates how each type of policy is built on different economic rationales and proposes distinct policy instruments. Then we present some evidence about different GVC policies in the Latin American context. Finally, by way of a conclusion, we present the trifecta of tasks, linkages, and firms to explain whether and how GVC-oriented policies differ from traditional public policies, and how they can contribute to sustain integration in GVCs in Latin America.

6.2. Objectives, Rationales, and Instruments of GVC-Oriented Policies

There is a growing appreciation in the academic community that GVCs add several layers of complexity to the link between international business and economic development, thus requiring new policy thinking. One group of scholars advocates that GVCs call for a new type of industrial policy which focuses on the development and attraction of fine-grained activities and emphasizes the importance of leveraging international supply chain linkages (Gereffi and Sturgeon, 2013; Milberg, Jiang, and Gereffi, 2014). Another group of researchers calls for governments to adopt a supply chain mindset in their thinking about trade and investment policies by focusing on how to allow domestic firms to establish rapid, efficient, and reliable linkages with their foreign value chain partners (Van Assche, 2017; Pietrobelli, 2021b). Yet a third group of studies argues that GVCs push policy away from the market fundamentalism of the Washington Consensus (Werner, Bair, and Fernandez, 2014), contending that their advent calls for a multi-scalar framework going beyond traditional approaches either focused on the nation-state or the firm (Pietrobelli and Staritz, 2018).

In a previous article, we have defined GVC-oriented policies as the spectrum of socio-economic tools and actions that governments use to influence GVCs and their actors so that they can secure local, regional, and national interests in a wide array of areas (Pietrobelli et al., 2021). We distinguish four types of GVC policies based on a mixture of objectives that are not necessarily complementary or compatible:

- *Participation policies* aimed at entering in and fostering the local economy's participation in GVCs;
- *Value-capture policies* intended for strengthening the local economy's value creation and capture within GVCs;
- *Inclusiveness policies* directed to improve the local social and environmental conditions in GVCs;
- *Resiliency policies* designed for strengthening the local economy's resiliency.

Each type of policy is characterized by different—implicit or explicit—rationales adopted by governments to justify their interventions and diverse instruments and actions to reach the different objectives.

Governments have different reasons to conduct public interventions, which can lead to different types of GVC-oriented policies. A first intention is the elimination of market distortions, such as tariffs and subsidies, that inhibit local GVC activities from reaching the envisioned goals. Another justification is to address externalities emerging in GVCs that interfere with the attainment of policy goals. For instance, risks, uncertainty, and incomplete information can limit private investments to join GVCs, to engage in transactions with suppliers, and to invest in innovation and learning activities aimed at upgrading. The uneven distribution of power and economic gains between lead firms and their suppliers can also generate GVC-related externalities by hindering the ability of domestic firms to capture economic and social gains from GVC participation (Pietrobelli and Staritz, 2018). Moreover, GVC-related externalities may take the form of coordination failures; for example, coordination among firms may be needed for industries related through backward and forward linkages.

The other differentiating dimension is represented by the different actions that the government can adopt to either buttress or harness GVCs. Horner (2017) identifies four different roles for the government: (i) as a facilitator, by eliminating market distortions through policies in areas such as trade, investment, and innovation; (ii) as a regulator, by restricting the negative externalities of private market transactions and by mitigating the unequal distributive impact of markets through, among other measures, rules concerning standards and labor conditions; (iii) as a producer, by directly engaging in state-owned production activities; and finally, (iv) as a buyer, by procuring products and services via state-led value chains, which may comprise distinct economic, social, and environmental requirements.

In the next section, we analyze in detail the four main categories of GVC-oriented policies introduced above, and in the following section we offer examples of different policies adopted in the Latin American context.

6.3. Types of GVC-Oriented Policies

GVC participation policies have gained great traction in policy circles in the past two decades for two main reasons. First, as already discussed, there is substantial empirical evidence that GVC participation is a powerful driver for economic performance (Stolzenburg et al., 2019; World Bank, 2019). Second, as explored below, policies to spur GVC participation encompass many of the liberal market-enabling and connectedness policies that policymakers have traditionally embraced.

Given the central roles of functional specialization and global connectedness in the GVC-growth nexus, the focus of GVC participation policies is concentrated on two policy pillars that attempt to reduce market distortions: *market-enabling policies* to give the private sector the incentives to align productive activities to a country's latent comparative advantage; and *connectedness policies* to reduce the costs related to linking domestic firms to foreign value chain partners. Both policies are generally horizontal in nature, because they do not imply targeting specific sectors (Crespi, Fernandez-Arias, and Stein, 2014; Pietrobelli, 2021a).

Market-enabling policies are aimed at addressing the market distortions that prevent the allocation of private resources toward comparative advantage sectors and value chain activities. Eliminating such market distortions is thus considered instrumental to facilitating GVC participation and promoting a country's functional specialization in those activities in which a country has a latent comparative advantage. They include the deregulation of factor markets and the strengthening of competition, as well as the removal of barriers to business creation and operation and policies to ensure an enabling business environment for foreign direct investments (FDI).

Connectedness policies aim at improving GVC participation by reducing the cost for local firms to receive or transfer goods and information across borders, thus turning them into more attractive GVC partners. On the goods side, there are policies that reduce trade costs, such as the elimination of tariff and non-tariff barriers and of the costs related to delays and uncertainty through customs reforms, as well as policies aimed at the introduction of competition in transport services and at the improvement of port structure and governance. On the information side, there are policies that strengthen companies' ability to transfer data cheaply, freely, and safely across borders, such as those aimed at fostering competition in the telecommunications sector and at improving the quality of the wireless network infrastructure.

Empirical relevance about how a cocktail of market-enabling and connectedness policies can help countries to increase their returns to intangible assets in GVCs is provided by Jaax and Miroudot (2021). The authors combine the Organisation for Economic Co-operation and Development (OECD) Trade in Value Added dataset with data on factor income to show that trade and investment openness, intellectual property protection, and competition enforcement are all positively associated with returns to intangible assets in GVCs.

A careful observer will note that the market-enabling and connectedness policies to boost GVC participation bear important similarities with traditional development strategies built around the so-called Washington Consensus (Gereffi, 2019b). Indeed, neoliberal convictions about comparative advantage, competitiveness, transaction costs, and minimalist state intervention are all easily accommodated within GVC participation policies. This explains why many national governments and international organizations have promptly adopted them.

Nonetheless, several features differentiate GVC participation policies from traditional trade policies. First, specialization is considered to take place at the disaggregated task level instead of the industry level. Second, connectedness policies are put on a higher pedestal. There are several reasons why reducing trade costs is considered disproportionately important in a GVC setting. In GVCs, the same component often crosses borders multiple times, therefore compounding the effect that trade costs have on the final price. Adding to this, production delays associated with trade impediments can have cascading effects throughout the chain. Keeping trade costs at bay is thus considered critical for GVC participation. Third, connectedness policies provide more room for unilateral state action than traditionally thought. Whereas eliminating trade costs on the export side generally requires governments to negotiate a reciprocity of concessions with other countries, reducing tariffs and non-tariff barriers on the import side can be done one-sidedly. 'Behind the border' measures that improve port and telecommunications infrastructure can also be unilaterally addressed.

GVC value-capture policies go far beyond the relatively minimalist, facilitative, and horizontal GVC participation policies (Gereffi, 2019b). While this research recognizes the possibility for firms and locations to effectively learn and develop from GVC participation, it cautions that the presence of multiple market and coordination failures implies that market forces do little to guarantee that GVC participation will go together with increased value capture (Pietrobelli and Staritz, 2018). For these scholars, governments thus need to adopt far more interventionist GVC value-capture policies to ensure a strong nexus between GVC participation and industrialization through structural transformation (Mayer and Phillips, 2017). Since these policies tend to target specific sectors, tasks, or firms, they are often more vertical in nature compared to GVC participation policies.

The argument is that GVC participation generates the biggest bang for its buck if it can improve the development of production and innovation capabilities, so that firms and countries can boost the value added that they can create and appropriate within a GVC through local learning and innovation (Pietrobelli and Rabellotti, 2011). In the GVC literature, this process has been termed 'economic upgrading' and refers to strategies that countries and firms might implement to move towards higher value-added activities (Gereffi et al., 2005).

The policy challenge is that market and coordination failures render the link between GVC participation and economic upgrading a highly uneven process, with up- and downgrading sometimes coexisting (Ponte and Ewert, 2009) and with economic upgrading outcomes varying across firms within countries, often leaving smaller and rural firms behind (Martinez-Covarrubias, Lenihan, and Hart, 2017).

First, it has been stressed that the quality of international knowledge flows critically depends on the governance patterns that lead firms adopt with their suppliers, as well as their bargaining power (Schmitz and Knorringa, 2000). For example, lead firms are generally willing to tolerate or even support upgrading by their suppliers along the dimensions of quality, flexibility, and productivity if it helps strengthen the complementarities between value chain partners. In contrast, they may discourage and even hinder the acquisition of technological capabilities by their suppliers if this type of upgrading risks encroaching on their core competence (Navas-Aleman, 2011).

Second, the quality of international knowledge flows also depends on local firms' ability to absorb, master, and adapt the knowledge and capabilities that the leading firms transfer to them (Morrison et al., 2008). These firm-level processes often suffer from important failures, especially in developing countries, where firms have low R&D and innovation capabilities. In these circumstances, an easy shortcut is to buy or borrow foreign technologies requiring little absorptive capacities, or to specialize in less technically sophisticated methods or assembly manufacturing. In such instances, effective forms of government policy should include various ways to cultivate R&D and innovation capabilities (Lee, 2013).

Thus, there is a clear role for policies aimed at enhancing the capture of value produced in GVCs as, first, power asymmetries between leading firms and their suppliers might hinder the ability to seize economic gains from GVC participation; second, upgrading in GVCs involves costs, risks, and uncertainty, with the potential of generating spillovers to the domestic economy; and third, there is a need for coordination of different actors investing along the chain (Pietrobelli and Staritz, 2018).

At the macro level, there is an issue related to identifying which parts of the GVC should be targeted with interventions to foster both short- and long-term growth through economic upgrading. Gereffi and Sturgeon (2013) argue that industrial policy in the age of GVCs must go beyond recreating entire supply chains within a national territory and needs to explicitly utilize extraterritorial linkages that affect a country's positioning in GVCs. However, this says little about the type of tasks that need special promotion.

Employing an input–output product space (IO–PS) framework to evaluate the effectiveness of industrial policies on specific GVC tasks over time in the automotive chain in South Africa, Bam, De Bruyne, and Laing (2021) argue that industrial policies can boost capacity development by (i) vertically supporting economic upgrading within GVCs, and (ii) horizontally unlocking opportunities in tasks that are close in technological space but not necessarily part of the same GVC. Both need to be considered when predicting the impact of industrial policy on GVC tasks.

Another array of policies which can impact economic upgrading is the introduction of local content requirements, typically explained with the logic of infant industries, granting the temporary breathing space to local firms to enable them to learn and catch up after the initial disadvantage. But local content policies need to go hand in hand with policies to promote domestic capability-building. Without the latter, the former lose their economic reason, as shown by Anzolin and Pietrobelli (2021) with a focus on the extractive industries.

At the meso and micro levels, value-capture policies are aimed at strengthening and deepening innovation and production ecosystems by facilitating the process of building the firm-level production and innovation capabilities that are necessary for capturing such gains (Sako and Zylberberg, 2019). Giuliani, Pietrobelli, and Rabellotti (2005) show how the processes of upgrading at the firm level may be enhanced by the collective efficiency prevailing in local small and medium enterprise (SME) clusters. Based on detailed Latin American case studies, they also suggest that relational forms of GVC governance favor value capturing through firm-level upgrading, and that GVC integration often helps product and process upgrading, but rarely functional upgrading. These upgrading processes in turn also depend on the prevailing innovation systems, that interact and sometimes co-evolve with GVC governance in ways that may promote or hinder the development of innovation capabilities in firms (Pietrobelli and Rabellotti, 2011; Lema et al., 2019).

De Marchi and Alford (2021) present a detailed account, enriched by many examples across industries and countries, of policies aimed at value capturing. Among them, there are those aimed at building and improving different types of logistical, digital, and productive infrastructure, which can help to attract GVCs and also facilitate upgrading within them. Besides improving countries' knowledge infrastructure, enhancing local capabilities to meet the changing and growing demand of local manufacturers is another important area for value-capturing policies. This implies the development of education and training projects creating the specific skills that local firms need for their integration into and upgrading within GVCs, and establishing links between universities, vocational centers, and the firms involved in the chains. The provision of advisory services in the areas of standards, metrology, testing, and certification is also particularly helpful in targeting value capture, because they can support local suppliers in developing the necessary capabilities for upgrading.

To conclude, value-capture policies imply a much more interventionist stance, with vertical interventions on specific sectors and even firms. The balance moves from the establishment of market-friendly conditions—by remedying market distortions to restore conditions favorable to the attraction of and integration into GVCs—to much greater selectivity and addressing of externalities. In addition, the focus of industrial policy is currently much more on the role of tasks and nodes than on entire productive sectors. This requires a different approach relative to the industrial policies of the 1980s and 1990s—that mainly focused on raising barriers (Morris and Staritz, 2019)—towards a multi-scalar perspective, accounting for sector specificities, inter-firm relations, and localized value-creation.

GVC inclusiveness policies are aimed at addressing sustainability challenges. Today's economic and governance systems are poorly equipped to target issues related with social inclusiveness and environmental sustainability without the help of the private sector. Market forces, for one, have done little to narrow income inequalities within and across countries, to overcome deeply entrenched social discrimination by race and gender, or to protect the natural environment (Sachs and Sachs, 2021). The global nature of many sustainability challenges has furthermore eroded the ability of countries to address these market failures (Scherer and Palazzo, 2011). For these reasons, there has been growing research investigating how GVCs can be better harnessed through policy to enhance social and environmental upgrading.

GVC participation and economic upgrading do not automatically foster social and environmental upgrading. Even if they create significant economic progress, the benefits often leave many behind (Locke, 2013; Lund-Thomsen and Lindgreen, 2014; Mayer and Gereffi, 2010; Posthuma and Nathan, 2010). Barrientos et al. (2011) show that economic upgrading can, but does not necessarily, lead to social upgrading which implies accessing better work and enhancing working conditions, protection, and rights. Similarly, there could be tensions between economic and environmental upgrading, defined as any change in the value chain resulting in the reduction of firms' ecological footprint, such as in their impact on greenhouse gas emissions, on biodiversity losses, and on natural resources overexploitation (De Marchi et al., 2019). Economic, social, and environmental upgrading are clearly interlinked, but the evidence available on how they interrelate is still rather limited. De Marchi et al. (2019) report about cases in which the three types of upgrading are part of a virtuous cycle, like in the coffee value chain studied by Giuliani et al. (2017) in several Latin American countries. However, they also report on value chains in which economic upgrading coincided with environmental downgrading, as among Kenyan farmers investigated by Krishnan, te Velde, and Were (2018).

At the same time, there is a growing acknowledgement that lead firms—if properly harnessed—can be a powerful vector to promote social and environmental upgrading. Lead firms have the corporate power to define the terms and conditions of GVC membership and can use their authority to promote social standards and environmental stewardship among their suppliers. This compliance can cascade down to lower-tier suppliers if GVC participation is made conditional on promoting sustainability standards further down the chain (Narula, 2019). Distelhorst and Locke (2018) find that firms reward suppliers for complying with social standards, supporting the notion that lead firms can play a key role in promoting social upgrading.

The ability of lead firms to dictate the terms under which lower-level actors operate in a GVC has led to a vibrant academic debate about the role of private governance in filling gaps in global regulation. Many MNEs have implemented corporate social responsibility (CSR) initiatives in their supply chains as a way of independently regulating labour issues, including the establishment of codes of conduct and the implementation of third-party monitoring of working and environmental conditions. While several scholars have pointed out the positive role that private governance can play in addressing market failures that public governance has difficulties tackling (Scherer and Palazzo, 2011), others have warned that it is relatively ineffective (Locke et al., 2019) and may weaken state regulation and create parallel regulatory systems (Seidman, 2009; Rossi, 2019).

How to push lead firms to promote sustainability throughout their GVCs nonetheless remains an area of scholarly contention. A first concern is that many Multinational Corporations (MNCs) are unmotivated to address sustainability challenges. They either threaten their suppliers with too small a stick, or cajole with too small a carrot, to incentivize the adoption of social standards and environmental stewardship. Indeed, several scholars have blamed lead firms of heaping the costs of compliance upon the suppliers without installing effective cost-sharing, monitoring, or penalty systems (Bird and Soundararajan, 2020; Contractor and Kundu, 1998; Locke et al., 2009). Moreover, lead firms are alleged to go ahead with such ineffective governance schemes since they care more about 'looking good' rather than 'doing good' (Lund-Thomsen, 2020), undermining the ability of GVC participation to render social upgrading. Ponte (2020), for example, draws from empirical evidence on the coffee and wine value chains and shows that the mainstreaming of sustainability has allowed the global lead firms to accumulate 'green' profits by extracting value from suppliers in the Global South. This has been possible because suppliers have been made responsible for the risks and paying for the costs of sustainability compliance.

A second concern is that lead firms do not have the capabilities to push suppliers to adopt higher social and environmental standards (Goerzen and Van Assche, 2020). The diverse socio-economic and cultural contexts of employment in which suppliers are embedded make it difficult for them to understand the bottlenecks that prevent compliance with social standards imposed from overseas (Lund-Thomsen and Lindgreen, 2014).

Taken together, GVC studies have firmly established that lead firms can be a powerful vector to promote social and environmental upgrading through their linkages with their suppliers and sub-suppliers. However, the literature is much less clear about which policies targeting lead firms and their linkages can most effectively promote sustainability along GVCs.

GVC resiliency policies have emerged as a fourth priority area in the wake of recent system-wide crises. In today's globally-interconnected economies, a disruption in one part of the economic system can turn into a severe global economic downturn, and GVCs often play an important role in the transmission (Miroudot, 2020). Recent history provides us with several examples. During the global financial crisis of 2008–2009, negative liquidity shocks in one country caused a chain reaction of financial difficulties throughout GVCs, as firms relied on each other for credit (Bems, Johnson, and Yi, 2013). In the immediate aftermath of the 2011 Tohoku earthquake and tsunami, the production of many Japanese automotive and electronics components dried up, creating a disruption of international supply chains that affected the price and availability of cars and computers around the world (Escaith et al., 2011). In the early months of the COVID-19 pandemic, confinement efforts in China led to the closure of factories across the globe as companies could not access parts (Foldy, 2020).

In policy circles, these events—combined with recent shortages in essential goods such as vaccines and medical equipment—have raised the concern that excessive international division of labor has overly heightened countries' reliance on foreign suppliers and GVCs, thus endangering governments' ability to deliver societal well-being (Dallas, Horner, and Li, 2021; Evenett, 2020). Assertions have been made that GVCs had become too complex and that they were not designed to operate in today's turbulent geopolitical landscape. Calls have therefore become increasingly loud for GVC policies that would make countries more resilient to global economic shocks.

A country's resilience is generally defined as its ability to rapidly return to delivering societal well-being in the wake of an economic disruption (Miroudot, 2020). In this respect, a country's participation in GVCs can influence resilience by affecting both the severity of a disruption's initial economic impact and the ability to rapidly bounce back post-disruption.

Current debates often equate resilience with self-sufficiency, but this can be misleading (OECD, 2020). It is of course true that fully localized production reduces a country's exposure to shocks that disrupt foreign production or trade (e.g., the Suez Canal blockage or the Ukrainian conflict). However, it also heightens a country's vulnerability to local disasters that curtail domestic production (e.g., Hurricane Katrina). In other words, building resilience implies that countries should avoid putting all apples in the same basket, and GVCs can play an important role in ensuring this does not happen.

A more pertinent resilience-related concern for policymakers is thus how to ensure that a society's ability to deliver essential goods and services is sufficiently resistant to both local and foreign disruptions (Miroudot, 2020). First, is a country's supply base of essential goods sufficiently diversified so that they are not excessively dependent on GVC links with specific countries (including the home country) that are prone to production or trade disruptions? During the COVID-19 pandemic, for example, an often-heard concern was that several countries were excessively dependent on China for the supply of essential medical equipment (Evenett, 2020). During the 2021 Texas power failure, then again, critics argued that the US state was insufficiently connected to the country's electricity grid, making it overly vulnerable to local shocks. Second, does a country have ready-to-access substitutes in case a disruption to an existing GVC linkage occurs? This can be in the form of domestic or regional buffer stocks, or a country's ability to rapidly switch to domestic or foreign supply alternatives (even if they are not yet in use) to compensate for the disruption. During the COVID-19 pandemic, for example, the US government was criticized for its poor stockpiling of medical masks pre-pandemic, but also praised for its ability to rapidly ramp up domestic production of masks (Gereffi, 2020).

Any policy response to these questions needs to acknowledge that companies generally grasp many of the risks related to international supply chain shocks and have already developed sophisticated risk management strategies to deal with them. Many firms have added agility to their supply chain by diversifying their supplier base, increasing manufacturing capacity and creating buffer stocks (Christopher and Peck, 2004). Well before the start of the 2018 Sino-US trade war, for example, many companies have adopted a China Plus One strategy, where they duplicated production in China and at least one other country to reduce their vulnerability to supply chain disruptions and currency fluctuations in any individual country. Gereffi et al. (2021) offer new evidence about firms' resilience in mitigating supply chain disruptions through the reconfiguration of their GVCs. As the US-China trade war unfolded, they found that many affected firms in the apparel, automotive, and electronics sectors were able to bypass newly imposed trade restrictions through two main strategies: (i) switching production locations, end markets, and/or suppliers; and (ii) upgrading value chain activities. They thus suggest that the adoption of risk-mitigation strategies in GVCs has undercut the effectiveness of traditional trade policies.

The ability of market forces to naturally push firms to develop their own risk-mitigation strategies suggests that governments should resist the temptation to go too far in their efforts to enhance resilience. The key resilience-related policy question that governments face is thus to what extent there are market failures in a society's ability to deal with domestic or foreign disruptions in the delivery of essential goods and services, and how to address them.

Indeed, there are several direct interventions that governments can conduct *ex ante* to enhance resilience. First, governments can develop buffering strategies such as stockpiling for essential products. Second, they can subsidize local production of essential goods or promote state ownership. Third, they can push for extra diversification of the supply base through their public procurement strategies.

Dialogue with the private sector and possibly even the organization of public–private platforms at the level of GVCs are needed to develop the appropriate government interventions (Hoekman, 2021). Simchi-Levi and Simchi-Levi (2020) have in this respect come up with an interesting proposal: like bank stress tests that were imposed after the Great Recession of 2008–2009, governments should work together with industries that provide essential goods to establish stress tests that capture a country's ability to deal with demand or supply disruptions. These stress tests should consider the government's own stockpiling strategy, the speed with which both local production and imports can be ramped up, the diversification of import sources, and the impact of potential export restrictions by other countries.

Finally, international cooperation should be an integral part of any resilience strategy. From the perspective of government authorities, agreements to share essential goods, to conduct joint procurements at a bilateral or regional level, and to limit export restrictions can facilitate diversification and risk sharing.

6.4. Some Examples of GVC-Oriented Policies in Latin America

Two-thirds of all trade in LAC countries occurs under trade agreements, and trade agreements themselves are an element of a GVC-oriented policy. Indeed, depending on their coverage, they may have an impact on the four taxonomic categories: participation, value capture, inclusiveness, and resiliency. Deep trade agreements go beyond simple market access, and include a wide-ranging set of border and behind-the-border policy areas regulating investment, services trade, customs procedures, regulatory measures, and intellectual property rights protection (Rocha and Ruta, 2022). In Latin America they influence countries' trade in different ways. In countries like Chile, Honduras, and Mexico, 95% of the trade is based on deep trade agreements, whilst in other countries in the Mercosur only about 25% of trade is accrued to trade agreements.

Deep trade agreements offer examples of GVC participation policies because they allow locally-produced goods to be exported and become inputs for other countries' exports, furthering GVC integration. A recent econometric analysis looks at the impact of trade facilitation policies on GVC firms' decisions on the extensive margin (whether trade occurs or not) and the intensive margin (the level once trade occurs) (USAID, 2021). The study covers Peru's trade during 2000–2017 with firm-level data and identifies three kinds of firms: bilateral GVC firms (the ones who import from and then export to the same countries), traditional exporters (using domestic inputs but exporting to other countries), and GVC firms that import intermediate inputs and then export. It tests the hypothesis that GVC firms will grow exports more than traditional firms as trade facilitation policies improve border efficiency and transparency. The evidence confirms that GVC firms benefit more than traditional firms, and even more so when they import from preferential trading area (PTA) partner countries. Reduced trade costs and uncertainties both at home and abroad bring about efficiency benefits (USAID, 2021).

Investment attraction has been traditionally a major focus of policies in developing countries, trusting to benefit from FDI by multinational corporations (MNCs) in the form of increased employment, investments, access to markets and technology, and so forth. With the fragmentation of production and the organization of transactions following the logic of GVCs, this area of policy activity also needs to be reconsidered. To this aim, Costa Rica offers an insightful example of FDI selective attraction measures in the spirit of GVC-oriented policies (Pietrobelli, 2021).

In their analyses of Costa Rica, Bamber and Gereffi (2013) and Gereffi et al. (2019) study the electronics and the medical devices sectors and their experience of upgrading. As far as the latter sector is considered, they argue that a key dynamic that facilitated firm upgrading was 'The identification by lead firms themselves of critical 'GVC gaps' in Costa Rica's technical capabilities, which was followed by targeted FDI recruitment efforts by national development institutions (CINDE and COMEX)' (Gereffi et al., 2019).[2] This suggests that a new consideration of the role and organization of GVCs needs to encompass the activities of investment attraction agencies.

The medical devices sector is one of a few sectors targeted by Costa Rica, through CINDE, to attract FDI. The sector has been expanding at healthy rates since Baxter first came to Costa Rica in 1987 and reached nearly $1.5 billion in exports in 2014. However, medical devices range across various levels of complexity, from simple disposable devices (such as catheters) to surgical and medical instruments (such as biopsy forceps), to therapeutic devices (such as heart valves), to complex medical equipment (such as MRI machines).

As of 2007, Costa Rica has been highly successful in attracting multinationals to the sector. But they are mainly producing low-complexity disposables, and not, for example, heart valves or other cardiovascular devices. A careful analysis to 'discover' the likely solution reveals that they need to go through the process of sterilization, not available locally at the time. Producing them in Costa Rica would have required shipping them to the United States to have them sterilized, and then shipping them back for packaging—complicating the logistics and adding greatly to the costs.

Why did sterilization activities not develop in the country? With no heart valves and other similar products in production, there was no demand for sterilization services, and with no demand, there would be no supply: a typical 'chicken-and-egg' problem. CINDE quickly realized that the market would not solve the problem by itself. Yet, having a sterilization process in the country would have helped the more complex links of the value chain to develop. CINDE's efforts paid off in early 2009, with the arrival of BeamOne, a contract sterilization processor headquartered in the United States, followed by Sterigenics in 2011. Within three years of inauguration of the BeamOne facility, Costa Rica has successfully

[2] CINDE (*Coalicion Costarricense de Iniciativas de Desarrollo*) is the Investment attraction agency of Costa Rica, and COMEX is Costa Rica's Foreign Trade Ministry.

attracted several companies in the cardiovascular sector, including Boston Scientific in 2009, Abbot Vascular in 2010, and St. Jude Medical in 2010. In 2013, Costa Rica exported nearly $300 million in the therapeutics category of medical devices, and an additional $500 million in surgical and medical instruments. The share of disposables fell from 90% in the early 2000s to less than half.

Why did CINDE target sterilization? Because it adopted the logic of GVCs and of a 'discovery' process and realized that a segment of the value chain was missing, and that the market alone would have not solved the problem. Moving Costa Rica into the more profitable sections of the value chain, and allowing them to capture more value, required selectively attracting foreign investors in that specific segment. This GVC-oriented policy made it possible for other local firms to discover and develop into new and higher-value stages of the GVC.

Although not necessarily focused on promoting insertion and value capture in GVCs, many Latin American countries have created public–private cooperation bodies, particularly in the form of sectoral tables or forums (Devlin and Moguillansky, 2013; Devlin and Pietrobelli, 2019; Cornick et al., 2018; Obaya and Stein, 2021; Schneider 2013). Unfortunately, a common denominator has been that the policy support of the central authority has been highly variable (Gonzalez, Hallak, and Tacsir, 2021). However, a recent case of continuity in this type of public–private cooperation is the experience of the *Mesas Ejecutivas* (Executive Boards) in Peru, which has often adopted a value chain approach. These boards have managed to transcend several government changes (Ghezzi, 2019). Moreover, they have connected the national and subnational levels, and in Peru they took the form of Regional Strategic Export Plans, through which priority was given to selected productive chains that receive support and technical assistance.

In addition, within the framework of such public–private coordination bodies, some instances have occurred of allocating competitive funds for projects to promote export competitiveness and strengthen value chains, as well as the integration of national firms. Funds of this type were the funds eligible under the Programme to Support the Competitiveness of Conglomerates and Productive Chains (PACC) of Uruguay, in which the value chains were selected through open and competitive calls and received funding and technical assistance (Rius and Isabella, 2014).

Finally, several countries in Latin America have a long tradition of supplier development programmes, which are aimed at helping suppliers enter and capture the gains from integration into GVCs. One example is the programme to support suppliers' networks (*Red de proveedores*) currently operating in Chile.[3]

[3] Information is available at Corfo.cl (accessed 13 April 2023).

6.5. Concluding Remarks: How Novel Are GVC-Oriented Policies?

Careful observers will notice that the distinction between GVC-oriented policies and traditional public policies does not lie in their social or economic objectives. Policymakers were using public policy tools to boost trade integration and to strengthen specialization in higher value-added industries well before they started paying attention to GVCs. Redistributive and resiliency concerns have also been on the agenda in traditional international business policy discussions.

In GVC-oriented policies, the novelty comes from the elevated role that is given to the trifecta of *tasks*, *linkages*, and *firms*, which pushes local, regional, and national governments to change the *economic rationales* for conducting policy interventions and which alters the range of *instruments* they can use to attain policy goals.

GVC-oriented policies put the spotlight on the development of fine-grained GVC *tasks* instead of the traditional focus on entire industries. A central objective of GVC policies aimed at increasing participation is to boost functional specialization so that countries can concentrate on those tasks in which they have a comparative advantage. A key goal of policies at value capturing within GVCs is to help countries create and appropriate more value by conducting the existing activities better or by functionally upgrading into higher value-added tasks. In both cases, policymakers are pushed to adopt a more granular view of the type of activities that they should target to promote economic development through structural transformation.

GVC-oriented policies also lay greater emphasis on the role of *linkages* than traditional development policies. This has been a traditional concern for Latin American policymakers. A key insight from GVC studies is that a firm's economic performance and the social conditions that it offers to its workers are heavily influenced by its value chain connections. Inter-firm linkages to foreign partners can act as a powerful conduit for accessing foreign knowledge and resources that can be leveraged to improve technological and operational capabilities. Decent work parameters imposed by foreign value chain partners can incentivize firms to improve their local work conditions. Economic shocks to foreign value chain partners can be transmitted to local firms through supply chains. A focal concern of policymakers is thus how to properly regulate, deepen, and strengthen GVC linkages so that they can promote both economic and social upgrading while at the same time guaranteeing a country's economic resilience.

GVC-oriented policies finally elevate the role of *firms*, both lead firms and their suppliers, and a fine-grained microeconomic focus is called for. GVC scholarship recognizes the essential role that lead firms play in defining the terms and conditions of GVC integration and thus considers harnessing their behavior to be a potent approach to accomplish policy objectives. Some GVC-oriented policies in this respect may promote a partnership between public and private actors in which policymakers collaborate with GVC lead firms to upgrade local suppliers, ensure fair treatment of workers, adopt environmentally sustainable business practices, and build resiliency (Gereffi, 2019). Furthermore, GVC-oriented policies recognize the essential objective of supporting suppliers' efforts to enter—and nurture—profitable relationships with lead firms, exploiting the potential offered by these relationships for their own learning and capability development.

The GVC literature's emphasis on the trifecta of *tasks*, *linkages*, and *firms* has exposed a new set of market failures that provide a potent narrative for new policy *rationales* (Pietrobelli and Staritz, 2018). The non-rival and partially excludable nature of intangibles—which are at the heart of some of the highest value-added and therefore most desirable tasks in a GVC (e.g. R&D and marketing)—create public good problems that need to be addressed through government intervention (Van Assche, 2020; Jaax and Miroudot, 2021). Market externalities abound in lead firms' willingness to share knowledge through their GVC linkages and the development of suppliers' capabilities to absorb it (Guerrieri and Pietrobelli, 2006; Pietrobelli and Staritz, 2018). Market forces do little to engender social upgrading, environmental upgrading, and economic resilience. For these reasons, there is a loudening call among GVC scholars for moving beyond the traditional development policies built around the so-called Washington Consensus, which focuses on minimalist state intervention, and to adopt more potent trade, industrial, and innovation policies (Neilson, 2014; Werner et al., 2014).

Moreover, an increasingly prominent viewpoint is that the global scope of GVCs has hampered countries' capacity to address some key GVC-related market failures (Kobrin, 2015). This produces two main consequences. On the one hand, supra-national policies and institutions need to be reformed to address the GVC-related market and coordination failures that individual countries' governments cannot fix. The G7 agreement reached in June 2021 for a minimum global corporate tax rate to close cross-border tax loopholes is a good example of this. On the other hand, governments are also being forced to partner up with the private sector to address 'governance gaps' (Scherer and Palazzo, 2011; Eberlein, 2019; Goerzen et al., 2021). That is, there is a growing call for private actors such as lead firms and non-governmental organizations to play an active role in filling gaps in global regulation and in resolving global public good problems. To reconcile private-sector interests, policy-makers should take on a brokering role in 'value chain coalitions', facilitating dialogues between public and private stakeholders (Morris et al., 2012).

The trifecta of *tasks*, *linkages*, and *firms* at the heart of GVC-oriented policies also implies that governments need to rely on new *instruments* and actions to reach their policy goals. In some cases, it provides policymakers with new levers in their policy toolbox. Many state-led export credit agencies, for example, have expanded the type of firms to which they can provide trade financing to reflect the growing reality of GVCs (Van Assche and Gangnes, 2019). Whereas in the past they relied on push strategies that provided financing to support the export sales of domestic firms, they now increasingly adopt pull strategies where they give loans and export credits to large foreign companies, insofar as this helps facilitate the integration of domestic firms into GVCs. In other cases, existing policy instruments are rendered less potent. For example, GVCs allow firms to circumvent trade policy barriers (Ma and Van Assche, 2014) more easily. To avoid a country-specific trade policy, a lead firm no longer must relocate its entire value chain to another country, but only a single value chain stage, often final assembly. Gereffi et al. (2021) indeed found that many firms in the apparel, automotive, and electronics sectors were able to bypass trade restrictions related to the US-China trade war by switching production locations, end markets, and suppliers.

Redesigning policy instruments for new GVC realities, however, is often easier said than done. Once the trifecta of *tasks*, *linkages*, and *firms* is considered, it becomes clear that policymakers need to take into consideration the complementarities between various at-the-border and beyond-the-border policies. The operation of a GVC makes it necessary to look at trade promotion, innovation, and industrial policies to support local suppliers, at training policy to produce the required skills, at infrastructural policy to facilitate exports and imports, at the availability of advisory services in the areas of standards and certifications, as well as at labor, social, and environmental regulations. Each policy needs to be assessed considering its systemic scope and influence, moving beyond the traditional 'silos' approach where each government ministry and agency pursues its own objectives independently. This will be a major but necessary challenge for Latin American governments. Moreover, the frontier has had to be moved beyond national borders to interact with global buyers, thus overcoming the traditional distinction between policies for the domestic and the foreign market. Therefore, even if many elements of policy were already present a long time ago, the advent of GVCs has forced governments to rethink them in such a deep fashion that the whole set of policies oriented to GVCs has now become a truly different concept.

References

Antràs, P., and Chor, D. 2021. 'Global Value Chains', WP 28149, NBER, Cambridge MA, https://www.nber.org/system/files/working_papers/w28549/w28549.pdf.

Anzolin, G., and Pietrobelli C. 2021, 'Local Content Policies: Why Mining Need Consistent Policy Packages to Support Capabilities Development', *The Extractive Industries and Society*, 8(1), 395–399. https://doi.org/10.1016/j.exis.2020.11.013.

Bam, W. G., De Bruyne, K., and Laing, M. 2021. 'The IO–PS in the Context of GVC-Related Policymaking: The Case of the South African Automotive Industry', *Journal of International Business Policy*, 4(3), 1–23.

Bamber, P., and Gereffi, G. 2013. 'Costa Rica in the Medical Devices Global Value Chain: Opportunities for Upgrading', GVC Center, Duke University, Durham, NC, August. https://gvcc.duke.edu/cggclisting/costa-rica-inthe-medical-devices-global-value-chain-opportunities-for-upgrading-chapter-2/ (accessed 10 April 2023.

Barrientos, S., Gereffi, G., and Rossi, A. 2011. 'Economic and Social Upgrading in Global Production Networks: A New Paradigm for a Changing World', *International Labour Review*, 150(3–4), 319–340.

Bems, R., Johnson, R. C., and Yi, K. M. 2013. 'The Great Trade Collapse', *Annual Review of Economics*, 5(1), 375–400.

Bird, R. C., and Soundararajan, V. 2020. 'The Role of Precontractual Signals in Creating Sustainable Global Supply Chains', *Journal of Business Ethics*, 164(1), 81–94.

Buckley, P. J. 2009. 'The Impact of the Global Factory on Economic Development', *Journal of World Business*, 44(2), 131–143.

Christopher, M., and Peck, H. 2004. 'Building the Resilient Supply Chain', *The International Journal of Logistics Management*, 15(2), 1–14.

Constantinescu, C., Mattoo, A., and Ruta, M. 2019. 'Does Vertical Specialisation Increase Productivity?', *The World Economy*, 42(8), 2385–2402.

Contractor, F. J., and Kundu, S. K. 1998. 'Modal Choice in a World of Alliances: Analyzing Organizational Forms in the International Hotel Sector', *Journal of International Business Studies*, 29(2), 325–356.

Cornick, J., Dal Bó, E., Fernández-Arias, E., Rivas, G., and Stein, E. 2018. *Building Capabilities for Productive Development*. Washington, DC: BID.

Crespi, G., Fernández-Arias, E., and Stein, E. 2014. 'Investing in Ideas: Policies to Foster Innovation', in Gustavo Crespi, Eduardo Fernández-Arias, and Ernesto Stein, eds., *Rethinking Productive Development*. New York: Palgrave Macmillan, 61–106.

Dallas, M. P., Horner, R., and Li, L. 2021. 'The Mutual Constraints of States and Global Value Chains during COVID-19: The Case of Personal Protective Equipment', *World Development*, 139, 1–13.

De Marchi, V., and Alford, M. 2021. 'State Policies and Upgrading in Global Value Chains: A Systematic Literature Review', *Journal of International Business Policy*, 5(1), 88–111.

De Marchi, V., Di Maria, E., Krishnan, A., and Ponte, S. 2019. 'Environmental Upgrading in Global Value Chains', in G. Gereffi, S. Ponte, and G. Raj-Rechert, eds., *Handbook on Global Value Chains*. Cheltenham, UK: Edward Elgar, 310–323.

Devlin R., and Moguillansky, G. 2013. 'What's New in the New Industrial Policy in Latin America?', in J. Stiglitz and J. Lin, eds., *The Industrial Policy Revolution I*. New York: Palgrave Macmillan, 276–317.

Devlin, R., and Pietrobelli, C. 2019. 'Modern Industrial Policy and Public–Private Councils at the Subnational Level: Mexico's Experience in an International Perspective', *L'Industria. Rivista di Economia e Politica Industriale*, 4(October–December), 761–791.

Distelhorst, G., and Locke, R. M. 2018. 'Does Compliance Pay? Social Standards and Firm-Level Trade', *American Journal of Political Science*, 62(3), 695–711.

Escaith, H., Keck, A., Nee, C., and Teh, R. 2011. 'Japan's Earthquake and Tsunami: International Trade and Global Supply Chain Impacts', *VOXEU*, April, 28. https://voxeu.org/article/japans-earthquake-and-tsunami-global-supply-chain-impacts.

Evenett, S. J. 2020. 'Chinese Whispers: COVID-19, Global Supply Chains in Essential Goods, and Public Policy', *Journal of International Business Policy*, 3(4), 408–429.

Fernandes A., Nievas G., and Winkler D. 2021. 'Trade and Global Value Chain Integration in Latin America: Stylized Facts', Background Paper. Washington, DC: The World Bank.

Findlay, C., and Hoekman, B. 2020. 'Value Chain Approaches to Reducing Policy Spillovers on International Business', *Journal of International Business Policy*, 4, 390–409.

Foldy, B. 2020. 'Coronavirus Pinching Car Industry Supply Chains', *Market Watch*. https://www.marketwatch.com/story/coronavirus-pinching-car-industry-supply-chains-2020-02-14?mod=mw_quote_news.

Gereffi G., Frederick S., and Bamber P. 2019. 'Diverse Paths of Upgrading in High-Tech Manufacturing: Costa Rica in the Electronics and Medical Devices Global Value Chains', *Transnational Corporations*, 26(1), 1–29.

Gereffi, G. 2019a. 'Economic Upgrading in Global Value Chains', in G. Gereffi, S. Ponte, and G. Raj-Reichert, eds., *Handbook on Global Value Chains*. Cheltenham, UK: Edward Elgar, 240–254.

Gereffi, G. 2019b. 'Global Value Chains and International Development Policy: Bringing Firms, Networks and Policy-Engaged Scholarship Back', *Journal of International Business Policy*, *2*(3), 195–210.

Gereffi, G. 2020. 'What Does the COVID-19 Pandemic Teach Us about Global Value Chains? The Case of Medical Supplies', *Journal of International Business Policy*, 3(3), 287–301.

Gereffi, G., Humphrey, J., and Sturgeon, T. 2005. 'The Governance of Global Value Chains', *Review of International Political Economy*, 12(1), 78–104.

Gereffi, G., Lim, H. C., and Lee, J. 2021. 'Trade Policies, Firm Strategies, and Adaptive Reconfigurations of Global Value Chains', *Journal of International Business Policy*, 4(4), 1–17.

Gereffi, G., and Sturgeon, T. 2013. 'Global Value Chain-Oriented Industrial Policy: The Role of Emerging Economies', in D. Elms and P. Low, eds., *Global Value Chains in a Changing World*. Geneva: WTO Publications, 329–360.

Ghezzi, P. 2019. 'Mesas ejecutivas en Perú: Una tecnología para el desarrollo productivo', Documento para discusión del BID, Núm. 711. Washington, DC: BID.

Giuliani, E., Ciravegna, L., Vezzulli, A., and Kilian, B. 2017. 'Decoupling Standards from Practice: The Impact of In-House Certifications on Coffee Farms' Environmental and Social Conduct', *World Development*, 96, 294–314.

Giuliani, E., Pietrobelli, C., and Rabellotti, R. 2005. 'Upgrading in Global Value Chains: Lessons from Latin American Clusters', *World Development*, 33(4), 549–573.

Goerzen, A., and Van Assche, A. 2020. 'Global Value Chain Governance: A MNC Capabilities View', in K. Mellahi, K. Meyer, R. Narula, I. Surdu, and A. Verbeke, eds., *The Oxford Handbook of International Business Strategy*. Oxford: Oxford University Press, 421–434.

Goerzen, A., Iskander, S. P., and Hofstetter, J. 2021. 'The Effect of Institutional Pressures on Business-Led Interventions to Improve Social Compliance among Emerging Market Suppliers in Global Value Chains', *Journal of International Business Policy*, 4(3), 1–21.

González, A., Hallak, J. C., and Tacsir, A. 2021. '¿Quién tracciona la estrategia sectorial para la inserción internacional? Desafíos de coordinación post-COVID-19 en cadenas agroindustriales de América Latina', *Revista Integración y Comercio*, 47, 1–87. BID-INTAL.

Guerrieri, P., and Pietrobelli, C. 2006. 'Old and New Forms of Clustering and Production Networks in Changing Technological Regimes: Contrasting Evidence from Taiwan and Italy', *Science, Technology and Society*, 11(1), 9–38.

Hallak, J. C., and López, A. 2022. '¿Cómo apoyar la internacionalización productiva en América Latina? Análisis de políticas, requerimientos de capacidades estatales y riesgos', Banco Interamericano de Desarrollo, Sector de Integración y Comercio, N° IDB-TN-02629, December, http://dx.doi.org/10.18235/0004650.

Horner, R. 2017. 'Beyond Facilitator? State Roles in Global Value Chains and Global Production Networks', *Geography Compass*, 11(2), e12307.

Horner, R. 2021. 'Global Value Chains, Import Orientation, and the State: South Africa's Pharmaceutical Industry', *Journal of International Business Policy*, 5(1), 1–20.

Jaax, A., and Miroudot, S. 2021. 'Capturing Value in GVCs through Intangible Assets: The Role of the Trade–Investment–Intellectual Property Nexus', *Journal of International Business Policy*, 4(3), 1–20.

Kobrin, S. J. 2015. 'Is a Global Nonmarket Strategy Possible? Economic Integration in a Multipolar World Order', *Journal of World Business*, 50(2), 262–272.

Krishnan, A., te Velde, D. W., and Were, A. 2018. 'Kenya–UK trade and investment relations', in Aarti Krishnan, Dirk Willem te Velde and Anzetse Were, eds., *Taking Stock and Promoting Exports to the UK*. London: Overseas Development Institute (ODI), 1–78.

Lee K., 2013. 'Capability Failure and Industrial Policy to Move beyond the Middle-Income Trap: From Trade-Based to Technology-Based Specialization', in J. E. Stiglitz and J. Y. Lin, eds., *The Industrial Policy Revolution I. The Role of Government Beyond Ideology*. Basingstoke, UK: Palgrave Macmillan, 244–272.

Lema R., Pietrobelli C., and Rabellotti R. 2019. 'Innovation in Global Value Chains', in G. Gereffi, S. Ponte, and G. Raj-Reichert, eds., *Handbook on Global Value Chains*. Cheltenham, UK: Edward Elgar, 370–384.

Locke, R. M. 2013. *The Promise and Limits of Private Power: Promoting Labor Standards in a Global Economy*. Cambridge: Cambridge University Press.

Locke, R., Amengual, M., and Mangla, A. 2009. 'Virtue out of Necessity? Compliance, Commitment, and the Improvement of Labor Conditions in Global Supply Chains', *Politics & Society*, 37(3), 319–351.

Lund-Thomsen, P. 2020. 'Corporate Social Responsibility: A Supplier-Centered Perspective', *Environment and Planning A: Economy and Space*, 52(8), 1700–1709.

Lund-Thomsen, P., and Lindgreen, A. 2014. 'Corporate Social Responsibility in Global Value Chains: Where Are We Now And Where Are We Going?', *Journal of Business Ethics*, 123(1), 11–22.

Ma, A., and Van Assche, A. 2014. 'Vertical Specialization, Tariff Shirking and Trade,' in B. Ferrarini and D. Hummels, eds., *Asia and Global Production Networks: Implications for Trade, Incomes and Economic Vulnerability*. London: Asian Development Bank and Edward Elgar, 148–178.

Martinez-Covarrubias, J. L., Lenihan, H., and Hart, M. 2017. 'Public Support for Business Innovation in Mexico: A Cross-Sectional Analysis', *Regional Studies*, 51(12), 1786–1800.

Mayer, F. W., and Phillips, N. 2017. 'Outsourcing Governance: States and the Politics of a "Global Value Chain World"', *New Political Economy*, 22(2), 134–152.

Mayer, F., and Gereffi, G. 2010. 'Regulation and Economic Globalization: Prospects and Limits of Private Governance', *Business and Politics*, 12(3), 1–25.

Milberg, W., Jiang, X., and Gereffi, G. 2014.' Industrial Policy in the Era of Vertically Specialized Industrialization', in José M. Salazar-Xirinachs, Irmgard Nübler and Richard Kozul-Wright, eds., *Transforming Economies: Making Industrial Policy Work for Growth, Jobs and Development*. Geneva: International Labour Organisation, 151–178.

Miroudot, S. 2020. 'Reshaping the Policy Debate on the implications of COVID-19 for Global Supply Chains', *Journal of International Business Policy*, 3(4), 1–13.

Montalbano P., Nenci S., and Pietrobelli C., 2018. 'Opening and Linking up: Firms, Global Value Chains and Productivity in Latin America', *Small Business Economics*, 50(4), 917–935, https://doi.org/10.1007/s11187-017-9902-6.

Morris, M., and Staritz, C. 2019. 'Industrialization Paths and Industrial Policy for Developing Countries in Global Value Chains', in G. Gereffi, S. Ponte, and G. Raj-Reichert, eds., *Handbook on Global Value Chains*. Cheltenham, UK: Edward Elgar, 506–520.

Morrison, A., Pietrobelli, C., and Rabellotti, R. 2008.' Global Value Chains and Technological Capabilities: A Framework to Study Learning and Innovation in Developing Countries', *Oxford Development Studies*, 36(1), 39–58.

Narula, R. 2019. 'Enforcing Higher Labor Standards within Developing Country Value Chains: Consequences for MNEs and Informal Actors in a Dual Economy', *Journal of International Business Studies*, 50(9), 1622–1635.

Navas-Alemán, L. 2011. 'The Impact of Operating in Multiple Value Chains for Upgrading: The Case of the Brazilian Furniture and Footwear Industries', *World Development*, 39(8), 1386–1397.

Neilson, J. 2014. 'Value Chains, Neoliberalism and Development Practice: The Indonesian Experience', *Review of International Political Economy*, 21(1), 38–69.

Obaya, M., and Stein, E. 2021. 'El diálogo público-privado para la formulación de políticas productivas: La experiencia de las mesas sectoriales en Argentina (2016–2019)', Nota Técnica TN--2120, BID.

OECD. 2020. 'Shocks, Risks and Global Value Chains: Insights from the OECD METRO Model', http://www.oecd.org/trade/documents/shocks-risks-gvc-insights-oecd-metro-model.pdf.

Pahl, S., and Timmer, M. P. 2020. 'Do Global Value Chains Enhance Economic Upgrading? A Long View', *The Journal of Development Studies*, 56(9), 1683–1705.

Pietrobelli, C. 2020. 'Modern Industrial Policy in Latin America: Lessons from Cluster Development Policies', in A. Oqubay and J.Y. Lin, eds., *The Oxford Handbook of Industrial Hubs and Economic Development*. Oxford: Oxford University Press, 783–798.

Pietrobelli, C. 2021. 'New Industrial Innovation Policies in a World of Global Value Chains', in K. Lee, J. D. Lee, S. Radosevic, D. Meissner, and N. Vonortas, eds., *The Challenges of Technology and Economic Catch-Up in Emerging Economies*. Oxford: Oxford University Press, 436–458.

Pietrobelli, C. 2022. 'Cross-Border Innovation and Global Value Chains: The Role of Public Policies', in D. Castellani, A. Perri, V. Scalera, and A. Zanfei, eds., *Cross-Border Innovation in a Changing World: Players, Places and Policies*, Oxford: Oxford University Press, 251–271.

Pietrobelli, C., and Rabellotti, R. 2011. 'Global Value Chains Meet Innovation Systems: Are There Learning Opportunities for Developing Countries?', *World Development*, 39(7), 1261–1269.

Pietrobelli, C., and Staritz, C. 2018. 'Upgrading, Interactive Learning, and Innovation Systems in Value Chain Interventions', *The European Journal of Development Research*, 30(3), 557–574.

Ponte, S. 2020. 'The Hidden Costs of Environmental Upgrading in Global Value Chains', *Review of International Political Economy*, 29(3), 1–26.

Ponte, S., and Ewert, J. 2009. 'Which Way Is "Up" in Upgrading? Trajectories of Change in the Value Chain for South African Wine', *World Development*, 37(10), 1637–1650.

Posthuma, A., and Nathan, D. 2010. *Labour in Global Production Networks*. Oxford: Oxford University Press.

Rius, A., and Isabella, F. (2014), 'Una memoria analítica del Programa de Competitividad de Conglomerados y Cadenas Productivas: 2006–2014', Instituto de Economía, Udelar. Montevideo, Uruguay.

Rocha, N., and Ruta M., 2022. *Deep Trade Agreements: Anchoring Global Value Chains in Latin America and the Caribbean*. Washington, DC: World Bank. https://openknowledge.worldbank.org/entities/publication/12214b54-7161-5595-be96-c50d58e5c60e.

Rossi, A. 2019. 'Applying the GVC Framework to Policy: The ILO Experience', *Journal of International Business Policy*, 2(3), 211–216.

Sachs, J. D., and Sachs, L. E. 2021. 'Business Alignment for the "Decade of Action"', *Journal of International Business Policy*, 4(1), 22–27.

Sako, M., and Zylberberg, E. 2019. 'SupplierSstrategy in Global Value Chains: Shaping Governance and Profiting from Upgrading', *Socio-Economic Review*, 17(3), 687–707.

Scherer, A. G., and Palazzo, G. 2011. 'The New Political Role of Business in a Globalized World: A Review of a New Perspective on CSR and Its Implications for the Firm, Governance, and Democracy', *Journal of Management Studies*, 48(4), 899–931.

Schmitz, H., and Knorringa, P. 2000. 'Learning from Global Buyers', *Journal of Development Studies*, 37(2), 177–205.

Schneider, B. R. 2013. 'Institutions for Effective Business-Government Collaboration: Micro Mechanisms and Macro Politics in Latin America', *Documento de trabajo del BID*, No. 418. Washington, DC: BID.

Seidman, G. W. 2009. *Beyond the Boycott: Labor Rights, Human Rights and Transnational Activism*. New York: Russell Sage Foundation.

Simchi-Levi, D., and Simchi-Levi, E. 2020. 'We Need a Stress Test for Critical Supply Chains', *Harvard Business Review*. https://hbr.org/2020/04/we-need-a-stress-test-for-critical-supply-chains

Stolzenburg, V., Taglioni, D., and Winkler, D. 2019. 'Economic Upgrading through Global Value Chain Participation: Which Policies Increase the Value-Added Gains?', in G. Gereffi, S. Ponte, and G. Raj-Reichert, eds., *Handbook on Global Value Chains*. Cheltenham, UK: Edward Elgar, 483–505.

Tokatli, N. 2012. 'Toward a Better Understanding of the Apparel Industry: A Critique of the Upgrading Literature', *Journal of Economic Geography*, 13(6), 993–1011.

USAID. 2021. 'Trade Facilitation Transparency in Peru: Comparative Best Practices and Recommendations', April. https://www.apec.org/docs/default-source/publications/2021/4/trade-facilitation-transparency-in-peru/221_cti_trade-facilitation-transparency-in-peru.pdf?sfvrsn=59ed5ad6_1.

Van Assche, A. 2017. 'Global Value Chains and the Rise of a Global Supply Chain Mindset', in S. Tapp, A. Van Assche and R. Wolfe, eds., *Redesigning Canadian Trade Policies for New Global Realities*. Montreal: McGill-Queen's University Press: 183–208.

Van Assche, A. 2020. 'Trade, Investment and Intangibles: The ABCs of Global Value Chain-Oriented Policies', *OECD Trade Policy Papers*, No. 242. Paris: OECD Publishing.

Van Assche, A., and Gangnes, B. 2019. 'Global Value Chains and the Fragmentation of Trade Policy Coalitions', *Transnational Corporations Journal*, 26(1), 31–60.

Van Assche, A., and Van Biesebroeck, J. 2018. 'Functional Upgrading in China's Export Processing Sector', *China Economic Review*, 47, 245–262.

Werner, M., Bair, J., and Fernández, V. R. 2014. 'Linking up to Development? Global Value Chains and the Making of a Post-Washington Consensus', *Development and Change*, 45(6), 1219–1247.

World Bank. 2019. *World Development Report 2020: Trading for Development in the Age of Global Value Chains*. Washington, DC: World Bank.

7
Innovation and Competitiveness
The Regional Dimension

Carlos Azzoni and Milene Tessarin

7.1. Introduction

An often-overlooked aspect of processes around innovation, competitiveness, and capabilities building concerns the spatial context in which they occur. This chapter illustrates the importance of labour pool and geographical concentration as essential factors that help shape pathways for innovation, and influence the speed with which technological change can occur.

Seeking to establish an association between inputs for innovative activity and regional innovative performance, we propose an approach based on human capital and the skills of workers who contribute to innovation. Human capital has a significant impact on diffusion and innovation. It is involved in interactive learning, such as learning by doing, learning by interacting, and learning by using, which increase production operations efficiency, promote cooperation between users and producers, and generate incremental innovations. We aim to include workers broadly involved in innovative activities, essential for innovation in traditional industries, and complementary R&D professionals in sectors with higher technological content.

Being able to capture this broader range of professionals is crucial to assess regional innovation in emerging countries such as those in Latin America, as their productive structure concentrates on lower technological-content industries and innovative activities not centred on formal R&D. Human capital is one of the elements behind the concept of innovative capabilities, and involves several actors, such as universities, research centres, financing institutions, firms, and workers, all acting to create and internalize knowledge to stimulate technological progress and innovation. According to Lundvall et al. (2009), innovative capabilities are needed to generate and manage technical matters and reflect on what actors know and what they can learn. In this process, the creation and accumulation of capabilities are related to the competencies of the persons involved, in the sense that capabilities are not only science-based but also experience-based. In this sense, local characteristics, especially the interaction of

Carlos Azzoni and Milene Tessarin, *Innovation and Competitiveness* In: *Innovation, Competitiveness, and Development in Latin America*. Edited by: Edmund Amann and Paulo N. Figueiredo, Oxford University Press. © Oxford University Press 2024. DOI: 10.1093/oso/9780197648070.003.0007

human capital in the process of knowledge accumulation, are crucial to provide a broader view of the innovative performance of developing countries.

Brazil is very heterogeneous spatially in terms of development and location of innovative activity. Although Pintec—the National Innovation Survey (IBGE, 2020)—has advanced in providing standardized and periodic data on innovative activity, it still does not allow analyses with a detailed regional disaggregation level.[1] Simões et al. (2005) used patent data, skilled labour, and R&D from 2000 to locate high-tech activities in Brazil. Gonçalves and Fajardo (2011) used patent data from the National Institute of Industrial Property (INPI) for 1999–2001 to verify the relationship between geographic and technological proximity as drivers of regional innovation. Sobrinho and Azzoni (2016) created a measure of the innovative potential of the Brazilian industrial sector based on workers' skills, with data from 2003 to 2012, at a granular regional level (cities and clusters).

To contribute to this literature, we created a new measure of innovative potential that can be used at different levels of regional disaggregation and with greater temporal frequency. We seek to work with the concept of innovative potential because it involves innovation inputs and not outputs. Given innovation characteristics in Latin American and other developing countries, traditional measures of innovation outcome—such as patents or R&D expenditures—may not accurately capture the effort involved in achieving innovation and technological change in such countries. Innovative potential includes several elements of the regional innovation system, especially the interaction between human capital, firms, and knowledge that shapes innovative capabilities.

The regional units used in this study are Labour Market Areas (LMA), created by the Brazilian statistical office (IBGE) based on commuting to work and study. We work with 374 relevant regions spread across all states in the country. We also use data from the Annual Report of Social Information (RAIS) on occupations in the Brazilian formal labour market from 2003 to 2018. Other variables we use to assess regional innovative potential include gross domestic product (GDP) per capita, university professors in STEM (science, technology, engineering, and mathematics) fields, size of firms, and the share of manufacturing, all at the regional level not yet displayed in the literature.

The chapter is based on a comparative analysis between regions to identify their innovative potential. It seeks to identify elements that represent innovation input and that help explain the regional innovative performance. It also seeks to understand whether the dynamics of increasing spatial disparities in innovative

[1] Regionally, Pintec covers 15 of the 26 Federation Units in Brazil (IBGE, 2020). Those not included in the survey are located in the North and North-East regions of the country, which invest the least in innovation.

potential—that is, the dark side of innovation—occurred in Brazil during the period covered by this study. In this sense, the role of public policy in influencing the spatial distribution of innovation is also considered in this chapter. Although innovative activities are heavily concentrated in a few regions, empirical evidence suggests that a shift has occurred since the early 2000s, with lagging regions making progress faster.

Nonetheless, such convergence is still slight, given the size of the discrepancies between the leading and lagging regions' innovative performance. Factors related to the previous capacities of the regions, such as the stock of workers with the necessary skills to develop innovative activity, the share of the manufacturing sector in the economy, and the presence of large firms, have a positive association with future innovative activity. Thus, we can confirm that path dependence matters for innovative development.

The structure of this chapter is as follows. Following this introduction, section 7.2 presents the theoretical background to the discussion. Methods and an empirical model are specified in section 7.3, while descriptive and statistical results are presented in section 7.4. Finally, section 7.5 offers a conclusion and policy implications.

7.2. Theoretical Background

7.2.1. Growth, Innovation, and Human Capital

Economists have long identified knowledge as a key factor explaining the growth of countries and regions. The Marshallian approach (Marshall, 1920) argued that spillovers of local knowledge, local labour pools, and non-tradable local inputs are central factors promoting regional agglomeration. The Jacobian tradition (Jacobs, 1969) also sees knowledge transfer in a diverse environment regarding workers and economic activities as an input for local growth. Modern growth theory (Lucas, 1988; Romer, 1990) also emphasizes human capital in explaining economic growth. Here, individuals accumulate new skills and know-how that impact productivity and general human capital levels, leading to growth.

Recently, researchers in Evolutionary Economic Geography have started to argue that factors other than geographic proximity explain the growth of regions (Boschma, 2005; Neffke, Henning, and Boschma, 2011; Pinheiro et al., 2022). For these authors, geographic proximity enhances the effects of institutional, cognitive, and structural factors in the regions. Together, the various dimensions of proximity reduce coordination costs and uncertainty and facilitate interactive learning, information and knowledge flow, and innovation (Boschma, 2005). Thus, regions are understood as a unique repository of specific characteristics that cannot be easily reproduced elsewhere (Gertler, 2005). These particularities define development and growth trajectories.

Human capital is one of the elements that permeate all these theories. Technology is embedded in both human and physical capital (Lucas, 1988; Romer, 1990), and the interaction between them and among workers is the primary means of technology diffusion. Some studies especially reinforce the importance of professionals in the STEM fields for the firms' innovation. Graduates in the STEM fields are recognized for their technological creativity and innovation, which may generate significant benefits for firm innovation performance (Rodríguez-Pose and Lee, 2020), since these fields expose their professionals to technological developments, critical thinking, and analytical skills during training, boosting their technical knowledge and expertise (Hsieh et al., 2022). Furthermore, STEM graduates are more likely to engage in individual patenting activities. In this sense, the stock of STEM workers has become vital for innovation and growth and a standard component of almost all innovation policies (Atkinson and Mayo, 2010).

In addition, recent evidence highlights a broader range of creative professionals with skills to identify and solve problems that also contribute to the development and diffusion of technical and organizational innovations (Rodríguez-Pose and Lee, 2020; Tessarin et al., 2020). Lundvall (1992) showed that engineers and scientists are critical in inventing and developing innovations. Additionally, some technical professionals work in the second stage of innovation, in which the innovation process and the technological adaptations are explored. For example, Schneider, Günther, and Brandenburg (2010) used the number of engineers, scientists, and managers to relate them to the product innovation of firms in Germany. Rodríguez-Pose and Lee (2020) compared the contribution of STEM professionals and creative workers (geeks versus hipsters) to the innovative potential of US cities. According to Rodríguez-Pose and Lee (2020), the interdependence of these two groups, in addition to producing general innovations, increases radical innovations, particularly to the market. In the Brazilian context, Gusso (2006) and Araújo, Cavalcante, and Alves (2009) used the number of engineers, technicians, and personnel linked to R&D to measure the innovative and technological capacity of the productive sectors in Brazil, while Simões et al. (2005) evaluated mid-level (technical) and higher-level workers. These authors confirm that creative and STEM occupations work together to expand the region's innovative potential.

Bell (2009) highlights that the construction of innovative capabilities is strongly linked to human capital. Although educational institutions provide the knowledge and skills needed in creative and manufacturing processes, firms are the locus where specific knowledge takes shape and turns into technological change. Firms increase workers' knowledge by transmitting productive and creative knowledge developed internally. Such development may involve acquiring new knowledge via externally trained human capital. The combination of internal and external knowledge results in incremental improvements and in new innovative activities.

Depending on the type of most frequent innovation in a particular industry, some professionals are more relevant than others for promoting innovation. Learning by doing and using are recognized drivers of incremental changes. Learning by doing, interacting, and using increases efficiency in production operations and promotes interaction between users and producers (Lundvall, 1992). According to Bell (1984), the interactive learning process can occur in two ways: on the one hand, passively without significant costs, generating incremental innovations continuously; and on the other hand, in an intentional and targeted way, using an internal feedback system that involves evaluating, reviewing, interpreting, and improving the experiences carried out. Radical change requires creating new knowledge that results in differentiated products and processes. In the end, product innovation, together with the accumulation of incremental innovations over the years, is responsible for a large part of the productivity growth and technological dynamism of countries.

7.2.2. The Geography of Innovation

Regions differ in their ability to accumulate knowledge, produce innovations, and promote growth. One of the main theoretical arguments that explains why companies choose certain locations comes from Marshall's (1920) agglomeration theory. Marshallian or agglomeration externalities suggest that firms tend to concentrate in dense urban areas to take advantage of externalities such as lower transport costs, skilled and abundant labour supply, and the existence of suppliers of specialized inputs (Caragliu, De Dominicis, and De Groot, 2016). Firms' agglomeration of the same economic activity results in regional specialization and produces positive externalities. Suppliers, workers, support institutions, and infrastructure, focused on regional specialization, are concentrated and facilitate the exchange of information and other benefits arising from geographic proximity (Torre and Gilly, 1999; Panne, 2004).

For innovation, agglomeration and geographic proximity also have their benefits. Knowledge spillovers, especially tacit knowledge, are geographically limited since this type of knowledge is acquired through social interaction (Panne, 2004). The agglomeration facilitates the interaction between agents, the exchange of information, and knowledge spillovers, producing positive effects on the interactive learning process (Gertler, 2005).

Jacobs (1969), on the other hand, argues that knowledge can spread across complementary rather than similar industries, as ideas developed by one industry can be applied in other industries, thus generating diversification, or Jacobian externalities. In this scenario, diversified rather than specialized regions stimulate the cross-fertilization of ideas, the addition of new information, and problem-solving (Jacobs, 1969), factors that drive the emergence of new types of jobs/industries (innovation, ultimately) and growth.

Several authors have investigated in depth whether agglomeration or diversification externalities are more relevant for regional innovation. Glaeser et al. (1992) argue that although most cities are specialized and generate Marshallian externalities, there are also activities outside the primary core, suggesting other externalities operating in cities. Feldman and Audretsch (1999) concluded that diversification rather than regional specialization is the element that has promoted innovative activity in the United States. But most studies (Paci and Usai, 1999; Panne, 2004; Caragliu, De Dominicis, and De Groot, 2016; Antonelli et al., 2017) highlight that specialization and diversification are important roles for innovation, which vary depending on the economic activity and the urban agglomeration characteristics. Regions with a greater number of high-tech industries depend more on diversification, while regions that concentrate on traditional industries depend more on agglomeration externalities to have more innovative results. Thus, agglomeration and diversification are relevant elements for promoting innovation in regions.

Seeking to understand the factors that lead regions to follow vibrant trajectories or to be stuck in low-growth trajectories, authors of evolutionary economic geography have built a theoretical and empirical framework to show that history matters in terms of where and how regions evolve (Neffke, Henning, and Boschma, 2011; Pinheiro et al., 2022). These authors argue that externalities of diversification (composition of activities) and specialization (size and intensity of clusters) have a fine connection since diversification does not go in any direction but to nearby areas. Diversification tends to occur more frequently for related industries, that is, industries that share knowledge (or technologies), skills, infrastructure, and similar institutions (Boschma and Frenken, 2018). Thus, industries in the regions take advantage of shared factors to diversify into nearby industries. 'The more related the variety of industries is vis-à-vis the new industry, the more likely a region can be successful in that new industry. Hence, the existing set of industries conditions the likelihood of new industries emerging, and in that sense, there exists regional path dependence' (Boschma and Frenken, 2018, pp. 8–9). When regional diversification moves towards unrelated industries—that is, which share few characteristics and therefore are rarer events—it means that an expansion of local capacities and the addition of new knowledge have occurred (Boschma and Frenken, 2018; Balland et al., 2019), the purest sense of Jacobian externalities.

In such an approach, regional development depends on the ability of regions to change paths over the time (Gertler, 2005). In this context, several dimensions of proximity are considered to explain the trajectories of regional evolution, such as technological, institutional, cognitive, and social proximity (Boschma, 2005). In Brazil, Tessarin et al. (2020) showed that innovative activity is positively associated with cognitive and technological proximity among workers. Galetti, Tessarin, and Morceiro (2021) also concluded that cognitive proximity between workers is correlated with diversification and the entry of new industries in Brazilian regions. The proximity between the portfolio of existing technologies in a region was also pointed out by Antonelli et al. (2017) as an element that stimulates the development of innovative activities among European regions. Other articles focused on the US regions also showed that proximity in the technological base has a positive association with patents (Kogler, Rigby, and Tucker, 2013; Boschma, Balland, and Kogler, 2015; Balland et al., 2019).

Therefore, evolutionary economic geography argues that the prior knowledge base and competencies established in a region will determine the future paths that the region can follow, that is, path dependence matters (Neffke, Henning, and Boschma, 2011). On the one hand, regions that concentrate fewer diversified and complex activities (backward regions) tend to perpetuate a trajectory of low technological dynamism for a long time. On the other hand, diversified regions with complex industries and knowledge (advanced regions) have a wider range of knowledge and technologies that can be (re)combined, resulting in innovations. Pinheiro et al. (2022) show that the process of regional industrial and technological diversification can be vigorous for advanced regions. However, the dark side of this process is that it increases spatial inequality, as lagging regions tend to have a smaller set of accumulated capabilities and complex industries to stimulate technological dynamism than advanced regions. In this sense, the gap between advanced versus lagging regions tends to increase, resulting in what has become known as the dark side of the geography of innovation (Pinheiro et al., 2022).

The literature has sought to understand the geographical unevenness of innovation. In general, innovation is even more concentrated in space than production (Pike, Rodríguez-Pose, and Tomaney, 2017), as few advanced regions tend to concentrate a variety of complex industries that patent, while lagging regions specialize in less-complex industries that rarely patent (Boschma, Balland, and Kogler, 2015) when they diversify. So, income disparities across regions are more likely to be reinforced, not reduced, according to Pinheiro et al. (2022), due to path-dependence mechanisms on regional processes of structural transformation.

Other characteristics present in investigations explaining regional innovation refer to the profile of the companies (mainly, activity type and size). According to Pintec (IBGE, 2020), 87.5% of private companies that implemented some type of innovation between 2015 and 2017 are part of the manufacturing industry—this share remains relatively constant compared to previous years. Therefore, manufacturing industries tend to be largely responsible for Brazilian innovation. High-tech firms, by definition, spend more on innovative activities,[2] especially R&D. On the other hand, less technologically intensive firms focus on incremental innovations and expenditures on other innovative activities (such as the acquisition of machinery and equipment with an innovative purpose or project development) (Morceiro et al., 2011; Tessarin, Suzigan, and Guilhoto, 2020). This type of innovation must be taken into account because, according to the Organisation for Economic Co-operation and Development (OECD, 2005), dissemination mechanisms and incremental changes account for most innovations carried out in developing countries.

Lastly, size also matters for innovative activity since large firms tend to spend more resources on innovation (Symeonidis, 1996). Schumpeter's theory is based on the oligopolistic entrepreneur's argument (Schumpeter, 1942) that innovation increases more than proportionately with firm size, since the costs involved in innovative activity are high and uncertain and can only be covered if the firm's sales are high. Thus, large firms have the greater financial capacity to invest in high-risk activities and to be involved in more than one project simultaneously (Symeonidis, 1996). In Brazil, around 80% of expenditures made in internal R&D activities by innovative companies in 2017 correspond to companies with more than 500 employees (IBGE, 2020). Bastos and Britto (2017) indicated that larger Brazilian firms (over 500 employees) are better prepared to obtain financing and tax incentives to engage in innovative activities. In addition, the authors showed that the innovation rate among large Brazilian companies is higher than in small companies. In terms of technological diversity, large firms tend to present a wide range of technological domains, producing positive effects on their innovative activity through the cross-fertilization of ideas from different areas.

7.2.3. Regional Innovation in Brazil

The ability to generate innovations differs between regions because it depends on unevenly distributed spatially factors, particularly with territorial

[2] The traditional OECD industrial classification by technological intensity computes the total expenditure on R&D in proportion to the sector's revenue to classify companies into four groups of technological intensity.

dimensions and structural inequalities such as those in Brazil. Among the elements that lead to spatial inequalities, we can mention the concentration of companies, productive activity and knowledge spillovers (Audretsch and Feldman, 1996); type of sectoral regional specialization (Glaeser et al., 1992); appropriate technological infrastructure, institutions, and knowledge proximity (Boschma, 2005); scale and urban amenities (Panne, 2004); knowledge diversity (Gertler, 2005); among others. For these reasons, although we have noticed a moderate de-concentration of industrial production in recent decades and the emergence of new innovative regions, this movement is still concentrated in a few directions. This is true for Latin American countries and for regions within Brazil. Innovation indicators in Latin America are strongly led by only one country—Brazil—and show a practically null evolution over the past few decades, contrary to the trend seen in developed countries as well as in China and India (ECLAC, 2022).

Previous studies show that the concentration of innovative activity is quite intense in Brazil, especially in the South–South-East axis. Diniz (1999) highlighted the concentration of technological activities in the South-East region, mainly in São Paulo State. The author pointed out that even after São Paulo lost relative importance in the distribution of productive activities between the 1970s and the 1980s, it retained technological leadership due to a dense and complex urban and technical-scientific network.

Diniz and Gonçalves (2000) also pointed to a strong concentration of techno-scientific inputs in a few locations. The authors identified that only five cities located in the South-East concentrate 49% of researchers, 50% of national scientific articles, and 64% of international scientific articles. Such authors indicate that Brazil can be divided according to the capacity for technical-scientific development: the dynamic region includes metropolises and medium-sized cities in the South-East and South regions; the backward region has large cities in the North-East at a disadvantage compared to cities in the Center-South to attract and develop knowledge-intensive companies; and the empty region, specialized in the production of commodities, some with low potential for technological development.

Silva and Simões (2004) crossed information from scientific publications and the number of employees in the industrial sectors. They also found a concentration of productive and scientific clusters in the South-East region. For the authors, this region presents more significant technological opportunities than other country regions, which explains the maintenance of technological concentration in this country's axis.

Albuquerque et al. (2009) found that only five states of the federation in the South and South-East region account for 70% of GDP, 84% of patents, 79% of scientific publications, and 69% of researchers in the country. This indicates that the concentration of scientific and technological results is even greater than GDP in five of the 27 UF of the country. In addition to the innovation system being spatially unequal, these authors note that it is also immature compared to the ones from advanced countries. Rodriguez and Gonçalves (2017) investigated the regional distribution of patents in several technological domains using a regional classification by urban scale. As a result, they found that urban agglomerations in the South and South-East (except Espírito Santo) led the hierarchy and concentration ranks in all of the 28 technological patent domains. For technological domains related to high technology, the concentration was even more evident in the urban agglomerations of São Paulo, Campinas, and Rio de Janeiro. Such findings align with the literature on evolutionary economic geography, which shows that few wealthier urban areas concentrate the most complex industries in the United States (Balland and Rigby, 2017; Balland et al., 2020) and European countries (Pinheiro et al., 2022).

Sobrinho and Azzoni (2016) adopted a skills-based approach to assess the innovative potential of Brazilian regions. They calculated indexes for regions, states, and municipalities from 2003 to 2012 to show that the South and South-East regions still have the potentially most innovative industry. The authors identified 15 innovation clusters across the country. Although the concentration in the South-East is notorious, the São Paulo cluster showed slower growth than others in the South (Curitiba-Joinville) and North-East region (Recife and Salvador). By focusing on Brazilian microregions, Galetti, Tessarin, and Morceiro (2021) also observed that microregions in the South and South-East have a higher average skill-relatedness density than the rest of the country's micro-regions. This means that workers with similar skills are present in the same region, and in the end, this encourages the entry of new related firms in that region, reinforcing local specialization and the concentration of productive and technological activity.

In general terms, what is observed in Brazil, as well as in other Latin American countries, is that efforts in science, technology, and innovation do not appear sufficiently aligned with capacity-building to spread innovative potential across all regions (Badia-Miró, Nicolini, and Willebald, 2020). On the one hand, public resources for innovation are mainly concentrated in universities and research centers to promote basic research. On the other hand, applied research that is led by the private sector receives a much smaller share of resources for innovation (ECLAC, 2022). As for companies, due to the lack of public resources available, many focus their innovative strategy on regions that offer more benefits and facilities in terms of infrastructure, specialized suppliers, skilled workers, and so on, reinforcing the regional concentration of innovative potential.

7.3. Methods

7.3.1. Innovative Potential by Regions

Our method centres on using a worker-based approach to capture innovative potential in Brazil. Workers contribute to innovative activities by applying knowledge and skills obtained through formal education and practical learning (learning by doing, learning by interacting, etc.). They also contribute to organizational change, one of the main elements of the innovative dynamic in less advanced countries (OECD, 2005), such as the Latin American countries.

A growing number of studies analyse the impact of workers' skills on the performance of firms and countries (Bacolod, Blum, and Strange, 2009; Acemoglu and Autor, 2010; Neffke and Henning, 2013). Following such studies, we create a proxy for innovative potential by selecting skills linked to innovation and the subsequent occupations that perform tasks to promote innovative activities. A similar approach was proposed by Tessarin, Galetti, and Morceiro (2022) to identify innovative occupations and their association with the increasing specialization of innovative activity in Brazilian regions.

We selected Brazilian employment data from the Annual Social Security Information Report (RAIS)—from the Brazilian Labour Secretary, Ministry of Economy—which contains the number of occupations by industries and regions. This broad database provides information about 50 million workers in the nationwide formal labour market.[3]

To identify the occupations' skills content, we use a crosswalk table elaborated by Maciente (2013), who linked the North-American occupation list (O-NET) with the Brazilian occupation classification (named CBO). O-NET provides a comprehensive classification that describes occupations' attributes and required skills. With the correspondence table, it was possible to connect all 2,514 Brazilian occupations to 263 skills. Then, following the strategy adopted by the literature, we made an accurate assessment of the skills' textual definition (Bacolod, Blum, and Strange, 2009; Acemoglu and Autor, 2010; Autor and Dorn, 2013; Frey and Osborne, 2017) to sort out six skills relevant to performing innovative tasks. Applying a Principal Component Analysis (KMO) (Hair et al., 1998) we have reached an innovative skills index. Table 7.1 shows the skills selected and the PCA results.

Thus, all CBO occupations now have an index referring to innovative potential. We weight the number of occupations in each region by their corresponding

[3] 'Formal' here refers to workers covered by social security. In Brazil, nearly 65% of all employees are formally employed in this sense (Ulyssea, 2018).

Table 7.1 Innovative Skills and PCA Results

Skill	Description	KMO
Innovation	Job requires creativity and alternative thinking to develop new ideas for and answers to work-related problems.	0.8908
Active learning	Understanding the implications of new information for both current and future problem-solving and decision-making	0.8125
Design	Knowledge of design techniques, tools, and principles involved in production of precision technical plans, blueprints, drawings, and models	0.8219
Engineering and technology	Knowledge of the practical application of engineering science and technology. This includes applying principles, techniques, procedures, and equipment to the design and production of various goods and services.	0.7425
Technology design	Generating or adapting equipment and technology to serve user needs	0.5303
Updating and using relevant knowledge	Keeping up to date technically and applying new knowledge to your job	0.5498
Factors Resulting from PCA		**Proportion**
Factor 1	Creativity and problem-solving	0.6630
Factor 2	Technical knowledge	0.3687

Source: Authors' elaboration, based on O-NET description.

PCA Principle Component Analysis

KMO Kaiser Meyer Olkin Test value

O-NET North-American occupation list

index to obtain the innovative potential proxy for each Brazilian region. Therefore, we will call innovative jobs those with an index of innovative potential above the national average.

The regions, or spatial units, considered in the study are Labour Market Areas (LMA). The configuration of such areas is defined by the Brazilian Statistical Office (IBGE) based on commuting to work and study. To the 294 regions identified by IBGE, we added 80 urban areas that are representative in terms of the number of jobs but do not show conurbation with other cities. We ended up with 374 relevant regions, accounting for 64.2% of the national population in the 2010 census and 78% of all formal jobs in 2018.

Table 7.2 Descriptive Statistics

	Min	Q1	Med	Avg	Q3	Max
Innovative jobs	0	107	503	3,881	1,833	423,130
Innovative jobs weighted	0	99	477	4,070	1,875	451,560
All jobs	14	5,230	18,807	92,041	59,716	7,717,382
STEM faculty	0	0	6	237	84	124,435
Share of manufacturing	0.01	0.11	0.20	0.23	0.31	0.82
Per capita GDP	1,274	9,241	15,749	19,108	25,419	135,586

Source: Author's elaboration.

As the literature informs, agglomeration influences innovations (Paci and Usai, 1999; Panne, 2004; Gertler, 2005). Therefore, besides estimating the regression using all 374 LMAs, we restricted the estimations to LMAs with at least 500 and 1,000 innovative jobs to do alternative tests (see Table 7.3 in section 7.4). The 214 LMA with 500 innovative jobs or more account for 98.5% of all innovative jobs, and the 160 LMAs with more than 1,000 innovative jobs account for 96.5% of innovative jobs. The data show that innovative jobs are more concentrated than overall jobs. Only 44 regions (12% of the total) concentrate on more than 80% of innovative jobs, while 111 regions (30% of the total) concentrate on the same percentage of overall jobs.

As the descriptive statistics show (Table 7.2), the indicator of the regional innovative potential shows concentration, with few areas hosting most of the innovative jobs—as the third quartile still has very few jobs (1,833 jobs in the Q3) when we compare the maximum (423,130 jobs). In terms of all jobs, concentration is also high but relatively smaller than in innovative jobs (Q3 amount has a higher proportion of jobs when compared to the maximum value of this group). We can also observe that, on average, the share of manufacturing represents around a quarter of the economic activities of the regions. For per capita GDP, regional concentration also takes place, as well in the case of jobs.

7.4. Empirical Analysis and Results

This section investigates the trends in this concentration from 2003 to indicate possible changes in the concentration scenario. Employment data come from RAIS dataset; per capita GDP and manufacturing share comes from IpeaData; and data on STEM professors were collected from the Brazilian Higher Education

Table 7.3 Regression Results

	All LMAs	InJ >500	InJ >1,000
$ShInJ_0$	−0.1908564***	−0.2061811***	−0.2286148***
	(0.0141677)	(0.0192741)	(0.0225727)
Y_0	0.0000001***	0.0000001**	0.0000001*
	(0.00000003)	(0.00000004)	(0.00000005)
$STEMFaculty_0$	0.0000001	0.0000001	0.0000001
	(0.0000001)	(0.0000001)	(0.0000001)
$ShManuf_0$	0.0049546**	0.0066693**	0.0089107**
	(0.0020944)	(0.0033283)	(0.0042262)
$ShLargeFirms_0$	1.7145750**	2.7865740*	3.1923050
	(0.7678640)	(1.670306)	(2.074421)
# Observation.	1,496	824	640
R^2	0.1138	0.1339	0.1526
Adjusted R^2	0.1090	0.1254	0.1418
Resid std error	0.0083	0.0097	0.0106
D of freedom	1,487	815	631

Source: Author's elaboration.
Note: The dependent variable is the share of innovative jobs at the time *t*.
LMA Labour Market Areas.

Census. We regress the regional growth of innovative jobs over the period on the initial levels of this variable in each region, such as:

$$InJ_{r,t} = \alpha + \beta_1 InJ_{r,to} + \beta_2 y_{r,to} + \beta_3 EdSTEM_{r,to} + \beta_4 LgFirms_{r,to} + \beta_6 Ind_{r,to} + FE_t$$

In which:

$InJ_{r,t}$ is the share of innovative jobs in region *r* in year *t*, at the end of the period.

$InJ_{r,to}$ is the share of innovative jobs in region *r* at the beginning of the period. This variable represents the initial levels of innovative jobs in the regions.

$y_{r,to}$ is the per capita value of the regional GDP. It is included in the regression to represent the initial development levels of the regions. It is expected that more affluent areas are more likely to have innovative potential.

$EdSTEM_{r,to}$ is the initial number of university professors in the region in STEM areas, at both the undergraduate and graduate levels. It represents the regional capacity to produce STEM professionals.

$LgFirms_{r,to}$ is the share of firms with more than 1,000 employees in the region at the beginning of the period. The idea is to verify whether the presence of sizeable firms in the region is associated with the change in the regional share of innovative jobs.

$ShManufct_{r,to}$ is the initial share of manufacturing in the regional value-added. It informs about the sectoral composition of the regional production. It is expected that regions with larger shares of manufacturing will be related to a more intense demand for innovative jobs.

FE_t are fixed effects for each period. They capture overall macroeconomic conditions in each period.

The equation was estimated as a time panel. We defined four periods of four years and related the growth of the share of innovative jobs over each period to the respective initial value. As per data availability, the initial time is 2003 and 2018 is the last year. We have chosen four non-overlap periods to avoid possible specific time fluctuations. Examining the data on how jobs with innovative potential are distributed across Brazilian LMAs and comparing with GDP per capita in 2003 and 2018, it becomes clear that the most innovative regions are also those with the highest per capita income. Figures 7.1 and 7.2 allow us to make a correlation analysis of the share of innovative jobs by LMAs. The vertical axis indicates the percentage of innovative jobs in relation to all jobs, by region, in 2018, and the horizontal axis indicates the same variable in 2003. The regions above (below) the 45° dashed line showed growth (fall) in the share in 2018 compared to 2003.

Figure 7.1 shows all LMAs, over a period of 16 years, evidencing a slight increase in the share of innovative employment in most regions—as they are located close to the dashed line. It is also evident that innovative jobs are heavily concentrated in a few LMAs, while the vast majority have a low share of innovative jobs.

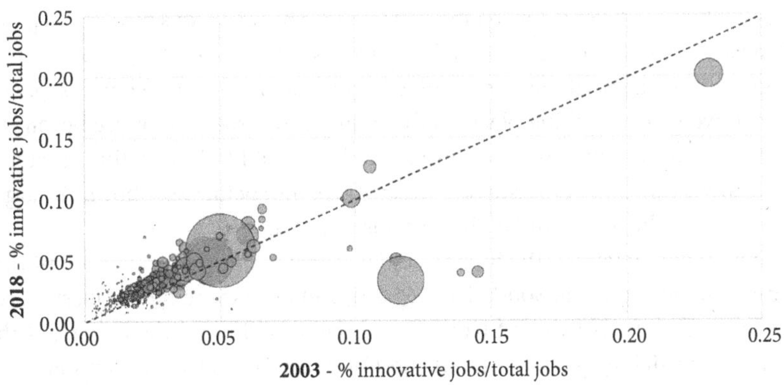

Figure 7.1. Change in the share of innovative jobs by regions: all regions (2003–2018).
Source: Author's elaboration. *Note:* bubble size represents the number of innovative jobs by region in 2003.

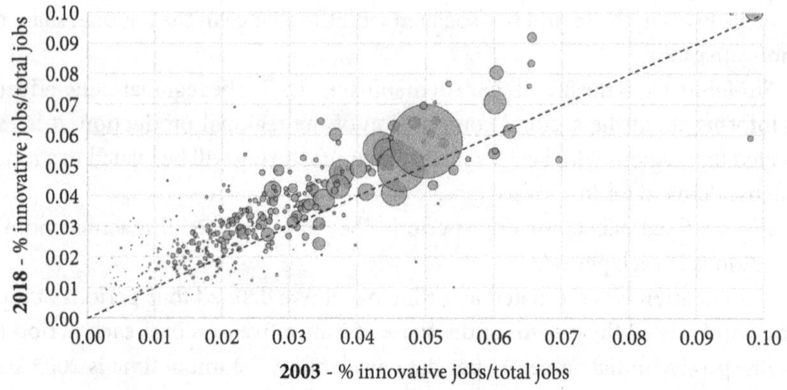

Figure 7.2. Change in the share of innovative jobs by regions: selected group (2003–2018).

Source: Author's elaboration. *Note:* The bubble size represents the number of innovative jobs by region in 2003. Includes only regions with up to 10% of innovative jobs.

Furthermore, while most regions showed a small increase in their share, a few regions with a higher share of innovative jobs experienced a decline.

To check in detail this large set of LMAs with a low share of innovative jobs, we have considered only LMAs that have up to 10% of innovative jobs in relation to the total number of jobs (Figure 7.2). When we look only at this set of LMAs, it becomes clearer that small regions had a (positive) variation in the share of innovative jobs relatively greater than in large regions. As we will see, the econometric results follow the same direction as the descriptive statistics, pointing to a relative de-concentration.

We also performed an econometric test, with results displayed in Table 7.3. As the negative coefficients for the initial share of innovative jobs indicate, regions with larger initial shares presented lower shares at the end of the period, and regions with small initial shares presented larger final shares. Such change suggests that convergence is taking place, as the shares of innovative jobs are becoming more similar. Although the conclusion is valid for all LMA sizes, this process is more intense in larger LMAs, as a comparison of the coefficients shows. As larger LMAs tend to be more similar, this result is expected.

Our results show that the highest initial shares of innovative jobs are mostly located in the South and South-East regions, and LMAs with the smallest shares are located in the North and North-East regions, following the pattern of the country's spatial inequality (Azzoni and Haddad, 2018; Bucciferro and Ferreira de Souza, 2020). So, rather than reinforcing spatial disparities—that is, a dark side of the geography of innovation—as preliminary evidence points to in European regions (Pinheiro et al., 2022), the opposite happened in Brazil. This convergence among Brazilian regions is probably associated with the policies implemented by the federal government that benefited the poorest regions relative to the richest. These include a real increase in the minimum wage, the creation of universities and technical institutes in peripheral regions, and the acceleration of social programmes that made it possible for a large part of the population to enter education and the job market.

As for the other variables, the initial per capita income level, the initial share of manufacturing, and the initial share of large firms appeared with positive signs. This indicates that more prosperous regions, where manufacturing plays a vital role and where large firms are located, tend to present larger shares of innovative jobs at the end of the period. Such a conclusion aligns with the evolutionary economic geography argument that history (path-dependence) matters for the future trajectory (Neffke, Henning, and Boschma, 2011; Pinheiro et al., 2022). In our case, the previous regional structural characteristics imply the future development of the innovative potential.

As previously indicated, the manufacturing sector performs around 70% of corporate R&D and an even higher percentage of other innovative activities in Brazil (IBGE, 2020). In addition, large companies concentrate innovative activity, according to Schumpeter (1942), especially in the manufacturing sector (Bastos and Britto, 2017). The manufacturing sector has a high capacity to promote regional development as locations where new industries are installed undergo major transformations (Greenstone, Hornbeck, and Moretti, 2010; Macedo and Monasterio, 2016). However, the profound and accelerated process of deindustrialization of the Brazilian economy (Morceiro and Guilhoto, 2022) is a worrying factor that is putting in question the ability of manufacturing to continue playing a vital role in the regional innovative potential.

Turning to the coefficients for the STEM faculty in the region, these proved positive but were not statistically different from zero. Therefore, there seems to be no association between the regional capacity to produce STEM professionals and the employment of these professionals at the local productive structure. This fact can be explained by the mobility of workers, who can move away from the regions they graduated from in search of employment with the best benefits. Thus, professionals trained in one region will not necessarily work in the same region. Lastly, many regions, especially the peripheral ones, still do not have universities. In summary, our results show that some previous local characteristics (found in the initial period) explain the future regional innovative potential (ending period). The regional convergence observed apparently has minor effects regarding catch-up at the national level since the leader regions are too far removed from the other regions in terms of innovative levels. The pace of convergence needs to be faster to promote effective changes within the bottom group so as to promote the innovative success of the country as a whole.

7.5. Conclusions and Policy Implications

Innovation depends on a wide range of factors. Several elements that can explain the innovative potential must be considered when analysing such a phenomenon from the regional point of view. Identifying the inputs and interaction among the elements which shape the regional innovative capabilities allows us to have a broader view of the innovative performance of emerging regions such as Latin America. For this reason, many studies have sought to explore how different factors can promote better innovative performance. The Latin American context is even more intriguing, as its countries are often far from the technological frontier and concentrate on less technologically intensive industries. They also tend to have companies with innovative strategies focused on diffusion and count on many multinational companies in high-tech sectors. These traditionally locate R&D activities in the home country rather than among subsidiary companies in developing countries.

In terms of GDP, Latin American countries have shown a slow but robust process of regional convergence, including in the period of state-led industrialization (until the late 1970s) and the liberalization period of the 1980s and 1990s (Badia-Miró, Nicolini, and Willebald, 2020). Notwithstanding, that innovative performance has been stagnant for decades in the region. Brazil leads the innovation indicators of Latin America (accounting for 62% of Latin American R&D expenditure), some way ahead of followers, such as Uruguay, Cuba, and Argentina (ECLAC, 2022). Convergence regarding innovative performance among Latin American countries remains a distant goal.

Brazil has one of the most diversified production structures among its Latin American neighbours. In addition, it also exhibits marked regional inequality in terms of the distribution of productive activity, labour, infrastructure, and income. Such characteristics also reflect on the innovative activity, which is relatively concentrated in a few regions located in the South and South-East regions. Our results point to some elements that explain the regions' innovative potential, such as per capita income, the degree of industrialization, and the proportion of large companies. These factors have a positive association with the regions' innovative potential in the future, and therefore contribute to the growth of regional innovative activity.

The initial share of innovative jobs is an important element in our results explaining the innovative potential of the regions in the future. Regions with a higher initial share of innovative jobs tend to grow at lower rates in the future, while regions with a lower share tend to develop a relatively higher growth rate. Therefore, a convergence movement of the regional innovative potential has slightly reduced the deep spatial inequality. This result is quite interesting, as it goes against the grain of the initial research carried out for European regions; this pointed to the dark side of the geography of innovation, that is, an even greater concentration of innovation in leading regions (with well-established technological capabilities) to the detriment of lagging ones. We believe that redistributive policies were vital for such spatial de-concentration, but the continuity of these policies ran out of steam from mid-2016 onwards.

Innovative capabilities are built little by little, and their evolution is decisive for regional innovative performance, especially for regions with less innovative potential (lagged regions). In Brazil, backward regions face major physical, social, and technological infrastructure bottlenecks. However, appropriate infrastructure is a necessary condition to attract firms from overpopulated advanced regions, which face increasing urbanization negative externalities (such as diseconomies of agglomeration, pollution, congestion, rising housing prices, and price inflation for key inputs). In its turn, enforcement and coordination of public policies are essential to provide infrastructure in such backward regions.

As manufacturing, especially where it involves large companies, is positively associated with the regional innovative potential, the challenge is to attract them to the backward regions so as to maintain the convergence process and reduce the deep spatial disparities currently present. To this end, we suggest policy approaches based on the local—according to the evolutionary economic geography literature—and people-based—according to the urban economics literature. In the first case, regions with less innovative potential could explore diversification opportunities for new industries related to existing industries in the same area with greater innovative potential. However, diversification towards more innovative industries is not a spontaneous process and, therefore, should be promoted by local public policies.

As for the second focus, it is vital for the less advanced regions to expand and improve the education system and professional training and create mechanisms to attract and retain professionals with innovative skills. In this sense, establishing partnerships and research collaborations with excellent education and training institutions domestically and abroad is a possible path. Finally, given the advance of deindustrialization in the South and South-East regions, especially in industries sensitive to the high labour cost, designing policies to attract manufacturing companies to peripheral locations is another option to be explored.

Although we have identified convergence in the innovative potential of Brazilian regions, the movement is too slow to indicate a deep transformation that would raise the country as a whole to the levels of developed nations. A strategy to bring about an unequivocal convergence between Brazilian regions depends on public policies focused on regional development projects centered on underperforming areas. If consistently and successfully pursued, these could not only resolve regional inequality; they could also unlock growth potential, contributing to an exit from the middle-income trap.

References

Acemoglu, D., and Autor, D. H. 2010. 'Skills, Tasks and Technologies: Implications for Employment and Earnings'. *NBER Working Paper Series* no. 16082. Cambridge.

Albuquerque, E. da M., Simões, R., Baessa, A., Campolina, B., and Silva, L. 2009. 'A distribuição espacial da produção científica e tecnológica Brasileira: Uma descrição de estatísticas de produção local de patentes e artigos científicos', *Revista Brasileira de Inovação*, 1(2), 225–251.

Antonelli, C., Crespi, F., Mongeau Ospina, C. A., and Scellato, G. 2017. 'Knowledge Composition, Jacobs Externalities and Innovation Performance in European Regions', *Regional Studies*, 51(11), 1708–1720.

Araújo, B. C., Cavalcante, L. R., and Alves, P. 2009. 'Variáveis proxy para os gastos empresariais em inovação com base no pessoal ocupado técnico-científico disponível na Relação Anual de Informações Sociais', *Radar IPEA: Tecnologia, Produção e Comércio Exterior*, 5, 16–21.

Atkinson, R. D., and Mayo, M. J. 2010. *Refueling the US Innovation Economy: Fresh Approaches to Science, Technology, Engineering and Mathematics (STEM) Education*. Washington, DC: The Information Technology & Innovation Foundation.

Audretsch, D. B., and Feldman, M. P. 1996. 'R&D Spillovers and the Geography of Innovation and Production', *American Economic Review*, 86(3), 630–640.

Autor, D. H., and Dorn, D. 2013. 'The Growth of Low-Skill Service Jobs and the Polarization of the US Labor Market', *American Economic Review*, 103(5), 1553–1597.

Azzoni, C. R., and Haddad, E. A. 2018. 'Regional Disparities', in E. Amann, C. R. Azzoni, and W. Baer, eds., *The Oxford Handbook of the Brazilian Economy*. Oxford: Oxford University Press, 1–27.

Bacolod, M., Blum, B. S., and Strange, W. C. 2009. 'Skills in the City', *Journal of Urban Economics*, 65(2), 136–153.

Badia-Miró, M., Nicolini, E. A., and Willebald, H. 2020. 'Spatial Inequality in Latin America (1895–2010): Convergence and Clusters in a Long-Run Approach', in Daniel A. Tirado-Fabregat, Marc Badia-Miró, and Henry Willebald, eds., *Time and Space: Latin American Regional Development in Historical Perspective*. Cham: Palgrave Macmillan, 343–374.

Balland, P. A., and Rigby, D. L. 2017. 'The Geography of Complex Knowledge', *Economic Geography*, 93(1), 1–23.

Balland, P. A., Boschma, R., Crespo, J., and Rigby, D. L. 2019. 'Smart Specialization Policy in the European Union: Relatedness, Knowledge Complexity and Regional Diversification', *Regional Studies*, 53(9), 1252–1268.

Balland, P. A., Jara-Figueroa, C., Petralia, S. G., Steijn, M. P. A., Rigby, D. L., and Hidalgo, C. A. 2020. 'Complex Economic Activities Concentrate in Large Cities', *Nature Human Behaviour*, 4, 248–254.

Bastos, C. P., and Britto, J. 2017. 'Inovação e geração de conhecimento científico e tecnológico no Brasil: Uma análise dos dados de cooperação da Pintec segundo porte e origem de capital', *Revista Brasileira de Inovação*, 16(1), 35–62.

Bell, M. 1984. '"Learning" and the Accumulation of Industrial Technological Capacity in Developing Countries', in M. Fransman and K. King, eds., *Technological Capability in the Third World*. London: Palgrave Macmillan, 187–209.

Bell, M. 2009. *Innovation Capabilities and Directions of Development*. Brighton: STEPS Centre.

Boschma, R. 2005. 'Proximity and Innovation: A Critical Assessment', *Regional Studies*, 39(1), 61–74.

Boschma, R., and Frenken, K. 2018. *Evolutionary Economic Geography*, in Vol. 1. G. L. Clark, M. P. Feldman, M. S. Gertler, and D. Wójcik, eds., New Oxford Handbook of Economic Geography, Chapter 11. Oxford: Oxford University Press, 213–229.

Boschma, R., Balland, P. A., and Kogler, D. F. 2015. 'Relatedness and Technological Change in Cities: The Rise and Fall of Technological Knowledge in US Metropolitan Areas from 1981 to 2010', *Industrial and Corporate Change*, 24(1), 223–250.

Bucciferro, J. R., and Ferreira de Souza, P. H. G. 2020. 'The Evolution of Regional Income Inequality in Brazil, 1872–2015', in H. Tirado-Fabregat, D. A. Badia-Miró, and M. Willebald, eds., *Time and Space. Palgrave Studies in Economic History*. Cham: Palgrave Macmillan, 131–156.

Caragliu, A., De Dominicis, L., and De Groot, H. L. F. 2016. 'Both Marshall and Jacobs Were Right!', *Economic Geography*, 92(1), 87–111.

Diniz, C. C., and Gonçalves, E. 2000. 'Possibilidades e tendências locacionais da indústria do conhecimento no Brasil', in *Encontro Nacional de Economia*. Campinas: Anais da ANPEC, 1–24.

ECLAC. 2022. *Innovation for Development: The Key to a Transformative Recovery in Latin America and the Caribbean*. Santiago: Economic Commission for Latin America and the Caribbean (ECLAC).

Feldman, M. P., and Audretsch, D. B. 1999. 'Innovation in Cities', *European Economic Review*, 43(2), 409–429.

Frey, C. B., and Osborne, M. A. 2017. 'The Future of Employment: How Susceptible Are Jobs to Computerisation?', *Technological Forecasting and Social Change*, 114(1), 254–280.

Galetti, J. R. B., Tessarin, M. S., and Morceiro, P. C. 2021. 'Skill Relatedness, Structural Change and Heterogeneous Regions: Evidence from a Developing Country', *Papers in Regional Science*, 100(6), 1355–1376.

Gertler, M. S. 2005. 'Tacit Knowledge, Path Dependency and Local Trajectories of Growth', in G. Fuchs and P. Shapira, eds., *Rethinking Regional Innovation and Change*. New York: Springer-Verlag, 23–41.

Glaeser, E. L., Kallal, H. D., Scheinkman, J. A., and Shleifer, A. 1992. 'Growth in Cities', *Journal of Political Economy*, 100(6), 1126–1152.

Gonçalves, E. 2007. 'O padrão espacial da atividade inovadora Brasileira: Uma análise exploratória', *Estudos Econômicos*, 37(2), 405–433.

Gonçalves, E., and Fajardo, B. 2011. 'A influência da proximidade tecnológica e geográfica sobre a inovação regional no Brasil', *Revista de Economia Contemporanea*, 15(1), 112–142.

Greenstone, M., Hornbeck, R., and Moretti, E. 2010. 'Identifying Agglomeration Spillovers: Evidence from Winners and Losers of Large Plant Openings', *Journal of Political Economy*, 118(3), 536–598.

Gusso, D. A. 2006. 'Agentes da inovação: quem os forma, quem os emprega?', in J.A. De Negri, F. De Negri, and D. Coelho, eds., *Tecnologia, Exportação e Emprego*. Brasília: Ipea, 397–444.

Hair, J. F., Black, W. C., Babin, B. J., and Anderson, R. E. 1998. *Multivariate Data Analysis*. 5th ed. Hoboken, NJ: Pearson Prentice Hall.

Hsieh, T.-S., Kim, J.-B., Wang, R. R., and Wang, Z. 2022. 'Educate to Innovate: STEM Directors and Corporate Innovation', *Journal of Business Research*, 138, 229–238.

IBGE. 2020. *Pesquisa de inovação: 2017*. Rio de Janeiro: Instituto Brasileiro de Geografia e Estatística.

Jacobs, J. 1969. *The Economy of Cities*. New York: Random House.

Kogler, D. F., Rigby, D. L., and Tucker, I. 2013. 'Mapping Knowledge Space and Technological Relatedness in US Cities', *European Planning Studies*, 21(9), 1374–1391.

Lucas, R. 1988. 'On the Mechanics of Economic Development', *Journal of Monetary Economics*, 22(1), 3–42.

Lundvall, B.-Å. 1992. *National Systems of Innovation: Towards a Theory of Innovation and Interactive Learning*. London: Pinter.

Lundvall, B.-Å., Joseph, K. J., Chaminade, C., and Vang, J. 2009. *Handbook of Innovation Systems and Developing Countries*. Cheltenham, UK: Edward Elgar.

Macedo, G., and Monasterio, L. 2016. 'Local Multiplier of Industrial Employment: Brazilian Mesoregions (2000–2010)', *Revista de Economia Política*, 36(4), 827–839.

Maciente, A. N. 2013. 'The Determinants of Agglomeration in Brazil: Input-Output, Labor and Knowledge Externalities'. Dissertation, University of Illinois at Urbana-Champaign.

Marshall, A. 1920. *Principles of Economics*. London: Macmillan.

Morceiro, P. C., Faria, L., Fornari, V., and Gomes, R. 2011. 'Why not low-technology?', in *9th GLOBELICS International Conference*. Buenos Aires, 15–17.

Morceiro, P. C., and Guilhoto, J. J. M. 2022. 'Sectoral Deindustrialization and Long-Run Stagnation of Brazilian Manufacturing', *Brazilian Journal of Political Economy*, 42(3), 418–441.

Neffke, F., and Henning, M. S. 2013. 'Skill Relatedness and Firm Diversification', *Strategic Management Journal*, 34(3), 297–316.

Neffke, F., Henning, M. S., and Boschma, R. 2011. 'How Do Regions Diversify over Time? Industry Relatedness and the Development of New Growth Paths in Regions', *Economic Geography*, 87(3), 237–265.

OECD. 2005. *Oslo Manual: Guidelines for Collecting and Interpreting Innovation Data*. 3rd ed. Paris: OECD Publishing.

Paci, R., and Usai, S. 1999. 'Externalities, Knowledge Spillovers and the Spatial Distribution of Innovation', *GeoJournal*, 49, 381–390.

Panne, G. Van Der. 2004. 'Agglomeration Externalities: Marshall versus Jacobs', *Journal of Evolutionary Economics*, 14, 593–604.

Pike, A., Rodríguez-Pose, A., and Tomaney, J. 2017. *Local and Regional Development*. 2nd ed. London: Routledge.

Pinheiro, F. L., Balland, P. A., Boschma, R., and Hartmann, D. 2022. *The Dark Side of the Geography of Innovation: Relatedness, Complexity, and Regional Inequality in Europe*. Utrecht University Department of Human Geography.

Rodríguez-Pose, A., and Lee, N. 2020. 'Hipsters vs. Geeks? Creative Workers, STEM and Innovation in US cities', *Cities*, 100, 1–45.

Romer, P. 1990. 'Endogenous Technological Change', *Journal of Political Economy*, 98(5, Part 2), S71–S102.

Schneider, L., Günther, J., and Brandenburg, B. 2010. 'Innovation and Skills from a Sectoral Perspective: A Linked Employer-Employee Analysis', *Economics of Innovation and New Technology*, 19(2), 185–202.

Schumpeter, J. A. 1942. *Capitalism, Socialism and Democracy*. London and New York: Routledge.

Silva, L., and Simões, R. 2004. 'Oportunidades tecnológicas e produção científica: Uma análise microrregional para o Brasil', *Revista Latinoamericana de Estudios Urbano Regionales*, 30(90), 85–102.

Simões, R., Oliveira, A., Gitirana, A., Cunha, J., Campos, M., and Cruz, W. 2005. 'A geografia da inovação: Uma metodologia de regionalização das informações de gastos em P&D no Brasil', *Revista Brasileira de Inovação*, 4(1), 157–185.

Sobrinho, E. M. G., and Azzoni, C. R. 2016. 'Potencial inovativo da indústria nas regiões brasileiras', *Revista Brasileira de Inovação*, 15(2), 275–304.

Symeonidis, G. 1996. 'Innovation, Firm Size and Market Structure: Schumpeterian Hypotheses and Some New Themes', OECD Economics Department Working Papers No. 161. Paris.

Tessarin, M. S., Morceiro, P. C., Chagas, A. L. S., and Guilhoto, J. J. M. 2020. 'Proximidade setorial na indústria de transformação brasileira', *Nova Economia*, 30(3), 771–801.

Tessarin, M. S., Suzigan, W., and Guilhoto, J. J. M. 2020. 'Cooperação para inovar no Brasil: Diferenças segundo a intensidade tecnológica e a origem do capital das empresas', *Estudos Econômicos*, 50(4), 671–704.

Tessarin, M. S., Galetti, J. R. B., and Morceiro, P. C. 2021. '*Skill-relatedness, structural change and innovative activity: evidence from a developing Country. Papers in Regional Science*, 100(6) 1355–1376.

Torre, A., and Gilly, J.-P. 1999. 'On the Analytical Dimension of Proximity Dynamics', *Regional Studies*, 34(2), 169–180.

Ulyssea, G. 2018. 'Firms, Informality, and Development: Theory and Evidence from Brazil', *American Economic Review*, 108(8), 2015–2047.

8

The Extractive Sector and Development in Latin America

The Rising Role of Transparency in Natural Resource Governance

Paul Fenton Villar, Elissaios Papyrakis, and Lorenzo Pellegrini

8.1. Introduction

The extractive sector has marked the past five centuries of Latin American history. Starting with the colonial period and up to the nineteenth century, the region became a major source of gold and silver, underpinning the political and economic growth of European superpowers (Hamilton, 1934). Subsequently, the postcolonial era then coincided with the global expansion of industrialization, and a global increase in energy and commodities consumption. For example, the expanding world economic system saw Chile become a leading exporter of copper, Peru and Bolivia as producers of tin, while Venezuela, Brazil, Mexico, and Colombia became major global exporters of oil in the first half of the twentieth century.

Due to the relative geological rarity and high value associated with coveted commodities (such as oil, gas, gold, and other mined materials), these materials are regularly linked to the generation of wealth and prosperity (Pellegrini, 2018). However, evidence of the inferior socio-economic performance of resource-rich countries in Latin America and beyond has engendered a literature, widely known as the 'resource curse' or the 'paradox of plenty', offering formal and empirical descriptions of how resource abundance might undermine countries' development (Sachs and Warner, 2001). Some of the key factors that may offset the economic benefits of extraction, if any, in the long run concern the fiscal, institutional, social, and environmental issues often associated with it.

Nevertheless, since the turn of the millennium, a nuanced understanding of these considerations has also been gaining currency. Some authors argue that with appropriately implemented governance frameworks, resource-rich countries may mitigate some of the negative externalities associated with natural-resource extraction (Stevens, Lahn, and Kooroshy, 2015; Lahn and Stevens,

Paul Fenton Villar, Elissaios Papyrakis, and Lorenzo Pellegrini, *The Extractive Sector and Development in Latin America* In: *Innovation, Competitiveness, and Development in Latin America.* Edited by: Edmund Amann and Paulo N. Figueiredo, Oxford University Press. DOI: 10.1093/oso/9780197648070.003.0008

2017). This might be especially true in combination with macroeconomic policies prescribed to counteract the economic externalities of extraction (e.g. see Davis, Fedelino, and Ossowski, 2003; Frankel 2012; Venables, 2016; Le Billon and Good, 2016). This chapter extends this discussion by focusing on the role that transparency in the extractive sector may have on resource governance in Latin America. In particular, this chapter is concerned with the Extractive Industries Transparency Initiative (EITI) and its potential role in improving development outcomes arising from the operation of the extractive sector.

After 15 years of advocacy and promotion, the EITI is now the leading financial and contractual transparency initiative within the extractive sector, and it is widely recognized as the sector's hallmark anti-corruption scheme. The initiative currently has more than 55 members, including 10 Latin American countries (Argentina, Colombia, Dominican Republic, Ecuador, Guatemala, Guyana, Honduras, Mexico, Peru, and Suriname). However, while the growing levels of interest and advocacy to ensure global standards of transparency in the extractives sector are commonplace in governing systems across the region (in particular those embodied in the EITI),[1] there has been surprisingly limited discussion of members' actual experience with the initiative in Latin America.

In this chapter, we review the role of the EITI in natural-resource governance and Latin American countries' progress with the initiative. The structure of this chapter is as follows. Following this introduction, section 8.2 describes further the literature on extraction-led development in Latin America. A key area of discussion here concerns the likelihood that institutional environments may be conducive to securing good governance of natural resources in Latin America. This explains the rising demand for increased levels of transparency, driven by the global standards of the EITI. In section 8.3, we review the operation, uptake, and performance of EITI in Latin America. Finally, section 8.4 concludes with a summary of our discussion and reflections for future research.

8.2. The Extractive Sector and Development in Latin America

While the first evidence on the resource curse was based on cross-country comparisons (Sachs and Warner, 2001), more recent evidence provides support to a more localized resource curse utilizing sub-national data on

[1] For example, the Inter-American Development Bank's (IDB) expert advisory group on anti-corruption, transparency, and integrity in Latin America and the Caribbean considers that there is a greater need to ensure that the public has access to accurate and credible information on political and public finances involving natural resources (and appropriate channels to participate in public affairs) (Engel et al., 2018).

mineral dependence and economic development indicators (Gilberthorpe and Papyrakis, 2014; Papyrakis and Gerlagh, 2007; Pellegrini, Tasciotti, and Spartaco, 2021). Focusing on sub-national evidence from Latin America, studies highlight the damaging historical legacy of resource extraction within the region. In particular, Dell (2010) shows that the social and economic effects of *mita*, a forced mining labour system implemented in Peru and Bolivia from the sixteenth century to the early nineteenth, persist to this day. Alternatively, another study by Usui (1997) (for the 1970s and 1980s) has also noted that an oil boom resulted in excessive borrowing, an overheated economy, and the decline of industrial production in the case of Mexico (see Usui, 1997).

Looking at more recent evidence, Perry and Olivera (2009) continue to find that high levels of oil production in the early years of the twenty-first century have been negatively correlated with GDP per capita growth among municipalities in Colombia. Other studies also fail to identify significant positive effects of mining activities in Latin America. For example, Arellano and Yanguas (2010) find that mining revenues do not relate with material or social welfare improvements in contemporary Peru. Indeed, they argue that welfare effects might have been negative if we take into consideration the environmental degradation generated by mining. This point rests on the contention that resource extraction corresponds to a decline in the stock of natural capital, which is not captured by standard measures of economic development (Neumayer, 2004; Arsel, Pellegrini, and Mena, 2019). Some of the mechanisms explaining the resource curse are particularly relevant to the case of Latin America. These include the possibility that natural-resource extraction fosters a higher incidence of political and social conflict, economic volatility, deindustrialization, fitful fiscal spending, environmental degradation (and its associated health risks), together with corruption (Papyrakis and Pellegrini, 2019).

8.2.1. Extractive-Led Development: Financing Domestic Market Growth

Despite the troubling evidence concerning the resource curse, today an emerging consensus known as the 'Extractive-Led Development Agenda' (ELDA) highlights the opportunities extraction poses to resource-rich countries in the region (Stevens, Lahn, and Kooroshy, 2015; Lahn and Stevens, 2017). Several economic arguments endorse the premise for extraction-based development. For example, Jacob Viner (1952), Arthur Lewis (1955), and Walter Rostow (1961) supported the view that natural-resource extraction can help finance the growth of domestic markets. In particular, Rostow's (1961) hugely influential five-stage model of economic development infers that resource rents can provide the investible funds or capital needed to industrialize and 'take off' in traditional economies.

Other well-known arguments suggest that resource revenues may finance infant industries (Balassa, 1980). At early stages of development, domestic industries often do not have access to markets that can generate economies of scale necessary to be competitive in the global market. Revenues arising from natural-resource production may generate funds to finance the industrial investment necessary to expand and become competitive on an international scale. A related argument, based on the Harrod-Domar model, also suggests that resource windfalls could be used to fill the financing gap and start a self-sustaining process of capital accumulation and economic growth (Easterly, 1999).

Furthermore, aside from providing capital to assist domestic markets to grow, common arguments favouring natural resources as a motor of development also regularly consider the public revenues that they generate may also offer more direct means to relieve income poverty. For instance, resource revenues could directly reduce poverty by funding social security or (conditional) cash transfers (Moss, Lambert, and Majerowicz, 2015). Segal (2012) shows that Mexico could almost eliminate extreme poverty by introducing a universal citizen dividend financed by resource revenues. Alternatively, resource revenues may finance improvements in local infrastructure (such as transport links, the electricity network, or housing stock) or to support public services in areas such as education and health (Collier and Laroche, 2015).

The positive historical experience of specific countries also supports the hypothesis that natural capital can stimulate economic growth. Following the discovery of North Sea oil during the 1960s and 1970s, Norway increased its GDP per capita level from 5% below the Organisation for Economic Co-operation and Development (OECD) average in 1970 to 70% above the OECD average by 2010 (Holden, 2013). Other countries, such as Australia and the United States, are also illustrative examples of places where natural resources may have been instrumental in economic development. Meanwhile, even within Latin America, there is some evidence suggesting that mining can also generate positive local economic impacts. Looking at the case of the Yanacocha gold mine in northern Peru, for example, Aragón and Rud (2014) find that the mine significantly increased local household incomes.

8.2.2. The 'Extractive-Led Development Agenda' (ELDA) and Institutions

The ELDA does, however, acknowledge that while positive examples do exist, many parallel cases highlighted by the resource curse literature point to poor experiences with extractives-based development. Hence the agenda includes initiatives to introduce new governance and policy frameworks that help mitigate the negative externalities by extractive industries (Stevens, Lahn, and Kooroshy, 2015; Lahn and Stevens, 2017). For example, the 'Norwegian model' suggests establishing a professionally managed fund to store resource revenues. The fund can help smooth fiscal spending and support economic diversification by managing investments in infant industries at home or in foreign markets not well represented domestically (Stevens, 2003; Koh, 2017). 'Chile-style' fiscal-related strategies impose limits on borrowing against natural-resource capital and savings rules during boom periods, which can support counter-cyclical fiscal policy and prevent fitful fiscal spending (Frankel, 2012).

Within this agenda, increasingly attention is being devoted to whether particular types of institutional environments are more conducive to preventing the resource curse. Here Acemoglu and Robinson (2012) make a distinction between *inclusive* and *extractive institutions*. Inclusive institutions benefit large segments of the population and support sustained growth by fostering competition and technological innovation. Extractive institutions, instead, generate limited (and often temporary) prosperity for the benefit of a small elite (and strong grievances from other groups that lose out in the distribution of extracted wealth). They are designed to safeguard the uneven distribution of resources for the benefit of a few and maintain the power structures that permit this. Helwege (2015) further describes how the lack of clearly defined rights and norms of redistribution of mining revenues commonly cause local social divisions. Arellano-Yanguas (2011) also provides a notable example of instances in Peru where 'jockeying' for control of resource rents has exacerbated local political conflicts.

Another possible consequence of resource abundance is that the vast sums of public revenues generated can incentivize rent-seeking and corruption (Williams and Le Billon, 2017). For example, the 'Petrobras (or Lava Jato) case' has shown the systemic nature and sheer scale of bribery and money laundering in Brazil's state-owned oil company and may have caused a loss of US$2 billion of public funds. Similarly, the 2008 Peru oil scandal resulted in a public outcry and ultimately in the resignation of Prime Minister Jorge Del Castillo. At the more local level, Caselli and Michaels (2013) also explore the effects of rent-sharing among local governments in Brazil and show that the rise in municipal spending falls short of the increase in royalty payments, and also that this is not due to offsetting reductions in taxes or federal spending. They suggest that the incumbent mayors may be diverting the funds to feed self-enrichment and vote-buying activities. The authors also find that mayors of oil-rich municipalities are more likely to appear in news stories involving corruption, or to be investigated for corruption by the federal police.

It is now widely considered that the natural-resource sector's frequently opaque management has facilitated the incidence of such rent-seeking behaviour and extractive institutions in many contexts (Kasekende, Abuka, and Sarr, 2016). The role of democracy has, as a consequence, become central to these dicussions. For example, as Siegle (2009) suggests, the principles of democracy support political competition, popular participation, and the oversight of public officials. Taken together, these principles may negate patterns of self-serving behaviour and hold governing officials accountable. Critics, though, argue that even in functioning democracies, accountability may be a chimera when information is limited or largely inaccessible (Williams, 2011). Perry and Oliveria (2009) offer evidence that municipalities with better quality and more transparent institutions in Colombia can and do mitigate the incidence of the resource curse. These considerations have contributed to the international demand for transparency in the sector, spearheaded and exemplified by the EITI. We discuss these developments in greater detail next.

8.3. Policy Strategies to Combat the 'Curse of Natural Resources': A Closer Look at the Extractive Industries Transparency Initiative (EITI) in Latin America

The Great Commodity Depression of the late 1980s and 1990s favoured industrialized countries that experienced a sustained period of economic growth, while major commodity producers suffered economic setbacks. These circumstances helped to mainstream the resource curse hypothesis in academic circles, and motivated policy discussions on the macroeconomic and fiscal solutions to address commodity market slumps. However, as the millennium approached, a cycle of high commodity prices produced a shift in research and policy attention towards the potential for natural resources to generate prosperity.

The main obstacle to realizing the potential of extractives to fuel economic development was diagnosed to be institutional, and especially rooted in the rent-seeking behaviour of public officials. Short (2014) describes how journalists and campaigners depicted and fed the discontent among a growing audience during the late 1990s as, despite a strengthening resource sector, the economies of resource-dependent states failed to record marked improvements in growth. We proceed in this section by contextualizing the rise of the EITI following the commodity markets ascent at the beginning of the new millennium. We then further examine the progress of the EITI within Latin America.

8.3.1. The Rise of the EITI

One of the most telling parts of the story leading to the creation of the EITI includes a prominent case in Angola, where both the private oil and banking sectors were found complicit with politicians plundering public assets during the 1990s civil war (van Alstine, 2017), damaging the prospects of the country's development and contributing to entrenching inequalities as the distribution of wealth became concentrated among the political elite. In response to a campaign to ensure that private mining companies followed a policy of full transparency in Angola, British Petroleum (BP) published the payments it had made to the Angolan government, prompting a political backlash (Moberg and Rich, 2012). The Angola-BP experience made clear that disclosure must become a joint procedure to reduce conflict between businesses and states.

This episode, and other similar circumstances, helped to motivate the establishment of an international transparency norm (the EITI) following a meeting between civil society, company, and government representatives convened by the UK Department for International Development (DFID) in 2003. The idea came to fruition in 2009, following an inception period where some trailblazers (including Azerbaijan, Ghana, the Kyrgyz Republic, Nigeria, Peru, the Republic of Congo, Sao Tomé en Principe, Timor Leste, and Trinidad and Tobago) explored how a set of transparency principles may be implemented in the extractive industries. The agreed EITI standard initially focused on the regular publication of information relating to agreements concerning the extraction of natural resources, particularly revenues paid and received by companies and governments. It set out that both parties are to separately disclose this information, and any discrepancies in the information submitted would be made identifiable and would be published.

Significant updates in 2011, 2013, and 2016 have continued to expand the standards informational remit. It now also includes the disclosure of information concerning issues such as the sub-national distribution of revenues and beneficial ownership information. The standard also established that EITI country members should maintain a national multi-stakeholder group comprising private, public, and civil society representatives to enable monitoring of the initiative's implementation and to promote stakeholder dialogue. Furthermore, they are required to undergo regular independent audits (i.e. validation) of their progress and compliance with the standard. A global secretariat oversees the implementation of the EITI, the validation process, and coordinates international activity (such as conferences and training events).

This validation process has created different categories of members, with each category representing the proximity (or stage) of a country to becoming compliant with the initiative's standard. For instance, in the first stage, the government of the prospective participating country announces its commitment to the EITI. In the second stage, a country completes the application and becomes a formal candidate. Countries that prove compliance with the various requirements of the transparency standard graduate to the compliant member status. Members are required to re-validate their compliance periodically, at least every three years.

These steps are not a mere formality, and there is often a significant time gap between the expression of commitment and acknowledgement of candidature. Lujala (2018) reports that countries take, on average, 17 months to become formal candidates after making the initial commitment, and another four years to progress to full compliance. Since 2016 a more disaggregated and regular scoring system for new entrants, with specific timeframes for implementing countries, has been introduced. This new scoring system also clearly highlights that EITI affiliation will be removed (i.e. members will be 'de-listed') in case of lack of progress in implementation. This is a response to previous criticisms of mock-compliance (Öge, 2016). The initiative continues to review and update this process, and further changes are expected to be made to the validation scoring system in the coming years (Fenton Villar, 2021c).

While there is no universally accepted theory on the effects of transparency in natural-resource management (Rustad, Le Billon, and Lujala, 2017), the growth of demand for greater transparency globally has primarily stemmed from the idea that transparency may help to reduce public malfeasance through its 'sunshine effect'. That is, by diluting the agency problem caused by information asymmetry, higher levels of transparency may empower citizens to better identify misuse or exploitation of natural resources (Stiglitz, 2007; Van Alstine, 2017). Fenton Villar (2021a) further describes that transparency also acts as a deterrent to the possibility of corrupt activity as the risk of being uncovered increases.

Greater transparency may also incentivize more diligent management of natural resources (Fenton Villar, 2021c), and Brunnschweiler et al. (2021) highlight how public knowledge of resource revenue management enhances citizen interest in the sector. Active public and civil society actors can generate public scrutiny over government actions (Epremian, Lujala, and Bruch, 2016). Moreover, public officials often assert that disclosure may help them to address common public misconceptions concerning their agreements with private companies. Given the possible link between trust in public institutions and transparency, the latter may help remove barriers to oversight and inherently increase confidence in the public system of management (Fenton Villar, 2020).

More critical observers consider transparency as a necessary, but not a sufficient, condition to guarantee the effective management of extractive industries (Pellegrini, 2019). In fact, transparency may only work in tandem with accountability, which in turn rests on the effective working of democratic processes and, more generally, the possibility for the citizens to rely on mechanisms of redress in case of malfeasance. Thus, the conditions for accountability would include a fair electoral process with competitive political parties, capable and independent mass media, an effective judiciary, and citizens that are confident in the rule of law—just to mention a few. Thus, knowledge of mismanagement would be crucial only in countries with solid democratic institutions—a currency that is rare in Latin America and beyond.

Existing reviews of the EITI describe the perceived benefits associated with countries joining and complying with the initiative. These benefits include improved international reputation and increased receipt of aid and foreign investment (Neumann et al., 2016). However, studies offer contrasting conclusions on the initiative's effects on development outcomes (Rustad, Le Billon, and Lujala, 2017).

Papyrakis et al. (2017) show that perceptions about corruption are improving for EITI members compared to non-members and that EITI commitment can offset the largest part (approximately 70%–80%) of any corruption-increasing effect arising from natural-resource dependence. However, Sovacool et al. (2016) find that the EITI is not significantly related with improvements in perceptions of corruption, as well as a broader set of governance indicators concerning perceptions of accountability and rule of law. Kasekende et al. (2016) go as far as to suggest that EITI membership may increase the levels of corruption. An ongoing methodological debate attempts to explain this heterogeneity in empirical findings. It suggests that, due to the heterogeneity between EITI and non-EITI country characteristics, an analysis of the EITI warrants more sophisticated statistical techniques than those that have been typically applied (Lujala, 2018; Fenton Villar, 2021a).

Regional, country-specific, or even sub-national studies on the EITI are limited and focus mostly on African states. For example, Hilson and Maconachie (2009) provide an early review of the EITI in Sub-Saharan Africa. More recent studies have examined the experiences of specific countries: for example, Nigeria (Bature, 2014), Zambia (Fenton Villar and Papyrakis, 2017), and Liberia (Sovacool and Andrews, 2015). Others have looked at the experiences among the gas republics of Eurasia, such as Azerbaijan and Kyrgyzstan (e.g. see Sovacool and Andrews, 2015; Öge, 2015). However, only scarce examples are available concerning Latin America (as discussed further below).

8.3.2. The EITI in Latin America: An Overview of Progress and Findings

The uptake of the EITI in Latin America has been gathering momentum in recent years, although membership remains low with only approximately a third ($n = 10$) of Latin American countries joining the initiative (Table 8.1). Most notably, some of the region's most resource-dependent economies remain dissidents of the initiative (Chile and Venezuela). Likewise, Brazil, the

Table 8.1 EITI Uptake and Country Progress in Latin America

Country	EITI Member	Commit	Candidate	Compliant	2016+ Validation	Suspension	Suspension Lifted
Argentina	Yes	2017	2019		N/A		
Belize	No						
Bolivia	No						
Brazil	No						
Chile	No						
Colombia	Yes	2013	2014	2018	SP		
Costa Rica	No						
Cuba	No						
Dom. Rep.	Yes	2015	2016		MP		
Ecuador	Yes	2020	2020		N/A		
El Salvador	No						
French Gui.	No						
Guadeloupe	No						
Guatemala	Yes	2010	2011	2014	IP	2015 / 2020	2015 / NA
Guyana	Yes	2010	2017		N/A		
Haiti	No						
Honduras	Yes	2012	2013		MP	2020	

(*continued*)

Table 8.1 Continued

Country	EITI Member	Commit	Candidate	Compliant	2016+ Validation	Suspension	Suspension Lifted
Martinique	No						
Mexico	Yes	2015	2017		N/A		
Nicaragua	No						
Panama	No						
Paraguay	No						
Peru	Yes	2005	2007	2012	MP		
Puerto Rico	No						
St. Martin	No						
St.-Barthél.	No						
Suriname	Yes	2016	2017		MP	2019	2019
Uruguay	No						
Venezuela	No						

Data Source: EITI (2021)

Notes: 2016+ validation refers to the updated validation procedure introduced in 2016. IP = Inadequate Progress; MP = Meaningful Progress; SP = Satisfactory Progress; N/A = Not Available (due to not undertaking a validation using the new standard).

largest and most populous economy in the region, has not committed to the initiative either.

Bebbington et al. (2017) elaborate on the national politics that can play out during the decision to join (or not) the initiative. For example, in Bolivia, President Morales found the EITI to be too closely related to the World Bank and other Western powers, and the type of initiative that his predecessors would have joined. Bolivia sought alternative arrangements for promoting transparency, although progress has been 'patchy and largely driven by political settlement' (Bebbington et al. 2017, p. 840). While some progress has been made in recent years following commitments from countries such as Ecuador, Mexico, Argentina, and Suriname, there is still considerable ground to mainstream the EITI's international standards across Latin America.

As in other regions of the world, EITI members' journeys to compliance have been slow across Latin America. Following their commitment, it has taken 5 to 6 years for the three members that have managed to reach the compliant status to do so. Others, such as Guyana, have been committed to the EITI for nearly a decade and are yet to be validated as compliant because of a lengthy process of commissioning and deliberating over a scoping study before becoming a formal candidate. It will be interesting to see whether the implementation of the new validation process increases the speed at which the initiatives' recent and new joiners progress, as well as whether this will motivate or crowd out laggards.

Colombia currently leads the region as Latin America's most advanced EITI member, with the highest validation score—satisfactory progress—in 2018. Meanwhile, despite previously being designated compliant and widely considered an innovator among EITI members (as detailed below), Peru has most recently been validated as only making 'meaningful progress' (equivalent to a candidate score by previous standards). A point of interest in the coming years includes whether the threat of suspension will motivate Peru in meeting all of the EITI's standards.

The potential 'political embarrassment' of suspension has to some degree been successful so far in pushing EITI members to complete the actions that are required to maintain their status. For example, following suspension in 2015 for failing to submit the 2012 country report in time, Guatemala published the necessary information and got the suspension lifted in the same year. Similar events occurred again in Suriname in 2019. However, both Honduras and Guatemala were later suspended in 2020 after being found to have made inadequate progress during the validation process, an issue that is yet to be resolved (as both remain suspended).

Table 8.2 reports a summary of revenues from the extractives sector disclosed by governments in the EITI reporting procedure. Since several countries are new to the EITI, information remains relatively sparse—as of mid-2021—and in

Table 8.2 Summary of Disclosed Government Revenues from EITI reports (USD, Millions)

	Argentina	Colombia	Dominican Republic	Guatemala	Guyana	Honduras	Mexico	Peru	Suriname
2004								886 (0%)	
2005								1,758 (0%)	
2006								2,925 (0%)	
2007								3,122 (0%)	
2008								3,574 (0%)	
2009								2,965 (0%)	
2010				165 (100%)				4,358 (0%)	
2011				225 (100%)				5,884 (0%)	
2012				207 (0%)		184 (0%)		5,481 (0%)	
2013		18,910 (5%)		184 (0%)		12 (0%)		5,511 (0%)	
2014		14,131 (0%)		167 (5%)		13 (0%)		1,463 (0%)	
2015		5,098 (0%)	356 (32%)	108 (13%)		9 (11%)		2,285 (10%)	
2016		3,441 (10%)	323 (6%)			23 (5%)	19,689 (3%)	2,525 (11%)	90 (11%)
2017			361 (1%)		93 (38%)		19,865 (3%)		243 (37%)
2018	3,247 (43%)		219 (2%)		69 (33%)		24,989 (5%)		

Data Source: EITI (2021)

Notes: % of government revenues not reconciled from company disclosure reported in parentheses ().

some instances the latest data are several years old. Looking at the figures shown in parenthesis in Table 8.2, there are numerous cases where countries have not been able to fully reconcile information reported independently by governments and companies. For example, the Colombian government's disclosed revenues in 2013 and 2016 were 5% and 10% larger than those disclosed by companies. In 2015 and 2016, the Dominican Republic's government disclosures were 32% and 6% larger than companies' reported figures, and in Peru, they were 10% and 11% greater.

These issues bring into question the relevance and accuracy of EITI data. First, the time delay in the publication of information may undermine its use in current debates or ensure that current political leaders are held accountable. Changes in leadership or responsibilities occur regularly among the politicians and senior civil servants, and those currently in office may claim some degree of plausible deniability. Second, if companies do not provide complete and consistent information on transactions with the government, as may be the case when government receipts remain significantly higher than company disclosures, then the use of this reconciliation exercise may be undermined. Ensuring standardized systems of reporting between governments and mining companies (to provide more useful and reliable evidence) remains a challenge.

Table 8.3 summarizes details of information disclosure in each EITI country showing that, broadly speaking, members are performing well in maintaining records of licenses and contracts awarded. Significant progress is still required, though, to ensure the availability of information that may be of most interest to local stakeholders. For example, access to social expenditures and subnational transfers and payments could still be improved. Also, the rollout of new requirements concerning beneficial ownership information is still ongoing. For instance, Peru has published a 'road map' outlining the procedures they will take to make this disclosure possible. Future challenges in this space may exist, though, as reviews by some EITI countries such as Honduras find current laws do not permit mandatory disclosure of beneficial ownership data (EITI, 2021).

Evidence of the wider effects and the implications of the EITI in Latin America also remains limited. Even within the EITI Secretariat, there has been criticism over the lack of rigorous impact assessments (Arond, Bebbington, and Dammert, 2019). Using data from the World Bank's Enterprise Survey, Etter (2012) produced some early evidence of the effects of the initiative on perceptions of corruption in Peru using within-country variation in firms' interaction with the government and a cross-country comparison. It addresses concerns of selection bias matching the pre-EITI country and firm characteristics using pre-process techniques known as the Synthetic Control Method and Entropy Balancing. The results show a

Table 8.3 Summary of Further Information Disclosure in EITI Countries in Latin America.

	Argentina	Colombia	Dominican Republic	Guatemala	Guyana	Honduras	Mexico	Peru	Suriname
Are revenues from the extractive industry recorded in the government accounts/budget?	Yes	Yes	Yes	Yes	Yes	Partially	Yes	Yes	Yes
Is there a public register of licences?	Yes	Yes	Partially	Yes	Yes	Yes	Yes	Yes	No
Information about awarding and transfer of licences	Yes	Yes	Yes	Yes	Yes	Yes	Yes	Yes	No
Is information available about Beneficial Ownership?	Yes	Yes	No	No	Yes	No	No	No	No
Does the report address the government's policy on contract disclosure?	Yes	Yes	Yes	Yes	Yes	Yes	Yes	Yes	No
Are contracts disclosed?	Yes	Yes	Partially	Yes	Yes	Yes	Yes	Yes	No
Does the report address sale of the state's share of production or other sales collected in-kind?	N/A	Yes	N/A	N/A	N/A	N/A	Yes	No	Yes
Does the report address Infrastructure provisions and barter arrangements?	N/A	Yes	N/A	No	N/A	N/A	No	No	N/A
Does the report address social expenditures?	N/A	Yes	N/A	No	N/A	Yes	No	Yes	N/A
Does the report address Transportation revenues?	N/A	Yes	N/A	N/A	N/A	N/A	No	Yes	N/A
Does the report address sub-national payments?	N/A	Yes	Yes	Yes	N/A	Yes	No	No	N/A
Does the report address sub-national transfers?	N/A	Yes	Yes	Yes	N/A	N/A	No	No	N/A

Source: Elaborated from EITI data

Note: N/A = EITI data reports that the disclosure is not applicable.

14-percentage-point reduction in the prevalence of corruption reported by firms following their commitment to the EITI. It also shows that firms in Peru that interact with the government consistently report less corruption after the introduction of EITI than firms that are not interacting with the government.

However, a more recent analysis by López-Cazar et al. (2021) on the EITI's impact on several corruption measures in four Latin American countries (Colombia, Guatemala, Honduras, and Peru) casts doubt on how decisive the scheme has been in combating corruption. Their impact evaluation study focuses on three different types of institutional outcomes. First, it examines EITI impacts on the 'control of corruption' index of the World Bank's World Governance Indicators. This indicator measures 'the perception of the extent to which public power is exercised for private gain, as well as the capture of the state by elites and private interests', on a scale from −2.5 to 2.5. This is an index with a broad focus that captures perceptions of both petty and grand corruption. The authors adjusted the original scale so that larger values stand for higher levels of corruption (rather than its control).

Second, the authors evaluate the effect of participation in the EITI scheme on 'public sector corruption'. This index captures respondent perceptions regarding the extent to which 'public sector employees grant favors in exchange for bribes, kickbacks, or inducements, and steal, embezzle, or misappropriate public funds or other state resources for personal or family use' (López-Cazar et al. 2021, p. 5). This relates more closely to corrupt practices by low-ranked public officials. Third, the study examines EITI impacts on grand 'regime corruption'. This third outcome variable relates to the extent to which high-ranked (executive, legislative, and judicial) officials and politicians take advantage of their positions in office for own benefit. Both public sector and regime corruption are measured on a scale from 0 to 1 (with larger valued denoting a higher level of corruption) and come from the V-Dem dataset.

A summary of results from the evaluation by López-Cazar et al. (2021) is presented in Table 8.4. The table disaggregates the impact on corruption across the different stages of participation in the EITI scheme (i.e. during the commitment, candidature, and compliance stages). The synthetic control estimates suggest that, for most years, there was no statistically significant reduction in corruption following participation in the scheme (i.e. in relation to the counterfactual synthetic units). For regime corruption, this was only the case for Peru after EITI compliance. The size of the EITI effects (presented in Table 8.4 for the statistically-significant impacts) also appears to be relatively modest. The inability of the EITI scheme to reduce corruption in participating countries can be attributed to multiple factors (e.g. tensions between local communities and extractive companies, limited participation of civil society, chronic entrenched corruption in the extractive sector that leaves little room for improvement and

Table 8.4 EITI Impact on Corruption (Colombia, Guatemala, Honduras, and Peru).

Country	EITI Stage (Years)	Control of Corruption Impact	Regime Corruption Impact	Public Sector Corruption Impact
Colombia	Commitment (2013)	+	+	+ (0.09)*
	Candidate (2014–2017)	+	+	+ (0.07)**
Guatemala	Commitment (2010)	–	+	+
	Candidate (2011–2013)	–	+ (0.08)*	–
	Compliant (2014–2017)	+	+ (0.07)*	–
Honduras	Commitment (2012)	+	–	+
	Candidate (2013–2017)	–	+	+
Peru	Commitment (2005–2006)	+	+	+
	Candidate (2007–2011)	–	+ (0.10)*	+
	Compliant (2012–2017)	+	– (0.05)*	+

Notes: ** and * correspond to 5% and 10% levels of statistical significance. +/– denotes higher/lower corruption levels with respect to synthetic unit. Size of effect (in relation to counterfactual synthetic unit) presented in parenthesis (for statistically significant results).
Source: López-Cazar et al. (2021).

weak governance; see López-Cazar et al., 2021, for a detailed discussion at the country level).

Other evidence has examined the functioning of the Multi-Stakeholder Groups (a feature of the EITI process which has received criticism as a toothless accountability mechanism). Based on evidence from interviews with non-governmental organization (NGO) staff and key participants in the EITI process in Colombia and Peru, I et al. (2019) highlight the informants' belief that the groups have allowed more open dialogue between the industries' stakeholders, granting civil society greater access to decision-makers. In turn, company and government officials have had to include new indicators in their reporting or open new areas for debate to satisfy the requests of the other stakeholders. This indicates the potential role these groups can have in influencing changes in the public governance of natural resources.

However, Arond et al. (2019) also suggest that the EITI remains largely an elite platform in both countries because of the demand on resources and capacities required to effectively participate in these groups. In addition, Jayasinghe and Ezpeleta (2020) explain how in the Dominican Republic traditional gender norms (regarding gender-assigned roles in the household division of labour) effectively prevent women from participating in the EITI multi-stakeholder group and, hence, restrict their ability to influence spending of extractive revenues. Furthermore, there are signs of participative exhaustion or fatigue since the information brought forward by the EITI is too complex and lacks simple messages which may provide a more effective way to provide engaging and influential discussions in broader society (Arond, Bebbington, and Dammert, 2019).

Overall, significant room for improvement exists in expanding and mainstreaming the provision of information concerning the extractive industries in Latin America. Nevertheless, it is also important to highlight the significant innovations that Latin American countries are contributing to progressing the implementation of transparency standards globally. Perhaps chief among these have been Peru's experimentation with the sub-national implementation of the EITI. Supported by the World Bank, 4 out of 5 planned regions (in Arequipa, Moquegua, Piura, and Apurimac) have established regional multi-stakeholder groups and have published regional EITI reports. This paves the way for understanding how the EITI may be relevant at more local or meso-levels. Colombia has also launched an online training platform providing information about the extractive industries and explaining how citizens can participate in accountability processes. Further to this, they have experimented with inclusion of environmental information in their information disclosures.

The latter of these innovations build on a point brought forward by civil society groups during the inception of the EITI in Colombia. This suggested that local populations value access to environmental information at least as much as they value access to financial information (Monge, 2014). Enforcing environmental legislation concerning resource extraction is recognized as a challenge in the region and, for example, a recent study by Bornschlegl (2018) describes the difficulty in enforcing environmental laws in the hydrocarbon sector in Ecuador. Supporting local engagement through increased access to information may help to break cycles of low levels of enforcement and ensure follow-up. It is due to the steps taken by innovators such as Colombia that the EITI has taken the next step to include new provisions in its global standard to support the disclosure of environmental monitoring and environmental payments by companies (EITI, 2021).

8.4. Conclusions

Contemporary advancements in theory and understanding concerning the potential problems associated with natural-resource extraction are offering a more critical perspective on the extractive imperative in development. In particular, the premise of the rising Extractive-Led Development Agenda (ELDA) is that many of the negative externalities associated with natural-resource extraction are avoidable (or can be mitigated) with 'appropriate' public governance of the sector. A key area of discussion is the likelihood that institutional environments may be conducive to securing the good governance of natural resources in Latin America.

In this respect, the rise of the EITI's standards over the past two decades is now widely viewed as a major advancement in tackling issues that have historically plagued the governance of natural resources: corruption or diversion of resource funds to a combination of public self-enrichment and vote-buying activities. The links associating transparency and improvements in the governance of the extractive sector include diluting the agency problem, de- incentivizing (or increasing the risk of) public malfeasance and increasing public scrutiny by increasing demand for information.

While the evolution of the EITI globally has been significant, our review of the progress of the initiative in Latin America is somewhat less encouraging. Our findings show that membership in the region is growing, but it still remains limited and that progress among those countries that have joined has been slow. There are some unfolding contributions concerning the EITI's practical development of transparency standards in Latin America, including experimenting with the implementation of transparency standards at sub-national levels in Peru and environmental disclosure standards in Colombia. However, perhaps the most interesting question is whether the EITI can help to mark the departure from a history of misgovernance of natural resources in Latin America, or whether we are witnessing another extractive development failure in the making. The jury is still out here, but so far there is limited evidence of any Latin American country comprehensively improving its approach to the management of extractive industries as a consequence of the EITI.

Several reviews (in particular reviews of the EITI) have recently highlighted the need for some 'middle' theory that further links the association between transparency and good governance with more specific intervention actions and concrete objectives (e.g. see Acosta, 2014; and Rustad, Le Billon, and Lujala, 2017). Two key ambiguities concern (i) the type and format of the information that is required (or desired) by stakeholders, and (ii) determining an effective means of delivery of information. These points offer an interesting avenue for future research, and we expect future work to continue in this vein. For example, Pellegrini (2019) recently experimented with the dissemination of information on environmental liabilities generated by hydrocarbon extraction (oil spills, disposal of highly contaminated formation waters and drilling muds, etc.) in the Ecuadoran and Peruvian Amazon using inexpensive high-tech tools (such as mobile phones and online apps). The experiment finds that such tools may contribute to improvements in public awareness, but enhanced operational practices and environmental outcomes depend on the effectiveness of accountability mechanisms.

References

Acemoglu, D., and Robinson, J. 2012. *Why Nations Fail: The Origins of Power, Prosperity, and Poverty*. London: Profile Books.

Acosta, A. 2014. 'The Extractive Industries Transparency Initiative: Impact, Effectiveness, and Where Next for Expanding Natural Resource Governance', *U4 Brief*, (6), 1–16.

Aragón, F. M., and Rud, J. P. 2013. 'Natural Resources and Local Communities: Evidence from a Peruvian Gold Mine', *American Economic Journal: Economic Policy*, 5(2), 1–25.

Arellano Yanguas, J. 2010. 'Local Politics, Conflict and Development in Peruvian Mining Regions'. PhD thesis, Institute of Development Studies, University of Sussex.

Arellano-Yanguas, J. 2011. 'Aggravating the Resource Curse: Decentralisation, Mining and Conflict in Peru', *The Journal of Development Studies*, 47(4), 617–638.

Arond, E., Bebbington, A., and Dammert, J. 2019. 'NGOs as Innovators in Extractive Industry Governance: Insights from the EITI Process in Colombia and Peru', *The Extractive Industries and Society*, 6(3), 665–674.

Arsel, M., Hogenboom, B., and Pellegrini, L. 2016. 'The Extractive Imperative in Latin America', *The Extractive Industries and Society*, 3(4), 880–887.

Arsel, M., Pellegrini, L., and Mena, C. 2019. 'Maria's Paradox and the Misery of Missing Development Alternatives in the Ecuadorian Amazon', in P. Shaffer, R. Kanbur, and R. Sandbrook, eds., *Immiserizing Growth: When Growth Fails the Poor*. Oxford: Oxford University Press, 203–225. https://doi.org/10.1093/oso/9780198832317.001.0001.

Balassa, B. 1980. *The Process of Industrial Development and Alternative Development Strategies*. Princeton, NJ: Princeton University.

Bature, B. 2014. 'Transparency and Accountability: Adaptation and Implementation of Extractive Industries Transparency Initiative (EITI) Principles in Nigeria', *The Macrotheme Review*, 3(8), 107–114.

Bebbington, A., Arond, E., and Dammert, J. L. 2017. 'Explaining Diverse National Responses to the Extractive Industries Transparency Initiative in the Andes: What Sort of Politics Matters?', *The Extractive Industries and Society*, 4(4), 833–841.

Bornschlegl, T. 2018. 'Petro-Geographies and the Dialectic of the Everyday: Enforcing Environmental Laws in the Hydrocarbon Sector in Post-Neoliberal Ecuador', *Journal of Latin American Geography*, 17(3), 15–41.

Brunnschweiler, C., Edjekumhene, I., and Lujala, P. 2021. 'Does Information Matter? Transparency and Demand for Accountability in Ghana's Natural Resource Revenue Management', *Ecological Economics*, 181, 1–14.

Caselli, F., and Michaels, G. 2013. 'Do Oil Windfalls Improve Living Standards? Evidence from Brazil', *American Economic Journal: Applied Economics*, 5(1), 208–238.

Collier, P., and Laroche, C. 2015. *Harnessing Natural Resources for Inclusive Growth*. London: The International Growth Centre.

Davis, M. J. M., Fedelino, M. A., and Ossowski, M. R. 2003. *Fiscal Policy Formulation and Implementation in Oil-Producing Countries*. Washington, DC: International Monetary Fund.

Dell, M. 2010. 'The Persistent Effects of Peru's Mining Mita', *Econometrica*, 78(6), 1863–1903.

Easterly, W. 1999. 'The Ghost of Financing Gap: Testing the Growth Model Used in the International Financial Institutions', *Journal of Development Economics*, 60(2), 423–438.

Engel, E., Rubio, D. F., Kaufmann, D., et al. 2018. *Report of the Expert Advisory Group on Anti-Corruption, Transparency, and Integrity in Latin America and the Caribbean*. Washington, DC: Inter-American Development Bank.

Epremian, L., Lujala, P., and Bruch, C. 2016. 'High-Value Natural Resources and Transparency: Accounting for Revenues and Governance, in Thompson, ed., *Oxford Research Encyclopedia of Politics*. Oxford: Oxford University Press, 1–34.

Etter, L. 2012. 'Can Transparency Reduce Corruption? Evidence from Firms in Peru and Mali on the Impact of the Extractive Industries Transparency Initiative (EITI) on Corruption'. Presented at: The Doing Business Conference at Georgetown University. Washington, DC, 20–21 February.

Extractive Industries Transparency Initiative. 2021. Retrieved from https://eiti.org/homepage.

Fenton Villar, P. 2020. 'The Extractive Industries Transparency Initiative (EITI) and Trust in Politicians', *Resources Policy*, 68, 1–13.

Fenton Villar, P. 2021a. 'An Assessment of the Extractive Industries Transparency Initiative (EITI) Using the Bayesian Corruption Indicator', *Environment and Development Economics*, 27(5), 414–435.

Fenton Villar, P. 2021b. 'Is There a Mineral-Induced "Economic Euphoria"?: Evidence from Latin America', *Journal of Happiness Studies*, 23, 1403–1430.

Fenton Villar, P. 2021c. 'The Extractive Industries Transparency Initiative (EITI) and the Technical Reforms Model: Insights from the Global Performance Assessments Literature', *The Extractive Industries and Society*, 8(4), 1–9.

Fenton Villar, P., and Papyrakis, E. 2017. 'Evaluating the Impact of the Extractive Industries Transparency Initiative (EITI) on Corruption in Zambia', *The Extractive Industries and Society*, 4(4), 795–805.

Frankel, J. A. 2012. 'The Natural Resource Curse: A Survey of Diagnoses and some Prescriptions', John F. Kennedy School of Government, Harvard University.

Gilberthorpe, E., and Papyrakis, E. 2015. 'The Extractive Industries and Development: The Resource Curse at the Micro, Meso and Macro Levels', *The Extractive Industries and Society*, 2(2), 381–390.

Hamilton, E. J. 1934. *American Treasure and the Price Revolution in Spain, 1501–1650*, Vol. 1125. Cambridge, MA: Harvard University Press.

Helwege, A. 2015. 'Challenges with Resolving Mining Conflicts in Latin America', *The Extractive Industries and Society*, 2(1), 73–84.

Hilson, G., and Maconachie, R. 2009. 'The Extractive Industries Transparency Initiative: Panacea or White Elephant for Sub-Saharan Africa?', in J. Richards, ed., *Mining, Society, and a Sustainable World*. Cham, Switzerland: Springer, 469–491.

Holden, S. 2013. 'Avoiding the Resource Curse the Case Norway', *Energy Policy*, 63, 870–876.

Jayasinghe, N., and Ezpeleta, M. 2020. 'Ensuring Women Follow the Money: Gender Barriers in Extractive Industry Revenue Accountability: The Dominican Republic and Zambia', *The Extractive Industries and Society*, 7(2), 428–434.

Kasekende, E., Abuka, C., and Sarr, M. 2016. 'Extractive Industries and Corruption: Investigating the Effectiveness of EITI as a Scrutiny Mechanism', *Resources Policy*, 48, 117–128.

Koh, W. C. 2017. 'Fiscal Policy in Oil-Exporting Countries: The Roles of Oil Funds and Institutional Quality', *Review of Development Economics*, 21(3), 567–590.

Lahn, G., and Stevens, P. 2017. 'The Curse of the One-Size-Fits-All Fix: Re-evaluating What We Know about Extractives and Economic Development'. WIDER Working Paper. Helsinki: UN-WIDER.

Le Billon, P., and Good, E. 2016. 'Responding to the Commodity Bust: Downturns, Policies and Poverty in Extractive Sector Dependent Countries', *The Extractive Industries and Society*, 3(1), 204–216.

Lewis, W. A. 1955. *Theory of Economic Growth*. Homewood, IL: R. D. Irwin.

López-Cazar, I., Papyrakis, E., and Pellegrini, L. 2021. 'The Extractive Industries Transparency Initiative (EITI) and Corruption in Latin America: Evidence from Colombia, Guatemala, Honduras, Peru, and Trinidad and Tobago', *Resources Policy*, 70, 1–24.

Lujala, P. 2018. 'An Analysis of the Extractive Industry Transparency Initiative Implementation Process', *World Development*, 107, 358–381.

Moberg, J., and Rich, E. 2012. 'Beyond Governments: Lessons on Multi-Stakeholder Governance from the Extractive Industries Transparency Initiative (EITI)', in M. Pieth, ed., *Collective Action: Innovative Strategies to Prevent Corruption*. Basel: Dike, 113–124.

Monge, C. 2014. 'EITI and the Environment: Colombian CSOs Look to Broaden Their Reporting Content'. Retrieved from Natural Resource Governance Institute website: http://www.resourcegovernance.org/blog/eiti-and-environment-colombian-csos-look-broaden-their-reporting-content.

Moss, T., Lambert, C., and Majerowicz, S. 2015. *Oil to Cash: Fighting the Resource Curse through Cash Transfers*. Washington, DC: CGD Books.

Neumann, L., Silvestrini, S., Strauss, T., et al. 2016. *Assessing the Effectiveness and Impact of the Extractive Industries Transparency Initiative (EITI): Short Version Russian*. Bonn, Germany: GIZ.

Neumayer, E. 2004. 'Does the "Resource Curse" Hold for Growth in Genuine Income as Well?', *World Development*, 32(10), 1627–1640.

Öge, K. 2015. 'Geopolitics and Revenue Transparency in Turkmenistan and Azerbaijan', *Eurasian Geography and Economics*, 56(1), 89–110.

Öge, K. 2016. 'Which Transparency Matters? Compliance with Anti-Corruption Efforts in Extractive Industries', *Resources Policy*, 49, 41–50.

Papyrakis, E., and Gerlagh, R. 2007. 'Resource Abundance and Economic Growth in the United States', *European Economic Review*, 51(4), 1011–1039.

Papyrakis, E., and Pellegrini, L. 2019. 'The Resource Curse in Latin America', in W. R. Thompson, ed., *Oxford Research Encyclopedia of Politics*. Oxford: Oxford University Press, 1–20.

Papyrakis, E., Rieger, M. and Gilberthorpe, E. 2017. 'Corruption and the Extractive Industries Transparency Initiative', *The Journal of Development Studies*, 53, 295–309.

Pellegrini, L. 2018. 'Imaginaries of Development through Extraction: The 'History of Bolivian Petroleum' and the Present View of the Future', *Geoforum*, 90, 130–141.

Pellegrini, L. 2019. *Community Monitoring Of Socio-Environmental Liabilities with Advanced Technologies in the Ecuadorian and Peruvian Amazon, 3ie Grantee Final Report*. New Delhi: International Initiative for Impact Evaluation (3ie).

Pellegrini, L., Tasciotti, L., and Spartaco, A. 2021. 'A Regional Resource Curse? A Synthetic-Control Approach to Oil Extraction in Basilicata, Italy', *Ecological Economics*, 185, 1–13. https://doi.org/10/gjpv5n

Perry, G., and Olivera, M. 2009. 'Natural Resources, Institutions and Economic Performance'. *FEDESARROLLO Publications*, 15. Bogotá, Colombia.

Rostow, W. W. 1960. *The Stages of Growth: A Non-Communist Manifesto*. Cambridge: Cambridge University Press.

Rustad, S. A., Le Billon, P., and Lujala, P. 2017. 'Has the Extractive Industries Transparency Initiative Been a Success? Identifying and Evaluating EITI Goals', *Resources Policy*, 51, 151–162.

Sachs, J. D., and Warner, A. M. 2001. 'The Curse of Natural Resources', *European Economic Review*, 45(4–6), 827–838.

Segal, P. 2012. *Fiscal Policy and Natural Resource Entitlements: Who Benefits from Mexican Oil?* Oxford: Oxford Institute for Energy Studies.

Short, C. 2014. 'The Development of the Extractive Industries Transparency Initiative', *Journal of World Energy Law and Business*, 7(1), 8–15.

Siegle, J. 2009. 'Governance Strategies to Remedy the Natural Resource Curse', *International Social Science Journal*, 57(1), 45–55.

Sovacool, B., and Andrews, N. 2015. 'Does Transparency Matter? Evaluating the Governance Impacts of the Extractive Industries Transparency Initiative (EITI) in Azerbaijan and Liberia', *Resources Policy*, 45, 183–192.

Sovacool, B., Walter, G., Van De Graaf, T., and Andrews, N. 2016. 'Energy Governance, Transnational Rules, and the Resource Curse: Exploring the Effectiveness of the Extractive Industries Transparency Initiative (EITI')', *World Development*, 83, 179–192.

Stevens, P. 2003. 'Resource Impact: Curse or Blessing? A Literature Survey', *Journal of Energy Literature*, 9(1), 3–42.

Stevens, P., Lahn, G., and Kooroshy, J. 2015. *The Resource Curse Revisited*. London, England: Chatham House for the Royal Institute of International Affairs.

Stiglitz, J. E. 2007. 'What Is the Role of the State?' *Escaping the Resource Curse*, M. Humphreys, JD Sachs and JE Stiglitz, eds. New York: Columbia University Press, 23–52.

Usui, N. 1997. 'Dutch Disease and Policy Adjustments to the Oil Boom: A Comparative Study of Indonesia and Mexico', *Resources Policy*, 23(4), 151–162.

van Alstine, J. 2017. 'Critical Reflections on 15 Years of the Extractive Industries Transparency Initiative (EITI)', *The Extractive Industries and Society*, 4(4), 766–770.

Venables, A. J. 2016. 'Using Natural Resources for Development: Why Has It Proven So Difficult?', *Journal of Economic Perspectives*, 30(1), 161–184.

Viner, J. 1953. *International Trade and Economic Development*. Glencoe, IL: Free Press.

Williams, A. 2011. 'Shining a Light on the Resource Curse: An Empirical Analysis of the Relationship between Natural Resources, Transparency, and Economic Growth', *World Development*, 39(4), 490–505.

Williams, A., and Le Billon, P. 2017. *Corruption, Natural Resources and Development: From Resource Curse to Political Ecology*. Cheltenham, UK: Edward Elgar.

9

Environmental, Energy, and Sustainability Issues

Tereza Bicalho, Rodrigo A. Bellezoni, and Jose A. Puppim de Oliveira

9.1. Introduction

Environmental resources are related in various ways to the forms of policies for innovation and development styles historically prevailing in Latin America, with energy playing a key role in all natural or intervened processes in the biosphere, particularly in the functioning of the built environment, industrialization, and transport. Indeed, the relative importance of energy sources has varied with time and technological development, exerting a decisive influence on the forms and styles of development. In the context of sustainability transition and response to the challenges of climate change, countries are developing strategies in order to explore opportunities, risks, and benefits, based on the priorities and characteristics of each region, as there are several pathways to more sustainable energy system in the socio-technical transitions (Geels, 2004; Geels and Schot, 2007). The push for sustainability transitions under climate change could be an opportunity for Latin America to technologically leapfrog developed countries, as the region is well-positioned in terms of renewable energy. Indeed, Latin America ranked well in the carbon intensity of the energy sector as compared to other regions of the world historically (ESCAP et al., 2016).

A fundamental element in these transitions, and one that stands out as a consensus, is the role of innovation in the search for sustainable solutions in increasingly complex and dynamic energy systems. Therefore, in an environment where technology is a key factor in the insertion of any country in the global economy, mapping and understanding the key players, the legal and economic mechanisms, and the quality of the efforts in research, development, and innovation (RD&I) can be determinant in the success of the national sustainable development strategy (CEPAL/CGEE, 2020a). The socio-technical system can be disrupted in several ways to allow new energy transitions (Johnstone et al., 2020).

In the energy sector, industrial revolutions have generally been associated with an increase in efficiency and in the supply of energy produced from fossil sources such as coal, oil, and gas. The adverse effects of industrial development,

Tereza Bicalho, Rodrigo A. Bellezoni, and Jose A. Puppim de Oliveira, *Environmental, Energy, and Sustainability Issues*
In: *Innovation, Competitiveness, and Development in Latin America.* Edited by: Edmund Amann and Paulo N. Figueiredo, Oxford University Press. DOI: 10.1093/oso/9780197648070.003.0009

which was focused on rapid economic growth at the expense of scarce natural resources, caused various impacts on health and the environment, mainly through the release of local air pollutants (SO_x and NO_x) and greenhouse gases (GHGs), such as carbon dioxide.

However, twenty-first-century industrial revolutions, such as Industry 4.0 and low-carbon transitions, are, in essence, technological revolutions that prioritize environmental and social dimensions of development. This technological revolution can make possible a leap in economic growth and social development while reducing the impact on planetary health. Technological revolutions are opportunities for developing countries, mostly technology laggards, to leapfrog current leading countries in terms of economic development with social and environmental benefits.

This chapter discusses the lessons for Latin America from the successful ethanol transition in Brazil, by analysing the key factors of this transition from a multi-level perspective. It intends to illustrate how these factors interact with the social-technical system, with a focus on the political and technological dimensions of the Brazilian regional, national, and global landscapes, while considering relevant aspects of governance inherent to this process.

9.2. The Environmental and Sustainability Transitions in Latin America

For several decades, the growth of an urban and industrial society in Latin America had been structurally adapting in all aspects to an abundant, cheap, and secure supply of hydrocarbons, mostly coming from imports from the Middle East. The situation changed radically in the 1970s, entering an era of limited, expensive, and insecure supplies of fossil fuel–based energy. The oil crisis is in fact the crisis of the contemporary development style in one of its basic pillars: its fundamental energy source. As a region, Latin America had the highest relative levels of hydrocarbon consumption in the 1970s, which placed the region at the forefront in terms of vulnerability to the oil crisis (Sunkel, 1981).

Moreover, the value of its oil consumption as a percentage of its total oil production increased from 38.4% in 1965, to 43.8% in 1970, 72.7% in 1990, and 84.5% in 2020 (BP, 2021), showing an increasing dependency on oil imports. Another 'villain' fossil fuel, coal, represented only 5% of energy consumption in 1975 in Latin America (lower than 10% in 1950) and its possibilities as a major source of energy are much more limited than in the Organisation for Economic Co-operation and Development (OECD) countries (Sunkel, 1981). Moreover, the coal quality is low. Nowadays, Chile is the country with the largest share of coal in primary energy consumption in Latin America, accounting for 18.7%, followed by Colombia (15.2%), Brazil (4.8%), Mexico (3.2%), Peru (2.3%), and Argentina (1%). The region has contributed less than 1% of the world's coal consumption, ahead only of the Middle East (0.25%), which leads in terms of proven oil reserves (BP, 2021). Thus, this increasing external energy dependence, coupled with high oil prices and scarce production of low-quality coals in the region, has caused alternative energy sources to start playing an important role in Latin American energy security.

Between the 1970s and 1980s, hydroelectricity consolidated itself as the second-most important source after oil, representing 18.4% of primary energy consumption (OWD, 2022), and the rise in oil prices has stimulated a considerable boom in the construction of large hydroelectric dams. Hydropower now represents 22.8% of primary energy in the region, but is followed in similar proportions by natural gas (20.8%) (OWD, 2022). The potential increase in hydropower production has been very important, but large dams bring with them environmental and social problems in the basins that are not yet well known and have not been taken into account in most of these projects. Alternatively, the most modern hydropower plants are not dependent on large flooded areas for power generation (i.e. they are called run-of-the-river plants), precisely to avoid the associated social, land-use change, and emissions impacts.

Hydroelectric developments totalled only 41 Terawatt Hour (TWh) in Latin America in the year 1965. After the oil crises in the 1970s, there was a 586% increase (to 284 TWh in 1985) in hydroelectricity generation in the region between the years 1965 and 1985. Bioenergy also became part of the energy mix, but with only 6 TWh. Wind power started only in 1993 in the region (<1 TWh), while solar had its first projects installed only five years later, in 1998 (<1 TWh). In the early 2000s, renewable energy continued to predominate, with 556 TWh from hydro and 15 TWh from biomass, with large projects concentrated mainly in Brazil. By 2020, hydroelectric power had become predominant (660 TWh), followed by biomass (85 TWh), an increase of 19% and 471% compared to the year 2000, respectively. It is interesting to note a gradual acceleration in the pace of installation of wind (from 2007 on) and solar (from 2014 on) sources. These sources grew by 7,254% and 1,928% in the period, totalling 85 TWh and 23 TWh in 2020, respectively (OWD, 2022).

In terms of primary energy consumption by source in Latin America in the early 1970s, 10% of total energy came from hydropower, mainly installed in Brazil (25% of the country's primary energy), Colombia (14%), Peru (13%), and Chile (13%), while the global average was only 6% (OWD, 2022). This figure improves even more in the early 2000s, with hydroelectric primary energy consumption in the region reaching almost 30%, led by Brazil (39%), Peru (31%), and Colombia (28%). As of 2010, we observe the emergence of wind and solar sources, peaking in 2022 mainly in Chile (3.2% wind, 4.3% solar, and 2.4% other renewables) and Brazil (4.7% wind, 0.6% solar, and 1.8% other renewables). It is important to note, however, that the share of each source in primary energy consumption (and in this case, renewables) is relative to the total energy consumed by each country (including fossil sources) and as a comparison, for example, the largest country in Latin America, Brazil, consumes almost 7 times more energy than Chile and 3.5 times more than Argentina (OWD, 2022).

Similar to the oil crises, when the use of alternative energy sources such as biomass and vegetable fuels was intensified, particularly in rural populations or those with lower purchasing power, the current high price of crude oil due to the supply restrictions imposed by the Russia-Ukraine war may play a key role in the development of bioenergy (biomass and biofuels) as well as other renewable sources such as hydro, solar, and wind, especially in Latin American countries. Examining the evolution of biofuel production by region, output from South and Central America has more than doubled between 1990 and 2020. This region is now the second largest global producer, North America being the first (BP, 2021). Within the South and Central American region, Brazil is by far the largest producer, with Argentina coming a distant second (BP, 2021).

Brazil is a particular success story (which will be discussed in more detail below) regarding the exploitation of both sugarcane and oil-rich seed crops (e.g. soybeans) to produce (bio)ethanol and (bio)diesel as substitutes for gasoline and mineral diesel. In addition, sugarcane bagasse is used in the country to co-generate electricity (and heat) to be used in ethanol plants, and the surplus is exported to the national electricity grid. Most of the current global biofuel production is the result of targets and incentives that players such as Brazil, the United States, and the European Union have set up to diversify transport fuel supplies, in order to improve energy security and mitigate climate change (IRENA, 2016). Brazil could mitigate up to 13% of the greenhouse gas emissions from electricity using the sugarcane bagasse as a fuel to power thermal power plants (Souza et al., 2021).

Besides the energy and environmental aspects, traditional biofuel production may have many social benefits that can help developing countries grow in a more sustainable way. Some studies have highlighted the employment and income generation related to biofuel programmes in developing countries and their positive effects on living conditions (Moraes et al., 2010). Thus, as technological improvements emerge, the potential environmental and economic benefits of biofuels are becoming more evident, making them a promising renewable energy source.

It is noteworthy that biofuels can be produced from different raw materials, generating sources of energy with distinct characteristics. Traditional biofuels use conventional food and feed crops, also known as 'flex-crops' or 'flex-commodities'. Flex-crops are agricultural crops that can be used for food, feed, fuel, and industrial material. First-generation biofuels (1G) usually refer to ethanol produced from sugar-rich (e.g. sugarcane, sugar beet, sweet sorghum) and starch-rich flex-crops (e.g. corn, wheat, cassava, rice), and to biodiesel made from oilseed crops (e.g. soybeans, rapeseed, sunflower, palm) or animal fat (Gasparatos and Stromberg, 2012). However, the production of 1G biofuels intensifies the exploitation of natural ecosystems and introduces competition with food production in land and water use (Bellezoni et al., 2018). Hence, 1G biofuel production can be a source of direct and indirect land use change (dLUC and iLUC) that is driven by biofuel feedstock production. These emissions take place at the beginning of the biofuel life cycle and can abruptly transform their GHG balances to higher emission levels than those associated with fossil fuels (Fargione et al., 2008; Searchinger et al., 2008; Lapola et al., 2010).

To overcome some adverse impacts, some biofuels are now made from non-edible biomass and cellulose, hemi-cellulose, and lignin, biomass-to-liquids (BTL), and bio-synthetic natural gas, the so-called second-generation biofuels (2G) (FAO, 2008; OECD/IEA, 2010). Typical lignocellulosic feedstocks are agricultural by-products (e.g. cane bagasse), forestry residues (e.g. treetops and branches), perennial grasses (e.g. switchgrass), short-rotation coppice (e.g. eucalyptus), and municipal waste (HLPE, 2013). Lignocellulosic feedstocks often do not compete for high-quality land with food crops due to their high yields and growing capacity on land poorly suited to food crops. Finally, third-generation (3G) biofuels (i.e. algae-based biofuels that do not compete with either food crops or with arable lands) are not yet cost-effective because of their current early stage of development. Several countries have now intensified their research and development efforts into both 2G and 3G biofuels due to their technical, economic, and environmental potential (IRENA, 2016).

Therefore, the urgent search for cheaper energy sources implies new impacts on the environment that are rarely taken into account in national programmes and projects, especially from a perspective of integration of different economic sectors. On the other hand, Latin America is shaped by an agricultural context, with a large supply of unskilled labour and low levels of investment in research, development, and industrial technology. The region has been historically suffering from the 'natural resource curse' and living under the hope and promise of being the future of sustainable development and renewable energy—a future that may never become reality, given the weakness of institutions, high corruption levels, poor infrastructure, over-reliance on commodities exports, and lack of articulation between sectors. However, some Latin American authors have persistently indicated possible paths for a prosperous and sustained development of the region (Sunkel, 1981; Sachs, 2004; Gudynas, 2011; Gligo et al., 2020; CEPAL, 2020, 2022). For this to occur, there needs to be a lean, clean, active, planning state capable of unveiling the future. According to Sachs (2004), who more than 30 years ago laid some of the foundations of the contemporary debate on the need for a new development paradigm (based on the convergence of economics, ecology, cultural anthropology, and political science), the national state has three main functions. These can be understood as key three elements for the transition to sustainability (Sachs, 2004, p. 11):

(a) The articulation of development spaces, from the local level (which must be expanded and strengthened) to the transnational level (which must be the object of a cautious policy of selective integration, subordinated to an endogenous development strategy);
(b) The promotion of partnerships among all interested actors around a negotiated sustainable development agreement;
(c) The harmonization of social, environmental, and economic goals, through strategic planning and day-to-day management of the economy and society, seeking a balance between different sustainability (social, cultural, ecological, environmental, territorial, economic, and political) and the five efficiencies (allocation, innovation, Keynesian, social and eco-efficiency) (Sachs, 2004, p. 11).

A fourth and fundamental element for the transition to sustainability in Latin America is the creation of an enabling environment for the development of innovations and, therefore, the emergence of disruptive technologies that enable or assist a sustainable energy transition. In this context, CEPAL's Big Push project (CEPAL/CGEE, 2020b) developed an overview of RD&I investments in energy in Brazil from 2013 to 2018. The figures reveal that the global resources for energy innovation in the country are mostly directed to fossil fuel technologies, due to the weight of the programmes regulated by the National Agency of Petroleum, Natural Gas and Biofuels (ANP). Public investments in energy R&D in Brazil reached their peak in 2014, with a total of R$1.1 billion. Moreover, most public investments are directed toward renewable energy, which accounted for 47% of the total in 2015, although publicly directed investments, which are the bulk of energy investments, are mostly dedicated to fossil sources.

Among renewable energy sources, biofuels received the highest volume of investments. Public spending on RD&I in energy, including specific investments in innovation in renewable energy, has been falling, from R$696 million in 2014 to R$217 million in 2018. This is due to both the economic crisis and deep cuts in federal spending. Furthermore, public and publicly directed RD&I investments in renewable energy technologies fell from R$966.44 million in 2014 to R$488.60 million in 2018, even with the recovery in total energy RD&I spending observed from 2016 to 2018.

During a visit to Chile, Carlo Rubbia, Nobel Prize winner in Physics, highlighted that innovation, driven by R&D, is key to finding a solution to the energy problem in general and to climate change in particular (CEPAL, 2011). It is therefore vital to encourage the development of renewable energy and to advance the formulation of policies to promote energy efficiency. However, the use of a particular renewable energy source will depend on the particular conditions of each country and the competitive advantages that its territory can offer. While biofuels have great potential in Brazil, solar, wind, and geothermal resources are more abundant in Chile; Uruguay has great wind potential, and Peru and Ecuador, geothermal.

The oil crisis has served to highlight the issues related to the finite nature and increasing cost of non-renewable natural resources, and therefore the importance of directing scientific and technological activities toward the use of renewable resources. It has, of course, led to recognition of the fact that energy—and therefore the natural resources from which it can be conveniently obtained—constitutes a crucial element in development. Another issue that the oil crisis highlights is the precariousness of the development strategies followed in Latin America. These base the processes of industrialization, urbanization, and modernization on the specialized use of a few natural resources, with a serious risk of depleting the best-quality non-renewable resources and deteriorating the renewable ones through over-exploitation, since the deterioration of natural resources can have serious economic and social consequences. However, Latin America's development planning can learn from cases within the region where innovation has led to increasing social, political, and governance capacities to promote a more sustainable, resilient, and just energy transition. A prime example here is the bioethanol transition in Brazil.

9.3. Brazilian Ethanol: A Case of Successful Energy Transition

Brazil is a pioneering country in the use of ethanol as transportation fuel at a large scale (Puppim de Oliveira, 2002). It is currently the second largest 1G ethanol producer, exceeded only by the United States, accounting for nearly 27% (27 billion litres) of the global ethanol production (RFA, 2017). The country had 384 ethanol mills, producing about 334,000 m^3 a day, with sugarcane being the feedstock used in 97% of the authorized mills in 2017 (ANP, 2017). Sugarcane is

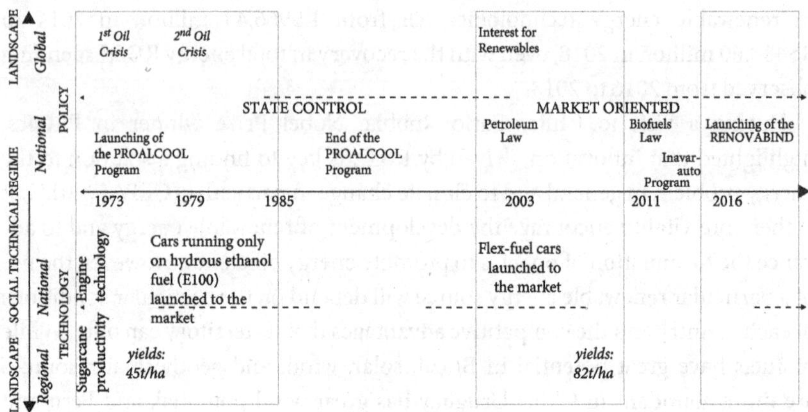

Figure 9.1. Historical overview of the Brazilian ethanol transition from a multi-level perspective.
Source: Authors.

cultivated in many Brazilian states, being the top crop in terms of raw biomass production and third in terms of area, after soybeans and corn (IBGE, 2017). The largest sugarcane-producing area is the Centre-South region, accounting for more than 90% of the country's production; within that region, São Paulo State produces 56% of the total in Brazil (IBGE, 2017; UNICA, 2017).

Brazil is also the largest sugar producer in the world and the biggest sugar exporter (respectively, 15% and 29% of the world total in 2019) (FAO, 2022). Figure 9.1 illustrates the flexible nature of sugarcane ethanol production, which is adjusted to more or less ethanol, according to sugar prices in the international market.

More importantly than consolidating its position as a leader in the global ethanol market, Brazil was able to effectively transition to use ethanol in large scale in its energy matrix in a few decades. The production and use of liquid biofuels in Brazil have long contributed to reducing GHG from the transport sector, besides contributing to agricultural development and reducing oil import dependency. By the late 1980s, energy produced from ethanol matched that derived from gasoline for road vehicles. Subsequently, ethanol-derived energy has continued to grow; however, not at quite at the same pace as that from gasoline consumption for road vehicles (EPE database[1]). This may be partly reflective of Brazil's ramping up of oil production from the 1990s onwards.

[1] https://www.epe.gov.br/pt/publicacoes-dados-abertos/dados-abertos/dados-do-anuario-estatistico-de-energia-eletrica.

9.3.1. Key Factors in the Brazilian Ethanol Transition

Brazil has a long history of sugarcane cultivation that initiated in 1532. In 1905, sugarcane was used for the first time as a source for experiments with ethanol-fueled vehicles, offering the roots of the ethanol transition. The sugarcane ethanol remained, however, a minor alternative to automobile use until the 1970s because the availability and low cost of petroleum derivatives inhibited the use of ethanol as a fuel source. From the 1970s, the use of ethanol became a mainstream energy policy to produce energy domestically (Goldemberg, 2008).

The use of ethanol as an alternative fuel in Brazil expanded after the first oil crisis, with the National Alcohol Programme (Proálcool) in 1975. First it was employed as an octane booster to gasoline and later as a complete substitute in properly adapted engines. The programme has attracted significant investment in agricultural and industrial processes related to 1G ethanol production, stimulating sugarcane growing and the construction of ethanol plants in the country. Additionally, an important domestic ethanol market was consolidated through a huge investment cycle focusing on promoting flex-fuel engines, which gives to consumers the choice of fueling their cars with petrol or ethanol in any proportion, according to their selling prices.

Thus, the present study takes into account the recent history of the ethanol transition, differentiating it into two major periods. The first, lasting from the early 1970s to 2000, saw ethanol production climb as a response to the global oil crisis. During this period ethanol supply and demand were primarily controlled by the government through subsidies and technological policies. The second period (continuing today), is market-oriented, where government plays a different and smaller role compared to the past. Energy security in this period is still an important driver in the transition, but it has also a large component of climate policy, as explained in the following sections.

9.3.2. The Political Economy Dimension

This section introduces the key factors that have conditioned the ethanol transition within the political economy dimension. Political power plays a key role in energy transitions (Ahlborg, 2017), even in the private sector, as different players try to define the rules of the game (Andrade and Puppim de Oliveira, 2015). The world oil crisis and the establishment of the Proálcool policy[2] emerged as key political and economic drivers in the first period of the Brazilian ethanol transition

[2] 'Proálcool' being the term used for the framework of policies designed to promote ethanol production and usage.

(1970–2000). In the second (still ongoing) period, the climate change debate and the world interest in renewables arise as key drivers.

9.3.2.1. Sugarcane Ethanol for Energy Security (1st Period, 1970s–2000)

The world oil crisis raised concerns about energy security and naturally led to the world's interest in alternative sources of energy. In Brazil, the government started promoting ethanol through Proálcool in 1970s as a response to the world oil crisis, when the fuel prices quadrupled, resulting in adverse impacts on the Brazilian trade balance (Amorim and Lopes, 2005; Puppim de Oliveira, 2002). At that time, 80% of the oil consumed in Brazil was imported, raising Brazil's expenses on oil imports from US$600 million in 1973 to US$2.5 billion in 1974 (Giacomazzi, 2012).

In the first period of the transition, as a measure for energy security, the Brazilian government supported the ethanol industry through a set of interventions undertaken under the Proálcool (see also 9.3.1). The Proálcool was, in addition, an alternative to support the sugarcane economy that was suffering from low sugar prices and huge surpluses in sugarcane production and processing capacity (Puppim de Oliveira, 2002).

The primary measure of the programme was to incorporate a mixture of up to 20% of anhydrous[3] alcohol to gasoline (by volume). In addition to ethanol mandates, the programme relied on tax incentives for new vehicles and controlled prices to make ethanol cheaper than gasoline (Puppim de Oliveira, 2002; Matsuoka, Ferro, and Arruda, 2009). Through controlling taxes, the government was able to set the price of hydrous ethanol[4] at 65% of the value of gasoline. Taxes applied to new car purchases were also lower for ethanol-fuel than for gasoline-fuel cars (Furtado et al., 2010). In 1980, the production of cars running on ethanol reached 95% of the light vehicles in the national fleet (Amorim and Lopes, 2005). In the years 1985–1986, the ethanol market started to weaken in the wake of stabilization in the oil market. Government support was, until 1985, key to increasing ethanol demand and supply, as well as providing the infrastructure and know-how for ethanol fuel.

9.3.2.2. Sugarcane Ethanol as a Climate Policy (2nd Period)

In 1986, as oil became cheaper and sugar more expensive, the Brazilian government was not able to maintain its support to the sector and loans for increasing

[3] Obtained in Brazil through the fermentation of sugarcane molasses. It has an alcoholic content of 99.3° INPM. The anhydrous ethanol is used in mixtures with gasoline A, for producing gasoline type C, in proportions defined by applicable law (ANP Resolution no. 19, of 15/4/2015).

[4] Motor vehicle fuel obtained in Brazil through the fermentation of sugarcane molasses. When free from hydrocarbons, it has an alcoholic content between 92.6° and 93.8° INPM. Used in Otto cycle internal combustion engines, specifically in alcohol-powered vehicles for road transportation (ANP Resolution no. 19, of 15/4/2015 and Resolution no. 681, of 5/6/2017).

capacity. Between 1989 and 1990, some 28 ethanol distilleries financed by Proálcool declared bankruptcy. The volume of old ethanol-fueled vehicles being scrapped surpassed the production of new ones, threatening the economic viability of more than 25,000 filling stations (Furtado, Scandiffio, and Cortez, 2010). There was a mismatch between the ethanol supply and the continuous production of alcohol-fueled cars. In 1990, the closure of the Institute of the Sugar and Alcohol (IAA), and governmental autarchy that led the ethanol boom, marked the end of Proálcool. The ethanol market share in the road transportation declined from 19.4% in 1988 to 12.2% in 2003, while the gasoline market share for the same period increased from 18.7% to 26.1% (Kamimura and Sauer, 2008). The crisis caused by the ethanol shortage in the late 1980s compromised all the infra-structure created during the second phase of Proálcool, but did not represent the collapse of the system.

From the beginning of the 2000s, a broad consensus on the need to prevent catastrophic and irreversible consequences of global warming has been reached worldwide. Several initiatives on the subject have put climate change at the top of the international agenda. Actions to reduce the consumption of fossil fuels and related GHG emissions started being promoted to encourage biofuel production and consumption worldwide.

Sugarcane ethanol produced in Brazil has been considered as one of the most promising biofuels to mitigate climate change because its carbon balance is considered superior compared to other biofuels, the so-called advanced biofuels (CARB, 2009; EC, 2009; EPA, 2010). Biofuel policies such as the European Directive 2003/30/EC (2009) and the Renewable Fuel Standard (RFS) established under the Energy Policy Act of 2005 (2010) encourage efforts from governments to promote biofuels and from industry to reduce life-cycle GHG emissions of ethanol production (Pacini and Strapasson, 2012). Brazilian sugarcane ethanol is, in fact, a major alternative to reduce GHG emissions from transport under these regulatory schemes. According to the US Environmental Protection Agency (EPA, 2010), Brazilian sugarcane ethanol, designated as an 'advanced biofuel', is able to reduce GHG emissions by up to 61% compared to gasoline. As an example, sugarcane ethanol life-cycle GHG emissions' estimates range from 23.97 to 66.40 gCO_{2eq}/MJ, while for US corn ethanol it ranges from 77.56 to 89.71 gCO_{2eq}/MJ (CARB, 2009; EC, 2009; EPA, 2010). Brazilian companies also benefited tremendously from the carbon projects coming from the Clean Development Mechanism (CDM) projects from the electricity generators that burned bagasse, giving enormous incentives for building new generators and improving the competitiveness of the biofuel sector (Costa-Júnior, Pasini, and Andrade, 2012).

The Paris Agreement (UN, 2015) established under the United Nations Framework Convention on Climate Change developments is key to the undergoing expansion of ethanol fuel. The Brazilian commitment to the mitigation efforts adopted under the Paris Agreement includes the reduction of GHG emissions by 43% in comparison to 2005 levels, and a 45% share of renewables in the primary energy mix by 2030. This must be achieved by increasing biofuels in the energy matrix to approximately 18% by 2030, especially through ethanol supply (BRASIL, 2016). However, sugarcane production can be a source of land use change, as it typically takes place on cropland previously used for growing food or feedstock, and hence, the displaced agricultural production may need to be grown in land not formerly cultivated such as grasslands and forests. The sugarcane planted area expanded 125% (3.1 million hectares) in São Paulo State between 2000 and 2015, which resulted in a significant reduction of other crops such as orange and corn.

Cattle ranching has particularly diminished by 20% in the state, while it increased in Brazil as a whole over the same period (Caldarelli and Gilio, 2018). Some studies demonstrate, for instance, that the expansion of sugarcane production is associated with deforestation in the Amazon, as it tends to push cattle grazing to the Amazon frontiers (Lapola et al., 2010). A similar process was witnessed in the expansion of palm oil production in Southeast Asia, which led to deforestation in the wake of the EU demand for biofuels to fill its mandates (Moreno-Peñaranda et a., 2015). Therefore, concerns about impacts of biomass growth for biofuel production emphasize the importance of national planning for biofuel development (Gasparatos et al., 2021), where crop expansion considers the land-water-food-climate-biodiversity nexus (Bellezoni et al., 2018).

Aiming to recognize the strategic role of biofuels in Brazil, the National Biofuel Policy 'RenovaBio' was established (Federal Law 13,576/2017) in December 2017 (Brasil, 2017), with the adoption of compulsory goals to reduce GHG emissions from biofuels, including individual targets addressed to the biofuel producers and sustainability of the production processes. Its main goals are:

- to promote the proper expansion of biofuels in the Brazilian energy matrix, with emphasis on the regularity of fuel supply, and
- to ensure predictability in the fuels market by inducing energy-efficiency gains and GHG emission reductions in the production, marketing, and use of biofuels.

To meet these goals, the RenovaBio has been designed to introduce two basic market mechanisms to recognize the potential of each biofuel in reducing GHG emissions, individually and by each processing plant:

- establishment of national emission reduction targets for the fuel matrix, determined for a 10-year period, whereby national targets will be turned into

individual targets. These targets are important for establishing some predictability and, therefore, enabling private players to undertake their planning and investment analyses in an environment with less uncertainty, and
- certification of biofuel production, with different scores being attributed to each producer (the higher the producer's score, the higher the net energy produced with less CO_2 emissions in the life cycle).

The connection between these two instruments is expected to occur through the creation of biofuel decarbonization credit (CBIO), a financial asset traded on the stock exchange and issued by the biofuel producer from biofuel sales (invoices). In summary, the RenovaBio's trading scheme is based on national emission-reduction targets that, in order to be met, are shared among regulated players, such as fossil fuel distributors; these distributors, in turn, must meet their individual targets to reduce emissions by purchasing the CBIO credits issued by certified biofuel producers/importers, thus ensuring that the fossil fuel producers themselves contribute to GHG emissions reduction.

Therefore, RenovaBio will promote the expansion of biofuel supplies in Brazil and seek efficiency and productivity. The growing scenarios for ethanol under the RenovaBio are very optimistic. Brazil's annual ethanol capacity could rise from 27 billion today to 54 billion litres by 2030 or, in a more conservative scenario, to 49 billion litres by 2030 (EPE, 2017).

9.3.3. Technological Factors

There are two technological advancements that conditioned the ethanol market expansion along with the political factors presented above:

(i) agricultural and industrial technology—resulting in an increasing productivity in the agricultural and processing stages (sugarcane and ethanol yields), both undertaken by the sugarcane industry, one of the most traditional in Brazil, and
(ii) vehicle technology, resulting mainly from efforts of the automotive industry, which has played a major role in Brazilian industry for decades (Vaz et al., 2017).

9.3.3.1. Innovation in Sugarcane and Ethanol Productivity

The competitiveness of sugarcane ethanol is closely related to sugarcane and ethanol productivity, as increase in cane and ethanol yields enable ethanol costs to be cut and production to increase. Yield associated with crops refers to the biomass produced in an area, expressed in units of fresh and dry weight at a given moment (e.g. dry tons per hectare per year). In sugarcane, crop productivity is variable, depending on local climate, seed varieties, and cultural practices. As an example, Macedo et al. (2008) consider an average yield of 87.1 tons per hectare of sugarcane, but minimum and maximum values range between 51.3 and 119.8 tons per hectare. The increase in cane yields has been obtained mainly by developing new varieties that are better adapted to Brazilian weather and soil, and also more resistant to plant diseases (Furtado, Scandiffio, and Cortez, 2010). From the beginning of the Proálcool in the 1970s until 2009, the evolution trend in cane productivity was continuous, from 45 tons per hectare to more than 80 tons per hectare (Macedo, Seabra, and Silva, 2008).

Cane productivity increased until 2011 and then began to fall[5] due especially to financial issues: gasoline prices pushed down the price of hydrated ethanol, reducing its margins. This margin reduction in an already indebted sector in turn jeopardized investment in the replanting of sugarcane fields, investment that was fundamental to ensuring productivity to meet demand for the coming years. This reduction also jeopardized investment in technological development and in adopting new sugarcane varieties.

Besides the financial crisis, the rapid implementation of mechanization motivated by the burning legislation[6] is also a key factor leading to productivity losses and increased production costs from 2009 to 2014.[7] Introduced initially in São Paulo (Law 11.241/2002), and subsequently in other states, this law generated improved work conditions and significant environmental benefits by reducing emissions. However, the implementation of mechanized harvesting and planting technologies caused important impacts in the sector due to the lack of appropriate soil preparation during planting, insufficient qualification of the operators, and the incompatibility of sugarcane varieties to the mechanical cutting. The losses occurred during this implementation period have been recovered with improved agricultural techniques in view of the learning curve resulting from the knowledge accumulated in the period and also to the introduction of precision agriculture (CEPEA, 2018; Delgado et al., 2017b).

[5] Sugarcane productivity has varied since 2010 from 77 t/ha in 2010/2011, to 67.1 t/ha in 2011/2012, 74.8 in 2013/2014, 76.9 t/ha in 2015/2016, and, finally, to 72.6 t/ha in 2016/2017 (EPE, 2017b). In the 2017/2018 and 2018/2019 seasons, yields were around 72 kg/ha, while in the 2019/2020 and 2020/2021 seasons, this figure rose back to around 76 kg/ha (CONAB, 2020).

[6] The State Law number 11241 from 2002 establishes that pre-harvest burning practice should be gradually banned by 2021 for most of São Paulo State (terrain slope less than or equal to 12%). Official data from the Brazilian Institute for Space Research shows that the burning legislation succeeds with shares of burnt fields in sugarcane crop area decreasing from 65.8% in the year 2006/2007 to 27.4% in 2012/2013 (Canasat, 2022).

[7] Other factors contributed to this scenario, such as the implantation of new plants carried out in a disorganized manner and the occurrence of adverse climatic conditions (droughts) (Delgado et al., 2017b)

In this century, the most important innovations in sugarcane cultivation have been in cane harvesting (Macedo et al., 2008), which had been moving from burned cane manual harvesting to mechanical harvesting of unburned cane[8] (see section 9.3.3.2). In order to facilitate harvest, it was a common practice in Brazil to burn the crop at the harvest stage and to manually cut the remaining standing stalks.

Yield associated with ethanol production corresponds to the conversion efficiency in a factory, usually expressed as the volumetric production of ethanol per unit mass (e.g. litres of ethanol per ton of feedstock). In the industrial stage, significant advancements have been achieved to increase ethanol productivity,[9] such as improving sugar extraction, vinasse recovery, and fermentation. In addition, co-generation of electric power from sugarcane bagasse has been increasingly relevant. Sugarcane mills are able to produce sufficient energy for their own consumption and to trade the surplus volume. Since 2013, they generate more electricity for the grid (roughly 60% of the electric power from sugarcane bagasse) than for their own plants. The supply of energy by the sucrose-energy sector in 2020 was 36.8 TWh, corresponding to 5.88% of national electricity supply (EPE, 2020). As a whole, over 70% of the biomass-based electricity generation in Brazil is fuelled by bagasse (EPE, 2020).

9.3.3.2. Innovation in Vehicle Technology

Important technical innovations occurred in the early 1970s (e.g. electronic fuel injection, improving performance and reducing emissions). The development of a 100% ethanol-powered car in 1979 is, definitely, the first technical element introduced by the automotive industry that can be considered key in the ethanol transition, as it changed the entire Brazilian car market (Freitas and Kaneco, 2011). The early ethanol engines presented problems starting at low temperatures, so the use of hydrated ethanol required the development of a new engine with a higher compression ratio and the development of new corrosion-resistant materials (Yu et al., 2010). The ethanol market declined in the subsequent years, becoming unstable with the recovery in the domestic market for automotive vehicles with new cars running on gasoline blended with anhydrous ethanol while sales of new cars fuelled with hydrated ethanol remained very low (Goldemberg, 2008). However, private actors responded dynamically, increasing expenditure and participation in R&D (Tromboni de Souza Nascimento et al.,

[8] GHG emissions from pre-harvest burning in sugarcane fields is particularly sensitive since it significantly affects total ethanol GHG emissions. It has been estimated as 941 $kgCO_{2eq}$/ha per year, which corresponds to 30% of the total GHG emission in sugarcane biomass production (Oliveira Bordonal et al., 2013) and about 19% of the total GHG ethanol life-cycle emissions (Macedo, Seabra, and Silva, 2008).

[9] According to Macedo, Seabra, and Silva (2008), ethanol yield varies between 78.9 and 94.5 litres of ethanol per ton of sugarcane.

2009). Local engineers and technology developers were the ones who believed in the flex-fuel car, and started influencing other key actors initially reticent about the technology[10] (Vieira do Nascimento, 2014). Petrobras also become more flexible in mixing ethanol with gasoline in order to control ups-and-downs in ethanol supply.

The introduction of flex-fuel technology from 2003 onwards has become dominant in the Brazilian automotive sector. Since their release, sales of flex-fuel vehicles have reached impressive levels, surpassing the sale of gasoline vehicles after just three years. Brazilian flex-fuel cars can run with pure gasoline, pure (hydrated) ethanol, or with any mix proportion of both, because their sensors can detect the proportion and adjust the ignition electronically (Goldemberg, 2008). Currently, anhydrous ethanol is employed as an oxygenated additive to gasoline (from a blend of 25% to 27% blending of gasoline-ethanol, also called gasohol). Hydrous ethanol is employed in dedicated engines or in flex-fuel engines (up to E100). According to Freitas and Kaneko (2011), the domestic consumption of hydrous ethanol increased from 236.82 million litres in 2003 to 1,317.62 million litres in 2010 thanks to the introduction of flex-fuel cars.

In the last decade, the most important technical factor related to vehicle technology advancements seems to be the efficiency improvements achieved in flex-fuel engines. In principle, as flex-type engines are gasoline engines that also operate with ethanol (thanks to software adjustments that control the engine), they were not designed to take full advantage of the properties of ethanol and its total calorific value (Goldemberg, 2008; Yu et al., 2010). However, most of the flex engines sold in the market today already show higher efficiency with ethanol than with gasoline. Thanks to a more generalized use of direct injection and turbos, about 85% of the flex-fuel cars sold in 2015 showed higher efficiency with ethanol, which represents a great advance compared to 2014, when only 25% were more efficient with ethanol (Delgado et al., 2017a).

9.4. Lessons for Latin America from the Brazilian Transition

This section discusses the innovation policy lessons for Latin America from the technological transitions towards sustainable energy systems using insights from the case of ethanol in Brazil. There have been two elements conditioning the success of the Brazilian ethanol arising from the key factors

[10] The alcohol industry was against the idea to give the choice to consumers to decide between ethanol and conventional fuel; the government wanted to avoid risks regarding lack of fuel supply and credibility towards society; and even the car manufacturers, without support from the government, were more concerned about the cost involved in the process than the introduction of the technology itself (Vieira do Nascimento, 2014).

examined above: policy response to global pressures and multi-sectoral technology interactions.

The technological driver towards energy sustainability changed over time. Figure 9.1 summarizes the historical overview of the Brazilian ethanol transition from a multi-level perspective. Crucial global and national market dimensions are represented at the left side of the figure within a multi-level perspective. The political and technological dimension and key related factors of the system are indicated along the chronological line in the figure. A key element was the transition from a state- to a market-driven approach, which was turbulent in the case of ethanol in Brazil. This transition was facilitated by the alignment between domestic and global trends, and the connection among different sectors in the economy.

9.4.1. Policy Alignment with the Global Landscape (Response to Global Pressures)

The alignment of the national technological policies in the energy sector with global developments in the energy sector was fundamental in driving the technological transitions. Energy technological systems need to align with global demands, being driven by a combination of state and market pressures. The national policy responses to global pressures in the Brazilian ethanol transition culminated in two main drivers of this transition: (i) the establishment of the Proálcool as a measure for energy security, and (ii) the Brazilian engagement on climate change mitigation focused on ethanol. In both cases there were an alignment between the global landscape and the national agenda, allowing a shift in the emergence, following by the strengthening, of ethanol in the energy mix. The international energy crisis in the 1970s compelled countries to search for energy alternatives and to strengthen energy security, which led Brazil to pursue the ethanol policy. The high prices of oil made the ethanol industry competitive after the initial push by the government. At the same time, the ethanol policy aligned economic and political interest groups (sugarcane producers and military nationalists) (Puppim de Oliveira, 2002). In the early 2000s, with the global climate agreements and mechanisms, the Brazilian climate policies have relied on the strengthening of ethanol production, including electricity production from bagasse, as the main strategy for mitigating GHG emissions.

9.4.2. Moving to a Market-Oriented Model

The changing global landscape in the energy sector, driven by sustainability concerns, facilitated the transition from state -to market-led innovation processes. Until 1985, government support was key to increase ethanol demand and supply, as well as to provide the infrastructure and know-how for the built internal ethanol market. In the second period of the transition (early 2000s), the insertion of flex-fuel technology completely redesigned the ethanol market scenario from a market-oriented perspective. This transformation involved a process of learning that oscillates in more or less challenging periods over time (Rodríguez-Morales, 2018). Instead of compromising the ethanol transition, the falling stages of the ethanol served as a springboard for a new rise in the transition.

The continual technological innovation and the crucial transformations surrounding it (section 9.3) reflect a system that learned from economic crisis and technological limits. Particularly, by moving from a dominant government intervention to a more market-oriented model (with government coordination), key players of the transition (suppliers of the automotive industry in partnership with research institutions) were able to make the supply and demand of ethanol more reliable and resilient, as the flex-fuel technology emerged in the early 2000s through the sharing of capabilities and interaction among them.

9.4.3. Multi-Sectoral Technology Interactions: Catalyzing the Technological Transition

Another key lesson for Latin America from the ethanol case in Brazil is the need to innovate in different fronts and connect the innovation to potential sectors that will further drive the innovative process. Connecting sectors can strengthen the market drive for certain technologies, facilitating the transitions from state-to market-led innovation.

Technological innovations in the field of ethanol have a clear multi-sectoral character. As described in section 9.3, technological innovations in sugarcane and ethanol productivity, as well as in vehicle technology, have significantly occurred along the historical line of the ethanol transition. These advancements have been essential for the success of the transition and for its survival during ethanol downturn periods. The major technological transformations that occurred in the ethanol transition involving the automobile industry and the agricultural sector also have different natures, and involve different kinds of innovations:

(i) The shift from ethanol to flex-fuel technology (product-based innovation): The progressive importance of ethanol as a substitution fuel for gasohol in the domestic market is directly connected with fleet growth based on flex-fuel technology starting in 2003, being the main reason for the increase in ethanol demand (Freitas and Kaneco, 2011), which boosted the resurgence of the country's interest in the industry. Growth in the Brazilian automobile fleet based on this technology is a major driving factor of long-run ethanol demand. Flex-fuel vehicles account today for more than 70% of the light vehicles in the national fleet.

(ii) Gains of sugarcane productivity (process-based innovation) as a result of mechanization and burning regulation: Losses in productivity that occurred earlier in the process of implementing mechanization have been recovered with the improvement of agricultural techniques.

As the driver of change has moved towards climate policies, the opportunity to gain carbon credits through the Clean Development Mechanism (CDM) in electricity generation allowed a series of innovations in the sector. Sugarcane bagasse could co-generate electricity and heat to be used in ethanol plants and also feed the national electricity grid, as well as gaining carbon credits. The connection of the liquid fuel ethanol sector with bagasse-powered electricity generation, particularly in the state of São Paulo, triggered a series of incremental innovations in the electricity sector to adapt generators to the new bagasse fuel.

9.5. Conclusions

This chapter has presented the elements explaining the factors that influence an environmental and sustainable transition in the energy sector in Brazil, with potential lessons for Latin America. Brazil has successfully implemented the world's first policy for large-scale use of biomass as a liquid fuel in the transportation sector.

There are key elements that we can draw as lessons for a sustainable energy transition. First, the state was fundamental in forcing the introduction of ethanol, both on the demand and supply sides. However, over time the state-centred and central planning system showed limitations, illustrated by the ethanol shortage in the 1990s. Thus, the market also must play a role in the later stages of the technological innovation and diffusion process. The transition from state-led to market-led is key for long-term innovation policy. Second, the alignment between governance at global and national levels can facilitate technological transitions. Global opportunities, such as high oil prices or carbon markets, can create market incentives so that technological transitions are less reliant on the actions of the state. Third, the connection between sectors can catalyze innovation processes in each. Innovation in the ethanol sector relied on innovations in manufacturing, the vehicle industry in particular. Later, the electricity sector was connected to ethanol production by the carbon market.

Latin America is a region endowed with a large potential for the production of sustainable energy. This is particularly valuable in an era where climate change has become such a relevant global policy issue. This new environment is already generating significant incentives for those engaged in sustainable energy. The region has to develop its capability to further use its potential to harness the natural endowments it has in the energy sector. The ethanol case in Brazil shows that this is possible, despite the limitations the region has faced in terms of development outcomes in the past decades.

References

Ahlborg, H. 2017. 'Towards a Conceptualization of Power in Energy Transitions', *Environmental Innovation and Societal Transitions*, 25, 122–141.

Amorim, H. V., and Lopes, M. L. 2005. 'Ethanol Production in a Petroleum Dependent World: The Brazilian Experience', *Sugar Journal*, 67, 11–14.

ANFAVEA (Brazilian Automotive Industry Association). 2020. 'Brazilian Automotive Industry Yearbook 2020'. ANFAVEA, Brasília. Available at: https://www.anfavea.com.br/anuario2020/site/anuario_2020.pdf.

Andrade, J. C. S., and Puppim de Oliveira, J. A. 2015. 'The Role of the Private Sector in Global Climate and Energy Governance', *Journal of Business Ethics*, 130(2), 375–387.

Bellezoni, R. A., Sharma, D., Villela, A. A., and Pereira Junior, A. O. 2018. 'Water-Energy-Food Nexus of Sugarcane Ethanol Production in the State of Goiás, Brazil: An Analysis with Regional Input-Output Matrix', *Biomass and Bioenergy*, 115, 108–119. https://doi.org/10.1016/j.biombioe.2018.04.017.

BP. 2021. *BP Statistical Review of World Energy 2021: All Data, 1965–2020*. 70th ed. London: BP. Available at: https://www.bp.com/en/global/corporate/energy-economics/statistical-review-of-world-energy.html.

Brasil. 2016. 'Brasil RF: Pretendida Contribuição Nacionalmente Determinada para Consecução do Objetivo da Convenção-Quadro das Nações Unidas sobre Mudança do Clima, 2016'. Brasilía: Federative Republic of Brazil.

Brasil. 2017. 'Casa Civil Presidência da República. Law n. 13.576: Política Nacional de Bicombustíveis, 2017'. Brasilía: Federative Republic of Brazil.

Caldarelli, C. E., and Gilio, L. 2018. 'Expansion of the Sugarcane Industry and Its Effects on Land Use in São Paulo: Analysis from 2000 through 2015', *Land Use Policy*, 76, 264–274. doi:10.1016/J.LANDUSEPOL.2018.05.008.

Canasat: Monitoramento da Cana-de-açúcar. 2009. http://www.dsr.inpe.br/laf/canasat/colheita.html (accessed 27 May 2022).

CARB. 2009. 'California's Low Carbon Fuel Final Regulation Order'. Sacramento, Ca: California Air Resources Board.

CEPAL (Comissão Econômica para a América Latina e o Caribe). 2011. 'O sol, uma energia renovável de grande potencial na América Latina e no Caribe', *Notas da CEPAL, Em Foco*. https://www.cepal.org/notas_p/68/EnFoco_4.

CEPAL (Comisión Económica para América Latina y el Caribe). 2020. 'Una mirada regional a la acción por el clima en los Planes Nacionales de Desarrollo de América Latina y el Caribe, Notas de Planificación para el Desarrollo, No. 9, 2020', https://observ

atorioplanificacion.cepal.org/es/nota/una-mirada-regional-la-accion-por-el-clima-en-los-planes-nacionales-de-desarrollo-de-america.

CEPAL (Comissão Econômica para a América Latina e o Caribe)/CGEE (Centro de Gestão e Estudos Estratégicos). 2020a. 'Um grande impulso para a sustentabilidade no setor energético do Brasil: Subsídios e evidências para a coordenação de políticas', Documentos de Projetos (LC/TS.2020/51; LC/BRS/TS.2020/3), Santiago.

CEPAL (Comissão Econômica para a América Latina e o Caribe)/CGEE (Centro de Gestão e Estudos Estratégicos). 2020b. 'Panorama dos investimentos em inovação em energia no Brasil: Dados para um grande impulso energético', Documentos de Projetos (LC/TS.2020/62; LC/BRS/TS.2020/4), Santiago.

CEPAL (Comisión Económica para América Latina y el Caribe). 2022. 'Una década de acción para un cambio de época (LC/FDS.5/3)', Santiago, https://repositorio.cepal.org/bitstream/handle/11362/47745/S2100985_es.pdf?sequence=4&isAllowed=y.

CEPEA. 2018. *Mercado de Trabalho do Agronegócio Brasileiro: A dinâmica dos empregos formais na indústria sucroenergética de 2000 a 2016*. Piracicaba, SP: CEPEA.

CONAB (Companhia Nacional de Abastecimento). 2020. *Acompanhamento da safra brasileira: Cana-de-açúcar, v. 7: Safra 2019/20, n. 2: Segundo levantamento*. Brasília: CONAB, 1–64.

CONAB (Companhia Nacional de Abastecimento). 2021. *Levantamentos de Safra: cana-de-açúcar. Acompanhamento da safra brasileira de cana-de-açúcar*. Brasília: CONAB. www.conab.gov.br.

Costa-Júnior, A., Pasini, K., and Andrade, C. 2012. 'Clean Development Mechanism in Brazil: An Instrument for Technology Transfer and the Promotion of Cleaner Technologies?', *Journal of Cleaner Production*, 46, 67–73. doi:10.1016/J.JCLEPRO.2012.09.044.

Delgado, F., Costa, J. E. G, Febraro, J., and da Silva, T. B. 2017a. *Caderno FGV Energia: Carros Elétricos*. Rio de Janeiro: Fundaao Getúlio Vargas.

Delgado, F., de Sousa, M. E., and Roitman, T. 2017b. *Caderno FGV Energia: Biocombustíveis*. Rio de Janeiro: Fundaao Getúlio Vargas.

EC. 2009. European Parliament Council of the EU. 'Directive 2009/28/EC of the European Parliament and of the Council of 23 April 2009 on the Promotion of the Use of Energy from Renewable Sources and Amending and Subsequently Repealing Directives 2001/77/EC and 2003/30/EC 2009'. https://www.legislation.gov.uk/eudr/2009/28/contents

EPA. 2010. *EPA. Renewable Fuel Standard Program (RFS2) Regulatory Impact Analysis*. Washington, DC: EPA.

EPE (Empresa de Pesquisa Energética). 2017. *Nota Técnica PR 04/18: Potencial dos Recursos Energéticos no Horizonte 2050*. Rio de Janeiro: EPE.

EPE (Empresa de Pesquisa Energética). 2017b. *Nota Técnica EPE-DPG-SGB-Bios-NT-01-2017-r0: RenovaBio: Biocombustíveis 2030: Papel dos biocombustíveis na matriz*. Rio de Janeiro: EPE/MME.

EPE. 2018. 'Projeções de Oferta e Demanda de Etanol, Gasolina, Biodiesel e Diesel. O Planej. Energético da Matriz Veicular do Bras. até 2030, Sindaçúcar-PE, Recife, Pernambuco', http://www.epe.gov.br/sites-pt/sala-de-imprensa/noticias/Documents/EPE_Jos%C3%A9%20Mauro_Proje%C3%A7%C3%B5es%20de%20Oferta%20e%20Demanda_26mar.pdf; 2018 (accessed 27 May 2022).

EPE (Brazilian Energy Research Office). 2020. *Brazilian Energy Balance 2020 Year 2019: Empresa de Pesquisa Energética*. Rio de Janeiro: EPE.

EPE (Empresa de Pesquisa Energética). 2021. 'Nota Técnica EPE/DPG/SDB/2021/03: Análise de conjuntira dos biocombustíveis, ano 2020', https://www.epe.gov.br/

sites-pt/publicacoes-dados-abertos/publicacoes/PublicacoesArquivos/publicacao-615/NT-EPE-DPG-SDB-2021-03_Analise_de_Conjuntura_dos_Biocombustiveis_ano_2020.pdf (accessed 9 June 2022].

ESCAP, UNU, UNEP, IGES. 2016. *Transformations for Sustainable Development: Promoting Environmental Sustainability in Asia and the Pacific*. Bangkok: United Nations, https://www.unescap.org/publications/transformations-sustainable-development-promoting-environmental-sustainability-asia-and.

FAO (Food and Agriculture Organization of the United Nations). 2008. *The State of Food and Agriculture. Biofuels: Prospects, Risks and Opportunities*. Rome: FAO.

FAO (Food and Agriculture Organization of the United Nations). 2017. 'Statistics Division (FAOSTAT)', online database, http://www.fao.org/faostat/en/#home. (accessed 9 June 2022).

Fargione, J., Hill, J., Tilman, D., Polasky, S., et al. 2008. 'Land Clearing and Carbon Debt', *Science*, 319(5867), 1235–1238.

Freitas, L. C., and Kaneko, S. 2011. 'Ethanol Demand under the Flex-Fuel Technology Regime in Brazil', *Energy Economics*, 33, 1146–1154. doi:10.1016/J.ENECO.2011.03.011.

Furtado, A. T., Scandiffio, M. I. G, and Cortez, L. A. B. 2011. 'The Brazilian Sugarcane Innovation System', *Energy Policy*, 39, 156–166. doi:10.1016/J.ENPOL.2010.09.023.

Gasparatos, A., and Stromberg, P. 2012. *Socioeconomic and Environmental Impacts of Biofuels: Evidence from Developing Nations*. Cambridge: Cambridge University Press.

Gasparatos, A., Lee, L., Maltitz, G. P. V., et al. 2013. 'Catalysing Biofuel Sustainability International and National Policy Interventions', *Environmental Policy and Law*, 43(4–5), 216–221.

Geels, F. W., and Schot, J. 2007. 'Typology of Sociotechnical Transition Pathways', *Research Policy*, 36(3), 399–417.

Geels, F. W. 2004. 'From Sectoral Systems of Innovation to Socio-Technical Systems: Insights about Dynamics and Change from Sociology and Institutional Theory', *Research Policy*, 33(6), 897–920.

Gligo, N., Alonso, G., Barkin, D., et al. 2020. *La tragedia ambiental de América Latina y el Caribe*, Libros de la CEPAL, No. 161 (LC/PUB.2020/11-P). Santiago: Comisión Económica para América Latina y el Caribe (CEPAL.

Giacomazzi, E. 2008. *A Brief History of Brazilian PróÁlcool Programme and Developments of Biofuel and Biobased Products in Brazil*. OECD Glob. Paris: Forum Biotechnol.

Goldemberg J. 2008. 'The Brazilian Biofuels Industry', *Biotechnology for Biofuels*, 1, 1–7. doi:10.1186/1754-6834-1-6.

Gudynas, E. 2011. *Debates sobre el desarrollo y sus alternativas en América Latina: una breve guía heterodoxa, Más allá del desarrollo, Grupo Permanente de Trabajo sobre Alternativas al Desarrollo*, M. Lang y D. Mokrani (comps.), Quito: Fundación Rosa Luxemburgo/Abya Yala.

HLPE (High Level Panel of Experts). 2013. *Biofuels and Food Security. A Report by the High-Level Panel of Experts on Food Security and Nutrition of the Committee on World Food Security*. Rome: FAO.

IRENA (International Renewable Energy Agency). 2016. 'Boosting Biofuels: Sustainable Paths to Greater Energy Security', http://www.irena.org/DocumentDownloads/Publications/IRENA_Boosting_Biofuels_2 016.pdf.

Johnstone, P., Rogge, K. S., Kivimaa, P., et al. 2020. 'Waves of Disruption in Clean Energy Transitions: Sociotechnical Dimensions of System Disruption in Germany and the United Kingdom', *Energy Research & Social Science*, 59, 1–13.

Kamimura, A., and Sauer, I. L. 2008. 'The Effect of Flex Fuel Vehicles in the Brazilian Light Road Transportation', *Energy Policy*, 36, 1574–1576. doi:10.1016/J.ENPOL.2008.01.016.

Lapola, D. M., Schaldach, R., Alcamo, J., et al. 2010. 'Indirect land-Use Changes Can Overcome Carbon Savings from Biofuels in Brazil', *Proceedings of the National Academy of Sciences*, 107(8), 3388–3393.

Macedo, I. C, Seabra, J. E. A, and Silva, J. E. A. R. 2008. 'Green House Gases Emissions in the Production and Use of Ethanol from Sugarcane in Brazil: The 2005/2006 Averages and a Prediction for 2020', *Biomass and Bioenergy*, 32, 582–595. doi:10.1016/J.BIOMBIOE.2007.12.006.

Matsuoka, S., Ferro, J., and Arruda, P. 2009. 'The Brazilian Experience of Sugarcane Ethanol Industry', *In Vitro Cellular and Development Biology*, 45, 372–381. doi:10.1007/s11627-009-9220-z.

Moraes, M. A. F. D., Costa, C. C., Guilhoto, J. J. M., et al. 2010. 'Externalidades sociais dos combustíveis', in E. L. L. Sousa and I. C. Macedo, eds., *Etanol e bioeletricidade: A cana-de-açúcar no futuro da matriz energética*, São Paulo: ÚNICA, 48–75.

Moreno-Peñaranda, R., Gasparatos, A., Stromberg, P., et al. 2015. 'Sustainable Production and Consumption of Palm Oil in Indonesia: What Can Stakeholder Perceptions Offer to the Debate?', *Sustainable Production and Consumption*, 4, 16–35. doi:10.1016/J.SPC.2015.10.002.

Nascimento, P. T. de S, P., Sin Oih Yu, A., Quinello, R. S., et al. 2015. 'Exogenous Factors in the Development of Flexible Fuel Cars as a Local Dominant Technology', *Journal of Technology, Management and Innovation*, 4, 110–119. doi:10.4067/S0718-27242009000400009.

OECD/IEA. 2010. *Sustainable Production of Second-Generation Biofuels, Potential and Perspectives in Major Economies and Developing Countries.* Paris: Anselm Eisentraut, http://www.iea.org/publications/freepublications/publication/second_generation_biofuel s.pdf.

Oliveira Bordonal, R., Barretto de Figueiredo, E., Aguiar, D. A., et al. 2013. 'Greenhouse Gas Mitigation Potential from Green Harvested Sugarcane Scenarios in São Paulo State, Brazil', *Biomass and Bioenergy*, 59, 195–207. doi:10.1016/J.BIOMBIOE.2013.08.040.

OWD (Our World in Data). 2022. 'Renewable Energy Generation, South & Central America', https://ourworldindata.org/renewable-energy.

Pacini, H., and Strapasson, A. 2012. 'Innovation Subject to Sustainability: The European Policy on Biofuels and Its Effects on Innovation in the Brazilian Bioethanol Industry', *Journal of Contemporary European Research*, 8, 367–397.

Puppim de Oliveira, J. 2002. 'The Policymaking Process for Creating Competitive Assets for the Use of Biomass Energy: The Brazilian Alcohol Programme', *Renewable and Sustainable Energy Reviews*, 6, 129–140. doi:10.1016/S1364-0321(01)00014-4.

RFA. 2017. *Building Partnerships: Growing Markets: 2017 Ethanol Industry Outlook.* Ellisville, MO: Renewable Fuels Association.

Rodríguez-Morales, J. E. 2018. 'Convergence, Conflict and the Historical Transition of Bioenergy for Transport in Brazil: The Political Economy of Governance and Institutional Change', *Energy Research and Social Science*, 44, 324–335. doi:10.1016/J.ERSS.2018.05.031.

Sachs, I. 2004. *Desenvolvimento includente, sustentável, sustentado.* Rio de Janeiro: Garamond.

Searchinger, T., Heimlich, R., Houghton, R. A., et al. 2008. 'Use of U.S. Croplands for Biofuels Increases Greenhouse Gases through Emissions from Land-Use Change', *Science*, 319(5867), 1238–1240.

Souza, N. R. D., Duft, D. G., Bruno, K. M. B., et al. 2021. 'Unraveling the Potential of Sugarcane Electricity for Climate Change Mitigation in Brazil', *Resources, Conservation and Recycling*, 175, 1–12. (https://www.sciencedirect.com/science/article/abs/pii/S0921344921004870#!).

Sunkel, O. 1981. *La Dimensión ambiental en los estilos de desarollo de América Latina*. CEPAL: Santiago de Chile. E/CEPAL/G.1143.

United Nations. 2015. Paris Agreement. https://unfccc.int/files/meetings/paris_nov_2015/application/pdf/paris_agreement_english_.pdf?gclid=EAIaIQobChMIr6G4won9gQMVRo2DBx3AhQqMEAAYASABEgLi7PD_BwE.

Vaz, C. R, Rauen, T. R. S, and Lezana, Á. G. R. 2017. 'Sustainability and Innovation in the Automotive Sector: A Structured Content Analysis', *Sustainability*, 9, 880, 1–23. doi:10.3390/su9060880.

Vieira do Nascimento, D. M. 2014. 'The Brazilian Experience of Flex-Fuel Vehicles Technology: Towards Low Carbon Mobility', *WIT Transactions on the Built Environment: Urban Transport XX*, 138, 545–553. doi:10.2495/UT140451.

Yu, A. S. O, Nascimento, P. T. de S., Nigro, F. E. B., et al. 2010. *The Evolution of Flex-Fuel Technology in Brazil: The Bosch Case*. Phuket, Thailand: Portland International Center for Management of Engineering and Technology.

10
Energy Transition in Brazil
Contributions from Technological Leapfrogging in the Sugarcane Bioethanol Sector

Paulo N. Figueiredo

10.1. Introduction

Developing economies are expected to play an active role in climate change mitigation, but most lack the technological capabilities to engage in low-carbon innovations (IPCC, 2014; United Nations Economic and Social Commission for Asia and the Pacific [ESCAP], 2016). These economies are responsible for more than 50% of the world's total carbon emissions (World Bank, 2010) and nearly 50% of the global GDP. Since 2000, annual CO_2 emissions from developing countries have more than doubled to nearly 14 gigatonnes per year (Gt/y), with most coming from China, India, and Brazil (IPCC, 2014). Thus, meeting the set targets seems to be ever more challenging, particularly from the standpoint of developing countries.

However, the most influential approaches for meeting low carbon development (LCD) targets rarely consider businesses in developing economies and their technological limitations. For example, it is argued that those targets cannot be met without the full engagement of businesses because of their indistputably large contribution to greenhouse gas (GHG) emissions and their technological capabilities, although governments need to regulate business activities (Moussu, 2016; Inter-Agency Task for on Financing for Development [IATF], 2016). However, these approaches are generally designed for businesses that are global industry leaders from advanced economies, and their technological capabilities to deliver low-carbon innovations are taken for granted, whereas most businesses in developing countries still need to build up their capabilities for engaging in innovative low-carbon activities (Bell, 2012).

Additionally, in climate change parlance, low carbon innovations are deemed to derive from research, development, and demonstration (RD&D) capabilities, which reside in public institutions, such as government agencies and universities, and are delivered to the industry. Furthermore, these RD&D capabilities and innovation are considered the determinant for emission-reduction policies

Paulo N. Figueiredo, *Energy Transition in Brazil* In: *Innovation, Competitiveness, and Development in Latin America*. Edited by: Edmund Amann and Paulo N. Figueiredo, Oxford University Press.
DOI: 10.1093/oso/9780197648070.003.0010

(Dechezleprêtre et al., 2016; International Energy Agency [IEA], 2016). However, such approaches downgrade the importance of incremental-type innovations for climate change mitigation (Rock and Angel, 2005; Rock et al., 2009; Bell, 2009, 2012).

These perspectives are reflected in the influential academic literature on sustainability and innovation systems, based on industries from advanced economies. It is argued that climate change mitigation depends on science-based breakthrough innovations, implemented by renewing the capabilities from different dimensions of innovation systems (Geels and Schot, 2007; Raven and Geels, 2010;; Foxon et al., 2008; Uyarra et al., 2016; Robertson, 2016;) or on the *deployment* of advanced low-carbon technologies and corresponding government regulations (Meadowcroft, 2011;). Therefore, while the abovementioned approaches and studies are relevant for highly industrialized contexts, they leave unexplored the intricacies of the context of developing countries.

From the perspective of developing countries, there has been a growing debate on the relationship between technological innovation and sustainable development (Altenburg, 2008; Mathews, 2008; World Bank, 2010; Berkhout, 2012;) and the role of institutional frameworks in supporting industrial innovation to mitigate GHG emissions (Mathews et al., 2011; Pueyo et al., 2011;). A considerable number of studies have examined the role of international technology transfer in the local development of low-carbon technologies (Bell, 1990, 2012;; Altenburg, 2008; Ockwell et al., 2008; Ockwell et al., 2010; Lema and Lema, 2012), while others have addressed the role of local industry-level capabilities in tackling climate change from different angles (Lewis, 2007, 2011; Marigo et al., 2010; Huenteler et al., 2014). Indeed, there is a need to deepen and expand evidence on the role of the local firm- and industry-level innovation capability accumulation process in contributing to transitions into sustainable industrial development (Hansen and Ockwell, 2014; Figueiredo, 2017).

A special issue of *Industrial and Corporate Change* has generated a valuable contribution in that direction by providing insights relative to opportunities for green development in emerging economies, how these opportunities emerge in different renewable energy sectors, and their implications for the global green economy (see Lema et al., 2021). However, we still know little about the learning processes underlying phases of the process of technological leapfrogging, proxied as innovation capability accumulation related to a novel technology, in renewable energy industries as drivers of energy transition in developing economies. This chapter seeks to discuss this theme by drawing on evidence from the Brazilian sugarcane bioethanol industry. Much has been written about the Brazilian sugarcane bioethanol industry from technical, economic, and innovation perspectives, including its contribution to greening Brazil's energy matrix. Furthermore, the Brazilian government's industrial innovation programme to support the second generation of sugarcane bioethanol has even been referred to as an example of a successful 'mission-oriented policy' (Mazzucato and Penna, 2015, 2016). However, extant studies and policy proposals related to the Brazilian sugarcane bioethanol industry tend to neglect the firm- and industry-level accumulation of innovation capability and learning processes as vital inputs for industrial innovation and development.

10.2. Relevance of Brazil and Its Sugarcane Bioethanol Industry

As the world's seventh-largest GHG emitter, Brazil is one of only five countries with the greatest potential to reduce its emissions over the coming decades. It plays a significant role in global climate change with a number of implications for research and policy actions (World Resources Institute, 2015). Moreover, Brazil is the world's largest sugarcane bioethanol producer. Among the several opportunities to expand the worldwide use of bioenergy, liquid biofuels capable of providing high energy density for air, marine, and heavy freight transport are responsible for the bulk of global petroleum (International Renewable Energy Agency [IRENA], 2016).

Brazil took a leading role in the energy transition process with the use of renewable energies in the BRICS bloc, which also includes Russia, India, China, and South Africa. By 2021, Brazil's energy matrix consisted of more than 45% of renewable sources and 54% of fossil sources. The numbers surpass the countries of the BRICS bloc in terms of the use of renewable energy to mitigate carbon emissions (Losekann and Tavares, 2021).

The use of biofuel currently represents 7% of Brazil's energy matrix; wind and solar reach a share of 4.5%; and biomass 4%. The country's expansion process in the use of renewable sources has gradually compensated for losses in the participation of hydroelectric plants in the energy policy model. The energy matrix of the other BRICS countries is highly concentrated on the use of fossil energies. The highest percentage was registered in South Africa, with the energy matrix formed by 97% of fossil energy, followed by Russia (94%), which is characterized by the high use of oil, India (92%), and China (87%) (Losekann and Tavares, 2021).

Almost half of Brazil's energy production, or 46.1%, comes from renewable sources, which, in terms of sustainability, places the country well above the global average, which is 14.2%. In addition to hydroelectric plants, sugarcane products play an important role. Biofuels represent about 7% of the Brazilian energy matrix, with sugarcane bioethanol being the most used product in this category in the country.

Sugarcane bioethanol may contribute to climate change mitigation, given that it (i) adds oxygen to gasoline, which helps reduce air pollution and harmful emissions in tailpipe exhaust; and (ii) reduces GHG emissions better than any other liquid biofuel produced today at commercial scale by cutting CO_2 emissions by 90% on average. As a high-octane fuel, bioethanol helps prevent engines from knocking and generates more power in higher compression engines. As a clean, affordable, and low-carbon biofuel, sugarcane bioethanol has become the leading renewable fuel for transport (Goldenberg, 2007; Goldenberg et al., 2008).

Sugarcane bioethanol represents one of the best alternatives for fossil fuels in transport: every litre of petrol replaced with sugarcane bioethanol reduces emissions by 90%. Additionally, the by-products of sugarcane bioethanol production (bagasse and straw) are sources for bioelectricity co-generation. The residues are burned in boilers in the sugarcane mills, producing steam and thus self-sufficient electricity. Surplus electricity is then sold to distribution companies. In 2014, sugarcane mills supplied approximately 19,000 gigawatt hours (GWh), or 4% of Brazil's electricity demand. According to estimates, sugarcane bioelectricity could reach 175,000 GWh by 2023 if all potential sources are fully developed. That would be enough energy to supply 23% of Brazil's electricity demand (Brazilian Sugarcane Industry Association, Unica, 2016).

10.3. The Brazilian Sugarcane Bioethanol Industry: A Brief Overview

10.3.1. Sugarcane Bioethanol Technology

Sugarcane bioethanol is a type of biofuel. There are three biofuel generations: (i) the 'first generation' uses feedstocks, such as sugar or starch (e.g. sugarcane, maize) to produce bioethanol, and oilseed or waste oil to produce biodiesel (these are currently the only commercially-available large-scale biofuels); (ii) the 'second generation' uses non-food feedstock (so-called lignocellulosic biomass, such as crop residues) to obtain diesel, jet fuel, and gasoline that can be used without blending in existing vehicles (i.e. a 'drop-in' replacement for fossil fuels); (iii) the 'third generation' is not yet cost-effective and involves the production of diesel and jet fuel from feedstocks such as microalgae. Because of their technical complexities, second- and third-generation biofuels involve intense R&D efforts (International Renewable Energy Agency [IRENA], 2016), different production processes and different plant configurations.

Sugarcane bioethanol is a biofuel produced from the fermentation of sugar cane juice and molasses. Bioethanol can be (i) blended with gasoline at levels ranging from 5% to 27%, reducing petroleum use, or (ii) used as pure bioethanol (85%–100% bioethanol) for powering specific engines. Sugarcane bioethanol helps prevent engine knocking and generates more power in higher-compression engines. It has become a leading renewable fuel for transport, as it is a clean, affordable, and low-carbon biofuel. It also contributes to climate change mitigation: (i) it adds oxygen to gasoline, reducing air pollution and harmful tailpipe emissions; (ii) it reduces GHG emissions more than any other liquid biofuel commercially produced today, by cutting CO_2 emissions by 90% on average (Goldenberg, 2007; IRENA, 2016). Additionally, every litre of petrol replaced with sugarcane bioethanol reduces emissions by 90%. The by-products of sugarcane bioethanol production (bagasse and straw) can be sources for bioelectricity cogeneration. In 2014, sugarcane mills met approximately 4% of Brazil's electricity demand (Unica, 2016).

Furthermore, the sugarcane bioethanol technology and industry offer opportunities for the exploration of new technological activities such as biotechnology, nanotechnology, bioinformatics, biology, agronomy, chemistry, synthetic chemistry, mechanical and electric engineering, pharmaceuticals, and nutrition through interaction between research institutes, universities, specialized suppliers, and others (IEA, 2011; Sousa and Macedo, 2010).

10.3.2. The Sugarcane Bioethanol Industry in Brazil

Brazil has been using sugarcane for sugar exports and alcohol for the pharmaceutical and beverage industries since the sixteenth century. However, it was not until 1920 that sugarcane bioethanol began to be used for transport purposes following the country's inception of the automotive industry. Originally, Brazil produced anhydrous bioethanol gasoline blending based on imported sugarcane varieties and other technologies. However, by the early 1920s, the sugarcane mosaic disease devastated all of Brazil's sugarcane plantations. This crisis forced Brazil to engage in the development of indigenous sugarcane varieties and related technologies. Brazil's first sugarcane variety programme was set up in the early 1920s at the Piracicaba Sugarcane Experimental Station (EECP), in the state of São Paulo. By 1935, all resources within EECP were transferred to the Campinas Agronomic Institute (IAC). The first Brazilian sugarcane variety was introduced to the market by IAC in 1941 (CB41-76).

As a global leader and producer of sugarcane bioethanol for transportation, Brazil has developed a sectoral system that involves not only production firms and suppliers, but also a reputable group of public and private institutions. These include universities, such as the Luiz de Queiroz College of Agriculture, the Inter-university Network for the Sugarcane Industry's Development, and research institutes, such as the Campinas Agronomic Institute, the Sugarcane

Technological Centre, and the Brazilian Bioethanol Science and Technology Laboratory (Figueiredo, 2017). These institutions perform research, recognized globally, on sugarcane and its functions, while reflecting a specific type of R&D governance that provides firms with scientific and technological support for productive sugarcane bioethanol production.

The Cooperative of Sugarcane, Sugar and Bioethanol Producers (Copersucar), created in the early 1950s, oversaw the sugar and bioethanol supply chain, including production, storage, transport, and trade activities.[1] In 1969, Copersucar created the Sugarcane Technological Centre (CTC) to develop technologies for the improvement of sugarcane and derived products. In 1971, the Brazilian government sponsored the creation of the National Programme for Sugarcane Breeding (Planalsucar) to engage in R&D efforts to develop new sugarcane varieties for all Brazilian regions. Since the 1970s, several government policies have been implemented to support the sugarcane bioethanol industry in Brazil (see Table 10.1).

In 1973, as a response to the first oil crisis, President Geisel's government created the National Alcohol Programme (Proálcool) to increase bioethanol production for automotive fuel based on hydrous bioethanol. During the 1970s and 1980s, the Proálcool also contributed to developing new and better sugarcane varieties, and R&D activities in agricultural, grinding, fermentation, distillation, and energy co-generation processes and equipment.

However, because of the structural reforms of the 1990s, the Proálcool became defunct. The Planalsucar was transferred to the Inter-university Network for the Development of the Sugar and Bioethanol Industry (RIDESA), a network of local universities. By the late 1990s, following the initiative of Copersucar and the CTC, a partnership was constructed between the São Paulo Research Foundation, universities, and firms to develop the Sugarcane Genome Project. This involved 240 researchers from 22 institutions and was implemented between 1999 and 2002. This project mapped 238,000 expressed sequence tags (ESTs) of sugarcane genes and created a basis for the development of new sugarcane varieties that are more productive and resistant to drought and poor soil.

The automobile industry's introduction of flexible-fuel vehicles (FFV) in Brazil in 2003 created a new demand for Brazilian sugarcane bioethanol (Law 10,336), contributing to the industry's revival. In 2010 the first second-generation bioethanol mill started production, and the Cana-Vertix Programme was created to develop a specific sugarcane variety with energy features. Brazil ranks as the world's largest sugarcane and sugarcane bioethanol producer. Brazil has 8.8 million hectares (Mha) of sugarcane plantations (about 3.9% of Brazil's total arable area).

[1] In 2011, it engaged in logistics through the creation of an integrated bioethanol distribution system, with the construction and development of multi-use pipelines, interconnecting the production regions to the biggest consumer centres.

Table 10.1 Evolution of the Main Public Policies Related to the Sugarcane Bioethanol Industry

1974	Creation of the Proalcool programme
1977	Addition of 4.5% of anhydrous bioethanol to gasoline
1979	Addition of 15% anhydrous bioethanol to gasoline
1983	Cars powered by hydrated bioethanol account for more than 90% of total sales
1985	Percentage of anhydrous bioethanol in gasoline changes to between 20% and 25%
1990s	Percentage of anhydrous bioethanol in gasoline changes to between 20% and 25%
2003	The first cars with flex technology (bioethanol + gasoline) enter circulation
2005	Start of the National Biodiesel programme; ANP's attributions are expanded
2008	Mandatory addition of biodiesel to petroleum diesel
2010	The mandatory percentage of biodiesel increases (B5)
2011	ANP assumes bioethanol regulation (Law 12,490)
2014	The mandatory percentage of biodiesel increases up to 27.5%
2014	The Support Plan for Agricultural Technological Innovation in the Sugar-Energy Sector, PAISS Agricultural, is a joint initiative between the Brazilian Innovation Agency (FINEP) and the National Bank for Economic and Social Development (BNDES) with the aim of coordinating actions to foster innovation and improve the integration of support instruments available for project financing for the sugar-energy sector.
2017	RenovaBio is the National Biofuels Policy, established by Law No. 13,576/2017, with the following objectives: • Provide an important contribution to the fulfilment of the commitments determined by Brazil under the Paris Agreement. • Promoting the adequate expansion of biofuels in the energy matrix, with emphasis on the regularity of fuel supply; and • Ensure predictability for the fuel market, inducing gains in energy efficiency and reduction of greenhouse gas emissions in the production, marketing, and use of biofuels.

Source: Author's elaboration.

Nevertheless, biofuels such as sugarcane bioethanol have been criticized for potential GHG emissions and competition with food crops (Pereira and Ortega, 2010). In this industry, the harvesting of sugarcane through burning and the storage and transportation of residues can produce GHG emissions. Some approaches can mitigate these effects, for example sugarcane harvesting without burning, using renewable fuels instead of fossil fuel, and optimizing the transportation of products and inputs (Ometto and Roma, 2010).

Regarding sugarcane burning in Brazil, Federal Decree 2661 of 1998 established a gradual elimination of sugarcane burning over a 20-year period. The state of São Paulo, in South-East Brazil, responsible for most of Brazil's bioethanol production, enacted the Agri-environmental Protocol in 2002, which established the progressive elimination of burning from 2007 to 2014. Such measures increase the availability of straw as a biomass source for cellulosic bioethanol production. Additionally, harvesting mechanization maintains organic material concentrations in the soil, increasing CO_2 sequestration (Oliveira et al., 2015).

Another important measure involves the treatment of residues such as vinasse.[2] Several improvements in vinasse storage and transportation methods have emerged: biogas generation through anaerobic digestion of vinasse (Bernal et al., 2017); development of new technologies to reduce vinasse volumes by increasing the bioethanol concentration during fermentation (Lopes et al., 2016). The implementation of these innovations depends on the firms' technological capabilities.

During the 1970s and 1980s in Brazil, the expansion of bioethanol replaced some areas once dedicated to food crops, especially in São Paulo. However, since the 1990s, these impacts have been reduced as the food crop area has not decreased and the sugarcane plantations have expanded over pasturelands (Goldenberg, 2009). Brazil's total area consists of 58% forests and native vegetation, 40% arable land, and 2% other land types. Of the total arable land, 30% is unutilized and potentially available for sugarcane plantation expansion. Currently, sugarcane plantations occupy less than 3% of Brazil's arable land and are primarily located in the North-East coastal and South-East regions, more than 2,000 kilometers away from the Amazon rainforest.

This low proportion of arable land occupation reflects average sugarcane productivity growth, which has increased from 45 tonnes per hectare (t/ha) (in 1975) to 78 t/ha (in 2015), whereas bioethanol productivity has increased from 3,800 litres per hectare (L/ha) (1970s) to the current 7,000 L/ha. This productivity increase reflects the development of new sugarcane varieties and improvements in agricultural practices (Goldenberg, 2009; Unica, 2016).

The participation of sugarcane products in Brazil's primary energy production increased from 16.6% (2006) to 17.6% (2015) (Ministry of Mines and Energy, 2016). For the 2013–2014 crop, the sugar and bioethanol industry represented approximately 2% of Brazil's GDP, milled 640 million tonnes of sugarcane, produced 27 billion litres of bioethanol, co-generated 43,919 gigajoules (GJ) of bioelectricity, employed 4.5 million people, and generated US$6.3 billion in

[2] This is a liquid residue derived from sugar and bioethanol production that may cause GHG emissions. It is used in ferti-irrigation of sugarcane crops because it contains a high organic matter content and several chemical components beneficial to sugarcane nutrition, thus reducing chemical fertilizer costs (Lopes et al., 2016). However, vinasse transport and application are expensive and require careful procedures to avoid contamination of table waters and soil saturation with cations (Oliveira et al., 2015).

taxes (ProCana, 2014). Their annual revenue in 2019 ranged from US$10.4 billion for sugarcane. The industry involves many vertically integrated firms, with an bioethanol production capacity of 271,340 m^3/d (National Agency for Oil, Natural Gas and Biofuels [ANP], 2013). The largest 10 producers contribute less than 40% of the total milled sugarcane (ProCana, 2014).

10.4. Technological Leapfrogging and the Brazilian Bioethanol Industry

10.4.1. Technological Leapfrogging: Concept and Operationalization

One of the key technological characteristics of firms operating in developing and emerging economies, which are referred to as latecomers, is their lack of innovation capability and their distance from the international innovation frontier. The narrowing of the innovation capability gap between latecomers and global leaders is known as technological catch-up.

However, the term 'catch-up' suggests a single pathway, with different firms distributed along it, with a clearly defined 'frontier'. Specifically, the notion of a frontier tends to be associated with that of all firms following the same specific technological path (towards the same end-point) as that previously followed by global technological leaders. In reality, the process of technological development of latecomers cannot be represented using the analogy of a race along a fixed track, because of the possibility of successful overtaking by latecomers moving in new directions, and of the emergence of radical discontinuities that open up opportunities for them (see Bell and Figueiredo, 2012). By such means, latecomer firms may accumulate capabilities by which they may pursue significantly new *directions* of innovation that depart from the trajectories previously mapped out by earlier innovators, thus opening *qualitatively different segments* of the international innovation frontier. In this chapter, the notion of catch-up therefore also encompasses so-called overtaking. In addition, rather than deeming the technological frontier to be an end-point or even a moving target, it is considered here to be a fluid area or horizon to be explored.

Since the 1970s, researchers have examined firms' technological catch-up through different frameworks (Bell, 2006; Bell and Figueiredo, 2012). Lee and Lim (2001) introduced a perspective on technological catch-up beyond the notion of latecomers following global leaders' paths. Their nuanced framework identifies variations in catch-up patterns: *path-following* (latecomers follow forerunners' path), *stage-skipping* (firms follow forerunners' path but skip some stages), and *path-creating* (firms explore their own technological development path). Entering path creation may not always mean creating a new path *after* having attained a significant level of innovation capability in the dominant technology, as reflected in Lee and Lim's (2001) schema and related studies. Firms can engage in path-creation processes during the *early stages* of the industry and initial stages of innovative capability development. When unable to replicate dominant technologies, firms may seek *alternative options* and path-creation searches. We refer to these processes as *technological leapfrogging*.

The orientation of innovation towards cleaner technologies and production systems that reduce both costs and environmental damage is of interest to research into technological capability-building in developing economies (Ely and Bell, 2009). These concerns arise from the potential environmental damage derived from economic and industrial growth in low- and middle-income countries. It has been argued that mitigation of this environmental burden of growth depends largely on the accumulation of indigenous capabilities for innovative activities within firms in developing economies—'latecomer firms' (Bell, 2009, 2012). Indeed, the accumulation of innovative capabilities in latecomer firms is intrinsically linked to sustainable industrial development (Berkhout, 2012; Ockwell and Mallet, 2012). Industrial development that encourages innovative capability accumulation for environmentally friendly technologies may produce production modes beyond the fossil-fuel industrial mode (Lee et al., 2014).

Over the past four decades, many studies have emerged that investigate firm-level capability-building in developing economies and industries (see reviews by Figueiredo, 2001; Bell, 2006; Bell and Figueiredo, 2012), including clean technology industries (Marigo et al., 2010; Lewis, 2011). However, some issues remain poorly explored. For instance, heterogeneity of capability accumulation processes is expected between and within firms (Bell and Pavitt, 1995; Figueiredo, 2001), but this issue has received little empirical treatment. Although studies have examined inter-firm differences in *current* technological capabilities (Hansen and Ockwell, 2014;), less attention has been paid to differences between and within firms in the *processes* by which they accumulate diverse levels and types of technological capabilities, especially regarding renewable energy industries. Additionally, few studies exist that explicitly tackle the time scales involved in the capability-building process (Figueiredo, 2001; Ariffin, 2010).

In contrast, considerable studies exist that assume that the industrial innovative capabilities of developing economies are associated with breakthrough innovations from research institutions (United Nations Framework Convention on Climate Change [UNFCCC], 2009; Raven and Geels, 2010; World Bank, 2010). Such studies assess innovative capabilities via cross-sectional studies using standard proxies such as R&D indicators and patents (Walz and Marscheider-Weidemann, 2011; Wu and Mathews, 2012). However, these proxies cannot completely capture a firm's innovative capability, particularly for firms with capabilities other than R&D (Bell and Pavitt, 1995; Bell, 2012). Nevertheless, judgements about 'dynamics' are made, generally indicating the absence of change or false negative conclusions (Ariffin, 2010).

Standard proxies also neglect some capabilities required for diverse innovative activities (Patel and Pavitt, 1994; Bell, 2009). For example, Rock et al. (2009) demonstrated the importance of engineering-based, incremental innovations for sustainable technological development for firms in Malaysia; Huenteler et al. (2014) demonstrated the importance of local and engineering-based technological capabilities for renewable electricity cost reduction in Thailand. Therefore, considering that firms' technological capability-building processes change slowly, short-term observations, 'snapshots', or statistical indicators cannot encompass the movement and time scales involved (Bell, 2006).

Therefore, this chapter is concerned with technological catch-up, understood as the closing of the innovative capability gap between latecomer firms and global industry leaders in advanced economies. Firms' capabilities reflect what a firm can do (Nelson and Winter, 1982; Jacobides and Winter, 2012): a firm is capable of something due to the possession of a reliable capacity to bring that thing about because of intended action (Dosi et al., 2000). Such reliable capacity or stock of resources (capability) involves dimensions such as human capital, techno-physical systems, and organizational systems (Bell and Pavitt, 1995; Leonard-Barton, 1995; Teece, 2012). In the operationalization of the capability construct, we draw on the 'revealed capability' approach (Sutton, 2012), the observable outcome reflecting the symbiotic relationship between these capability dimensions in terms of firms' innovative technological activities. In line with studies that take this approach (see review in Bell and Figueiredo, 2012) and drawing on technical literature and industry experts, the tailored framework examines capability accumulation in the sugarcane bioethanol industry (Figure 10.1).

Specifically, we operationalize the technological capability accumulation construct through a 'revealed capability' approach, in which a firm's implemented technological activities reflect its technological capability level. Consistent with studies taking this approach (see Bell and Figueiredo, 2012; Figueiredo and Cohen, 2019; Figueiredo et al., 2020), the capability maturity framework in Figure 10.1 identifies five technological capability levels that firms may accumulate over time: one for 'production' (or operational) capability, and 'basic', 'intermediate', 'advanced', and 'world-leading' for innovation capability. This framework highlights the capabilities internal to the firm while recognizing

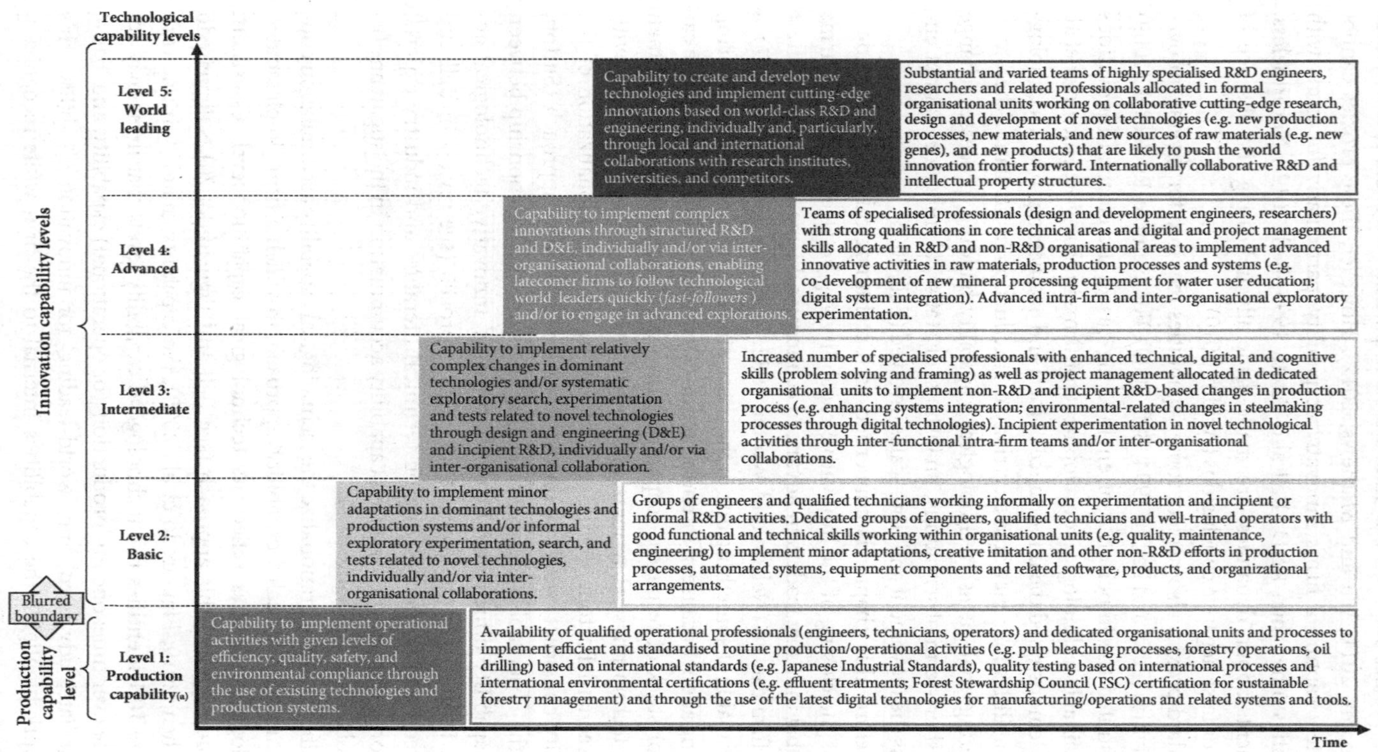

Figure 10.1. Maturity model for firm-level technological capability accumulation in latecomer process industries.

Sources: Adapted from Lall (1992), Bell and Pavitt (1995), Figueiredo (2001, 2011, 2017), Bell and Figueiredo (2012), Figueiredo and Cohen (2019).

that a substantial part of a firm's capability lies in other organizations outside the firm, that is, suppliers, users, specialized consulting firms, competitors, research institutes, and universities.

10.4.2. Technological Leapfrogging in the Brazilian Sugarcane Bioethanol Ecosystem in Brazil

In this chapter, the focus is on one specific technological function: that of *feedstock*. It involves sugarcane silviculture, sugarcane variety development through genetic breeding, and transgenics. In light of the framework in Figure 10.1, Figure 10.2 illustrates the process of technological leapfrogging in the Brazilian sugarcane bioethanol industry.

10.4.3. Emergence Phase

Although Brazil began using sugarcane bioethanol for transportation and developed indigenous sugarcane varieties in the 1920s, it was not until the early 1970s that the sugarcane bioethanol industry became formally organized. During the emergence phase, the ecosystem simultaneously accumulated incomplete Levels 2 and 3 innovation capabilities (Figure 10.2), while Level 1 production capabilities were only based on trials and pilot runs. Given the in-house shortage of higher capability levels to develop the desired technology, the ecosystem jumped into the creation of elements of Level 5 innovation capability. External R&D was created to offset the firm-level shortage of innovation capabilities. In 1969, the Sugarcane Technological Centre (CTC) was created to develop

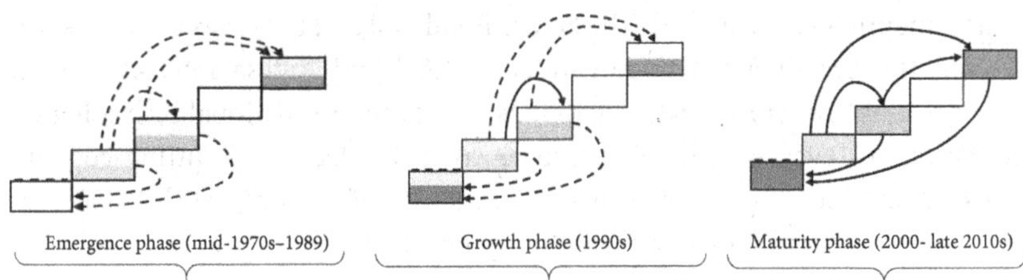

Figure 10.2. Phases of the technological capability accumulation in the Brazilian sugarcane bioethanol industry: technological leapfrogging.

Key: (a) Black arrows within each figure represent the movements of technological capability accumulation levels: continuous arrows represent a completed accumulation process, while dotted ones imply an incomplete accumulation process; (b) colour fill levels in each step illustrate the completeness of the capability level accumulation.

technologies and products using sugarcane. In 1971, the Brazilian government created Planalsucar to pursue R&D for new sugarcane varieties. In 1973, as a response to the first oil crisis, the government created Proálcool to increase bioethanol production for hydrous bioethanol-based automotive fuel. The CTC and the Campinas Agronomic Institute entered into a cooperative agreement for the joint use of the germplasm bank. Two producing companies implemented their own genetic improvement programmes. The cooperation between producing companies, universities, and research institutes remained the same as in the background period. The producing companies implemented pruning disinfection techniques in their seedling nurseries. These efforts contributed to obtaining new varieties using conventional genetic improvement methods and creating germplasm banks.

The creation of Planalsucar, CTC, and Proálcool contributed to the Brazilian bioethanol industry by implementing innovative activities of complex changes based on applied R&D. During the 1970s and 1980s, Proálcool contributed to the development of new and improved sugarcane varieties. During the 1990s, Proálcool was discontinued and Planalsucar was transferred to RIDESA, created in 1991. These changes led to a period of relative stagnation in the industry. However, the introduction of FFVs to Brazil's automobile industry in the early 2000s created new demand for Brazilian sugarcane bioethanol, contributing to the industry's revival.

10.4.4. Growth Phase

During the growth phase, there were intense efforts to accumulate Level 5 innovation capability for the sugarcane bioethanol technology. In parallel, as they completed the accumulation of Levels 2 to 4 capabilities as well as Level 1 production. R&D efforts sought to explore the technological route of transgenics and genetic mapping of sugarcane. The end of Proálcool and the crisis at Copersucar affected the Brazilian bioethanol industry. IAC and Ridesa intensified their efforts to implement innovative activities along the international technological frontier. CTC, even with the Copersucar crisis, implemented cutting-edge innovative activities (e.g., transgenic sugarcane). In other words, at this stage, the Brazilian bioethanol industry began to explore the technological route of transgenic development of a new feedstock.

For instance, the São Paulo Research Foundation created the SucEST Project. In this project, innovative activities were carried out with world-class R&D (e.g. mapping the sugarcane genome). The producing companies have implemented heat-treatment techniques in the management of their seedling nurseries. The way in which technological capabilities were accumulated in the industry remained almost unchanged, with high dependence on the efforts of research institutes and universities, and a supporting role for producing companies.

10.4.5. Maturity Phase

During the maturity phase, there was the consolidation of Level 5 innovation capability around the sugarcane bioethanol technology. More intense efforts were made to collaborate with different research institutes, universities, and biotechnology companies to apply biotechnological tools in the process of obtaining new varieties. The relationship between producing companies and research organizations has evolved. Producing companies started more participatory efforts in the process of obtaining new varieties. The producing companies began their participation in genetic experiments and implemented more complex phytosanitary techniques, such as roguing and polymerase chain reaction (PCR) molecular diagnostics.

New organizations were created (e.g. Embrapa Agroenergia and CTBE), which collaborated with IAC, Ridesa, and CTC to generate innovative activities with cutting-edge R&D (e.g. sugarcane generation for second-grade bioethanol generation, use of biotechnological tools, etc.). Biotechnology companies have also initiated collaborative efforts with the CTC. For example, BASF and Bayer worked cooperatively to generate transgenic varieties. Collaborations between a producing firm, the IAC, and RIDESA led to the development of a new sugarcane variety, 'Cana-Vertix', for second-generation bioethanol industrial processes.

10.5. The Role of Learning Strategies in Technological Leapfrogging in the Brazilian Sugarcane Bioethanol Feedstock

10.5.1. Technological Learning Strategies: Concept and Operationalization

Technological capabilities are not automatically 'acquired from the market'; their creation and accumulation by specific firms depend on deliberate and costly efforts in learning strategies (Bell and Pavitt, 1993; Bell and Figueiredo, 2012). Technological learning processes involve costly, deliberate efforts to create and accumulate capabilities for production and innovation activities. We follow previous research (Bell and Figueiredo, 2012; Figueiredo et al., 2020) and operationalize firms' learning process constructs through external and internal learning mechanisms.

External learning mechanisms involve actions to identify and acquire knowledge and skills from external sources. Internal learning includes intra-firm efforts toward creating, sharing, integrating, and codifying knowledge. Drawing on Bell and Figueiredo (2012), Figueiredo and Cohen (2019) and Figueiredo et al. (2021) identify a broad set of external and internal learning mechanisms, which are applied in this chapter. Regarding external learning mechanisms, this framework identifies the possible partners with which each firm can potentially collaborate in some of its external knowledge search-and-acquisition strategies. Furthermore, learning mechanisms can identify possible outputs in terms of capabilities and innovative activities.

10.5.1.1. Emergence Phase

Before the emergence phase, the bioethanol industry in Brazil had already formed a body of highly trained researchers, agronomists, and technicians, as well as a base of scientific knowledge in the areas of biology, agronomy, and genetic improvement. This knowledge and human resources created in the background period served as a basis for the industry to continue and expand its learning efforts and, consequently, its technological capabilities in the emergence phase.

Essentially, the Brazilian bioethanol industry improved the combination of learning mechanisms in relation to the background period. The industry continued to use training mechanisms (e.g. it set up a course at the University of Mauritius to train professionals), operational and laboratory experimentation (e.g. advances in genetic improvement programmes contributed to the creation of new knowledge about plant biology) and started to use the applied R&D mechanism (e.g. genetic improvement programmes started to study the phenotypic and genotypic characteristics of the plant to improve the process of obtaining new varieties; a new method of evaluating the quality and robustness of promising varieties) in relation to the background period. The improvement of the combination of learning mechanisms contributed to the accumulation of innovation capabilities during this phase (see Table 10.2).

10.5.1.2. Growth Phase

The industry further improved the combination of learning mechanisms used in the growth phase versus the emergence phase. The industry used a new combination of technological learning mechanisms, continuing to use the applied R&D mechanism (e.g. collaborations with universities and research institutes in the US and France to create knowledge in the area of genetic manipulation; expansion of studies of identification of species and expansion of the number

Table 10.2 Technological Learning Strategies Supporting the Technological Capability Accumulation in the Brazilian Sugarcane Bioethanol Industry: Emergence Phase

Training programmes	The industry improved its training efforts, for example: • Copersucar created technical committees to carry out technical visits. These technical visits aimed to prospect foreign technologies in Australia, USA (Hawaii), Cuba, and South Africa. • CTC created specific courses for local professionals. This was one of the mechanisms that contributed to the creation of basic technological knowledge for the beginning of the genetic improvement program at the Copersucar Technology Centre in the early 1970s. Specifically, these courses were important for disseminating knowledge in the agricultural and industrial areas and creating knowledge for carrying out genetic experiments on sugarcane. • Organizations such as Planalsucar, IAC and CTC offered training to producing companies to pass on technical knowledge about sugarcane varieties. There were lectures, courses and training given by the researchers and technicians of the institutions aiming to transfer the procedures, concepts and criteria for creating and monitoring experiments with clones to interested companies. • These organisations trained the producing companies to work with phytosanitary techniques, such as heat treatment, asepsis of cutting instruments and disinfection of the cutting edge. These techniques enable controlling and combatting diseases like ratoon rickets and scalds. In these events, results of promising clones were also presented, and opinions and feedback were collected from agronomists of the producing companies. • These efforts were essential for homogenising basic and operational knowledge for implementing and operating nurseries with quality and disease control in producing companies.
Experimentations	The industry improved its operational and laboratory experimentation efforts, for example: • CTC, Planalsucar and IAC used operational experimentation in genetic improvement to expand knowledge about obtaining new sugarcane varieties by conventional methods, plant biology and the adaptability of varieties to different environments. • The efforts on operational and laboratory experimentation contributed to the producer companies to create and assimilate technical and operational knowledge for the management of experimentation nurseries as multiplication nurseries. Teams of researchers, agronomists and technicians conducted genetic experiments and tests to evaluate the performance of new sugarcane varieties. These experimentations contributed to the development of several sugarcane varieties.
Applied R&D	The CTC created its germplasm bank in the Northeast state of Bahia with thousands of genotypes of different species. An agreement was signed between the IAC and the CTC that allowed the IAC program to use the experimental crossing station in Bahia, where the world's largest number of sugarcane genotypes is located. Researchers from the CTC and IAC carried out R&D activities individually and in cooperation to create and assimilate knowledge about the biology of sugarcane, its phenotypic and genotypic characteristics, and species identification. They studied the adaptability and performance of species and new varieties. This learning effort contributed to improving genetic programs for obtaining new sugarcane varieties.

of species available and catalogued in germplasm banks) and started the use of basic R&D (e.g. the formation of the SucEST Project which initiated studies for the mapping of the sugarcane genome). The use and combination of the learning mechanisms outlined in Table 10.3 proved effective in the accumulation of innovation capabilities during the growth phase.

10.5.1.3. Maturity Phase

The industry used essentially the same combination of mechanisms as compared to the growth phase, but especially the experimentation and applied R&D mechanisms were used in a different way (Table 10.4). The industry has improved the use of mechanisms for training programmes and operational experimentation (e.g. implementation of joint analysis and testing of promising varieties between producing companies and research organizations. Applied R&D (e.g. CTC/BASF/Bayer cooperation on transgenics to create new varieties that are more resistant to drought and diseases; IAC/Ridesa/Sigma cooperation in the Cana-Vertix Programme to create a specific variety for second-generation bioethanol) and basic (e.g. the SucEST-Fun Project has advanced knowledge about the sugarcane genome for the development of molecular markers and biotechnological tools to be used in genetic improvement programmes) in relation to the growth phase. Therefore, improving the combination of learning mechanisms contributed to the industry's progress in its technological capabilities from basic production (Level 1) from the growth phase (1990–1990) to advanced production (Level 2) in the maturity phase (2000–2014) and to sustain its world-leading innovation capability (Level 6).

10.6. Conclusion

Much has been written about the importance of technological innovation and corresponding capabilities in different renewable energy sectors to achieve greener industrial and economic development in emerging economies. Also, it has extensively been argued that the accumulation of innovation capabilities in cleaner technologies in emerging-market firms can mitigate the environmental damage associated with economic growth. However, we still know little about the learning processes underlying phases of the process of technological leapfrogging, proxied as innovation capability accumulation related to a novel technology, in renewable energy industries as drivers of energy transition in developing economies. This chapter sought to contribute to exploring this gap by briefly examining the process of technological leapfrogging—measured in terms of innovation capability accumulation—and the underlying learning strategies

Table 10.3 Technological Learning Strategies Supporting the Technological Capability Accumulation in the Brazilian Sugarcane Bioethanol Industry: Growth Phase

Training programmes	Training programmes to disseminate knowledge of genetic experimentation involved and facilitated: Transfer of the basic concepts to create and conduct a genetic improvement trial: researchers and technicians from IAC, CTC, and Ridesa offered courses in the classroom and in the field for agronomists and technicians from producing companies. The courses carried out by CTC, Ridesa, and IAC (Sugarcane Phytotechnical Group) aimed at transferring knowledge to increase the absorption capacity of agronomists and technicians of the companies to participate more actively in the process of generating new varieties. These training mechanisms were important for the creation, assimilation, and dissemination of knowledge of phytosanitary techniques for conducting tests such as heat treatment, asepsis of cutting instruments, and disinfection of the cutting edge. Universities linked to Ridesa expanded the number of undergraduate and graduate courses related to sugarcane cultivation, contributing to the training of human resources both to work in producing companies and to the creation of researchers to work in research organizations.
Experimentations	Operational and laboratory experimentation mechanisms contributed to the continuation of the CTC, Ridesa, and IAC genetic improvement programmes. The combination of the operational and laboratory experimentations with the applied R&D contributed to the industry obtaining more than 30 new sugarcane varieties in a decade.
Applied R&D	The CTC carried out more robust applied R&D efforts to create and assimilate knowledge on genetic manipulation, and new processes for obtaining new varieties and transgenics. The CTC has also established collaborations with foreign organizations for research into transformation methods, such as collaborative applied R&D efforts between CTC, Texas A&M, Cornell, and INRA, which contributed to the development of the first transgenic sugarcane in Brazil. Furthermore, the combination of operational and laboratory experimentation mechanisms and applied R&D contributed to Ridesa developing 20 new sugarcane varieties while CTC and IAC launched dozens of new varieties
Basic R&D	The industry carried out basic R&D to create and expand knowledge about the sugarcane genome, genotypic traits, molecular markers, quantitative trait loci, and other biotechnological tools, including a consortium composed of different universities, research institutes, and companies, which was organized to form the SucEST Project. This consortium, which involved 240 researchers from more than 40 institutions, 17 of them from abroad, evaluated the sugarcane transcriptome and organized a vast database on the plant's genetic material. One of the results of the project was the creation and training of qualified scientists and researchers in biotechnology, bioinformatics, genetics, biology, etc. The SucEST Project resulted in the SucEST-Fun Project, which marked the beginning of research into molecular markers for sugarcane in Brazil.

Table 10.4 Technological Learning Strategies Supporting the Technological Capability Accumulation in the Brazilian Sugarcane Bioethanol Industry: Maturity Phase

Training programmes	The bioethanol industry in Brazil changed the way it used training, for example: • Researchers linked to Ridesa participated in courses, seminars, and international congresses on genetic improvement, leading to the dissemination of advances made by the Ridesa genetic improvement programme and the exchange of information between genetic improvement programmes in different parts of the world. • The focus of training programmes shifted to enabling producer companies to participate in the final phases of the IAC and Ridesa genetic improvement programmes. • These training and courses contributed to the management of the experimental fields implemented in the companies' crops with the most advanced techniques for treating and preventing diseases, such as molecular PCR diagnosis, serology, nitrogen fertilizer splitting, and microscopy.
Experimentations	IAC and Ridesa began to conduct experimentations in a cooperative manner with producing companies to expand knowledge about the process of obtaining new varieties of sugarcane by conventional methods, plant biology, and the adaptability of varieties to different environments. Experimentations centred on the increased responsibilities of technicians and agronomists of producing firms in the process of obtaining new varieties. Producing firms also started joint activities with Ridesa and IAC for analysis, testing, and selection of promising clones in the final stages of the improvement process. They benefited from this new practice mainly by accumulating technical knowledge of promising varieties.
Applied R&D	These efforts by CTC, Ridesa, and IAC contributed to the creation and assimilation of knowledge about the biology of sugarcane, its phenotypic and genotypic characteristics, and species identification, and carried out studies of adaptability and performance of species and new varieties. Ridesa, CTC, and IAC established applied R&D collaborations with foreign institutions to exchange varieties to be researched in different countries. These collaborative applied R&D efforts contributed to the expansion of Ridesa's germplasm banks and, consequently, the expansion of the diversity of germplasm to be used in obtaining new varieties of sugarcane. CTC, Ridesa, IAC, and Sigma made efforts in applied R&D with the objective of creating and assimilating knowledge in genetic modification, genetic improvement using transgenic techniques, and genetic improvement of new raw materials. For example, this contributed to the CTC implementing R&D activities to create transgenic sugarcane varieties with multinationals BASF and Bayer. The industry has also relied on applied R&D efforts to obtain specific varieties for second generation of bioethanol – e.g., the Cana-Vertix Programme. It was the first effort to obtain a new variety specifically for the manufacture of second-generation bioethanol.

Table 10.4 Continued

Basic R&D	Basic R&D efforts contributed to the expansion of knowledge about the sugarcane genome, expressed sequence markers, quantitative character loci, molecular markers, and other biotechnological tools. The SucEST Project, which had the purpose of carrying out activities for mapping the sugarcane genome and developing biotechnological tools, was carried out with basic R&D collaborations between local and international research institutes (e.g. CTC, Cold Spring Harbor Laboratory (US) etc.), local universities and producing companies. These efforts have contributed to advancing the knowledge of the use of biotechnological tools for the genetic mapping of sugarcane, the understanding of its genotypic characteristics, and the use of biotechnology to accelerate the process of obtaining new varieties of sugarcane.

in the Brazilian bioethanol industry and its consequent contribution to the country's energy transition.

Renewable sources have been playing an increasingly important role in Brazil's energy matrix. At least within the bloc of BRICS countries, Brazil stands out, with more than 45% of its energy matrix originating from renewable sources. Within that energy matrix, sugarcane bioethanol has been demonstrating an important and growing proportion. Through an effective technological leapfrogging process, Brazil was propelled towards being the world leader in production, technological innovation, and large-scale use of low-carbon biofuel based on sugarcane bioethanol.

The evidence in this chapter has explored the deliberate qualitative changes in the different learning processes and mechanisms that were needed to support the effective technological leapfrogging in the Brazilian sugarcane ethanol industry. These learning efforts involved a combination of initiatives from different components of the sectoral system, such as producing firms, suppliers, lead users, universities, and research institutes. There was also a convergence of the private-sector and government efforts around a common objective. One of the key characteristics of this technological leapfrogging process was the wide spectrum of innovation capabilities accumulated by different stakeholders of the sectoral system, but to meet the needs and demands of producing firms. This experience tends to differ from policy approaches that tend to emphasize research activities located in universities and research institutes as the main sources of industrial innovation and development.

Therefore, firm- and intra-industry learning processes underlying the accumulation of significant innovation capability levels should be placed at the centre of the policy debate and proposals related to energy transition in developing economies. Although much has been proposed in terms of a more 'entrepreneurial' role of the governments and related policy actions towards achieving low-carbon industrial innovation and in developing economies, there is a scarcity of concrete policy mechanisms oriented to achieve effective firm- and intra-industry-level learning processes underpinning innovation capability accumulation and related assessments.

Finally, the discussion in this chapter also draws attention to the opportunities opened by natural-resource-intensive industries in terms of technological catch-up, learning and innovation and their positive impacts on climate change mitigation. Indeed, the evidence in this chapter suggests that the development of high-level innovation capability accumulation, including science-based capabilities, contributes to reconciling or mediating the exploitation of natural resources with the need for natural resource preservation and technological catch-up and economic growth.

References

Altenburg, T. 2008. 'New Global Players in Innovation? China's and India's Technological Catch-up and the Low Carbon Economy', in H. Schmitz, D. Messner, eds., *Poor and Powerful: The Rise of China and India and the Implications for Europe*. Bonn: German Development Institute, 26–39.

Bell, M. 1990. *Continuing Industrialisation, Climate Change and International Technology Transfer*. Brighton: Science Policy Research Unit, Sussex University.

ANP. 2013. 'Brazilian Bioethanol Industry', http://www.anp.gov.br (accessed 16 November 2016).

Ariffin, N. 2010. 'Internationalisation of Technological Innovative Capabilities: Levels, Types And Speed (Learning Rates) in the Electronics Industry in Malaysia', *International Journal of Technological Learning, Innovation and Development*, 3(4), 347–391.

Bell, M. 2006. 'Time and Technological Learning in Industrializing Countries: How Long Does It Take? How Fast Is It Moving (if at All)?', *International Journal of Technology and Management*, 36, 25–39.

Bell, M. 2009. 'Innovation Capabilities and Directions of Development', *STEPS Working Paper 33*. Brighton: STEPS Centre.

Bell, M. 2012. 'International Technology Transfer, Innovation Capabilities and Sustainable Directions of Development', in D. Ockwell and A. Mallet, eds., *Low-Carbon Technology Transfer: From Rhetoric to Reality*. London: Routledge, 20–47.

Bell, M., and Pavitt, K., 1993. 'Technological Accumulation and Industrial Growth: Contrasts between Developed and Developing Countries', *Industrial and Corporate Change* 2(1), 157–211.

Bell, M., and Pavitt, K. 1995. 'The Development of Technological Capabilities', in *Trade, Technology and International Competitiveness*. Washington, DC: World Bank.

Bell, M., and Figueiredo, P. N. 2012. 'Building Innovative Capabilities in Latecomer Emerging Market Firms: Some Key Issues', in E. Amann and J. Cantwell, eds., *Innovative Firms in Emerging Market Countries*. Oxford: Oxford University Press, 24–109.

Berkhout, F. 2012. 'Green Growth and Innovation: Home-Grown Technology and Innovation in the Developing World Are Key to Achieving Sustainable Growth', *Human Dimensions of Wildlife* (1), 18–21.

Bernal, A. P., Santos, I. F. S., Silva, A. P. M., et al. 2017. 'Vinasse Biogás for Energy Generation in Brazil: An Assessment of Economic Feasibility, Energy Potential and Avoided CO_2 Emissions, *Journal of Cleaner Production*, 151, 260–271.

Consoni, F., and Quadros, R. 2006. 'From Adaptation to Complete Vehicle Design: A Case Study of Product Development Capabilities in a Carmaker in Brazil, *International Journal of Technology Management*, 36(1–3), 91–107.

Dechezleprêtre, A., Martin, R., and Bassi, S. 2016. *Climate Change Policy, Innovation and Growth*. London and Seoul: The Grantham Research Institute and Global Green Growth Institute.

Dosi, G., Hobday, M., and Marengo, L. 2000. *Problem-Solving Behaviours, Organisational Forms and the Complexity of Tasks*. Pisa: Sant'Anna School of Advanced Studies.

Ely, A., and Bell, M. 2009. 'The Original "Sussex Manifesto": Its Past and Future Relevance'. *STEPS Working Paper 27*.

Figueiredo, P. N. 2001. *Technological Learning and Competitive Performance*. Cheltenham, UK: Edward Elgar.

Figueiredo, P. N. 2011. 'The Role of Dual Embeddedness in the Innovative Performance of MNE Subsidiaries: Evidence from Brazil', *Journal of Management Studies*, 48(2), 417–440.

Figueiredo, P. N. 2017. 'Micro-Level Technological Capability Accumulation in Developing Economies: Insights from the Brazilian Sugarcane Bioethanol Industry', *Journal of Cleaner Production*, 167(C), 416–431.

Figueiredo, P. N., Cabral., B. P., and Silva, F. Q. 2021. 'Intricacies of Firm-Level Innovation Performance: An Empirical Analysis of Latecomer Process Industries', *Technovation*, 102302, 1–21.

Figueiredo, P. N., and Cohen, M. 2019. 'Explaining Early Entry into Path-Creation Technological Catch-Up in the Forestry and Pulp Industry: Evidence from Brazil', *Research Policy*, 48(7), 1694–1713.

Figueiredo, P. N., Larsen, H., and Hansen, U. E. 2020. 'The Role of Interactive Learning in Innovation Capability Building in Multinational Subsidiaries: A Micro-Level Study of Biotechnology in Brazil, *Research Policy*, 49(6), 103995.

Figueiredo, P. N., and Piana, J. 2016. 'When "One Thing (Almost) Leads to Another": A Micro-Level Exploration of Learning Linkages in Brazil's Mining Industry', *Resources Policy*, 49(3), 405–414.

Foxon, T. J., Köhler, J., and Oughton, C. (eds). 2008. *Innovation for a Low Carbon Economy: Economic, Institutional and Management Approaches*. Cheltenham: Edward Elgar.

Geels, F. W., and Schot, J. 2007. 'Typology of Sociotechnical Transition Pathways', *Research Policy*, 36(3), 399–417.

Goldenberg, J. 2007. 'Bioethanol for a Sustainable Energy Future', *Science*, 315, 808–810.

Goldenberg, J., Coelho, S., and Guardabassi, P. 2008. 'The Sustainability of Ethanol Production from Sugarcane', *Energy Policy* 36(6), 2086–2097.

Goldenberg, J. 2009. 'The Brazilian Experience with Biofuels (Innovations Case Narrative)', *Innovations*, 4(4), 91–107.

Hansen, U. E., and Ockwell, D. 2014. 'Learning and Technological Capability Building in Emerging Economies: The Case of the Biomass Power Equipment Industry in Malaysia', *Technovation*, 34, 617–630.

Huenteler, J., Niebuhr, C., and Schmidt, T. S. 2014. 'The Effect of Local and Global Learning on the Cost of Renewable Energy in Developing Countries', *Journal of Cleaner Production* 128, 6–21.

Inter-Agency Task for on Financing for Development–IATF. 2016. Inaugural Report of the Inter-agency Task Force on Financing for Development–Addis Ababa Action Agenda: Monitoring Commitments and Actions.

Intergovernmental Panel on Climate Change–IPCC. 2014. *Climate Change 2014: Impacts, Adaptation, and Vulnerability*. Geneva: IPCC.

International Energy Agency–IAE. 2016. *Energy Technology Perspectives 2016: Towards Sustainable Urban Energy Systems*. Paris: IEA.

IRENA. 2016. *Boosting Biofuels: Sustainable Paths to Greater Energy Security*. IRENA.

Jacobides, M., and Winter, S. 2012. 'Capabilities Structure, Agency and Evolution', *Organization Science*, 23(5), 1365–1381.

Lall, S. 1992. 'Technological Capabilities and Industrialization', *World Development*, 20(2), 165–186.

Lee, K., Juma, C., and Mathews, J. 2014. 'Innovation Capabilities for Sustainable Development in Africa', Wider/UNU Working Paper 062.

Lee, K., and Lim, C. S., 2001. 'Technological Regimes, Catching-Up and Leapfrogging: Findings from the Korean Industries', *Research Policy*, 30(3), 459–483.

Lema, R., and Lema, A. 2012. 'Technology Transfer? The Rise of China and India in Green Technology Sectors', *Innovation and Development* 2(1), 23–44.

Lema, R. 2014. 'Offshore Outsourcing and Innovation Capabilities in the Supply Base: Evidence from Software Firms in Bangalore', *International Journal of Technological Learning, Innovation and Development*, 7, 19–48.

Lema, R., Quadros, R., and Schmitz, H. 2015. 'Reorganising Global Value Chains and Building Innovation Capabilities in Brazil and India, *Research Policy*, 44(7), 1376–1386.

Lema, R.; Fu, X.; Rabellotti, R. 2020. Green windows of opportunity: latecomer development in the age of transformation toward sustainability, Industrial and Corporate Change, Volume 29, Issue 5, October 2020, Pages 1193–1209, https://doi.org/10.1093/icc/dtaa044.

Leonard-Barton, D. 1995. *Wellsprings of Knowledge: Building and Sustaining the Sources of Innovation*. Boston: Harvard Business School Press.

Lewis, J. 2007. 'Technology Acquisition and Innovation in the Developing World: Wind Turbine Development in China and India', *Studies in Comparative International Development*, 42(3–4), 208–232.

Lewis, J. 2011. 'Building a National Wind Turbine Industry: Experiences from China, India and South Korea', *International Journal of Technology and Human Interaction*, 5(3–4), 281–305.

Losekann, L., and Tavares, A. 2021. 'Transição energética e potencial de cooperação nos BRICS em energias renováveis e gás natural', IPEA, *Texto para Discussão* n. 2680. Brasília, DF, Brasil: IPEA.

Lopes, M. L., Paulillo, S. C. L., Godoy, A., et al. 2016. 'Bioethanol Production in Brazil: A Bridge between Science and Industry', *Brazilian Journal of Microbiology*, 47, 64–76.

Mathews, J. A. 2008. Towards a Sustainably Certifiable Futures Contract for Biofuels', *Energy Policy*, 36, 1577–1583.

Mathews, J., Hu, M., and Wu, C. 2011. 'Fast-follower Industrial Dynamics: The Case of Taiwan's Emergent Solar Photovoltaic Industry', *Industry and Innovation*, 18(2), 177–202.

Marigo, N., Foxon, T., and Pearson, P. 2010. 'Chinese Low-Carbon Innovation: Developing Technological Capabilities in the Solar Photovoltaic Manufacturing Industry', *Journal of Knowledge-Based Innovation in China*, 2(3), 253–268.

Mazzucato, M., and Penna, C. C. R. 2015. *Mission-Oriented Finance for Innovation: New Ideas for Investment-Led Growth*. London: Rowman & Littlefield International.

Mazzucato, M., and Penna, C. C. R. 2016. *The Brazilian Innovation System: A Mission-Oriented Policy Proposal*. Brasília, DF: CGEE.

Meadowcroft, J. 2011. 'Engaging with the Politics of Sustainability Transitions', *Environmental Innovation and Societal Transitions*, 1(1), 70–75.

Ministry of Mines and Energy. 2016. *Brazilian Energy Balance 2015*. Brasília, DF: Brazil's Ministry of Mines and Energy.

Moussu, N. 2016. The Role of the Business Sector in Climate Negotiations. European Commission–Research & Innovation, available at https://ec.europa.eu/research/social-sciences.

Nelson, R. R., and Winter, S. G. 1982. *An Evolutionary Theory of Economic Change*. Cambridge, MA: Belknap Press of Harvard University Press.

Ockwell, D., Watson, J., Mackerron, G., Pal, P., and Yamin, F. 2008. 'Key Policy Considerations for Facilitating Low Carbon Technology Transfer to Developing Countries', *Energy Policy*, 36(11), 4104–4115.

Ockwell, D., Haum, R., Mallett, A., and Watson, J. 2010. 'Intellectual Property Rights and Low Carbon Technology Transfer: Conflicting Discourses of Diffusion and Development', *Global Environmental Change*, 20(4), 729–738.

Ockwell, D., and Mallet, A., eds. 2012. *Low-Carbon Technology Transfer: From Rhetoric to Reality*. London: Routledge.

Oliveira, B. G., Carvalho, J. L. N., Cerri, C. E. P., et al. 2015. 'Greenhouse Gas Emissions from Sugarcane Vinasse Transportation by Open Channel: A Case Study in Brazil', *Journal of Cleaner Production*, 94, 102–107.

Ometto, A. R., and Roma, W. N. L. 2010. 'Atmospheric Impacts of the Life Cycle Emissions of Fuel Bioethanol in Brazil: Based on Chemical Exergy', *Journal of Cleaner Production*, 18(1), 71–76.

Patel, P., and Pavitt, K. 1994. 'The Continuing, Widespread (and Neglected) Importance of Improvements in Mechanical Technologies', *Research Policy*, 23, 533–545.

Pereira, C. L. F., and Ortega, E. 2010. 'Sustainability Assessment of Large-Scale Bioethanol Production from Sugarcane', *Journal of Cleaner Production*, 18, 77–82.

Pueyo, A., García, R., Mendiluce, M., and Morales, D. 2011. 'The Role of Technology Transfer for the Development of a Local Wind Component Industry in Chile', *Energy Policy*, 39(7), 4274–4283.

Procana. 2014. *Bioethanol Information Centre* (in Portuguese), http://www.jornalcana.com.br/procana-brasil/ (accessed 30 May 2017).

Raven, R. P. J. M., and Geels, F. W. 2010. 'Socio-Cognitive Evolution in Niche Development: Comparative Analysis of Biogas Development in Denmark and the Netherlands (1973–2004)', *Technovation*, 30(2), 87–99.

Robertson, S. 2016. 'A Longitudinal Quantitative-qualitative Systems Approach to the Study of Transitions Toward a Low Carbon Society', *Journal of Cleaner Production*, 128, 221–233.

Rock, M. T., and Angel, D. P. 2005. *Industrial Transformation in the Developing World*. Oxford: Oxford University Press.

Rock, M., Murphy, J. T., Rasiah, R., et al. 2009. 'A Hard Slog, Not a Leapfrog: Globalization and Sustainability Transitions in Developing Asia', *Technological Forecasting and Social Change*, 76(2), 241–254.

Sousa, E. L. L., and Macedo, I. C. 2010. *Etanol e Bioeletricidade. A Cana-de-açúcar no Futuro da Matriz Energética*. São Paulo: Luc Projetos de Comunicação.

Sutton, J. 2012. *Competing in Capabilities: The Globalization Process*. Oxford: Oxford University Press.

Teece, D. J. 2012. 'Dynamic Capabilities: Routines versus Entrepreneurial Action', *Journal of Management Studies*, 49(8), 1395–1401.

UNFCCC. 2009. *The Copenhagen Accord*. Copenhagen: UNFCCC.

United Nations Economic and Social Commission for Asia and the Pacific–ESCAP. 2016. *Transformations for Sustainable Development on its Third Session*. Bangkok.

Uyarra, E., Shapira, P., and Harding, A. 2016. 'Low Carbon Innovation and Enterprise Growth in the UK: Challenges of a Place-blind Policy Mix', *Technological Forecasting & Social Change*, 103, 264–272.

UNICA. 2016. *The Role of Cleaner Fuels after COP21*. São Paulo, SP, Brasil: ÚNICA.

Walz, R., and Marscheider-Weidemann, F. 2011. 'Technology-Specific Absorptive Capacities for Green Technologies in Newly Industrializing Countries', *International Journal of Technology and Globalization*, 5(3–4), 212–229.

World Bank. 2010. *World Development Report 2010: Development and Climate Change*. Washington, DC: World Bank.

World Resources Institute–WRI. 2015. *Bridging the Gap Between Energy And Climate Policies in Brazil: Policy Options to Reduce Energy-Related GHG Emissions*.

Wu, C.-Y., and Mathews, J.A. 2012. 'Knowledge Flows in the Solar Photovoltaic Industry: Insights from Patenting by Taiwan, Korea, and China', *Research Policy*, 41(3), 524–540.

11
Digitalization in Latin America
A Divide in the Making?

João Carlos Ferraz, Julia Torracca, Gabriela Arona, and Wilson Peres

11.1. Introduction

This chapter addresses a much-debated subject: the extent to which the diffusion of digital-related technologies may contribute to development catching-up processes of nations, with particular attention paid to the Latin American region. We start from the realization that Latin America is a region marked by the coexistence of significant differentials of capabilities and performance among countries, and economic sectors and agents; this constitutes one of the most important facets of the region's structural heterogeneity (ECLAC, 2007, 2022). As the structuralist school argues, such differentials constitute a relevant constraint to be overcome towards a sustainable development trajectory for the region.

In this sense, given their inherent features, could digital technologies contribute to the breaking up of long-standing development lock-ins and represent a new window of opportunity for a catching-up process in the Abramovitz (1986) sense? Are these technologies contributing to increase efficiency levels? And, in the face of outstanding income and capability differentials, over time, are productivity gaps between formal and informal sectors evolving alongside the diffusion of new technologies? Are we observing digital progress, or a digital divide in the making? These are the motivating questions we discuss in this chapter.

We propose these questions because, to the best of our knowledge, economic transformations arising from digital technologies are potentially immense. Yet the evidence and the literature about possible gains, especially those of an efficiency nature, are not conclusive. From an empirical, development perspective, there are those who argue that Solow's (1987, p. 36) qualified intuition—'You can see the computer age everywhere but in the productivity statistics'—still stands (Acemoglu et al., 2014). Others (Van Ark et al., 2020; Brynjolfsson, Rock, and Syverson, 2017) argue that time lags are the most important reason for the slow emergence of productivity effects

João Carlos Ferraz, Julia Torracca, Gabriela Arona, and Wilson Peres, *Digitalization in Latin America* In: *Innovation, Competitiveness, and Development in Latin America.* Edited by: Edmund Amann and Paulo N. Figueiredo, Oxford University Press. DOI: 10.1093/oso/9780197648070.003.0011

derived from the diffusion of digital technologies. Nevertheless, a certain scepticism prevails among many authors as they argue that during the recent period of rapid technological change, economic and social inequalities have been on the increase. As Qureshi (2022, p. 1) argues, 'over the period of the boom in digital technologies . . . many are being left behind, across industries, across the workforce, and across different segments of society'. In the context of developing nations, these trends are even more worrisome, as digital progress falls behind trends observed in the developed world (UNIDO 2019; Andreoni, Chang, and Labrunie, 2021).

In search for answers to our questions, we review the main contributions and arguments put forward by specialists and compile and analyse the available evidence. The chapter starts with an analysis of the nature of digital technologies and their economic relevance, together with an evaluation of the essential requirements needed to increase the probability of people and organizations profiting from such technical progress.

Having set the analytical scene, we then address the relations between digitalization and economic efficiency from two perspectives. Firstly, we review the specialized literature to discuss the extent to which digital progress leads to economic gains, including in the context of developing nations. Secondly, we focus our attention on the Latin American region. Our analysis covers two angles: firstly, how the region's digital progress fares against other regions, and, secondly, how the recent evolution of digital access to the productivity gap contrasts between the formal and informal sectors of selected Latin American countries. We finalize the chapter with analytical reflections about our findings and related policy implications.

Our efforts are aimed at contrasting digital progress and economic efficiency in an exploratory manner. We are aware that digitalization is a complex process, changing not only efficiency parameters, but also opening the way for new products, services, markets, modes of organizing institutions and even ways of life. We also acknowledge that economic efficiency is influenced and mediated by other factors beyond the adoption of digital technologies.

With such caveats, our interest is with the direction of the evolution of digital adoption and efficiency curves over time. We also address one of the outstanding features of the Latin American region: its structural differences represented by a significant informality in labour relations and modes of functioning of business organizations. For that, and based on available data, we analyse the digital gap between the region vis-à-vis other parts of the world, and we juxtapose the local digital adoption trends with the evolution of the formal and informal sector efficiency gaps. In short, even in the face of the continuous transformation of the digital phenomenon and the lack of reliable and sound evidence, we hope that our chapter brings to attention important economic, social, and technological research and policy issues.

11.2. A Digital Revolution in the Making?

11.2.1. The Economic Relevance of Digital Technologies

Advanced digital technologies—perhaps the most outstanding example of general purposes technologies (GPT)—can be defined as a group of technologies based on microprocessors with increasing capacity to generate, manipulate, and interconnect information. As the neo-Schumpeterian literature convincingly argues, the potential of transformation of the digital solutions, is determined by:

- (i) their constitution as the result of the convergence and blending of different technologies;
- (ii) their complementary manifestation as tangible and intangible assets;
- (iii) the observed steady decrease in costs and the simultaneous growth in processing capacity (Moore's Law);
- (iv) the ever-increasing surge of new digital solutions and their pervasiveness, vastness of utilization while being, at the same time, solution-specific where they are applied; and,
- (v) their interactive capacity with other non-digitally based technologies[1] (Dosi, 1982; Freeman and Perez, 1988). The transformative potential of digital technologies is becoming even more pronounced because of the continuous improvement in costs and benefits of these technologies—especially at their very heart, the microprocessors, and related devices[2]—leading to increasing effectiveness in computer capacity to process the massive availability of data created by new modes of production and consumption.

Pervasive connectivity leads the digital economy to a new level: the digitalized economy.[3] The effectiveness of digital technologies, such as internet of things

[1] An example of such interactive character is the use of new materials discovered by nanotechnology that will enable the production of high-performance semiconductors which, in turn, supports more sophisticated computer processors for the application of more complex AI software/algorithms.

[2] Evidence indicates that the average cost of sensors for IOT was $1.30 in 2004 and reached $0.44 in 2018, or for instance the US$/KWh cost of lithium-ion batteries dropped from $1,000 in 2010 to $209 in 2017 (IEL/CNI, 2018; MICROSOFT DYNAMICS, 2019).

[3] By 'digital economy' is meant the use of global digital platforms as a business model. The term 'digitalized economy' refers to the incorporation of digital technologies (particularly AI solutions) into the production, organization, and consumption patterns of the whole economy (ECLAC, 2021).

(IOT), artificial intelligence (AI), big data, blockchain, among others, relies on the speed and low latency of internet connections; that is, a reliable communication infrastructure is a necessary condition for the dissemination of new digital technologies. Instant response time and stability of connections are prior conditions to enable any digital solution. Contrarywise, low speed is a serious impediment to the supply of digital services and applications. This requires the existence of increasingly efficient transmission networks, made for example of fibre optic cables, or based on high-speed mobile connections. The most advanced transmission technologies (e.g. 5G) can enhance the download speed by roughly 200 times and the upload by 100 times when compared to 4G networks (OECD et al., 2017; OECD et al., 2020). In short, communication technologies have advanced in the past and will evolve in the coming years according to two parameters: speed and latency. This will enable ever-increasing innovations in all productive and social dimensions of life, making almost ubiquitous the presence of the internet in the life of peoples and organizations.

The growing economic importance of digital technologies is readily observable in the statistics on data transmission and storage. Between 2010 and 2025, world generated data are predicted to rise from 2 to 180 *zettabytes*.[4] In line with such growth, data-storage capacity is expected to grow at an annual rate of 19.2% between 2020 and 2025 (STATISTA, 2021a). In the same vein, World Economic Forum (WEF) (2018) estimates that in 2021, global internet data traffic exceeded 125 times the volume of traffic registered in 2005.

Such impressive growth in data capacity has a direct correspondence with the economic relevance of digital technologies. Correspondingly, there has been a sharp increase in information and communications technology (ICT) goods-related spending—such as software, digital services, data centre systems, and communication services. This has risen from just about US$2.5 trillion in 2005 to US$4.47 trillion worldwide in 2022. Mićić (2017) goes even further to suggest that just before the second decade of the twenty-first century, about a quarter of total global business could be directly related to the so-called digital economy.

The exponential growth of digital technologies is revealed by the number of publications, patents, and expansion of market size of different solutions (Table 11.1). In AI, over 400 thousand publications were produced between 1996 and 2018, while 116.6 thousand patents were registered in the same period. Correspondingly, AI market size is expected to increase more than 10-fold between 2017 and 2024, to US$191 billion. The market size of IOT is also expected to grow at a similar scale, from US$130 billion in 2018, to US$1.5 trillion by 2025, representing about half of the total revenue generated by the most relevant

[4] At *zettabyte* is a unit of information or memory, corresponding to 10^{21} bytes.

Table 11.1 Current and Expected Importance of Selected Digital Technologies

Digital Technologies	Publications (1996–2018)	Patents (1996–2018)	Market Size (US billion)	Major users
Artificial intelligence	4,03,596.00	1,16,600.00	$16 (2017) $191 (2024)	Retail, banking, discreet manufacturing
IOT	66,467.00	22,218.00	$130 (2018) $1,500 (2025)	Consumer, insurance, health-care, providers
Blockchain	4,821.00	2,975.00	$0.708 (2017) $61 (2024)	Finance, manufacturing, retail
3D printing	17,039.00	13,215.00	$10 (2018) $44 (2025)	Discreet manufacturing, healthcare, education
Robotics	2,54,409.00	59,535.00	$32 (2018) $499 (2025)	Discrete manufacturing, process manufacturing, resource industry
Big data	73,957.00	6,850.00	$32 (2017) $157 (2026)	Banking, discrete manufacturing, professional services
Nanotechnology	1,52,359.00	4,293.00	$1 (2018) $2.2 (2025)	Medicine, manufacturing, energy

Source: Arona (2021), adapted from UNCTAD (2021), with data collected from Elsevier's Scopus database, PatSeer database.

* Market size data are rounded.

advanced digital technologies. The production of papers and patents and the market size of blockchain, robotics, 3D printing, and big data are to follow a similar trajectory.

Despite this huge advance, in 2022 slower global growth and higher inflation, as well as the persistent tension between the United States and China, disproportionally hit the consumer-internet companies. From January 1 to November 11, 2022, the Nasdaq 100 Technology Sector Stock Index fell more than 35%,[5] while the Dow Jones Industrial Average, made up of fewer tech firms, was down by around 10%. Moreover, it is estimated that US tech companies had already shed more than 45,000 jobs in 2022 alone.[6] It remains to be seen whether these recent trends are just a hiccup, an adjustment process after a strong expansionary period, or whether the economic forces in play may lead to a loss of steam for some digital business models.

11.2.2. New Economic Activities and Business Models Enabled by Digital Technologies

Digital technologies have been around or a long time. But, since the 1980s, with rapid improvements in the capacity of microprocessors, they have been progressively transforming economies and societies. In the productive sector, digital solutions coupled with fast and reliable connectivity induce the emergence of new business models, the so-called platformization and/or servitization of business, or changes in existing organizations. According to ECLAC (2022), worldwide there were around 600 operational IOT platforms in Ban, a threefold increase since 2015, providing US$9 billion worth of solutions to a variety of markets, from manufacturing to mobility.

Digital goods and services are blended alongside and/or even substitute for long-standing ones (OECD et al., 2020). By way of illustration, one can mention how digital streaming has redefined the musical sector, how internet booking has changed the relations between consumers and the tourism industry, or how the so-called social media have impacted the traditional printed media. And there are further examples. New platform-based firms have emerged to explore and facilitate trade transactions (Amazon, Alibaba, Mercado Libre), provide financial services (Ant Financial, Avant, Mercado Pago), expand communication services, and create social networks (Facebook, Skype, WhatsApp) or facilitate the search for jobs (Laborum, LinkedIn, Workana, Freelancer). In short, internet

[5] https://www.marketwatch.com/investing/index/ndxt?countrycode=xx.

[6] https://www.economist.com/business/2022/10/31/what-went-wrong-with-snap-netflix-and-uber.

connections and digital platforms play a key role in approximating, in real time, demand to supply, thus reducing transaction costs, increasing efficiency gains in the use of assets, creating new markets, and enabling new business opportunities.

At the enterprise level, the advantages presumed by the implementation of digital technologies are associated with a greater aggregation of value along value chains, the reconfiguration of competitive drivers, the modernization of traditional sectors, and/or the creation of new market opportunities. At the production level, horizontal integration can be brought by innovations such as machine learning or IOT that enable instant machine-to-machine communication, as well as real-time forward and backward logistics. As a result, response time to suppliers and end consumers are reduced, operational errors and accidents are minimized, and more efficient allocation of resources associated with greater control of the production process is achieved. At the decision-making level of companies, more assertiveness and minimum downtime are brought about by big data analytics.

In a nutshell, technical progress is offering the capacity to manipulate an ever-increasing amount of information at a correspondingly smaller amount of time, while costs per unit of information are falling, and new applications are exponentially growing. While the process of digitalization is undeniably reaching all facets of life, its transforming potential depends, to a great extent, on the related digital capabilities of people, organizations, and private and public institutions.

But all is not so rosy for the digital firms. By late 2022, three business models are displaying issues: the movers (which shuttle people or things around cities), the streamers (which offer music and TV online), and the creepers (which make money by watching their users and selling eerily well-targeted ads). Over the past year, the firms that epitomize these business models—Uber and DoorDash; Netflix and Spotify; Snap and Meta (which has fallen out of the trillion-dollar club)—have lost two-thirds of their market capitalization on average. These businesses models suffer from similar problems: too much faith in network effects, low barriers to entry, and a dependence on other firms' platforms.[7] Moreover, concerns about content moderation played its part in the hostile take-over of Twitter. The effects of these new trends, as well their persistence, will take time to be duly assessed.

11.2.3. The Capabilities Challenge

The digital qualification of peoples and organizations will be a decisive factor in fostering or impeding the fulfilment of the potential promises of a digital economy. For that, significant and permanent investments in the transformation

[7] https://www.economist.com/business/2022/10/31/what-went-wrong-with-snap-netflix-and-uber.

of the qualification profile of workers, citizens, and organizations are necessary: effective digitalization requires digital citizens, digital organizations, and digital governments.

Such qualification starts with a sound basic education in national languages and mathematics. But it certainly must go beyond basic education. The very education and vocational training systems must be overhauled to also incorporate digitalization in their conceptual design and practices.

New technologies require computational thinking-based solutions that aim to streamline daily living conditions and/or work processes by identifying patterns to achieve more efficient and comfortable ways of living, producing, and solving problems. Such solutions may pave the way for improvements in the lives and works of peoples, including the facilitation of daily and strategic decision-making processes at home, in leisure times, and at work. To enable a trajectory along these lines, the Organisation for Economic Co-operation and Development (OECD et al., 2020) calls for substantive investments in the 'digital literacy' of the population, not only forming a workforce capable of dealing with new digital technologies, but also reaching the development of values promoting their innovative usage. Thus, digital capabilities should allow for the understanding of technology potentialities regarding the reconfiguration of work methods, easing workers with the appropriate skills to participate in this paradigm. In this sense, the stimulation of trivial digital skills, such as the use of mobile applications—to ensure familiarity with new technological means—is relevant. In short, the effective adoption of a digital technology implies investments in organizational capital and skills (GAL et al., 2019).

And, correspondingly, the more extensive and intensive a digitalization drive is, the higher the needs for adaptation and/or requalification of workers and consumers. From this perspective, adopting and adapting these new technologies induce the creation of new functions and professions in labour markets, such as robotics engineers, software developers, data scientists, systems analysts, materials scientists, and web designers, among others. Beyond the usage dimension, the fostering of advanced skills, such as data interpretation and high-level programming for cutting-edge technologies, is very important for the generation of new solutions.

In terms of the organization of businesses, the evolution has been towards the incorporation and exploration of the voluminous flow of data generated by digital platforms. When duly processed—with the support of AI—the 'big data' provide more, reliable, and real-time information for decision-making and greater agility to production processes, leading to superior competitive performance. For this reason, developing the appropriate capabilities of data interpretation and manipulation are of quintessential importance for the effective usage of digital technologies. These technologies are becoming cheaper and more accessible, but to no avail if organizations do not have strategic commitments to change and the capabilities to understand, interact, manipulate, and even evolve alongside technical progress.

In its turn, a digitalized business sector cannot survive without a digitalized market and society. The quality and the costs of digital devices and related infrastructures are necessary conditions for its efficient and effective deployment. Thus, the dissemination of frontier digital technologies demands permanent and fast access to broadband internet through which people can use digital services, even in areas away from large urban centres. Above all, digital education and capabilities, at the level of each and every organization, and at the level of households and individuals, are of the essence.

Likewise, in civil society, even if individuals hold the latest communication devices and enjoy access to the necessary digital infrastructure at reasonable costs, if digital ignorance prevails and consumers do not have the proper knowledge and capacity to use the potentials provided by new technologies, their 'usage effectiveness' is much lower, relatively to those capable of doing so. In other words, not only the lack of access but also the lack of digital literacy and digital capabilities of organizations and individuals may divide those who can and those who cannot benefit from the digital promised land, strengthening existing social, cultural, political, and economic inequalities.

Moreover, digitalization may contribute to the breaking of formal barriers between the work and non-work or home and off-home spaces. The necessary flexibility to navigate in and around these spaces demands digital capabilities from citizens, combined with complementary soft skills to entitle them to new and emerging social interactions. Thus, to follow the constant technological changes of the digital paradigm, competencies such as creative reasoning, adaptability, and the ability to learn become of fundamental importance.

11.3. Digitalization and Development

11.3.1. Is the Solow Paradox Still Standing?

Solow's 1987 proposed paradox still hounds analysts today. Theoretically, if extensively and intensively disseminated, new digital technologies are expected to induce positive efficiency effects to the performance of all types of organizations and, in aggregation, to the productivity of countries. Such improved performance, in turn, would lead firms (and, in aggregation, countries) to a better insertion in the local and international markets, giving rise to more demand and income. Such a trajectory would engender, consequently, quality-based long-term economic growth and development prospects.

Naturally the determinants of efficiency and growth are mediated by other relevant factors. To put it simply, it is not easy to isolate the effects of productivity gains or losses due to the adoption, or not, of digital technologies. Even so, what is the available evidence?

Some authors argue that the existence of economically-relevant digital-intensive sectors positively contributes to productivity growth in advanced economies[8] (Van Ark et al., 2020). According to these authors, during the 2007–2018 period, in the United States, most of the contribution to aggregate productivity growth came from 'digital-producer' sectors; a similar result was found for the Euro Zone and the United Kingdom for the same period. Other empirical evidence collected by Gal et al. (2019), Evangelista et al. (2014), Solomon and Klyton (2020), and Aly (2020) also reveal positive contributions of the adoption of digital technologies on different economic variables, either at firm or country level.

Others are more cautious. Acemoglu et al. (2014, p. 394), when analysing the usage of digital technologies in IT-intensive sectors after the 1990s, found that 'the evidence for faster productivity growth in more IT-intensive industries is somewhat mixed and depends on the measure of IT intensity used'. For them, the reasons for the observed productivity growth in IT-intensive sectors were to be found in the concurrent decline in employment and in output, not in IT usage: 'If IT is indeed increasing productivity and reducing costs, at the very least it should also increase output in IT-intensive industries'. Also problematizing the relation between digital technologies and their implications, Autor (2022, p. 41) issues words of caution: 'Fundamentally, technological change expands the frontier of human possibilities, but we should expect it to create many winners and losers, and to pose vast societal challenges and opportunities.'

The literature points out some justifications for such a paradox, starting with the very nature of the diffusion processes, which implies gradual improvements over time, the spawn of secondary or incremental products/processes, and the inherent differences in dissemination of its applications across multiple sectors of the economy. Thus, for the gains to be reflected in statistics, a long period of time from the very first introduction of digital technologies to their widespread dissemination would be required. In this sense, the full effects of digital technologies wouldn't be realized until a sufficient stock of assets of new technologies is accumulated, including the realization of waves of complementary innovations. This wide dissemination takes time and implies adjustment hurdles, such as learning costs associated with organizational changes. For many

[8] Digital-intensive sectors are those with relatively higher proportions of investments in tangible and intangible ICT assets, as well as a high share of ICT specialists in total employees, of robots per 100 employees, and of turnover from online sales (Van Ark et al., 2020).

authors, gaps in time would be one of the main causes of the contradiction between the fast diffusion of digital technologies and low productivity growth (Brynjolfsson, Rock, and Syverson, 2017).

Additionally, the importance of the temporal lag, complementary investments combined with an ever-increasing emergence of new and more sophisticated digital technologies, and the increased participation of intangible assets—like tacit knowledge and organizational capital—also contribute to delays hindering catching-up processes of latecomer firms, industries, or countries (Sturgeon, 2017; Andrews, Criscuolo, and Gal, 2016). Econometric analysis at the level of the firm carried out by Gal et al. (2019), for 20 European countries, from 2010 to 2015, demonstrates that the adoption of digital technologies is associated not only with a company's productivity growth, but also with an increased variability of productive performance among firms. This effect happens because the contribution to productivity does not occur at the same intensity, at the same time, for all firms, being more significant in (i) previously more productive firms, (ii) those with abundance of routine-intensive activities, and (iii) those operating in more digitalized environments. On the contrary, the effects of digital technologies on productivity rates are less significant in firms lacking these characteristics.

Under these circumstances, if the diffusion process is a gradual one, regardless of the sources of gradualism, what does emerge as a reasonable possibility is that the variability in the adoption process manifests itself as a factor inducing productivity disparities within an economy. From such a perspective, in firms, industries, or nations where pronounced differences in capabilities and performance subsist over time, the process of digital uptake may increase asymmetries and even may reinforce further existing imbalances among economic agents (Ferraz et al., 2019).

Within the digital era, Autor (2022) has detected a concurrent trend of rising inequalities with slower productivity growth within advanced countries, and most major emerging economies. According to this analysis, at its very roots, the recent slowdown in productivity of OECD economies reflects a growing inequality in productivity performance among firms. Between 2000 and 2015, productivity growth for firms at the technological frontier rose by around 45%, while among non-frontier firms the increase was well below 10%. One possible consequence for such divergent inter-firm productivity growth would be a rising inequality trend among different groups of workers. This is because the process of digitalization changes the relative demand for different types of workers. The demand for digital-related higher-level skills levels increases and pushes away the demand for middle-skill to lower-skill, lower-productivity, and lower-wage jobs, with consequent skill premium and wage differentials.

Hence, the deceleration of aggregate productivity of the past decade would be associated not only with the limits of technological diffusion, but also with widening existing gaps. This would occur as the product of an accumulated deployment of digital technologies by organizations forging ahead vis-à-vis those lagging behind. In other words, regardless of the positive and noticeable evolution of diffusion of digital technologies, only a limited group of users (companies, organizations, people) with previous accumulated capabilities, and/or with a positive stand towards new technologies, would benefit. Such partial capacity to accrue gains from digital technologies would then be revealed in the limited evolution of aggregate productivity.

From a capability perspective then, the 'Solowian' gaps may exist for two reasons:

(i) because of the straightforward differences in access to new technologies among economic agents and to their digital drivers and enablers (a have/have not condition); and
(ii) even if access is not a barrier, divergence may exist among economic agents in terms of their capability to effectively use digital technologies. If this is so, capability-weak countries, industries, organizations, and segments of the population may lag and distance themselves even more so from those with a higher capacity to effectively take up digital adoption.

11.3.2. Digital Progress in the Context of Developing Economies

All waves of technological change, from the first industrial revolution to the digital age, have been accompanied by progress, but also by the maintenance and even deepening of inequalities within and between countries, including the widening of disparities in the access to products, services, and public goods, in the most diverse sectors of societies (UNCTAD, 2021). This invites us to consider some outstanding socio-economic features of developing nations so as to question whether the digital progress could potentially lead to catching-up processes.

There is ample evidence that the most productive countries are those with a well-developed technological and knowledge base, and with an economically significant proportion of income and workforce related to high-value-added economic activities. To the contrary, developing countries, like those of Latin America, have a specialized production structure—either in low-skilled labour or in capital-intensive/natural-resource-related activities. Such a structural pattern can imply production systems concentrated in low-value-added sectors, exports with low technological content, and limited forward and backward linkages and activities with little potential production and technological spillovers.

At the microeconomic level, part of the heterogeneity problem arises from the fact that the knowledge economy is confined to islands of progress, while the large majority of economic activities operate with old technologies and thus lower efficiency levels (Andreoni and Anzolin, 2019). A recent comparative exercise based on surveys of 1,212 firms of various sizes and sectors in manufacturing, carried out between 2017 and 2019 in Brazil, Argentina, Ghana, Thailand, and Vietnam, shows that large firms from high- and medium-high-technology industries are seemingly better placed to move digitalization forward, compared to their small- and lower-technology-intensity peers (Kupfer, Ferraz, and Torracca, 2019). It is within such a context that Cirera et al. (2021) argue that differences in technology adoption are an important determinant of the widening productivity gap between leader and laggard firms in developing countries.

These features may affect the structure of labour markets, as the presence of unfavourable specialization patterns and a 'low-quality' international trade profile fosters the expansion of the informal sector (ECLAC, 2007). Indeed, in the Latin American region, in 2019, half of the working population (above 15 years old) was employed in low-productivity sectors with a strong propensity to be holding informal jobs. In relative terms, informality in Latin America is very high: informal sector output in relation to total output averaged 35.5% between 2000 and 2018, while in East Asia and Pacific countries it stood at 26.5% during the same period (Abramo, 2021).

In this context, a marked feature of developing economies is the wide variation in labour productivity between and within production sectors. In 2016, in Latin America, the productivity of micro, small, and medium-size enterprises relative to that of larger firms stood at 6%, 23% and 46%, respectively. In contrast, for that same year, in the European Union, the corresponding figures were at 42%, 58%, and 76%, respectively (OECD et al., 2020).

Such dispersion of productivity among firms quite possibly will imply weak productivity growth rates at the aggregate level (Andrews, Criscuolo, and Gal, 2016). Also, the simultaneous existence of a formal and a pervasive informal sector is seen as a peculiar form of structural heterogeneity that hinders the development of the region, since having a higher concentration of the workforce in the least-productive sector drags overall productivity down (Cimoli et al., 2006).

These structural conditions contribute to erratic trajectories for economic growth, implying limited absorption of labour in formal jobs, except in the face of inclusive public policies and/or periods when international trade and financial conditions are favourable. Along these lines, Rodrik (2022, p. 65) argues that during the 1990s and early 2000s, 'developing countries as a group were growing more rapidly than the advanced nations', but that more recently such performance was reverting. In this sense, a closed and negative loop seems to exist between erratic growth and informality which constitute a systemic obstacle for the acquisition of skills and assets necessary for sustained economic development (UNCTAD, 2021).

The digital economy also may induce new and informal work arrangements in the labour market, in association with the emergence of the 'gig' economy and the new digital platforms.[9] As fluid labour relationships become prevalent, workers in such market niches face performance-based forms of remuneration and usually do not fully participate in social security systems. Neither formal employment contract standards, nor labour-related regulatory rules apply to these occupations, which, according to Abramo (2021), in general imply the deprivation of basic rights and income instability. As a result, digitalization would be contributing to higher labour income inequality, affecting the structure of employment and ultimately income distribution within countries (Brambilla et al., 2021).

The above discussion brings us to the central questions of this chapter: Are advanced digital technologies opening windows of opportunities for peoples, firms, and nations? Alternatively, are they reinforcing structural features at play, such as the long-standing productivity gaps between formal and informal sectors? If so, is this leading to a limited caching-up for the few with the necessary assets and capabilities to take advantage of the digital revolution, thus reaffirming their historically dominant position? If this is so, will those lacking income, resources, and capabilities still be able to fully enjoy the benefits of the digital age, or would they appropriate just marginal gains?

11.4. Digitalization in Latin America

11.4.1. The Inter-Region Perspective: Is Latin America Catching Up or Lagging Behind?

Consistent with our narrative, it should be expected that the adoption of frontier technologies would be unequally experienced by countries due to their structural conditions. More advanced economies have gathered significant capability levels in association with complex and dynamic industrial structures, allowing the accumulation of economic resources needed to invest in innovation and more sophisticated infrastructure. It would be expected, then, that such structural conditions of developed countries would facilitate their digitalization drive vis-à-vis developing regions. Addressing this, this section examines four digital enabling factors: (i) the extent of internet access; (ii) the quality of the ICT

[9] By way of illustration, in 2021 Uber's 3.5 million drivers served 93 million customers in 10,000 cities around the world (https://backlinko.com/uber-users).

infrastructure; (iii) the relative ICT costs; and (iv) the digital capabilities from an international comparative perspective. It rounds off with an experimental exercise to contrast indicators of economic performance and digital uptake, also from a comparative country-level perspective.

The percentage of the population with access to the 4G mobile network in 2020, by region, is shown in Table 11.2. It reveals that the Sub-Saharan region is undeniably lagging—with just about half of the population with 4G access—whereas other developing regions are at 10 percentage points below the access levels of developed regions, which are almost at saturated diffusion levels. This first piece of evidence then is quite straightforward: the Latin American region does not lag much behind other regions in terms of mobile access to digital technologies.

Data on the average download speed of fixed broadband networks provide an indicator of the quality of the ICT infrastructure essential for the provision of advanced digital services such as IOT-based solutions. The data suggests that, between 2007 and 2020, average internet download speed in South Asia, Latin America, and Sub-Saharan Africa rose but was increasingly lagging that of other regions, such as Europe, the Middle East, North Africa, East Asia, Pacific Asia, and, especially, North America (ECLAC et al., 2020). The uneven evolution of internet speed implies different capacities to potentially enjoy the benefits of digitalization by different societies (WEF et al., 2018). This second set of evidence shows that the current widespread access to a relatively advanced mobile

Table 11.2 Percentage of Population with 4G Mobile Network Coverage

Region	2020
North America	99.7%
Europe & Central Asia	97.4%
Middle East & North Africa	90.5%
East Asia & Pacific	88.1%
Latin America & Caribbean	80.4%
South Asia	80.7%
Sub-Saharan Africa	58.3%

Source: Authors' elaboration based on ITU Digital Development data, World Telecommunication/ICT Indicators Database (2021).

Note: Continent classification by World Bank Country Classification (2020).

Annual data for each region were calculated from the average % of the population for each country.

network is not enough; the quality of the infrastructure allowing such digital access also matters.

The third set of evidence is related to the cost of access. In high-income economies, the monthly cost of a 1.5 GB connection speed is, on average, below 2% of the gross national income (GNI) per capita. In middle-income economies, a similar access cost ranges from 5% to 10% of the GNI per capita and, in low-income economies, such connections can represent more than 20% of the prevailing GNI per capita (UNCTAD, 2021). Still from the same perspective but with a slightly different angle, ECLAC (2022, p. 183) estimates that, in Latin America, the cost of a basic digital basket 'can represent up to 33% of the average income of households in the poorest quintile'. This evidence indicates that even if universal access is enabled and a quality infrastructure is available, the relative costs of devices and services constitute a significant barrier to the potential digital benefits.

The fourth and final set of evidence to be examined is related to the capabilities of the population. If the influence of the previous set of factors (access, infrastructure, and income) was positive, one remaining factor can be decisive in setting up the proper conditions for any person to benefit from the digital era: his/her knowledge and skill base. In this respect, according to OECD (2017), by 2012, even wealthy countries were struggling to foster the proper skills for this new digital era: by then, only 6% of the population of all OECD countries had advanced digital skills.

If the situation was already critical by 2012, as the years passed, digital skill inequalities among countries remain an international well-marked feature, and not all developed nations fare well. As shown in Figure 11.1, in 2020, the percentage of the population of selected countries, from various regions, with advanced digital skills varies considerably. In one extreme, the percentage is higher for the United Arab Emirates (17.4%) and Malaysia (11.1%). Between 7% and 8% of the population from Spain, Ireland, Singapore, and Mexico have advanced skills, while the figure is around 5% for Hong Kong, Cuba, and Malta. Brazil, Ecuador, Thailand, and Ukraine have 3.5% or less of their population with those digital skills. Regardless of the proportion for each country, this evidence indicates that digital capabilities are a challenge for all selected countries.

All countries face digital challenges, but in different 'proportions'. Even with some progress, especially in relation to internet access, developing countries face higher digital costs, lower-quality digital infrastructure, and limited digital skills. Most countries in North America, in Western Europe, in East Asia (South Korea, Japan), and a few Arab nations are relatively more 'advanced', not only for their sophisticated economic structure and greater wealth, but also because they are relatively further ahead in their capacity to capture the benefits of technical progress,

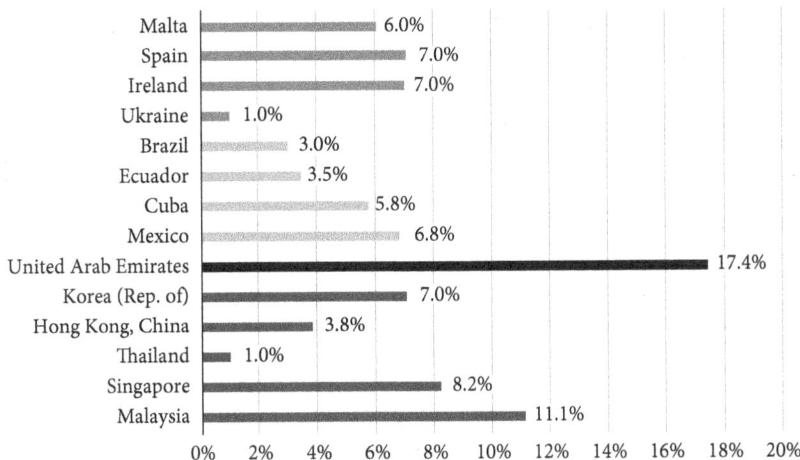

Figure 11.1. Percentage of total population with advanced digital skills: selected countries, 2020.

Source: Authors' elaboration based on ITU Digital Development data, World Telecommunication/ICT Indicators Database (2022).

even with challenges of their own, especially in relation to digital skills. Do these striking differences reveal themselves in different economic gains?

In Figure 11.2, an attempt is made to contrast labour productivity (GDP per worker) with an ICT index[10] of countries grouped according to their income level (high, upper middle, lower middle, and low),[11] for 2013 and for 2019. Three readings can be made. Firstly, the data suggest important country differences: countries with higher labour productivity also show higher ICT access levels, and vice versa. Secondly, such association becomes more pronounced over time (2019 vs. 2013). Thirdly and contrary wise, between these two years, while the productivity position of low- and medium-low-income countries remains unchanged, some digital progress can be observed; that is, their digital progress outpaces their productivity advance.

[10] The ICT access index is one of the 80 indicators used by the Global Innovation Index. It is a composite index that weights five ICT indicators (with a weight of 20% for each one): (1) fixed telephone subscriptions per 100 inhabitants; (2) mobile cellular telephone subscriptions per 100 inhabitants; (3) international internet bandwidth (bit/s) per internet user; (4) percentage of households with a computer; and (5) percentage of households with Internet access (Cornell University et al., 2020).

[11] The World Bank Country Classification (2020) divides countries into four income groups using the 2019 Gross National Income (GNI) per capita, calculated according to the World Bank Atlas Method. The groups are low income (GNI per capita of US$1,035 or less); lower middle income ($1,036–4,045); upper middle income ($4,046 – $12,535), and high income ($12,536 or more).

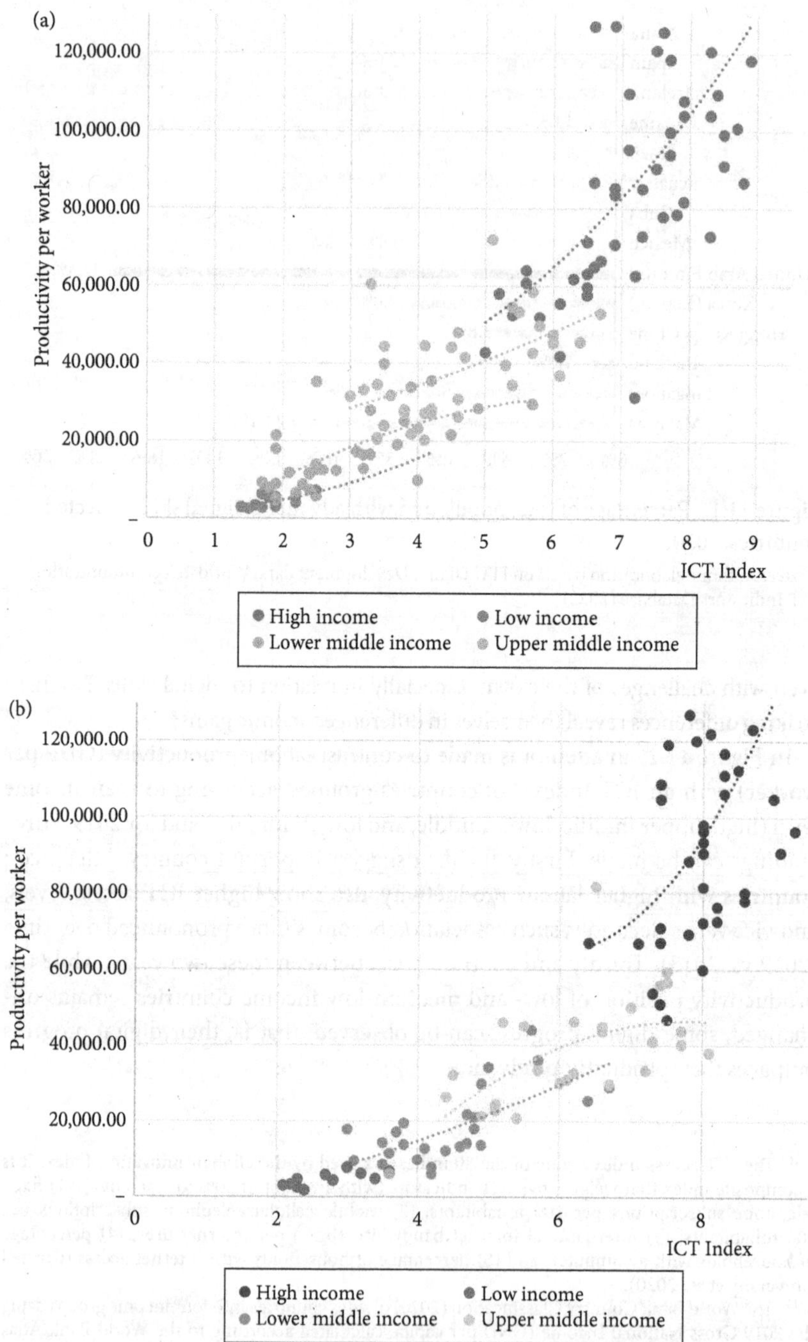

Figure 11.2. Labour productivity (GDP per worker in USD) vs. access to ICT (ICT Index) in 2013 (a) and 2019 (b).

Source: Arona (2021) with data from World Bank (2021) and GII INDEX.

Notes: Productivity is measured in PPC dollars of 2017 prices. Countries are classified according to World Bank Country Classification (2020).

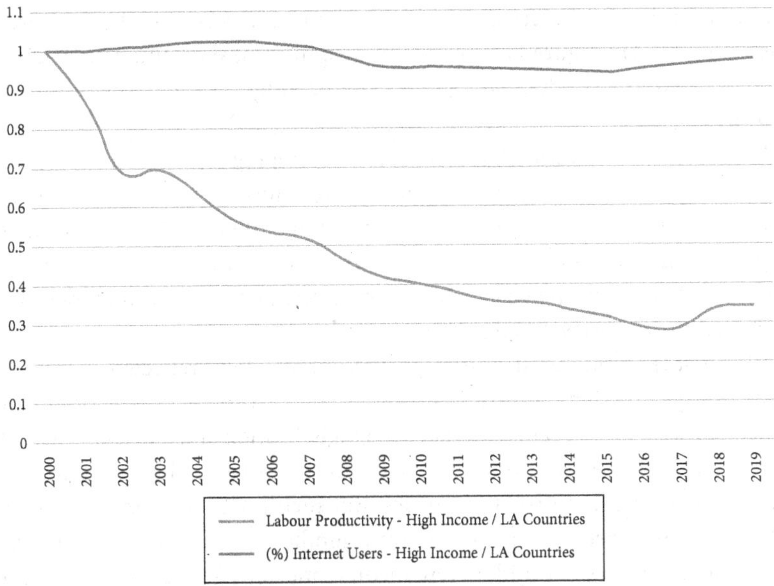

Figure 11.3. The productivity gap vs. the internet user gap between high-income countries and Latin American countries in time (2000–2019).

Source: Authors' elaboration based on data from World Bank (2021) and ITU (2021).

Note: Labour productivity is measured in GDP per worker in PPC dollars at constant 2017 prices.

The comparison between digital progress and economic efficiency can be further and closely observed in Figure 11.3, where two curves were drawn up for a 20-year period (2000–2019) comparing Latin American countries and high-income ones. The first curve relates the labour productivity of high-income countries to the labour productivity of Latin American countries.[12] The second curve relates the digitalization of high-income countries to the digitalization of Latin American countries, measured as the percentage of total population of each region with internet access.[13]

To provide a comprehensible visualization of the evolution of the two series, both indicators were normalized. Therefore, the closer to 1 in the vertical axis, the greater the productivity gap or the digital gap between high-income

[12] The classification for high-income countries follows the criteria legitimated by the World Bank. Latin American countries that are considered by the World Bank as high-income were reclassified as Latin American countries.

[13] The country classification was obtained from the World Bank Country Classification (2020). To estimate the productivity gap between the categories, a ratio was established between the annual average labour productivity of high-income countries and the annual average labour productivity of the Latin American countries.

countries and Latin American countries. Figure 11.3 stresses what was previously suggested in Figure 11.2: while a very significant shortening of the digital gap occurred, the productivity gap was reduced by only 2.1% between 2000 and 2019.

In summary, this section has shown that developing nations, including Latin America, were able to significantly extend the most basic form of digitalization (internet access) to an important proportion of their population, while still lagging behind in costs, skills, and infrastructure relatively to higher-income countries. More comprehensive digital advances, in turn, run in tandem with improved efficiency levels (and vice versa).

With a note of caution (digital progress is not only to be reflected in efficiency gains, and productivity growth has sources and drivers far beyond the digital dimension), such divergent paths between digitalization and efficiency open the way for an initial set of reflections. Firstly, in recent years, digital progress has certainly been achieved by all countries. But such progress seems to be qualitatively different between high- and even middle-high-income countries, and those situated in low- or middle-low-income brackets. Secondly, these marked disparities also imply differences in the capacity of countries to enjoy the benefits of the digital era. In short, it seems that the relative 'development position' of most developing nations has not changed over time.

After the country-level comparative analysis, a new question arises: If we examine each developing country, with their internal striking economic and social differences, will we find equivalent digital gaps? This is the subject matter of the following sub-section.

11.4.2. The Intra-Region Perspective: Digitalization in the Face of Long-Standing Economic Disparities

In this section we maintain our focus on the contrast between indicators of digital progress and those associated with economic performance. But, in terms of the latter, we propose an outstanding feature of most Latin American countries' structural conditions as a reference to develop the efficiency indicator: the relative importance of the informal sector.

For the purposes of this chapter, we assume that productivity differentials are inherently related to the type of occupation of workers. That is, we suppose that high-productivity economic activities also have a significant proportion of formal jobs. In contrast, as argued by ECLAC (2007), informal jobs (non-professional salaried workers, unpaid family work, and employees in micro enterprises) are more likely to be associated with low-productivity economic activities.

According to Maurizio (2021), by the end of the 2010s, the region's rate of informality was around 50%. In the face of such a reality, it is important to review the productivity indicators of the formal and informal sectors and to relate one to the other.[14] In doing so, a country-level productivity gap can be estimated, and it can then by compared alongside a proxy indicator of digital progress (internet users).[15] We then plotted the two curves over the 2000–2018 period, as shown in Figure 11.4. To allow a better visualization of their evolution over time, both indicators were transformed into index numbers, with 2011 serving as the base year.

Given the evidence of the previous section, the positive evolution of the indicator of digital access (internet users in relation to total population) of the selected Latin American countries (Figure 11.4) comes as no surprise. The curve depicting the percentage of internet users grows steadily along time. In the base year (2011), about 41% of the inhabitants of eight selected Latin American countries (Argentina, Bolivia, Brazil, Chile, Colombia, Costa Rica, Mexico, and Peru) were internet users, while back in 2000 this figure stood at only 5.5% of their total population. In contrast to the first year of the series, by 2019 the percentage of the internet population had increased 14 times, to 70.5%. For the whole Latin American (and Caribbean) region, ECLAC (2022) estimates that in 2021 the internet users as a percentage of total population were close to 80%, just 8 percentage points below the European Union. It is quite clear that, regarding access to internet usage, Latin American countries experienced a significant progress in the recent past.

One word of caution, though. As argued previously, internet access is just one of the components of the process of digitalization, which would have to include other dimensions such as affordability, reliability and speed of infrastructure, and skills, as argued by Katz et al. (2013). For most developing countries, and those from Latin America are no exception, progress in these dimensions (which would represent a more comprehensive perspective of the process of digitalization) is lower and slower than the increase of the internet population. For example, although a large proportion of the population has access to the internet, the quality of such access may be limited by hardware (basically mobile phones, which are hardly suitable for multi-tasking) and the costs of connection to higher speeds.

[14] Methodological notes: Labour productivity estimates are based on UN/ECLAC data in 2010 US dollars. The informal sector includes the following categories: domestic service, non-professional salaried workers, unpaid family work, and employees in microenterprises (with fewer than five workers). Labour productivity of the informal sector was estimated based on the average income of informal workers. Such income is considered a good proxy for the value-added generated by the informal sectors, due to the nature of the activities carried out in those sectors.

[15] Internet users: ITU et al. (2021a) estimates for the proportion of individuals to total population (above 5 years old) using the internet, based on data from national household surveys.

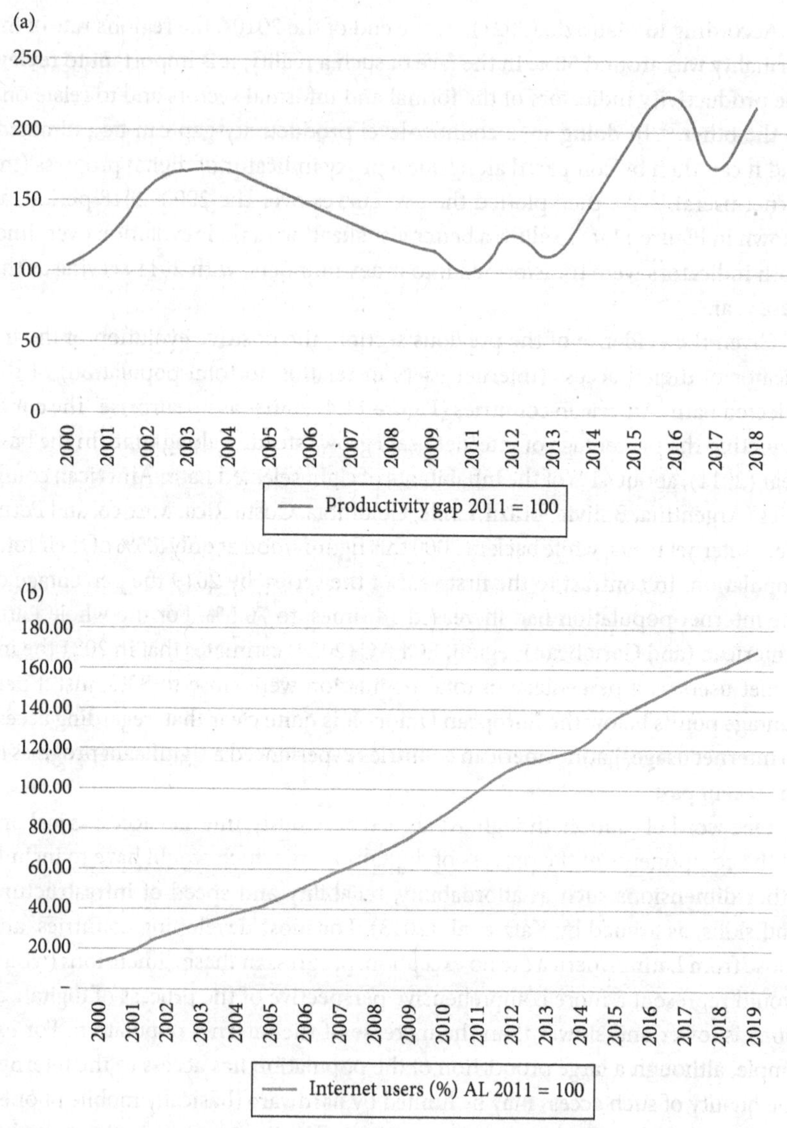

Figure 11.4. The evolution of internet users and the formal/informal sector productivity gap in selected Latin American countries, 2000-2019. (a) Formal/informal productivity gap. (b) Internet users (% population).

Source: Authors' elaboration based on ECLAC and ITU data.*

Notes: Data on the proportion of internet users is an annual average for eight Latin American countries (Argentina, Bolivia, Brazil, Chile, Colombia, Costa Rica, Mexico, Peru). These are also the countries for which the average productivity gap was estimated.

* The data were extracted from household surveys, which may not be uniform across Latin American countries or even within a country over time.

In contrast to the path of internet usage, the evolution of the productivity differentials between the formal and the informal sectors (Figure 11.4a) follows a different pattern. After increasing in the beginning of the 2000, there was a decrease in the productivity gap between 2004 and 2011 when the gap was quite like that in the first year of the series. From then onwards, the productivity gap increases sharply and steadily. The actual gap behind these trend lines is even more staggering. Over the years, between 2000 and 2018 the average labour productivity of the informal sector, for these selected Latin American countries, was situated between 8% and 9% of the productivity levels of the formal sector. Ohnsorge et al. (2021) argue that, in one of the dimensions of informality, that associated with the business sector, a significant reliance on unskilled labour and the lack of managerial abilities, in association with limited economies of scale, and restricted access to infrastructure and services by micro and small firms, create a difficult scenario for the reaping of efficiency gains provided by digital assets.

11.5. Conclusions: Can Digital Technologies (Partially) Unleash Development Processes?

11.5.1. Points of Departure

In this final section we want to reflect on the main findings and arguments made, and to discuss the related policy implications, or policy challenges. For the former, two issues will be discussed regarding the comprehensive nature of digital progress and its relation to economic efficiency. For the latter, we want to enunciate the digital-related policy challenges facing Latin American countries.

Economic transformations arising from digital technologies are potentially immense. In view of that, we debate whether digital technologies may represent a new window of opportunity for catching-up processes in developing countries, with a special focus on the contrast between the evolution of digital adoption and efficiency levels. Moreover, considering the outstanding income and capability differentials prevailing in most developing countries and, in particular in Latin America, we have made an effort to ascertain whether the productivity gaps between formal and informal sectors are evolving alongside the diffusion of digital technologies.

In search for answers to our questions, we reviewed the main contributions and arguments put forward by specialists, and we compiled and analysed the available evidence. Ours is an exploratory exercise, and we are fully aware of three interrelated factors that may play a relevant role in determining the potential outcomes of digitalization. Firstly, digital technologies change not only efficiency parameters but also pave the way for new products, services, markets, modes of organizing institutions, and even ways of life. Secondly, economic efficiency is influenced and mediated by other factors beyond the adoption of digital technologies. Thirdly, to be reflected in statistics, a long period of time from the very first introduction of digital technologies to their widespread dissemination would be required. In this sense, the full effects of digital technologies would not be realized until a sufficient stock of assets of new technologies is accumulated, including the realization of waves of complementary innovations

With such caveats, our interest lies more in the direction of the evolution of digital adoption and efficiency curves over time. For that, and based on available data, we analyse the digital gap between the region vis-à-vis other parts of the world, and we juxtapose the local digital adoption trends with the evolution of the formal and informal sector efficiency gaps.

11.5.2. A Divide in the Making?

Latin America is a region marked by the coexistence of significant differentials of capabilities and performance among economic sectors and agents. Our findings are not at odds with this reality. We found that developing nations, including Latin America, were able to significantly evolve and to extend the most basic form of digitalization (internet access) to an important proportion of their population, while still lagging in costs, skills, and infrastructure relative to higher-income countries. We detected that, in Latin America, the productivity gap of the informal sector, in comparison to its formal counterpart, has increased along the first two decades of the twenty-first century, despite substantial progress in the expansion of digital access in all selected countries of the region. The region's digital progress has been limited, as the lowering of costs, the expansion of a fast and reliable infrastructure, and improvement in digital skills are still behind the global frontier. A consolidation of progress along these lines would increase the likelihood of a positive contribution of digital technologies to economic efficiency. These stylized findings lead to four reflections.

Firstly, and in answer to our first question (can digitalization open new windows of opportunity for the development of Latin American countries?), Latin American digital progress is real; it has happened, and quite significant proportions of peoples and organizations have access to internet services. So, we can state that relative to the past, there are significant advances. But, relative to developed nations, such progress is limited, as the latter are capable of engaging in more comprehensive and deeper processes of digital adoption. In short, in absolute terms, there was progress; in relative terms, the digital development position of Latin American countries has not improved significantly. If such a trend continues, it is fair to argue that, despite their immense transformation potential, digital technologies' contribution to development catching-up will still be insufficient.

Secondly, what of our second and third questions: Over time, is the diffusion of new technologies evolving alongside efficiency levels? Are digital technologies contributing to shorten the productivity gaps between the formal and the informal sectors? We can reasonably argue that the harnessing of digital dividends is greater for the formal sector in comparison to the informal sector, due to the nature of the capabilities typically associated with the former. By reaping the efficiency-related benefits from digital progress, the formal sector is likely to increase the productivity distance from its informal counterpart.

Thirdly, there are risks that the nature of the ongoing trajectory of digitalization in Latin American countries may accentuate the existing intra-country economic and social disparities. That is, in the absence of a broad improvement in the quality of digital access, with corresponding improvements in digital capabilities for those with current limited access, digitalization may benefit mainly those with accumulated tangible and intangible assets. As a result, aggregated productivity is not fully affected by the potential positive effects of the digital technologies.

Fourthly, at this point it is important to remember that there are other important elements mediating the process of leveraging productivity. Such circumstances suggest that, even if a comprehensive process of digitalization were to take place, such a process alone may not constitute a sufficient strategy to sustain catching-up processes. But, in the absence of any efforts to induce improvements in the quality of infrastructure in digital skill levels and in costs of access, the chances of a successful development catching-up trajectory are meagre.

11.5.3. Policy Alternatives and Challenges

In light of the discussion so far, we conclude that public policies are of the essence to better capture the potential gains in productivity and economic growth from the adoption of digital technologies. Although policy objectives are clear, public policies face all types of constraints, from access to fiscal and financial resources to the capabilities of public institutions to effectively implement and monitor policy directives.

11.5.3.1. The Policy Direction: Digital Inclusion; the Policy Challenge: to Choose, Prioritize, and Implement Actions

Given the digital divide in Latin America, digital inclusion can be justified as the policy goal. Advanced digital capabilities are confined to islands of progress; in the business sector they are represented by larger firms and those from high- and medium-high-technology industries; in the civil society, by its formal segments. Small and lower-technology businesses and peoples engaged in informal activities should then be the policy targets. But this is quite a challenge.

From a demand-side perspective, in order to build an inclusive digital society, ECLAC (2020) estimates that a basic basket of technological products, comprising a laptop, a smartphone, and a tablet, can be provided to households that do not have digital devices at an annual cost of less than 1% of GDP. This basket should be complemented with a subsidy to payment for a fixed connection and a mobile connection for offline urban households and payment for a mobile connection for rural households, which would cost less than 0.4% of GDP. In both cases, costs vary significantly across countries. In the current fiscal stance in the region, these figures are quite demanding.

From a supply-side approach, fostering digital transformation in the business sector implies different types of policies (ECLAC, 2022). For firms near the international productivity frontier, polices should: (i) define and adopt Industry 4.0 standards to enable intelligent and autonomous data-driven equipment and technologies to function interoperably, transparently, and securely; (ii) support the incorporation of cutting-edge digital technologies into production processes through science parks, incubators, accelerators, and innovation laboratories; and (iii) promote digital entrepreneurship through financing mechanisms that facilitate the creation of emerging and technology-based companies.

For micro and small firms, actions should be oriented towards: (i) providing technical assistance and low-cost financial incentives to firms unable by themselves to catch up with their digitally advanced peers; and (ii) implementing policies suited to the specificities of the target firms and industries, in terms of production capabilities, management, and linkages with the local area.

For the informal sector, granularity and direct contact with potential beneficiaries are essential; thus, access to support programmes should include dialogue mechanisms based on direct interaction between policy implementers and their beneficiaries, rather than on formal protocols and written communications. Moreover, close collaboration is needed to implement policies that address a wide variety of issues, especially those concerning the quality of life of the population in the informal sector (e.g. food, health, and security). Finally, given the huge size of the informal sector in the region, policies must be applied with a massive scope if they are to produce significant effects. This implies that policy measures must be simple, easy to understand, and with very low unit-management costs.

Even if well-designed comprehensive and coordinated policies, as well as implementation-capable organizations, were available, digital policies would have to compete for scarce fiscal resources with other equally justifiable policy demands. In this sense, policy choices are of political nature, and the vision and commitments of political leaders are what matters, in the last instance. However, developing countries face not only enormous challenges, but also a sort of 'policy competition' with other nations: the United States is mobilizing right now US$250 billion in just one of its programmes, the Innovation and Competition Act.[16] The Italia Domani, a recovery and resilience-building programme, involves more than US$200 billion for the support of new technologies.[17]

From a broader social perspective, digitalization policies should aim at the facilitation of citizens' access to public goods. Some examples are: (i) public services capable of extending social safety nets to protect vulnerable groups, including those under atypical jobs and working on digital platforms, adapting, if necessary, administrative procedures, benefits, and contributions to their capacity; (ii) labour regulations based on the guarantee of the recognition and protection of workers' social and labour rights; (iii) regulatory initiatives and institutions aimed at simplifying registration procedures and encouraging the formalization of micro firms and workers through formalization systems; and (iv) investments in the expansion of job training and skill-development infrastructure with proper alignment with the needs of productive areas.

In this respect, again, most countries have initiatives of this sort, with the most advanced solutions being implemented in the tax systems, for obvious reasons. But, for their nature, the health and education systems would be almost 'natural' areas for a public commitment to digitalization. However, the complexity involved in the digitalization processes of education and health systems is highly demanding, not only in terms of significant resources invested over a long period, but also institutions capable of implementing the relevant policies.

In the last instance, the tackling of new policy challenges demands new approaches to the policymaking process. In this sense, from a normative perspective, it is at the political domain where choices are made to guide a new policy agenda—that is, actions towards digital inclusion of specific population segments. Decisions must then resonate in policy directives, and mandated executive agencies must have the resources and the capabilities to design, implement, and monitor policy priorities. Policy initiatives often have more effective results when they are based on solid and long-term customized and well-coordinated programmes in a supportive institutional and economic environment.

16 https://www.congress.gov/bill/117th-congress/senate-bill/1260.
17 https://italiadomani.gov.it/en/home.html.

References

Abramo, L. 2021. 'Políticas para enfrentar los desafíos de las antiguas y nuevas formas de informalidad en América Latina', serie *Políticas Sociales*, No. 240 (LC/TS.2021/137). Santiago: CEPAL.

Abramovitz, M. 1986. 'Catching Up, Forging Ahead, and Falling Behind', *The Journal of Economic History*, 46(2), 385–406

Acemoglu, D., Autor, D., Dorn, D., Hanson, G. H., and Price, B. 2014. 'Return of the Solow Paradox? IT, Productivity, and Employment in US Manufacturing', *American Economic Review*, 104(5), 394–99. doi:10.1257/aer.104.5.394.

Aly, H. 2020. 'Digital Transformation, Development and Productivity in Developing Countries: Is Artificial Intelligence a Curse or a Blessing?', *Review of Economics and Political Science*, 7(4), 238–256. doi:10.1108/REPS-11-2019-0145.

Andreoni, A., and Anzolin, G. 2019. 'A Revolution in the Making? Challenges and Opportunities of Digital Production Technologies for Developing Countries', *UNIDO Inclusive and Sustainable Industrial Development Working Paper Series, No. 7*, pp. 1–71. Vienna.

Andreoni, A., Chang, H., and Labrunie, M. 2021. 'Natura Non Facit Saltus: Challenges and Opportunities for Digital Industrialisation across Developing Countries', *The European Journal of Development Research*, 33, 1– 41. doi:https://doi.org/10.1057/s41287-020-00355-z.

Andrews, D., Criscuolo, C., and Gal, P. N. 2016. 'The Best versus the Rest: The Global Productivity Slowdown, Divergence across Firms and the Role of Public Policy', *OECD Productivity Working Papers, No. 5*, pp. 1–77. Paris.

Arona, G. N. 2021. 'O impacto das tecnologias digitais na produtividade do trabalho: Uma análise a nível internacional'. Final BSc degree work, Instituto de Economia, UFRJ.

Autor, D. 2022. 'The Labor Market Impacts of Technological Change: From Unbridled Enthusiasm to Qualified Optimism to Vast Uncertainty', in D. Autor, K. Baus, Z. Qureshi, and D. Rodrik, eds., *An Inclusive Future? Technology, New Dynamics and Policy Challenges*. Global Economy and Development at Brookings. Washington, DC: Brookings Institution, 234–253.

Brambilla, I., César, A., and Falcone, G. 2021. 'The Asymmetric Risks of Automation in Latin America', *Revista de ciencias sociales*, 62(235), 234–253.

Brynjolfsson, B., Rock, D., and Syverson, C. 2017. 'Artificial Intelligence and the Modern Productivity Paradox: A Clash of Expectations and Statistics', *National Bureau of Economic Research*, No. 24001, pp. 1–46.

Calvino, F., Criscuolo, C., and Marcolin, L. 2018. 'A Taxonomy of Digital Intensive Sectors', *OECD Science, Technology and Industry Working Papers*, No. 2018/14. Paris: OECD Publishing, https://doi.org/10.1787/f404736a-en.

Cimoli, M., Primi, A., and Pugno, M. 2006. 'A Low-Growth Model: Informality as a Structural Constraint', *CEPAL Review*, 88, April 2006, 85–102.

Cirera, X., Comin, D., Cruz, M., et al. 2021. 'Anatomy of Technology in the Firm', *NBER Working Paper Series*, 28080. Cambridge, MA: National Bureau of Economic Research.

Cornell University/INSEAD/WIPO. 2020. *The Global Innovation Index 2020: Who Will Finance Innovation?* Dutta, S., Lanvin, B., and Wunsch-Vincent, S., eds. Ithaca, Fontainebleau, and Geneva. https://www.wipo.int/edocs/pubdocs/en/wipo_pub_gii_2020.pdf. (accessed 27 October 2021).

Dosi, G. 1982. 'Technological Paradigms and Technological Trajectories: A Suggested Interpretation of the Determinants and Directions of Technical Change', *Research Policy* 11, 147–162.

ECLAC. 2007. 'Progreso Técnico y Cambio Estructural en América Latina', *IDRC-UN-División de Desarrollo Productivo*, LC/W.136. Santiago: CEPAL.

ECLAC. 2020. 'Universalizing Access to Digital Technologies to Address the Consequences of COVID-19', Special Report COVID-19, No. 7, Santiago, 26 August.

ECLAC. 2021. *Digital Technologies for a New Future*. Santiago: ECLAC.

ECLAC. 2022. *Towards Transformation of the Development Model in Latin America and the Caribbean: Production, Inclusion and Sustainability*. Santiago: ECLAC.

ECLAC. 2018. 'Informe de la sexta conferencia ministerial sobre la sociedad de la información de américa latina y el caribe', in *Conferencia Ministerial Sobre la Sociedad de la Información de América Latina, 2018*. Santiago de Chile: Cartagena de Indias, 1–35.

ECLAC. 2020. *Tracking the Digital Footprint in Latin America and the Caribbean: Lessons Learned from Using Big Data to Assess the Digital Economy*. Santiago: ECLAC.

Evangelista, R., Guerrieri, P., and Meliciani, V. 2014. 'The Economic Impact of Digital Technologies in Europe', *Economics of Innovation and New Technology*, 23(8), 802–824.

Ferraz, J. C., Kupfer, D., Torracca, J., et al. 2019. 'Snapshots of a State of Flux: How Brazilian Industrial Firms Differ in the Adoption of Digital Technologies and Policy Implications', *Journal of Economic Policy Reform*, 23(4), 390–407. doi:10.1080/17487870.2019.1578651

Freeman, C., and Perez, C. 1988. 'Structural Crises of Adjustment: Business Cycles and Investment Behavior', In G. Dosi, R. Freeman, R. Nelson, G. Silverberg, and L. Soete, eds., *Technical Change and Economic Theory*. London: Pinter Publishing, 38–66.

Gal, P., Nicoletti, G., and Renault, T. 2019. 'Digitalisation and Productivity: In Search of the Holy Grail: Firm-Level Empirical Evidence from EU Countries', *OECD Economics Department Working Papers*, No. 1533. Paris: OECD. doi:https://dx.doi.org/10.1787/5080f4b6-en.

IEL/CNI. 2018. *Industry 2027: Risks and Opportunities for Brazil in the Face of Disruptive Innovations. Final Report: Building the Future of Brazilian Industry*. Brasília: IEL/CNI.

ITU. 2021a. 'Internet Users (%): ITU Statistics', https://www.itu.int/en/ITU-D/Statistics/Pages/stat/default.aspx.

ITU. 2021b. 'ITU Digital Development Data: ITU Statistics', https://www.itu.int/en/ITU-D/Statistics/Dashboards/Pages/Digital-Development.aspx.

Katz, R. L., Koutroumpis, P., and Callorda, F. 2013. 'The Latin American Path towards Digitization', *Info*, 15(3), 6–24. https://doi.org/10.1108/14636691311327098.

Kupfer, D., Ferraz, J., and Torracca, J. 2019. 'A Comparative Analysis on Digitalization in Manufacturing Industries in Selected Developing Countries: Firm-Level Data on Industry 4.0', *UNIDO: Department of Policy, Research and Statistics, Working Paper, No. 16*. Vienna.

Maurizio, R. 2021. 'Employment and Informality in Latin America and the Caribbean: An Insufficient and Unequal Recovery', *Technical Note, Labour Overview Series, Latin America and the Caribbean 2021*. Geneva: IOL.

Mićić, L. 2017. 'Digital Transformation and Its Influence on GDP', *De Gruyter*, 5(2), 135–147. doi:10.1515/eoik-2017-0028.

Microsoft Dynamics 365. 2018. *Manufacturing Trends Report*. https://info.microsoft.com/rs/157-GQE-382/images/EN-US-CNTNT-Report-2019-Manufacturing-Trends.pdf.

Nolan, A. 2021. 'Artificial Intelligence, Its Diffusion and Uses in Manufacturing', *Going Digital Toolkit Note*, No. 12, https://goingdigital.oecd.org/data/toolkitnotes/No12_ToolkitNote_AI&Manufacturing.pdf.

OECD. 2017. *The Next Production Revolution: Implications for Governments and Business*. Paris: OECD Publishing. doi:https://dx.doi.org/10.1787/9789264271036-en.

OECD. 2020. *Perspectivas económicas de América Latina 2020: Transformación digital para una mejor reconstrucción*. Paris: OECD Publishing. doi:https://doi.org/10.1787/f2fdced2-es.

Ohnsorge, F., and Shu Yu, E. 2021. *The Long Shadow of Informality: Challenges and Policies*. Washington, DC: World Bank Publications.

Qureshi, Z. 2022. 'Overview: Combating Inequality and Building Inclusive Prosperity in the Digital Era', in D. Autor, K. Baus, Z. Qureshi, and D. Rodrik, eds., *An Inclusive Future? Technology, New Dynamics and Policy Challenges*. Global Economy and Development at Brookings. Washington, DC: Brookings Institution, 1–17.

Rodrik, D. 2022. 'Prospects for Global Economic Convergence under New Technologies', in D. Autor, K. Baus, Z. Qureshi, and D. Rodrik, eds., *An Inclusive Future? Technology, New Dynamics and Policy Challenges*. Global Economy and Development at Brookings. Washington, DC: Brookings Institution, 65–82.

Solomon, M., and Klyton, A. 2020. *The Impact of Digital Technology Usage on Economic Growth in Africa. Utilities Policy*, Elsevier, 67(C), 1–12. doi:https://doi.org/10.1016/j.jup.2020.101104.

Solow, R. M. 1987. '"We'd Better Watch Out": Review of *Manufacturing Matters: The Myth of the Post-Industrial Economy*, by Stephen S. Cohen and John Zysman', *New York Times*, 12 July 1987, p. 36.

Sturgeon, J. 2017. 'The "New" Digital Economy and Development', *UNCTAD Technical Notes on ICT for Development*, No. 8, pp. 1–41.

STATISTA. 2021a. 'Global IT Spending', *Statista Research Department*, https://www.statista.com/statistics/203935/overall-it-spending-worldwide/.

STATISTA. 2021b. 'Evolution of the Volume of Data Created, Captured, Copied, and Consumed Globally', *Statista Research Department*, https://www.statista.com/statistics/871513/worldwide-data-created/.

UNCTAD. 2021. *Technology and Innovation Report 2021: Catching Technological Waves: Innovation with Equity*. Geneva: United Nations Publications.

UNIDO. 2019. 'Industrializing in the Digital Age', *Industrial Development Report 2020*. Vienna.

Van Ark, B., de Vries, K., and Erumban, A. 2020. 'How to Not Miss the Productivity Revival', *National Institute of Economic and Social Research, Discussion Paper, No.* 518, pp. 1–21.

WEF. 2018. 'Financing a Forward-Looking Internet for All', *World Economic Forum*, 1–34. https://www3.weforum.org/docs/WP_Financing_Forward-Looking_Internet_for_All_report_2018.pdf.

World Bank. 2021a. 'GDP per Person Employed', *The World Bank Data*, https://data.worldbank.org/indicator/SL.GDP.PCAP.EM.KD.

World Bank. 2021b. 'TCdata360: ICT Access', *The World Bank Data*, https://tcdata360.worldbank.org/indicators/107eb4d1?country=BRA&indicator=40372&viz=choropleth&years=2020.

SECTION III
COUNTRY EXPERIENCES

12
Argentina
Building New Capabilities and Competitive Advantages in a Challenging Macroeconomic Landscape

Bernardo Kosacoff and Mariana Fuchs

12.1. Introduction

The goal of this chapter is to analyse the main characteristics of Argentina's economic development and the ways in which the country attempted—sometimes successfully and sometimes not—to approach structural constraints impeding sustained and inclusive growth. The focus centres on consistency problems in macroeconomic management, and the role of the public policy in the development of firm capability-building.

Argentina's economy has followed what is in many ways an unusual, perhaps unexpected, development path over the past four decades. When comparing the evolution of the country's GDP per capita in relation to the economies of developed countries, what becomes obvious is a lack of convergence. Not only did Argentina try—and fail—to close the income per capita gap; the gap itself has widened considerably since the early 1980s. The divergence of the Argentinian growth experience from that of developed countries is one dimension of a broader story. Since the end of the import substitution industrialization (ISI) process, in the late 1970s, Argentina has been characterized by a number of distinctive features which have frustrated attempts to improve economic outcomes.

In first place, the country has experienced marked bouts of volatility, with periods of expansion that have not been sustained, and which led to deeper still crises. This has accompanied secular stagnation, and deterioration in living standards. Second, fiscal deficits, accompanied by an absence of sustainable sources of public-sector finance, have resulted in significant external debts and unsustainable monetary issuance. This has led to successive macroeconomic crises and, in some cases, International Monetary Fund (IMF) intervention. Part of the problem here has been that public spending and employment have experienced periods of surge, without strengthening the capacity to implement and evaluate public policies. Thus, opportunities to generate better outcomes have been foregone.

Bernardo Kosacoff and Mariana Fuchs, *Argentina* In: *Innovation, Competitiveness, and Development in Latin America.* Edited by: Edmund Amann and Paulo N. Figueiredo, Oxford University Press. © Oxford University Press 2024.
DOI: 10.1093/oso/9780197648070.003.0012

Accompanying this, Argentina has periodically suffered from large current account deficits. These have partly sprung from poor export dynamism. This has seen the country lose participation in world trade. The situation here has not been helped by restrictions in foreign exchange availability, whether as a result of market outcomes or public policy. Difficulties in finding a macreconomic framework that delivers stability has had consequences beyond growth and inflation, extending to the firm and sector level. Economic uncertainty and volatility help explain why Argentina has suffered from low investment levels, meagre spending on R&D, and an educational deterioration that led to significant losses in productivity. This has been accompanied by the disappearance of many firms, causing a fall in formal private employment. This in turn has contributed to a growth in poverty, particularly among young people.

One phenomenon characterizing contemporary Argentina can be argued to be growing economic and social disparities. This leads some to talk of the coexistence of 'three different Argentinas': (i) a modern sector, responsible for exports, R&D expenses, and the recruitment of highly qualified personnel, but accounting for only 20% of the economically active population; (ii) a sector with long evolutionary processes oriented to the domestic market, with key assets, but far from the best international practices; and (iii) an informal and excluded sector oriented to the so-called popular economy (characterized by informality in the labour market and increasing inequalities).

Against this challenging backdrop, this chapter attempts to analyse the attempts which have been made to tackle the structural impediments the Argentinian economy has been facing. Relatedly, alongside this, the chapter also concerns itself with attempts to build productive capabilities, elements which are indispensable in any attempt to engineer a step change in growth, and break out of the middle-income trap. The structure of this chapter is as follows. In section 12.2, the main stages of Argentine industrial development are described. Section 12.3 addresses today's challenges and opportunities for the Argentine productive sector. The section analyses traditional activities and the emerging ones, in terms of new sources of export growth, and the pursuit of competitiveness. Section 12.4 focuses on competitiveness and productive development policies in Argentina. Finally, section 12.5 offers some concluding remarks, pointing towards a new strategy of development.

12.2. The Stages of Argentine Industrial Development

Argentina's present industrial structure is the result of a long series of developments that started over a century ago. The ensuing industrial activities did not merely produce goods, but led, at the same time, to the growth of learning processes, to the incorporation of technology, to continuous improvements in skills and training, to the development of business skills, and to the setting up of institutional and regulatory frameworks. The Argentine economy became recognized for its significant degree of industrialization within the Latin American context. However, when comparing with the economies of more advanced countries, the central features of Argentina's economy clearly define it as a 'semi-industrialized' one.

Three major periods can be identified in Argentina's industrialization process (see Table 12.1). The first one begins around 1880, when the country made a radical shift into becoming integrated with the rest of the world as an agro-export economy. This position continued until the crisis of 1930. The second period, extending up until the late 1970s, refers to the ISI model within a semi-closed economy framework, and it includes, in its five-decade period, various phases. The third period starts with the failure of the 1979–1981 economic openness policy and the lengthy macroeconomic disruption of the country which lasted from the 1970s until today.

12.2.1. The Agro-Export Model and the ISI

The Argentine agro-export model was based on specializing in the production of grains and meat through exploiting the country's abundant and competitive natural resources. Once it had gotten its institutional structure settled, Argentina vigorously won a place for itself in the international economy as a dynamic exporter of primary goods and as an importer of capital and manufactured goods. It operated as an open economy, regulated by the gold standard. Its economic fluctuations were linked to weather conditions (which affected total agricultural output) and to the British business cycle (as Britain was its main international trading partner). At the same time, conditions began to arise which were favourable for the incipient industrialization of the country. These conditions largely took the form of the 'stimuli' which Hirschman described for Latin America (Hirshman, 1968).

Among them the following can be mentioned: (a) the existence of competitive goods in the primary sector that had to be processed in some way before being exported (meat, tannin, leather, wool, flour, etc.); (b) a flow of European immigrants who already possessed industrial skills; (c) the early development of widespread education and technical and professional specialization; (e) difficulties in external supply during World War I; (f) derived demands from primary production and from infrastructure needs (e.g. agricultural machinery, large railway maintenance networks, cement, etc.); (g) transportation costs and natural protective barriers; and (h) sustained rapid growth in the size of the domestic market. All these factors contributed to the gradual development of the

Table 12.1 Stages of Industrial Development in Argentina, 1880–2022

Stages of Development Type of Context and Firm	Agro-Export Stage with Incipient Industrialization	Import Substitution Model (ISI) Focused on Internal Market	Economic Openness Model with Restructuring and Globalization		
International Scenario	**1880–1929**	**1930-1978**	**1979–1990**	**1991–2001**	**2002-2022**
General framework	Industrial consolidation. British hegemony in production and finance	Fordist production US hegemony and rise of NICs Protected markets	Flexible organization of production. Dynamic growth of science and technology-based goods. Restructuring of emerging markets Economic blocs. Overt regionalism Financial globalization		Improvement in terms of trade. Commodities. Industry 4.0 Digitalization. Robotics Artificial Intelligence Growth of China and Asian countries Covid 19 Pandemic Dynamism of technology companies
Foreign Direct Investment	Focused on infrastructure, financing, raw materials, and primary resources	Focused on production for the protected domestic market. Attracted by factor prices Multi-plant structure of firms	Strong growth of globalization and privatization Mergers and acquisitions. Strategic alliances Systemic networks (resources, industry, services) Global value chains		Growing importance of knowledge-based services
LOCAL CONDITIONS General framework	Agro-exports integrated into the world economy stimulate incipient industry. Build-up of institutions.	Import substituting industry. Strong state participation in the economy. Government regulation. Stagnation of natural resources.	Continuous efforts and measures aiming to achieve stabilization. Trade and financial openness. Transformation of the industrial structure with growing heterogeneity	Stabilization-privatization-openness and deregulation. Expansion of natural resources. Improvement in the terms of trade. Structural unemployment	Macroeconomic instability. GDP stagnation. Loss of participation in the world. Poverty growth

Industry - Dynamic sectors	Food and textiles and others for domestic consumption	Automobiles, other metal products and machinery sectors chemicals	Steel and aluminium, petrochemicals, pulp and paper, vegetable oils	Automobiles, consumer durable goods, differentiated food products	Bioeconomy. Natural resources Knowledge-based services Pharmaceutical. Autom industry 4x4 vehicles
- Destination markets	Export markets for agro-industrial goods. Domestic market	Domestic market.	Export and domestic markets	MERCOSUR, domestic and export markets	China Brasil Domestic market
- Origin of Technology	Imported	Adapted and locally developed technologies far from 'best practice' standards. Short production series with technological lags. 'Idiosyncratic' Fordist production.	Imported and adapted to local conditions. Narrower technical gap in some sectors.	Imported foreign technology with little local adaptative input	Imported foreign technology with little local adaptative input
- Technical and productive organization	Dual: State-of-the-art technologies in export sectors and semi-artisanal ones for the domestic market.	Short production series with technological lags. 'Idiosyncratic' Fordist production. high integration with few experienced providers	Heterogeneity: sectors with Fordist organization and technology. Attempts at flexibilization and new forms of organization.	Modernization of product technology. Increased assembly of imported inputs and parts. Weak development of technologies on processes	Growing heterogeneity. Modern sector associated with exports. Loss of competitiveness of domestic production

(*continued*)

Table 12.1 Continued

Stages of Development Type of Context and Firm	Agro-Export Stage with Incipient Industrialization	Import Substitution Model (ISI) Focused on Internal Market	Economic Openness Model with Restructuring and Globalization		
International Scenario	1880–1929	1930-1978	1979–1990	1991–2001	2002-2022
Companies	Export-oriented local business groups. Semi-artisanal small and medium-sized enterprises (SMEs).	State-owned enterprises. Subsidiaries of transnational corporations. Small and medium-sized enterprises (SMEs).	National holding companies. Some small and medium-sized enterprises (SMEs)	National companies. Natural resources. Basic supplies	Subsidiaries of transnational corporations. National companies. Natural resources, basic inputs
- Transnational companies	With modern plants to facilitate agro-industrial exports. Railways and infrastructure	Growing participation in the industry. Greenfield investments Structural change. Development of adaptive technological capabilities	Loss of importance. Poor integration in global value chains	High participation in acquisitions processes. Less local technology	Brazilian firms. Poor FDI. Decrease in share in world trade

Source: Authors' elaboration.

most significant industrial structure in the region which, even before the crisis of the agro-export model, already had a share of 20% of GDP and consisted of over 50,000 industrial establishments.

The end of the expansion of the agricultural frontier, together with the 1929 international crisis and the conflictive three-sided relationship between Argentina, the United Kingdom, and the United States, caused the demise of the agro-export model. The imposition of foreign-exchange control in 1931 and of import permits in 1933, and the splitting into two of the foreign exchange market and the raising of import tariffs (measures mainly taken for fiscal reasons) are illustrative of the new way the economy worked.

The result of the closed-economy scheme was that foreign trade gradually became less and less important in terms of its share of GDP. These were, in fact, the conditions in which the first sub-period of ISI developed. The substitution process was based on the incipient industrialization already achieved in the first stage and it advanced very quickly into the 'easy' sectors of manufacturing production. Industries which produced consumer goods (food, textiles, clothing, etc.), household electrical appliances, simple machinery, and straightforward metal products, as well as those industrial activities associated with construction, were the most dynamic activities during this sub-period, which continued until Perón took office in 1945. Industrialization quickly deepened during this decade. This was basically due to the expansion of existing activities, the intensive utilization of labour, and the broadening of the domestic market to incorporate the entire population. Industry had clearly specialized in producing consumer goods exclusively for the domestic market, but constraints on its dynamic further growth were found as the level of technological obsolescence increased, and as the business community found itself unable—either due to entrepreneurial or technological limitations—to move towards more complex kinds of manufacturing, in a context where continuous restrictions were imposed by the balance of payments.

In 1958 the last ISI sub-period started, which lasted until the mid-1970s. It was based on the petrochemical industry and on the complex of metal products and machinery industries (the motor vehicles industry being the most representative sector), as well as the base for capital accumulation. The empty cells of the input-output matrix were progressively filled in, and this involved some extensive participation by subsidiaries of transnational corporations through 'greenfield' strategies. This took place in the framework of a highly protected economy and was a response to the explicit policy goal of raising the level of national economic self-sufficiency.

These changes led to a process of rapid technological development based on installing technologies which had been developed in more advanced countries, yet adapting them significantly to the local environment, but with a capital/

labour ratio quite different from the one in the developed world. This meant copying 'Fordist' production-line methods, yet incorporating a strong local component into them. However, this led to various problems. The output of these plants was generated in short production series and was exclusively oriented to the local market so that the scale of output from these plants was, on average, some 10 times lower than that of similar plants operating at the technological frontier; the level of vertical integration was notably high due to the weak development of specialized suppliers and subcontractors in a context where transaction costs were high; and the production mix was also markedly diversified. These were only some of the problems of international competitiveness affecting the Argentine industrial structure. In addition, Argentina's macroeconomic constraints were an obstacle for financing the transfer of income to industrial activities. Furthermore, it was industry's own trade deficit that restricted the possibilities of achieving industrial growth over any sustained period without engendering a balance-of-payments crisis.

The perception of these problems led to a search for policy solutions within the framework of the ISI model. On the one hand, incentives programmes to export manufactured goods were introduced. Their aim was simultaneously to generate scarce foreign currency, to expand the overall market (because the domestic market was showing signs of saturation), and to stimulate the overall competitiveness of industry. The results were quite visible: while in 1960 exports of non-traditional goods were practically non-existent, in 1975 they represented a quarter of the country's exports. On the other hand, the attempt was made to deepen the extent of the ISI model by reducing the country's heavy dependence on imports of basic industrial inputs such as steel, aluminium, paper, and petrochemicals. This led the government to promote some major industrial projects to produce these inputs locally. The promotion was based on (i) the amount of foreign currency savings these projects would produce, and (ii) the prospect that these projects would also lead to the broadening of the domestic market through the forward linkages that the new factories would have with high-value-added and employment-generating activities. Meanwhile the government also continued to operate its existing promotional mechanisms, as well as using the purchasing power and investment programmes of public-sector and state-owned enterprises as significant instruments of industrial policy throughout this subperiod.

12.2.2. The Breakdown of the ISI Model

The economic policy launched in April 1976 by the military regime in government profoundly changed the guidelines and directions which the Argentine industry had been engaged with until then. The new authorities' full confidence in the resource-allocation capabilities of market forces and in the state's subsidiary role were the philosophical underpinnings for a programme of market liberalization, followed by external openness. It aimed to eliminate the entire set of regulations, subsidies, and privileges established in the past to modernize and increase the efficiency of the economy (Sourrouille, Kosacoff, and Lucangeli, 1985). As far as industrial policy is concerned, two distinct sub-periods can be identified, with a dividing line around late 1978. The first period—called 'getting the macroeconomics in order'—started with reducing import tariffs (Berlinsky, 1977). Furthermore, the financial reform approved in 1977 liberalized the interest rate and created a totally different mechanism for the allocation of credit.[1] The second sub-period began in late 1978 with the detailed application of a policy which was based on the monetarist school's model of the open economy (i.e. the monetary approach to the balance of payments).

In this context, the coexistence of several negative factors produced the deepest crisis for the Argentine industrial sector in its entire history. The most important issues were that both domestic demand and export demand for locally produced industrial goods were low: domestic demand for these goods had been hit by the influx of competitive imported products, and export demand for them had been reduced by the exchange-rate policy. The investment processes and productive changes associated with increasing industrial exports were not verified. In 1981, the failure of this reform programme led to a deep macroeconomic and social crisis. The revaluation of the exchange rate and the newly imposed restrictions on imports (brought in because of the huge foreign-debt burden) created conditions that signified renewed protection for the industrial sector. The import coefficient of the Argentine economy once again approached the levels registered before the economic-openness policy was applied.

The local macroeconomic framework was the key determinant of most of the transformations that occurred between 1982 and 1990 (Machinea, 1990). The huge ensuing level of foreign indebtedness generated macroeconomic instability and uncertainty for the whole next decade. The instability encompassed both fiscal and external disequilibria, plus a very fragile financial system. 'Stabilization'—which the economy needed—was not merely a constant goal of policymakers throughout this period, but became an utterly unavoidable priority once the economy began to suffer a series of major disturbances, among which the hyperinflationary episodes in 1989 and 1990 were the most evident.

[1] From the 1930 crisis until today, the Argentine financial system was characterized by the Central Bank's regulation of re-discounting facilities for the granting of credit at highly negative interest rates. Industrial firms had a favored treatment in terms of the credit allocations made under this system.

Foreign investment led the 1990s productive reconversion process, particularly in those aspects that modernize the process. It is remarkable to observe the high correlation between the most dynamic sectors of local production and the increase in share of foreign capital in such sectors. Even if the strategies had a clear focus on taking advantage of the domestic or subregional market, affiliates made investments also aimed to achieve an efficient use of its physical and human resources and, much more selectively, joining in a more active way the corporation's international structure. It is possible to identify two stages in the behaviour of foreign direct investment (FDI) flows towards Argentina. Between 1990 and 1993, more than half of foreign investment income corresponded to public assets privatization and concession operations. Subsequently, mergers and acquisitions of private companies acquired a key role in Argentina's foreign investments. To sum up, unlike previous periods which had been characterized by strategies of the 'greenfields' type, most FDI funds were devoted to buying existing assets, both state-run and private.

However, the contribution of foreign-capital companies in the generation of productive linkages, spreading externalities, and achieving an active incorporation into international trade dynamic networks remained weak. Local conglomerates' behaviour in the 1990s was highly heterogeneous and changing. The strategies followed show some common features: a tendency to specialization in a reduced group of activities related to the past, an expansion to other markets by means of direct investment and in the concentration of productive activities in sectors with higher natural advantages or lower tradability, and scarce presence in the most internationally dynamic sectors based on knowledge and technological innovation. For another group of companies, internationalization through direct investment is essential for their own survival and expansion in the new economic context (Kosacoff, 1999).

The main elements that characterized the 1990s microeconomic performance were: (i) the decreased number of productive establishments; (ii) increase in trade opening (with the focus on imports); (iii) an investment process based on the acquisition of imported equipment; (iv) a more concentrated and 'foreign-oriented' economy; and (v) the sudden drop in the added-value coefficient. In addition, there was a higher adoption of foreign state-of-the-art product technologies, an abandonment of most of local technological efforts in the generation of new products and processes, a break in the vertical organization of activities based on the substitution of local added-value in favour of foreign supplies. A decreased mix of production, along with a higher complementation with foreign supply, growing outsourcing of activities in the service sector, a higher internationalization of companies, and increased importance of regional trade agreements in business strategies were also noted. But the most salient feature in the 1990s productive organization was heterogeneity. Clearly, all economic agents equally faced the challenge of moving from a 'workshop stage' to a 'company stage': new production strategies in which local production went hand in hand with foreign supplies and finished goods, with the purpose of making full use of the new rules of the economic game.

Between 1998 and 2001, the return to the extreme volatility of the environment seriously affected production and investment decisions and gave rise to growing doubts about the solvency of a big number of companies. The problems of Argentina's economy generated financial and trade turmoil. The negative consequences at a business stage had already been shown, and nobody knew how the economic agents would react facing the return of high macroeconomic uncertainty.

12.2.3. Industrial Development after the Convertibility Plan (2002–2022)

The abandonment of the convertibility system was marked by great turmoil, not only economic, but also in the social and political spheres. The costs of leaving a regime without 'escape mechanisms' and which turned out to be unsustainable, were in fact very high. However, the ensuing recovery was equally intense. The tendency to economic normalization allowed for the recovery of the pre-crisis activity levels and the notable creation of jobs. The current account of the balance of payments and the balance of trade show surpluses. The recomposition of the investment process was higher than expected and already has reached the record values in the 1990s. This was especially significant in agriculture, tourism, mining, construction, and within the whole of small- and medium-sized companies. Also, the international context of high raw material prices—related to the expansion of China and India—and the decreased interest rates had been very favourable for Argentina in the past few years, with forecasts of remaining so in the medium term, providing the country with a window of opportunity.

The devaluation at the beginning of 2002 caused a radical change in the relative prices of the economy, generating returns in favour of the production of tradable goods. Since then, the Argentine economy has experienced rapid growth between 2002 and 2007 (Fernández Bugna and Porta, 2007). Industry led this reactivation process, characterized by a relatively early recovery and high growth rates, reversing the process of relative deindustrialization of the past decade. It can be pointed out that the industry had a remarkably dynamic performance between 2003 and 2008, with a growth rate of 11% per year. Likewise, the annual rate of growth of employment was close to 6%, based on the growth of intensive sectors in the use of labour, with industry recovering after 30 years its capacity to generate employment. In turn, a notable growth of exports and imports is verified, and consequently of the international insertion of the manufacturing sector.

As a result of the profound modification of the production function in the 1990s—with a growing incorporation of imported inputs, a trend that has not changed in this period—a process of import substitution was not generated. On the contrary, the balances of industry's foreign trade were increasingly negative. In terms of export dynamism, the participation of a group of companies with greater capacity for engineering activities (such as agricultural machinery, compressed natural gas equipment, medical instruments, medicinal laboratories, among others), but with still little weight, was verified as an auspicious fact, enough to modify the pattern of productive specialization (Tavosnanska and Herrera, 2008).

The process of foreign investment that took place in the previous decade was not reversed, but this time the dynamism of acquisitions was articulated by the subsidiaries of Brazilian companies, which displaced corporations from developed countries in that role. The industrial dynamism was basically financed with the firms' own resources, in a context of scarce domestic financial deepening and foreign financing. Consequently, the financial exposure of the companies, their delinquency levels, and the functioning of the payment chain unfolded without disturbances.

Finally, the investment process was decisive in sustaining growth. However, the existence of radical investments that underpin a dynamic of structural change was not verified. Faced with a very sustained demand, a preference was observed to accelerate imports to supply it, postponing investment decisions. Although many sectors that had fully or partially recovered lost ground in the framework of a more favourable macroeconomic and incentive framework, the sectoral configuration of the industry did not change significantly. The impacts of the 2008 international crisis, associated with negative domestic expectations after the 'absurd and unnecessary' crisis between the government and the agricultural sector, and the deterioration of macroeconomic consistency, interrupted this cycle of growth in production and employment. Between 2009 and 2011, a new industrial dynamism is observed, associated with durable consumer goods, but without job creation. This recovery was interrupted in 2011, when a long cycle of stagnation and difficulties began, which has lasted until 2022.

The performance of the Argentine economy from 2012 up to the first quarter of 2022 has been weak. The macroeconomic difficulties determined the drop in GDP per inhabitant, the non-generation of formal private employment in a labour market with growth in public employment, the fall in real wages, a high level of inflation, the deterioration of social conditions, a strong contraction in investment, and stagnant productivity, among other consequences. Uncertainty and the difficulty to identify the long-term income trend disturbed consumption and investment decisions (Dal Poggetto and Kerner, 2021). The evolution of the macroeconomic aggregates in the period 2012–2018, considering their average annual growth per capita, shows an average annual decrease in GDP per inhabitant of 1.1%. This contraction is deeper in investment with 2.1%, and even more so in exports with an average annual fall of 2.6%. Meanwhile, consumption decreases by only 0.1% at an annual average, and the only growth is in imports with 0.2%. As a result, global supply has declined less than GDP at an average annual rate of 0.9%. In short, on the one hand, there is a drop in GDP, with a strong negative impact on the sources of growth coming from investments and exports. On the other hand, there is a greater preponderance of consumption, supplied by the growth of imports, explaining the fact that the global supply decreases less than GDP. In turn, the growth in imports associated with a sharp contraction in exports negatively affected the external trade surplus and job creation (Fanelli, 2018).

The disappointing behaviour of investments in this recent stage accentuates a structural feature of the economy in the long term. The annual average coefficient of the series of investments at current prices from 1950 to 2018 as a percentage of GDP is only 16.61%. At the beginning of the new government's administration in December 2015, the so-called investment shower was expected. The figures showed a very different process. These low aggregate investment performances, however, can be identified in two heterogeneous groups of sectors: (i) competitive sectors with regulatory frameworks, with a proactive investment attitude; (ii) sectors with far from best international practices.

(i) *Competitive sectors with regulatory frameworks*: These are characterized by strong developments of previous competitive capacities that have a high value market position and very significant sunk specific assets (machinery and equipment, technological assets, brands, human resources, etc.) that place them close to international best practices. Their business strategy combines valuing this market position, together with the flow of expected returns. If they stop investing, they lose competitiveness, and the wealth value of the company erodes rapidly. These sectors explain a large part of exports and innovation expenses and recruit the most highly qualified employees. Simultaneously, the government adjusted the incentives and provided regulatory frameworks that have given it longer and more predictable horizons, with more favourable incentives and institutions. In this sense, it is worth highlighting the following: (a) regulatory frameworks, markets, prices, union agreements, in unconventional oil and gas and renewable energies; (b) renewal and expansion of incentives for knowledge-based services; (c) development of airport infrastructure and aviation for tourism; (d) permissions for exports of meat and grains, with the development of international negotiations; (e) regulation of the automotive industry; (f) promotion of mining projects (lithium, gold, copper, uranium); (g) expansion of infrastructure: telecommunications, railways, ports, urban mobility, roads.

(ii) *Less competitive sectors*: These are characterized by being far from the best international practices, with problems of scale and economies of specialization, factors that have worsened since 2011 due to the lack of dynamism in investments and productivity improvements. They have specific assets, with unvalued market positions, that require strong investment processes. For its update, the individual effort of the company is not enough. Likewise, the aggravation of systemic conditions had a negative influence. Increases in logistics costs, strong growth in tax pressure, increased labour absenteeism and litigation costs, and few specialized suppliers are among other factors that interfere in investment decisions. In turn, all business strategies require financing, and the capital market is far from providing instruments, rates, and access for the investment process. Simultaneously, it is necessary to articulate a message that improves confidence and expectations and a strategy to strengthen these sectors.

The disturbances in the international financial market and the deep drought in agricultural areas in the first quarter of 2018 altered the fragile macroeconomic consistency, and the crisis deepened notably, leading to the request for assistance from the IMF of almost US$57bn, which prevented the default of the economy. In their implementation they failed to resolve the imbalances and led to a new period of stagnation and rising inflation. With the change of government in 2020, Argentina was facing a set of economic and social challenges that were aggravated by the pandemic, with the need to attend to the health situation. Since 2011, the manufacturing sector's level of activity dropped, losing competitiveness, within a scenario of falling physical volumes of production, job creation, R&D spending, exports of industrial goods, and investment.

In this context of deep crisis, the manufacturing sector in 2021 has had a greater recovery process than other activities. In 2020, the restructuring of the private external debt was achieved, followed in April 2022 by the agreement with the IMF. The agenda of economic stabilization of the economy, macroeconomic consistency, structural reforms, productive transformation, and solutions to the poverty problems are the key issues defining the difficult starting point to consider a development strategy and international insertion of the country. Currently, Russia's invasion of Ukraine is having a significant impact in the food sector as well as the energy sector around the world, with strong implications in the case of Argentina, given the country's specialization pattern.

12.3. Challenges and Opportunities for the Argentine Productive Sector: Established and Emerging Sectors

The Argentine productive structure is today characterized by its high heterogeneity. In this section we will very briefly detail the activities that have managed to converge to international productivity levels and that could play a significant role in the recovery of a growth path, the increase of exports, the improvement of productivity, the strengthening of innovation, job creation, and poverty reduction. The existence of highly competitive production organization models with significant development potential stands out, generating dynamic competitive advantages in long evolutionary processes, in some cases of more than a century. The determinants of these behaviours are very specific in each situation, but in all of them the entrepreneurial ability to develop its strategy based on the assets that were built and the ability to adapt to contexts of high local uncertainty and strong changes in the market are key features. Systemic aspects have played a fundamental role and, in turn, public policies and regulatory frameworks have affected their performance. There are very few developing countries that have managed to build these activities of excellence.

The 'competitive' universe is currently made up of just under 400 exporting companies—out of a universe of around 9,000—that export more than US$10 million worth of products and explain the export pattern; 600 companies that develop R&D activities and define the group of intensive knowledge activities; 11 unicorns that are listed in 2020 for a collective value of US$80,000 million on the New York Stock Exchange and are the most significant group of the new knowledge-based services (KBS). In turn, they are characterized by recruiting the most qualified workforce, but they represent only 20% of employment. They are made up of activities that are based on natural resources, industrial and KBS, which are a base to promote growth, but require an expansion of their specialization in the transition of their production from that characterized by a high presence of 'commodities' towards productive chains, that expand externalities with goods with greater incorporation of technological content and creation of qualified employment. The Argentine Ministry of Production is carrying out a series of studies, analysing some of these sectors.[2]

Argentina's international insertion was quantified and analysed in a study carried out jointly by the UIA (Unión Industrial Argentina) and ILO (International Labor Office) in 2019.[3] This report identifies the asymmetries between sales and purchases abroad in terms of technological intensity,

[2] See https://www.argentina.gob.ar/produccion/cep/consejo-cambio-estructural/documentos.

[3] UIA-OIT (2019), 'Una nueva inserción comercial argentina. El papel de la diversificación y la complejización. para crear más y mejor empleo'.

differentiation by quality, and complexity. Likewise, it evaluates the possibilities for improvement, both in the short term, by diversifying destinations and products where there is already the capacity to compete, and in the medium term, identifying potential for sectoral upgrading. The analysis uses the conceptual and methodological frameworks referring to the revealed comparative advantages (RCA) of Bela Ballasa, of technological intensity of the OECD and Sanjaya Lall, of the economy of complexity (Hidalgo and Hausmann, 2009) and the product space (Hausmann and Klinger, 2006). For the period between 1996 and 2016, the export of low-technology products represents 52% of all exports (associated with natural resources and to a lesser extent with manufactures) and the import of medium-high-technology industrial products, 54% of total imports.

In relation to economic complexity, Argentina is positioned at an intermediate point in the global context: in 2014, its export basket was more complex than that of 41% of the countries in the world (87th out of a total of 147 countries), placing Argentina in the range occupied by medium-developed countries. Even though its global performance has not been satisfactory in recent decades, the average complexity of the national export basket presents an encouraging result, given that it has managed to develop a broad set of activities with revealed comparative advantages, some of which are highly sophisticated, in multiple items. This diverse productive structure constitutes an asset when thinking about development strategies and offers multiple potentialities to improve the country's international insertion, based on the consolidation and empowerment of the RCAs with greater than average sophistication and with better use of the supply chain of value generating higher-quality employment.

Likewise, in the analysis contained in the report mentioned above, evidence of important opportunities emerges, which is an optimistic predictor of future RCAs of greater complexity. Argentina has possibilities to expand advantages in goods and services with high added-value in numerous production chains: the agri-food complex, primary products, chemicals and pharmaceuticals, machinery, steel, metalworking, plastics, non-metallic minerals, and textiles, to name a few (see Table 12.2). From a long-term view, structural limitations can be transformed into opportunities.

Considering the previous analysis, some selected sectors are presented below.

12.3.1. Natural Resources-Based Sectors

The availability of a wide range of natural resources, with evolutionary developments located on the international technical frontier, is one of Argentina's most important sources of growth. These sectors have a huge capacity to expand

Table 12.2 Comparative advantages in the Product Space Sectors with Potential (Selected Examples)

PRIMARY PRODUCTS, FOOD, AND BEVERAGES: powdered milk, cheese, milk, and egg proteins. Cornstarch, corn, flax, and soybean oil, glycerol, balanced food, glucose, chocolate, wine, flours, and extracts.
CHEMISTRY, PETROCHEMISTRY, PHARMACEUTICAL: benzene, chalk, vitamins, and derivatives. Hormones, albumins, various organic compounds. Vaccines for veterinary use. Paints, fungicides. Medicines, deodorants, essential oils, fertilizers.
RUBBER AND PLASTICS: polyamides, belts, styrene, polyethylene and other polymers, rubber tubes, films, plastic containers
METALWORKING AND AUTOMOTIVE: knives, semi-finished steel, aluminium and steel tubes, bars, wires, and cables. Engines, valves, pumps, agricultural machinery, and parts. Equipment for drums, scales, refrigerators, vehicles and auto parts, gearboxes, sailboats, medical instruments
OTHER INDUSTRIAL PRODUCTS: leather, paper, and cardboard. Wood and textiles, glass. Leather goods, fibres, wood pulp and panels, paper, coils, towels, high-resistance fabrics, candles, clothing

Source: Authors' elaboration based on UIA-OIT (2019).

and by being increasingly based on the importance of knowledge and innovation as a competitive factor. Moving forward to developing productive chains and generating positive externalities in employment and competitiveness, considering environmental sustainability, can be defined as one of the central axes of the country's immediate challenges.

12.3.1.1. Bioeconomy

In Argentina, where the availability of biological resources, the capacity of its human resources, and a good stock of technologies linked to agricultural value chains constitute its greatest comparative advantages, the productive use of the bioeconomy represents a window of opportunity as part of a broader strategy of genuine and sustainable development, as many authors point out (Bisang and Trigo, 2017). The bioeconomy is based on the sustainable production of plant, animal, and microbial biomass, taking advantage of photosynthesis to produce, in addition to food, energy and a wide range of environmentally friendly biomaterials. Agriculture is no longer seen only as a source of employment for labour and food production, but is also seen as an activity strongly integrated into industrial processes and services. The bioeconomy appears as an alternative development guide for structural change based on local natural endowments, the previous accumulation (from technological/genetic capacities to business routines) of assets, the smaller competitive distance of several of these activities, and the (potential) global opportunities as a space for massive accumulation mediated by commercial exchange.

Based on this, while traditional approaches emphasize products and value chains, bioeconomy also highlights the interrelationships that exist between the different production chains, the provision of natural resources, and the production of ecosystem services. Within this approach, the opportunities to improve productivity are highlighted—through the enhancement of all externalities. This emphasizes the potential for recycling, circularity, and cascade approaches, which during the processing stage plays a determining role in the identification and development of opportunities at the territorial level (Bisang and Trigo, 2017).

This perspective gives a strategic value to increasing efficiency in the use of natural resources, generating innovation options, and opening new business opportunities. It involves as well new sources of growth in terms of regional income and job creation, while contributing to recompose strategic balances in energy and territorial matters. Additionally, this productive approach results in a greater multiplier effect of the activity on the economy in general, tending to increase the density of the industrial fabric and closely articulating both spheres, primary and industrial. The concept of bioeconomy appeared and was raised around capturing the social and economic benefits related to taking advantage of the innovation opportunities associated with new biological technologies. Subsequently, it has been mutating towards a broader and more ambitious vision for sustainable development, and to put into practice the strategies of decarbonization of the economy.

Until the 1980s, agricultural production was a synonym of food, and the rural producer was the supplier of wheat, corn, meat, fruit, and vegetables. It was completed with the food industry and the commercial system. The 'exportable balances' were also part of the basic basket: meat, corn, and wheat dominated exports. They were key elements in the agro-export model. During the ISI model they continued to explain almost all foreign sales. However, its production remained stagnant at 20 million tons per year. The sector became more dynamic through mechanization and fertilization, distinctive characteristics of the so-called green revolution, which was already present several decades ago in the best world producers. With great surprise, since the mid-1990s, a remarkable transformation process has begun that increased grain production to about 160 million tons in 2021, associated with the introduction of innovation that places the country in the best levels of international efficiency.

Changes are currently being verified in the producer´s behaviour, in the way of organizing activities and their technological intensities and routines. Food production is also expanding towards materials for industry/inputs and bioenergy. Primary production—agriculture and/or traditional livestock—is complemented by the coverage of inputs and industrial chains. Thirty-one agro-industrial productive chains explain, in 2020, 14% of the national GDP and employ 2.2 million people. It is noteworthy that 89% is used—directly or indirectly—for human consumption, around 10% goes to the manufacturing industry and/or biological inputs, while just over 1% of the total Value added (VA) feeds the national energetic matrix.

In recent decades, the organization of the agricultural production model has been evolving towards another, framed within 'agricultural network production', with totally different structural features and relational impacts with the rest of the economy. The new form of organization of agricultural activity is built on a number of 'columns': (i) the owners of land (who exploit it and/or give it up for exploitation); (ii) agricultural production companies that pool or capture financial resources, hire services, lease land, and bear the risk of production; (iii) service contractors (who by their own action and on behalf of agricultural production companies carry out various agricultural activities); (iv) suppliers of inputs (seeds, fertilizers, agricultural machines, technical consultants, public technology agencies) who also provide technologies and tacit knowledge; (v) financing providers; (vi) the transport network and other support services. Several of these agents existed in some way in the previous model, but their evolution, the new technologies that are being implemented, and the high yields that are being obtained have modified and integrated them under a new form of joint organization, mixed between the primary sector, industry, and services. The construction of new public and private strong institutional entities is essential for the consolidation of the productive ecosystem.[4]

The bioeconomy appears as a timely development path since it implies the beginning of a structural change towards a sustainable productive matrix in environmental and social terms. It is about applying the structural change approach to the technological, productive, and trade realities, identifying and promoting, early and with certain advantages, activities that (i) have growing demands; (ii) base their competitiveness on dynamic advantages (in this case, natural resources and applied biotechnology); (iii) enter the international market; (iv) generate positive externalities on other sectors, amplifying the multiplier effect; and (v) take special care of environmental and social sustainability. A review of the sector indicates that, in the face of new local and international conditions, the industrialization of 'biology', which is already being carried out

[4] Bioceres is one among several interesting cases of national entrepreneurship by a group of farmers. It is a public-private asociation, including universities and science and technology institutions from the province of Santa Fe. The company made important technological developments in modern biotechnology, generating a significant impact on exports and construction of knowledge networks and technological synergies, being able to value the technological advances achieved in the company, for example, by applying the HB4 event to the germplasm developed by others, or in the development of gene therapies for human health. Since 2021, Bioceres is listed on the NASDAQ. It is one of best performing Argentine 'Unicorns', with a valuation over US$5,000 million in March 2022. https://bioceressemillas.com.ar.

in traditional manufacturing branches, can make significant advances that give new answers to the demand for growth and development. Biofuels, which are the most outstanding development to date, can make a significant contribution to the generation of an energy matrix that is less dependent on fossil fuels and more sympathetic to environmental issues (Bisang and Trigo, 2017).

This leads necessarily to the review of policies and instruments of policy and fundamentally of the criteria for allocating resources in favour of the new model, especially in horizontal policies. Another relevant area regards policies for these new markets related to the bioeconomy: establishment of technical standards for products and processes for bio-products; security, marketing, and so on. A third level is the induction of consumption guidelines towards bio-products; in this case, although the market allocates private consumption via prices, the reason for the interventions is that such prices usually do not consider positive and negative externalities. Communication towards society and towards consumers plays a role in this regard.

Policies to promote the development of new production facilities should also be considered. Briefly, it is necessary to re-think state policies for the construction of public goods necessary for the bioeconomy. The recent Russian invasion of Ukraine and the conflict that emerged have had a strong impact on the food industry and put the focus on Argentina's potential to help provide a solution to the current international food crisis. The same can be said concerning the energy and the mining sectors, as discussed in the following subsection.

12.3.1.2. Energy (Bioenergy, Oil and Unconventional Gas, Renewable, Eolic, Solar, Green Hydrogen)

Bioenergy

Bioenergy production appears as an important new activity based on its sustained development over the past decade in Argentina and in the main countries of the world. Its initial impulse was given by the opportunities of the external biodiesel market, and later it evolved associated with a promotional regulatory framework in various aspects (compulsory use as a mixture of fossil fuels, differential prices and tax treatments, subsidies for the formation of installed capacities, promotion of the exports). For specific cases of countries with abundant biomass production, biofuels appear as a window of opportunity to balance their trade balances in terms of energy and additionally industrially develop their potential on genuine bases. Argentina falls within this group of countries (it has abundant generation of biomass, controls the associated biotechnologies, shows energy imbalances, although the development of unconventional gas and oil in Vaca Muerta could help reduce them).

In the case of Argentina, this activity is based on genuine sources of competition since it begins with the supply of inputs on a large scale and competitive prices (soybeans, corn, sugarcane) and takes advantage of the pre-existence of complementary facilities (milling capacity, development of commercial channels, installations of various livestock farms previously fed with other inputs). Added to this is the self-generation and use of energy in closed production circuits. Likewise, biofuels tend to mitigate the energy imbalance both in terms of final fuels and in the generation of gas and/or electricity, replacing fossil fuels. Due to their location, they offset any differences in generation costs (with respect to fossil fuels) with savings in energy transportation costs.

At present there are several hundred companies—considering those where the main production is biofuels—responsible for biologically-based industrial complexes of different magnitudes. Many authors describe the indirect impacts on employment and the development of suppliers of capital goods (the machinery and equipment industry and other inputs required by this activity). This is a sector in full development, highly sensitive to regulatory conditions at different levels: technical standards for production, marketing, and use, price distortions for raw materials and products (differential tax rates, taxes on foreign trade), and systems of regulated prices of the biofuels used in the cuts.[5]

Oil and Unconventional Gas

Global supply and demand for energy are facing profound changes. While traditional sources, mainly fossil fuels, are experiencing a relative decline in the energy balance, the use of alternative sources is developing, at the same time as investment in technologies to improve energy efficiency in general is growing. In the global context of energy supply and demand that is currently facing profound changes, the use of alternative sources is developing. The appearance of unconventional gas reserves and technologies that allow their recovery has given rise to the so-called gas revolution (or boom) (Advanced Resources International, 2013). Argentina is among the countries with the largest recoverable reserves of unconventional oil and gas. The Vaca Muerta[6] formation reservoir is the most important in the country, located in the Neuquén Basin, with an area of approximately 30,000 km^2.

Many authors highlight the presence of interregional spillover effects because of the development of unconventional hydrocarbons. In addition, the development of Vaca Muerta is requiring certain qualifications of the labour force due to the introduction of new production technologies (e.g. the need to import drilling and/or maintenance services; development of suppliers) and would also allow the development of related industries (e.g. plastic inputs, fertilizers, electricity).

[5] For more details, see https://www.argentina.gob.ar/economia/energia/hidrocarburos/biocombustibles.

[6] For more details, see https://www.argentina.gob.ar/economia/energia/vaca-muerta.

However, it is worth weighing the environmental impacts, such as the water consumption of the activity, the contamination of groundwater, the seismic risks, and the dangers due to the use of chemical additives (López et al., 2021).

The exploration and production of oil and gas in the oceans have had an extraordinary development in the last decade, finding important accumulations of these hydrocarbons. Argentina has a great potential in its offshore basin, with resources that could equal those in Vaca Muerta. The big formation of unconventional hydrocarbons in southwestern Argentina and its development could generate 'profound change', transforming the country into an exporter of energy to the world, with a potential to generate 200,000 barrels of oil per day, a volume like what is currently produced in Argentina by YPF, the country's largest oil company. It is estimated that for its development, investments would amount to more than US$6,000 million with a very positive impact on the local supply chain and on job creation. In the development phase, 22,000 direct jobs could be generated.

Although Argentina has had offshore exploration and production platforms since the 1970s in the southern basin (off the coast of Tierra del Fuego and Santa Cruz), the recent authorization to start exploration in the northern basin (coast of Buenos Aires and Río Negro) put the sector in the centre of the scene. The exploratory potential for hydrocarbons over a surface area consists of more than 1.2 million square kilometers, of which some 590,000 are prospective. It is an extension like the basins of the North Sea.

Argentina has also a great potential to develop the hydrogen economy in all its varieties. From the grey hydrogen (which is currently produced but without capture technologies carbon), to cleaner hydrogens like blue (based on natural gas), pink (based on energy nuclear), or green (based on renewable energies). Regarding green hydrogen, the North-West region has high levels of solar radiation, almost twice the world average, with 2800 kilowatt hour (kWh) per cubic meter annual. Patagonia, due to the strong winds, has huge potential from wind power as well (Consejo Económico y Social, 2021).

Mining (Lithium, Copper, Gold, Silver)

Despite having the Andes Mountain range along its extensive border, until the 1990s Argentina only extracted non-metallic minerals. The law of promotion and fiscal security was the beginning of the development of the sector, which has enormous reserves of copper, silver, gold, potassium, and the recent white gold-lithium, among other minerals. According to World Bank estimates of natural resource accounting, mining is several times larger than the agricultural sector.[7]

The case of lithium has become well-known in the past decade. Lithium is currently the material chosen for the manufacture of electric batteries, the key

[7] https://www.argentina.gob.ar/eiti/mineria.

component in the transition towards electromobility and in the diffusion of efficient storage systems for renewable energies such as solar or wind power. Argentina is the 4th producer of lithium and the 3rd reserve in the world. There are 2 mines in operation, 6 under construction, and 28 advanced projects. Income from exploration and prospecting activities, as well as from the construction and operation of lithium carbonate production projects, can have a significant impact on the fiscal resources and employment at the level of provinces. The generation of local productive linkages could help to enhance these impacts, with the opportunity offered by lithium for Argentina to become a relevant player in the development of technologies applied in the different stages of the value chain (Schteingart, 2021).

Fisheries

Argentina has an extensive maritime coastline, some 5,000 kilometers in length. In this territory, there are living and mineral resources that have not yet been fully exploited and that reflect great potential for the future. The Argentine fishing sector is structurally in surplus in terms of foreign trade. The growth in the value of exports in recent years is mainly explained by the increase in crustaceans and shrimp. Argentina has become the world's leading exporter, known worldwide for the unique quality of its shrimp. The potential for additional generation of foreign currency in the sector is necessarily due to the greater value-added within current volumes. This is very difficult and requires long-term planning, since it is linked to innovative processes involving alternative production methods, new business strategies, greater links with other production sectors, and the incorporation of advanced technology. Among the production methods that can be complemented with capture fishing, aquaculture stands out, scarcely exploited in Argentina to date. The link with other productive sectors and the incorporation of technology present high potential both for the environmental dimension and for the strictly economic one. In summary, it is concluded that technological, productive, and commercial innovation is necessary to expand the export potential of the Argentine fishing sector without putting the sustainability of the resource at risk.[8]

Forestry

The forestry sector has great potential, given the wide availability of land and important linkages. Argentina's forested land consists of 1.3 million hectares of forest plantations and 53.6 million hectares of native forests. Argentina has at least 3.7 million ha of forest land available to expand forest plantations that do not affect sites of high conservation value, nor do they compete with native forests or crops. The forestry and industrial forestry sector in Argentina is a source of growth for the country on a renewable and low-carbon-intensity basis. It is one

[8] https://www.argentina.gob.ar/sites/default/files/dt_2_-_el_sector_pesquero_argentino.pdf.

of the sectors with the greatest ability to increase regional development in a sustainable manner, providing jobs in both rural and urban areas. The opportunities in the forest-industrial chain are found in the sustainable management of native forests, the possibility of growing in forested areas while preserving ecosystems of high conservation value, advancing in industrialization and innovation, and the comprehensive use of all products and by-products, being fundamental the concretion of the necessary investments to add value to the forestry production.

The potential of the current forest-industrial chain is enormous, for example: in the development of new technologies and high value-added products (green chemistry, nanotechnology, biorefineries, provision of capital goods, etc.) in stimulating domestic consumption to increase demand in technological updating and optimization of current processes for efficient use of the resource in the use of by-products of primary transformation for alternative sources of energy (thermal and electrical) in the certification of wood to open access to sustainable markets, among others.[9]

12.3.2. Knowledge-Based Service Sector

This knowledge-based service (KBS) sector has been gaining weight in the Argentine economy in the past 20 years in terms of employment and in exports. The important export development of these activities and their direct impact in employment reflects today's systemic effects as well as their potential since they present a significant capacity of helping increase other productive activities competitiveness (Lachman and López, 2022). This dynamism of the KBS industry in Argentina is mainly driven by the outstanding talent of human resources, a favourable time zone, and a high-quality local technological infrastructure. These services comprise almost 10% of total national exports. Argentina is also the only country in the region that has a trade surplus in the KBS category.

Although there have been companies dedicated to the production of software in Argentina since the 1970s, the software and computer services sector has grown significantly in Argentina since the beginning of the new millennium. At the end of 2018, there were 5,300 companies that directly employed nearly 100,000 people, compared to 2,000 companies and 25,000 jobs in 2000. The sector's exports reached more than US$1,900 million in 2018. This good performance was based both on the business capacities accumulated locally in previous decades, and on the availability of human capital at competitive costs, which allowed several large multinationals in the sector to begin developing locally and

[9] https://www.argentina.gob.ar/sites/default/files/2021/04/plan_estrategico_foresto_industrial_2030.pdf.

exporting computer services. Public policies supported this process, both with tax measures and with others linked to innovation and training of human resources, although a more rigorous evaluation of the costs and benefits of these policies is still a pending issue (López, 2018). There is still a significant chance to expand the links between the sector and the rest of the economy since Argentina could export more sophisticated products and develop locally more complex activities such as in the area of agribusiness technology services (AgTech), and it is gaining ground in the FinTech and videogame industry.[10]

12.3.3. Industrial Activities

As noted in previous sections, basic inputs were a central element at the end of the ISI process. Aluminum, steel, paper, and petrochemicals were pillars of industrial development. Argentina has plants on the international technical frontier. For example, the Techint Organization is the world's largest exporter of seamless steel tubes, the largest steel producer in Latin America, and operates extensively in the oil sector.[11] Today there are many possibilities to boost these industries. This is the case of the revitalization of projects, which, with the appearance of raw materials (in this case, gas from Vaca Muerta), opens the door to carrying out projects with significant spillovers in terms of job creation and development of specialized suppliers, achieving productivity levels like those in the United States in a few years. One example is the expansion of a urea production plant, owned by the company Profertil (owned by the national oil company YPF and Canadian Nutrien), which incorporates more environmentally friendly technology. This is the urea plant in the Bahía Blanca petrochemical complex.[12]

In the metalworking field, Argentina had a leadership position in Latin America during the ISI period. Several subsectors managed to continue developing capabilities of excellence. The automotive industry developed a specialization in 4×4s; the Toyota firm stands out, with a production of almost 200,000 4×4 vehicles per year, mainly for export.[13] Volkswagen also has a global gearbox plant, export oriented, as well as manufacturing engine valves. Another interesting case is Basso, a local company that started manufacturing valves for combustion engines in the 1960s and is currently exporting its products to five continents. The company's international character deepened after the acquisition, in 2002, of a valve factory in the United States, exporting valves to Mexico. Basso financed

[10] https://www.argentina.gob.ar/produccion/datos-productivos/observatorio-de-la-economia-del-conocimiento.

[11] https://www.techintgroup.com/en.

[12] https://www.profertil.com.ar/index.php/en/about-us.

[13] https://autohistoria.com.ar/index.php/marcas-de-autos/toyota/.

during 2020 a project to adapt classrooms and laboratories for training in Industry 4.0 at the Rafaela Technological Institute, in the province of Santa Fe.

Likewise, the competitiveness of agricultural machinery, sports sailboats, medical instruments, and machinery for the gas industry, among many other sectors, is highlighted. Among other highly competitive activities, the following sectors must be mentioned: (i) pharmaceutical sector, in R&D;[14] (ii) high-quality wines;[15] (iii) high-design clothing;[16] and (iv) the food industry, with sophisticated nodes the production matrix (Kosacoff et al., 2014). As an example of new emerging sectors, the space industry is one of the high-tech sectors where Argentina has generated its own innovation capabilities and has reached a relevant level of international recognition. This accumulation of capabilities is the result of a process of more than two decades during which the country was able to design and put into orbit different observation and telecommunications satellites.

In Argentina, as in other nations with a space industry, the state was the initial promoter. The accumulation of previous technological capabilities that led to the emergence of the space industry occurred in two sectors: the nuclear industry and the aeronautics industry (López, Pascuini, and Ramos, 2017). At present, there are two main players in this industry. On the one hand, CONAE, created in 1991—with antecedents in the National Space Research Commission (CNIE), established in 1960 under the Argentine air force—as a civil organization, is one of the main actors in the current 'ecosystem' of the space industry.[17] The second central player in the Argentine space industry is INVAP. The company was born in 1972 within the framework of the Applied Physics group (composed of several graduates of the Balseiro Institute), precursor of the later Applied Research programme of the Bariloche Atomic Center. Formal activity was launched in 1976 under the figure of a state company, through an agreement between the province of Río Negro and the National Atomic Energy Commission (CNEA). INVAP is a state company fully owned by the province of Río Negro, with technical areas focused on Nuclear Projects, Space Projects and Government, Industrial Projects and Alternative Energies, and ICTs and Technological Services (López, Pascuini, and Ramos, 2017).[18]

[14] https://www.argentina.gob.ar/sites/default/files/sspmicro_cadenas_de_valor_farmacia_0.pdf.

[15] https://coviar.ar/plan-estrategico-vitivinicola-argentina-2020/.

[16] http://www.ciaindumentaria.com.ar.

[17] https://www.argentina.gob.ar/ciencia/conae/.

[18] INVAP is a world leader in research reactors, manufacture of fuel elements for these reactors, radioisotope production plants. Argentina constructed three nuclear plants; https://www.argentina.gob.ar/economia/energia/energia-electrica/nuclear/centrales. The company exported large nuclear projects all around the world, based on strong capabilities in management, design, construction, and provision of services for nuclear facilities. Among them, the design and construction of radioisotopes reactors for medical use in Egypt, Australia, and the Netherlands in recent years should be mentioned; this last, still in construction involving a more than $US400 million investment, in partnership with the Pallas Foundation in Petten. https://www.invap.com.ar.

ARSAT is another main agent of the space industry ecosystem in Argentina. Its statute provides that the company's corporate purpose is: (a) the design, development, construction in the country, launch and/or commissioning of geostationary telecommunications satellites in orbital positions or resulting from international coordination procedures before the International Telecommunications Union (ITU), and associated frequency bands; and (b) the corresponding exploitation, use, provision of satellite facilities, and/or commercialization of satellite and/or related services. These major players in the industry work with several local public and private providers (https://www.arsat.com.ar/satelital/).

Argentina is part of a select group of countries that develop their own technologies in the satellite industry, and design and produce geocommunications satellites. Additionally, it plans to dominate the technology of space launchers. This is one of the high-tech areas where Argentina has internationally recognized skills, which are the result of a process of learning and capacity development carried out over several decades. The company Satellogic is an example in this field. It is an Earth observation platform, offering solutions for agriculture, defense, energy, oil and gas, and forestry, among others. Recently Satellogic announced its collaboration with the Ukraine government, allies, and humanitarian organizations to protect citizens affected by the Russian invasion. In partnership with geospatial and AI analysis software company Astraea, Satellogic offers a direct stream of high-resolution satellite imagery collections over Ukraine as well as neighbouring areas.

Satellogic started trading on the Nasdaq in January 2022 and plans to launch up to 12 additional spacecraft later this year to reach a constellation of 34 commercial satellites in orbit by the first quarter of 2023 and up to 200 satellites by 2025 (https://satellogic.com/).

12.4. Competitiveness Policies and Productive Development in Argentina

It is well known, from the analytical point of view, that correct implementation of economic policies has a key role in achieving improvements in competitiveness and productivity. Successful experiences in many countries prove it. Argentina has a long experience in the implementation of this kind of policies. However, a very critical view of the real impacts that have been generated arises. The recent history of productive development in Argentina is characterized by a large set of instruments and policies, creation of agencies without coordination and enforcement capacities, along with a set of shortcomings.

Analysing the institutions and instruments involved, we can mention: (i) lack of a clear 'country' strategy with monitoring mechanisms, and coordination spaces; (ii) limited impact of instruments due to an absence of articulation among institutions; (iii) scarce and discontinuous budgetary resources; and (iv) even if the private sector has developed some programmes to enhance competitiveness, the necessary articulation of these efforts with the public sector is still erratic and not systematic. Among the most important aspects to be mentioned is the absence of impact evaluation tools, and the lack of accountability that allows for adjustments and corrections and for a better impact of the programmes (Baruj, Kosacoff, and Ramos, 2009).

However, this does not mean that there are not some examples where policies have performed well. In this sense, in terms of public-private cooperation, two successful experiences, among others, can be mentioned: (i) the case of wine industry transformation toward higher-quality links in the province of Mendoza, where private wineries interact with the public sector and share knowledge with university laboratories and public Science and Technology (S&T) institutions; and (ii) the development of INDEAR (research and development services company; https://www.indear.com/en/about-us/) in the field of agricultural biotechnology, by the Bioceres group in cooperation with the scientific-technological system.

In terms of technological policies, the case of the Argentine Technology Fund (FONTAR) deserves to be described. This Fund is charged with designing and implementing Productive Development Policies (PDPs) that support business-oriented technological innovation and R&D. These instruments deal mostly through financing and subsidizing technological modernization, R&D, the provision of technological services to private firms, and the provision of local technological public goods that enhance the technological capabilities of small and medium-sized enterprises (SMEs). It has managed to survive over time, despite threats posed by macroeconomic in stability since its inception in the mid-1990s.

As an example of sectoral policy in recent years, in 2019, the so-called Knowledge Economy Law was approved. This law replaced the Software Law enacted in 2004. The new law partially reformulates the tax benefits scheme of the Software Law and extends them to a wide range of high-tech and/or creative activities (including audiovisual, biotechnology, bioeconomy, nanotechnology, aerospace, nuclear, R&D, engineering, automation, and professional services for export, among others).

Regarding the impacts, we can briefly analyse the tax expenditures associated with the policies. Taking 2022 as a reference year, these expenditures barely reach 0.54% of GDP and appear highly concentrated in one specific programme of fiscal regime, which concerns the development, in the province of Tierra del Fuego (the southernmost-territory of Argentina), of electronic products assembly plants, very far from urban centres and concentrating two-thirds of these contributions.[19] These are simple assembly processes without externalities that justify the fiscal subsidy and the enormous cost for consumers, also generating unfair competition with the continent and monopolistic positions that are the main economic distortions, to which is added the lack of an impact evaluation of the policy and control customs incentives (Feinstein, 2021).

In March 2022, the government launched the 'Plan Argentina Productiva 2030' (https://www.argentina.gob.ar/produccion/argentina-productiva-2030). This Plan seeks to transform the productive and technological structure of the country to guarantee sustainable growth, and thus generate quality jobs. It focuses on 10 productive missions. These so called missions are aim to focus accurately on their objectives, fostering productive development with regional and social equity. However, this takes place in a context of lack of macroeconomic consistency and fragility of public and private organizations responsible for the implementation of the policies. These organizations do not consider horizontal actions over systemic issues that involve logistics, characteristics of the financial system, tax pressure and labour market aspects, among others, with a very negative impact on productive development.

Likewise, the productive heterogeneity of Argentina needs a development strategy. It requires not only focusing on the sectors with the greatest potential for productivity improvement, but also on the productive apparatus that needs a general improvement in productivity and investment processes, with job creation in domestic market-oriented activities. This must go together with an approach related to the new productive structure that involves the informal sector of the Argentine economy and the so called '\popular economy—a new concept born after the 2001 crisis, including subsidized poor sectors—that obviously have a significant impact in terms of employment and social issues.

12.5. Conclusions: Towards a New Strategy for Development

This chapter has analysed the competitiveness and the specialization pattern of Argentina, a country of intermediate development, characterized by macroeconomic volatility and inconsistency, low institutional quality, high social and productive heterogeneity, in an increasingly uncertain context.

During the ISI stage, a significant evolutionary path towards the construction of technological assets and the development of competitive advantages was identified. But at the same time, the existence of reduced economies of scale and

[19] The tax expenditures data can be found in: 'Informe sobre gastos tributarios. Estimación para los años 2020–2022', Dirección Nacional de Investigaciones y Análisis Fiscal, Subsecretaría de Ingresos Públicos, Secretaría de Hacienda. Ministerio de Economía, República Argentina (2021)

specialization and a strong orientation to the internal market, with a significant gap to the best international practices, characterized this period. At the end of the 1970s, there occurred a transition from a semi-closed economy to a more open one. This was accompanied by notable changes in the international techno-productive paradigm, notably the information revolution and the expansion of global value chains.

Argentina lacked the capacity to respond adequately to this change of economic regime. This resulted in macroeconomic inconsistencies, secular stagnation, and a notable deterioration in welfare and income equality. Macroeconomic imbalances were enhanced due to the absence of a development strategy that safeguarded previously built productive assets and overcame their competitive restrictions. The challenge now faced centres on constructing a shared public-private vision of economic development, making use of the enormous assets that Argentina has built up. This will involve the implementation of consistent macroeconomic frameworks to sustain external, fiscal, and financial balances.

At the same time, attention must be focused on the most important issue: inclusive development. Long-term investment decisions, the development of dynamic competitive advantages, and achieving greater social cohesion through equal capacities and opportunities must be encouraged. Successful long-term growth is largely explained by the ability to incorporate, generate, and disseminate knowledge and technology. In this sense, education and training of the workforce, changes in the organization of production, and institutional quality are key elements. In short, the future should be about developing local capacities to close the productivity gaps that separate Argentina from the advanced nations. As is well known, value and employment are generated at the firm level. A development strategy must therefore include the strengthening of business capacities, with incentives and rules of the game that promote long-term investment decisions. Attention here must also focus on increased productivity, the development of dynamic competitive advantages, and job creation.

The pattern of specialization is a determinant for sustainability. Strengthening Argentina's internal market is essential to develop competitive advantages, create jobs, and become integrated into the global economy in an intelligent way. This will require adopting an open economy model, with regional competitive integration. The growth of exports will prove essential to overcome external restrictions, secure additional demand for production, and develop the business base in competitive environments. This in turn should generate more positive externalities to sustain development. The natural resources sector and established industries can form a base for advancing towards the production of differentiated goods that are more intensive in the incorporation of innovation processes. This will involve the generation of domestic technological capacities, the better qualification of human resources, and business strengthening. All of this should occur in a collective exercise of building networks of knowledge and production capacities.

References

Balassa, B. 1965. 'Trade Liberalisation and "Revealed" Comparative Advantage'. The Manchester School.

Baruj G., Kosacoff B., and Ramos A. 2009. 'Las políticas de promoción de la competitividad en la Argentina: Principales instituciones e instrumentos de apoyo y mecanismos de articulación público-privada', Proyect Document No. 257. Santiago de Chile: CEPAL.

Berlinsky, J. 1977. *Protección arancelaria de actividades seleccionadas de la industria manufacturera Argentina*. Buenos Aires: Ministerio de Economía.

Bisang, R., and Trigo E. 2017. 'Bioeconomía Argentina: Modelos de negocios para una nueva matriz productiva', Bolsa de Cereales. Ministerio de Agroindustria de la Argentina y Grupo Bioeconomía.

Coatz, D., Grasso, F., and Kosacoff, B. 2011. 'Industria Argentina: Recuperación, freno y desafíos para el desarrollo en el Siglo XXI', Consejo Profesional de Ciencias Económicas de Buenos Aires.

Consejo Económico y Social. 2021 'Hacia una estrategia Nacional Hidrógeno 2030'. Buenos Aires: Government of Argentina. https://www.argentina.gob.ar/noticias/el-consejo-economico-y-social-realizo-el-foro-hacia-una-estrategia-nacional-hidrogeno-2030.

Dal Poggetto, M., and Kerner, D. 2021. *Tiempo perdido: La herencia, el manejo de la herencia de la herencia*. Buenos Aires: Editorial Perfil.

Dirección Nacional de Investigaciones y Análisis Fiscal, Subsecretaría de Ingresos Públicos, Secretaría de Hacienda, Ministerio de Economía, República Argentina. 2021. 'Informe sobre gastos tributaries: Estimación para los años. 2020–2022'. https://www.argentina.gob.ar/economia/ingresospublicos/gastostributarios.

Fanelli, J. M. 2018. 'Crecimiento, productividad y empleo: La competitividad es la llave', IEI (Instituto de Estrategia Internacional, CERA).

Feinstein, O. 2021. 'El desarrollo de capacidades nacionales de evaluación', *Estado Abierto. Revista sobre el Estado, la administración y las políticas públicas*, 6(1), agosto-noviembre, 109–121.

Fernández Bugna, C., and Porta, F. 2007. 'El crecimiento reciente de la industria argentina. Nuevo régimen sin cambio estructural', CEPAL-UN. Buenos Aires.

Hausmann, R., and Klinger, B. 2006. 'Structural Transformation and Patterns of Comparative Advantage in the Product Space', *SSRN Electronic Journal*. CID Working Paper 128, 1–39.

Hidalgo, C., and Hausmann, R. 2009. 'The Building Blocks of Economic Complexity', *Proceedings of the National Academy of Sciences*, 106(26), 10570–10575.

Heymann, D., and Kosacoff, B. 2000. *La Argentina de los noventa: desempeño económico en un contexto de reformas*. Buenos Aires: Eudeba.

Hirschman, A. 1968. 'La economía política de la industrialización a través de la sustitución de importaciones', *El Trimestre Económico*, XXXV(140), 1–32.

IICA. 2020. 'Bioeconomía: Una estrategia de desarrollo para la argentina del siglo XXI. Impulsando Impulsando a la bioeconomía como modelo de desarrollo sustentable: entre las políticas públicas y las estrategias privadas'. San José, Costa Rica: Instituto Interamericano para Cooperación para la Agricultura.

Kosacoff, B., Forteza, J., and Barbero, M. 2014. *Globalizar desde América Latina: El caso ARCOR*. Mexico City: McGraw-Hill.

Kosacoff, B., ed. 2000. *Corporate Strategies under Structural Adjustment in Argentina*. Basingstoke, UK: Macmillan/St. Antony's Series.

Kosacoff, B. 1999. 'Las multinacionales argentinas', in D. Chudnovsky, B. Kosacoff, and A. López, eds., *Las multinacionales latinoamericanas: Sus estrategias en un mundo globalizado*. Buenos Aires: Fondo de Cultura Económica.

Katz, J., and Kosacoff, B. 2000. 'Import-Substituting Industrialization in Argentina, 1940–80: Its Achievements and Shortcomings', in E. Cárdenas, J. A. Ocampo, and R. Thorp, eds., *An Economic History of Twentieth-Century Latin America*, Vol. 3: *Industrialization and State in Latin America: The Post War Years*. Oxford: Palgrave/St. Antony'sCollege, 36–57.

Lachman, J., and López, A 2022. 'Los servicios basados en conocimiento en Argentina. Tendencias, oportunidades y desafíos'. Documento no. 34, Ministerio de la Producción, República Argentina.

Lall, S. 2000. 'The Technological Structure and Performance of Developing Country Manufactured Exports, 1985–98', *Oxford Development Studies, Taylor & Francis Journals*, 28, 337–369.

López, A., Fuchs, M., Lachman, J., and Pascuini, P., comp. 2021. *Nuevos sectores productivos en la economía argentina*. Buenos Aires: Eudeba.

López, A., Pascuini, P., and Ramos A. 2017. 'Al infinito y más allá: Una exploración sobre la economía del espacio en Argentina'. Serie de documentos de trabajo del IIEP. Instituto Interdisciplinario de Economía Política (UBA-CONICET).

Machinea, J. L. 1990. 'Stabilization under Alfonsin's Government: A Frustrated Attempt', CEDES Document No. 42. Buenos Aires.

Schteingart, D., and Coatz, D. 2015. '¿Qué modelo de desarrollo para la Argentina?', Techint; Boletin Informativo.

Schteingart, D., and Rajzman, N. 2021. 'Del litio a la batería: Análisis del posicionamiento argentino', Documento de Trabajo No. 16, octubre 2021. Ministerio de la Producción de la República Argentina.

Sourrouille, J. V., Kosacoff, B., and Lucangeli, J. 1985. *Transnacionalización y política económica en la Argentina*. Buenos Aires: Centro Editor de América Latina.

Tavosnanska, A., and Herrera, G. 2008. 'La industria argentina a comienzos del siglo XXI: Aportes para una revisión de la experiencia reciente'. Mimeo. Buenos Aires.

UIA-ILO. 2019. 'Una nueva inserción comercial argentina: El papel de la diversificación y la complejización para crear más y mejor empleo.' https://www.ilo.org/wcmsp5/groups/public/---americas/---ro-lima/---ilo-buenos_aires/documents/publication/wcms_677631.pdf.

Vispo, A., and Kosacoff, B. 1991. 'Difusión de tecnologías de punta en Argentina: Algunas reflexiones sobre la organización de la producción industrial de I.B.M.', Doc. Trabajo 38. CEPAL-Naciones Unidas, Buenos Aires.

13
Brazil
Economic Crisis, Structural Change, and Breaking Out of the Middle-Income Trap

Edmund Amann

13.1. Introduction

The past four decades have proven a tumultuous period for the Brazilian economy, the largest in Latin America and one of the world's leading emerging markets. Following a half century of inward-orientated state-driven industrialization strategy, Brazil in the late 1980s switched course, embarking on an ambitious programme of liberal reforms (Baer, 2013). These were aimed at opening up the economy to global trade and investment and, in so doing, exposing previously protected sectors to the winds of competition. Simultaneously, through privatization programmes and de-regulation, the scope of the state in the economy was targeted for reduction.

All of these bold measures, carried out at a time of rapid democratization, were intended to address long-standing structural constraints. The idea was to escape the legacy of volatile growth, inflation, and external vulnerability that had come to saddle the Brazilian economy by the last quarter of the twentieth century. Almost 40 years on from the start of this reform process, it is clear that the challenges it was intended to tackle very much remain in place. As detailed later in this chapter, Brazil has yet to embark on a path of sustained or sustainable, inclusive growth. Put more broadly, Brazil's growth and development trajectory has not enabled it to close the gap with the advanced industrialized countries of Europe and North America. In stark contrast, other emerging market economies, notably in East Asia, have proven capable of breaking with past legacies, propelling growth and living standards inexorably upwards.

Recognizing Brazil's difficulties in emulating this experience, administrations from the early 2000s on have engaged in policy experimentation, albeit broadly aligned with the underlying agenda of global economic integration. During the terms of the PT (Workers' Party) Presidents Lula (2003–2010) and Rouseff (2011–2016), Brazil cautiously rowed back on liberal reform, increasing economic and industrial interventionism. Over this period Brazil enjoyed a brief

Edmund Amann, *Brazil* In: *Innovation, Competitiveness, and Development in Latin America*. Edited by: Edmund Amann and Paulo N. Figueiredo, Oxford University Press. © Oxford University Press 2024.
DOI: 10.1093/oso/9780197648070.003.0013

commodities boom-induced growth spurt, as this strategy appeared to bear fruit. The evaporation of the commodities boom and the onset of economic crisis during 2014–2017 revealed the limitations of such an approach (Borges, 2016). Reacting to this, the Bolsonaro administration (2019–2022) attempted to reinvigorate liberal reform. However, in the teeth of the COVID-19 pandemic it only achieved limited results both in terms of policy innovation and effects on the ground. At the time of writing, President Lula was commencing a third term in office, with his pronouncements indicating a renewed emphasis on the state as a driver of social and economic development.

Reviewing these events, it becomes clear that policymakers in Brazil are still in search of a formula that works. Given the four-decade-long common consensus that integration with the global economy is both desirable and unavoidable, the policy conundrum centres on the strategies that can best take advantage of the opportunities that this presents. How might Brazil better leverage the potential of the global economy in which it is embedded to secure the accelerated development it craves but has so far yet to achieve? To put it bluntly, what pathways potentially exist for Brazil to break out of what appears to have become a middle-income trap? The purpose of this chapter is to shed light on this question, focusing on the structural constraints that have been holding Brazil back and the potential means for overcoming them. To achieve its objectives, this chapter adopts the following structure. The next section (section 13.2) characterizes the dimensions of the middle-income trap in the Brazilian context. Next, in section 13.3, the key structural factors which are argued to underpin the trap are elucidated. Section 13.4 then considers options for breaking out of the middle-income trap; finally, section 13.5 draws together the main arguments of the chapter.

13.2. Frustrated Growth and Development: A Brazilian Middle-Income Trap?

Before examining the factors which may be impeding Brazil's repeated attempts to break with the past and close the gap with the advanced industrial world, it is worth characterizing the dimensions of the problem. In what senses could Brazil said to be caught in a middle-income trap? Do, in fact, key data support the contention that Brazil is so ensnared? In the course of Chapter 1, the conceptual nature of the middle-income trap was set out. It was argued that countries afflicted by the trap very often have undergone a partial process of structural transformation and modernization (as indeed Brazil had under import substitution industrialization in the mid-twentieth century).

However, for a variety of reasons, the pace of transformation cannot be sustained, and the cost advantages in the newly established sectors begin to erode.

Partly in response to this, economies are forced to fall back on areas of established competitive advantage, reinforcing traditional modes of integration into the international division of labour. Under these circumstances, the accelerated growth and development that had been experienced are confined to the past (Gill and Kheras, 2015). Moreover, economic progress becomes more episodic as economies experiencing greater external vulnerability are buffeted by exogenous shocks, often those associated with swings in commodities prices.

By contrast, economies which have succeeded in escaping the middle-income trap are able to overcome the erosion of their cost advantages by adding value to existing activities or by diversifying into new ones (Gill and Kheras, 2015). Diversification and the pursuit of added value not only allow for the direct propulsion of growth and employment; they also open up new avenues for technical progress, productivity gains, and reduced exposure to commodity price shifts. This in turn facilitates sustained growth over the long term, together with progressive increases in living standards.

Having very briefly laid out the key conceptual foundation for the discussion, is there any broad empirical basis to suggest that Brazil is in fact caught in a middle-income trap? Table 13.1a offers some interesting insights relating to the course of GDP growth both in overall and per capita terms. Two key trends can be observed.

In first place, in terms of growth of annual real GDP, the post–World War II period broadly divides into two periods: that preceding the liberal reform period ushered in by the debt adjustment crisis of the 1980s, and that which followed. During the rapid industrialization phase engendered by import substitution industrialization (ISI) between the late 1940s and the 1960s, annual GDP growth rarely stood below 5% (Amann, 2021). By the late 1970s and early 1980s, it was clear that the growth dynamism was ebbing as Brazil headed towards the debt adjustment crisis and the 'lost decade' of the 1980s. In the wake of that crisis, ISI was largely abandoned and Brazil, as mentioned, adopted a strategy of accelerated integration with the global economy and a reduced role for the state.

Reflecting on the period of broadly liberal reform which has followed, it is interesting to note that, whatever the expectations might have been, average growth performance has not matched that encountered in the 'take-off phase' of ISI during the initial postwar period (Amann, 2021). Only in four years (1994, 2004, 2007, and 2010) has GDP growth exceeded 5%. Moreover, the period since the 1980s has witnessed multiple sharp recessions in which economic output significantly contracted. In very recent years, Brazil appears to have entered a crisis period with the steepest recession in its history between 2013 and 2016, followed by a further contraction in 2020 as the economy responded to the impacts of COVID-19.

Table 13.1a GDP Growth, Brazil, 1961–2021 (% p.a.)

1961	8.6	**1983**	−2.9	**2005**	3.2
1962	6.6	**1984**	5.4	**2006**	4.0
1963	0.6	**1985**	7.9	**2007**	6.1
1964	3.4	**1986**	7.5	**2008**	5.1
1965	2.4	**1987**	3.5	**2009**	−0.1
1966	6.7	**1988**	−0.1	**2010**	7.5
1967	4.2	**1989**	3.2	**2011**	4.0
1968	9.8	**1990**	−4.4	**2012**	1.9
1969	9.5	**1991**	1.0	**2013**	3.0
1970	10.4	**1992**	−0.5	**2014**	0.5
1971	11.3	**1993**	4.9	**2015**	−3.5
1972	11.9	**1994**	5.9	**2016**	−3.3
1973	14.0	**1995**	4.2	**2017**	1.3
1974	8.2	**1996**	2.2	**2018**	1.8
1975	5.2	**1997**	3.4	**2019**	1.2
1976	10.3	**1998**	0.3	**2020**	−3.9
1977	4.9	**1999**	0.5	**2021**	4.6
1978	5.0	**2000**	4.4		
1979	6.8	**2001**	1.4		
1980	9.2	**2002**	3.1		
1981	−4.2	**2003**	1.1		
1982	0.8	**2004**	5.8		

Set beside the disappointing average annual growth rates of the past four decades lies an important second trend: the volatility of that growth which has been realized. As Table 13.1a indicates, Brazil's growth trajectory has been anything but smooth, with considerable year-on-year variation, as opposed to constant progress, being the order of the day. Tracing the events which underlie the observed volatility, one obvious candidate explanation is represented by gyrations in commodity prices (Table 13.1b). In the case of the short-lived boom experienced between 2009 and 2013, and the subsequent recession, their role appears obvious. However, vulnerability to external commodity-related shocks is only part of the story and one which will be examined in further detail below. For the time being, suffice to say, the notion that Brazil's growing relative dependence on exports of natural-resource-intensive products is necessarily a driver of below par, volatile growth is one which needs at least some critical qualification. Domestic macroeconomic policy missteps, changes in the availability of international credit, and periods of acute political uncertainty have also played a role.

Taking examples of these factors at work, consider the crisis and recession period that endured between 2013 and 2018. While Brazil was certainly facing the fallout from a global commodities slump, the fact that the country endured a deeper recession than many of its Latin American counterparts points to the operation of specific local factors, notably the Jet Wash corruption scandal that helped propel the impeachment of President Rousseff in 2016 (Lapper, 2021). This had, among other effects, a negative impact on foreign investor confidence and, more directly, a freezing of capital formation in the petroleum sector as the latter came under intense scrutiny in the corruption probes.

Besides political turbulence, the growth trajectory in Brazil has also suffered at times from domestic macroeconomic policy errors. For example, President Collor de Melo's counter-inflation plan in 1990–1992 supplemented the negative effects of the international recession on the Brazilian economy with an ill-considered monetary freeze (Baer, 2013). This instilled a badly timed demand shock which failed to bring inflation under control, yet severely impacted GDP growth. Almost a decade later, the misalignment of the Real—Brazil's then relatively new national currency—forced the authorities to concede a maxi-devaluation against the US dollar. This destabilizing event placed Brazil at a disadvantage in coping with the global macroeconomic fallout from the technology stocks bust of the early 2000s.

While conjunctural factors—whether commodity prices, domestic political developments, or macroeconomic policy phenomena—have certainly influenced growth outcomes, our key concern is with long-term structural drivers which, it is argued, are the most critical issues to tackle if Brazil is to improve its growth performance over the long term. Before embarking on this

Table 13.1b UNCTAD Commodity Price Index, annual (2015 = 100), Growth Rate Year on Year, All Commodities

1996	8.7
1997	–4.2
1998	–20.2
1999	7.0
2000	36.7
2001	–8.5
2002	–2.1
2003	20.1
2004	20.5
2005	34.9
2006	15.3
2007	10.5
2008	33.4
2009	–31.6
2010	24.3
2011	28.6
2012	–3.0
2013	–3.7
2014	–7.9
2015	–36.2
2016	–9.4
2017	17.3
2018	16.1
2019	–7.5
2020	–15.8
2021	54.7
2022	39.5

Source: UNCTAD Stat.

Table 13.2a Real GDP Per Capita, Brazil, India, and China, 1980–2017 (US$)

	Brazil	India	China
1980	7,566.66	879.40	523.95
1990	10,344.86	1,754.86	1,526.41
2000	11,370.97	2,495.05	3,700.74
2010	14,537.57	4,404.70	9,525.82
2017	14,103.45	6,426.67	15,308.71

Source: IPEA/World Bank.

discussion, it is worth highlighting the evolution of living standards in comparative context, as these provide further evidence of the apparent middle-income trap into which Brazil seems to have fallen.

As Table 13.2a reveals, living standards in Brazil, as measured by GDP per capita, roughly doubled between 1980 and the end of the 2010s. What is notable about this trend is the fact that such improvements as have been realized were strongly concentrated in the period between the mid-1990s and the early 2010s. Subsequently, income per capita has struggled to resume a healthy upward trend, a situation reminiscent of the 1980s. The sense of stalled progress becomes amplified when one compares the experience of Brazil to that of other leading emerging economies. Examining the cases of India and China, for example, one finds an 8-fold increase in income per capita over the same period for the former and no less than 30-fold for the latter. For both these countries, despite the challenges in the international economy that Brazil also faced, the latter part of the 2010s proved not to be a period of profound economic crisis. Instead, income per head remained headed on an upward path in China and India, to the extent that China managed to overtake Brazil as its GDP per head passed the US$15,000 mark.

Another interesting insight into the evolution of living standards is offered by the UNDP's Human Development Index (HDI). Between 1990 and 2021, Brazil's HDI rose from 0.610 to 0.754. However, reflecting stronger improvements in other countries, its overall ranking with respect to this index actually fell from 79th to 87th place. By contrast, over the same period, China's ranking rose from 108th to 79th place, while India saw its rank falling by 16 places in the face of a more modest than average improvement in its HDI score. Examining the evolution of these data over time, what becomes strikingly evident is the fact that improvements in the index, which for Brazil had been considerable between the mid-1990s and the early 2010s, levelled off after around 2012.

Table 13.2b Evolution of Brazil's Human Development Index, 1990–2021

HDI rank	Human Development Index (HDI) Value								Change in HDI Rank	Average Annual HDI Growth (%)			
	1990	2000	2010	2015	2018	2019	2020	2021	2015–2021	1990–2000	2000–2010	2010–2021	1990–2021
87	0.610	0.679	0.723	0.753	0.764	0.766	0.758	0.754	1	1.08	0.63	0.38	0.69

Source: UNDP.

The same cannot be said for China, where the value of the HDI has continued its upward ascent. The sense that the momentum behind accelerated social development has slackened off over the past decade is undoubtedly among the factors driving the increasing polarization of Brazil's political environment. This heralds the possibility of a negative feedback loop whereby inadequate progress on economic and social development helps drive political instability, which in turn rebounds adversely on the investment climate and, in due course, economic performance.

All of the preceding discussion suggests that Brazil is locked in something of a low growth and development trap from which it is struggling to escape. While conjunctural and macroeconomic policy factors have played their part, there are in reality a range of structural impediments to accelerated growth which Brazil will need to overcome if it is to realize fully its potential and close the yawning gap with the advanced industrialized economies of the North.

13.3. Structural Drivers of the Middle-Income Trap

In examining the development of Brazil's economy over the long term, it becomes apparent that, despite noteworthy achievements such as relative price stability and—for a period—poverty alleviation, a range of key challenges have yet to be properly tackled. These challenges centre on a range of ingrained structural economic characteristics. Over the decades these have, among other things, restricted supply-side responsiveness, retarded the pace of technical change, and prevented Brazil from fully capitalizing on emerging opportunities in the global export marketplace. Collectively, these unmet challenges have acted as a drag on the speed at which the economy could grow and, by extension, on the ability of Latin America's largest economy to close the standard-of-living gap with the advanced industrial economies (Bonelli and Veloso, 2016). The key challenges which we will examine here, beginning with the issue of productivity, have long formed a central concern. For structuralist economists such as Osvaldo Sunkel, they have been viewed as no less than the fundamental drivers of Latin American underdevelopment (Sunkel, 1993).

Among these drivers, the question of low productivity growth has long been an important concern for policymakers in Brazil and has been the subject of a variety of initiatives in the post-ISI era, starting with the *Programa Brasileira de Qualidade e Produtividade* (Brazilian Programme of Quality and Productivity) in the 1990s. More broadly, the entire thrust of microeconomic policy from the return to civilian rule in 1985 until well into the first couple of Lula administrations was aimed at boosting productivity and competitiveness by encouraging more rapid integration into the global economy, whether by trade or market liberalization.

Given the prominence of the issue, and the twin imperatives of boosting lethargic growth rates and global competitiveness, it is perhaps surprising to discover that Brazil has endured something of a productivity crisis over recent decades.

In terms of total factor productivity (TFP), Quian et al. (2018) estimate that between 1996 and 2015, TFP growth in Brazil stood at a negative 1%, with the country's 2.6% average annual GDP growth being predominantly accounted for by increases in labour and capital inputs, plus increased human capital per unit of labour. Over the same period, by contrast, human capital growth in the United States stood at 0.93% per annum. The contrast highlighted in TFP performance between the United States and Brazil is especially surprising given the greater level of development in the former and, hence, supposedly fewer unrealized opportunities for productivity gains than might be expected in a less mature economy.

Data presented in Amann (2021, pp. 49–55) indicate that, as might be expected, Brazil's productivity problem extends beyond TFP and to single-factor measures. The picture presented is stark. Between 1991 and 2018, industrial output per employee in real terms changed very little. While the failure of productivity to take off here finds its analogue in other Latin American countries (e.g. Argentina), the same is not true in two of the emerging market world's largest economies: China and India. Over the same period, in these two countries, output per employee in industry rose by 2-fold and 10-fold, respectively (Amann, 2021). Turning to the services sector, labour productivity growth was also disappointing for Brazil. However, in marked contrast, in agriculture, forestry, and fishing, Brazil experienced something of a productivity boom. Here, between 1991 and 2018, output per employee rose by a factor of 4, a performance only outstripped by Chile among the countries surveyed in the study (Amann, 2021).

The failure of productivity to take off in all but the natural-resource-intensive sector represents a clear concern since it places obvious limits on the degree to which growth might be accelerated without increasing factor inputs. All of this, of course, raises a further issue: What factors are holding productivity growth back? We will return to this question later. First, it is worth reflecting on another supposed driver of Brazil's middle-income trap issue: the re-primarization of the economy.

The concept of re-primarization relates to the idea that, over time, a newly industrialized economy such as Brazil, having moved on from formal import substitution in industrial and manufactured products, may find itself falling back on exports of natural-resource-intensive products. This happens as underlying comparative advantage in this area makes itself felt in a more liberalized environment. Here, falling barriers to trade may render less competitive (industrial) sectors incapable of holding their own domestically, let alone in the global marketplace. However, where established comparative advantages exist (as they do in natural-resource-intensive sectors), greater market access (whether to export opportunities or key inputs) enables them to thrive.

To gain some quantitative insight as to whether an economy may be in the throes of re-primarization, one obvious place to look is the composition of exports. De Paula and Oreiro (2022) calculate that the share of manufactured goods in total exports 'fell from more than 50% in 1981–2007 to 29% in 2020' (De Paula and Oreiro, 2022, p. 11). A more granular picture of the issue may be gleaned from examining data on revealed comparative advantage (RCA). This indicator, developed by Bela Belassa (1965), divides the share of a product category in a country's total exports by its share in total world exports. If the resulting value is greater than one, then a country would enjoy a revealed comparative advantage in that product.

Examining Table 13.3, it becomes apparent that increases in the value of the RCA have become strongly evident in natural-resource-intensive products such as vegetable and mineral products. By contrast, in the non-traditional export sectors of capital goods and transportation equipment, the value of the RCA actually declined between the start of the 1990s and the end of the 2010s. The data suggest competitive struggles in the industrial sector, which is a concern, but is the reversion to exports focused on natural-resource-intensive products necessarily problematic? Does it constitute a factor binding Brazil into the middle-income trap?

The answer here is a firm 'not necessarily'. Recalling the earlier discussion, it will be noted that the natural-resource-intensive sectors were notable for their superior productivity performance. This, in turn, reflects not so much the legacy of long-established comparative advantage as continuing innovation, both in process and product terms and, in some cases, success in ascending the value chain. As Mueller and Mueller (2016) suggest, the agriculture sector, in particular, has been the subject of something of a technological, managerial, and logistical revolution. This has enabled it to engage in product diversification, downstream processing, and improvements in cost efficiency. All of this has enabled producers to capture effectively global markets, while subtly changing the position of Brazil in the global division of labour within the natural-resource-intensive products sector. In sum, therefore, characterizing the recent re-primarization of the Brazilian export economy as regressive, or as a fetter on growth and development, would be highly inaccurate.

Table 13.3 Revealed Comparative Advantage by Export Product Category in Brazil, 1990–2017

Product Group	1990	2000	2010	2017
All products	1	1	1	1
Capital goods	0.35	0.59	0.43	0.36
Consumer goods	0.56	0.75	0.44	0.41
Intermediate goods	1.75	1.64	1.29	1.26
Raw materials	1.84	1.89	2.94	3.59
Animal	0.8	1.88	3.48	2.89
Chemicals	0.62	0.72	0.57	0.53
Food products	4.46	4.68	4.22	2.98
Footwear	1.95	3.24	1.08	0.65
Fuels	0.03	0.19	0.61	0.83
Hides and skins	1.62	1.85	1.51	1.54
Mach and elec	0.32	0.41	0.28	0.22
Metals	2.89	1.72	0.91	1.03
Minerals	10.26	10.37	10.77	8.81
Miscellaneous	0.17	0.21	0.33	0.4
Plastic or rubber	0.5	0.77	0.57	0.55
Stone and glass	0.56	0.85	0.36	0.56
Textiles and clothing	0.67	0.35	0.28	0.2
Transportation	0.35	1.12	0.88	0.86
Vegetable	2.61	3.67	3.85	4.97
Wood	0.95	2.27	2.13	2.57

Source: Author's Elaboration from WITS Database.

Reflecting on the question of sectoral change and export specialization, the focal point of the challenge Brazil faces lies in ensuring that some of the productivity and efficiency gains encountered in the natural-resource-intensive sectors are, in the future, felt more broadly. In particular, this applies to industrial and manufacturing activities which have seen their participation in Brazil's export profile decline since the abandonment of ISI in the 1990s.

Attempts to boost productivity and build capabilities across the board cannot, of course, be realized without paying attention to the need to invest in human and physical capital. In relation to this critical issue, there has been much policy debate around two key aspects: investment in infrastructure and attempts to improve Brazil's stock of human capital. It is to the latter issue to which we turn first.

There has long been concern that, compared to advanced industrial economies, average levels of attainment in education or vocational training, or access to them, have lagged well behind the advanced industrial countries or indeed the emerging economies of East and South-East Asia. Responding to this, policymakers have made significant attempts to address the situation, especially in the first two Lula administrations (2003–2010) (Moura Castro, 2018). How effective have these efforts been?

Examination of data from the Organisation for Economic Co-operation and Development's (OECD) Programme for International Student Assessment (PISA) indicates the extent of the attainment gap which exists between Brazil and the majority of the OECD and partner economies, whether in reading, science, or mathematics (OECD 2019a, 2019b). The issue is particularly significant in terms of the preponderance of the student group characterized as 'low performers' (OECD 2019a, 2019b). While, in international terms, Brazil clearly has some way to go to close the education performance gap, this should not obscure the significant progress which has been made in recent years, relative to the country's own record on educational attainment. Data released by the educational foundation *Todos para Educação* show significant declines in illiteracy between 2001–2002 and 2018. Importantly, while Brazil's PISA scores have more or less remained stable (even showing a small improvement in one or two categories), this has taken place against a background of sharply rising enrolment rates, the latter being driven by the rollout of the *Bolsa Familía* conditional cash transfer programme. The *Bolsa* and its successor, the *Auxilío Brasil*, directly incentivize parents to keep their offspring in school via the benefits system.

Turning to vocational education, Brazil's track record is strong by regional standards, with long-established technical training and apprenticeship programmes run by both private- and public-sector bodies, notably Serviço Nacional de Aprendizagem Industrial (SENAI, 'National Service for Industrial Training) and Programa Nacional de Acesso ao Ensino Técnico e Emprego (PRONATEC, National Programme for Access to Technical Education and Employment). Under the Lula and Rousseff administrations, federal spending in the vocational education and training areas rose sharply, to around 0.2% of GDP (Amann, 2021, p. 89). However, relative to OECD countries, participation rates by relevant age groups in vocational education and training remain quite low (Amann, 2021) and skills shortages remain a serious concern in an economy which is now, under a new Lula administration, beginning renewed efforts to technologically upgrade itself, as Chapter 2 describes.

Another key issue commonly acknowledged to be restricting Brazil's ability to become more competitive and respond to changing global market opportunities centres on infrastructure. Compared to its emerging market peers, Brazil spends remarkable little on infrastructure, typically around 2% of its annual GDP versus approximately 7% in China and 5.5% in India (WEF, 2019). As a proportion of overall GDP, Brazil's infrastructure capital stock has actually fallen over the years, from 58.2% in 1983 to 36.2% in 2018 (Canuto, 2020, p. 1). The deficiencies of the squeeze on infrastructure spending have been well documented in what has become an extensive literature and have been experienced in such diverse sectors as ports, highways, railroads.

Collectively, these have impeded the ability of Brazil to export in a timely and cost-efficient manner and have more general negative implications for the supply-side responsiveness of the economy. As a result of this, the infrastructure issue has become a key policy focus, not least for multilateral organizations including the World Economic Forum (WEF), the Inter-American Development Bank, and the International Monetary Fund (IMF), which have all published reports on the issues involved. The solutions proposed—and which have only been partially adopted—centre on reforming regulatory models and improving the availability of finance. In regard to the latter, much of the focus has recently been placed on promoting public-private partnerships and, under the recent administration of President Bolsonaro, accelerating the privatization programme. It seems likely that the new administration of President Lula will adopt a more state-led approach, perhaps similar to the *Programa de Crescimento Acelerado* (growth acceleration programme) followed by the Rousseff administration in the 2010s.

Another central and long-running focus of concern among international analysts and, most of all, domestic industry associations is the so-called *Custo Brasil* or Brazil Cost. The concept of the Brazil Cost centres on the idea that a range of cost impediments have converged on producers to render them uncompetitive in international markets. This is despite whatever efforts have been made by enterprises to rise up to the challenges posed by trade and market liberalization. The CNI (*Confederação Nacional de Indústria*) or National Industrial Confederation has been especially vocal for many years in promoting the concept[1] and deploying it to lobby for reform and, where appropriate, accelerated investment. The Brazil Cost is argued to be multidimensional. Beyond the aforementioned issues of education, training, and infrastructure, it also embraces the costs and frictions associated with what the CNI sees as excessive bureaucracy, inefficiency of public sector processes, and the weight and compliance costs associated with direct and sales taxes. A particular concern has come to centre on Brazil's complex system of indirect taxes which are associated with high compliance costs for business and regressive distributional impacts. Among the measures the incoming Lula administration is studying is a long-awaited proposal to consolidate indirect taxes into a unified, European-style value-added tax.

[1] See https://www.portaldaindustria.com.br/industria-de-a-z/o-que-e-custo-brasil/.

13.4. Options for Breaking Out of the Middle-Income Trap

The previous section outlined the ways in which growth performance in Brazil has been constrained by a complex of intertwined structural factors. Charting a course out of these constraints represents a clear policy priority for the new Lula administration, at least as much as it should have been for its predecessors. As Chapter 2 indicates, the evidence so far suggests that the challenges are being taken very seriously with firm attempts being made to reinvigorate technology policy. In what follows, this chapter now sets out some of the fruitful steps that might be taken to break out of the middle-income trap. First, the potential of sector-specific initiatives is explored. Second, the discussion moves on to consider more generic policy interventions which might ignite accelerated, inclusive, and sustainable growth.

In decades gone by, under ISI, the policy consensus held that the secret to unlocking Brazil's growth potential lay in promoting non-traditional industrial activities, rather than building on existing sources of comparative advantage (Baer, 2013). Looking ahead, should any strategy promoting accelerated growth embrace this approach, perhaps seeking the reverse the deindustrialization which has characterized the past three decades? The answer here is almost certainly no, for two main reasons. In first place, the notion, implicit in earlier structuralist analysis, that there exists some binary divide between the industrial sector on the one hand, and the natural-resource-intensive sectors on the other, does not reflect present-day realities. As a seminal study by Harvey (2002) made clear, formal innovation processes, the use of information technology, and logistical planning are increasingly common to productive activities, whether they are focused on industry, services or agriculture. It is also the case that services activities are frequently bundled with industrial products when sold to end users.[2] Thus, prioritizing 'industry' above 'services' or 'agriculture' may not make much sense given the common innovative processes, routes to value creation, and interdependencies that bind sectors together.

Second, the idea that a resumption of more favourable growth performance requires a reversion to an industrialization-focused development model would ignore the significant efficiency gains and export success achieved by the natural-resource-intensive sectors. These achievements were noted earlier in this chapter and were especially notable in the agriculture and agribusiness sectors. In these areas, Brazil has built competitiveness and has been able to carve out fresh niches in the global marketplace. This has occurred as a result of an interplay between natural comparative advantages, significant public- and private-sector

[2] Consider, for example, the case of aero engines, where service and monitoring packages are sold alongside the engines themselves, representing the bulk of the value in the contract.

investment in product and process innovation, and selected investments in training, infrastructure, and logistics provision. Thus, looking ahead, any growth-promotion strategy aimed at prising Brazil from the middle-income trap will have to recognize that opportunities for growth and competitive transformation are as likely to exist in natural-resource-focused areas as much as, for example, business services or high-technology manufacturing. With all of this in mind, in sectoral terms, where might future policy usefully focus its efforts?

Following previous discussion, it should be obvious that continued investment and innovation in the natural-resource-intensive sectors should continue to be recognized as a priority area. This stems from their demonstrated dynamism, whether in terms of productivity growth, capture of global market share, or ability to add value and shift the basis on which Brazil competes. An ample literature (see e.g. Figueiredo and Piana, 2018) has developed in which case studies of successful development of activities within this sector are documented and analysed. Particular examples worthy of note in this regard comprise the pulp and paper complex, biofuels, steel, and meat production and processing. The common elements which contribute to success include underlying comparative advantage, strategic investment in technology (often in association with publicly funded research institutes such as EMBRAPA), a robust entrepreneurial corporate culture, and, in some cases, an effective track record in attracting high-quality inward foreign direct investment.

In select cases (e.g. biofuels), sectors have flourished thanks to effective sector-wide policies reminiscent of more traditional industrial strategy. In others, however, the role of such policies is more muted and the positive trajectory realized appears to rest to a greater degree on effective response to global market signals. This seems to be the case in much of Brazilian agriculture, according to Mueller and Mueller (2016). What the evidence points to is the scope that still exists for investment and technological upgrading in natural-resource-intensive sectors and that, once made, this can propel productivity growth, capture of global market share, and added value. In the context of concern over climate change and deforestation, the need for such continued innovative effort and investment will only increase.

In particular, Brazil's rise as a leading exporter of agricultural products has been in part the result of an extension of cultivated or grazed land, which has had negative consequences for the scope of important biomes such as the natural rainforest and semi-arid *Cerrado* grasslands (Viola and Franchini, 2018). Given the commitment of the new Lula administration to rapidly slow the place of deforestation, maintaining the growth trajectory of the agricultural sector will require even more focus on driving productivity and yields up. More generally, right across the natural-resource-intensive sectors, the need to limit carbon emissions will require innovation and fresh approaches to be adopted. This is especially true in energy-intensive sectors such as minerals processing and metals production.

A central criticism that could be levelled at continued attempts to promote the development of the natural-resource-intensive sectors is that this would simply reinforce existing patterns of specialization and, by extension, render Brazil yet more vulnerable to fluctuating global commodities demand. To what extent is this argument valid? In first place, policies supportive towards the development of natural-resource-intensive activities need not come at the expense of efforts to promote others, such as in services or manufacturing. Indeed, many more generic policies designed to support productive activities—for example, investment in basic education or the achievement of price stability—should benefit investment, enterprise, and innovation across the board. Secondly, as should be clear from the discussion so far, the story of the development of natural-resource-intensive sectors in Brazil has been one of consistent efficiency improvements and subtly shifting the basis of comparative advantage through added value. Thus, while vulnerability to the commodities cycle remains a valid concern, there is reason to believe that the natural-resource-intensive sectors as they have developed are progressively allowing the Brazilian economy to cope better with shifts in global demand and prices for their products.

Whatever the strengths and potential of the natural-resource-intensive sectors, unlocking Brazil's growth potential and, in particular, driving up low average productivity will require attention be paid to other sectors. Traditionally, this would have been addressed through a comprehensive industrial strategy of the kind both Presidents Rousseff and Lula tried to develop during their previous terms in office (2003–2016). It is possible that the new Lula administration, elected in 2022, will attempt to reboot this. However, a singular focus on industry might divert attention away from opportunities which are emerging in other parts of the economy. Two particularly promising areas here that would be worth further exploring for their potential are Fintech and green energy.

Traditionally, Brazil's financial sector has been dominated by a select few private-sector commercial and investment banks, on the one hand, and a handful of extremely large public-sector institutions, especially the BNDES (a development bank), the Banco do Brasil (a full-service retail and commercial bank), and the Caixa Econômica Federal (a savings and mortgage bank). This concentrated financial landscape produced high interest rate spreads which, combined with already elevated base rates, resulted in very high borrowing costs, especially for small businesses and retail customers. Over the past decade, however, a combination of technological change and a more flexible regulatory climate have seen the emergence of numerous new financial institutions, collectively known as Fintechs. The Fintechs have used internet and smartphone technologies to bring down intermediation costs while improving their customer knowledge and risk assessments (Lisboa et al., 2018). As a result, consumers and businesses now enjoy much greater choice and, in some cases, lower borrowing costs. Besides offering more traditional banking services such as credit and loans, some Fintechs offer electronic payment systems and retail investment platforms. In regard to the latter, one enterprise, XP, has changed the landscape for small investors by offering an accessible portal into the financial markets (Silva et al., 2020).

Perhaps the most important long-term potential benefit of the Fintechs, in terms of catalysing accelerated growth and productivity gains, is the possibility that, through improved access to cost-effective finance, they stimulate challenger enterprises right across the productive sector. Particularly in the industrial sector, where productivity problems are long-standing, market structures can be highly oligopolistic, this partly reflecting the historical difficulty many enterprises have faced in securing capital. With appropriate support and regulatory reform, it is possible that financial innovation, such as that embodied by Fintechs, could stimulate the development of challenger enterprises in these sectors. This increased market contestability holds out the prospect of improving competitiveness and productivity, raising growth rates in the longer term. This effect would, of course, potentially be supplemented by direct impact on GDP growth by the expansion of the financial sector itself.

Another emerging sector that has the possibility of creating new sources of growth, while, at the same time, ensuring that growth itself becomes more environmentally sustainable, is green energy. By international standards, Brazil has long relied on an energy mix in which the role of renewables—principally hydroelectric power—has played a very significant role. Brazil stands as the second-largest hydroelectricity producer in the world; taken together, hydroelectric power, sugarcane-derived energy sources, and other renewable sources account for around 40% of the country's annual energy needs (Matriz Energética e Energia, 2022). Despite the advances Brazil has made in the energy field—especially its pioneering use of biofuels to power road vehicles—there is clear scope to expand the use of renewables, especially since the relative importance of fossil fuels in electricity generation has been growing in recent years (Viola and Franchini, 2018, p. 110). Particularly promising in this regard is the potential of increasing investments in the solar and wind energy complexes where Brazil already ranks among the world's most significant producers.[3] The pressure to unlock fresh sources of renewable energy will be especially acute given the potentially adverse consequences for deforestation of expanding sugarcane cultivation or installing further hydroelectric dams in ecologically sensitive areas.

The argument so far has tended to stress the growth potential implicit in areas of the natural-resource-intensive services and energy sectors. What of industry and

[3] 7th and 14th in terms of installed capacity for wind and solar energy, respectively.

manufacturing, the focus of so much determined policy intervention in the mid- to late twentieth century? As a large and expanding literature attests, within the industrial sector, elements of technological capability, built up initially during the import substitution period, have gone on to provide a springboard for the emergence of new industrial activities (Amann and Figueiredo, 2012). Some of these have become world leaders in their field. Perhaps the most prominent here are civil aerospace (the Embraer family of regional jetliners), flex-fuel vehicles (pioneering the use of ethanol in road transport), and the technologies surrounding oil exploration and production in deep waters (Petrobrás) (Reynolds, Schneider, and Zylberberg, 2019). Amann and Figueiredo (2012) suggest that the experience of cases such as these shows that, given the right mix of implicit and explicit technology and industrial policies, it is possible to develop industrial and manufacturing competences (and associated technologies) that are competitive at a world level. This can happen in sectors that are not always necessarily linked to existing natural comparative advantages, or even pre-existing capabilities (although the presence of these is likely to help).

However, Amann and Figueiredo (2012), along with Chapter 10 in the present volume, highlight the significant complexities and firm-level specificities surrounding the capability-building process. The creation of capabilities is a costly and risky undertaking, and cases abound where firms or sectors have stalled, or even have seen capabilities depletion in the face of financial headwinds. Consequently, it is vital that policy is configured with an eye to the difficulties, complexities, and specificities of capabilities creation. This implies that vertical as well as horizontal policies are present and correctly configured.

Looking ahead, with a view to boosting future growth rates and strengthening Brazil's position in the international division of labour, what does all of this imply? At the very least, the presence of such competences in non-traditional, high technology export sectors suggests that future policies (whether trade or technology policies) must be configured in such a way as to maintain and, if possible, build on what has already been developed in terms of high-technology sectors. More fundamentally, though, Brazil's industrial success stories illustrate the potential that always exists to identify fruitful, if ambitious, opportunities and then to develop a supportive policy framework within which they might be pursued. The challenge, as always, lies in selecting which opportunities to follow. Given changes in the technology policy framework over recent years (see Reynolds et al., 2019), in the future more of the decision-making process here is likely to reside in the hands of the private sector.[4]

[4] For a more detailed discussion of Brazil's technology policy and potential future developments around it, see Chapter 2.

13.5. Final Remarks

Despite significant, mainly liberal, economic reform over the past four decades, Brazil has yet to find an effective formula which would enable it to build on its strengths and move forward on a path of accelerated, inclusive, and sustainable growth. With a new administration under President Lula having taken office at the start of 2023, an opportunity has opened up for a constructive discussion around the elements needed to generate such a formula. This chapter has suggested that fruitful approaches here are unlikely to centre on forced attempts to reverse the so-called re-primarization of the Brazilian economy.

While re-primarization might superficially appear responsible for locking Brazil into the volatile and low growth performance of recent years, the reality is much more complex. It turns out that the natural-resource-intensive sector has been the scene of notable productivity gains and technological dynamism. Brazil will need to build on this further to improve future growth performance. In fact, many of the economy's growth and productivity challenges lie outside the natural-resource-intensive sector, in industry and services. The chapter has argued that these need to be addressed, and that good starting points centre on tackling shortcomings in human capital formation, infrastructure, the availability of finance, and the regulatory environment. Confronting these successfully would have economy-wide benefits. Still, what of the potential of individual sectors to act as lead elements in any Brazilian growth renaissance? Beyond the clearly demonstrated potential of the natural-resource-intensive sectors, this chapter pointed to the promising opportunities presented by Fintech, green energy, and advanced manufacturing. Such sectors have benefited from advantageous sector-specific policies in the past. The new administration would do well to revisit existing policy frameworks with a view to enhancing their effectiveness.

References

Amann, E. 2021. *The Brazilian Economy: Confronting Structural Challenges*. Abingdon, UK, and New York: Routledge

Amann, E., and Figueiredo, P. 2012. 'Brazil', in E. Amann and J. Cantwell, eds., *Innovative Firms in Emerging Market Countries*. Oxford: Oxford University Press, 210–247.

Baer, W. 2013. *The Brazilian Economy: Growth and Development*. Boulder, CO: Lynne Rienner.

Belassa, B. 1965. 'Trade liberalization and "revealed" comparative advantage', *The Manchester School*, 33(2), 99–123.

Borges, B. 2016. 'Bad luck or bad policy: Uma investigação das causas do fraco crescimento da economia brasileira nos últimos anos', in R. Bonelli and F. Veloso, eds., *A crise de crescimento do Brasil*: Rio de Janeiro: Elsevier, 19–40.

Canuto, O. 2020. 'Brazil Is in Dire Need of More and Better Investments', *Policy Centre for the New South Policy Brief*, PB20/06, January.

De Moura Castro, C. 2018. 'The Development of Brazilian Education: A Tale of Lost Opportunities', in E. Amann, C. Azzoni, and W. Baer, eds., *Oxford Handbook of the Brazilian Economy*. New York: Oxford University Press, 489–510.

Figueiredo, P., and Piana, J. 2018. 'Innovative Capability and Learning Linkages in Knowledge Intensive Service SMEs in Brazil's Mining Industry', *Research Policy*, 58, 21–33.

Gill, I., and Kheras, H. 2015. 'The Middle Income Trap Turns Ten', *World Bank Policy Research Working Paper* 7403, August.

Harvey, M. 2002. *Exploring the Tomato*. Cheltenham, UK: Edward Elgar.

Lapper, R. 2021. *Beef, Bible and Bullets: Brazil in the age of Bolsonaro*. Manchester, UK: Manchester University Press.

Lisboa, E, R. Godinho, and L. da Silva. 2018. 'Fintechs in Brazil: Opportunities or Threats?', *International Association for Management of Technology IAMOT 2018 Conference Proceedings*, 1127–1143.

Mueller, B., and C. Mueller. 2016. 'The Political Economy of the Brazilian Model of Agricultural Development: Institutions versus Sectoral Policy', *Quarterly Review of Economics and Finance*, 62(C), 12–20.

OECD. 2019a. *Education at a Glance, 2018*. Paris: OECD.

OECD. 2019b. *Education at a Glance: Brazil Country Note, 2018*. Paris: OECD.

Paula, L. F. de, and Oreiro, J. L. 2022. 'Strategies for Economic Development in Brazil: A Structuralist-Keynesian Approach', paper prepared for the 26th FMM Conference, Berlin, 20–22 October.

Quian, R, J. Araújo, and A. Nucifora. 2018. *Brazil's Productivity Dynamics*. Washington, DC: World Bank.

Reynolds, E. B, Schneider, B. R., and Zylberberg, E., eds. 2019. *Innovation in Brazil: Advancing Development in the 21st Century*. Abingdon, UK: Routledge.

Silva, D., Assis, V., and De Oliveira, J. P. 2020. 'De uma pequena corretora a um banco múltiplo estudo de caso sobre a XP investimentos', *Brazilian Journal of Development*, 6(11), 87593–87605.

Sunkel, O. 1993. *Development from Within: Toward a Neostructural Approach for Latin America*. Boulder CO.: Lynne Rienner.

Viola, E., and Franchini, M. 2019. *Brazil and Climate Change: Beyond the Amazon*. Abingdon, UK: Routledge.

World Economic Forum. 2019. *Improving Infrastructure Finance in Brazil*. Geneva: World Economic Forum in Cooperation with the Inter-American Development Bank.

14

Colombia's Growth since the 1990s

From Reform to the Risk of the Middle-Income Trap

Ivan Luzardo-Luna

14.1. Introduction

In the early 1990s, and after a long decade of slow economic growth, Colombia's government implemented a set of structural reforms, the so-called *economic opening* (la Apertura Económica), aimed at integrating itself into the world economy, consolidating its macroeconomic stability, and boosting its economic growth. The range of these reforms was wide—from an independent central bank to a partial liberalization of international trade—which is why there were high expectations regarding Colombia's economic performance over the following decades. These reforms were followed by a second generation of structural reforms in the first decade of the twenty-first century, intended to increase private participation in the oil industry and boost international trade via free trade agreements with world economies such as the United States, the European Union, and Canada.

Three decades after the beginning of these ambitious reforms, Colombia has witnessed substantial progress and has outperformed most Latin American large economies in terms of economic growth. However, Colombia still stands far behind advanced economies. Although the evolution of economic growth since the early 1990s has certainly been positive and has brought about a substantial reduction in poverty, it still has not had the 'power' to perform economic miracles such as those observed in the 'Asian Tiger' countries in the late twentieth century. Moreover, since 2012, Colombia's economy has slowed down, and its GDP per capita, compared to that of the United States, has remained essentially constant at approximately 24%. After almost a decade of relative stagnation, the risk of falling into the so-called middle-income trap has emerged. This is why it is relevant to examine the fundamentals of the Colombian economy, and whether they are strong enough to allow a complete transition from a middle- to a high-income economy.

This chapter examines the constraints preventing dynamic economic growth over the past three decades. Low productivity growth and the deep financial

Ivan Luzardo-Luna, *Colombia's Growth since the 1990s* In: *Innovation, Competitiveness, and Development in Latin America*. Edited by: Edmund Amann and Paulo N. Figueiredo, Oxford University Press.
DOI: 10.1093/oso/9780197648070.003.0014

crisis of the late 1990s emerge as immediate reasons behind Colombia's lack of global convergence during this period. However, institutional flaws, specifically violence and poor levels of rule of law, are identified as Colombia's main barriers to higher levels of growth.

Within Latin America, Colombia has outperformed other large economies over the past three decades, and this has intensified since the mid-2010s. This fact indicates that despite its constraints, the Colombian economy has established some essential preconditions that have enabled its progress, and these conditions should be preserved to maintain its expansion. This chapter hypothesizes that the structural reforms initiated in Colombia in the early 1990s have now paid off, and have allowed a relatively better evolution in terms of growth than that of other countries in Latin America, where reforms were implemented with lower intensity or were reversed early on. However, Colombia still needs to see substantial institutional progress for the reforms from the early 1990s to exert their full potential and boost economic growth, which would allow the country to converge with the more advanced economies. In other words, Colombia has substantially progressed in the past few decades, but to overcome the recent slowdown in terms of growth and to avoid falling into the middle-income trap, substantial improvements in the quality of its institutions need to be achieved.

14.2. Colombia's GDP Evolution since the Early 1980s

Figure 14.1 shows the evolution of Colombia's real GDP per capita between 1980 and 2021. After four years of stagnation in the early 1980s in the context of a Latin American sovereign debt crisis, the so-called lost decade, Colombia's economic growth resumed by 1984, and this continued for almost a decade. By the mid-1990s, and a few years after implementing an ambitious set of economic reforms intended to promote international trade and macroeconomic stability, Colombia had moved into another period of economic stagnation, only to fall into a deep recession in 1999 as a result of the East Asian financial crisis. The recession was initially followed by a slow recovery, but by 2003, economic growth had started to accelerate, boosted by the so-called commodity boom, which for a decade allowed considerable progress in development, such as a substantial reduction in poverty and improvements in the country's healthcare and education systems. After a decade of sustained growth, in 2014, Colombia entered into a period of economic slowdown, where it essentially remains to this day, except for 2020–2021, when the country experienced the impact of the COVID-19 pandemic and its subsequent recovery.

The persistent low economic growth after the booming decade of 2003–2013 has raised concerns that Colombia could be falling into the middle-income trap

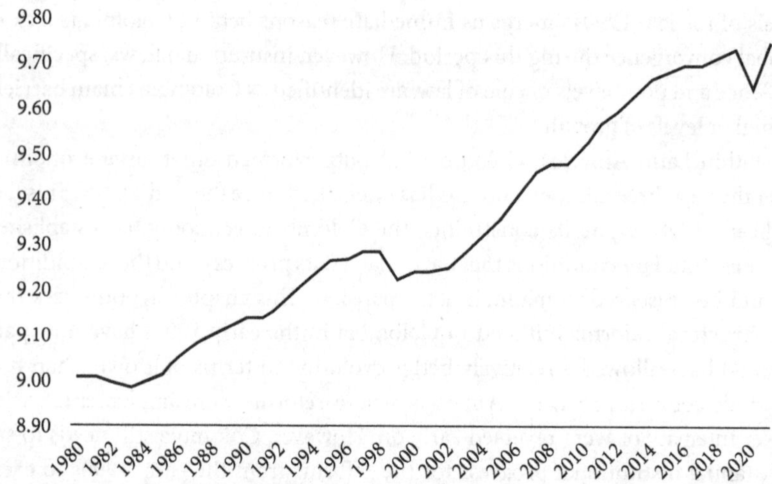

Figure 14.1. Natural logarithm of the real GDP per capita – PPP (2021 = 100).
Source: Author's elaboration based on Conference Board data.

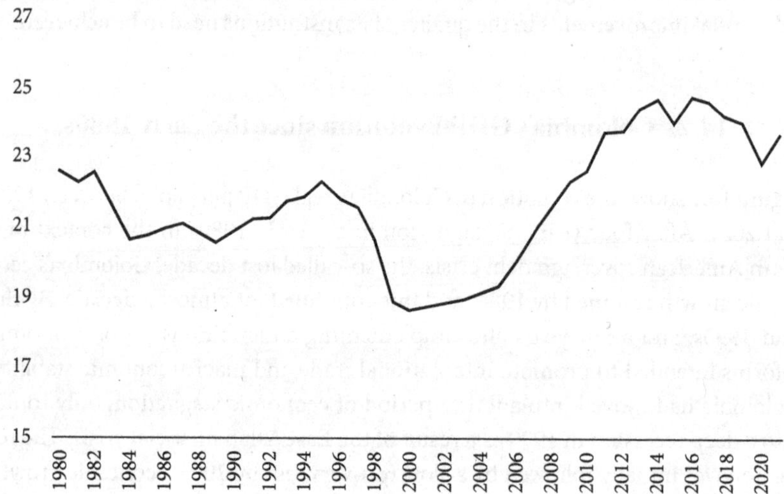

Figure 14.2. GDP per capita relative to that of the United States, 1980–2021.
Source: Author's elaboration based on International Monetary Fund data.

due to its gap with the advanced economies, which has remained constant since the mid-2010s. Figure 14.2 shows the evolution of Colombia's GDP per capita relative to that of the United States, the global economic leader in the study period, between 1980 and 2021. Between 1980 and 1995, Colombia's GDP per capita accounted for approximately 21.5% of that of the United States. From the mid-1990s, but particularly with the onset of the East Asian financial crisis, Colombia's relative GDP per capita saw a substantial decline until it reached a nadir in 2000. Colombia's relatively poor economic performance since the mid-1990s contrasted with the 'roaring nineties' in the United States, which increased the gap between the two countries. This declining trend was reversed in the twenty-first century, especially between 2005 and 2014, when most countries in Latin America benefited from the so-called *commodities boom*. This progress, however, stalled in 2014, and Colombia's relative GDP stabilized with a new plateau of approximately 24% that of the United States, raising the question as to whether Colombia has fallen into the middle-income trap.

The commodities boom, which propelled Latin American economic growth between the first decade of the twenty-first century and the mid-2010s via prices for oil, coal, copper, soy, and other primary goods in international markets, led many contemporary policymakers to dream of a second 'take-off'[1] that would finally permit Latin American countries to escape the middle-income trap, which shaped the continent's economic history during the twentieth century. These hopes, however, vanished by the mid-2010s, when commodity prices declined, and most countries in the region moved into either a long-lasting recession or a substantial economic slowdown, following a long-lasting pattern where commodity prices determine the continent's business cycle. Despite Colombia entering into a stage of low economic growth and ceasing its path to convergence with the United States, it displayed a better outcome than most of the other Latin American countries. Since the mid-2010s, Colombia has certainly avoided falling into secular stagnation, which has characterized several other large economies in the region, but it has not yet managed to avoid the risk of falling into the middle-income trap.

Comparing Colombia's GDP per capita relative to that of the average of Latin America's seven largest economies,[2] by 2012, Colombia's GDP per capita was approximately 76% of the regional average, substantially lower than that of upper-middle-income countries in the region at that time, such as Brazil or Mexico. Almost a decade later, in 2021, however, Colombia's GDP per capita reached 97% that of the average for the largest of the Latin American economies, which essentially reflected a regional convergence. Colombia clearly outperformed the rest of Latin America over the past decade, which points to the fact that there were elements beyond the high commodity prices that enabled a long period of sustained growth, despite the remaining gap with the industrial leader. The lack of global convergence highlights the fact that Colombia is still missing some

[1] The first 'take-off' would be the late nineteenth/early twentieth century, when most Latin American economies made their transition to modern economic growth.

[2] These economies are Argentina, Brazil, Chile, Ecuador, Mexico, Peru, and Venezuela.

preconditions necessary for converging with more advanced economies and escaping the middle-income trap. At the same time, Colombia fulfilled other missing preconditions that are not observed in the other large economies in Latin America, such as persisting in the structural reforms from the 1990s. In summary, for the past 30 years, Colombia's economic growth has been characterized by both a regional outperformance, particularly since the mid-2010s, and a lack of global convergence.[3]

14.3. Structural Breaks

14.3.1. Crisis, Acceleration, and Resilience

Are these changes in the evolution of the relative GDP for Colombia structural? If so, when and why did these changes occur? Answering these questions is essential in establishing the reasons behind Colombia's lack of global convergence and its regional outperformance. To identify the number of structural breaks in Colombia's relative GDP per capita and the years when these occurred, a Bai and Perron (1998) test for unknown structural breaks was implemented. As there were many domestic and international events with the potential to impact the aggregate economy during the analysed period, an unknown structural break test was opted for, rather than the use of the Chow test, which requires prior knowledge of the potential break points. During the period between 1980 and 2021, several events had the potential to impact the relative GDP of Colombia, such as economic liberalization in 1990, the East Asian financial crisis in 1997–1998, and the consolidation of the oil industry, which became Colombia's main export in the twenty-first century, a role that had historically been played by coffee. However, the relative importance of each of these influences cannot be a priori established.

Table 14.1 shows the number of structural breaks and the expected break years. The null hypothesis, which assumes that the relative GDP for Colombia is constant, is rejected for both series. In the case of Colombia's GDP relative to that of the United States, the test finds at least three structural breaks, with the estimated break years being 1998, 2006, and 2012. As observed in Figure 14.2 and confirmed by the results of the structural break test, Colombia was heavily affected by the East Asian financial crisis, which led to a divergence relative to the GDP of the United States.

This crisis was followed by a slow recovery, and it was only almost a decade later, in 2006, when Colombia resumed its path to convergence. The acceleration

[3] Taking the United States as the benchmark.

Table 14.1 Structural Breaks and the Expected Break Years

	Colombia's GDP per Capita Relative to that of the United States	Colombia's GDP per Capita Relative to That of the United States
Detected number of breaks (1% critical value)	3	2
Detected number of breaks (5% critical value)	3	3
Test for multiple breaks at unknown break dates		
Break 1	1998	1987
Break 2	2006	2014
Break 3	2012	

Source: Bai and Perron (1998), elaborated by author.

in economic growth between 2006 and 2012, which was probably related to improvements in security and the 'commodities boom' era, allowed Colombia to close its gap with the United States. In addition to high commodity prices, Colombia persisted with the structural reforms from the 1990s, and even moved into a second generation of structural reforms in the early 2000s, characterized by a deepening in international trade through the negotiation of free trade agreements and the increase in the private sector's share in the oil industry, which is why the good economic performance of the second half of the first decade of the twenty-first century was not only commodity-driven. In 2013, when international commodity prices declined, the global convergence trend ceased. Regardless of the reason for its relatively good performance in the early twenty-first century, these forces did not have the power to sustain Colombia's convergence beyond 2012.

Table 14.1 also displays the results for Colombia's GDP relative to those of the seven largest economies in Latin America. In this case, the Bai and Perron test finds two structural breaks at 99% significance. The estimated break years are 1987 and 2014. Throughout the 1980s, during the so-called lost decade, when Latin America was immersed in a profound sovereign debt crisis, Colombia reduced its gap with regard to the regional average. The reason behind this convergence was probably a milder recession and lower inflation (Caselli et al., 2021), with Colombia being the only large economy in the region that did not default on its sovereign debt and that maintained its access to international credit. Colombia's outperformance in the 1980s came to an end in 1987, when other countries in the region resumed their growth and overcame the worst of the 1980s crisis. According to the results presented in Table 14.1, between 1987 and 2014, Colombia grew at a pace similar to that of the average for large Latin American economies. From 2014 onwards, and despite its economic slowdown, Colombia was able to continue growing in the context of a region that witnessed an important stagnation in large economies, such as Argentina and Brazil, or an economic collapse, as was the case for Venezuela.

After examining the results for the structural break tests, at least four questions arise: Why was the shock of the East Asian financial crisis strong enough to stop Colombia's global convergence for almost a decade? What were the reasons behind the acceleration of economic growth between 2006 and 2012? Why did the Colombian economy, unlike most Latin American economies, continue to expand from 2014, despite the end of the commodities boom? Why did Colombia's global convergence stall after 2012?

14.3.2. From Reforms to a Crisis: The Painful Impact of the East Asian Financial Crisis

After six decades under the import-substitution model, in the early 1990s, Colombia implemented a set of reforms that were aimed at liberalizing its economy and increasing its integration into the world economy. The reforms were ambitious and ranged from reducing tariffs and opening up the financial sector to foreign investment to reforming the central bank to conducting an independent monetary policy with the aim of controlling inflation. This set of structural reforms, and despite the institutional challenges of that decade, generated positive expectations for a higher potential growth for the Colombian economy. The full benefits of the reforms, however, could not be quickly observed in the 1990s due to the strong shock caused by the East Asian financial crisis.

In 1998, Colombia was heavily impacted by the East Asian financial crisis, which caused a sudden stop to capital inflow and a decline of more than 4% in the real GDP in 1999. The problems in the East Asian financial markets increased international investors' risk aversion, and these investors reduced their positions in developing countries, spurring the crisis to spread rapidly toward Russia and Latin America by 1998. Despite the crisis originally being an external shock, there were also weaknesses in Colombia's fundamentals, particularly the institutional deterioration related to security and persistent fiscal deficit, which amplified the crisis (Luzardo-Luna, 2019). Between 1994 and 1998, public expenditure increased from 12.8% to 17% of the GDP. However, the government's revenue did not increase at the same pace. This led to a substantial increase in public debt, and this affected Colombia's credibility once it impacted Latin America in 1998. By September 1998, in the middle of the financial crisis, Colombia's EMBI+

Table 14.2 Drivers of Economic Growth, Average 1990–2021 (%)

Variable	1990–1997	1998–2005	2006–2011	2012–2021
Labour quantity contribution	2.19	1.24	1.57	0.09
Labour quality contribution	0.81	0.47	(0.27)	0.84
Total capital contribution	2.02	0.96	3.20	1.92
Total factor productivity	(1.05)	(0.56)	0.25	(0.01)
GDP	3.97	2.12	4.75	2.83

Source: Elaborated from Conference Board data.

sovereign bond spread[4] was 1,090 basic points (Kaminsky and Reinhart, 2001), indicating that Colombia was perceived as a 'riskier' country than the average for other developing countries.

In addition to the deterioration in public finance, by the late 1990s, Colombia was suffering a particularly violent period that impacted the quality of its institutions. Beginning in the 1980s, as a result of the rise of drug cartels and insurgent groups, Colombia saw a substantial deterioration in its security conditions. Bonilla (2009) found that the homicide rate (per 100,000 people) increased from 20 in 1979 to more than 80 in 1991. After its peak in 1991, the homicide rate declined during the mid-1990s, before starting to rise again until 2002, after which it started to consistently decline again.

Both the sustainability of public finance and the deterioration in security are elements that explain the intensity of the crisis. However, the East Asian financial crisis also impacted Colombia's economic growth through its slow recovery, and its relative GDP compared to that of the United States only returned to pre-crisis levels in 2007. To establish the reasons behind Colombia's slow recovery throughout the early 2000s, it is useful to examine the drivers behind economic growth for different periods, defined according to the results of the structural break test, as presented in Table 14.2.

The slower economic growth between 1998 and 2005 was mainly input-driven, although productivity decline also played an important role. The onset of the crisis led to a substantial and long-lasting decline in the investment rate, which is mainly explained by a collapse in the housing sector. One of the

[4] This is an indicator developed and published by J. P. Morgan that compares a country's spread relative to the weighted sum of a group of developing countries.

mechanisms through which the financial crisis transmitted into the real estate sector was the rise in the mortgage interest rate, which at that time was mostly variable. Higher interest rates, in the context of a recession and high unemployment, led to a sharp increase in delinquent mortgages, affecting the solvency of the banking sector, which led to a vast contraction in the construction industry. By 2019, 20 years after the start of the crisis, the volume of mortgages as a percentage of the GDP was still lower than the pre-crisis level, although the construction industry enjoyed a strong recovery from 2010 onwards (Cuellar et al., 2020).

Between 1998 and 2005, productivity had a negative impact on economic growth, reducing GDP growth by an average of 0.56 basic points. Following Colombia's slow recovery from the late 1990s, the financial and economic crisis presented a profound challenge for the economy to use its inputs in an efficient way. Considering that technological decline is very unlikely to occur, the causes behind the decline in productivity observed in Colombia in the early twenty-first century are probably related to a misallocation of resources, both between industries and within industries. However, it is worth noting that the productivity decline between 1998 and 2005 was lower than that of 1990–1997, which is why it can be assumed that Colombia saw some improvements in its input misallocation.

The reforms of the 1990s created a basis for macroeconomic stability, particularly regarding monetary policy, through the establishment of the independent central bank. However, the full benefits of these reforms could not immediately be observed in the 1990s due to the strong shock of the East Asian financial crisis, which was probably amplified by substantial fiscal deterioration, as well as the rise in violence in Colombia. The East Asian financial crisis led to a collapse in the investment rate, which in turn delayed Colombia's global convergence for almost a decade between the late 1990s and early 2000s.

14.3.3. The Resumption of Economic Growth and Global Convergence

The sharp fall in GDP in 1999 was followed by three years of low economic growth until 2003, when economic expansion started to gain momentum again. However, it was not until 2006 that Colombia's growth rate was high enough to resume its path to convergence, reaching 24.7% of the United States' GDP per capita in 2014, its highest point since 1940. Importantly, this evolution was not exclusive to Colombia; rather, it was a general pattern that was observed across the large Latin American economies, as observed in Figure 14.2, and mainly explained by a boom in international commodities prices.

Between 2003 and 2014, Latin America underwent a decade of economic expansion, propelled by a strong and sustained increase in commodity prices. Fuel, minerals, and agricultural goods experienced a super-cycle of high prices, brought about by the strong demand from the Asian economies. According to Ocampo (2017), between 2003 and 2013, the terms of trade increased by approximately 50%, which allowed a substantial increase in exports. Colombia saw a gradual increase in the relative importance of export goods with the consolidation of the oil and coal industries. However, it was from 2003 onward that the country experienced a major acceleration in exports, although that acceleration was compensated for by a dynamic expansion in the value of imports.

While the commodity boom certainly helped Colombia's economic growth in the early twenty-first century, there were also other drivers in its domestic economy. As Table 14.2 shows, capital growth was the main driver of economic growth between 2006 and 2011. This fact is in line with the evolution of fixed gross capital formation, which, by 2006, had regained its level from the early 1990s.

Colombia's strong performance between 2006 and 2011 was mainly due to the rise in investment. The average investment rate increased to 22.5% of the GDP between 2006 and 2011, up from 17% between 1998 and 2005. Understanding the reasons behind the recovery in investment is essential for explaining the positive economic performance in this period. Investment was propelled not only by domestic savings but also by foreign investment. In 2001 there was already a gap between gross capital formation and gross savings, which consolidated in 2006. This gap could be sustained due to the contribution of foreign investment. Turning to net inflows of direct foreign investment as a share of the GDP, between 2006 and 2011, that indicator was 3.82% of the GDP, and excluding 2010, the percentage was 4.13%, substantially higher than the 2.24% and 1.67% observed in 1999–2004[5] and 1980–1998, respectively. What is different here is that after 2006, Colombia was able to increase its capacity to attract foreign investment in a substantial and persistent way. This persistence is particularly relevant because, before the first decade of the twenty-first century, there were short cycles of rapid increases in foreign investment, but they were also followed by sharp contractions.

Considering the evolution of capital inflows from the early 2000s onward, it seems that something structural changed in Colombia's ability to attract foreign investment, which highlights the improvement in institutional elements. Finding the determinants of foreign investment in Colombia during the first two decades of the twenty-first century would require a detailed study, but two elements appear to be particularly relevant: the consolidation of the fuel industry

[5] The year 2005 was exceptional, with a net inflow of foreign investment of 7% of the GDP, mostly due to the fuel industry.

and improvements in security. Between 2002 and 2008, Colombia saw a notable reduction in its homicide rate, which continued to decline thereafter, though at a slower pace. This improvement in security, despite Colombia still being a country with a high level of violence, could have had a positive impact on Colombia's ability to attract foreign investment.

In addition to investment, productivity also contributed to economic growth. Unlike the periods before and after, the period of productivity between 2006 and 2011 contributed to economic growth. Due to its contribution being very moderate, the relevance of productivity needs to be assessed in context, as it did not reduce economic growth as it did between 1990 and 1997. The increase in foreign investment may have impacted Colombian firms through their ability to adopt better technologies, as well as the mobilization of resources toward more productive areas of the economy.

In addition to improvements in security and persisting in the structural reforms of the 1990s, Colombia embarked on a second generation of structural reforms in the early 2000s. One of the most relevant of these reforms was the establishment of the Agencia Nacional de Hidrocarburos (National Hydrocarbons Agency) as a new regulator of the oil industry, a function until then fulfilled by Ecopetrol, the state-owned oil enterprise. This change was intended to increase private participation in the oil industry by promoting competition. A second relevant structural reform was the stepping up of the free trade policy by pursuing free trade agreements with some of world's largest economies, such as the United States and the European Union. The reforms from the early 2000s were certainly less ambitious than those of the *economic opening*, but they were essential in reinforcing the transition that started in the early 1990s.

14.3.4. Moderation and Survival after the Commodities Boom

Commodity-driven growth came to an end in 2013 due to a fall in prices from that year onward. This fact led to a substantial economic slowdown, which effectively stopped the convergence of Colombia's relative GDP with that of the United States. Despite this economic slowdown, Colombia's economy managed to continue growing, unlike the majority of the large economies in Latin America, which moved into a long-lasting period of stagnation. Up to 2014, Colombia's GDP per capita was approximately 20% lower than that of the weighted sum of Latin America's six largest economies. However, by 2021, that gap had essentially closed.

In analysing the drivers behind economic growth presented in Table 14.1, the economic slowdown from 2012 onward is explained by the reduction in the contribution of capital and the null contribution of the quantity of labour and productivity. In addition to investment, the quantity of labour accounted for approximately one-third of Colombia's GDP growth between 2006 and 2011. Over these years, the employed population grew by an average of 2.7% per year, while the total population expanded by 1.2%. A higher proportion of the population participating in the labour force certainly contributed to economic growth in this period. However, by the mid-2010s, this engine of economic growth essentially disappeared.

Between 2012 and 2021, the size of the labour force made a marginal contribution to economic growth. Even excluding 2020 and 2021 to control for the effects of the crisis brought about by the COVID-19 pandemic, the contribution of the size of the labour force was on average only 0.5%. As the gap between the employed population and total population growth narrowed, so did the possibility of growth due to the increasing share of the population in the labour force. However, labour contributed to Colombia's growth for the period from 2012 to 2021, mainly through its quality, not quantity.

The quality of labour made a positive contribution to economic growth. Between 2012 and 2021, the improvements in the level of education of the labour force contributed approximately 0.84% to GDP growth. In this sense, it is important to consider the advancements in higher education that Colombia achieved in the first two decades of the twenty-first century. Considering the evolution of gross enrolment in tertiary education between 1970 and 2019, between 2006 and 2017, Colombia witnessed a mass expansion of higher education uptake, which increased from approximately 32.7% to 56.4% of the population in the age group that corresponds to that level of education.

To the same extent that the population completed professional or vocational education, these educated workers were gradually incorporated into the labour force. In Colombia, a professional career usually requires five years of study; therefore, it is plausible to assume that students who enrolled in universities by the first decade of the twenty-first century entered the labour market in approximately 2010–2011. Regardless of the specific timing, the relevant fact is that the labour force of the decade commencing in 2010 was different from that of the previous decade, as professional and highly skilled workers accounted for a larger proportion in the second decade of the twenty-first century.

Despite its contribution to economic growth, it was not the improvements in human capital that explained Colombia's out-performance of the largest economies in Latin America after the commodity boom. Table 14.3 shows the average annual growth rate and its drivers between 2014 and 2021. The main reason that Colombia managed to continue growing after the decline in international commodities prices was that it did not see a decline in productivity but, instead, experienced a marginal increase. When these prices declined, most of Latin America entered into a long-lasting period of productivity decline,

Table 14.3 Annual Average GDP Growth Rates and Their Drivers for Latin America's Six Largest Economies, 2014–2021 (%)

Country	Contribution of Labour Quantity to GDP Growth	Contribution of Labour Quality to GDP Growth	Contribution of Total Capital to GDP Growth	Total Factor Productivity	GDP Growth
Argentina	0.06	0.21	0.73	(1.56)	(0.57)
Brazil	(0.13)	0.95	0.84	(1.86)	(0.20)
Chile	(0.71)	0.31	2.20	0.29	2.09
Colombia	(0.17)	0.71	1.77	0.13	2.44
Ecuador	0.77	0.02	2.03	(2.55)	0.27
Peru	0.27	0.37	2.51	(0.80)	2.36
Mexico	0.63	0.08	0.92	(0.52)	1.11
Venezuela	0.44	0.08	(3.29)	(15.81)	(18.58)

Source: Author's elaboration based on Conference Board data.

except for Chile and Colombia. Again, the determinants of productivity growth are beyond the scope of this chapter. However, a plausible explanation is that both Chile and Colombia displayed higher flexibility in regard to mobilizing resources and transitioning toward those industries with higher returns and away from industries with low or even negative returns. The fall in commodity prices certainly reduced the returns in these industries, which could have had a deeply negative impact on their productivity. However, in most Latin American economies, there was no rapid reallocation of resources to industries with higher potential growth. In the particular case of Colombia, the relative faster reallocation could be boosted by the second generation of structural reforms.

Table 14.4 presents the same information as Table 14.3, but for the commodity boom period (2003–2013). During that decade, productivity increased in several countries that experienced long-lasting stagnation after 2013, such as Argentina and Ecuador, and even in Venezuela, which experienced one of the greatest economic collapses in recent history. The high international commodity prices probably increased the returns and therefore productivity in the industries within the commodities sector. However, when the returns in these firms fell, the economy did not have the flexibility to allow a structural change and increase the proportion of firms and industries with high potential returns.

Finally, an additional reason behind Colombia's relatively good economic performance between 2014 and 2021 is the contribution of capital, which was on average higher than that of Argentina, Brazil, and Mexico, although lower than that of Chile and Peru. Gross capital formation in the decade commencing in 2010

Table 14.4 Annual Average GDP Growth Rates and Their Drivers for Latin America's Six Largest Economies, 2003–2013 (%)

Country	Contribution of Labour Quantity to GDP Growth	Contribution of Labour Quality to GDP Growth	Contribution of Total Capital to GDP Growth	Total Factor Productivity	GDP Growth
Argentina	1.11	0.16	1.95	1.92	5.15
Brazil	0.66	0.86	2.19	(0.02)	3.68
Chile	1.00	0.49	4.28	(1.22)	4.56
Colombia	1.38	0.38	2.64	0.24	4.63
Ecuador	0.57	0.18	2.92	0.91	4.57
Peru	0.93	0.54	3.87	0.67	6.01
Mexico	0.92	0.14	1.31	(0.23)	2.13
Venezuela	1.02	0.26	1.50	1.55	4.33

Source: Author's elaboration based on Conference Board data.

remained at a level similar to that of around 2005, despite the decline in gross savings. For that reason, what allowed Colombia to maintain its investment rate was essentially foreign investment inflows, which continued to enter the country despite the decline in the attractiveness of industries within the commodities sector. In explaining how Colombia could have preserved its attractiveness for capital inflows, it is probably important to consider that in 2011, the country recovered its investment grade from the rating agencies, which it had lost during the East Asian financial crisis.

14.4. The Reasons behind the Stall in Global Convergence and the Risk of Falling into the Middle-Income Trap

The previous section identified the different periods related to Colombia's global and regional convergence, as well as their proximate causes. However, identifying the ultimate reasons behind Colombia's lack of global convergence goes beyond the decomposition in GDP between inputs and productivity, which, after all, are outcomes rather than fundamental changes. Likewise, the recent stagnation in Colombia's global convergence, after a period of rapid economic growth, raises concerns that the country could become another example of the middle-income trap. This possibility is particularly interesting due to the magnitude of structural reforms implemented in the early 1990s and the following decade, which were considered essential for propelling Colombia's economic growth by several policymakers and observers. In that context, it is worth exploring why structural reforms could not sustain Colombia's global convergence.

The impact of supply-side structural reforms, particularly those implemented in the late 1980s and early 1990s in Latin America that were put in place to promote macroeconomic stability and international trade, on long-term economic growth has been extensively discussed in the literature (Lora and Panizza, 2002; Rajagopal, 2006; Lora, 2012). Analysing the case of middle-income economies between 1960 and 2014, Lee (2019) maintains that convergence success is associated with improvements in human capital, effective rule of law, trade openness, and a high level of high-tech exports.

This section aims to identify the impact of the persistence of the structural reforms implemented in Colombia in the early 1990s and early 2000s—which were put in place to promote the transition from the import-substitution model toward a mostly open economy with macroeconomic stability—on Colombia's subsequent economic growth. To achieve this purpose, use is made of the synthetic control method that follows the methodology of Abadie and Gardeazabal (2003).

The synthetic control used is based on other countries in Latin America (donor pool), where similar reforms were adopted in the early 1990s, but where these reforms were either rapidly reversed after the East Asian financial crisis, or did not move forward with a second generation of structural reforms in the early 2000s. For that reason, the econometric model aims to capture the cumulative effect of structural reforms from the 1990s after surviving the East Asian financial crisis. The countries included in the donor pool were Argentina, Brazil, Bolivia, Ecuador, Paraguay, Uruguay, and Venezuela, which, on average, maintained and preserved substantial elements from the import substitution era, such as high tariffs and large state-owned enterprises (SOEs) after the East Asian financial crisis, or only embodied the first generation of structural reforms.

Naturally, it is not possible to directly measure the degree to which each of these countries persisted or implemented new structural reforms aimed at leaving the import substitution model. Thus, use is made of a proxy variable centring on the fact that these countries have not signed a free trade agreement with the United States. It is assumed that this proxy variable, although it only focuses on international trade, loosely captures whether a country persisted in the structural reforms implemented to transition out of the import-substitution model after the East Asian financial crisis.

In the model, it will be assumed that the treatment country, Colombia, persisted in its structural reforms of the early 1990s, and moved forward to a second generation of structural reforms in the first decade of the twenty-first century. It will be assumed that the treatment started in 2012, when the free trade agreement between Colombia and the United States entered into force. It is worth clarifying that the model does not aim to measure or test the impact of that particular free trade agreement on economic growth, but Colombia's willingness to persist in the structural reforms from the 1990s. In other words, the fact that Colombia signed a free trade agreement with the United States signals its willingness to maintain and step up the structural reforms from the 1990s.

More formally, within a set of countries in Latin America j = 1 . . . , N over T periods, Colombia received a treatment (initiating negotiations for a free trade agreement with the United States) in period t_0 (2004). For a given value of reform $R_j \in \{0, 1\}$, the potential outcome is $Y_{j,t(0)} = 0$ if the country did not implement the reform and $Y_{j,t(1)} = 1$ if the country did implement the reform. $Y_{j,t(1)}$ is Colombia, and $Y_{j,t(0)}$ is the 'synthetic Colombia' based on other countries in Latin America that did not reform.

Equations (1) and (2) represent the vector of weights W = (w2 . . . , wn + 1) and $D_{1,t}$ represents the treatment effect:

$$\hat{Y}_{1,t}(0) = \sum_{j=2}^{j+1} \omega_j Y_{j,t} \qquad (1)$$

$$\hat{D}_{1,t} = Y_{1,t}(1) - \hat{Y}_{1,t}(0) \qquad (2)$$

Table 14.5 presents the control country weights, and Figure 14.3 maps Colombia's and synthetic Colombia's GDP per capita evolution between 1991 and 2019. I excluded 2020 and 2021, in order to avoid the distortion caused by the COVID-19 crisis and recovery. According to the results presented in Figure 14.3, the persistence in the first generation of reforms from the 1990s and the adoption

Table 14.5 Country Weights and Goodness of Fit

Country	Weight
Argentina	0.106
Brazil	0.132
Ecuador	0.152
Venezuela	0.114
Bolivia	0.214
Paraguay	0.161
Uruguay	0.120
RMSPE	0.037

Source: Author's elaboration.

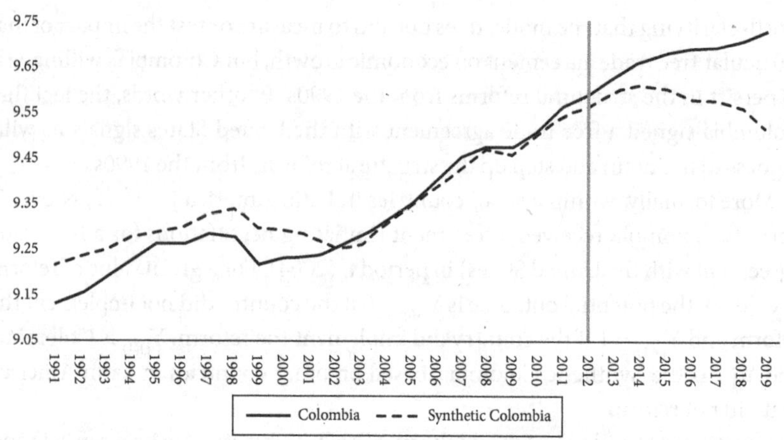

Figure 14.3. Effect of persisting in the structural reforms from the early 1990s (treatment begins 2012).

of a second generation of structural reforms paid off for Colombia, which achieved a GDP 19.3% higher than that of synthetic Colombia by 2019.

It is important to note that the structural reforms from both the early 1990s and the following decade have not been enough to allow Colombia's economy to converge globally. Results presented in Table 14.1 signalled that Colombia has not met all the required preconditions for closing its gap with the United States, at least since 2012. This chapter hypothesizes that violence and a weak rule of law, even relative to the rest of Latin America, are relevant reasons behind Colombia's lack of more dynamic growth, despite its willingness to implement structural reforms, and are major risks for falling into the middle-income trap.

To test this hypothesis, use is made of the syntactic control method again; this time, the treatment is the high level of violence, which was a factor in Colombia in the last three decades. In this case, the donor pool is composed of countries in Latin America that implemented similar structural reforms in the early 1990s, and persisted in them throughout the following decade but had homicide rates substantially lower than those of Colombia. These countries are Chile, Costa Rica, Dominican Republic, and Peru. In this case, it will be assumed that the treatment started in 2006, when there began a slowdown in the decline of its national homicide rates. Table 14.6 presents the country weights, and Figure 14.4 shows the evolution of both Colombia's and synthetic Colombia's GDP per capita between 2001 and 2019. According to these results, high levels of violence reduced Colombia's GDP per capita by 18.3% by 2019.

The Worldwide Governance Indicators constructed by the World Bank evaluate countries' formal institutions in six dimensions since 1996: voice and accountability, political stability and absence of violence, government effectiveness,

Table 14.6 Country Weights and Goodness of Fit

Country	Weight
Costa Rica	0.115
Dominican Republic	0.245
Peru	0.564
Chile	0.077

Source: Author's elaboration.

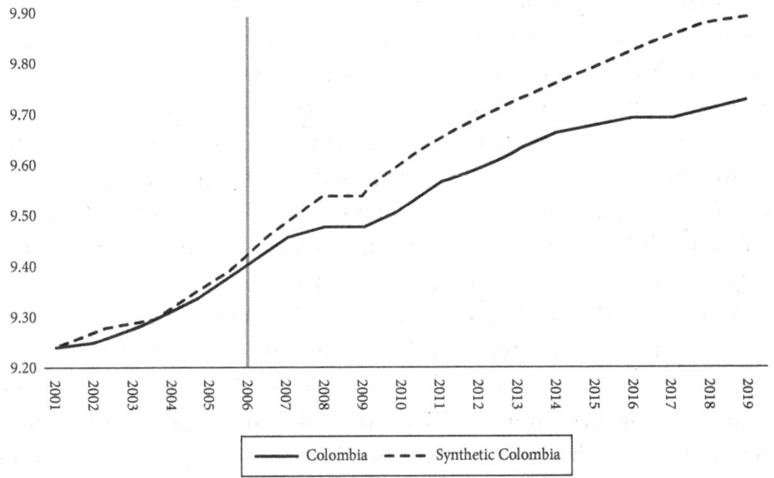

Figure 14.4. Effect of persisting in the structural reforms from the early 1990s (treatment begins 2006).
Source: Author's elaboration.

regulatory quality, rule of law, and control of corruption. In most cases, Colombia presents an outcome similar to the regional average indicators, such as voice and accountability and government effectiveness, and even outperforms Latin America in terms of quality of regulation. However, Colombia displays substantially worse results in terms of political stability and absence of violence, and to a lesser extent in rule of law. The rule of law dimension, which measures agents' confidence in contract enforcement, property rights, the police, and the courts, saw a decline between 2015 and 2019, which contrasts with the improvements between 2000 and 2015. According to the Worldwide Governance Indicators, Colombia's lack of global convergence from 2013 onwards could be associated with a stall in progress and even a reverse in terms of rule of law, as well as the country's chronic problem of violence. This latter issue, despite continued improvement in the second half of the 2010s, still falls well short of the regional standards.

14.5. Conclusions

In the early twenty-first century, Colombia saw substantial progress in terms of economic growth and development. This improvement allowed the country to reduce its income gap with advanced economies, as well as its poverty level, even outperforming most of the large economies in Latin America since 2014. The reasons behind this regional outperformance are probably related to the persistence of structural reforms implemented in the early 1990s, reinforced by a second generation of reforms in the early twenty-first century, which allowed Colombia to better navigate the international environment of the post-commodity boom period. Despite the economic slowdown, Colombia managed to continue growing in the second half of the 2010s, which contrasted with the stagnation seen in other Latin American countries, where growth halted with the end of the commodities boom. A positive, although small, evolution of productivity from 2003 onward signals a higher level of flexibility for reallocation of resources in the productive sectors and industries relative to other large economies in the region that did not persist with or build upon the economic reforms from the 1990s.

Beyond Latin America, however, Colombia's economic convergence with the global economic leader, the United States, stalled in the mid-2010s. Structural reforms implemented hitherto have not had enough power to maintain Colombia on the path toward convergence. In other words, Colombia has continued progressing, but not at a pace rapid enough to converge with advanced economies, which is why Colombia risks falling into the middle-income trap.

Despite the positive effect of economic reforms in the past three decades, Colombia's persistent institutional problems, particularly its high level of violence and weak rule of law, remain the main constraints for more dynamic economic growth. This chapter shows that other countries in Latin America that persisted with similar structural reforms to transition from the import substitution model but had lower levels of violence achieved a significantly higher income per capita. For this reason, Colombia's pathway to overcome the middle-income trap probably lies in improving its institutions and reducing violence, as well as persisting in, and naturally improving, the economic framework established in the early 1990s.

The relationship between institutions and economic growth has been largely documented by the economic literature, although other elements, such as human capital (Glaeser et al., 2004) and competitiveness in high-value sectors, such as the high-tech industry (Lee, 2013), have also been identified as essential for boosting economic growth, particularly for the transition toward high-income from middle-income status. Colombia's recent experience highlights that supply-side structural reforms certainly contribute to economic growth. However, such reforms can only express their full potential benefits in the context of a high-quality institutional environment. Reforms without institutional improvement could be a pathway toward the middle-income trap.

References

Abadie, A., and Gardeazabal, J. 2003. 'The Economic Costs of CONFLICT: A CASE STUDY of the Basque Country', *American Economic Review*, 93(1), 113–132.

Bai, J., and Perron, P. 1998. 'Estimating and Testing Linear Models with Multiple Structural Changes', *Econometrica*, 66(1), 47–78.

Bonilla-Mejía, L. 2009. 'Revisión de la literatura económica reciente sobre las causas de la violencia homicida en Colombia', *Documentos de Trabajo Sobre Economía Regional y Urbana*, No. 114.

Caselli, F., Faralli, M., Manasse, P., and Panizza, U. 2021. 'On the Benefits of Repaying', CEPR Discussion Paper 16539.

Conference Board Total Economy Database, April 2022. https://www.conference-board.org/data/economydatabase/total-economy-database-productivity.

Glaeser, E. L., La Porta, R., Lopez-de-Silanes, F., and Shleifer, A. 2004. 'Do institutions cause growth?', *Journal of economic Growth*, 9(3), 271–303.

International Monetary Fund. 2021. *The World Economic Outlook (WEO)*. Washington, DC: IMF.

Kaminsky, G., and Reinhart, C. 2001. 'Financial Markets in Times of Stress', *NBER Working Paper Series*.

Lee, J. W. 2020. 'Convergence Success and the Middle-Income Trap', *The Developing Economies*, 58(1), 30–62.

Lora, E. 2012. 'Structural Reform in Latin America: What Has Been Reformed and How It Can Be Quantified (Updated Version)', No. IDB-WP-346. *IDB Working Paper Series*.

Lora, E., and Panizza, U. 2002. 'Structural Reforms in Latin America under Scrutiny', *Annual Meetings of the Board of Governors, Inter-American Development Bank and Inter-American Investment Corporation*. Washington, DC.

Luzardo-Luna, I. 2019. 'The Lost Decades, 1980–2000: External Debt, Structural Reforms, and a Deep Financial Crisis', in I Luzardo-Luna, ed., *Colombia's Slow Economic Growth*. Cham, Switzerland: Palgrave Macmillan, 107–128.

Manasse, P., Panizza, U., Caselli, F. G., and Faralli, M. 2021. 'On the Benefits of Repaying', No. 2021/233. International Monetary Fund.

Ocampo, J. A. 2017. 'Commodity-Led Development in Latin America', in Gilles Carbonnier, Humberto Campodónico, Sergio Tezanos Vázquez, eds., *Alternative Pathways to Sustainable Development: Lessons from Latin America*. Nijhoff: Brill, 51–76.

Rajagopal, D. 2006. 'Where Did the Trade Liberalization Drive Latin American Economy: A Cross Section Analysis', *Applied Econometrics and International Development*, 6(2), 89–108.

World Bank. 2021. *World-Development-Indicators*. Washington, DC.

15
Moving up the Value Chain in Mexico
FDI, Learning, Clusters, and the Creation of New Capabilities

Clemente Ruiz Durán and Moises Balestro

15.1. Introduction

There are two often-neglected issues in the debate about creating technological capabilities for latecomers, particularly in Latin American countries. One is the missing link between structural transformation as an exit from the middle-income trap. Another is the politics embedded in the collective action and institutions needed to build such capabilities. Therefore, this chapter explores the strengthening of Mexican clusters in knowledge-intensive industries and the challenge of developing and scaling up new capabilities to exit the middle-income trap.

In contrast to other Latin American countries that went through the import substitution period, Mexico avoided deindustrialization by strengthening its linkages to the new global value chains (GVCs) that enabled the development of new production clusters in different regions. There was a critical juncture for this move from import-substitution to export-led manufacturing with the North America Free Trade Agreement (NAFTA) in 1994.

The essential industrialization of Mexico began in the late nineteenth century with the emergence of textiles and steel. The railway system developed industrial projects in the Northern states (Nuevo Leon) and coastal areas (Veracruz). The import substitution industrialization (ISI) model, developed in Central Mexico, created a network of educational institutions that supported the rise of new industrial activities (steel industry, auto, electronics, pharmaceuticals, among others). Public policy fostered infrastructure investment, allowing more trade in the territory, supported by creating industrial parks in the central states of Mexico, Querétaro, and Puebla; in the West, Jalisco, Aguascalientes, Guanajuato, San Luis Potosí; and in the North in Nuevo León and Saltillo. In the 1960s, a parallel model developed in the border states based on industries serving the US market and subject to special customs arrangements. The industries that resulted here were termed the *maquiladoras*.

Clemente Ruiz Durán and Moises Balestro, *Moving up the Value Chain in Mexico* In: *Innovation, Competitiveness, and Development in Latin America.* Edited by: Edmund Amann and Paulo N. Figueiredo, Oxford University Press.
 DOI: 10.1093/oso/9780197648070.003.0015

Eventually, the debt crisis of the 1980s destroyed the basis of the older ISI model. There then emerged a new model of industrialization focused on export industrialization. The new model took advantage of the old facilities to promote export-oriented industrialization supported by a trade agreement with the United States and Canada (NAFTA). Geography was redrawn, in the border *maquila* models of Baja California, Sonora, Chihuahua, and Tamaulipas, mixed with industrial states of Coahuila and Nuevo León. In Central Mexico, a new wave of investment encouraged the reconfiguration of Mexico City, the state of Mexico, Puebla, and a North-West-Central complex that combined the states of Jalisco, Aguascalientes, Guanajuato, Querétaro, and San Luis Potosí (Bajio). Such investments promoted GVCs in electronics, the auto industry, and software, bringing small and medium enterprises (SMEs) into the process and pushing them to upgrade (Pietrobelli and Rabellotti, 2006).

Due to special zones and specific agreements for foreign direct investment (FDI) in manufacturing, the industrial clusters lay at the core of the Mexican manufacturing structure, including the auto industry, electronics, medical devices, pharmaceuticals, and software. The clusters led to interactive cities, whose linkages pushed the emergence of new forms of industrial organization and technological development (Ruiz, in press). Notwithstanding the production of value-added manufacturing, one of the main problems of cluster development was the lack of innovation.

The Mexican Economic Complexity Index increased from 0.7 in 1995 to 1.22 in 2020 (Growth Lab at Harvard University, 2022). Differently from other industrialized countries in Latin America, such as Brazil, Argentina, and Colombia, Mexico has solid regional agglomeration, which traces back to the location of US multinationals in the border states of Mexico at the beginning of the 1960s. In this sense, there has been a decisive role of FDI in the country's industrial development, which goes beyond the ISI.

Among the most industrialized countries in Latin America, Mexico is the only country with increasing economic complexity due to the larger share of manufacturing in its exports. Mexico has not gone through early deindustrialization like Brazil and Argentina. The share of manufacturing in the Mexican economy has been relatively stable for more than 50 years, ranging between 15% and 22% of GDP.

The *maquila* argument labeling Mexico as an assembly manufacturing economy competing on low wages and a low-skilled workforce and highly dependent on multinational corporations (MNCs) is only part of the picture. When the analysis of the structure of the Mexican economy occurs on a macro level without considering the regional development associated with the clusters, the *maquila* argument gains more evidence. However, when delving into the clusters and examining specific industries such as auto, electronics, medical devices, and aerospace, Mexican manufacturing presents a different landscape.

As a corollary of this cluster development, the domestic value-added embodied in the foreign demand for Mexican exports went from US$60 billion in 1995 to US$304 billion in 2018 (as seen in OECD, 2022). Moreover, although slower, the Mexican gross exports grew from US$214 billion in 2005 to US$494 billion in 2021; manufacturing exports rose from US$175 billion in 2005 to US$436 billion in 2021. An increase in the export of intermediate goods reflects a better position within the GVC. By using data from 15 states with industrial clusters in Mexico between 1999 and 2019, it was possible to identify high significant correlations between FDI, R&D as a percentage of the state GDP, federal government spending on science and technology, the number of scientific and technological organizations, and the graduate students of engineering.

15.2. Learning and the Creation of New Capabilities

The concept of productive and technological capabilities became widely known because of Lall's seminal article in 1992. When Lall wrote about the technological capabilities at the firm and the national levels, there was already considerable literature on the main characteristics of the newly industrialized countries and the different paths of catching-up and upgrading processes. Technological change at the firm level is broadly defined to encompass activities fitting the efforts to innovate, such as a continuous process to absorb or create technical knowledge coming from external inputs (learning by acquiring new technology) and the past accumulation of skills and knowledge (Lall, 1992).

The technological learning required to build up capabilities demands absorptive capacity. Such capacity has two elements: the existing knowledge base from firms and the intensity of effort (Kim, 2000). The intensity of effort relates to the time and commitment that organization members deploy to solve problems. The more demanding the embodiment of knowledge in products and services, the greater the need for systematic problem-solving, as in the in-house R&D, moving away from learning by doing.

So, capabilities are built out of learning processes at different levels, moderated by absorptive capacity, the firm, the region, and the national level. Song et al. (2018) suggest two dimensions to the concept by updating the absorptive capacity. The first dimension concerns the effort to build knowledge by searching, identifying, and acquiring external knowledge. The effort implies using knowledge search routines, boundary-spanning learning, and a direct interface with external knowledge. Then there is the dimension of the absorptive knowledge base with knowledge-processing routines and learning through experimentation and experience (Song et al., 2018). Both dimensions go beyond implementation capabilities (Lee et al., 2019) and contribute to leveraging cluster knowledge spillovers.

Katz (1987), quoted by Lall, claimed the weight of learning by doing, experience, and search efforts for latecomers. However, there is no cleavage between imitation, technology absorption, and innovative activities. Katz (1987) points out that acquiring certain technologies can demand tacit knowledge that is difficult to imitate and requires learning by doing and R&D efforts. Drawing on Lall (1992), it is possible to claim that countries like Mexico require a transition from intermediate capabilities with technology transfer to local suppliers to an innovative technological capability with R&D and the development of their technology.

As Lee et al. (2019) remind us, most middle-income countries fail to develop design capabilities, becoming locked into implementation capabilities. Design capabilities require learning-by-building with experimentation and creativity. By directly relating the middle-income trap to innovation, the authors mention a middle-innovation trap or capability-transition failure (Lee et al., 2019).

The absorptive capacity embeds itself in the institutional context, and the institutional voids or limits on institutions' work in emerging countries also affect the absorptive capacity at the firm level. As a result, there are higher risks and fewer innovative incentives (Cuervo-Cazurra and Rui, 2017). Due to political and economic instability, economic actors tend to overlook long-term planning and long-term gains. Therefore, the incentives to cooperate with other firms and organizations are small, creating barriers to enhance trust within and between firms. Political instability is a moderate, central, and severe obstacle to 59% of firms.[1]

As the recent Mexican experience with electric cars reveals, multinational corporations can provide incentives to increase the absorptive capacity when the Trans National Corporation (TNC) affiliates leverage the knowledge resources from local firms and local institutions. However, this process is far from spontaneous (Alfranca, 2015). As Paus (2017, 2020) claims, coordination and capabilities failures entail a proactive state to support the development of local firm capabilities, to set a critical level of absorptive capacity, and to provide economic incentives conducive to capability accumulation.

More recently, there has been a lively debate on the relationship between building capabilities, especially innovation capabilities, and exiting the middle-income trap. Although the middle-income trap is a relatively new concept coined

[1] World Bank Mexico 2010 Enterprise Survey Dataset.

in 2005 (Gill and Kharas, 2015), Fagerberg (1987) mentioned the link between economic growth and the technology gap. He saw that both imitation and innovation could contribute to narrowing the gap. However, the scope for imitation has decreased, and the costs of imitation have increased compared with the 1960s (Fagerberg, 1987). Such a claim needs cautious regard when considering the recent Chinese experience, where imitation in the 1990s contributed to moving up the value chain in the following decades. Exiting the middle-income trap calls for a transition in which institutions and political leadership can strengthen the firms' and regions' capabilities while increasing domestic actors' absorptive capacity.

According to Lee (2019), three elements complement learning and capability-building at the firm level. One is designing a working innovation or technological learning system. Developing countries not only have problems in the linkages between the actors integrating this system, but also require context-specific solutions. The second element encompasses the specific institutional settings with financial systems, educational systems, norms, and regulations. Lee's third element concerns the links and interactions among actors constituting the system.

Less knowledge-intensive innovation efforts such as R&D play a prominent role in increasing productivity. That is why overestimating the weak R&D investments in countries caught in the middle-income trap is often tricky. For example, Figueiredo et al. (2021) claim that labour productivity increases stem from the accumulation of non-R&D technological capabilities. However, the room for labour productivity increases from technological diffusion and learning-by-doing is larger for mature industries and middle-level technology. Although this is the case for countries like Brazil, Colombia, and Argentina, this does not seem to be the case for Mexico.

On the other hand, the aggregate data on labour productivity growth rate and output per person employed in Mexico reveal the need to reduce the asymmetries within and between different industries. In this sense, the scale-up of economic efficiency and technological development still requires learning by interaction and learning-by-doing so that the absorption of externally acquired knowledge and skills paves the way for innovation capabilities (Figueiredo, Cabral, and Silva, 2021).

Even for developing countries in a catching-up process, learning became more complex, demanding what Nooteboom (2000) calls 'interactive learning'. This type of learning implies interacting with other firms and research organizations, business associations, and other types of actors. Interactive learning means a socially-embedded process that must consider the institutional and cultural context (Lundvall, 2010). In this sense, as most of Mexico's production and technological development takes place in the industrial clusters, there is more room for collective and interactive learning. However, albeit important, geographical proximity is not a sufficient condition for creating institutions providing incentives for actors to interact with each other in a culture of cooperation and mutual trust. Social cohesion and trust, enabling knowledge flows, depend on institutions.

As foreign patterns arrived at the different regions, there was a process of supplier development where foreign firms pushed for suppliers' development in the auto, electronics, medical devices, and chemical-pharmaceutical products. As an ecosystem of innovation developed, public investment was allocated to build infrastructure, upgrade education, and promote research institutions through funds of the *Consejo Nacional de Ciencia y Tecnología* (CONACYT). Mexican clusters reveal that FDI is conducive to innovation measured by patents, utility models, and industrial designs. As evidence shows in Figure 15.1, regions with higher FDI also have more innovative indicators.

For upgrading and leapfrogging, firms cannot rely solely on increasing efficiency featuring the phase of implementation capabilities (Lee et al., 2019). There is also a need to explore knowledge (March, 1991). Exploration includes elements such as search, variation, risk-taking, experimentation, play, flexibility, discovery, and innovation. The author adds that returns from exploration are systematically less certain, more remote in time, and organizationally more distant from the locus of action and adaption. From this perspective, one can say that knowledge exploration requires interactive learning as a collective, diverse, and socially embedded enterprise.

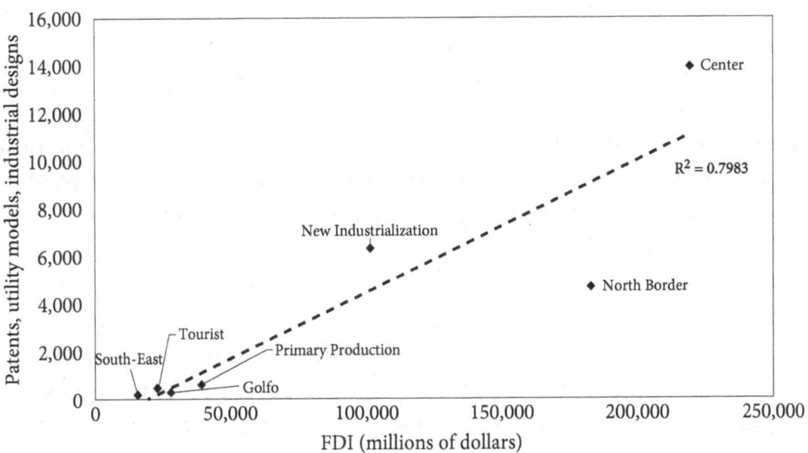

Figure 15.1. Foreign direct investment and emergence of knowledge regions.
Source: Authors' elaboration based on World Bank Database and IMPI (2022).

To build innovation capabilities and knowledge exploration tools for latecomers, it is necessary to establish independent R&D efforts, as latecomer firms struggle to acquire technology licences from well-established foreign firms when it comes to entering a highly profitable or value-added-oriented market, which is usually dominated by more advanced countries; thus R&D may allow latecomers to develop technological capabilities and find ways to absorb advanced technologies.

However, for such a process to occur, it is necessary to transition from the continuous production of low-end goods to high-end goods that allow higher wages and other advantages; otherwise the firm will be stuck in the middle-income trap (Lee, 2020). It is worth remembering that catching-up has an evolutionary nature and does not stick to a continuous imitation of the forerunners. However, it demands building capabilities to create different products and technologies. It implies opening new trajectories, as in the leapfrogging process, which takes advantage of emerging technologies driven by 'windows of opportunity' (Malerba and Lee, 2021).

As a dynamic evolutionary process, catch-up requires building capabilities to take advantage of the windows of opportunity which stem from heterogeneous actors with different rationales. Moreover, such capabilities must deal with different responses and strategies by firms and countries (Malerba and Lee, 2021).

The complexity arising from the need to coordinate heterogeneous actors with different rationales and, sometimes, conflicting interests is inevitable. Moreover, this complexity calls for a political economy approach from capabilities because there is room for public policy, a vocational system, a financial system, knowledge infrastructure, and relations among domestic and foreign actors to address coordination and capabilities failures (Malerba and Lee, 2021). Moreover, various responses and strategies provide causal complexity (Ragin, 2014), where more than one combination of causal conditions leads to catching-up or leapfrogging. One example is Mexican firms involved in the manufacturing of components for electric cars, as well as the cooperation initiatives from multinational enterprise (MNE) subsidiaries with local Mexican universities and institutes in applied research to electric cars. In many aspects, this process means stage-skipping, not a path-following strategy.

The standards and technologies for electric vehicles are still emerging. So, there is more room for a short cycle time of technology (CTT) than in established industries. As Lee et al. (2021) put it, shorter CTTs have rapid obsolescence of knowledge, demanding local knowledge production, and less reliance on patents owned by foreign MNEs. The authors bring evidence that countries with rapid economic catch-up that specialized in short CTT sectors increased their levels of knowledge localization and diversification.

15.3. The Roots of Technological Development: Manufacturing and Learning

The roots of Mexico's transformation into a learning economy trace back to the renewal process brought in by the creation of knowledge institutions at the end of the revolutionary process in the early twentieth century. In its third article, the new Constitution acknowledged the right to education of all citizens, supporting a national system of public education with one national university and a system of universities in each of the thirty-two federal states. As a result, Mexico founded a subsystem of technical institutes; the largest is the National Polytechnic Institute and 254 local technological institutes, and 882 private universities. In addition, Mexico introduced in the 1970s a dual education system at the undergraduate level to promote technical secondary schools. As a result, students could continue their path to higher education or go directly to work upon graduation; today, there are 21,414 technical secondary schools.[2] Under this knowledge framework, Mexico began its renewed trajectory of industrialization in the 1930s, which has been called the 'import substitution process' and continued for 50 years.

Traditional industries renewed their technology, such as food processing, textiles, basic metal, steel, and petrochemical, all supported by trained professionals who earned bachelor's degrees from universities and technical schools. The government also pushed for a renewed innovation process in the health system. In this sense, President Lazaro Cardenas promoted universal vaccination, reduced child deaths, and promoted national vaccine development and production. In addition, the health system spurred research in the private sector to develop medical drugs, as Syntex company did. To perform these synthetic transformations, Syntex conducted chemical research between 1932 and 1942, using the 'barbasco,' endemic species of Mexico, as vegetal raw material.

State-owned enterprises, such as Pemex, created the Instituto Mexicano del Petroleo (IMP) in the 1960s. Research on oil products promoted a petrochemical industry. Likewise, Comision Federal de Electricidad (CFE), in charge of electricity generation, pushed for research on nuclear energy and developed the first nuclear plant in Laguna Verde, Veracruz, in 1990.

Engineering research helped to develop infrastructure in the twentieth century. Created in the 1940s, the National Autonomous University of Mexico's Institute of Engineering developed research in a wide range of areas: geotechnical, environmental engineering, system engineering, mechanics and energy,

[2] SEP, Sistema de Educación Dual, Impulso a la Educación Dual en la Educación Media Superior, Abril 2022.

computing systems, structure and materials, electricity and computing, hydraulics, industrial processing, and seismological engineering.

15.3.1. Early Initiatives to Promote Industrial Parks

In the 1940s, the impetus for economic and industrial development in Mexico supported the creation of industrial parks; operations began in Central Mexico, with the industrial zone of Vallejo, in Mexico City (1944) and Ciudad Sahagun (1951) in Hidalgo, followed by Querétaro. The concept of industrial parks implied that the concentration of industries could bring economies of scale and help develop research activities. Later in 1964, the first large export *maquiladora* industry was created, with facilities and logistics similar to the industrial parks that already existed in the United States, to counteract the unemployment that arose after the cancellation of the Bracero Program with the neighbouring country.

There was a simultaneous process on the border with the National Border Program (PRONAF) that stimulated regional economies by creating the first industrial park in Ciudad Juárez, Chihuahua. It also included in its plan the emergence of more industrial parks with the support of public resources from Nacional Financiera (NAFINSA). In 1986, the Mexican Association of Industrial Parks (AMPIP) was born after 40 years of non-organized industrial parks development. Its main objective was to regulate and promote best practices in infrastructure, logistics, sustainability, and social responsibility. The industrial park concept stemmed from the Italian industrial districts, where agglomeration increased communication and dialogues, leading to best practices exchange and helping develop new technologies.

Today there are more than 512 industrial parks distributed throughout the Mexican Republic. During the ISI period (1930–1980), industrial parks allowed the emergence of national technologies in electro domestic (Mabe), steel (Altos Hornos de Mexico, TAMSA), and shipbuilding (Astilleros Unidos and Fundiciones Rice). However, they were unable to set a path for massive innovation. As a result, in 1964, a parallel process was set up on the border with the United States (PRONAF) to take advantage of low-wage production through the *maquila* industry.

15.4. From Import Substitution to Export-Led Growth through FDI Learning Clusters

The financial crisis of the 1980s led to a change in the industrialization paradigm. Unlike other industrialized countries in Latin America, Mexico replaced traditional import substitution with export-led industrialization based on the low-wage paradigm. The first wave took place in the northern border states of Baja California, Sonora, Chihuahua, Coahuila, Nuevo León, and Tamaulipas.

As Carrillo and De Los Santos (2020) pointed out, the trajectory of Nuevo León is a successful case of industrial upgrading. It moved from heavy industry based on raw materials to medium-technology goods (machinery and equipment, auto parts, and household appliances) to high-technology industries in biotechnology and nanotechnology. Nuevo León has a dense fabric of institutions and organizations at the local level, such as the Innovation and Technology Transfer Institute (I2T2) and the Research and Technological Innovation Park (PIIT), with more than 50 public and private research centres and relevant university institutes (Carrillo and De Los Santos, 2020).

The second stage of industrial development reached the central northern states, Jalisco, Aguascalientes, Guanajuato, Querétaro, and San Luis Potosí. Central states, the stronghold of ISI, also adopted the *maquila* model: Mexico City, state of Mexico, Puebla, Morelos, and Tlaxcala. However, the rest of the country kept its specialization in non-manufacturing low-added-value activities. In this second stage, Querétaro stands out as a learning cluster. This cluster combined the promotion of new investment with the development of human resources with a high concentration of scientists and technicians and a knowledge infrastructure with different types of technological parks (automotive, biotechnology, and a promising centre for research and certification of composite materials for the aerospace industry) (Carrillo and De Los Santos, 2020). Querétaro also houses the leading Mexican firm in household appliances with Mabe headquarters and its R&D centre.

The enactment of NAFTA in 1994 reinforced export-led growth, which led to further specialization of the regions. As a result, export-led specialization evolved into a complex process of transforming regions into knowledge clusters, led by the development of electronics, auto, and medical devices, providing diversity in the Mexican manufacturing landscape. According to the Technology Achievement Index (TAI) (Desai et al., 2002), Mexico had an enormous increase in the diffusion of the newest technologies, measured by internet hosts and the share of medium- and high-technology exports between 2000 and 2018, from 0.05 to 0.50.

However, the country did not perform so successfully in the other two indicators composing the TAI: the creation of technology (patents by residents at their national offices and receipts of royalty and licence fees) and human skills (based on years of schooling and tertiary science enrolment). Technology indicators stood at 0.03 between 2000 and 2018, and human skills barely changed from 0.34 to 0.36 in the same period.[3]

15.4.1. Learning Clusters

As NAFTA was enacted, there was a flow of investment from the United States and Canada to reinforce the already existing capacities in Mexico. Therefore, the strategy demanded the development of vital industries and their supply chains (foreign and local). It took place pari passu with the development of universities and technical schools, providing engineers and trained workers for operations, and the development of a research network that could support scaling-up the operations in Mexican plants. Central Mexico was, up to then, the main area of manufacturing production and the most extensive research network. However, under the decision to increase the linkages with United States and Canada, new clusters needed to become self-sustainable knowledge clusters with the capacity to innovate and deliver high-quality goods abroad.

The asymmetries in the knowledge bases from firms and other types of organizations in latecomers entail forming embryonic core capabilities to combine simple knowledge bases in different organizations. As part of a transition process, this former stage is a precondition to building complex knowledge repositories, which demand the coordination of different learning processes simultaneously (Dutrénit, 2004). The clusters facilitate firms' engagement, whether large or medium-sized, in deliberate efforts to use and manage the various learning mechanisms akin to external organizations such as buyers, producers, suppliers, research institutes, and consulting firms (Bell and Figueiredo, 2012). Following this path, agglomerations in Mexico have been able to develop linkages among the different sizes of businesses and to support research promoting patent registration by nationals. In what follows, the characteristics of the various key clusters that have emerged are identified.

15.4.1.1. The Bajio Cluster

Bajio is a geographical, historical, economic, and cultural region that comprises part of the states of Aguascalientes, Jalisco, Guanajuato, Querétaro, and San Luis Potosí. Within this region, the industries that have shaped the clusters have been a combination of electronics, software, digital creative industries, auto, and aeronautics, all interacting within the supply chain. The cluster has 1,598 businesses, 831 in the auto industry, 372 in electronics, 371 in medical devices, and 24 in

[3] Available at https://zenodo.org/record/3955182#.YnCTANPMKUk (accessed 2 May 2022).

aeronautics. As a result, the region's exports in 2021 reached US$89.99 billion, mainly accounted for by the auto industry and electronics exports. Employment reached 280,536 persons, with 56% in the auto industry and 39% in electronics (INEGI, 2018).

The region, taking advantage of the existing knowledge capacities, decided to engage in new research activities through the creation of centres in different areas of knowledge, such as the Western Biomedical Research Center (C.I.B.O.) and CINVESTAV Guadalajara on research in computer science, automatic control, electronic design, electrical power systems, and telecommunications.

The knowledge infrastructure also included the C.I.A.T.E.J. Center for Research and Assistance in Technology and Design of the state of Jalisco in Guanajuato, the Center of Optics Research in optics and photonics in Querétaro, the C.I.A.T.E.Q., the A. C. Centro de Tecnología Avanzada, the Centro de Ingeniería y Desarrollo Industrial, and the Mabe innovation centre with projects in energy efficiency and technology development in connected products, through schemes such as the internet of things. In addition, research contributed to developing electronics manufacturing services (EMS) in Jalisco, Guadalajara. Both host 12 original equipment manufacturers (OEM) and more than 380 specialized suppliers like Plexus, I.M.I., I.K.O.R., Flex Ltd., V-TEK, InterLatin, Sanmina, QSS, J.A.B.I.L., Molex, O.M.P. Mechtron, and Talos.

Bajio houses one of the largest auto industry clusters in the country, with facilities in El Salto, Jalisco: Honda; Aguascalientes: Nissan I and II, Mercedes Benz, Infinity; Guanajuato: GM, Volkswagen (VW), Mazda, Honda, Toyota; San Luis Potosí: GM and BMW; and in Querétaro, which has become a manufacturer of critical components such as wire harnesses manufactured in San Juan del Rio, Querétaro; VW has developed a motor plant in Silao, Guanajuato, where they have invested US$7.1 billion for the production of electric motors for their vehicles factories in Puebla, one in Puebla City and the Audi plant in San José Chiapa, and to export to the plant in Chattanooga, Tennessee.

Querétaro has one of the most significant aero clusters in the country, made up of 85 companies and organizations: 24 companies, TR1, TR2, and TR3; 8 specialized process companies; 4 OEM; 5 MRO (maintenance, repair, and operations); 12 research and design centres; 19 specialized services companies; 6 companies providing raw materials, and 7 academic institutions (Internacional Metalmecanica, 2018). Bombardier and Safran are the largest companies in the cluster. To encourage the development of the cluster, the local government supported the development of the Universidad Nacional Aeronautica de Querétaro.

The lack of compliance with international certification in the aeronautics industry is a significant shortcoming in developing the Bombardier supply chain with Mexican SMEs (Carrillo and De Los Santos, 2020). Meeting these compliances constitutes an opportunity to build domestic organizational and technological capabilities in Mexican firms.

Querétaro has also become the house of the domestic electronics network. The main plant was Mabe, which in 1986 entered a critical joint venture with General Electric (GE) to produce appliances for the US market. GE entered the joint venture with a 48% minority stake to move away from controlling Mexican operations. As a result, while GE gained access to Mexico's low-cost labour pool, Mabe had greater access to the world's largest consumer market through GE's US distribution network. Thus, two-thirds of all gas stoves and refrigerators imported into the United States are designed and manufactured by Mabe.

Mabe produces 95% of gas stoves and refrigerators sold under the General Electric brand in the San Luis Potosí plant, the world's largest kitchen plant. As the company grew, exports and production remained concentrated in Latin America. As a result, Mabe dominates the market in Mexico, while it commands a 70% market share in home appliances in Latin America. The group also joined several joint ventures and alliances with other regional manufacturers. NAFTA reinforced the Central Mexico home appliance network, with investments from Asian companies, in Querétaro with Daewoo and Samsung, in Guanajuato with Whirlpool, and in the San Luis area with Onnera Solutions. Besides home appliances, the area houses electronic components for the auto and aeronautic industries.

15.4.1.2. The Baja California Cluster

Baja California has been intertwined with the United States since the nineteenth century, when it became a centre for Chinese migration after the California railway construction ended. Due to its location at the frontier, multiple cities have flourished. Tijuana, Tecate, and Mexicali became industrial poles when the Mexican government initiated the Border Industrialization Program in 1965 as a response to the demise of the 'Bracero Program' by the US government in 1964. The state government decided to support the project with the creation of higher education institutions; the backbone of the project was the Universidad Autonoma de Baja California. This university developed areas of scientific research in engineering. It formed more than 1,422 engineering graduates up to 2022 and had 25 registered patents (IMPI, 2022).

The campuses in nearby cities (Mexicali, Ensenada, and Tecate) allowed the development of a regional research network supported by the creation of other higher education institutions in the area, including Instituto Tecnologico de Tijuana, el Colegio de la Frontera Norte, Universidad Iberoamericana, and CETYS, among others. In addition, they have developed research linkages with universities in California, mainly with the University of California in San Diego. Thanks to these efforts, the Baja cluster has registered 231 patents from 1999 to

2020, 64 of them from national firms. Additionally, the location and well-trained workforce attracted foreign investment in the area from 1999 to 2020. FDI poured US$19.6 billion into manufacturing activities in the region, increasing its export capacity to US$48 billion in 2021.

Success in operational practices has pushed Baja to maintain a high volume of the export manufacturing base in Mexico. As a result, the region has become a manufacturing powerhouse for many industries; these include medical devices, electronics, aerospace, automotive, and semiconductors. The main areas developed have been:

(a) *Medical devices*: This cluster of manufacturing industry is 30 years old and maintains an established local supply-chain network, making this city the most prominent medical device manufacturing hub in the country. Some of the most recognizable medical device firms include Welch Allyn, BD Beckton Dickinson (US), Cardinal Health (US), Carl Zeiss (Germany), Flex (US), Essilor (France), Fisher & Paykel (New Zealand), Integer (US), H3 Tijuana (US), Haemonetics (US), Medtronic (US), Ossur (Iceland), Outset Medical (US), Demant (Denmark), Stryker (US), Thermofisher (US), and Enovis, previously DJ Orthopedic (US). With some of these companies calling Tijuana home, the industry has named the northern Mexican city a 'Medical Device Cluster,' with 91% of the medical device industry's FDI coming from the United States (Co-Production International, 2016). The Medical Device Cluster supplies inputs such as medical, orthopaedic, and disposable equipment; the main Mexican supplier has been Laboratorios Baja Med.

(b) *The Tijuana electronics manufacturing cluster*: This produces a wide range of goods, spanning appliances, electrical components, media equipment, and semiconductors. In addition, Tijuana became a world leader in producing plasma, HDTV, and LCD television sets. Television manufacturing in Tijuana became a significant industrial activity during the 1980s, when, over that decade, production reached 30 million units each year. Although Tijuana lost ground to China for a time, in the past several years, the capital of the state of Baja, California, has regained its position as the world leader in manufacturing this product.

Among the developments that have resulted in the resurgence of television manufacturing in Tijuana was the opening of a Center for Digital Research and Technological Development in 2013 by Korean electronics giant Samsung. The purpose of creating the Center was to develop technologies aimed explicitly at serving Latin American markets. Samsung chose the city because television manufacturing in Tijuana had a long track record of success for more than 25 years as a driver of the border city's electronics sector and a significant employer of its manufacturing workforce (Tecma, 2015).

(c) *The Tijuana aerospace cluster*: Tijuana has developed an ecosystem of supply-chain and second-tier-level companies in aerospace over the past 40 years. More than 45 aerospace and defence companies have chosen Tijuana as a home (Tijuana EDC, n.d). Production focuses on electronic components, emergency and security communications, connectivity and wiring devices, product controls, industrial controls, drives, automation, and sensors. Due to the quality achieved by one plant, it was able to gain authorization by the Pentagon to produce switches for helicopters of the US Navy.

(d) *The Tijuana automotive cluster*: This is also a manufacturing powerhouse, specializing in truck chassis, stamped metal parts, seat belts, sound speakers, carbon fibre body kits, and electronic sensors. The automotive companies include Hyundai, Toyota, and Goodridge. Toyota produces the Tacoma pickup, and Hyundai–Kia produces trailer boxes and containers.

15.4.1.3. North-West Cluster: Sonora-Chihuahua

From 1999 to 2021, FDI worth US$32.5 billion poured into Sonora and Chihuahua, aimed at manufacturing activities. Manufacturing exports from this cluster reached US$79.3 billion dollars in 2021. Also, innovation in both states developed, with 164 patents registered between 1999 and 2020. Hermosillo, Nogales, Chihuahua, and Ciudad Juárez have become important cities in developing GVCs in North-West Mexico. The GVCs interact through various channels. One key sector where this takes place is the auto industry. Here, the Ford facilities in Hermosillo and Chihuahua interact—the first has a stamping and assembly plant, and the second has a motor plant. However, they are independent under the Ford production system. Both interact with Ford plants in the United States, the Hermosillo plant produces the Fusion hybrid model, and the Chihuahua plant manufactures gasoline and diesel motors. Although production was on the rise between 2010 and 2015, reaching 515,395 units, since then, there has been a continuous decrease, and in 2019 production reached only 249,605 units, a decrease of more than 50%, weakening the North-West cluster.

Nogales has become a key exchange hub between Arizona and Sonora, Mexico. Nogales, Arizona, is a service centre enabling businesses to quickly understand and navigate the various laws, regulations, and agreements governing cross-border trade. Nogales, Arizona, is also a logistics, warehousing, and service hub for manufacturing operations in Nogales, Sonora, known as *maquilas*.

While manufacturing may occur in Mexico, these operations have warehousing and distribution operations on the Arizona side of the border, first for receiving components and sub-assemblies to move into Sonora, and later for cross-docking and warehousing operations. This involves the transport of goods to parent companies or distribution sites. Many companies use third parties and customs brokers to manage logistics, while others operate their warehouses. *Maquilas* account for the direct regional economic impact of manufacturing. Truck crossings attributable to *maquilas* are about 500–600 northbound daily and 200–300 southbound daily. On a typical day in Nogales, Arizona, and Nogales, Mexico, chassis, motherboards, and mining equipment move south while manufactured products, including vehicles, move north.

The monetary impact of the *maquilas* for Nogales, Arizona, when considering direct and secondary activity, affects more than 1,100 jobs and generates $206.8 million. Nogales, Arizona, is highly integrated with Nogales, Sonora; nearly 35% of the *maquilas* in the southern city are owned and operated by out-of-Arizona parent companies, while 20% have a parent company in Nogales or Santa Cruz County (Sun Corridor Inc., 2022). Electronics has revamped; the West part of Mexico specializes in manufacturing aerospace, hi-tech, Information Technology (IT), and electronic sub-assembly parts; exports reached US$19,788 million in 2018; two-thirds came from Chihuahua, mainly from plants in Ciudad Juárez.

The Institute for Policy and Economic Development at the University of Texas at El Paso 'examined customer-supplier linkages between Cd. Juárez manufacturing operations and El Paso industry' (Tecma, 2013). The study considers the top manufacturing clusters in Juárez, Mexico, as follows: automotive industry, semiconductor electric parts, electrical equipment, medical equipment, communications equipment, printing ink, navigational, measuring, electromedical, and control instruments, audio and video equipment, plastics products, and household appliances. These clusters will continue growing due to the rising costs for manufacturers in United States and China, making Mexican clusters an attractive venue for nearshoring.

15.4.1.4. Northeast Cluster: Monterrey–Coahuila

Monterrey was one of the traditional manufacturing centres of Mexico; what the GVC era brought to the region was the consolidation of a joint cluster with Saltillo, the capital city of Coahuila. As a result, the region's exports reached in US$95 billion in 2021, half of which came from the auto industry and one-fifth from electronics.

The World Economic Forum recognized the effort to build strong capabilities to develop GVCs:

> The dynamism, productivity, location, talent base, and industrial diversity of Monterrey have attracted more than 2,200 foreign companies in the sectors of appliances, automotive, information technologies, aerospace, electric electronic, metal manufacturing, among others, making Monterrey an active

> player in the G.V.C.s of these sectors. Universities in Monterrey provide a solid soft connectivity platform, including the Tecnologico de Monterrey, the Universidad Autonoma de Nuevo Leon, and the Universidad de Monterrey. The average schooling in Monterrey is 11 years, 2.4 years above the national mean; 18% of the city's population has finished either a bachelor's or graduate degree. Nuevo Leon is the state with the second-highest number of students enrolled in master's and Ph.D. programs. (World Economic Forum, 2016, p. 12)

There were substantial efforts to support Monterrey's potential as an economic epicenter in the new knowledge economy and the G.V.C.s competitive arena.

In 2004, the Monterrey International City of Knowledge initiative was launched and aimed to promote technological development, position the education sector internationally, develop the necessary urban infrastructure, and reinforce the competitiveness of the public and private sectors. An Innovation and Technology Transfer Institute and the Technological Innovation Park, founded in 2009, is home to 34 public, private and academic research and development centers, 3,000 highly skilled jobs, two high-impact incubators, and a total investment of over $600 million. In addition, the technological parks initiative enabled the emergence of twelve strategic economic clusters in nanotechnology, biotechnology, aerospace, medical services, energy, automotive, electrical appliances, information technologies and software, agribusiness, logistics, transportation, sustainable housing, and multimedia and creative industries.

Monterrey, well located near the US border, has solid capabilities that can serve the North American market, but it is necessary to understand that the 'city needs to productively engage in the knowledge-based economy and a new institutional framework that enables the participation of all sectors' (World Economic Forum, 2016, p. 12).

Saltillo is rife with manufacturing activity due to its location, highly educated workforce, affordable labour, and advanced infrastructure. According to CoahuilaMex, the state of Coahuila has produced more than 578,000 vehicles and 49,000 tractor-trailer trucks. Additionally, there are more than 22 industrial parks in the area. As far as Saltillo is concerned, the city's automotive manufacturing sector is one of Mexico's most prominent, often referred to as the 'Detroit of Mexico'. Ninety percent of the city's economic base comprises automotive industry firms, and it is a crucial centre for servicing the global automotive industry.

Some notable manufacturers in the city include the Chrysler Motors plant (876 workers) and the Chrysler Motors Ramos Arizpe plant (1,552 workers); Chrysler assembly plant (2,479 workers); Chrysler van assembly plant (891 workers); Chrysler die plant (250 workers); Daimler-Freightliner assembly plant (3,802 workers); and General Motors Ramos Arizpe complex (3,800 workers). The extensive area's manufacturing sector comprises of 18 industrial parks, five industrial complexes, and one manufacturing community, the La Angostura Manufacturing Community, owned and operated by The Offshore Group. With many manufacturers located in Saltillo, businesses have access to a strong network of suppliers and larger OEM producers.

15.4.2. Agglomerations as a Source of Knowledge

Export promotion and links to GVCs have promoted the emergence of new knowledge clusters in Mexico. As new foreign investment arrived in *maquila*-oriented areas, there was a push for new knowledge institutions to develop, which led to the emergence of a trained labour force and the construction of new institutions for research and development jointly with business-developed patents. As shown in Figure 15.2, the Central, Bajio, and North regions, intensive in manufacturing activities, have had a high number of patents granted in comparison to other regions within the country. Investment in training and research avoided that export industries remained trapped in the *maquila* paradigm. In particular, government support of education at the national and local level and training of new engineers allowed enhanced production linked to research hubs throughout the territory, developing a partnership for innovation. A new reality has emerged, linked to the new information and communication

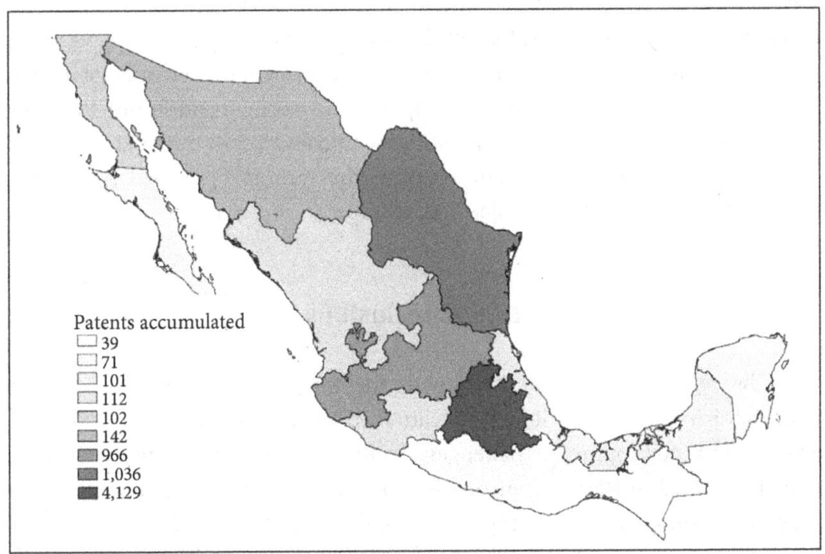

Figure 15.2. Patents granted, by Mexican region, 1993–2020.
Source: Authors' elaboration based on data recovered from IMPI (2022).

technology (ICT), allowing businesses to develop research networks in remote areas, strengthening GVCs.

15.5. The Missing Link: Scaling-up Productivity Growth and the Middle-Income Trap

Export-based manufacturing productivity growth did not exercise a multiplier effect on other sectors. While there were sharp investment coefficient increases in the automotive, electronic, pharmaceutical, and medical devices sectors, these have not spilled over to the rest of the economy. For instance, while in 2021 the investment coefficient (investment divided by output) for electrical devices stood at 78.7%, and for transport equipment at 67.7%, for primary activities the figure was just 3.2%. In fact, there is a considerable contrast between the investment coefficients in manufacturing (around 45%) and the overall economy (around 17%). Moreover, the aggregate capital accumulation rate is low, limiting aggregate productivity gains.

When production levels decouple from productivity, this contributes to the middle-income trap. Since the economy's structural transformation took place when Mexico reached its middle-income level, the continuing gains in productivity come from intra-sectoral technological growth or through moving up the value chain (Gill and Kharas, 2015). From 1991 to 2020, growth in output was, on average, 2.21%, while total factor productivity growth was 0.45%. Low productivity growth stems from insufficient domestic innovation capabilities, which is the outcome of the interactions between weak investment in non-manufacturing industries and public investment to spur innovation. In addition, the slow scaling-up of the technological capabilities within and across the clusters did not allow Mexico to overcome the 'enclave economy' technical progress. All this led the country to fall into the middle-income trap.

15.6. Conclusions

This chapter has concerned itself with the intricate dynamics of Mexican manufacturing and what light this can shed on the country's more general growth and development challenges. Examining specific industry types—notably regional clusters in transport equipment, machinery, equipment, chemistry, electronics, and computing—the chapter contests generalist claims about Mexican manufacturing. While liberalization and low wages were the main drivers forming and expanding *maquila* industrial clusters in Mexico, their path was not tied down by the need to maintain low comparative advantage cost. As

Dutrénit and Vera-Cruz (2007) suggest, while there were limits to the accumulation in the technical functions centred on products, the *maquilas* learned and accumulated the technical functions related to plant operation and expansion. Moreover, some *maquilas* evolved to attract global business, allowing them to accumulate further technical capabilities.

The evidence provided in this chapter also reveals a more nuanced picture of the state's role in public funding for technological development, R&D centres, and programmes across industrial clusters. The state's role in the federal budget for science and technology and the public research institutes targeting technology development becomes more explicitly apparent in the regional clusters than at the national level.

By joining NAFTA, Mexico substantially increased inward FDI. This went from US$3 billion in 1989 to US$14 billion in 1999. The bulk of this investment was directed at building and expanding geographically concentrated industrial plants. However, the evidence is ambiguous regarding the creation of technological capabilities. The chapter found evidence that, when embedded in the public knowledge infrastructure, FDI is a positive predictor for upgrading. Another outcome was the emergence of regional clusters, where local entrepreneurs managed to build capabilities to design local technology.

Albeit well established, Mexican manufacturing is essentially engaged in technological diffusion, and shares quite well in the exports of high- and medium-tech products. However, the sector is moving slowly, and even stagnating, in technological creation. This is challenging, considering that upgrading requires intensive knowledge and technological upgrading, and minor incremental innovation does not meet this transition. In contrast to other industrialized countries in Latin America, Mexico was fortuitous in maintaining its industrial structure. While Brazil and Argentina deindustrialized in the liberalization waves of the 1990s, Mexico took advantage of liberalization to maintain and expand its implementation capabilities. However, Mexican manufacturing is associated with marked heterogeneity in terms of performance. For example, productivity levels for the Monterrey–Saltillo and Bajío clusters are three times higher than in Sonora and Baja. There is a large variance in patents, utility models, and industrial designs between clusters with the same or similar types of industry.

Despite its industrial achievements, Mexico needs to make a new transition in order to exit the middle-income trap. Unlike the previous transition to export-led manufacturing, this fresh transition is far more demanding from business and political actors. It will require systematic attempts to address large swathes of the economy where productivity and innovation remain at stubbornly low levels. New capabilities will need to be created, new sources of demand will need to be tapped, and the growth potential of sectors besides manufacturing will have to be contemplated.

References

Alfranca, O. 2015. 'Intellectual Property Rights', in F. Wherry and J. Schor, eds., *The Sage Encyclopedia of Economics and Society*. London: Sage, 757–761.

Beckert, J. 2016. *Imagined Futures: Fictional Expectations and Capitalist Dynamics*. Cambridge, MA: Harvard University Press.

Bell, M., and Figueiredo, P. N. 2012. 'Innovation Capability Building and Learning Mechanisms in Latecomer Firms: Recent Empirical Contributions and Implications for Research', *Canadian Journal of Development Studies*, 33(1), 14–40.

Carrillo, J., and De Los Santos, S. 2020. "Industrial Hubs, Industrial Policy and Economic Development in Mexico', in A. Oqubay and J. Y. Lin, eds., *The Oxford Handbook of Industrial Hubs and Economic Development*. Oxford: Oxford University Press, 836–854.

Cuervo-Cazurra, A., and Rui, H. 2017. 'Barriers to Absorptive Capacity in Emerging Market Firms', *Journal of World Business*, 52(6), 727–742. https://doi.org/10.1016/j.jwb.2017.06.004

Desai, M., Fukuda-Parr, S., Johansson, C., and Sagasti, F. 2002. 'Measuring the Technology Achievement of Nations and the Capacity to Participate in the Network Age', *Journal of Human Development*, 3(1), 95–122.

Dutrénit, G. 2004. 'Building Technological Capabilities in Latecomer Firms: A Review Essay', *Science Technology and Society*, 9, 209, 209–241.

Dutrénit, G., and Vera-Cruz, A. O. 2007. 'Triggers of the Technological Capability Accumulation in MNCs' Subsidiaries: The *Maquilas* in Mexico', *International Journal of Technology and Globalisation*, 3(2–3), 315–336.

Fagerberg, J. 1987. 'A Technology Gap Approach to Why Growth Rates Differ', *Working Papers Archives* 1987002, Centre for Technology, Innovation and Culture, University of Oslo.

Figueiredo, P. N., Cabral, B. P., and Silva, F. Q. 2021. 'Intricacies of Firm-Level Innovation Performance: An Empirical Analysis of Latecomer Process Industries', *Technovation*, 105, 1–21.

Gill, I. S., and Kharas, H. 2015. 'The Middle-Income Trap Turns Ten', *Policy Research Working Paper* 7403, World Bank Group.

Growth Lab at Harvard University. 2022. *Atlas of Economic Complexity*. Cambridge, MA: Harvard University. http://www.atlas.cid.harvard.edu.

Instituto Nacional de Estadística y Geografía, INEGI. 2018. *Economic Census 2019*. https://en.www.inegi.org.mx/programas/ce/2019/.

Lall, S. 1992. 'Technological Capabilities and Industrialization', *World Development*, 20(2), 165–186. https://doi.org/10.1016/0305-750X(92)90097-F

Lee, J. D., Baek, C., Maliphol, S., and Yeon, J. I. 2019. 'Middle innovation trap', *Foresight and STI Governance*, 13(1), 6–18. https://dx.doi.org/10.17323/2500-2597.2019.1.6.18.

Lee, K. 2000. 'The Dynamics of Technological Learning in Industrialization', *International Social Science Journal*, 53(7), 297–308. doi:10.1111/1468-2451.00316

Lee, K. 2020. 'Innovation and the Three Detours for Economic Growth beyond the Middle-Income Stage', in J. Alonso and J. Ocampo, eds., *Trapped in the Middle-Developmental Challenges for Middle Income Countries*. Oxford: Oxford University Press, 48–68. 10.1093/oso/9780198852773.003.0003.

Lee, K., Lee, J., and Lee, J. 2021. 'Variety of National Innovation Systems (NIS) and Alternative Pathways to Growth beyond the Middle-Income Stage: Balanced, Imbalanced, Catching-up, and Trapped NIS', *World Development*, 144, 1–20. https://doi.org/10.1016/j.worlddev.2021.105472

Malerba, F., and Lee, K. 2021. 'An Evolutionary Perspective on Economic Catch-up by Latecomers', *Industrial and Corporate Change*, 30(4), 986–1010. https://doi.org/10.1093/icc/dtab008

March, J. G. 1991. 'Exploration and Exploitation in Organizational Learning', *Organization Science*, 2(1), 71–87. https://doi.org/10.1287/orsc.2.1.71.

Nooteboom, B. 2000. *Learning and Innovation in Organizations and Economies*. Oxford: Oxford University Press.

OECD. 2022. 'Origin of Value Added in Gross Exports', *OECD Statistics on Trade in Value Added* (database), https://doi.org/10.1787/data-00826-en (accessed 5 June 2022).

Paus, E. 2017. *Escaping the Middle-Income*. Manila: Asian Development Bank Institute.

Paus, E. 2020. 'Innovation Strategies Matter: Latin America's Middle Income Trap meets China and Globalization', *The Journal of Development Studies*, 56(4), 657–679, https://doi.org/10.1080/00220388.2019.1595600

Pietrobelli, C., and Rabellotti, R. 2006. *Upgrading to Compete: Global Value Chains, Clusters and SMEs in Latin America*. Washington, DC: Inter-American Development Bank.

Ragin, C. 2014. *The Comparative Method: Moving Beyond Qualitative and Quantitative Strategies*. Oakland: University of California Press.

Ruiz, C. In press. 'Cadenas de valor y surgimiento de ciudades interactivas', Facultad de Economía UNAM.

Song, Y., Gnyawali, D. R., Srivastava, M. K., and Asgari, E. 2018. 'In Search of Precision in Absorptive Capacity Research: A Synthesis of the Literature and Consolidation of Findings', *Journal of Management*, 44(6), 2343–2374.

Sun Corridor Inc. 2022. 'Community Overviews: Sonora', https://suncorridorinc.com/why-mexico/community-overviews/

Russel, A. 2013. 'Principal Clusters of Manufacturing in Ciudad Juárez, México', https://www.tecma.com/clusters-of-manufacturing-in-ciudad-juarez/.

Tecma. 2015. 'Television Manufacturing in Tijuana Is King', https://www.tecma.com/television-manufacturing-in-tijuana/.

Tecma. 2013. 'Principal Clusters of Manufacturing in Ciudad Juarez, Mexico', https://www.tecma.com/clusters-of-manufacturing-in-ciudad-juarez/.

Tijuana EDC. n.d. 'Manufacturing in Mexico', https://tijuanaedc.org/aerospace-manufacturing-in-mexico.

World Economic Forum. 2016. *Competitive Cities and Their Connections to Global Value Chains*. Davos, Switzerland: WEF.

16

Peru and the Search for a Development Model That Works

John Crabtree

16.1. Introduction

From the 1960s onwards, Peru had (belatedly) sought to emulate policies applied elsewhere in Latin America designed to promote domestic industrialization, to reduce dependence on the export of commodities, and to help diversify the structure of production. Though application of such policies waxed and waned, it was only in the 1990s—under the aegis of President Alberto Fujimori (1990–2000)—that Peru departed radically from this model, undergoing a 'neoliberal revolution'. The exhaustion of the import substitution model was in evidence well before the beginning of the 1990s, but it was the 'critical juncture' of the late 1980s that created the economic and political conditions that facilitated a radical change in policy direction.

In the wake of this, between 2003 and 2013, the Peruvian economy underwent an unusual period of expansion, both in terms of historical trends, and in relation to growth patterns elsewhere in Latin America.[1] The period became known as 'the Peruvian miracle'. Not only did output expand across economic sectors, but Peru's exports underwent a sudden surge. The increase in export demand went hand in hand with a rise in domestic demand, perhaps most visible in a construction boom. The period saw increasing real incomes and substantial reductions in rates of poverty. However, the structure of employment remained such that the country continued to have one of the region's largest percentages of the workforce in the informal sector.

The 'miracle' took place as the country benefited from the commodity super-cycle, with world prices for most of Peru's minerals enjoying unusually high market prices, a phenomenon closely connected with the emergence of China as its main market. The super-cycle coincided with a large increase in foreign

[1] Peru's growth spurt began in 2002 and reached its zenith in 2008 with an annual growth rate of 9.8%. The impact of the 2008 financial crisis led to a sudden drop (0.9%) in 2009, but recovery was rapid, averaging 6.7% between 2010 and 2013 (BCRP, 2016).

John Crabtree, *Peru and the Search for a Development Model That Works* In: *Innovation, Competitiveness, and Development in Latin America*. Edited by: Edmund Amann and Paulo N. Figueiredo, Oxford University Press.
 DOI: 10.1093/oso/9780197648070.003.0016

investment, most notably in the mining industry. This, in turn, was further stimulated by the process of liberalization and privatization that had taken place in the previous decade, and the introduction of legislation designed to make Peru a far more attractive destination for capital than it had been previously.

However, by 2014, the growth bonanza had come to an end and investment inflows had begun to taper off. The validity of the growth model imposed by Fujimori's autocratic regime, and followed by his more democratic successors, had increasingly become the subject of questioning and contestation. During the period of rapid growth, business confidence remained firm and key decision-making posts were securely in the hands of those most committed to the model. By the mid-2010s, and leading up to the election of Pedro Castillo as president in 2021, the limitations of the neoliberal model became increasingly evident. This occurred as the pattern of growth slowed, many failed to receive its benefits, and public confidence in the business class was sapped by corruption scandals.

These events reflect a long-standing reality: like many of its regional counterparts, Peru has been in constant search for a formula capable of delivering sustained and inclusive growth. By charting the recent history of economic management in Peru, this chapter aims to elucidate some of the unresolved problems bedevilling Peru's development model. In so doing, the discussion hints at fruitful ways in which the county may need to proceed if it is to overcome its growth and development impasse.

16.2. The Crisis of the Developmentalist State

Peru was a latecomer to the trend that began elsewhere in Latin America in the 1930s of state-led development and import substitutive industrialization (Thorp and Bertram, 1978). It was only in the 1960s that governments, particularly the military regime of General Juan Velasco Alvarado (1968–1975), sought to 'modernize' the country with a supposedly more autonomous state taking centre stage in providing the main motor of a strategy of social and economic transformation (Lowenthal, 1975). This strategy sought to reduce Peru's dependence on commodity exports and foreign investment and diversify production and ownership patterns (Fitzgerald, 1979). Of key importance was the nationalization of major export industries, a radical programme of agrarian reform, and the development of domestic industry in response to redistributive reforms stimulating local demand. State intervention and planning were at the heart of this transformative strategy.

The shortcomings and contradictions within this strategy soon became apparent, with the successor regime (led by General Francisco Morales Bermúdez, 1975–1980) reversing many of these reforms (McClintock and Lowenthal, 1983).

Liberalizing polices of structural adjustment were subsequently continued under the civilian government of Fernando Belaúnde (1980–1985), only to be reversed by Alan García in the late 1980s (1985–1990) (Crabtree, 1992).

The Velasco reforms thus failed to provide a solid financial base for the expansion of the state sector, relying excessively on foreign borrowing to make up the shortfall of private investment and the lack of an effective tax regime.[2] While Velasco antagonized the business elite, he failed to create an alternative political base, and his programme of industrial diversification failed to meet the expectations vested in it (Seminario, 2015). Well before the 1982 Mexican default triggered the debt crisis, and the adoption of liberalizing reforms elsewhere in Latin America, Peru ran into balance of payments problems in the mid-1970s. These hastened the resort to stabilization policies under the aegis of the International Monetary Fund (IMF).

However, the change of direction proved short-lived. While the Belaúnde administration started with a fanfare of reforms designed to reduce the role of the state, promote the private sector, and re-engage with the global economy, its reformist impulse ran into political and economic obstacles (Conaghan and Malloy, 1994). Faith in orthodox remedies waned as adjustment measures seemed to work in perverse ways, stimulating price inflation and reducing growth. Meanwhile the popularity of the Belaúnde government quickly dissipated as real incomes fell. Opposition swiftly built up to a government that failed to raise standards of living and curb the rise in poverty.[3] From 1982 onwards, policymaking became increasingly erratic as Peru sought, unsuccessfully, to stay within the macroeconomic parameters laid down by the IMF. The liberalizing agenda thus petered out, having largely failed to re-dimension the relationship between the private and public sectors, or to put the country firmly on to a path of export-led growth.

The return to more interventionist policies under García responded to frustration with orthodox remedies and growing voter disenchantment. With policies that harked back to *velasquismo*, García sought to revive the role of the state in pursuit of a development model that was at once socially redistributive and protectionist (Crabtree, 1992). Domestic demand became the main motor of growth, while Peru turned its back on debt servicing and export promotion. García believed that private industry would respond to increased domestic demand with investment, thus generating a virtuous cycle that government planners hoped would sustain development.[4]

[2] The foreign debt increased from US$737 million in 1968 to US$4.1 billion in 1976. The debt service ratio rose from 7% to 39%.

[3] Per capita incomes fell from the equivalent of US$1,232 in 1980 to US$1,055 in 1985.

[4] This was the basis of García's relationship with the so-called 12 apostles, the leaders of Peru's 12 largest business groups (Durand, 2003, Chapter 5).

However, the limitations of such a strategy soon became clear as fiscal pressures built up and balance of payments problems resurfaced. Politically, it ran into the buffers when, in 1987, García sought unsuccessfully to nationalize the country's commercial banks, provoking a major political backlash by the business elite.

The latter years of the García administration saw spiralling hyperinflation, engendered by and giving rise to a fiscal crisis of the state,[5] a crisis in which production and employment plummeted, and poverty rates surged. As the balance of payment crisis worsened, foreign reserves were exhausted, and having antagonized the IMF and international banks, Peru was unable to tap into foreign reserves. At the same time, the country experienced growing political conflict arising from the expansion of the Sendero Luminoso insurgency (Degregori, 2012), a phenomenon that intertwined with the fiscal crisis to place the very survival of the Peruvian state in jeopardy.

Neither state-led development nor more laissez-faire alternatives thus proved able to put Peru on an economically- or politically-viable development path. Peru in 1990 was poorer in terms of GDP per capita than it had been 30 years earlier, while policies to modernize the country, raise output, and provide adequate employment lay in tatters. This, therefore, was the critical juncture which enabled bold new policies to be introduced and gain traction. On taking office in 1990, Alberto Fujimori set about a liberalizing strategy which went far beyond the timid approaches of the Belaúnde period. In doing so, Peru took advantage of a situation in which anything seemed better than what had gone before.

The crisis of the developmentalist state (Wise, 2003) thus revealed the basic difficulties of this approach. It failed to provide a sustainable model by which state intervention would lead to the objectives formulated by the *velasquistas*. The return to a more liberal economic model after 1975 did little to remedy things, nor did the return to statism under García. Peru remained hobbled by an unpayable debt that limited policy options. Reliance on the private sector as the motor for growth proved unreliable. The quality of governance proved problematic, with inefficiencies and corruption afflicting the public sector (Quiroz, 2015, pp. 307–346). Governance was affected by over-centralization and the failure to embrace administrative reforms. Finally, it proved difficult to forge a unity of purpose in a highly unequal society between an economic elite, highly concentrated in Lima, and the rest of society whose living standards declined during these years.

[5] According to the Central Bank (BCRP, 1996), government tax income fell to 7% of GDP in 1989.

16.3. The Liberalizing 'Revolution'

The surprise election of a complete outsider, Alberto Fujimori, in the 1990 elections bore witness to the crisis of public confidence in Peru's political elite and its policy preferences. Though elected on a moderate, centre-left platform, Fujimori swiftly abandoned his initial stance in favour of a radical departure from interventionist policy. The economic correctives introduced in 1991 and 1992 were designed, with the support of the IMF, to stabilize the economy and to set the groundwork for a profound change in approach towards development. Peru underwent what was to be one of Latin America's most radical and rapid transformations; it began with the so-called Fujishock at the end of 1990, a classic stabilization package that swiftly gave way to a period of structural adjustment designed to deregulate the economy, reorient it towards export-led development, and shift the frontier between the private and public sectors through radical privatization of almost all public companies.[6]

Politically popular at the outset, the Fujimori administration resorted to ever more authoritarian modes of governance as it sought to deepen pro-business reforms and make those changes irreversible (Conaghan, 2005). Peru became a clear case in gainsaying the precept, highlighted by the Washington Consensus, that political and economic liberalism necessarily worked in tandem.

The initial stabilization package proved successful in reducing inflation rates, albeit at significant social cost. It provided a platform to reverse capital flight, prompt a recovery in investment, and encourage a return to growth. The reduction in inflation aided fiscal recovery and created a more stable basis for a turnaround in development strategy. During the 1990s, privatization led to the sale of some 150 public companies, yielding significant revenues to the state.[7] Policy sought to encourage trade and export-led growth, dismantling the protectionist legacies of the past. The legislation governing foreign investment was reformulated, not least in the key mining sector, where property restrictions were removed and special tax regimes introduced. Development of Peru's mining potential became a key objective in promoting growth. The government also sought to deregulate the domestic economy, reducing controls and barriers to private-sector activity, and liberalizing the financial sector (Arce, 2010).

As Table 16.1 shows, the macroeconomic effects of policy during these years led to the resumption of growth and the elimination of large fiscal

[6] For more detail as to policy and its effects in the 1990s, see Arce (2010), Wise (2003), and Gonzáles de Olarte (1998). The only major company to remain in state hands was Petroperú, the state petroleum company, but this ended up little more than a corporate shell, as private companies took over most of the production and distribution of hydrocarbons

[7] Revenues from privatization, mainly in the first half of the decade, totalled US$9.2 billion.

Table 16.1 Economic Indicators (1990–2000)

	1990	1991	1992	1993	1994	1995	1996	1997	1998	1999	2000
GDP growth (%)	−5.1	2.2	0.4	4.8	12.8	8.6	2.5	6.7	−0.6	1.6	3.5
GDP/cap (%)	−7.1	0.2	−2.3	2.9	10.8	6.7	0.7	5.1	−2.3	−0.7	1.4
Inflation (%)	7,649.60	139.2	56.7	39.5	15.4	10.2	11.8	6.5	6	3.7	3.7
Exports (% of GDP)	11.1	10	10.1	9.8	9.9	10.3	10.5	11.6	10.1	11.8	13
Exports (US$bn)	3.3	3.4	3.7	3.4	4.4	5.5	5.9	6.8	5.8	6.1	6.9
FDI (stock, % of GDP)	4.4	4	4.2	4.7	9.9	10.3	12	13.2	14.8	18.9	19.3
FDI (stock, US$bn)	1.3	1.4	1.5	1.6	4.4	5.5	6.7	7.8	8.4	9.8	10.3
Fiscal balance (% of GDP)	−8.7	−2.8	−3.9	−3.1	−2.8	−3.2	−1	0.2	−0.8	−3.2	−3.2
Net intern. reserves (US$bn)	0.5	1.3	2	2.7	5.7	6.6	8.5	10.2	9.1	8.4	8.2

Source: Central Bank Memorias (various years).

deficits. Export levels increased substantially in dollar terms, as well as in relation to GDP, as did (in the later 1990s) inflows of foreign direct investment. Production in the mining sector benefited from new investments and tax incentives (Abugattás, 1998). Notwithstanding the short-term effects of stabilization on incomes and employment, social conditions began slowly to improve, although high levels of poverty and inequality persisted. GDP per capita increased substantially in the mid-1990s. The hyperinflation that afflicted Peru at the end of the 1980s was brought under control, even though inflationary pressures remained until the middle of the decade. Poverty rates, which increased massively as a result of the economic dislocation of the late 1980s, declined over the 1990s, but not as much as in the subsequent decade.

Fujimori's privatization programme involved the return of all formerly state-owned mining companies to the private sector. New investment led to increased output, which advanced (albeit erratically) as the decade progressed. The most significant new investment was that of Yanacocha (co-owned by US-owned Newmont Mining), with gold production increasing fivefold over the decade. The impact on copper production was somewhat slower but nevertheless marked. Overall, mineral exports more than doubled over the decade. GDP in the mining sector, which had stagnated for much of the previous 20 years, more than doubled in the 1990s (Seminario, 2015, p. 1067).

The reforms thus brought a major change to the relationship between the state and the private sector. Businessmen were brought in to manage key areas of the state, especially in the all-important Ministry of Economy and Finance. As I have argued elsewhere (Crabtree and Durand, 2017), this prompted the effective 'capture' of the state by business elites. Recruitment into the public sector privileged business, with private consultancies and lobby groups, and gave rise to what came to be termed the 'revolving door' syndrome. The main business confederation, Confiep, became a highly influential actor in influencing policy decisions. The minister of economy and finance throughout much of the Fujimori period, from 1993 through to 1997, was Jorge Camet, a successful business entrepreneur from the construction industry who maintained the closest ties to Confiep. Policies of privatization added greatly to the opportunities open to the private sector.[8]

The Fujimori period also signified a marked improvement in relations with Peru's foreign creditors, and, in particular, with the Washington-based multilateral banks that had played a significant role in the design and adoption of liberalizing economic reforms. Indeed, it was the World Bank which, in 1990, persuaded Fujimori that the only viable way out of Peru's

[8] The impact of neoliberalism on business power is analysed in Durand (2005).

macroeconomic difficulties was the adoption of a radical liberalization of the economy.

Politically the first decade of the new millennium saw a return to more democratic, less authoritarian modes of governance. Still, even with Fujimori's fall in 2000, the economic model employed did not change substantially. The governments of Alejandro Toledo (2001–2006) and the return of Alan García to the presidency (2006–2011) reaffirmed Peru's commitment to pro-business policies based on adherence to the neoliberal agenda. Unlike other countries in Latin America, Peru saw no 'pink tide' or reversion to more state-led recipes of governance. The structural reforms engineered by Fujimori remained largely in place. The contrast between Peru and other countries became particularly clear during the second government of Alan García (2006–2011), in many ways the reverse image of his first administration in terms of economic policy. García took further steps to encourage foreign investment, signing the all-important free trade agreement with the United States and aggressively distributing mining and hydrocarbons concessions to the private sector.

During these years, Peru benefited enormously from the 'commodities super cycle', with prices for its minerals reaching new record highs. For successive years between 2002 and 2014, Peru scored one of the highest growth rates in Latin America. As Table 16.2 shows, this had the effect of raising GDP per capita substantially. Exports increased rapidly, and foreign investment became the cornerstone of Peru's development. Inflation remained low, with the maintenance of conservative fiscal and monetary policies.

On the back of this, poverty rates declined with large numbers joining the so-called middle class.[9] A building frenzy in middle-class areas of Lima and other cities attests to some of the positive social changes that took place as a result of the boom in growth rates during the commodity 'super-cycle'. At the same time, Peru's external accounts improved substantially, because of the increase in export earnings and the pattern of investments in the all-important mining industry. This was particularly notable in the second half of the decade when García was president. The country accumulated large foreign reserves which, in turn, buttressed confidence among international risk assessment agencies as to its ability to cover its foreign obligations. High growth rates also enabled successive governments to augment public spending on the back of increased tax receipts. The so-called Peruvian miracle became the object of lavish praise in the international financial media.

[9] The exact nature of this 'middle class' is, of course, debatable. Many of those 'escaping' poverty remained at risk of falling back below the poverty line once economic conditions deteriorated.

Table 16.2 Economic Indicators 2001–2010

	2001	2002	2003	2004	2005	2006	2007	2008	2009	2010
GDP growth (%)	0.6	5.5	4.2	5	6.3	7.5	8.5	9.1	1	8.5
GDP/cap (%)	–0.8	4	2.8	3.6	4.9	6.2	7.3	7.9	–0.1	7.2
Inflation	–0.1	1.5	2.5	3.5	1.5	1.1	3.9	6.7	0.2	2.1
Exports (% of GDP)	13	13.6	14.8	18.4	21.9	27.1	27.4	25.5	22.2	24.1
Exports (US$bn)	7	7.7	9.1	12.8	17.4	23.8	28.1	31	27.1	35.8
FDI (stock, % of GDP	21.9	22.1	21	19.1	20	23.3	26.2	26.5	28.4	28.9
FDI (stock, US$bn)	11.8	12.5	13.3	15.8	20.4	26.8	32.3	34.5	42.9	50.1
Fiscal balance (% of GDP)	–2.7	–2.2	–1.7	–1.1	–0.4	2.5	3.1	2.5	–1.4	–0.2
Net intern. reserves (US$bn)	8.6	9.6	10.2	12.6	14.1	17.3	27.7	31.2	33.2	44.1

Source: BCRP Memorias (various years).

The apparent solidity of the model was enhanced by the generalized acceptance, especially in better-off sectors of society, that economic liberalization was the only viable route to development. However, in less affluent circles, growing criticism emerged that the benefits of growth were far from equally shared. García's successor, Ollanta Humala (2011–2016), a nationalist, came to office on a wave of revulsion against the policies of neoliberalism. Still, he proved unable to shift policy far from the rules of orthodoxy. Within six months of taking office, he had sacked his more interventionist ministers in response to the pressures from Confiep, the association of mine owners (SNMPE), and other business organizations. His plans for 'the great transformation', involving a return to a more state-led model, were shelved, with the government siding with the interests of the investor community when it came to conflicts, for example, over major mining projects.[10]

The positive evolution of the economy persisted until the mid-2010s, but the ending of the commodity boom in 2013–2014 took its toll on the economic cycle, as Table 16.3 shows. Growth was curtailed while the previous rapid increase in exports and investment began to falter. The massive economic contraction in 2020 and its knock-on effects on GDP per capita were due to the onset of the COVID-19 pandemic, which hit Peru particularly hard.

The election of Pedro Pablo Kuczynski, an international financier, as president in 2016 upheld the centrality of orthodox economic management. But under his government the political consensus surrounding acceptance of neoliberalism began seriously to unravel. His government ended up being subsumed under the avalanche of corruption scandals unleashed by the Lava Jato (Car Wash) investigations in Brazil, and by an unrelenting political vendetta waged by Keiko Fujimori, the daughter of the jailed former president. Keiko was only narrowly defeated in both the 2011 and 2016 elections.

Lava Jato revealed with a wealth of detail the close, corrupt nature of ties between successive governments and a range of private-sector interests, both Peruvian and foreign (Durand, 2018). Successive presidents, beginning with Alberto Fujimori through to Kuczynski, faced charges of corruption. And, as the commodities super-cycle tailed off after 2014 and Peru's growth rate faltered, public disenchantment with the political and economic elite grew to proportions that raised doubts as to the sustainability of the economic model. This was finally brought into dramatic relief when, in 2021, Pedro Castillo, a left-wing rural schoolteacher who challenged the political establishment, narrowly won the presidential elections. The electoral power of the left had been marginalized during the Fujimori years but returned forcefully in 2021.

[10] The shift was triggered by a major conflict over the Conga mining project in Cajamarca by Yanacocha.

Table 16.3 Economic Indicators 2011–2020

	2011	2012	2013	2014	2015	2016	2017	2018(a)	2019(a)	2020(a)
GDP growth (%)	6.3	6.1	5.9	2.4	3.3	4	2.5	4	2.2	−11.1
GDP/cap (%)	5.5	5.4	5	1.4	2.1	2.4	0.7	2	0.3	−12.5
Inflation (%)	4.7	2.6	2.9	3.2	4.4	3.2	1.4	2.2	1.9	2
Exports (% of GDP)	27.1	24.6	21.2	19.5	18	19.1	21.2	21.8	20.6	20.7
Exports (US$bn)	46.4	47.4	42.9	39.5	34.4	37.1	45.4	49.1	47.7	42.4
FDI (stock, % of GDP)	29.7	33.3	36.7	38.6	45.1	47.9	46.6	47.4	49.8	56.7
FDI (stock, US$bn)	50.7	64.3	74.1	78	86.4	93.1	99.9	106.9	115	115.9
Fiscal balance (% of GDP)	2.1	2.3	0.9	−0.2	−1.9	−2.3	−3	−2.3	−1.6	−8.9
Net intern. reserves (US$bn)	48.8	64	65.7	62.3	61.5	61.7	63.6	60.1	68.3	74.7

Source: BCRP Memoria, 2020.
(a) Preliminary figures.

16.4. Unresolved Problems of Peru's Growth 'Model'

Peru's espousal of market-driven economic polices since the 1990s has been widely praised, not least in the international financial world. As we have seen, it led to a period of rapid growth on the back of export-oriented policies and the attraction of international capital. However, as we shall see in what follows, it was a growth model vulnerable to a number of interconnected contrary influences that raised questions as to sustainability over time. Indeed, as we will show, many of the country's traditional development problems persisted, masked by the positive outcomes achieved in more recent decades.

16.4.1. Primary Export Dependency

As we saw above, Peru remained a country dependent on primary exports later than most other major economies in Latin America. The adoption of policies to reduce that dependence, beginning in the early 1960s, sought to promote industrialization and the substitution of manufactured imports by products produced locally. The transformative effects of these policies were limited, and even at the end of the 1970s, the country remained highly dependent on primary exports, chiefly minerals, for its foreign exchange. The liberalizing polices of the 1990s accentuated that dependence once again through the reduction of import tariffs, the deregulation of markets, and the rewriting of contractual arrangements to attract foreign investment. The full implications of this about-turn in policy under the Fujimori government were felt only in the subsequent decade when inward investment flourished, exports took off, and the country's foreign reserves mushroomed.

The importance of the mining sector grew rapidly during these years. In the five years between 2014 and 2018, mining exports constituted nearly 60% of total exports (BCRP, 2018), the proportion peaking in 2017. Within the mix of mineral exports, the lion's share was copper, followed by gold. In 2017 and 2018, copper accounted for well over 30% of total exports. With international minerals prices notoriously volatile, this constituted a potential weakness for longer-term economic development. Indeed, as the commodity super-cycle ended around 2013, the fast pace of growth rates achieved in previous years came to an end and with it the rapid increase in GDP per capita (Table 16.3). Although attempts were made over these years to diversify the economy, they were aimed not at boosting industrialization or services, but mainly at agriculture.

While the market for Peruvian minerals changed significantly over the period since the early 1990s, the diversification of markets remained rather limited, with China taking over from the United States in 2011 as the prime market.[11] Chinese industrial expansion over these years led to voracious demand for minerals, particularly copper. So long as demand for copper held up, Peruvian mining prospered. However, the slowdown in Chinese growth rates was a major contributory factor for the deceleration of Peruvian growth in 2019.

Although the prospects for future demand for copper and other minerals once again appeared bright at the beginning of 2022 (in view of global initiatives to transform the energy sector), Peru's future growth remained perilously dependent on this sector for inward investment and export earnings. Predictions of future growth would perpetuate that dependency as the interest of new investors was confined largely to the mining sector. The coming on-stream in 2022 of a major new copper mine, Anglo American's Quellaveco in Moquegua region, an investment of over US$5 billion, was poised to substantially increase that reliance on copper output and sales.

China also became a growing market for other primary produce, notably niche agriculture. This is a sector that has witnessed considerable development in recent years, driven chiefly by export demand. Products include asparagus (for which Peru has become a world leader), blueberries, paprika, avocados, mangoes, and lemons. The effect was to diversify somewhat the country's range of exports and incorporate a degree of technification based on more sophisticated agricultural practices.[12] But the spillover effects into other, more traditional agricultural sectors were few, and the effect was to further widen regional disparities between irrigated coastal areas and the low productivity of peasant agriculture in the highlands. The main agricultural export remained coffee. This made a virtue of the lack of technification; it sold as organic only because most of its producers had historically been unable to afford fertilizer or other chemical inputs. Some service industries developed too, such as tourism (taking advantage of Peru's peculiarly rich historical and cultural heritage). This has led to the spin-off development of hotels and restaurants. However, as the COVID-19 pandemic showed, this was a sector highly dependent on the influx of foreign visitors in Peru.

16.4.2. Informality and Low Productivity

The primacy of the mining industry in Peru's pattern of development exposed the problem of low employment generation. Apart from the initial

[11] A free trade agreement with China was signed in April 2009. Ten years later, exports to China reached US$23.4 billion, of which 96.4% were 'traditional' exports (basically minerals and fish products) and 72.2% were copper exports. In 2019, China accounted for just under 30% of Peru's total exports.

[12] The emergence of what seems to be a dynamic agro-exporting capitalism was due, in the first instance, to the huge public investment made in coastal irrigation projects over previous decades, such as Majes, Olmos, and Chavimochic.

construction phase, modern mining is highly capital intensive, employing a few skilled workers and creating few backward or forward linkages to the rest of the economy. Investors in the mining sector have been repeatedly criticized for importing even the most basic goods rather than purchasing them locally. Arguably, niche agriculture has generated more employment. However, labour conditions remained poor, and the linkages between these enclaves and the wider economy weak.

Along with Bolivia, Peru has one of the largest informal sectors anywhere in Latin America, reinforcing high productive heterogeneity. Even before the COVID-driven downturn in 2020, it was estimated that around 70% of the workforce was informal, labouring in enterprises of extremely low levels of productivity.[13] The scale of informality thus remains a structural feature of the Peruvian economy. While the economic collapse of the late 1980s led to a substantial increase in informality, it did not fall again with the recovery under Fujimori. Informality is closely linked to persistent poverty, with those working in the sector enjoying little by way of job stability, welfare benefits, or pension entitlements.[14] Public policy to encourage 'formalization' of employment has had limited effects, not least in mining (Cano, 2021) where the environmental effects of informal gold extraction have proved highly damaging.[15]

Problems of low productivity are closely related to the scale of informality. According to Economic Commission for Latin America and the Caribbean (ECLAC) figures, labour productivity in Peru was significantly lower than the Latin American average in 2019, even though the gap had been reduced over the previous decade (OECD, 2021). The predominance of low-income employment impacts on patterns of domestic demand, restricting growth and productive diversification. Attempts by various governments to increase productivity, primarily through the Ministry of Production, have had positive impacts, but Peru lags badly in enhancing its value-added. Investment in research and development (R&D) has been low compared to the larger economies of Latin America, and the percentage of high-tech exports is close to zero. Particularly challenging are attempts to raise productivity levels within small and medium-sized enterprises, many working within the informal sector. Private-sector services dedicated to technological innovation are weakly constituted and in-work training largely deficient.

[13] ILO figures put informality in Peru at 70.1% in 2020, 66.5% for men and 74.9% for women. https://ilostat.ilo.org/topics/informality/.

[14] It should be pointed out that not all those working in the informal sector are necessarily poor, especially those involved in illicit activities like drug trafficking, contraband, illegal mining, and timber extraction.

[15] This is particularly the case in the Amazon, but informal gold mining is widespread throughout the Andes.

Despite some improvements in educational provision in recent years, the impact on raising levels of human capital have proved disappointing. Despite a rapid expansion in the number of universities, partly on the back of profits from mining, these generally provide poor educational outputs ill-attuned to the needs of new, more sophisticated industries. While areas of excellence exist (largely in elite private schools and universities), educational levels lag badly behind other countries at similar levels of development, particularly so in areas beyond the main urban hubs.[16] In terms of school attainment, Peru remains near the bottom of the Programme for International Student Assessment (PISA) league tables for educational attainment.[17]

Although industrial policy has taken a backseat in Peru in recent years, it remains questionable whether it is possible for Peru to catch up with the world's more advanced economies, or whether the more feasible policy is to build on the sustainable development of natural-resource processing, which itself depends on institutional development and that of a more sophisticated R&D capacity (Marin et al., 2015). One route to raising the technological content of exports is through regional integration, a policy that has gained little traction for Peru in recent years (OECD, 2021). To this end, the state has a clear responsibility to provide the necessary infrastructure to enable such activities to prosper.

16.4.3. Social and Regional Inequalities

Closely related to the problem of tackling informality and low productivity is the even greater one of building a development model conducive to bridging the marked inequalities that divide Peru both socially and geographically. It was in part this that the reforms of the Velasco period sought to ameliorate, but which the policies adopted signally failed to achieve. The deep divides in Peruvian society remained during the subsequent period, almost certainly made worse by the economic crisis of the late 1980s. While the Fujimori period saw an attempt to tackle poverty under the Foncodes programme (Francke, 2006), the state avoided policies to redistribute income or promote regional development. Poverty levels fell as a consequence of the export-led boom during the first years of the new millennium, but as growth rates faltered, at least some of those who had entered the so-called middle class began to sink back into poverty as economic growth

[16] Attempts by the state to regulate universities have met with strong opposition from politically influential lobbies from business groups that own highly lucrative private universities.

[17] The latest PISA survey is for 2018, http://gpseducation.oecd.org/CountryProfile?primaryCountry=PER&treshold=10&topic=PI.

tapered off.[18] Then the COVID-19 lockdown caused both levels of poverty and social inequality to rise sharply once again.

To tackle poverty, the Toledo government introduced a conditional cash transfer programme called Juntos in September 2005. But its scope was more limited than those of other larger Latin American countries like Mexico or Brazil. Its record in reducing social inequalities was relatively small. The Humala administration brought in additional programmes designed to target poverty, notably for families with young children (Cuna Más) and for the elderly (Pensión 65). But the effects of targeted social spending were less than those of economic growth. The sharp fall in Peru's poverty rate up until around 2014 became much less pronounced thereafter, even though poverty as a whole continued to decline. The achievements of the previous period were wiped out in 2020 as a consequence of COVID, which hit Peru particularly hard; 2020 saw a 14% contraction in those employed (one of Latin America's highest rates), with labour income dropping by 28% (the largest fall of the 13 countries studied).[19] COVID exposed not only the deficiencies of Peru's public health system, weakened by years of underspending, but also the scale of informality and the lack of social protection that made it impossible for people to self-isolate. As far as income inequality is concerned, ECLAC (2021) shows that Peru had the region's highest relative increase, both according to the Gini coefficient and the Atkinson index.

While the 'Peruvian miracle' reduced the numbers living in monetary poverty, it did little to reduce regional inequalities. Peru remained highly 'Lima-centric', with the capital accounting for most of the country's population, sources of employment, and GDP. In terms of share of GDP, Lima accounted for just under half the value of output (47.8%) in 2020, slightly more than in 2007, notwithstanding huge investments in mining. The next largest region in terms of GDP was Arequipa, with only 5.9%. Attempts to redress the balance proved largely ineffectual. The canon system, whereby mining rents were redistributed to regions, provinces, and districts, did little to offset the imbalance. Rather, lacking adequate oversight, it encouraged wasteful spending and corruption at the local level (Crabtree, 2014). Policies of decentralization, started under the Toledo government, proved disappointing in terms of creating a vibrant political culture at

[18] According to the head of INEI (La República, 2020), as of 2019, 6.6 million Peruvians (just over 20% of the population) faced monetary poverty, with a further 3.3 million falling into poverty in 2020. Added together, this is just under a third of the population. A further 11.2 million were believed to be 'vulnerable' to poverty, with income only just above the officially defined poverty line. These figures do not measure multidimensional poverty, which takes into account other measures of poverty than just income and shows levels that are considerably higher.

[19] According to ECLAC, labour income among lower-income groups fell 25% in 2020, followed by 22% in Colombia.

the subnational level; rather, they accentuated problems of poor administrative capacity and the disengagement of the state from society at the local level.

16.4.4. Institutional Deficiencies

The Peruvian state has not taken a key role in forcing the pace of alternative development. The function of state planning went out of vogue in the 1990s when the Fujimori government dismantled the National Planning Institute, and it has never properly returned. There has therefore been little by way of an overall strategy of development, other than policies conducted by individual ministries. These often conflict. Although the Ministry of Economy and Finance exercises more decisive influence than others, its agenda obviated notions of state planning. Although relations between the state and the private sector are arguably less antagonistic than in the past, there is little by way of strong partnerships emerging to push for the development of an alternative development model to that which has prevailed since the early 1990s.

As we have noted, the private sector has sought to minimize the extent of state intervention and even to 'capture' those areas of state involvement of most strategic interest to it. This is especially true of the regulatory agencies. The capacity of the state has been eroded by years of government austerity. Nowhere has this been more apparent than in the public health sector whose deficiencies were laid bare in 2020 by COVID: Peru suffered the world's highest death toll per head of population. And as we have seen, the efficacy of the state has also been undermined by corruption, badly affecting public confidence in its role and capacities.

State capacities have also been limited by low tax revenue. Tax reform, as mentioned above, has long proved a problematic area, both as a means to enhance public-sector solvency and as a way to improve income distribution. As in other countries, Peru's tax system remains skewed strongly in the direction of indirect taxation, with all the regressive impact that this implies. One of the more significant reforms of the Fujimori era was to overhaul the tax administration, SUNAT. For a brief period, at least, this helped reduce the scope for tax evasion both by individuals and firms. However, it proved hard to sustain over the longer term because of institutional backsliding. Although more solvent today than in the late 1990s, Peru's tax take remains very low by Latin American standards.[20] This is an obstacle to the state assuming a more activist role, let alone in tackling infrastructural deficits or providing quality public services in fields such as health, education, and pension benefits.

[20] Tax income was equivalent to 13.4% of GDP in 2018. See BCRP Memoria, 2020, Annex 38.

Decentralization to the regional level has been slow and uneven. In some areas, more enterprising regional governments have begun to engage in the planning of development strategies. These have on occasions led to the development of new industries. The growth of palm oil production in the San Martín region, for example, has brought benefits, providing new sources of revenues and employment. It has helped provide an alternative to production of coca. But such cases are few and far between; and even palm oil brings problems of its own, notably negative environmental consequences.

Public administration has also been compromised by corruption and a lack of public oversight. The problem of corruption at the national scale, identified above, continues to plague state institutions, diverting much-needed resources away from more economically and socially pressing objectives. Peru has been swamped by corruption cases, many dating back to the 1990s, with private companies bribing politicians to secure decisions and contracts that favour them. Key here have been the 'Lava Jato' bribes offered by Brazilian construction firms such as Odebrecht in the building of public infrastructure.[21] Politicians of all persuasions have become enmeshed in these scandals. This is particularly true of those of the right and centre-right, who have tended to occupy government posts since the 1990s. Of Peru's presidents since 1990, all are either in jail, have been in jail, or are subject to corruption investigations that could land them in jail.[22] It should be said that the prevalence of such cases—by no means limited to companies like Odebrecht—has had the effect of raising the salience of corruption in public life. This has led attorneys and prosecutors, backed by public opinion, to take a stand in confronting corruption.

16.4.5. An Absence of Consensus

A successful development strategy requires a degree of consensus that brings together the various sectors of society. This appears largely absent in contemporary Peru. In order to maintain a degree of stability (upon which business decisions can be made with a degree of certainty), there needs to be agreement on the rules of the game. Such rules need to enjoy acceptance in wider society.

[21] Francisco Durand, 'Odebrecht, la empresa que capturaba gobiernos', Oxfam/PUCP, 2018.

[22] Alberto Fujimori was jailed for 25 years in 2008 for corruption and crimes against humanity. At the time of writing, Alejandro Toledo was the subject of extradition proceedings from the United States for corruption. Alan García committed suicide in 2019 when police arrived to arrest him for corruption. Both Keiko Fujimori and Ollanta Humala spent lengthy periods in preventative detention pending investigations for corruption. Pedro Pablo Kuczynski was placed under house arrest in 2018 for alleged involvement in corruption as minister under Toledo's government.

However, problems of social and regional inequality have made it more difficult to build such a consensus.

While this may be the case, a consensus of sorts appeared in the 1990s around the liberalizing programme of Alberto Fujimori. This was a critical juncture in Peru's recent development history. Fujimori's re-election in 1995 owed much to a public view that there was, effectively, no alternative. The scale of the economic collapse of the late 1980s was such that few wanted to return to a status quo which had proved so painful. This was especially so for the poorest in society, and those least able to protect their living standards. Added to this was the absence of voices in society actively protesting against the measures introduced: the union movement, which had been relatively powerful a decade earlier, was weakened by both the effects of hyperinflation and the privatizing measures introduced by Fujimori.

By the early years of the following decade, however, disenchantment with the effects of the model were clearly present. The strong vote for Ollanta Humala in the 2006 presidential elections showed a growing level of disconformity, a public mood confirmed five years later when he narrowly beat Fujimori's daughter, Keiko, in the 2011 elections. Such disconformity was poorly articulated by Peru's fragmented political parties, deliberately debilitated by the Fujimori regime. These were no longer able to articulate public opinion through their presence in Congress. In such circumstances, it became difficult to engender public consensus around a development model, a key requirement for success. Civil society remained poorly integrated into the operations of the state, and—as successive surveys by the Latinobarómetro (Latinobarómetro, various years) have shown—Peru is among the countries in which faith in democratic institutions is among the weakest in Latin America.

By the end of the second decade of the new millennium, public disaffection had become even more palpable, fired up by the fall in annual growth rates, the eruption of the Lava Jato scandals, and other examples of egregious corruption. Faith in the political elite had plumbed new depths, and business elites were widely perceived as using their access to political decision-making with a view to further their own interests, rather than working in a disinterested manner for the goods of society. The public mood was further soured by the economic and social dislocations caused by the onset of the COVID-19 pandemic in March 2020. The surprise election of Pedro Castillo in the 2021 presidential contest, in which Keiko Fujimori narrowly lost for a third time, brought with it a polarization of public opinion and the return of left-wing politics that had been so notoriously absent in Peru during Latin America's 'pink wave'. Although once in office—rather like Humala before him—Castillo faced strong pressures from the business community to abandon his more radical proposals, his election showed that large swathes of public opinion no longer shared a conviction that business-oriented economic policies were bringing benefits to the whole country. However, after a disastrous few months in power, Castillo was impeached and removed from office at the end of 2022, leaving in his wake a nation more divided than ever.

16.5. Conclusions

As it moved into the 2020s, Peru faced major challenges in its pursuit of a development model that would, at once, prove economically sustainable, socially inclusive, and politically consensual. Economically, its dependence on mining had rendered it subject to volatile tendencies in the global economy, over which no government in Lima could exercise control. Socially, the country remained stratified, with most in the labour force working in precarious circumstances in the informal economy. And politically, the fragile consensus that seemed to prevail in the 1990s appeared to have broken down amid growing polarization between left and right and within a context of growing distrust in political and economic elites. The COVID-19 pandemic simply seemed to amplify these difficulties.

The previous 60 years had seen various contrasting attempts to tackle these development problems, ranging from the statist solutions proffered by the Velasco regime in the 1970s through to the hyper-liberal policies of the Fujimori era in the 1990s which sought to reduce state intervention to an absolute minimum. At the same time, the country has wrestled with governance approaches that have varied from authoritarian through to more participative and democratic models. What can be seen over this lengthy period are gyrations in access to political power and difficulties in establishing an institutional setting on which sustainable growth would ultimately depend.

This chapter has sought to identify how the building of such a model has been bedevilled by difficulties inherited from the past, and which reforms over recent decades have done little to resolve. While some productive diversification has been achieved, Peru's economy remains one characterized by low productivity. Only 'islands' of more technologically sophisticated productive activities exist. The incentives to broaden the country's economic base and to build new sources of productive employment have been largely missing. Meanwhile, the dynamics of democratization, and those of business prosperity, have proved difficult to reconcile, leading to an unsettled relationship over time. This has made it harder to build a lasting consensus around an economic model which might successfully combine sustainable growth with benefits for the broad mass of the population.

References

Abugattás, L. 1998. 'Stabilisation, Structural Reform and Industrial Performance', in J. Crabtree and J. Thomas, eds., *Fujimori's Peru: The Political Economy*. London: Institute of Latin American Studies, 61–88.

Arce, M. 2010. *El fujimorismo y la reforma del mercado en la sociedad peruana*. Lima: Instituto de Estudios Peruanos.

BCRP (Banco Central de Reserva del Perú). 1996. *Memoria*. Lima: BCRP.

BCRP (Banco Central de Reserva del Perú). 2018. *Memoria*. Lima: BCRP.

BCRP (Banco Central de Reserva del Perú). 2020. *Memoria*. Lima: BCRP.

Cano, A. 2021. *Formalización de la minería artesenal y de pequeña escala en la amazonía peruana: Lecciones aprndidas y prouestas de solución*. Lima: USAID.

Conaghan, C. 2005. *Fujimori's Peru: Deception in the Public Sphere*. Pittsburgh: University of Pittsburgh Press.

Conaghan, C., and Malloy, J. 1994. *Unsettling Statecraft: Democracy and Neoliberalism in the Central Andes*. Pittsburgh: University of Pittsburgh Press.

Crabtree, J. 1992. *Peru under Garcia: An Opportunity Lost*. Basingstoke, UK: Macmillan.

Crabtree, J. 2014. 'Funding of Local Government: Use and Abuse of Peru's Canon System', *Bulletin of Latin American Research*, 33(4), 452–467.

Crabtree, J., and Durand, F. 2017. *Peru: Elite Power and Political Capture*. London: Zed Books.

Degregori, C. I. 2012. *How Difficult It Is to Be God: Shining Path's Politics of War in Peru, 1980–1999*. Madison: University of Wisconsin Press.

Durand, F. 2003. *Riqueza económica y pobreza política*. Lima: Fondo Editorial de la Pontificia Universidad Católica del Perú.

Durand, F. 2005. *La mano invisible en el estado: Efectos del neoliberalismo en el empresariado y en la política*. Lima: DESCO, Friedrich Ebert Stiftung.

Durand, F. 2018. *Odebrecht, la empresa que capturaba gobiernos*. Lima: Oxfam/Pontificia Universidad Católica del Perú.

ECLAC (UN Economic Commission for Latin America and the Caribbean). 2021. *Social Panorama of Latin America 2020*. ECLAC: Santiago.

Fitzgerald, E. 1979. *The Political Economy of Peru, 1956–1978: Economic Development and the Restructuring of Capital*. Cambridge: Cambridge University Press.

Francke, P., 2006. 'Institutional Change and Social Programmes', in J. Crabtree, ed., *Making Institutions Work in Peru*. London: Institute for the Study of the Americas, 95–96.

Gonzáles de Olarte, E. 1998. *El neoliberalismo a la peruana*. Lima: Instituto de Estudios Peruanos.

La República. 2020. https://larepublica.pe/economia/2020/12/28/2020-un-ano-que-deja-a-99-millones-de-peruanos-en-la-pobreza/.

Lowenthal, A., ed. 1975. *The Peruvian Experiment: Continuity and Change under Military Rule*. Princeton, NJ: Princeton University Press.

Marin, A., Navas-Alemán, L., and Pérez, C. 2015. 'Natural Resource Industries as a Platform for the Development of Knowledge Intensive Industries', *Tijdschrift voor economische en social geografie*, 106(2), 154–168.

McClintock, C., and Lowenthal, A., eds. 1983. *The Peruvian Experiment Reconsidered*. Princeton, NJ: Princeton University Press.

OECD. 2021. *Latin American Economic Outlook, 2021: Working Together for a Better Recovery*. Paris: OECD Publishing, https://doi.org/10.1787/5fedabe5-en.

Quiroz, A. 2013. *Corrupt Circles: A History of Unbound Graft in Peru.* Washington DC: Woodrow Wilson Center Press with Johns Hopkins University Press.
Thorp, R., and Bertram, G. 1978. *Peru 1890–1977: Growth and Policy in an Open Economy.* London: Macmillan.
Seminario, B. 2015. *El Desarrollo de la economía peruana en la era moderna: Precios, población, demanda y producción desde 1700.* Lima: Universidad del Pacífico.
Wise, C. 2003. *Reinventando el estado: Estratégia eocoómica y cambio institucional en el Perú.* Lima: Universidad del Pacífico.

17

Uruguay

Public Policies in a Period of Inclusive Growth without Structural Change

Carlos Bianchi and Fernando Isabella

17.1. Introduction: A Small Democratic Middle-Income Country

During the past decades, Uruguay has followed an uneven development path, characterized by some long-run stylized facts and critical internal and external changes. Economists, historians, and social scientists have usually differentiated the Uruguayan development path within the Latin American context (e.g. Fajnzylber, 1990; Filgueira, 1983; Sunkel and Paz, 1979). Bértola and Ocampo (2012) show that, since the end of the nineteenth century, Uruguay has been part of a group of high-growth and high-income countries within Latin America. Traditionally, Uruguay was a small and open economy based on natural resources and enjoying a relatively egalitarian society. The political science literature highlighted the stability and quality of democracy in Uruguay as determinants of national development (Lanzaro and Piñeiro, 2017; Grassi, 2014).

However, the economic growth of the country during the first globalization process was not accompanied by intensive investment in capabilities. Although Uruguay had one of the best educational performances in the region, enrolment in education was low by advanced-country standards (Bértola and Ocampo, 2012).

In this context, during the twentieth century, Uruguay diverged from the rich world and the successive sets of catching-up countries from Australasia and Asia, but maintained singular features that differentiated it in the Latin American region (Bértola and Ocampo, 2012; Bértola and Porcile, 1998). In particular, the relationship between productive and institutional factors in the divergence process of the Uruguayan economy has been stressed (Álvarez et al., 2011). Its low growth dynamic and high volatility have been explained by the dependency on a small number of tradable products in which the country has Ricardian advantages. Those products include agro-based products like beef, dairy, grains, and, more recently, wood pulp. Despite the natural wealth and industrialization

Carlos Bianchi and Fernando Isabella, *Uruguay* In: *Innovation, Competitiveness, and Development in Latin America.* Edited by: Edmund Amann and Paulo N. Figueiredo, Oxford University Press. © Oxford University Press 2024.
DOI: 10.1093/oso/9780197648070.003.0017

initiatives, production has remained scarcely diversified (Bértola, Isabella, and Saavedra, 2014; Cimoli and Katz, 2003).

Meanwhile, public policies during the state-led industrialization process (approximately 1930–1970) played a critical role in building an urban and integrated society. Welfare has been mainly provided by the state through contributory policies focused on the formal labour of the home breadwinner, usually male (Filgueira et al., 2011). In this historical context, after the tragic civil-military dictatorship (1973–1985), the country experienced different industrial and technological policy orientations (Baptista, 2016). At the end of the past century, Uruguay partially introduced the Washington Consensus policies, which were softened by social and political expressions, in particular through direct democracy mechanisms (Moreira, 2004).

During recent decades, along with a sustained increase in commodity prices, industrial policies came back, now including a strong institutional push for innovation policies (Pittaluga et al., 2016; Bianchi, Bianco, and Snoeck, 2014). However, the end of the commodity boom seems to have revealed the limits of the policy efforts, in particular when considering the relatively unchanged productive structure of the country (Isabella, 2015; Bértola, Isabella, and Saavedra, 2014). The productive structure based on traditional sectors has not boosted the emergence of a critical mass of innovative firms, although there is evidence of a small core of innovative firms in the Uruguayan economy, which shows positive effects of innovation on productivity and job creation (Laguna and Bianchi, 2020; Crespi and Zuniga, 2012).

However, this evidence also shows that most firms in Uruguay do not conduct innovative activities, and there are few behavioural effects and spillovers from innovative to non-innovative firms (Bukstein et al., 2020; Berrutti and Bianchi, 2020). Thus, after a period of economic growth and active public policies, many problems exist related to the unchanged productive structure and the limits that the external conditions impose on a sustainable development path. In line with previous research, we argue that Uruguay's development process has been marked by better distributional than productive results (Fajnzylber, 1990). Moreover, recent experience reinforces that the country performs better in social and welfare policies than in productive and technological ones (Martínez Franzoni and Sánchez-Ancochea, 2014).

In analysing Uruguay's situation, we aim to contribute to the ongoing debate, both in the national and regional context, on the effects and limitations of the industrial and innovation policies implemented during the last period of economic growth. Our discussion especially focuses on the widespread concept of the middle-income trap applied to small open economies. Much recent research has shown that most Latin American countries seem to be trapped in this situation (e.g. Bianchi, Isabella, and Picasso, 2020; Suárez and Erbes, 2016; Paus, 2014).

This chapter adopts the following structure. After this introduction, section 17.2 reviews the concept of the middle-income trap, considering the Uruguayan case and evaluating the specific challenges of escaping the trap in democratic societies with a relatively broad welfare system. Next, section 17.3 addresses the hypothesis that Uruguay is facing a long-run middle-income trap despite its recent period of intensive economic growth. Section 17.3 lays out the main characteristics of the industrial and innovation policies in the recent period of inclusive growth and assesses their effectiveness. Finally, section 17.4 summarizes the key development challenges facing small, democratic middle-income countries.

17.2. On the Middle-Income Trap and the Role of Public Policies

The concept of the middle-income trap refers to a long-lasting, but perhaps not permanent, slowdown in economic growth in countries that have overcome the low-income thresholds but remain trapped for a relatively long period in middle-income levels. Despite criticisms (e.g. Bresser Pereira, Araújo, and Peres, 2020; Albuquerque, 2019), the concept of the middle-income trap offers an operational tool to understand growth slowdowns in middle-income countries. These have been associated with the challenges of structural change in countries that are highly dependent on commodities based on natural resources. Much research, from different perspectives, has discussed the limits of a productive specialization based on natural resources and the advantages of manufacturing and global services activities in the creation of value (Bértola and Lara, 2017; Martínez Franzoni and Sánchez Ancochea, 2014; ECLAC, 2014). Some of this has shed light on virtuous development processes based on the diversification of production from natural resources, calling for a non-fundamentalist approach to this topic (Andersen and Johnson, 2011; Pérez, 2010).

We acknowledge the contributions of these bodies of literature, recognizing the relevance of natural resources in the development strategies and the relevance of structural diversification of the economies. In this sense, we stress the problem associated with productive specialization in a small number of undifferentiated products. Several previous contributions have analysed positive experiences of product differentiation based on natural resources in Uruguay (Pittaluga et al., 2016; D'Albora and Durán, 2013) and other Latin American countries (Lebdioui, Lee, and Pietrobelli, 2021; Figueiredo and Cohen, 2019).

Following previous contributions (Bianchi, Isabella, and Picasso, 2020; Catela and Porcile, 2012), we assert that the limits of development strategies based on commodities are associated with an external restriction that strangles the growth of economies. Specialization in scarcely differentiated products makes such countries dependent on exogenously determined prices to sustain the path of growth. In particular, in Latin American economies, this constraint has been associated with growth cycles that are characterized by brief periods of upswings followed by deep crises, hindering sustainable growth paths (Cimini, Britto, and Ribeiro, 2021; Albuquerque, 2019; Bértola and Lara, 2017).

We have recently proposed a simple indicator to summarize many of these concepts for commodity-dependent countries, called the 'export margin' (Bianchi, Isabella, and Picasso, 2020). This indicator expresses the relation between commodities' export prices in local currency and internal prices as a proxy for production costs. Thus, it summarizes the conditions for price competition.[1] This variable is significant and is positively associated with economic growth for those countries in the middle-income trap, but not for advanced countries. This evidence shows that trapped countries, with unsophisticated and poorly diversified productive structures, can only grow when prices and costs conditions allow them to, while advanced countries do not depend on these mostly exogenous conditions, because they can grow based on innovation, upgrading, and quality competition (Bianchi, Isabella, and Picasso, 2020).

This cyclical process associated with productive specialization makes it possible to identify the increasing challenges that countries face on their development paths. For example, an economic growth trajectory that overcomes the middle-income trap under authoritarian and unequal distribution conditions seems normatively unacceptable for Uruguay in particular and for Latin America in general. Both need to face the challenge of building capabilities for the future in a pluralist political system. This implies discarding potential development strategies initially based on authoritarianism, even if democracy materializes after an accelerated growth process. This was the case with the Republic of Korea in the second half of the twentieth century (Lee, 2019). Most of the successful catching-up by Asian countries, to which Latin America is often compared, was based on non-democratic institutions.

Moreover, coevolution of economic growth and social structures which permit or favour internal redistribution (strong democracy) will trigger a generalized increase in wages and other costs of the national economy (e.g. taxes devoted to supporting social policies, basic non-tradable production inputs such as energy). What is more, the distributive process may foster the demand and profitability of economic sectors focused on the expanding internal market, reinforcing the increase in internal costs, reallocating investment flows, and subtracting

[1] Export margin $= \frac{PcE}{P}$, where Pc is the price of the commodities (exports), E refers to the exchange rate, and P refers to internal prices.

potential resources from tradable sectors that could promote structural productive changes (Agénor, 2017; Paus, 2014; Eichengreen, Park, and Shin, 2013).

On the other hand, an unchanged productive structure that is dependent on commodity production (with externally determined prices) will progressively lose competitiveness if the evolution of the internal costs surpasses the productivity increases in those activities. Therefore, the national economy is neither able to compete in the commodity markets where it had based the previous growth path, nor able to produce more sophisticated goods that fetch higher and more stable prices in the international market, which would, in turn, allow it to obtain the necessary resources to support the growing welfare of the population (Lee, 2019; Vivarelli, 2013).

Previous studies have shown that this process of improving the quality of life requires structural changes to be sustainable, and thus able to overcome the recurring cycles of brief stages of growth followed by deep crises (Porcile and Sánchez-Ancochea, 2021). The economic process previously described closely resembles the recent Uruguayan experience. The period of accelerated growth coincided with a change in the political orientation of the government, with a strong redistributive orientation to public policies becoming predominant.

Thus, an increase in real income is observed, associated with the reinstatement of collective bargaining systems and an increase of the minimum wage, together with a dense set of regulations designed to protect employees and various social policies that assist informal workers. Moreover, a tax reform oriented toward taxing personal income was implemented, together with the creation of the national health system and a strong increase in public expenditure on education, health, and social protection. These policies were effective in reducing inequality and improving the welfare of the population (Bértola and Lara, 2017; Martínez Franzoni and Sánchez-Ancochea, 2014). Moreover, this process aimed at expanding the public protection system while reducing the traditional stratification of the universal Uruguayan welfare system (Filgueira, 2005).

As can be seen in Figures 17.1 and 17.2, both fiscal pressure and real salaries have increased during the past 15 years. Also, the prices of some non-tradable production inputs (electric energy and fuels) remain among the highest in the region. What is more, together with a strong currency appreciation, these costs, measured in US dollars, have increased sharply.

However, the evolution of these indicators has not gone hand in hand with a deep structural transformation of the economy. The Uruguayan export dependence on primary products remains high (Figure 17.3) (UNCTAD, 2021) and has even increased, without showing clear signals of technological sophistication (Bértola, Isabella, and Saavedra, 2014), except for some new service activities.

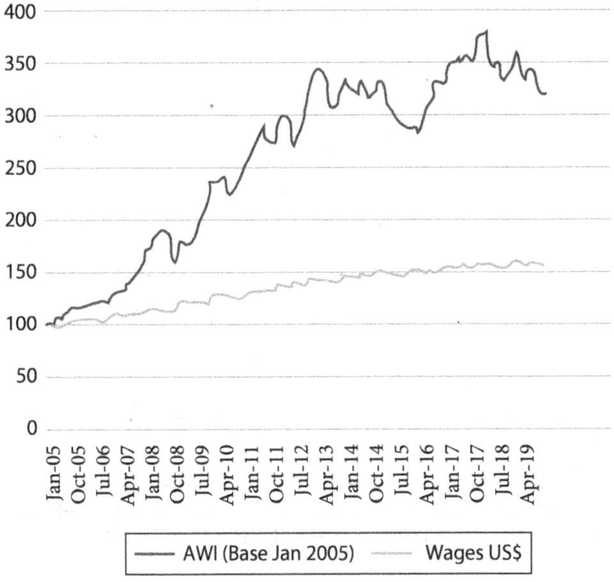

Figure 17.1. Uruguay evolution of salaries 2005–2019.
AWI: Average Real Wage Index; Wage US$: Real wages in US dollars.
Source: Authors, based on National Institute of Statistics, Uruguay.

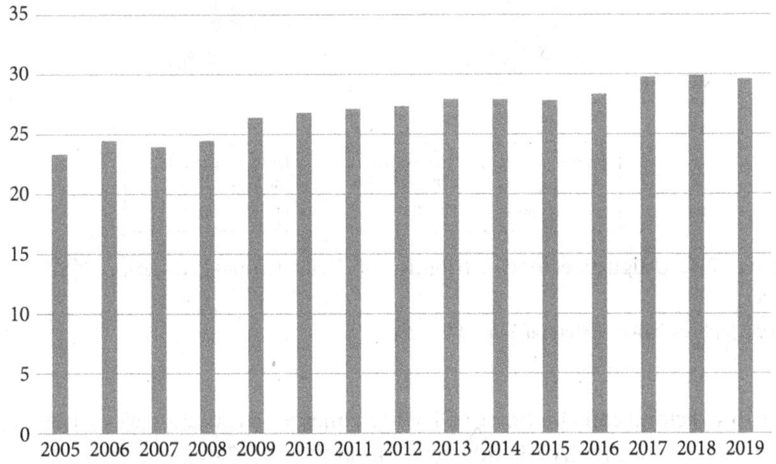

Figure 17.2. Uruguay tax burden 2005–2019 (percentage of GDP).
Source: Elaborated from CEPAL STAT.

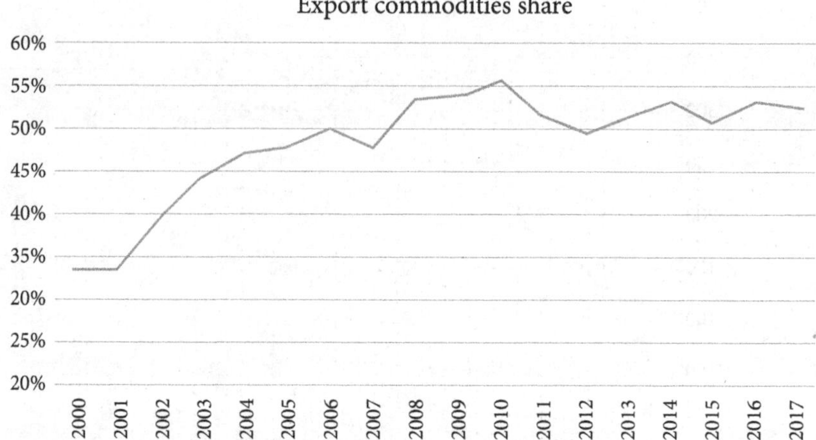

Figure 17.3. Uruguay export commodities share, 2000–2017.
Source: Authors, based on data from the Atlas of economic complexity (https://atlas.cid.harvard.edu/), using the commodity definition of Radetzki and Wårell 2020).

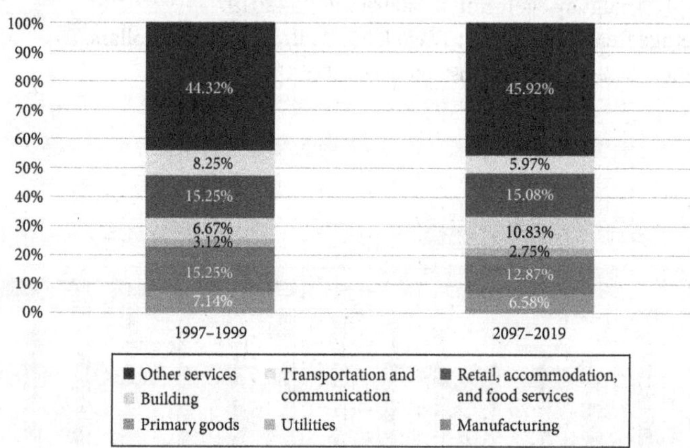

Figure 17.4. Uruguay sectoral distribution of GDP triennial averages, current prices.
Source: Authors, based on Central Bank of Uruguay.

Also, the sectoral contribution to GDP has remained strikingly stable, showing a slow but sustained path of deindustrialization (Figure 17.4).

Taking a closer look at manufacturing activities, it can be seen that only two branches show persistent and intense growth during the period: food and beverage, and wood and paper, which are both dependent on local primary products (Figure 17.5). This seems to be in line with a long-run trend of the

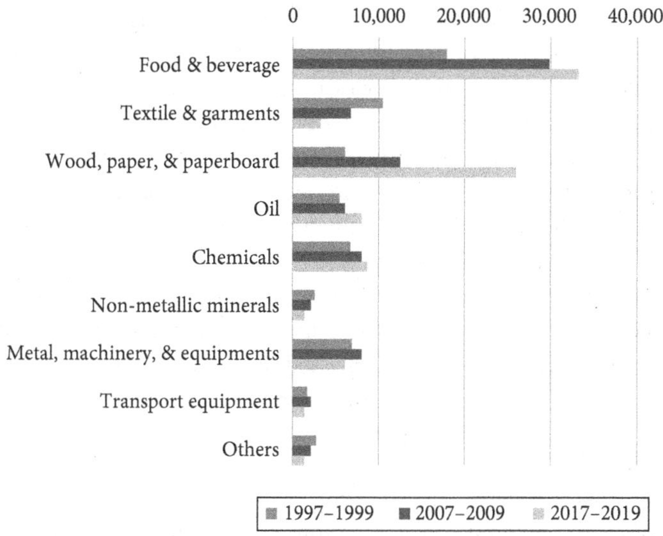

Figure 17.5. Uruguay manufacturing industry output constant prices of 2005 (US$ M).
Source: Authors, based on Central Bank of Uruguay.

Uruguayan economy, which has historically specialized in activities in which it enjoys comparative advantages based on its natural resource endowments. Manufacturing, therefore, has not been a source of generation of dynamic competitive advantages.

In this period, high disparity in productivity levels is also observed according to both activity sector and firm size. High productivity growth rates have been observed in manufacturing and communication activities, compared to the relatively stable productivity level of primary goods (Bértola, Isabella, and Saavedra, 2014).

Heterogeneous productivity is associated with a higher risk of falling into a trap-like situation. As mentioned above, countries that are dependent on mineral or food commodities are particularly exposed to economic growth volatility. Since the prices of these goods usually suffer sharp oscillations, these countries face a high risk of suddenly facing a middle-income trap because, during the expansive phase of the growth cycle, the profit margins are relaxed so the distributive process and the subsequent increase in internal costs are easier, faster, and deeper than in regular phases (Bianchi, Isabella, and Picasso, 2020). Nevertheless, the unexpected price-cycle reversion reveals the unsustainable situation, hampering potential gradual measures and boosting sharp macroeconomic adjustments that, in turn, usually destroy capabilities and increase social conflict (Porcile and Sanchez-Ancochea, 2021; Eichengreen, Park, and Shin, 2013).

This situation could be potentially avoided, without significant changes in the goods and services produced, through a strong intra-sectoral productivity growth that compensates for the increase in costs. In that situation, simultaneous and parallel productivity and internal cost increases would keep the unit cost stable and would not give rise to the conditions described previously. However, intra-sectoral productivity growth without inter-sectoral reallocation of resources from traditional to higher productivity activities hardly follows the intensity and sustainability of cost growth.

Focusing on the Uruguayan experience, we observe that the recent boom in commodity prices, even with gains in export margins in some markets (D'Albora and Durán, 2013), was surpassed by cost increases when measured in the same currency (Figure 17.6). This narrowed opportunities to redirect resources to structural transformation in a way that would have promoted accelerated growth.

A productive transformation allowing the growth process to be sustained would require the accumulation of capabilities across the economic system. The literature on the middle-income trap has highlighted the relevance of policies for building technological capabilities. Policies related to educational expansion are critical to improve the educational levels of the population and increase enrolment in tertiary and vocational education (Paus, 2014; Lee, 2013).

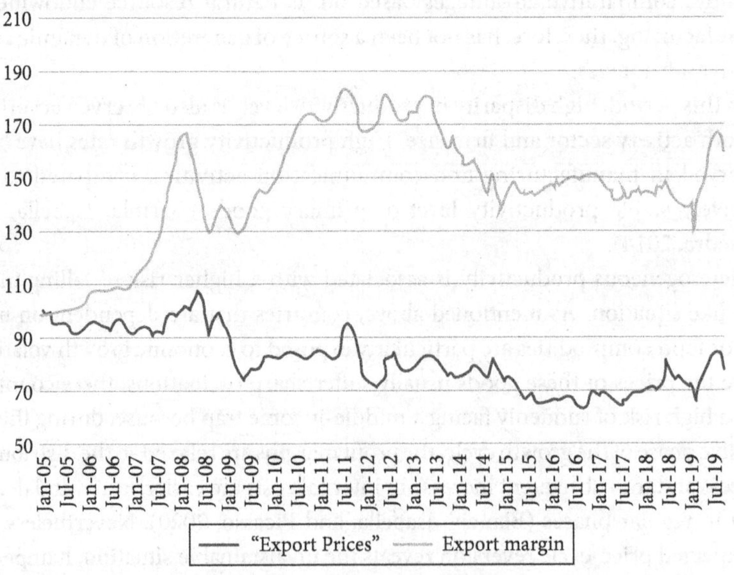

Figure 17.6. Uruguay export commodity price and export margin evolution, 2005–2021.

Source: Authors, based on Bianchi et al. (2020).

Moreover, the strength of the national innovation system (NIS), which entails a diverse and dynamic research community and regular linkages between the research base and the productive system, is also a critical dimension for a sustained growth process. Finally, such a process requires high levels of strategically driven public and private investment (Lee, Lee, and Lee, 2021; Paus, 2014).

However, recent research from Latin America has stressed the relevance of policy barriers that hamper the decision-making process of strategic selection and structural change (Donner and Schneider, 2016, 2020). These authors argue that a critical issue for middle-income countries relates to building the necessary support coalitions to manage the inherent conflict associated with the definition of strategic goals and productive and skills priorities in a process of structural change. This has been recently analysed, in particular referring to the recent boost of innovation policies in Latin American countries (Chiarini et al., 2020; Kang and Paus, 2020; Bianchi, Pittaluga, and Fuentes, 2018).

The barriers to the formation of support coalitions for development projects that involve strategic selections of winners and losers are a long-lasting issue in the political economy of Latin America (Hirschman, 1958). This not only is related to the inability to create consensus (Donner and Schneider, 2016), but also reflects a democratic reality where no authoritarian solutions can be imposed.

17.3. Uruguay in the Twenty-First Century: Industrial and Innovation Policies to Escape the Middle-Income Trap?

Latin American thinking on science, technology, and innovation (STI) has traditionally been discussed within the framework of national development strategies, in particular, according to the articulation or disarticulation of these policies with others, such as industrial, macroeconomic, educational, and, recently, socially inclusive policies (Sábato and Botana, 2021; Dutrénit and Sutz, 2014; Sagasti, 2005; Herrera, 1972). A classic concept from this body of literature distinguishes between policies that are explicitly oriented to promoting scientific and technological change and those that, being oriented to other areas, implicitly affect the development of technical change (Sagasti, 2005; Herrera, 1972).

An example of implicit STI policies is given by the relationship between macroeconomic policies and innovation policies. In Uruguay, during the period analysed in this chapter, macroeconomic policy aimed to promote macroeconomic stability and economic growth. Macroeconomic policy may affect innovation and industrial policies differently. For example, low exchange rates will affect the competitiveness of exports and facilitate the importation of products that are competitive with domestic production, potentially affecting the development of supply chains. The implication of this is that it is not enough to develop adequate explicit STI policies if these are not articulated appropriately with implicit policies (Cimoli and Katz, 2003).

More recently, a rich stream of research about the so-called policy mixes and instrument mixes has appeared in the international literature (e.g. Flanagan, Uyarra, and Laranja, 2011; Borrás and Edquist, 2013; Magro and Wilson, 2019). This is focused on the articulation at the micro level between STI policies, and between STI policies and other public policies, such as health, industrial, and environmental policies. The basic idea is similar to the concept of explicit and implicit policies, applied at the micro level. The policy mix refers to the concern that different policies and instruments may overlap or even produce substitution effects among one another. Moreover, different instruments may require some sequencing between them to obtain efficient results. On the contrary, an unbalanced policy mix may only be oriented to some types of problems or agents.

Based on these ideas, some research has applied the notion of implicit and explicit policies to analyse the extent to which the STI policies are articulated under a coherent rationale. Such research has been carried out in Brazil (De Melo and Rapini, 2012) and Uruguay (Aboal et al., 2015). We will now use this approach to analyse the micro-level articulation between STI policies and industrial policies during Uruguay's inclusive growth period. In doing so, we analyse the innovation and industrial policies as necessary conditions to generate structural change, which, in turn, is needed to sustain an inclusive growth strategy (Porcile and Sánchez-Ancochea, 2020; Ciarli, Savona, and Thorpe, 2021).

17.3.1. Institutional Setting and Governance

In the period under analysis, Latin American countries experienced a return of industrial policies (Pagés, 2010) and a progressive expansion of innovation policies (Crespi and Dutrénit, 2014). In the Uruguayan case, this process was characterized by the creation of ministerial cabinets to address sectoral agendas—that is, innovation, production, social inclusion, public security, and foreign trade—which aimed to facilitate a transversal approach to complex long-run development challenges in Uruguay.

Innovation policies had been framed by the first Strategic National Plan of STI (PENCTI by its Spanish acronym), established by law in 2006 and effectively approved in 2010 (Uruguay, 2006, 2010). This plan is based on the general premise that STI activities are a tool for social and economic development rather than an end in themselves. Aiming to stimulate the contribution of STI to development, the PECNTI defined five main goals. The first goal refers to consolidating the scientific-technological system and its links with productive and social needs; in relation to that, the second goal of the PENCTI refers to increasing the competitiveness of the productive sectors in the globalization scenario. In line with the development strategy that Uruguay followed in this period, the third and fourth goals, respectively, of the PENCTI refer to developing capacities and opportunities for the social appropriation of knowledge and 'inclusive' innovation, and to educating and training the human resources required to meet the demands for building a knowledge society. Finally, the PENCTI stated a fifth goal related to developing a system of prospective surveillance and evaluation as support for the achievement of the other proposed objectives and for the evaluation of public policies and STI instruments.

One pillar of this plan is the contribution of STI to structural change by promoting new activities or areas (i.e. biotechnology, nanotechnology, and ICTs), but also emphasizing the relevance of the technological convergence between these technologies and the main agricultural productive chains in the country (Bianchi and Snoeck, 2009).

Based on these strategic orientations, a number of institutional changes were introduced, which were based on three principles. First, the idea of STI as a development tool needs a transversal governance design that allows both the diffusion of the STI agenda in all government offices and, especially, the emergence of specific STI agendas based on the problems observed in the different government areas. Hence, a Ministry Cabinet of Innovation (GMI by its Spanish acronym) was created. The GMI consisted of four ministries (Economy, Agriculture, Industry, and Education) and the Planning Office. It was supposed that this design would facilitate the identification of problems and their translation to STI demands.

Meanwhile, by the same legal act, the National Council of Innovation, Science and Technology (CONICYT by its Spanish acronym) was reformulated, expanding its integration by including representatives of local governments, the education system, and labour unions, in addition to those already participating from the government, business, and universities (Uruguay, 2006). This change was based on the same rationale of transversal and participative policies that supported the creation of the GMI. By the extension of the integration of the CONICYT, a better and deeper articulation between the STI agenda and the productive and social problems was expected. In addition, the National Agency of Research and Innovation (ANII by its Spanish acronym) was created by the same law. The agency design—a model that is widely diffused in Latin America—is based on some postulates of the new public management ideas as to the importance of efficient management for the implementation of programs and instruments separated from the spheres of design and strategic orientation, which have been supposed to be reserved for the GMI (Bianchi, Bianco, and Snoeck, 2014; Angelelli, Luna, and Suaznábar, 2017).

Different authors point out that this institutional design faced several problems related to its governance. Among the major drawbacks detected, we can mention the displacement of the function of defining policies towards lower levels (as in the case of the ANII, given the ineffectiveness of the GMI). In terms of Donner and Schneider (2016), it is possible to assert that the Uruguayan government was not able to build a broad and strong enough coalition within the public authorities to support transversal policies. In addition, problems related to the design of policies have been observed, especially the PENCTI's lack of clear goals (Bértola and Lara, 2017).

Regarding industrial policies, several layers of policy instruments were deployed. Some previous sectoral subsidies—for example, automotive, beverage, and clothing—remain active jointly with horizontal regimes promoting investment. Moreover, in 2010, the Ministry of Industry launched the sectoral councils as the main policy instrument. These councils aimed to articulate the strategical articulation of previous instruments and the creation of new ones. Sectoral councils consisted of representatives from the sectoral chambers, the labour unions, the government, and, in some cases, the academy. The work methodology consisted of elaborating sectoral diagnoses, organized in a hierarchical set of problems and challenges, and defining a sectoral plan to address these challenges (Pittaluga et al., 2016). There were 19 sectoral councils that showed heterogeneous and uneven performances. In some cases, the councils remain as deliberative spaces, while others were able to define sectoral plans and reach some of the main goals (Bianchi, Pittaluga, and Fuentes, 2018).

This policy has also been conceived as part of the actions of a transversal Ministry Cabinet, the Productive Cabinet. Similar problems to those mentioned regarding innovation policy were observed in the Productive Cabinet. In spite of the transversal design, the sectoral advisory councils show little involvement from various ministries. Hence, this policy instrument was practically reduced to the initiative of the Ministry of Industry. As happened with the case of the ANII and the GMI in the innovation policies, this affected the strategic orientation of the councils. In addition, this problem revealed serious challenges to public-sector coordination, which is a basic element of a policy development coalition.

Industrial policies oriented to structural change have met resistance from private actors. For example, the public contracting subprogram for the development of the pharmaceutical industry, created by the Council of Pharmaceutics in 2014, was initially conceived as a way to promote changes in the national industry, but it finally provides a market reserve for national production in state pharmaceutical purchases without any counterpart from local firms beyond certifications in quality standards (Bianchi, 2021). Moreover, the model of advisory councils in some traditional sectors does not facilitate the definition of a strategic sectoral plan, but continues to focus only on the resolution of problems and bottlenecks that are very immediate, without being able to build longer-term strategies (Bertola and Lara, 2017). In some sectors, mainly traditional ones, this appears as a critical barrier to the articulation of industrial plans with the STI policy agenda, which, by definition, requires relatively long-term planning.

Uruguay has many other experiences of institutional design for public-private collaboration in productive and technological policies, mostly related to agricultural production. Sectoral institutes governed by public-private councils have played a critical role in promoting research and development in agricultural fields (Pittaluga et al., 2016). The agricultural innovation system was developed early in the twentieth century and has historically shown better functioning than the manufacturing system (Bianchi, Bianco, and Snoeck, 2014). Moreover, during this period some examples of technology convergence between high-tech sectors and agricultural sectors were developed, for example, the diffusion of electronic traceability in cattle production (Pittaluga et al., 2016). This can be considered a strategic tool for upgrading in the beef industry and gaining access to new and more demanding markets (D'Albora and Duran, 2013; Paolino, Pittaluga, and Mondelli, 2014). Relatedly, recent studies have identified opportunities for the development of high-tech services driven by the demand of dynamic agricultural sectors; however, these initiatives are still incipient, and their potential development relies strongly on public capabilities (Bisang et al., 2022).

One particular agro-based sector which has benefited from long-run public policies and constitutes a strong new export driver is the forest sector. Its development can be traced back to 1987, when a forest-oriented law was passed that promoted plantations in special locations based on the characteristics of the land (forest priority areas) through direct subsidies. Since then, a wide range of instruments have prompted the activity, which has evolved from just 26,000 hectares in 1987 to more than a million today (OPP, 2018). What is more, the sector also attracted huge industrial investment in the mechanical processing of wood (e.g. sawn goods, wood panels) and especially in paper pulp (cellulose), which constitutes the second-largest export of the country with around 20% of the country's exports. These investments also benefited from general promotion instruments like the Investment Promotion Regime (RPI by its Spanish acronym) and the free-zones regime. This experience is in line with the experience of other countries like Chile and Malaysia whose success is explained by new activities strongly dependent on natural-resource endowments (Lebdioui, Lee, and Pietrobelli, 2021). Moreover, within the innovation policy, some instruments oriented to research and innovation on strategic problems of forest activities have been implemented by the ANII.

There were other significant differences between innovation and industrial policies. First, the innovation policies became a new area in Uruguayan public policy that, until then, had not been formalized, and fewer activities were carried out in dispersed organizations (Rubianes, 2014). Meanwhile, industrial policy is a long-standing policy, with key instruments that were maintained and the creation of sectoral councils being the main institutional novelty, but not the most important instrument considering both the budget allocation and the demand from the productive agents.

Arguably, the main industrial policy was the RPI, which aims to provide a unique, coherent, and objective system of tax incentives for investments from both national and foreign investors (Uruguay, 1998, 2007, 2012). The Application Commission (COMAP by its Spanish acronym) is in charge of the implementation of this system. This commission assesses the contributions of the investment projects to some development goals defined in the legal framework, which are measured using a matrix of economic indicators linked to employment, innovation, promotion, and diversification of exports, decentralization in the countryside, and use of clean technologies (Llambí et al., 2018). Moreover, the creation of and support for the development of free trade zones has also been one of the most important industrial policies and has been applied in a sustained manner in recent decades in Uruguay (Ons and García, 2016; Bértola, 2018; Lavalleja and Scalesse, 2020). In the free zones of Uruguay, any type of activity—commercial, industrial, or services—can be developed and is exempt from any national tax. Under a strategy of attracting investment and integration into regional markets, other instruments were created to promote trade facilities, also based on tax-exemption mechanisms. Thus, together with the free zone policy and the RPI, the free port and free airport regimes and the Industrial Parks Law have been developed. These instruments have been essential for the development of so-called global services, which currently account for around 15% of Uruguayan exports (Uruguay XXI, 2022).

Another difference between STI and industrial policies is related to the creation of state capacities to conduct them. While the ANII was endowed with its own budget, other areas, such as the sectoral councils, the CONICYT, and the ministerial cabinets themselves, received almost no budget. This affected the creation and dedication of public capacities in those spaces and also affected the potential articulation of these policy agendas due to the relative imbalance between the staff of these organizations (Bianchi, Pittaluga, and Fuentes, 2018).

The transversal rationale that supported the creation of the ministerial cabinets began to be critically reviewed around 2015. In the first place, this type of design, although theoretically valid, had been shown to be ineffective in achieving the involvement of ministerial authorities. This meant, in the case of the STI policy, a shift of policymaking responsibilities to the ANII. In the case of industrial policy, the concentration of responsibility in the Ministry of Industry found the limits of its political capacity for public-sector and public-private articulation.

Furthermore, the articulation between these two agendas had not resulted in a coherent policy mix, but in an instrument mix more or less associated with different policies. In this context, between 2015 and 2017 the Uruguayan government promoted the creation of the National System for Productive Transformation and Competitiveness (SNTPC by its Spanish acronym), which operated from the end of 2017 until the change of government in 2020. The SNTPC replaced the ministerial cabinets for innovation and production, transferring responsibility for the articulation to the Ministerial Cabinet of Productive Transformation, which includes almost all ministers. In addition, a technical secretariat was created to coordinate the system, with the explicit aim of articulating the industrial, investment, and innovation policy agenda (Kefeli, 2020).

The SNTPC implemented a policy called *Transforma Uruguay* which maintained many of the guidelines of previous policies, with an emphasis on the coordination of policies and based on the action of a specialized secretariat that aims to overcome the previously observed problems of coordination. The first plan of *Transforma Uruguay* defines orientation guidelines, focusing on development objectives and productive sectors and activities, aiming to improve the impact of policy instruments, and seeking greater effectiveness in a scenario of limited resources. Moreover, the plan promotes the generalization of good practices in the design and application of public policies and the specialization of public institutions and inter-institutional articulation.

Even though the SNTPC did not mean a new strategic plan for STI, this system allows some incipient advances in the coordination between innovation and industrial policies and also in mapping the instrument mix related to these policies. An example of coordination efforts is the definition of the CONICYT as the consultative council in STI of the SNTPC, and the role of ANII as an executive agency in innovation instruments (*Transforma Uruguay*, 2018). However, the experience shows that the Secretariat collaborated with the agencies—for example, ANII—to obtain the necessary support for some instruments that agencies already had in their agenda, but was not able to enforce modifications in the operative plans of the agencies according to the national plan of productive transformation (Kefeli, 2020).

17.3.2. Types of Policies and Instruments

During the period under study, together with the return of the public policies oriented to promoting STI and industrial activities, the number of instruments in these areas showed a dramatic increase (Figure 17.7).

This increase seems to reflect a singular period in the Uruguayan public policy, characterized by the return of industrial policies and a unique explicit

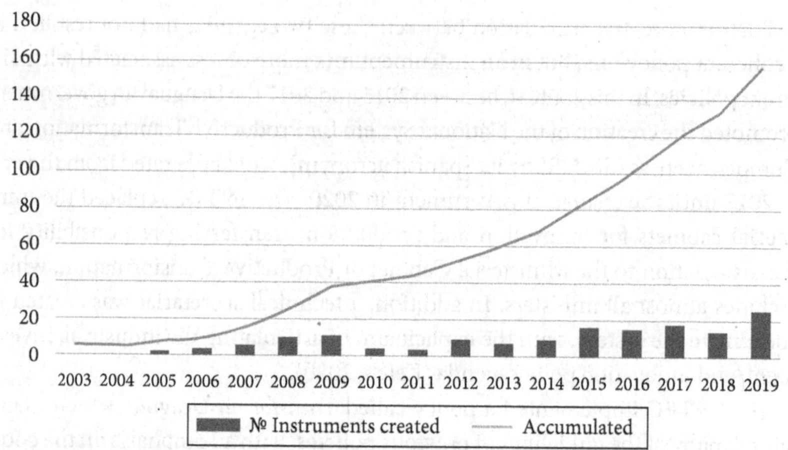

Figure 17.7. Uruguay STI and industrial policy instruments, 2003–2019.
Source: Authors, based on data from https://pcti.uy/.

promotion of the STI policies. In this context, a sort of policy experimentation (Leutert, 2021)—which does not mean experimental policies in the sense of policies based on experimental design (Bravo-Biosca, 2020)—has emerged, mostly guided by the creation of new policy instruments and with relatively little evaluation. An indicator of this experimentation process may be seen in the fact that around 30% of the instruments created in this period have been opened only for one edition (Bianchi et al., 2022).

Focusing on the instruments of STI policies, it is observed that most of the instruments created in this period have been oriented to promoting innovation, investment, or technology acquisition in firms, while the number of new instruments oriented to research activities has been comparatively low. However, the resources allocated in this period to research activities, basic and applied, have been greater than those allocated to innovation programs (Bianchi, Pittaluga, and Fuentes, 2018). This seems to reflect some characteristics of both the innovation system and the policy process. First, there is a consistent demand for public funds for research activities from the academic community. Conversely, because of the structural characteristics of the productive sector, there is little demand for public programs oriented to innovation. A small number of Uruguayan firms usually conducted some type of innovative activity and, within innovative firms, external acquisition of knowledge embodied in machinery prevails, rather than R&D or external cooperation (Bukstein, Hernández, and Usher, 2018; Berrutti and Bianchi, 2020). Precisely to address these lacks, the policy experimentation has mostly focused on the search for instruments oriented to mobilizing firms' innovation. In this context, many instruments have been implemented with the aim of creating incentives to change the traditional behaviour of Uruguayan firms (Bukstein et al., 2020). Second, in the Uruguayan context, this type of instrument arguably has a necessary component of experimentation because the instruments are oriented toward a non-fully-identified target population. Therefore, these instruments do not respond to an expressed demand of public support, but to create new demands of public support. Conversely, research instruments, as usually happens worldwide, already have a clearly identified demand from the academic community. Moreover, as research activities have increased during this period in Uruguay, demand for new resources and instruments have also increased.

In both industrial policies and innovation and research policies, the use of horizontal-type instruments has predominated. However, there were also vertical policies focused on specific sectors or problems and some initiatives to promote systemic linkages (Barrios, Gandelman, and Michelin, 2010; Álvarez et al., 2012; Peres, 2013; Bértola, Isabella, and Saavedra, 2014). Industrial policies were mostly based on tax credits and free zone regimes with the aim of attracting foreign direct investment and promoting national investment. These instruments were widely used and have contributed to additional effects on a large share of the private investment conducted in the period (Bértola and Lara, 2017; Llambí et al., 2018). However, they were conceived as horizontal instruments, in the sense that they did not focus on strategic sectors or activities but were available to any investment project regarding its contribution to some policy goals (employment, exports, etc.). What is more, as a consequence of their conception, which was mostly centred on corporate rent tax exemptions, they only benefited those sectors that were already profitable, rendering unchanged the situation of those activities that did not originally benefit from static comparative advantages. Vertical policies such as sectoral public procurement programs, on the other hand, had little development (Bértola, Isabella, and Saavedra, 2014).

Regarding innovation policies, the most used instruments were also based on tax credits or subsidies implemented in a horizontal way (Bukstein, Hernández, and Usher, 2018; Bukstein et al., 2020). According to the available evaluations, these instruments have had additional positive effects on the innovative firms' investments but hardly any effects on the innovation behaviour of the rest of the firms (Aboal and Garda, 2015; Bukstein, Hernández, and Usher, 2019; Berrutti and Bianchi 2020).

According to previous works, the tax credit delivered through the RPI represented almost 3% of yearly GDP (2012), which implies more than 12 times the budget delivered by ANII. The significant difference between the incentives given to industrial and innovation policies may operate as an implicit matrix of incentives that negatively affects the propensity to innovate in favour of following investment plans mostly based on the same type of production that firms have already done (Aboal et al., 2015)

The required capacities of the public sector to execute different types of instruments are also different. While the instruments that provide tax benefits and subsidies mainly require fund-management capabilities (controller role), in the instruments of technical assistance and associativity, articulation and facilitation capacities are necessary, in addition to the availability of technical personnel for implementation (executing role) (Bértola, Isabella, and Saavedra, 2014).

17.4. Final Remarks

Uruguay experienced an inclusive growth episode during the commodity price boom at the beginning of the twenty-first century. However, this experience was not accompanied by significant changes in the productive structure. This can be interpreted as a critical weakness with regard to sustaining economic growth in a democratic context, amid increasing demands for welfare provision. In line with the recent literature, the chapter found that structural change oriented to promoting the intensive use of knowledge is a necessary condition for sustaining an inclusive growth path. In turn, public policies are necessary to stimulate and orientate structural change.

The failure to generate sufficient structural change might lead one to conclude that the Uruguayan state was passive. This was not so. In fact, it deployed a broad set of policies and instruments aimed at promoting both innovation and industrial activities. This may be observed in other Latin American countries, especially those that applied more intensive and sophisticated policies for a more developed industrial and innovation system (Lebdioui, Lee, and Pietrobelli, 2021; Bresser Pereira, Araújo, and Peres, 2020).

However, policy action faced limits due to problems of articulation between different policy areas. At the macroeconomic level, the implemented policies successfully assured fiscal stability, promoted investment, and controlled inflation during the growth period. In the same vein, the expansion of the formal labour market, the regulation of wages, and focused social policies contributed to an inclusive model which increasingly demanded more resources.

At the micro and meso levels, however, the articulation between the industrial and STI agendas has not resulted in a coherent policy mix. Despite a certain evolution, the new initiatives faced important governance problems, budget constraints, lack of commitment from first-level authorities, and permanent public-sector articulation barriers. Horizontal industrial policies based on the promotion of investment and free zone regimes were the main tools employed. However, they did not promote sufficient structural change. Thus, despite some promising new activities, the need to overcome price competition in simple industries and to move towards an innovation-based competitive matrix of sophisticated activities has not been clearly addressed in the recent Uruguayan cycle.

Turning to the future, the extant evidence on the effects and impact of innovation and productive policies is too limited (Bianchi et al., 2022). Some public agencies and offices have recently incorporated the evaluation of programs and policies in their regular activities (Duran et al., 2020; Bukstein, Hernández, and Usher, 2018), but it is not possible to present a rigorous evaluation of the whole system. Together with the results of the new impact-evaluation programs, further research is needed which may benefit from incorporating the experience of policy design, particularly by considering both the recurrent effect of the price boom in commodity markets, and the barriers to public-sector and public-private articulation barriers that previous policy initiatives have faced.

New strategic development plans in the fields of innovation and development are needed which should systematically integrate the inputs from evaluations of policies and instruments in the design of experimental policies. In this sense, policy design should include *ex ante* not only the main goals and measurable results expected from the instruments, but also the potential barriers and the capacity required to overcome them.

References

Aboal, D., Angelelli, P., Crespi, G., López, A., Vairo, M., and Pereschi, F. 2015. 'Innovación en Uruguay: Diagnóstico y propuestas de política', *Uruguay +25 Documento de Trabajo*, No. 12. RedSur, Fundación Astur, Montevideo. https://www.cinve.org.uy/wp-content/uploads/2015/05/Documento-de-Trabajo-11.pdf.

Aboal, D., and Garda, P. 2015. 'Does Public Financial Support Stimulate Innovation and Productivity? An Impact Evaluation', *CEPAL Review*, 115, 42–62. http://hdl.handle.net/11362/38832.

Agénor, P. R. 2017. Caught in the Middle? The Economics of Middle-Income Traps', *Journal of Economic Surveys*, *31*(3), 771–791.

Albuquerque, E. 2019. 'Brazil and the Middle-Income Trap: Its Historical Roots', *Seoul Journal of Economics*, 32(1), 23–62.

Álvarez, R., Benavente, J., Contreras, C., and Contreras, J. 2012. 'Consorcios tecnológicos en Argentina, Chile, Colombia y Uruguay', *El Trimestre Económico*, 79(313), 227–256.

Álvarez, J., Bilancini, E., D'Alessandro, S., and Porcile, G. 2011. 'Agricultural Institutions, Industrialization and Growth: The Case of New Zealand and Uruguay in 1870–1940', *Explorations in Economic History*, 48(2), 151–168.

Andersen, A., and Johnson, B. 2011. 'Monocausalism versus Systems Approach to Development: The Possibility of Natural Resource-Based Development'. Aalborg, Denmark: Aalborg University. https://vbn.aau.dk/en/publications/monocausalism-versus-systems-approach-to-development-the-possibil-2

Angelelli, P., Luna, F., and Suaznábar, C. 2017. 'Agencias latinoamericanas de fomento de la innovación y el emprendimiento: Características y retos futuros', *Nota Técnica* No. IDBTN-1285, BID. http://dx.doi.org/10.18235/0000857.

Baptista, B. 2016. 'Revisión histórica de las políticas de ciencia, tecnología e innovación en Uruguay', *Documentos On-line /FCS-UM*, No. 46. https://hdl.handle.net/20.500.12008/27144.

Barrios, J. J., Gandelman, N., and Michelin, G. 2010. 'Analysis of Several Productive Development Policies in Uruguay', *IDB Working Paper Series*, No. IDB-WP-130. Washington, DC: Inter-American Development Bank (IDB. http://hdl.handle.net/10419/89157.

Berrutti, F., and Bianchi, C. 2020. 'Effects of Public Funding on Firm Innovation: Transforming or Reinforcing a Weak Innovation Pattern?', *Economics of Innovation and New Technology*, 29(5), 522–539. https://doi.org/10.1080/10438599.2019.1636452

Bértola, L., coord. 2018. 'Políticas de desarrollo productivo en Uruguay'. *Informes Técnicos*, 11. Lima: ILO. http://www.ciu.com.uy/innovaportal/file/87034/1/wcms_636583.pdf.

Bértola, L., and Lara, C. 2017. 'Política industrial en el ciclo de los commodities en Uruguay', in M. Cimoli, M. Castillo, G. Porcile, and G. Stumpo, eds., *Políticas industriales y tecnológicas en América Latina*. Santiago de Chile: CEPAL, 411–459. http://hdl.handle.net/11362/43939.

Bértola, L., and Ocampo, J. A. 2012. *The Economic Development of Latin America since Independence*. Oxford: Oxford University Press.

Bértola, L., and Porcile, G. 1998. 'Argentina, Brazil, Uruguay and the World Economy: An Approach to Different Convergence and Divergence Regimes'. *DOL (Documentos On-line) Reedición/FCS-UM*, No. 18. UR. https://www.colibri.udelar.edu.uy/jspui/bitstream/20.500.12008/4663/1/DOL%20UM%2018.pdf.

Bértola, L., Isabella, F., and Saavedra, C. 2014. 'El ciclo económico de Uruguay, 1998–2012', *Documentos On-line/FCS-UM*, No. 33. https://hdl.handle.net/20.500.12008/4678

Bianchi, C. 2021. 'Cadena de valor biofarmacéutica: Potencialidades y desafíos para el Uruguay', *Estudios y perspectivas*, No. 54. Montevideo: CEPAL. https://hdl.handle.net/11362/47362.

Bianchi, C., Bianco, M., and Snoeck, M. 2014. 'Value Attributed to STI Activities and Policies in Uruguay', in G. Crespi and G. Dutrénit, eds., *Science, Technology and Innovation Policies for Development*. New York: Springer, 133–155.

Bianchi, C. Bortagaray, I. Liurner, F. and Magallán, E. 2022. 'Desafíos para el Uruguay del siglo XXI: Políticas de ciencia, tecnología e innovación y el desarrollo sostenible', *Serie Ideas para agendas emergentes*, No. 4. Montevideo: UNDP-UN. https://www.undp.org/es/uruguay/publications/desaf%C3%ADos-para-el-uruguay-del-siglo-xxi-pol%C3%ADticas-de-ciencia-tecnolog%C3%ADa-e-innovaci%C3%B3n-y-desarrollo-sostenible .

Bianchi, C., Isabella F. Picasso S. 2020. 'La trampa de ingresos medios: nuevas exploraciones sobre sus determinantes', *Serie Documentos de Trabajo*, DT 18/2020. Instituto de Economía, Facultad de Ciencias Económicas y Administración, Universidad de la República, Uruguay. https://hdl.handle.net/20.500.12008/26898.

Bianchi, C. Pittaluga, L. and Fuentes, G. 2018. 'The Capacity Required by Innovation and Structural Change Policies in Uruguay', in E. Stein, J. Cornick, E. Fernández-Arias, E. Dal Bó, and G. Rivas, eds., *Building Capabilities for Productive Development*. Washington, DC: IDB, 81–109. doi:http://dx.doi.org/10.18235/0001182. 81-121

Bianchi, C., and Snoeck. M. 2009. *Ciencia, tecnología e innovación a nivel sectorial: Desafíos estratégicos, objetivos de política e instrumentos*. Montevideo: ANII. https://www.anii.org.uy/upcms/files/listado-documentos/documentos/libro-cti-anivelsect.pdf.

Bisang, R., Lachman, J., López, A., Pereyra, M., and Tacsir, E. 2022. 'Agtech: Startups y nuevas tecnologías digitales para el sector agropecuario. Los casos de Argentina y Uruguay', *Documento de Investigación*, No. 132. Montevideo: Universidad ORT Uruguay, Facultad de Administración y Ciencias Sociales. http://hdl.handle.net/20.500.11968/4645.

Borrás, S., and Edquist, C. 2013. 'The Choice of Innovation Policy Instruments', *Technological Forecasting and Social Change*, 80(8), 1513–1522.

Bravo-Biosca, A. 2020. 'Experimental Innovation Policy', *Innovation Policy and the Economy*, 20(1), 191–232.

Bresser-Pereira, L., Araújo, E., and Peres, S. 2020. 'An Alternative to the Middle-Income Trap', *Structural Change and Economic Dynamics*, 52, 294–312.

Bukstein, D., Hernández, E., Monteiro, L., Peralta, M., Reyes, C., and Usher, X. 2020. 'Evaluación de los programas de innovación empresarial de ANII, 2009–2018'. Montevideo: Agencia Nacional de Innovación e Investigación. https://www.anii.org.uy/institucional/documentos-de-interes/4/informes-de-evaluacion/.

Bukstein, D., Hernández, E., and Usher, X. 2018. 'Impacto de los instrumentos de promoción de la innovación orientada al sector productivo: El caso de ANII en Uruguay', *Estudios de Economía*, 45(2), 271–299. http://dx.doi.org/10.4067/S0718-52862018000200271.

Bukstein, D., Hernández, E., and Usher, X. 2019. 'Assessing the Impacts of Market Failures on Innovation Investment in Uruguay', *Journal of Technology Management & Innovation*, 14(4), 137–157. http://dx.doi.org/10.4067/S0718-27242019000400137.

Catela, Y., and Porcile, G. 2012. 'Keynesian and Schumpeterian Efficiency in a BOP-Constrained Growth Model', *Journal of Post Keynesian Economics*, 34(4), 777–802.

Chiarini, T., Cimini, F., Rapini, M., and Silva, L. 2020. 'The Political Economy of Innovation: Why Is Brazil Stuck in the Technology Ladder?', *Brazilian Political Science Review*, 14, 1–39.

Ciarli, T., Savona, M., and Thorpe, J. 2021. 'Innovation for Inclusive Structural Change', in J. D. Lee, K. Lee, D. Meissner, S. Radosevic, and N. Vonortas, eds., *The Challenges of Technology and Economic Catch-up in Emerging Economies*. Oxford: Oxford University Press, 349–376.

Cimini, F., Britto, J., and Ribeiro, L. C. 2021. 'Complexity Systems and Middle-Income Trap: The Long-Term Roots of Latin America Underdevelopment', *Nova Economia*, 30, 1225–1256.

Cimoli, M., and Katz, J. 2003. 'Structural Reforms, Technological Gaps and Economic Development: A Latin American Perspective', *Industrial and Corporate Change*, 12(2), 387–411.

Crespi, G., and Dutrénit, G., eds. 2014. *Science, Technology and Innovation Policies for Development: The Latin American Experience*. Cham: Springer.

Crespi, G., and Zuniga, P. 2012. 'Innovation and Productivity: Evidence from Six Latin American Countries', *World Development*, 40(2), 273–290.

D'Albora A., and Durán, V. 2013. '¿Ha mejorado la calidad de los productos agroindustriales exportados por Uruguay? Un análisis de los precios de exportación,' *Anuario OPYPA 2013*. Montevideo: MGAP.

De Melo, L., and Rapini, M. 2021. 'Innovation Finance and Funding in the National System Innovation: The Brazilian Case', in M. Kahn, L. M. de Melo, and M. G. P. de Matos, eds., (2020). *Financing Innovation: BRICS National Systems of Innovation*. Rio de Janeiro: Taylor & Francis, 21–77.

Doner, R. F., and Ross Schneider, B. R. 2016. 'The Middle-Income Trap: More Politics than Economics', *World Politics*, 68(4), 608–644.

Doner, R., and Schneider, B. R. 2020. 'Centripetal Politics and Institution Building in Exiting the Middle-Income Trap', in J. A. Alonso and J. A. Ocampo, eds., *Trapped in the Middle?: Developmental Challenges for Middle-Income Countries*. Oxford: Oxford University Press, 94–116.

Durán, V., Aguirre, E., Baraldo, J., Hernández, E., and Laguna, H. 2020. 'Resultados y aprendizajes de la evaluación de políticas agropecuarias en Uruguay', *Cuadernos del CLAEH*, 39(112), 103–117.

Dutrénit, G., and Sutz, J., eds. 2014. *National Innovation Systems, Social Inclusion and Development*. Cham: Springer.

ECLAC. 2014. *Cambio Estructural para la igualdad: Una visión integrada del desarrollo*. Santiago de Chile: ECLAC. http://hdl.handle.net/11362/36700.

Eichengreen, B., Park, D., and Shin, K. 2013. 'Growth Slowdowns Redux: New Evidence on the Middle-Income Trap', *National Bureau of Economic Research*, No. w18673.

Figueiredo, P., and Cohen, M. 2019. 'Explaining Early Entry into Path-Creation Technological Catch-up in the Forestry and Pulp Industry: Evidence from Brazil', *Research Policy*, 48(7), 1694–1713.

Filgueira, C. 1983. 'Estructura y cambio social: Tendencias recientes en Argentina, Brasil y Uruguay', *Seminario sobre Cambios Recientes en las Estructuras y Estratificación Sociales en América Latina*. Santiago de Chile: CEPAL.

Filgueira, F. 2005. 'Welfare and Democracy in Latin America: The Development, Crises and Aftermath of Universal, Dual and Exclusionary Social States'. Paper prepared for the UNRISD Project on Social Policy and Democratization, Geneva.

Filgueira, F., Gutiérrez, M., and Papadópulos, J. 2011. 'A Perfect Storm? Welfare, Care, Gender and Generations in Uruguay', *Development and Change*, 42(4), 1023–1048.

Flanagan, K., Uyarra, E., and Laranja, M. 2011. 'Reconceptualising the "Policy Mix" for Innovation', *Research Policy*, 40(5), 702–713.

Grassi, D. 2014. 'Democracy and Social Welfare in Uruguay and Paraguay', *Latin American Politics and Society*, 56(1), 120–143.

Herrera, A. 1972. 'Social determinants of science policy in Latin America: explicit science policy and implicit science policy', *The Journal of Development Studies*, 9(1), 19–37.

Hirschman, A. 1958. *The Strategy of Economic Development*. New Haven, CT, and London: Yale University Press.

Isabella, F. 2015. 'International Technological Dynamics in Production Sectors: An Empirical Analysis', *CEPAL Review*, 115, 23–39.

Kang, N., and Paus, E. 2020. 'The Political Economy of the Middle Income Trap: The Challenges of Advancing Innovation Capabilities in Latin America, Asia and Beyond', *The Journal of Development Studies*, 56(4), 651–656.

Kefeli, D. 2020. 'Capacidades estatales para el diseño e implementación del Sistema Nacional de Transformación Productiva y Competitividad'. Master's dissertation in public policies, FCS, UDELAR, Montevideo. https://hdl.handle.net/20.500.12008/30481.

Laguna, H., and Bianchi, C. 2020. 'Firm's Innovation Strategies and Employment: New Evidence from Uruguay', *Serie Documentos de Trabajo*, DT 06/2020. Instituto de

Economía, Facultad de Ciencias Económicas y Administración, Universidad de la República, Uruguay. https://hdl.handle.net/20.500.12008/24910.

Lanzaro, J., and Piñeiro, R. 2017. 'Uruguay: A Counterexample of Malaise in Representation: A Propitious Transformation of the Old Party Democracy', in A. Joignant, M. Morales, C. Fuentes, eds., *Malaise in Representation in Latin American Countries*. New York: Palgrave Macmillan, 211–231.

Lavalleja, M., and Scalese, F. 2020. 'Los incentivos y apoyos públicos a la producción en el Uruguay'. Montevideo: CEPAL. http://hdl.handle.net/11362/45107.

Lebdioui, A., Lee, K., and Pietrobelli, C. 2021. 'Local-Foreign Technology Interface, Resource-Based Development, and Industrial Policy: How Chile and Malaysia Are Escaping the Middle-Income Trap', *The Journal of Technology Transfer*, 46(3), 660–685.

Lee, K. 2013. *Schumpeterian Analysis of Economic Catch-Up: Knowledge, Path-Creation, and the Middle-Income Trap*. Cambridge: Cambridge University Press.

Lee, K. 2019. *The Art of Economic Catch-Up: Barriers, Detours and Leapfrogging in Innovation Systems*. Cambridge: Cambridge University Press.

Lee, K., Lee, J., and Lee, J. 2021. 'Variety of National Innovation Systems (NIS) and Alternative Pathways to Growth beyond the Middle-Income Stage: Balanced, Imbalanced, Catching-Up, and Trapped NIS', *World Development*, 144, 1–20.

Leutert, W. 2021. 'Innovation through Iteration: Policy Feedback Loops in China's Economic Reform', *World Development*, 138, 1–11.

Llambí, C., Rius, A., Carbajal, F., Carrasco, P., and Cazulo, P. 2018. 'Are Tax Credits Effective in Developing Countries? The Recent Uruguayan Experience', *Economía*, 18(2), 25–58. https://muse.jhu.edu/article/694083.

Magro, E., and Wilson, J. R. 2019. 'Policy-Mix Evaluation: Governance Challenges from New Place-Based Innovation Policies', *Research Policy*, 48(10), 1–10.

Martínez Franzoni, J., and Sánchez-Ancochea, D. 2014. 'The Double Challenge of Market and Social Incorporation: Progress and Bottlenecks in Latin America', *Development Policy Review*, 32(3), 275–298.

Moreira, C. 2004. 'Resistencia política y ciudadanía: plebiscitos y referéndums en el Uruguay de los 90', *América Latina Hoy*, (36), 17–45.

Ons, Á., and Garcia, P. 2016. *Análisis de los instrumentos de promoción de inversiones el caso de Uruguay*. Washington DC: BID. https://publications.iadb.org/es/publicacion/15644/analisis-de-los-instrumentos-de-promocion-de-inversiones-el-caso-de-uruguay.

Oficina de Planeamiento y Presupuesto (OPP). 2018. 'Oportunidades para el futuro de la bioeconomía forestal en Uruguay'. *Hacia una Estrategia Nacional de Desarrollo Uruguay 2050, Serie de divulgación, Volumen XII*. Montevideo: Dirección de Planificación, Oficina de Planeamiento y Presupuesto. https://www.opp.gub.uy/sites/default/files/inline-files/Oportunidades%20para%20el%20futuro%20de%20la%20bioeconomi%CC%81a%20forestal%20en%20Uruguay.pdf.

Pagés, C. 2010. *The Age of Productivity*. New York: Palgrave Macmillan. https://doi.org/10.1057/9780230107618.

Paolino, C., Pittaluga, L., and Mondelli, M. 2014. 'Cambios en la dinámica agropecuaria y agroindustrial del Uruguay y las políticas públicas', *Serie Estudios y Perspectivas*, No. 15. Montevideo: CEPAL. http://hdl.handle.net/11362/36780.

Paus, E. 2014. 'Latin America and the Middle Income Trap', *ECLAC, Financing for Development* Series (250). Santiago de Chile: ECLAC.

Peres, W. 2013. 'Industrial Policies in Latin America', in A. Szirmai, W. Naudé, and L. Alcorta, eds., *Pathways to Industrialization in the Twenty-First Century: New Challenges and Emerging Paradigms*. Oxford: Oxford University Press, 223–243.

Pérez, C. 2010. 'Technological Dynamism and Social Inclusion in Latin America: A Resource-Based Production Development Strategy', *CEPAL Review*, 100, 121–141. https://doi.org/10.18356/7dce2f27-en.

Pittaluga, L., Rius, A. Bianchi, C., and González, M. 2016. 'Cattle Traceability, Biotechnology, and Other Stories of Collaboration in Uruguay', in E. Fernández-Arias, C. Sabel, E. H. Stein, et al., eds., *Two to Tango: Public-Private Collaboration for Productive Development Policies*. Washington, DC: IDB, 237–294. https://publications.iadb.org/en/two-tango-public-private-collaboration-productive-development-policies-0.

Porcile, G., and Sanchez-Ancochea, D. 2021. 'Institutional Change and Political Conflict in a Structuralist Model', *Cambridge Journal of Economics*, 45(6), 1269–1296.

Radetzki, M., and Wårell, L. 2020. *A Handbook of Primary Commodities in the Global Economy*. Cambridge: Cambridge University Press.

Rubianes, E. 2014. 'Políticas públicas y reformas institucionales en el sistema de innovación de Uruguay', in G. Rivas and S. Rovira, eds., *Nuevas instituciones para la innovación: Prácticas y experiencias en América Latina*. Santiago de Chile: CEPAL, 221–257. http://hdl.handle.net/11362/36797.

Sábato, J., and Botana, N. 2021 [1968]. 'Science and Technology in the Future Development of Latin America', *Documento de Trabajo de CiTINDe* No, 1. Universidad de la República, Montevideo. https://citinde.ei.udelar.edu.uy/publicacion/la-ciencia-y-la-tecnologia-en-el-desarrollo-futuro-de-america-latina/ .

Sagasti, F. 2005. *Knowledge and Innovation for Development: The Sisyphus Challenge of the 21st Century*. London: Edward Elgar.

Suárez, D., and Erbes, A. 2016. 'Trapped in the Middle: Development, R&D and the National Innovation System', *IDEI Working Paper*, DT IDEI 19-2016, UNGS-IDEI, Los Polvorines.

Sunkel, O., and Paz, P. 1979. *El subdesarrollo latinoamericano y la teoría del subdesarrollo*. México, DF: Siglo XXI.

Transforma Uruguay. 2017. 'Primer Plan de Transformación Productiva y Competitividad', *Transforma Uruguay—Sistema Nacional de Transformación Productiva y Competitividad*. Montevideo. https://www.opp.gub.uy/es/noticias/plan-de-transformacion-productiva-y-competitividad.

Transforma Uruguay. 2018. 'Informe a la Asamblea General', *Transforma Uruguay—Sistema Nacional de Transformación Productiva y Competitividad*. Montevideo. http://www.diputados.gub.uy/docs/TransformaUruguay/Documento-TU-web.pdf.

Uruguay. 1998. 'Ley 16.906. Ley de Inversiones. Promoción Industrial'. Montevideo. https://www.impo.com.uy/bases/leyes/16906-1998.

Uruguay. 2006. 'Ley 18.084. Se establecen los cometidos y competencias de la Agencia Nacional de Investigación e Innovación'. Montevideo. https://www.impo.com.uy/bases/leyes/18084-2006.

Uruguay. 2007. 'Presidencia de la República, Decreto 455/007. Reglamentación de la metodología de evaluación de los proyectos de inversión'. Montevideo. https://www.impo.com.uy/bases/decretos/455-2007.

Uruguay. 2010. 'Presidencia de la República, Decreto 82/010. Aprobación del Plan Estratégico Nacional de Ciencia, Tecnología e Innovación'. Montevideo. https://www.impo.com.uy/bases/decretos/82-2010.

Uruguay. 2012. 'Presidencia de la República, Decreto 02/012. Reglamentación de la metodología de evaluación de los proyectos de inversión'. Montevideo. https://www.impo.com.uy/bases/decretos/2-2012.

Uruguay XXI. 2022. 'Servicios Globales en Uruguay'. Montevideo: Uruguay XXI. https://www.uruguayxxi.gub.uy/es/centro-informacion/articulo/servicios-globales-de-exportacion-2022/.

Vivarelli, M. 2016. 'The Middle Income Trap: A Way Out Based on Technological and Structural Change', *Economic Change and Restructuring*, 49(2–3), 159–193.

18

Costa Rica

The Challenge of Diversification in a Small-Country Context

Jeffrey Orozco and Keynor Ruiz

18.1. Introduction

For several decades, starting in the 1950s, Costa Rica developed a state apparatus focused on improving living conditions, attending at different times to the social demands of the population, and leading to the development policy becoming a key component in promoting a virtuous circle of economic growth with social equity. This style of development was inspired by Keynesian approaches and the ideas of the welfare state, which were reflected in expansive monetary and fiscal policies aimed at developing the industrial sector through public investments in infrastructure, tariff protection policies, and various incentives for industrial production. This all had clear features of an import substitution industrialization model (for a detailed analysis, see Arias and Muñoz, 2007).

This industrialization model achieved significant improvements in the living conditions of the population. However, the model began presenting several contradictions. Eventually there emerged a strong crisis that affected economic growth, political stability, and the possibility of continuing to improve the population's welfare in a sustained manner. As stated by Furst (1986) and Sojo (1984), the problems were connected to several factors, including the impact of higher oil prices after the creation of the Organization of the Petroleum Exporting Countries (OPEC), the external debt crisis, adverse conditions in the international economy, a growing fiscal crisis, and the inconsistency and lack of consensus in the management of economic policy, especially in the period 1978–1982. This set of internal and external challenges led to a deep recessionary crisis in the years 1979 to 1982. This underscored the urgency of a change in policies to promote the country's development (Arias, 1992).

As a result of the bilateral negotiation processes with the International Monetary Fund (IMF) and the World Bank (WB) during the 1982–1986 period, the objective was to obtain financial resources to promote the stabilization and reactivation of the country's economy. In 1982, with the signing of the first agreement with the

Jeffrey Orozco and Keynor Ruiz, *Costa Rica* In: *Innovation, Competitiveness, and Development in Latin America*.
Edited by: Edmund Amann and Paulo N. Figueiredo, Oxford University Press.
DOI: 10.1093/oso/9780197648070.003.0018

IMF, the country began a process of economic reforms structured on IMF and WB stabilization and structural adjustment programmes. A slow recovery of the main macroeconomic indicators was achieved (Herrero and Rodríguez, 1987) as a new development model was introduced, focused on promoting exports of non-traditional products to third markets (Arias and Muñoz, 2007). In addition, a programme of fiscal adjustment was introduced alongside exchange and interest rate policies designed to bring inflation under control.

18.2. Beginnings of the Export Promotion and Diversification Programmes

For many years, Costa Rica had been using tariff protection as part of the import substitution model. But it must be kept in mind that this type of protection also affects the export sector, since in practice it becomes a kind of two-way tax, raising the price of the intermediate goods that are protected, and therefore increasing the price of exports that use those intermediate goods. In turn, this causes an overvaluation of the exchange rate, which then reduces the purchasing power of the local currency that producers receive for each dollar exported (Willmore, 1997). Part of the change towards an export stimulus model was the gradual reduction of tariff protection. In the meantime, free-trade zones were created, offering fiscal incentives through the reduction of taxes on intermediate goods, as well as lower taxes on profits. Temporary admission regimes were also promoted, which allowed production plants located anywhere in the country to carry out assembly or *maquila* work using imported inputs, with the purpose of exporting them free of customs duties (Willmore, 1997).

In Costa Rica, direct subsidies were also provided to promote exports. The figure used was the tax credit certificate (CAT) for exporters. This instrument required a minimum value added (around 35%) of national origin in their products. As Willmore (1997) argues, by 1992 a large part of Costa Rica's non-traditional exports obtained these subsidies, but they were later eliminated in the early 2000s. Several authors analysed the incentive scheme and concluded that it had different types of problems. For example, Alonso and Alonso (1990) pointed to the high fiscal impact of CATs. Furst (1992) and Corrales and Monge (1990) argued that the instruments applied did not guarantee an authentic productive transformation capable of achieving a solid insertion of the Costa Rican economy in international markets. Corrales and Monge (1990) carried out a study in which they obtained important data. They showed that tax exonerations for raw materials and inputs were a factor of great relevance for 97% of exporting companies, 87% gave great importance to them, and 61% said that exoneration from national taxes was of great relevance.

Based on a more in-depth study of several companies in different branches of industrial activity, Orozco (1996) pointed out several risks of the CAT, since they were being applied without solving more general problems, such as lack of export infrastructure, complexity of export and import procedures, the protectionism of some target markets, and the complexity of the international legal system. In addition, Orozco concluded that many of the companies were not making significant transformations that would lead them to generate sustained competitiveness; the CAT came to account for more than 100% of their profits, so there was an imminent risk that when the incentive disappeared, the companies would not be able to survive. Still, Costa Rica's non-traditional exports to third markets (outside Central America) responded to the set of incentives and changes in trade policy.

One of the most relevant aspects of the economic reform process in Costa Rica was the gradual application of productive transformation measures. At the same time, the Costa Rican government managed to maintain the characteristics of the welfare state—the institutional framework and the network of public organizations aimed at addressing the social problems of a small economy in the process of development. Thus, the transition from an import substitution model to a more export-oriented model of insertion in the international market was carried out through a set of policies in which the state was setting the tone and generating greater participation spaces for the private productive sectors, while providing a social safety net. The model that emerged was characterized by productive diversification aimed at exports, both agricultural products and manufactures. At the same time, trade liberalization and encouragement of inward investment made Costa Rica an increasingly attractive space for economic growth and learning.

18.3. Changes towards Programmes to Attract Foreign Direct Investment Focused on High Technologies

As mentioned above, in the 1980s Costa Rica began to open its economy and create a series of institutions and policies to promote international trade and attract investment. Gradually, a more outward-oriented growth development model was adopted. The effort was accompanied by investment-promotion efforts aimed at guiding companies to reduce costs and improve efficiency (Dunning, 1993). In the early stages, much of the foreign direct investment (FDI) attracted to the country was focused on the textile and apparel industries and some agro-industrial activities. A major change occurred in 1997 with the arrival of Intel. This company paved the way for other multinational high-tech companies. Through this, Costa Rica developed a solid reputation as an investment destination. This opened further space to attract investments in other sectors such as business services and manufacturing. In the latter, key activities such as medical devices, aeronautics, and automotive parts were developed (Gómez, Zolezzi, and Monge, 2018).

As Monge and Zolezzi (2012) argue, the arrival of Intel in Costa Rica can be considered as the turning point of the country's insertion into global production chains, and as the beginning of a sector oriented to the production and export of sophisticated, high-tech manufacturing and value-added services. The example of Intel helped attract emblematic multinationals in other sectors, especially in business services. Much greater dynamism in FDI inflows occurred from the mid-1990s onwards. Starting in 1997, Costa Rica saw a pronounced increase in the number of firms operating in knowledge-intensive sectors, such as information technology (IT) and IT-enabled services, advanced manufacturing, and medical devices (Gómez, Zolezzi, and Monge, 2018).

The Dominican Republic-US-Central America Free Trade Agreement (CAFTA-DR), signed in 2004, brought significant changes. It led to a surge in FDI flows to the medical device industry, especially from US companies. The trade agreement provided for the reduction or elimination of tariffs and included investment-protection mechanisms with a secure and predictable framework. In addition, CAFTA-DR introduced liberalization of the telecommunications sector, which was gradually opened up. It also led to increasing investment and reinvestment of foreign companies in the business services sector, many with US capital (Gómez, Zolezzi, and Monge, 2018).

Many other internationally well-known companies opened operations in Costa Rica over time, such as Fiserv, which installed a captive centre dedicated to application development, quality assurance, technology documentation writing, and information security. P&G selected Costa Rica for its Financial Services Centre for the Americas, while in 2009 Hewlett Packard also invested in Costa Rica and established the first R&D centre outside the United States. Other companies, such as Baxter Healthcare, Hospira, Allergan, and Bridgestone, also made important investments in Costa Rica, generally using free-trade zone schemes. The number of companies has continued to grow (a detailed analysis can be found in Gómez, Zolezzi, and Monge, 2018).

As will be seen below, the country's efforts to attract foreign direct investment have been successful, and exports in modern services and high-tech manufacturing have been growing steadily. The origins of this policy date back to the second half of the nineteenth century when education was declared free and compulsory, using the resources that were previously used by the army. Subsequently, as summarized by Gómez et al. (2018), the country has invested in other organizations focused on education and training for the industrial sector.

Alongside this, a series of policies have been implemented to promote exports by modern service sectors. The most relevant groups of policies have been focused on competence and capability-building. Among them, we can highlight the efforts made by the Costa Rican Coalition of Development Initiatives (CINDE) to identify the competence and skills requirements of foreign multinational corporations (MNCs) established in the country, and those that have shown interest in investing in Costa Rica (Ruiz, 2020, p. 25). This initiative has made it possible to coordinate with vocational training organizations to introduce changes aimed at satisfying the demand for these skills. Another is the creation of new careers at the vocational secondary schools. An example is the *Cedes don Bosco*, which includes vocational training in graphic design, electronics, electromechanics, network computing, computer science in software development, and precision mechanics. The Instituto Nacional de Aprendizaje (INA, for its Spanish acronym) is one of the state organizations with the greatest scope of action in professional training, through face-to-face and virtual courses, as well as dual training. This organization has 54 training centres around the country and an important part of its training courses are related to the demands of the export services sectors. Projects have also been achieved with local universities in areas of computer engineering, mechatronics, electronics, project management, among others (Gómez, Zolezzi, and Monge, 2018). It is clear that capabilities, competencies, and skills of the labour force have been a central element of Costa Rica's relative success in attracting FDI (Salazar, 2022).

Another group of policies have focused on tax incentives, which are found in Law No. 7210 of the Free Zone Regime and its reforms. The main benefits of the regime encompass tax and duty exemptions for raw materials, processed or semi-processed products, and machinery and equipment. This provision also extends to work vehicles. In addition, there exist exemptions for a period of 10 years from the payment of capital tax and real estate transfer tax; exemption from sales and consumption tax on purchases of goods and services; exemption from taxes on fuels and oils; exemption from all taxes on profits, with differentiated percentages depending on the location of the company inside or outside the Greater Metropolitan Area (GAM); exemption for 10 years on all taxes and municipal patents; and exemption of all taxes on remittances abroad.

It can be considered that the main FDI attraction policy is centred on all the incentives contemplated in the Free Trade Zone Regime Law, but other policies have also been generated, among which is the negotiation of bilateral investment agreements (BITs). These in general have included investment chapters (there are more than 20 BITs, and 15 are in force).

Costa Rica joined the Central American Common Market (CACM) in the early 1970s. This was the country's first regional trade agreement. In the mid-1980s a unilateral reduction of tariffs and non-tariff barriers was applied and, as mentioned, the promotion of non-traditional exports was initiated. Entry into the General Agreement on Tariffs and Trade (GATT) and subsequent participation as a founding member of the World Trade Organization (WTO) took place in 1995. The first bilateral trade agreement was signed with Mexico and entered into force in 1995. Bilateral agreements were also signed with the Dominican Republic, Chile, and Canada. These entered into force in 2002. In addition, a free trade agreement was negotiated with the Community of Caribbean States (CARICOM). This treaty entered into force on different dates: for Trinidad and Tobago (2005); for Guyana and Barbados (2006); for Belize (2011); and finally for Jamaica (2015). With Panama, a treaty was negotiated at different times and finally entered into force in 2008.

One of the most important negotiation efforts was the Central America–Dominican Republic–United States Free Trade Agreement (CAFTA-DR), which was completed between 2003 and 2004. One of the most drastic changes brought about by this agreement was the opening of some service-sector activities. The Association Agreement between Central America and the European Union was also negotiated between 2007 and 2010. This agreement entered into force in 2013. Subsequently, trade agreements with China (2013), with Peru (2013), and with Colombia (2016) were put into force. A trade agreement with South Korea was negotiated in 2018. This high number of agreements has been favourable, particularly for the services sector, because of the clauses they contain regarding cross-border trade in services, financial services, telecommunications, and temporary entry of businesspersons. In addition, these agreements guarantee respect for the most favoured nation (MFN) and national treatment (NT) principles and include a series of preferential market access conditions (Gómez, Zolezzi, and Monge, 2018).

18.4. Main Institutional Changes Promoted in the New Model

In order to promote a stable and reliable country image, making it attractive for attracting investment and to promote investment in general, several institutional changes have been generated. In 2011, the Law for the Protection of the Person against the Processing of Personal Data was created, which was later complemented with other regulations. The Agency for the Protection of Personal Data (PRODHAB) was also created, with the function of overseeing compliance with the data-protection rules established in the national legislation. Similarly, emphasis has been given to the protection of intellectual property, based on internal regulations and on what has been negotiated in most of the free trade agreements, as well as with the signing of multilateral agreements.

Among the fundamental actions have been, as explained by Gómez et al. (2018), the pursuit of a strategy for the export of modern services, with concrete measures for the attraction of FDI focused on high-value-added services. This has been complemented by the negotiation of trade agreements and bilateral investment agreements. Likewise, actions have been proposed to take advantage of labour force capabilities and competencies and the benefits granted by the free trade zone regime. Export goals for this type of services began to be set for the period 2006–2010. This type of goal made it possible to evaluate the results with respect to the targets set and to periodically review the strategies designed to achieve them. As part of the strategy, coordination processes were initiated between various public and private actors. The Ministry of Foreign Trade (COMEX, for its acronym in Spanish) stands out, and within it the General Directorate of Foreign Trade and the Directorate of Investment. Of great relevance has been the Foreign Trade Promoter (PROCOMER), which functions as an export-promotion agency and as the executing arm of the policies defined by COMEX.

CINDE has also been playing a fundamental role, responsible for attracting FDI, and also as an executing arm of COMEX. The Ministry of Science, Technology, and Telecommunications (MICITT) has also played a role, as it is responsible for dictating policy that promotes the use of knowledge and innovation as mechanisms to improve competitiveness and welfare. Other entities, such as the Ministry of Labor and Social Security (MTSS), the Ministry of Public Education (MEP), the Central Bank of Costa Rica (BCCR), the National Learning Institute (INA), the Chamber of Information and Communication Technologies (CAMTIC), the Costa Rican Union of Chambers and Associations of the Private Business Sector (UCCAEP), and the Association of Free Zone Companies of Costa Rica (AZOFRAS), also participate as key players in the system, contributing from their specific fields of action. A strength of the strategy is that very effective coordination mechanisms have been achieved between the different public and private entities, including specific mechanisms such as the creation of working groups between exporting companies and government institutions (Gómez, Zolezzi, and Monge, 2018).

18.5. Achievement Indicators of the Promoted Programmes

Several stages that have marked the evolution of Costa Rica's international trade over the past 71 years. A first stage is clearly identified until the 1970s by the export of traditional products, mainly dominated by coffee and banana exports. As mentioned in section 18.1, between 1980 and 1982 there was a turning point, caused mainly by the severe crisis that led to a significant change in the growth model and greater interaction with the international market.

This was followed by a diversification of exports, always dominated by exports of agricultural products, although many of these were no longer traditional products. From the end of the 1980s and more markedly in the 1990s, the attraction of FDI gave way to the development of free trade zones. At this point, manufacturing industry, increasingly accompanied by services, began to play a more important role in national export dynamics. The dynamics of imports have been closely aligned with the evolution of exports. Imports have tended to exceed exports, but both share a common growth trend. As a result of this, Costa Rica ran a trade deficit from 1955 to 2021, except for 1999. This deficit has accelerated since 2000, when the trade deficit has accounted for up to one-third the value of total exports. In this sense, Ruiz (2012) points out that the trade deficit was financed by the growing income from FDI, which represented 98% of the country's current account balance for that period.

In addition, it is important to note that, when observing the evolution of exports and imports, different depressions can be seen in both series, most of which occurred during periods of world economic recessions, when there was a generalized decrease in economic activity, such as the international oil price crisis (1973–1974), the Latin American debt crisis (1980), the world dollar crisis (1985), the Asian crisis (1996), the subprime mortgage crisis and commodity prices (2008), and the global crisis of the COVID-19 pandemic (2020).

With the stabilization policies and the change to the export-promotion model, starting in 1992 there was a marked difference in the growth of exports and imports, boosted by the growth of certain agricultural products and the manufacturing industry. The participation of the free trade zones had a strong influence, which reached a key point in 1999 when, after many years and as an exceptional case in the balance of trade, exports exceed imports. However, this trend was cut short by the great contraction in 2000, when exports fell by 38% and imports by 13%, while imports fell by 1% in 2001. It is important to mention that, for the period prior to the year 2000, exports of services began to gain an important weight in Costa Rica's productive matrix, representing approximately 27% by the end of 2000. An important characteristic of Costa Rica's trade dynamics with respect to the evolution of traditional versus non-traditional exports is that the trend has stabilized and the structure, with some ups and downs, has been maintained throughout the past two decades.

The next drop in exports and imports occurred in 2008–2009, with the subprime mortgage crisis and the prices of raw materials in the international market. At that time, the world and the country began a recession due to a collapse of the economic and financial system, which had not been seen since the Great Depression of 1930. Costa Rica was also affected by this crisis, the best example being an 11% drop in exports in 2009, while imports registered a 26% drop in 2009. For its part, the State of the Nation Program Sustainable Human Development (2014) mentions the following in relation to exports of goods and services: 'Goods [exports] presented negative rates only in the years 2001 and 2009, while those of services in 2001, 2002 and 2009' (p. 12). This is due to the fluctuations of the world economy, especially with the economy of the United States, with which Costa Rica has an important commercial relationship.

Finally, there was a significant drop in imports of 4% in 2019 and 12% in 2020; this drop corresponds to the paralysis of world trade, due to the COVID-19 pandemic, where many economies of the world adopted lockdown measures to curb the contagion. In addition, there was also a positive decrease in exports due to the collapse of tourism and transportation, but the most affected were imports, as they registered negative annual growth rates.

Costa Rica's economy has experienced a significant transformation, with clear expansion, sophistication, and diversification of its export base, in which the growth of exports of modern services has played a role of relevance (Table 18.1). These have become one of the most dynamic in the national economy (Gómez, Zolezzi, and Monge, 2018). The marked growth achieved is impressive, with total services exports rising from US$488 million in 1991 to US$8,232 million in 2021.

Figure 18.1 shows the changes in the distribution of services exports by type between 2010 and 2021. The total amount of exports of services were US$5,021 million and US$8,991 million in 2010 and 2021, respectively, where business and management consulting (including public relations) shows the biggest change among those years, changing from 26% to 54%. Travel services lost participation in the structure of services exports from 45% in 2010 to 19% in 2021, while ICT services increased from 11% to 16% during the decade. It is relevant to note that R&D services were important around the beginning of the 2010s (9%) but then reduced their participation in the structure of services exports. They are increasing again in 2021, but at only 4% of total services exports.

The most important activities within service exports are those related to business and management consulting services. Other business services are also important, such as travel (accommodation, food, transportation), as well as telecommunications, computing, and information. Therefore, it can be affirmed that services exports in Costa Rica are quite diversified and that this has been an important result of the incentives and the new institutional framework in the country.

18.6. An Analysis of the Rationality of Export-Promotion Policies from Innovation System and Middle-Income-Trap Approaches

There has been a growing literature surrounding the phenomenon known as the 'middle-income trap', and the possible strategies to move towards high-income possibilities (Gill and Kharas, 2007). Most of the empirical literature

Table 18.1 Evolution of Costa Rica's Services Exports

Year	Services Exports (Costa Rica Colon)	Average Exchange Rate (Costa Rica Colon per US$)	Services Exports (US$) M	Growth Rate of Services Exports
1991	₡ 59,674.19	122.1	$ 488.73	20%
1992	₡ 84,210.99	134.3	$ 627.22	28%
1993	₡ 113,932.67	142.4	$ 799.86	28%
1994	₡ 137,948.31	157.0	$ 878.54	10%
1995	₡ 166,805.81	179.6	$ 928.61	6%
1996	₡ 210,797.60	207.7	$ 1,014.86	9%
1997	₡ 254,067.92	232.6	$ 1,092.30	8%
1998	₡ 366,390.26	257.2	$ 1,424.59	30%
1999	₡ 500,552.94	285.7	$ 1,752.15	23%
2000	₡ 645,141.55	308.2	$ 2,093.32	19%
2001	₡ 700,844.23	328.9	$ 2,131.07	2%
2002	₡ 754,487.02	359.8	$ 2,096.85	−2%
2003	₡ 898,439.01	398.7	$ 2,253.65	7%
2004	₡ 1,116,911.97	437.9	$ 2,550.43	13%
2005	₡ 1,401,339.81	477.9	$ 2,932.41	15%
2006	₡ 1,693,096.39	511.3	$ 3,311.68	13%
2007	₡ 1,961,942.11	516.6	$ 3,797.68	15%
2008	₡ 2,227,703.85	526.2	$ 4,233.28	11%
2009	₡ 2,210,574.22	573.3	$ 3,855.96	−9%
2010	₡ 2,467,352.69	525.8	$ 4,692.31	22%
2011	₡ 2,736,344.11	505.7	$ 5,411.39	15%
2012	₡ 2,933,181.91	502.9	$ 5,832.52	8%
2013	₡ 3,246,461.10	499.8	$ 6,495.95	11%
2014	₡ 3,577,063.87	538.3	$ 6,644.90	2%
2015	₡ 3,896,064.96	534.6	$ 7,288.28	10%
2016	₡ 4,388,232.14	544.7	$ 8,055.65	11%
2017	₡ 4,816,193.17	567.5	$ 8,486.49	5%
2018	₡ 5,271,813.62	577.0	$ 9,137.03	8%
2019	₡ 5,899,309.96	587.3	$10,044.89	10%
2020	₡ 4,312,213.15	584.9	$ 7,372.56	−27%
2021	₡ 5,110,506.61	620.80	$ 8,232.13	12%

Source: Elaborated by authors with data from Banco Central de Costa Rica, https://gee.bccr.fi.cr/indicadoreseconomicos/Cuadros/frmVerCatCuadro.aspx?idioma=1&CodCuadro=%205802;

https://gee.bccr.fi.cr/indicadoreseconomicos/Cuadros/frmVerCatCuadro.aspx?CodCuadro=367&Idioma=1&FecInicial=1991/01/01&FecFinal=2022/06/10.

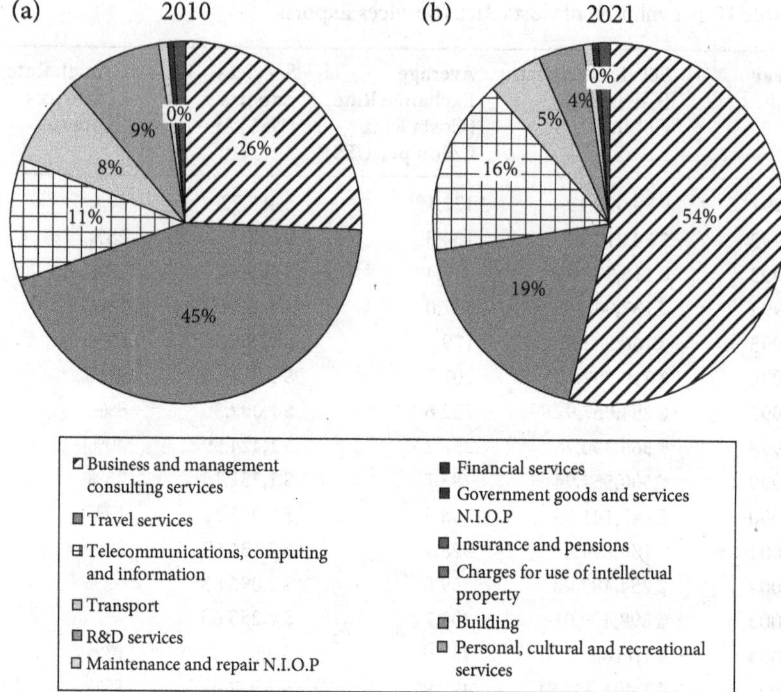

Figure 18.1. Distribution of Costa Rican services exports by category, 2010–2021.
Source: Elaborated by authors with data of Banco Central de Costa Rica (2010–2021).

on the middle-income trap suggests the relevant roles of capabilities, structural change, and technological progress as the key factors able to better positioning a middle-income country to meet the challenge (Vivarelli, 2014). As suggested by Perez-Sebastian (2007), Agenor and Canuto (2012), and Agenor et al. (2012), when some countries reach the middle-income level, the pool of unemployed and underemployed rural workers drains out, wages start to rise, but a significant problem is that benefits from imitation and importing foreign mature technologies decrease in importance. The result is then that the capital accumulation starts to show decreasing returns and difficulties to grasp further scale economies.

A key point in the literature is that changing the structure of the economy (diversification from low-productivity sectors into high-productivity ones) and on the types of product exported are the most important drivers in the strategies to overcome the middle-income trap (Gill and Bhattasali, 2007). Hidalgo and Hausmann (2009) understand economic development as a process based on building capabilities and learning capacities as the centre of the strategy to produce and export more complex and sophisticated goods through a continuous process of diversification, product differentiation, and product upgrading. It is important to consider that capability-building and catch-up by domestic firms depend greatly upon the nature and features of innovation systems, and it is necessary to consider the heterogeneous nature of the knowledge base, the specificity of the national, sectoral, and regional contexts, and the role of institutions in which innovative activities occur (Malerba and Lee, 2021). Strong efforts to promote innovation and structural change in the export sector are then necessary, and it is also necessary to strengthen the system of innovation.

In the innovation system approach, the set of interrelated components is understood as a system working towards a common objective (Carlsson et al., 2002). Therefore, the set of parts and aspects of the economic structure and institutional set-up that affect learning and research are understood as the innovation system (Lundvall, 1992). Innovation policy is then understood as an element of strategic coordination between the pressure of transformation, the ability to innovate and adapt to change, and the cost-benefits of that change with its respective social and spatial distribution (Lundvall, 2002). The comprehensive analysis of a national innovation system transcends the economic or financial sphere and reaches other institutional frameworks. The rationality of innovation policies refers to the background that is in this process and responds to why, when, and how to intervene in innovation processes (Lundvall, Chaminade, and Haneef, 2018).

Chaminade and Edquist (2010) understand innovation policies as those public actions that drive innovation processes, both for development and dissemination processes. They can be oriented to both economic and non-economic objectives. Edquist (2014, p. 191) and Borrás and Edquist (2018) suggest 10 basic objectives that an innovation system should fulfil. The rationality of innovation policies is based on trying to solve system problems. There are some failures in the system that hinder the possibility to reach these objectives. System problems in meeting those objectives can usually be understood as problems of infrastructure provision and investment problems; problems of transition; problems of 'lock-in'; institutional problems; network problems; skills and learning problems; exploration-exploitation imbalance; and complementarity problems (Chaminade and Edquist, 2010). Borrás and Edquist (2013) suggest a possible way to group policies and instruments to foster innovation, considering regulations (intellectual property, regulations), economic transfers (competitive funds, exemptions), and soft instruments (alliances, agreements). Orozco (2017) argues that to increase the efficiency of such policies and instruments, it is important to consider the geographical, sectoral, or firm-size specificities (there is a deeper analysis in Orozco, 2017, and in Orozco and Guillén, 2020).

Considering the analysis by Porter (1985), value chains have become a reference for the analysis of trade and industrial organization. One of the main characteristics is a global strategy to organize the full range of activities that firms and workers perform to bring a product or service from its conception to end-use and beyond. The whole range of activities (design, production, marketing, distribution, and support to the final consumer) can be contained within a single firm or divided among different firms. There is now a highly flexible and dynamic context. The location of different activities is a key issue. The location of the activities is based on decisions about choices related to country differences in the cost of input factors, competitiveness drivers, social and environmental conditions, as well as geographic and cultural proximity to the final consumer (Cattaneo et al., 2013).

One lesson in the global value chain (GVC) approach is the necessary paradigm shift from public to private impetus. In the new paradigm, trade and development policies should be increasingly designed and implemented in consultation and—where possible—in association with the private sector, moving from supply-side to demand-driven trade strategies. Three major intermediate objectives should be added to the trade competitiveness and development strategies: joining, maintaining participation, and moving up value chains (Cattaneo et al., 2013). The challenge is difficult, because of the heterogeneity of sectors, since the organization of GVCs tends to be sector-specific (and sometimes even firm-specific), and there are no one-size-fits-all policies (Sturgeon and Memedovic, 2011).

The rationality of policies in GVC approaches is aimed mainly at facilitating trade. According to the Organisation for Economic Co-operation and Development (OECD, 2012) and Cattaneo et al. (2013), the focus here should be on scaling down protectionist measures and improving infrastructure and communications. More specific to innovation and capacity-building, the approach recognizes that GVCs address capacity constraints, since a country does not need to develop a fully integrated industry to participate in international trade. But capacities and productivity remain key factors for foreign investors and lead firms. In the new trade paradigm, adaptability to the lead firms' requests, responsiveness, and capability to innovate are also key factors (World Bank, 2010).

The potential of a country for GVC participation is determined by different aspects, including capacity for scale production; availability of services necessary to support production and market integration; education and skills of the workforce matching the needs of global producers and buyers; and capacity for innovation in its multiple dimensions, including environmental sustainability (Cattaneo et al., 2013). In the new context, lead firms have to define strategies where innovation centres are decentralized. Lead firms need to innovate in developing countries, solving their specific needs, ultimately contributing to boosting developing-country exports (Govindarajan and Trimble, 2012). This requires the host developing country to generate innovation capacities, based on education and skills.

Stemming from this, there is a strong connection between the policy approaches of innovation systems and GVCs. It is clearer for the approach of sectoral systems of innovation. But it is also clear that for more geographical approaches of innovation systems, it is also necessary to consider both the challenges and the opportunities from the conditions of international trade. Most of the challenges for economic and social upgrading in GVCs require strong innovation systems. The main differences could be in the objectives to promote in both approaches, but the kind of policy instruments seem to be similar at the national level. However, it is necessary to consider the strong focus of GVC on international trade and on the role of the private sector and multinational firms.

Considering the rationality of both approaches, it is clear that Costa Rica's export-promotion and foreign-investment attraction policies have been mainly based on the GVC approach. Indeed, the strategy has focused on lowering barriers to international trade and consolidating an institutional framework to attract investment and promote new export products. From the point of view of the innovation-system approach, there are still many gaps in the country's policies, as will be discussed in the following section. These gaps have contributed to the maintenance of elements of the middle-income trap.

18.7. Conclusions

Despite Costa Rica's recent economic achievements, especially around export diversification, there remain structural challenges that need addressing if the country is to definitively exit the middle-income trap. Weaknesses persist around the capabilities of the financial system, coordination of different elements of development policies, and the integration of universities into the national system of innovation. Also, there is a need for stronger linkages between foreign and local firms in order to address challenges around the development of new technological capabilities and innovation. Without strategies to solve these problems, it will be difficult for the country to finally overcome the middle-income trap.

Several studies have analysed the functioning of the innovation system in Costa Rica (OECD, 2017; Orozco and Guillén, 2020; Orozco, 2021). The OECD concludes that the country's innovation system is very underdeveloped and highly fragmented, further stating that its actors have generally weak capacities to fulfil the functions that the system should address. The OECD study also states that funding schemes for technology and innovation have been weak, and that public research has suffered from a lack of focus on national problems. It also states that there are weak institutions and governance mechanisms. These do not contribute to an adequate articulation and implementation of effective policies. In this sense, it could be said that the interactions required in modern national innovation systems are not achieved. The OECD study also shows that there are great challenges to improve the quality of education. One of the aspects highlighted is the lack of coincidence between the demand and supply of labour force competences, and weaknesses around boosting individuals' general capabilities to integrate into the labour market.

An additional aspect that stands out is the weakness in advancing in mission-oriented research to solve the needs of the different sectors. The evidence is that Costa Rica confronts a series of characteristics that limit its capacity to promote innovation. These comprise: (a) weak priority given to science, technology, and innovation (STI) in national strategies and low budgets to STI; (b) institutional overlaps and legal/regulatory constraints hindering the effectiveness of STI policies, with high fragmentation; (c) ineffective governance practices, with weak coordination mechanisms and a legalistic approach; (d) inefficient procedures in the allocation of funds through STI programmes, (e) weak accountability of institutions/programmes in STI, with insufficient monitoring and evaluation; (f) underdeveloped statistical infrastructure for reporting STI and benchmarking policies, with imbalances in funding to different institutions with respect to universities; (g) absence of intermediary institutions for technology diffusion and business innovation; (h) weak absorptive capacity of domestic enterprise; low investments in R&D and technology adoption and weak industry-academia linkages; (i) increasing supply and demand mismatches of skilled personnel and weak vocational training; and (j) weak enforcement of the legal framework for intellectual property rights (OECD, 2017; Orozco, 2021).

There are also barriers around the functioning of the financial sector to promote innovation processes in the productive sectors. Thus, most companies depend on their own funds to promote their innovations (Orozco and Guillén, 2020). In response to so many weaknesses in the innovation system, a law was passed in 2021 creating the Innovation Agency. The entity began operating at the end of 2021 but is in a process of transition from its predecessor, CONICIT. There is still a long way to go in identifying the real contribution it will have in strengthening the country's innovation system.

Reflecting on the discussion so far, it is even more evident that the export-promotion and FDI-attraction strategy did not consider the innovation system as a whole, but was based on partial policies deriving from GVC approaches. Gómez et al. (2018) argue that a pending challenge for the new development model to be sustainable is to achieve economic growth based on increasing productivity. In addition, these authors highlight the need to increase the value of the domestic content of exports, for which it would be necessary to strengthen the linkages of exporting companies with the local production activities. These linkages cannot be built without increasing the technological capabilities of national companies and the competencies and capabilities of the labour force. Therefore, policies must be promoted from the logic of understanding the innovation system, supporting the existing linkages, and promoting new interrelations among actors.

Arias and Muñoz (2007) raise an issue that remains unresolved. They argue that there is an implicit contradiction in Costa Rica's export-promotion model, since due to exonerations and subsidies to stimulate exports, it has contributed to a structural fiscal deficit which has not been mitigated by a productive restructuring strategy in the other sectors of the economy. An associated issue that has been dragging on for a long time is the limited capacity to promote infrastructure, professional training, and R&D. All of these would, of course, require an increase in the fiscal burden (Garnier, 2005).

Thus, although export activity in Costa Rica remains very dynamic, it has not been able to consolidate itself as the engine of the economy, mainly due to the weak productive and technological integration with the national economy. This is an argument made by Mora (2000) and is still applicable today. He also made another argument that is still valid, namely, that a regulatory framework should be formulated to improve the international transfer of productive knowledge, technology transfer, and regional development. Despite the great dynamism of the export sector, and even considering the profound process of structural transformation, the economy's growth rates are still low and volatile. Problems such as informal employment and unemployment persist, largely due to the lack of linkages between the productive sectors and the rest of the economy. Important infrastructure problems, weaknesses in the educational system and personnel training, lack of an understanding and support to an innovation system are fundamental limitations (Salazar, 2020).

To grow at higher and sustained rates and reduce productive dualism, the country needs a new generation of productive development policies. These should have clear coordination between the public and private sectors and would have to draw on educational reforms, improvements in the vocational training system, and strengthening of the national innovation system (Salazar, 2022). It is important that the new institutions generated with the creation of the Agency of Innovation contribute significantly to promoting new initiatives. They should do this by facilitating interrelationships among actors and supporting capability-building in the innovation system. These new institutions would need to evolve proactive policies to consolidate the development model, advancing its environmental sustainability, and closing social gaps. As suggested by Monge (2020), the strategy to overcome the middle-income trap must include the development of an efficient National Innovation System (NIS). This implies the need to work in several areas: human resources (quality and quantity); financing (new instruments and hedging); governance of innovation policy (steering and execution of policies and programmes); and the creation of the institutions necessary for the correct attention of the typical market failures in terms of innovation.

Considering the experience of Costa Rica, we can summarize the most important policy lessons. First, as suggested by the middle-income trap literature, it is possible to move from low income to middle income, applying well-thought-out policies for structural change of the export sector. Second, however, it is much more difficult to move beyond this towards higher income levels. In Costa Rica the problem was that the policies adopted did not develop the system of innovation as a whole, and there was weak integration between the dynamic export sectors and the rest of the economy. Looking ahead, the third lesson is that it will not be possible to develop the necessary new sources of growth without addressing the latter and launching a holistic strategy to strengthen the system of innovation.

References

Agénor, P. R., and Canuto, O. 2012. 'Middle-Income Growth Traps, World Bank Policy Research', *Working Paper* 6210. Washington, DC: World Bank.

Agénor, P. R., Canuto, O., and Jelenic, M. 2012. 'Avoiding Middle-Income Growth Traps, Economic Premise', *Working Paper* No. 98. Washington, DC: World Bank.

Alonso, E. 1., and Alonso, E. 1. 1990. 'El contrato de exportación y el certificado de abono tributario en Costa Rica (CAT)', available at Consejo Superior Universitatio Centroamericano Library.

Arias, R. 1992. *Diagnóstico y evaluación de las principales limitaciones estructurales del sector industrial en la década de los ochenta*. Heredia: Universidad Nacional, Costa Rica.

Arias, R., and Muñoz, J. 2007. 'Pobreza: ¿Dónde estamos y cómo superarla? Reforma Económica y Modelo de Promoción de Exportaciones: Logros y vacíos de la política de desarrollo de las últimas dos décadas', *Ciencias Económicas* 5(1),15–40.

Banco Central de Costa Rica. 2022. *Exportaciones FOB acumuladas*. https://gee.bccr.fi.cr/indicadoreseconomicos/cuadros/frmvercatcuadro.aspx?idioma=1&codcuadro=%20467.

Banco Central de Costa Rica. 2022. *Importaciones CIF acumuladas*. https://gee.bccr.fi.cr/indicadoreseconomicos/cuadros/frmvercatcuadro.aspx?idioma=1&codcuadro=%20468.

Borrás, S., and Edquist, C. 2013. 'The Choice of Innovation Policy Instruments', *Technological Forecasting and Social Change*, 80, 1513–1522. https://www.sciencedirect.com/science/article/pii/S0040162513000504.

Borrás, S., and Edquist, C. 2018. 'The Design of Holistic Innovation Policy: Characterizing 22 Policy Problems', in Austrian Institute of Technology, ed., *Book of Abstracts EuSPRI Annual Conference Vienna 2017: The Future of STI—the Future of STI Policy*. Vienna: Austrian Institute of Technology, 9–10.

Carlsson, B., Jacobsson, S., Holmén, M., and Rickne, A. 2002. 'Innovation Systems: Analytical and Methodological Issues', *Research Policy*, 31(2), 233–245. https://www.researchgate.net/publication/222560405_Innovation_Systems_Analytical_And_Methodological_Issues.

Cattaneo, O., Gereffi, G., Miroudot, S., and Taglioni, D. April 2013. 'Joining, Upgrading and Being Competitive in Global Value Chains; A Strategic Framework', *The World Bank Poverty Reduction and Economic Management Network, International Trade Department*. https://openknowledge.worldbank.org/handle/10986/14444.

Chaminade, C., and Edquist, C. 2010. 'Rationales for Public Policy Intervention in the Innovation Process: Systems of Innovation Approach', in Ruud E. Smits, Stefan Kuhlmann, and Phillip Shapira, eds., *The Theory and Practice of Innovation Policy: An International Research Handbook*. Cheltenham, UK: Edward Elgar, 95–114. https://cristinachaminade.files.wordpress.com/2018/07/cham-edq-rationales-2010-postprint.pdf.

CEDES Don Bosco. 2022. *Oferta Técnica*. Publicación revisada el 18 de Octubre del 2022 en: https://www.cedesdonbosco.ed.cr/es/index.php/component/k2/item/9.

Corrales, J., and Monge, R. 1990. *Exportaciones no tradicionales de Costa Rica*. San José: Trejos Hermanos Sucesores.

Dunning, J. H. 1993. *Multinational Enterprises and the Global Economy*. Reading, MA: Addison Wesley.

Edquist, C. 2014. 'Systems of Innovation: Perspectives and Challenges', in J. Fagerberg and D. Mowery, eds., *The Oxford Handbook of Innovation*. Oxford: Oxford University Press, 181–208.

Furst, E. 1986. *Estabilización vs. industrialización: Crisis económica, medidas de estabilización y políticas industriales durante la administración Carazo; 1978–1982*. Heredia, Costa Rica: Universidad Nacional, Escuela de Economía. https://books.goog le.co.cr/books?id=5jMWnQAACAAJ&dq=inauthor:%22Edgar+F%C3%BCrst%22&hl=es&sa=X&redir_esc=y.

Furst, E. 1992. *Liberalización comercial y promoción de exportaciones en Costa Rica (1985–1990): Limitaciones y desafíos de la política de ajuste estructural reciente*. Maestría en Política Económica para Centroamérica y el Caribe, Universidad Nacional. Heredia, Costa Rica: Universidad Nacional, Escuela de Economía. https://books.google.co.cr/books?id=0chDAAAAYAAJ&q=politica+comercial+costa+rica&dq=politica+comercial+costa+rica&hl=es&sa=X&redir_esc=y

Garita, L. 1973. 'Algunas causas que han influido en el crónico desequilibrio de la balanza comercial de Costa Rica', *Revista de la Universidad de Costa Rica*, 35, 107–121.

Garnier, L. 2005. 'Importancia de la inversión social y de sus vínculos con una reforma fiscal', in M. Barahona and Y. Ceciliana, eds., *Reforma Fiscal en Costa Rica: Aporte a una Agenda Inconclusa*. San José, Costa Rica: Editorial FLACSO, 63–71.

Gill, I., Kharas, H., with Bhattasali D., et al. 2007. *An East Asian Renaissance: Ideas for Economic Growth*. Washington DC, World Bank.

Gobierno de Costa Rica. 20 October 1986. *Memorándum sobre el régimen de comercio exterior de Costa Rica*. World Trade Organization. https://docs.wto.org/gattdocs/s/GG/L6199/6050.PDF.

Gómez, A., Zolezzi, S., and Monge, F. 2018. *Gobernanza de la formulación e implementación de políticas públicas para las exportaciones de servicios modernos en Costa Rica*. San José, Costa Rica: UNCTAD.

Govindarajan, V., and Trimble, C. 2012. *Reverse Innovation: Create Away from Home, Win Everywhere*. Cambridge, MA: Harvard Business Review Press. https://hbr.org/2012/06/reverse-innovation-create-far.html.

Herrero, F., and Rodríguez, E. 1987. *La construcción del futuro a partir de la crisis: Asociación alternativas del desarrollo*. San José, Costa Rica: Centro de Estudios Democráticos de América Latina (CEDAL).

Hidalgo, C., and Hausmann, R. 2009. 'The Building Blocks of Economic Complexity', in *Proceedings of the National Academy of Sciences*, 106(26), 10570–10575.

Krugman, P., Obstfeld, M., and Melitz, M. 2012. *Economía internacional: Teoría y política*. Madrid: Pearson.

Lundvall, B. 1992. *National Systems of Innovation: Toward a Theory of Innovation and Interactive Learning*. London: Pinter Publishers. https://books.google.co.cr/books/about/National_Systems_of_Innovation.html?id=B_C3AAAAIAAJ&redir_esc=y.

Lundvall, B. 2002. *Innovation, Growth, and Social Cohesion: The Danish Model*. Cheltenham, UK: Edward Elgar. https://books.google.co.cr/books?hl=es&lr=&id=bixmAwAAQBAJ&oi=fnd&pg=PR1&dq=Lundvall,+B+(2002b).+Innovation,+Growth,+and+Social+Cohesion:+The+Danish+Model.+Edward+Elgar+Publishing.&ots=XnpR5vjZEL&sig=Ps7m9hB5-uOKTfeVxDcrQAfIz-k#v=onepage&q&f=false.

Lundvall B., Chaminade, C., and Haneef, S. 2018. *Advanced Introduction to National Innovation Systems*. Cheltenham: Edward Elgar. https://books.google.co.cr/books?hl=es&lr=&id=T2NaDwAAQBAJ&oi=fnd&pg=PT11&dq=Lundvall,+Chaminade+and+Haneef+(2018).&ots=sMyFlAu-qb&sig=I4rESTAyi6afH2bqcHOm2gQWY3g#v=onepage&q=Lundvall%2C%20Chaminade%20and%20Haneef%20(2018).&f=false.

Malerba, F., and Lee, K. 2021. 'An Evolutionary Perspective on Economic Catch-up by Latecomers', *Industrial and Corporate Change*, 30(4), 986–1010. https://doi.org/10.1093/icc/dtab008.

Monge-González, R. 2020. *Fortalecimiento del sistema nacional de innovación de Costa Rica como elemento clave para la mejora de la productividad y el crecimiento económico*. San José, Costa Rica: Academia de Centroamérica. doi:10.13140/RG.2.2.34847.38568.

Monge, R., and Zolezzi, S. 2012. 'Insertion of Costa Rica in Global Value Chains: A Case Study', *IDB Working Paper Series*, No. IDB-WP-373. Inter-American Development Bank, Integration and Trade Sector.

Mora, H. 2000. 'Capítulo V. Promoción de exportaciones y atracción de inversiones: Hacia un sistema nacional de innovación', *Economía y Sociedad*, February, 89–95.

OECD. 2012. *Managing Aid to Achieve Trade and Development Results: An Analysis of Trade-Related Targets*. Paris: OECD Publishing. https://www.oecd.org/dac/aft/VietnamCaseStudy.pdf.

OECD. 2017. *OECD Reviews of Innovation Policy: Costa Rica 2017*. Paris: OECD Publishing. http://dx.doi.org/10.1787/9789264271654-en.

Orozco, J. 2017. 'Políticas para promover la innovación: reflexiones para países en desarrollo', In J. Barrantes, O. Segura, and S. Alonso, eds., *Políticas económicas para el desarrollo sostenible*. Washington, DC: Global South Press, 101–125. https://www.revistas.una.ac.cr/index.php/politicaeconomica/article/view/10920.

Orozco, J. 1996. '¿Se está aumentando la productividad y la competitividad a niveles internacionales?', *Economía y Sociedad*, 1(02), 100–102. https://www.revistas.una.ac.cr/index.php/economia/article/view/6850.

Orozco, J. 2021. *Desafíos para Costa Rica en materia de Ciencia, Tecnología e Innovación (CTI) con la entrada a la OCDE*. La Revista, Costa Rica, San José.

Orozco, J., and Guillén, S. 2020. 'Objetivos e instrumentos de las políticas de innovación en Costa Rica', in *Revista política económica y desarrollo sostenible*. Centro Internacional de Política Económica para el Desarrollo Sostenible. Vol. 6(1), 1–24. https://www.revistas.una.ac.cr/index.php/politicaeconomica/article/view/14806.

Perez-Sebastian, F. 2007. 'Public Support to Innovation and Imitation in a Non-Scale Growth Model', *Journal of Economic Dynamics and Control*, 31, 3791–3821.

Porter, M. 1985. *Competitive Advantage: Creating and Sustaining Superior Performance*. New York: Free Press.

Programa Estado de la Nación Desarrollo Humano Sostenible. 2014. *Desempeño exportador y heterogeneidad estructural en Costa Rica*. Estado de la Nación, https://repositorio.conare.ac.cr/bitstream/handle/20.500.12337/903/949.%20Desempe%C3%B1o%20exportador%20y%20heterogeneidad%20estructural%20en%20Costa%20Rica.pdf?sequence=1&isAllowed=y.

Ruiz, H. 2012. *Algunos datos relevantes del Comercio Exterior de Costa Rica*. Universidad Estatal a Distancia de Costa Rica, https://www.uned.ac.cr/ocex/images/stories/boletines/Comercio%20Exterior%20de%20CR%20por%20HRH.pdf.

Ruiz, K. 2020. 'Cambio tecnológico y ocupaciones emergentes en Costa Rica', *Documentos de Proyectos* (LC/TS.2020/80). Santiago, Chile: Comisión Económica para América Latina y el Caribe (CEPAL). https://repositorio.cepal.org/bitstream/handle/11362/45894/S2000439_es.pdf?sequence=1&isAllowed=y.

Salazar Xirinash, J. M. 2020. 'Recomendaciones para el desarrollo productivo nacional y las regiones', in J. Vargas-Cullell, ed., *Pensar con sentido práctico: Un enfoque de resolución a problemas estratégicos del desarrollo nacional*. Washington, DC: Banco Interamericano de Desarrollo (BID).

Salazar Xirinash, J. M. 2022. 'El patrón de cambio estructural y de desarrollo de Costa Rica, 1950–2021 y retos futuros', in R. Bielschowsky, M. C. Castro, and H. E. Beteta (coords.), *Patrones de desarrollo económico enlos seis países de Centroamérica (1950–2018)* (LC/MEX/TS.2022/7). Ciudad de México: Comisión Económica para América Latina y el Caribe (CEPAL), 229–294.

Sojo, A. 1984. *Estado empresario y lucha política en Costa Rica*. San José, Costa Rica: EDUCA.

Sturgeon, T., and Memedovic, O. 2011. *Mapping Global Value Chains: Intermediate Goods Trade and Structural Change in the World Economy*. Vienna: United Nations Industrial Development Organization. https://open.unido.org/api/documents/4811381/download/Mapping%20Global%20Value%20Chains%20-%20Intermediate%20Goods%20Trade%20and%20Structural%20Change%20in%20the%20World%20Economy.

Vivarelli, M. 2014. 'Structural Change and Innovation as Exit Strategies from the Middle Income Trap', *Economic Change and Restructuring*, 49, 159–193.

Willmore, L. 1997. 'Políticas de promoción de exportaciones en Centroamérica', *Revista de la CEPAL* 62, 169–184.

World Bank. 2010. 'Innovation Policy: A Guide for Developing Countries', *Open Knowledge Repository: The World Bank*. https://openknowledge.worldbank.org/handle/10986/2460.

SECTION IV
FINAL REMARKS

19
Conclusions

Edmund Amann and Paulo N. Figueiredo

The Latin American development experience, stretching back almost half a century, has been a tale of repeated attempts to find a formula capable of delivering sustained and socially inclusive economic growth. The aim has been to escape from a legacy of economic volatility and disappointingly slow improvements in living standards and, ultimately, to close the gap with the advanced industrial economies. It is fair to say that success has proved elusive. Many have characterized the predicament in which Latin America finds itself as a middle-income trap. According to this interpretation, progress has stalled, with the region caught between a rock and a hard place. On the one hand, Latin America has developed to the point where it has lost many of its cost advantages. On the other, it has failed to carve out a fresh position in the international division of labour, capable of reconciling renewed economic dynamism with increased wage costs and elevated social expectations. This book has attempted to explore the nature of this apparently intractable bind, and to suggest ways out of it.

Latin America's present growth challenge comes amid complex and rapid change in the international economic environment. In the first two decades after the eruption of the region's debt crisis in the mid-1980s, the global economy experienced a period of rapid integration as trade barriers fell and obstacles to foreign direct investment reduced. These developments provided significant opportunities for Latin American economies—many of which were emerging from decades of import substitution—to deepen their international ties. The export, as opposed to the domestic market, became the motor for growth.

Fast forwarding to the mid-2020s, the nature of the international economic landscape appears far more ambiguous. The headlong rush towards ever-deeper globalization is no longer the given it once appeared. Protectionist forces have gathered pace, both internationally—as exemplified by the course of events in the United States under the Trump administration—and within Latin America itself. The region, meantime, has been subtly shifting the balance of its external economic focus away from traditional partnerships with Europe and North America, and towards that of China, and other economies in the Global South.

As the tectonic plates underpinning the region's interactions with the global economy have shifted, so have their analogues in the geo-political realm. The

Edmund Amann and Paulo N. Figueiredo, *Conclusions* In: *Innovation, Competitiveness, and Development in Latin America.* Edited by: Edmund Amann and Paulo N. Figueiredo, Oxford University Press. © Oxford University Press 2024. DOI: 10.1093/oso/9780197648070.003.0019

hemispheric North-South relationship with the United States is still most critical in terms of Latin America's international affairs. However, the primacy of the US relationship is now being challenged, both by the rise of China and the increasing engagement between Latin American countries and their peers in other emerging market regions. Over the course of the future, this ongoing realignment is likely to impart its own dynamic to the global economic opportunities that fall open to Latin American economies.

Not all the polar shifts affecting the economic environment—and hence Latin America's prospects for growth—are international in scope. It is also case that the region is experiencing internal political and ideological change. This is reshaping the policy environment and, relatedly, the very conceptualization of the growth challenge the region faces.

In the four decades spanning the end of World War II to the 1980s, economic policymaking in Latin America broadly aligned itself with the structuralist paradigm. This saw development problems as essentially the products of structural and institutional impediments that could be systematically addressed with well-thought-out policy interventions. The product of this was state-driven import substitution industrialization. With the emergence of the debt crisis in the early 1980s, a new development ideology took the place of structuralism. This, centred on the 'Washington Consensus', saw Latin America's central economic challenges couched in terms of market distortions, an over-mighty state, and too little integration with the global economy. Accordingly, the solution to the region's enduring economic problems was held to lie with greater openness and a reduction of the role of the state in the economy. Thus, privatization, together with trade and market liberalization, became the order of the day.

Partly influenced by the rise of the Latin American New Left, since the late 1990s the Washington Consensus has given way to a more nuanced view concerning the relative roles of state and market. Alongside this has surfaced a more sceptical assessment of the potential benefits of integration with the global economy. As a result, while import substitution may have not returned in earnest, selective trade protectionism is once again in evidence. Industrial policy has also made a comeback. Regarding the role of the state, in a certain sense, this has even expanded in comparison with the import substitution era: governments right across the region now actively pursue targeted anti-poverty programmes.

The recent ideological shift away from market fundamentalism has created the basis for a more pragmatic understanding of the region's economic challenges and possible solutions to them. This backdrop provides the context for this book's analysis of the nature of Latin America's middle-income trap, and potential exit routes from it. To recall, at the outset of this volume, three central questions were posed. In first place, what factors characterize Latin America's middle technology and income trap, and how do they impact the region's ability to break out of it? Second, how are these issues reflected in the experience of individual countries, as well as across the region? Third, nationally and across the region, which policies are proving effective in addressing the middle technology and income trap? Finally, given the region's current situation and the lessons of policy experience, what are the best ways forward for the future regarding Latin America's prospect of breaking out of the trap? In the remainder of what follows, these questions are variously addressed, through the optic of critical cross-cutting themes which have emerged among the preceding chapters. From this discussion arise important implications for the region's future course.

One of the key questions surrounding any development strategy surrounds the relative role of exports, of external versus internal demand. As previously noted, for most of the region, the second half of the twentieth century was dominated by strategies that sought to build up domestic industrial capacity behind protective barriers. Traditional reliance on exports (especially natural-resource-intensive products) was sidelined in favour of an approach which emphasized the domestic market and the instigation of rapid structural change. While this pathway to development and modernization led to initial success, it could not be sustained in the light of growing external disequilibria and the consequent need to draw in foreign savings.

Subsequently, from the 1980s on, the policy consensus across the region has shifted back in favour of higher priority accorded to exports. This is true even for countries such as Argentina and Brazil which later reintroduced selective import substitution policies under left-of-centre administrations in the first decade of the twenty-first century and the early 2010s. Yet, as the introductory chapter by Amann and Figueiredo makes clear, the movement back to a more internationally integrated approach has failed to deliver the sustained, accelerated growth many advocates of the 'Washington Consensus' had expected. Does this imply that policymakers should now downplay emphasis on exports and external demand as they seek to break out of the middle-income trap?

The evidence presented in this volume suggests that such an approach would be mistaken. In general terms, exports are good for growth and are likely to be essential for delivering sustained growth. This is not only because of the direct impact on aggregate demand; exports also offer the capacity to engage in learning and gain international market experience. This can be a first step on the road to internationalization and the emergence of home-grown multinational corporations. It is also the case that exports provide the foreign currency earnings required to import vital capital equipment and licence foreign technology. Access to both is essential to any strategy aimed at changing a country's position in the global division of labour, and boosting long-term growth rates.

Examining the evidence over the long term, in Chapter 4, Bravo-Ortega and Eterovic show how Scandinavia was able to drive up an income gap between it and Latin America as a result of its greater openness and superior export growth between the end of the nineteenth century and the end of the 1980s. Subsequently, at least up until about 2010, the income gap has tended to narrow. Comparing the cases of Chile and Sweden, the authors demonstrate a significant recent process of income catch-up flowing from liberal reforms in the former country, and a related rise in export demand. The comparison between Latin America and Scandinavia is particularly relevant and interesting. This is because the development process of both regions has featured a strong emphasis on exports of natural-resource-intensive products.

The authors suggest, that, aside from greater openness, Scandinavia's relative success over the long term in translating natural-resource-intensive exports into more sustained and dynamic growth stems from its efforts to build up human capital. This has allowed the region to establish more export sectors related to natural-resource-intensive activities, and to improve linkages between export sectors and the rest of the economy. The added-value activities which this has facilitated have allowed Scandinavia to mitigate its exposure to the global commodity market volatility. This, of course, is typically associated with a strong focus on natural-resource-intensive exports. Again, this serves as an important policy lesson from a Latin American perspective.

The sense that any focus on the role of exports needs to centre not just on their own growth potential, but on more qualitative, structural dimensions, is emphasized elsewhere in this volume. Particular attention is drawn to the issue of export connectedness. This theme has a long pedigree in structuralist theorizing around Latin America's development challenges. For structuralists, one essential weakness of the region's traditional, natural-resource-based, export-led model was that the lead export sectors—often highly competitive by global standards—had too little connection with the economies in which they were supposedly embedded (Kay, 1989). This disconnection implied, among other things, that there were too few learning opportunities, or scope for knowledge spillovers, between lead sectors and their counterparts in the economic hinterland. This limited the prospects for the emergence of new sources of export growth. The weak connectedness—as manifested in the lack of backward linkages—also meant that the lead export sectors were frequently obliged to source key inputs from abroad. This resulted in lower local value-added, strain on the current account balance, and forgone opportunities for the creation of new sources of domestic employment and output growth.

In the case of Mexico, Chapter 5 by Pineli and Narula digs beneath the country's apparent export success and highlights many of these issues at work. The Mexican economy since the debt crisis of the mid-1980s has pursued a policy of economic opening with a strong emphasis (via NAFTA and, latterly, the USMCA) on regional integration. Unlike its counterparts elsewhere in the region, non-traditional (especially industrial) exports have not gone into retreat. Instead, Mexico has proved very effective at developing higher-technology categories of exports, especially in terms of electronics and motor vehicles. As the authors point out, this (by Latin American standards) unusual export profile has co-evolved with distinctive patterns of inward foreign direct investment (FDI). The latter have seen foreign multinational corporations take advantage of Mexico's prime access to the United States and broader hemispheric markets.

However, does this promising mix amount to a recipe for success? Does it secure the basis for long-term, accelerated growth? Here, the authors sound a note of caution. It turns out that the higher-technology export-focused activities developed in Mexico have comparatively elevated import content, especially as concerns more technologically intensive components. Also, the authors suggest that there exist generally low levels of investment in innovation and limited learning opportunities. The failure to capture more of the value chain domestically, and to engage in processes of learning and capability-building, is likely to limit the long-term growth potential of the current Mexican 'model'. This will probably remain true even though the country has proven almost uniquely successful at resisting the region's slide into deindustrialization.

The concern that engagement in 'higher-tech' activities may not necessarily live up to their growth potential is echoed in Chapter 18 by Orozco and Ruiz on Costa Rica. Here, like Mexico, new industries (notably the production of integrated circuits) were established as a result of policies designed to attract inward FDI. While this certainly resulted in export diversification, there was weak productive and technological integration with the wider economy.

The Peruvian economy, despite being more natural-resource-focused in its export structure than Mexico, also illustrates a situation where growth opportunities are being missed. In Chapter 16 on the Peruvian experience, Crabtree reveals that the country has built up a dynamic mining sector which, until comparatively recently, was a prime mover in its economic success story. However, once again, there appears to be something of a disconnection between this lead sector and other parts of the economy. This has meant that the full potential benefits of the mining boom were never realized.

So far, the discussion might lead one to suppose that disarticulation between lead sectors and the rest of the economy is a fact of life in the region and will be very hard to overcome. This is far from the case. As will be seen later in this chapter, assisted by the development of capabilities accumulated under the import substitution regime, some countries have embarked on a modest path of productive and export diversification. This has often (though not always), involved building on the potential of natural-resource-intensive sectors. In line with this theme, it is first worth focussing on another aspect of Latin America's recent development experience: re-primarization, and its possible implications for growth, development, and breaking out of the middle-income trap.

In Chapter 3, concerning the implications of Latin America's growing economic ties with China, Jenkins highlights changes in patterns of trade which this relationship has helped to drive. He finds strong evidence that, in most countries across the region, patterns of exports have tilted notably in favour of natural-resource-intensive products. This 're-primarization' has occurred as the sidelining of import substitution industrialization drove a reversion to natural sources of comparative advantage. This saw many of the non-traditional industrial activities established under import substitution unable to compete in a more open economic environment, the competitive pressure made all the more acute by a surge in industrial exports from China.

At the same time, the astonishing economic expansion of that country drove unprecedented demand for the mineral and agriculturally-based products in which Latin American had long excelled. Two related questions emerge from these developments, one specifically relating to China, and the other rather broader in scope. The first concerns whether the rise of China itself represents an opportunity or a constraint in terms of breaking out of the middle-income trap. The second centres on whether reversion to a relatively greater reliance on natural-resource-intensive product exports is irreversible, and in of itself a backward developmental step.

Regarding the rise of China and its growing importance in terms of Latin America's international economic relationships, Jenkins points to some nuanced conclusions. In the first place, while it is true that Latin American exports directed at China have been dominated by natural-resource-intensive products, there is little evidence that this resulted—even during the commodities boom—in an outbreak of Dutch disease. In other words, there is little basis to suppose that intensified commodities-based exports to China have resulted in an overshooting of key Latin American currencies, resulting in competitive pressures on other elements of the region's tradables sectors. What appears to be more likely the case, as documented elsewhere in the volume (e.g. Brazil), is that competitive challenges in the non-natural-resource-intensive tradables sectors find their origin in structural impediments connected, for example, with under-investment in infrastructure, education, and innovation.

Still, the rise of China does pose particular challenges in the following two senses. In first place, at present at least, too much processing of Latin America's natural-resource-intensive exports takes place in China itself rather than upstream, close to points of extraction. This places limits on the growth and export potential engendered by Latin America's trade links with China. Second, the very competitiveness of China's industrial exports has made the global marketplace for these products a much tougher challenge for Latin American producers. When Latin American industrial exports first started to gain appreciable global market share in the 1960s and 1970s, they did not have to contend with anything like the suite of competitively priced industrial and manufactured products that China now offers to customers worldwide.

Despite these issues, Jenkins appears comparatively optimistic that Latin America is capable of benefiting more from its expanding economic relationship with China. Doing so will partly depend on better policy design in the region, especially in terms of the trade and industrial policies required to capture locally more of the value chain associated with Latin America's natural-resource-intensive products.

The second question surrounding re-primarization is far broader: Does Latin America's shift in the international division of labour towards natural-resource-intensive exports represent a regression? More specifically, is falling back on traditional sources of comparative advantage inevitable, and could it doom the region to the volatile, low average growth enshrined in the predictions of the Prebisch-Singer hypothesis? Drawing on the evidence set out in earlier chapters, the answer here would have to be at least a qualified 'no'. There are two reasons underpinning this conclusion.

In first place, there is no suggestion in the recent structural evolution of Latin America's economies and export profile that the re-primarization trend is either universal or irreversible. As the chapters on Costa Rica and Mexico made clear, thanks to FDI inflows, it has proven possible for economies in the region to maintain an elevated profile of non-traditional industrial and manufactured exports, to say nothing of the business services and tourism exports that are so important for many economies in the region. The role and potential of non-natural-resource-intensive sectors and their exports will be discussed at greater length later in this chapter. Suffice to say for the moment, however, that even if the re-primarization trend were seen as intrinsically undesirable, the capacity appears to exist in the region to buck it.

Is, however, the re-primarization trend as corrosive as the Prebisch-Singer hypothesis and related structuralist thinking might suggest? The evidence from this volume again suggests that on balance the answer is 'no'. As highlighted in the chapters on Argentina and Brazil, it would be a mistake to assume that natural-resource-based activities are necessarily technologically inert. Nor should it be thought that they lack the potential to catalyse the emergence of related sectors, whether as a result of conventional backward and forward linkages, or through knowledge spillovers.

In the case of Brazil, for example, key natural-resource-intensive activities around oil exploration and production, cellulose, soya, and ethanol have witnessed significant innovative effort and technological dynamism. In some cases (oil production, for example) these efforts have resulted in capabilities-building that have catapulted Brazil to the global frontier. In this field, Brazil holds the world deep-water drilling record. A significant industrial offshore sector has been established, partly on the basis of inward FDI. The success at translating innovative effort into success on the ground has underpinned striking gains in the productivity of Brazilian agriculture over the past four decades, helping the country capture global market share and additional components of the value chain.

In their chapters on the emergence of the sugarcane-derived ethanol complex, Figueiredo and Bicalho et al. show how the natural resources sector has been helping Brazil navigate the energy transition, developing sources of energy that reduce reliance on fossil fuels and limit the expansion of carbon emissions. Policies initially designed around energy security provided a basis for the development of a significant biofuels complex. The capabilities so acquired were later capitalized on in a more market-driven context, amid a drive to sustainability. Brazil was able to pioneer the use of pure ethanol and then flex-fuel vehicles, the technology used in the latter now being commonplace the world over. Chapter 10 by Figueiredo indicates the complexities of the process surrounding the accumulation of capabilities which made this all possible. In particular, he highlights the significant inter- and intra-firm variations in capability accumulation, a factor which would need to be taken account of in effective policy design in other contexts, elsewhere in the region. We will return to the issue of policy design later in this chapter.

Similar to the Brazilian case, in Argentina, capabilities have been built and progress made in the natural-resource-intensive sectors despite, at times, a very volatile political and macroeconomic backdrop. Structural diversification, both of the natural-resource-intensive sector and of its export profile, is a reality across the region. In the case of Peru, for example, it was shown how the country—whose exports have traditionally been dominated by mineral products—has successfully established exports of blueberries, avocados, paprika, mangoes, and lemons. Chile is well known as a centre for mining and is the world's largest copper producer. Yet, over recent decades it has established significant global market share in farmed salmon and wine.

Collectively, these experiences illustrate how fresh opportunities can be realized in productive activities conventionally considered 'traditional' but whose developmental potential has been recently enhanced by productivity gains and the ability to capture lucrative market niches. None of this would have been possible, however, without concerted effort and targeted policies. In the case of Brazilian agriculture, for example, considerable public resources have been directed into a sectoral system of innovation which has connected leading producers with research laboratories and technical institutes. These efforts have contributed to the rise of Brazil as an agricultural superpower, able to compete around the world on quality and availability, as well as price. As Brazil's natural resources sector has undergone a step change in its competitiveness over the past four decades, so a number of home-grown multinationals have expanded their global activities, among them JBS (in meat products), Vale (in mining), and Petrobrás (in oil and gas).

This is indicative of another potential benefit of the acquisition of capabilities and export market share in the natural-resource-intensive sectors: the possibility that they can result in the creation of what Dunning would term 'ownership advantages'. As the international business literature makes clear, these lie at the root of what drives the instigation and expansion of multinational corporations (Dunning and Lundan, 2008). In terms of their contribution to Latin America's escape from the middle-income trap, the growth in home-grown multinationals may open promising avenues. These might include strengthening the external balance through reductions in the traditional deficit registered in the income balance. However, they might also extend to providing enhanced opportunities for learning and international knowledge transfer. This could occur as a result of strategic asset seeking-focused outward FDI.

A possible downside of any development strategy in which natural-resource-intensive products play an important part centres on its potential negative externalities, especially in terms of corruption, clientelism, and political instability. This, the so-called resources curse, has received much attention in the literature, and was one of the focal points of Acemoglu and Robinson's famous 2008 book, *Why Nations Fail*. In the course of their contribution to the current book, Villar, Papyrakis, and Pellegrini argue that much scope exists to mitigate the risks of such a curse materializing. In particular, this might be achieved through the adoption of externally-mediated monitoring mechanisms designed to improve transparency around the governance of natural resource extraction. The authors focus on the case of one such initiative, EITI. While some positive results have been achieved, especially in Colombia and Peru, it appears that, considering Latin America as a whole, progress has been slow and needs to be speeded up.

Having reviewed the phenomenon of re-primarization, its opportunities and potential downsides, what of a more conventional structuralist response to overcoming growth challenges: the promotion of 'non-traditional' export activities? Throughout the 1950s, 1960s, and 1970s, structural transformation through the establishment of new, higher-technology industries was commonly seen as the route to accelerated, sustained growth. This view underpinned both import substitution strategies practiced in Latin America and export-orientated industrialization approaches implemented in East and South-East Asia. Does such a conceptualization of this way forward any longer hold relevance in Latin America?

While the natural-resource-intensive sectors will clearly have a critical role to play, there is no doubt that in selected areas, non-traditional sectors have achieved noteworthy breakthroughs, and could continue to do so in the future. As noted previously, Argentina, Costa Rica, and Mexico have achieved a measure of success in promoting such activities, the latter especially so in the consumer durables, electronics, and automotive sectors. Perhaps surprisingly, as Ruiz Durán and Balestro indicate in Chapter 15, Mexican *maquila* enterprises were able to acquire productive and technological capabilities. The challenge, as we have seen, lies in extending linkages from these sectors to others in the economy, capturing greater parts of the value chain, and establishing related sectors. Also necessary is the ability to facilitate knowledge spillovers from these 'lead sectors' to others in the economy. Were such spillovers to become more the rule than the exception, then the potential is held out for accelerated productivity growth in the Latin American 'economic hinterland', a domain typically characterized by a lack of dynamism and formal innovation.

Among Latin America's economies, it is arguably Brazil which has gone furthest and achieved most in terms of establishing selective non-traditional activities embodying home-grown technology and extended local value chains. Beyond the aforementioned oil exploration and production-related capital goods sector, Brazil has famously established significant production and innovative capabilities in the aerospace sector. The Brazil-based Embraer, alongside Airbus and Boeing, ranks as one of the world's three largest producers of civilian jet transport aircraft. Brazil's expertise in manufacturing extends into the automotive and capital goods sectors where, for example, Marco Polo and Weg rank among the largest global producers in their sectors (respectively, passenger buses and electric motors).

In the realm of financial services, Brazil stands among the global pioneers of Fintech, a new business model which employs web-based technologies to reduce the cost of financial intermediation. Aside from the growth potential implicit in the expansion of Fintech enterprises themselves, the rise of these institutions, through lowering borrowing costs, holds out the possibility of catalysing business investment. Equally important, more cost-effective access to capital for small entrepreneurs makes it more likely that a new generation of enterprises can be launched, challenging incumbents and exploring new sectors.

What factors account for success, where it has been achieved? In brief, the answer here would appear to be a combination of capabilities inherited from the state-driven industrialization epoch, entrepreneurial vision, and, in selected cases, the application of consistent government policy towards the sectors in question.

While the Brazilian experience may seem highly positive from this description—even possibly a model for the region—the reality is rather more nuanced. It should be borne in mind that the successful non-traditional sectors—aerospace, Fintech, and so on—are not representative of the technological dynamism or efficiency encountered in much of Brazilian industry. Here, low levels of innovation and underinvestment in human and fixed capital are the order of the day and help account for sluggish productivity growth. The challenge for Brazil (and indeed for the rest of the region) lies in broadening the base of competitive, dynamic, non-traditional sectors, whether in industry or services. As will be argued shortly, the role of policy design here is critical.

Whether in the natural-resource-intensive, industrial, or services sectors, digital technologies are reshaping the ways in which production is undertaken, business conducted, and innovation realized. In Chapter 11, Ferraz, Torracca, Arona, and Peres point to the possibilities of digitization opening new technological windows and growth paths for Latin America, potentially addressing issues such as the productivity problem and poor inter-sectoral linkages. However, the authors find that for the region relative to the developed economies, progress has been slow in terms of access to digital technologies and the availability of high-quality infrastructure. Again, it would appear that a combination of better policy design and accelerated investment are required if the full growth-propelling potential of digitization is to be realized.

Another aspect, often overlooked in terms of the potential for innovation to spur structural change and growth, concerns its spatial dimensions. In Chapter 7, Azzoni and Tessarin argue that geographical dispersion of innovative capability could go a long way to addressing regional inequality in terms of income and growth within countries. They point to evidence from Brazil pointing to progress in this direction, attributing the success that has been achieved to policy design. Further progress, both within Brazil and across Latin America as a whole, is required. Were it realized, the authors argue, an important contribution could be made towards addressing the middle-income trap.

One recurrent theme that emerges throughout the chapters centres on the importance of effective policy design. In order that the middle-income trap be effectively addressed, it has been argued that new sources of growth need to be identified, existing capabilities leveraged, investment in fixed and human capital boosted, and emerging opportunities in the global marketplace seized. While entrepreneurial vision and an openness to fresh ideas will always prove indispensable in achieving these outcomes, an effective, carefully designed policy framework will also need to be in place.

Over the course of the 1980s and 1990s there occurred something of a paradigm shift in respect of approaches taken to promoting competitive and structural change across the region. In general terms, horizontal forms of industrial and technology policy found favour. These emphasized the creation of generic conditions deemed necessary for a resurgence of investment, competitiveness, and capabilities creation. Among other things, this new policy environment stressed the importance of macroeconomic stability, access to cost-effective finance, assistance with export promotion, and the provision of training. Relegated was the previous emphasis on 'picking winners' and relatedly, confecting policy frameworks with the needs of particular sectors in mind.

More recently, with a return to interventionism gaining ground across the world, the consensus surrounding the design of optimal policy interventions has been changing. Part of the shift in perspective can be attributed to the rise of interest in 'mission-orientated policies'. These aim to coalesce policies and capabilities around tackling 'frontier challenges', whether in terms of archetypical objectives (such as putting a man on the moon) or, in the contemporary context, tackling complex, socially entwined issues such as climate change (Mazzacato, 2018).

The changing intellectual and philosophical approach of recent years has seen consideration of more vertical, sector-specific policy approaches move back into favour. These have perhaps achieved their most high-profile expression in the policy framework established by the current US administration towards the promotion of the electric vehicle sector in that country. Turning to Latin America, it would seem that scope also exists to countenance the expansion of such policies given the structural challenges the region now faces. In Chapter 17 on Uruguay, Bianchi and Isabella argue that the country, although seemingly successful for a while in achieving an inclusive growth resurgence, was unable to escape the middle-income trap. A central reason for this is that insufficient fresh sources of sustained growth were created. This was because policies were framed with an emphasis on horizontal, generic interventions. In the Uruguayan case, so the authors argue, vertical industrial and technological policies will need to accompany appropriately designed horizontal interventions to tackle key challenges revolving around particular sectors.

One key objective here might involve tackling the lack of backward and forward linkages around lead export sectors. This challenge appears especially pressing in the cases of Brazil, Costa Rica, and Mexico. Another related and critical area where effective policy articulation is required centres on global value chains (GVCs). In Chapter 6, Pietrobelli, Rabellotti, and Van Assche suggest that better policy frameworks have a vital role to play in helping Latin American economies capture more nodes on GVCs. If achieved, this would help in the generation of more local value-added, positively impact the import coefficient, and increase the likelihood of effective knowledge spillovers from abroad.

The argument that a successful articulation of horizontal and vertical policies can achieve results seems to find support in the context of the region's experience, exceptional though the instances may be. It can be argued that Brazil's policy towards the ethanol fuel and transportation complex represents such a positive example, hence the high profile accorded to it in this volume. Also in the Brazilian context, the country's aerospace and agribusiness sectors stand out as compelling cases. To a more limited extent, the same might be said to be true of Mexico's automotive sector and Argentina's oil and gas and agribusiness sectors.

This book has argued that Latin America indeed faces pressing growth constraints, but that the ingredients exist to enable the region to overcome them and embark on a more dynamic path. Despite the apparent fragmentation of the global economy and growing geopolitical tensions, the region will, and should, be able to take advantage of opportunities presented by astute international integration. To realize this potential and catalyse growth, imaginative policy design is needed. Investment in fixed and human capital will need to be mobilized. This will involve profound societal choices and associated opportunity costs. In order to address these, it is essential that countries across the region succeed in building a political consensus behind the design and implementation of appropriate policy frameworks. Still, however compelling the way forward may appear, the practical difficulties involved in assembling a coalition of interests in favour of realizing it should not be underestimated.

Focussing on the political and institutional dimensions of overcoming Latin America's growth and development challenges, Mahrukh Doctor in Chapter 2 argues that inequality and low levels of social cohesion have characterized the region's political reality. She suggests that these have not proven conducive to the formation of a consensus around much-needed change. This point also emerges in John Crabtree's chapter on Peru. There, decades of instability and (under Fujimori) authoritarian rule created a fractured society and polity. This prevented the creation of the consensus needed to accomplish the structural changes necessary for sustained growth. Even with this unpromising political backdrop, Peru was still—for a while—able to deliver accelerated growth; it even engaged in some natural-resource-intensive sector diversification. This points to the resilience of elements of Latin America's productive sector, and what might be possible if the political environment were more favourably configured.

Turning to issues of institutional design, independence, and accountability around the articulation and implementation of policies, the current situation is far from ideal. In this connection, it is worth highlighting the case of Brazil. Here, the region's largest corruption scandal for many years—the Car Wash scandal—revealed nefarious financial relationships between the government, large enterprises, and political parties (Lagunes and Svejnar, 2020). In the course of the scandal, industrial policy—especially around the building up of the domestic oil and gas equipment sector—became a conduit for the illicit channelling of public funds into the hands of political parties.

The Car Wash scandal exemplifies a clear and present danger in societies with a history of corruption, clientelism, and lack of probity in public office. This is that horizontal and vertical policy frameworks can become subverted by malfeasance. In turn, their credibility and effectiveness can be undermined, leaving vital structural challenges unmet. The sense of the rule of law (or absence of it) as a long-term influence on economic performance and ability to break out of the middle-income trap strongly emerges in the case of Colombia. In Chapter 14 on that country, Luzardo-Luna shows how high levels of violence and a weak rule of law remained key obstacles for a resumption of growth after the initial success which followed economic reforms in the 1990s.

As Latin America looks forward to the second quarter of the twenty-first century, this book suggests that, despite many frustrations, key elements for success are already in place. Capabilities built up over the long term can be unleashed. The entrepreneurial spirit of the region is undoubted and can be channelled into new ventures. At the same time, opportunities in a more complex and troubled global economy are there for the taking and can be seized. All of this can unfold on the basis of a pragmatic approach to blending the region's advantages in natural-resource-intensive sectors with emergent activities, many of which are linked to the knowledge economy. Fundamental to success in all these dimensions will be well-considered policy frameworks. Also required will be the allocation of resources into priority areas, especially around investment in people and productive assets. Whether or not Latin America grasps the opportunities within its reach will depend on societal choices and the political processes that underpin them. With the future of the region at stake, it must be hoped that a consensus in favour of positive, mutually beneficial change can at last be realized.

References

Acemoglu, D., and Robinson, J. 2012. *Why Nations Fail: The Origins of Power, Prosperity and Poverty*. New York: Crown Business

Dunning, J., and Lundan, S. 2008. *Multinational Enterprises and the Global Economy*. Cheltenham, UK: Edward Elgar.

Kay, C. 1989. *Latin American Theories of Development and Underdevelopment*. Abingdon, UK: Routledge

Lagunes, P., and Svejnar, J. 2020. *Corruption and the Lava Jato Scandal in Latin America*. Abingdon, UK: Routledge.

Mazzacato, M. 2018. 'Mission-Orientated Industrial Policies: Challenges and Opportunities', *Industrial and Corporate Change*, 27(5), 803–815.

Index

For the benefit of digital users, indexed terms that span two pages (e.g., 52–53) may, on occasion, appear on only one of those pages.

Note: Tables and figures are indicated by *t* and *f* following the page number